introductory philosophy

introductory

philosophy

ROBERT PAUL WOLFF

Department of Philosophy
University of Massachusetts at Amherst

PRENTICE-HALL, INC., ENGLEWOOD CLIFFS, N.J. 07632

Library of Congress Cataloging in Publication Data
Main entry under title:

Introductory philosophy.

    Bibliography: p.
    1. Philosophy—Addresses, essays, lectures.
I. Wolff, Robert Paul.
B21.I57   108   78–11615
ISBN 0–13–500876–X

INTRODUCTORY PHILOSOPHY
Robert Paul Wolff

© 1979 by Prentice-Hall, Inc., Englewood Cliffs, N. J. 07632

Printed in the United States of America

10 9 8 7 6 5 4 3 2 1

Editorial/production supervision by Fred Bernardi
Interior design by Linda Conway and Fred Bernardi
Cover design by Linda Conway
Manufacturing Buyer: John Hall

PRENTICE-HALL INTERNATIONAL, INC., *London*
PRENTICE-HALL OF AUSTRALIA PTY. LIMITED, *Sydney*
PRENTICE-HALL OF CANADA, LTD., *Toronto*
PRENTICE-HALL OF INDIA PRIVATE LIMITED, *New Delhi*
PRENTICE-HALL OF JAPAN, INC., *Tokyo*
PRENTICE-HALL OF SOUTHEAST ASIA PTE. LTD., *Singapore*
WHITEHALL BOOKS LIMITED, *Wellington, New Zealand*

contents

CHAPTER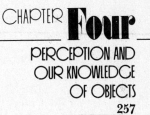

PERCEPTION AND
OUR KNOWLEDGE
OF OBJECTS
257

CHAPTER **Seven**

GOD AND RELIGIOUS
EXPERIENCE
497

preface

Let me address these few opening words to you, the students who will be using this book in an introductory course in Philosophy. As the semester or quarter goes by, you will be listening to your instructor, asking questions, arguing with him or her about some of the issues raised in this book, and arguing as well with your fellow-students. But I will not be there to join in the discussion. My contribution is finished before you even begin to study Philosophy. So this is my chance to talk directly to you.

Why study Philosophy? Why, indeed! The course you are taking may be required for graduation, although these days that is unlikely. More probably, it is one of a number of courses that satisfy some sort of distribution requirement. But that simply pushes the question back one step. Why require a philosophy course, or count it towards a distribution requirement? What *is* Philosophy anyway, and what can you, as students, hope to gain from puzzling over it?

Well, the oldest answers to these questions, surprisingly enough, are still the best. Philosophy is the love or pursuit of wisdom, and the only really good reason for studying Philosophy is that it may help you to become wise. (Notice, I did not say that studying Philosophy would make you wise. Only you yourself can do that. But studying Philosophy can help, if you will let it). Wise doesn't mean smart, or clever, or knowledgeable, although there is nothing wrong with being any of those. Wise means reflective, self-aware, conscious of the standards and principles you use in judging, choosing, and acting. Wise also means self-critical, ready to subject your own life to examination, to face up to the implications of your beliefs and the consequences of your actions.

Wisdom, in one form or another, is prized by virtually all the great cultural traditions of mankind. In many societies, wisdom is thought to come simply with age—and with the experience that age brings. In some cultures, wisdom is thought to come from meditation, or from the denial of the flesh, or from the taking of special drugs. The central conviction of western Philosophy, running all the way from the ancient Greeks to our contemporaries in the twentieth century, is that *reason* is the key to true wisdom. Arguments, analyses, reasonings and counter-reasonings—these, rather than age or meditation or drugs, are the true road to insight and self-understanding.

Now, you may have your doubts about the value of reason as a key to wisdom. Indeed, you may even have your doubts about wisdom! But for the duration of this Philosophy course, I ask you to give Philosophy a try. You are going to find it difficult, unusual, even a trifle painful, just as you would a new set of exercises before you were quite used to them. Your instructor, and the authors of the selections in this book, may ask questions, pose problems, or worry about difficulties that at first you have trouble understanding. All of that is to be expected. Countless thousands of Philosophy students before you have experienced the same initial puzzlement—and the same excitement as things become clear and you first see what Philosophy is driving at.

Studying Philosophy is different from studying anything else. I had better warn you now, so that you will be prepared for what is to come. First of all, Philosophy is not a collection of facts or theories that you must learn up and spit back in papers or on exams. Philosophy is an activity. You are going to learn *how to philosophize*. Obviously, the only good way to learn how to do something is to do it. You learn tennis on a court and swimming in a pool. The first time you swing a racket, you are going to look pretty clumsy. Only practice can improve your stroke, and it will be a while before you are able to pull off a killing overhead smash. In the same way, the first time you try to present a philosophical argument, you are liable to make a botch of it. But don't despair. Trying is the only way you'll learn. Naturally, your Philosophy instructor will come right back at you with a counter-argument, just as a tennis instructor will return your volley. And also naturally, his or her counter-argument will be classier than your argument. After all, you are the beginner, the instructor is the pro. But no one ever got to be a first-class tennis player by refusing to play until he could win, and no one got to be a philosopher that way either.

So far, learning Philosophy sounds rather like learning a sport or a musical instrument. But now we come to the special feature of Philosophy that makes it unique. When I study the piano, it is understood that there is a right way to play, and my piano teacher knows it. That is why I am taking lessons. But Philosophy is the activity of rational self-criticism and analysis. When you engage in it, *no one* can ever take your place as the judge of what is true or false, valid or invalid, right or wrong. You must be your own judge in those matters, for if you give up the final say to someone else—to a teacher, a parent, or a minister—then you will only seem to be wise, you will not actually be wise.

Don't be misled! I am not saying that any opinion is as good as any other. Only a fool would think such a thing. But I am saying that you must accept the responsibility of judging for yourself. So your Philosophy instructor can be your guide, your coach, your helper along the path to wisdom and self-knowledge, but you will have to decide which path to take.

The philosophers represented in this book have all ventured in search of wisdom. Some followed false trails and ended up in tangled confusions and contradictions. A few achieved genuine wisdom. (Here too, of course, you must judge for yourself which are which). All of them have in common three characteristics that mark the philosopher. First, they are careful, precise reasoners, who strive for clarity and logical rigor. Second, they all put their faith in the power of reason, even though only a few of them could, in the technical sense of the term, be called "rationalists." And third, all of them are seekers of the *truth*, whatever it may be and wherever it may lie. If you will attempt to acquire those three traits, then you too can become philosophers. And some few of you, like the best of the philosophers in this book and in the world, may achieve wisdom.

Good luck! Work hard at being a philosopher, insist always on clear thinking and rigorous arguments, never be afraid to ask a question or raise an objection, and most important of all, never say "I see" until you really *do* see. I hope the book challenges and stimulates you to wonder about things you might otherwise have ignored. From here on in, it is up to you, your classmates, and your instructor to make your first Philosophy course a successful quest.

Northampton, Mass.   ROBERT PAUL WOLFF
August, 1978

CHAPTER ONE

PERSONS AND THINGS

(Focal Issues)

1. *What Is a Person?*

2. *Do I Know Myself in the Same Way That I Know Other Persons?*

3. *What Are the Roles of Reason, Goal Orientation, Consciousness, and Memory in the Definition of a Person?*

INTRODUCTION

"Know thyself!" was the message of the Delphic Oracle in Ancient Greece, and for more than two thousand years since that time, philosophers have been wrestling with the problem of the nature of the self and the possibility of self-knowledge. What am I? What is a human being? What is a person? Is there something about persons that sets them off from all other beings, that makes them different, special? If there is, does it follow that we ought to treat human beings differently from the way we treat other things, living or dead?

Let us suppose that we have just landed on a planet in a distant solar system (thanks to an as yet undiscovered way of traveling faster than the speed of light), and that we find ourselves facing some sort of—well, some sort of things. What would it take to convince us that we had been *met* by a reception committee, and not simply that we had landed in a field of objects?

First of all, if we saw *people,* ordinary men and women just like the men and women we had left back on Earth, and if those people stepped forward and greeted us with a welcoming speech in English, we would conclude that we were indeed facing entities like ourselves. It would be something of a puzzle how they had gotten there, of course, but so long as they looked like us, talked like us, responded roughly as we ourselves might, gave coherent answers to our questions in colloquial English, and asked coherent questions in turn, we would have very little doubt that we were talking to people. It would follow, I think we can agree, that we would be wrong to kill these creatures idly, as we might swat flies or break up rocks. Depending on our moral convictions, we might also agree that we ought not to lie to them in our conversations, or make false promises to them, or cause them needless, pointless pain.

But now suppose that the "things" we encountered were *not* completely like ourselves. What then should we conclude? In true science fiction fashion, we can imagine a sort of continuous scale or spectrum of creatures, ranging all the way from people indistinguishable from ourselves to "things" *very* different indeed! If the reception committee merely had pointed ears, say, and greenish skin, but in every other way (including speaking English) were like ourselves, we would surely conclude that they were persons, just as we are. Their physical characteristics could be pretty bizarre without shaking our belief in their "personhood," so long as they spoke understandable, colloquial English and gave comprehensible, coherent replies to our questions. Indeed, we would probably be equally sure that they were, in some sense, people even if they spoke a very odd language that took the linguists among us a long time to learn.

The question would become very confusing if the creatures with which we communicated did not have *bodies* in the sense that we do. For example, we might discover after a while that it was the *breeze* with which we were communicating, not the lumpy objects squatting in front of us. We might discover this by tapping out a numerical sequence, such as "one tap, two taps, three taps," and then noticing that the breeze blew in four gusts, five gusts, six gusts. Would we, *could* we, believe that on this planet the breeze was a person? Or would we feel forced to conclude that some creature was *using* the breeze to communicate with us, even though we could never observe anything but the breeze? Would we feel obliged to be truthful and forthright with the breeze?

To go back for a moment to the original reception committee of ordinary-looking men and women, what would we think if they spoke colloquial English but gave irrelevant answers to our questions? More bothersome still, what would we think if we somehow discovered that beneath their quite ordinary-looking skin were masses of transistors, wires, gears, and levers? If I make a solemn promise to such a "man," am I released from its binding force by the discovery that he has a nuclear energy unit where I have a stomach, and a tiny computer where I have a brain? Would I agree that *he* had been released from *his* promise to *me* merely because it turned out that I had blood vessels where he had copper tubing?

We have introduced the problem of the nature of *persons* by means of an example from science fiction, but the problem itself remains puzzling and important even if we ignore such fancies. Historically, it is our religious beliefs that have posed the issue in the most pressing manner. The Christian tradition teaches that human beings have value, have significance in the scheme of things, because they have *souls*. In some fundamental sense, it is claimed, I *am* my soul. The soul is the seat of life, and after the body has died and decomposed, the soul lives on, either blissfully or in eternal torment. According to other religions, the soul moves from body to body, leaving one body and being reborn into another. In all of these views, the soul is a thing of some sort (though not a physical or material thing). So to a believer, the relevant question to ask of the creatures on another planet would not be whether they looked like us, or spoke like us, or even could communicate with us, but simply whether they had souls.

We have touched on a number of the themes that turn up repeatedly in philosophical discussions of the nature of persons. In the science fiction example, we focused mainly on the ability to *communicate,* because that is the way in which the problem would

3

present itself to us most naturally as space explorers. But a little reflection on what it means to communicate will reveal at least three characteristics that are centrally important in our notion of what it is to be a person.

First of all, if I can truly communicate with a creature, then it must be able to *think*—that is, it must be able to understand a question and select a suitable or relevant answer (even though the answer may be false!). If I ask (using English, or taps, or breezes, or whatever), "Is this your native planet?" and the creatures replies, "No, we come from far away," then whether it is telling the truth or not, I can tell that it has understood me, for its answer is a relevant or suitable or appropriate answer to my question. On the other hand, if I ask my question and it sends back a sign that I thought we had agreed upon for the number five, then I will have grave doubts that I am in touch with a thinking being!

Another way to say that the creature can think is to say that it is *rational.* Part of what we mean by this, of course, is that it can reason, i.e., it can draw conclusions from premises, inferring things that are implied but not explicitly stated. For example we might say, "There were twenty of us when we began our long journey, but two died on the way." If it replied, "Then you are now eighteen; but only seventeen are present—where is the other one?" we would know that it had carried out a two-stage reasoning process (first, that we were twenty minus two, or eighteen; second, that one was absent, inasmuch as only seventeen were present). Similarly, if at one time we told our new friends that we had an oxygen-based metabolism, and later told them that we did *not* have an oxygen-based metabolism, and if they then replied that one of our statements must be wrong, we would conclude that they understood and could employ the notion of contradiction, which is one of the marks of the power to reason. So communication implies rationality, and rationality is at least part of what we mean by "being a person."

Second, communication seems to imply the *having of purposes, intentions, goals.* Communicating is an activity. When I try to communicate, I start doing something, at a specific moment in time, with the aim of conveying a thought or a question to some other being. Typically, I complete my act of communication and then wait for a reply. There is an appropriate sequence to a communicative exchange: a question is followed by an answer, for example, not preceeded by it. Insofar as I am attempting to communicate, there must be some state of affairs I am trying to bring about—namely, a reply, or at least the receipt of my communication. So I must be able to conceive of a future state of affairs, adopt it as my end, and then choose some action that I believe is a means to that end.

There are several component parts to the having of a purpose. There is the end, the goal at which I am aiming. It may be some rearrangement of physical objects in my vicinity (such as the building of a stone wall), or an experience (such as the pleasure from eating a piece of chocolate cake), or a rather complicated combination of states of affairs and experiences (such as the general enjoyment that results from my telling a good joke), but in any case I must be able in some manner to envision it as a situation that I wish to bring into being. Another component to the having of a purpose is the network of beliefs about the world in general, and situations like this one in particular, which I call upon in reflecting on the best way to achieve my end. Typically, this network includes a number of beliefs about what the results will be if I *do* something, such as lifting a rock, or saying some words, or putting a piece of cake in my mouth and chewing it. Still another component is my doing of one of the things that my beliefs tell me will help to bring about my goal.

All of these—and much more—are involved in the having of purposes, intentions, or goals. Insofar as someone or something communicates with me, I can be sure that it and I both are creatures capable of purposive behavior. Now, you might object that somewhere in the universe I could come upon a perfectly rational creature that simply had no interest in communicating, or in doing anything else, for that matter. It might have the *ability* to engage in purposive activity, but no interest in doing so. Quite true. But then I would never know it! For either such a self-sufficient creature would choose not to do anything at all, in which case I would have no way of telling that it was anything but a nonpurposive, nonrational entity, or else it *would* choose to do something (perhaps just to let me know, by a single act of communication, that it existed but did not choose to act), in which case it would, by that single act, have forfeited its standing as a nonactor. (This, of course, is the problem with the traditional theological conception of God. If God is really perfect and fully self-sufficient, then He won't *do* anything, because He won't lack anything that He wants or needs, and then we won't know that He exists. But if He lets us know of his existence, by so much as a single act of revelation, then it can only be because there *is* something He wants—namely, that we should know of His existence—in which case He cannot be perfect.)

The third characteristic involved in being a person is *being conscious,* or more precisely, being *self-conscious.* Most of the time (when I am awake), I am aware of things around me, but at least some of the time I am also aware of myself. I can notice my own thought processes (as when I observe that I am not thinking too clearly on an exam, or reflect on the fact that my foot has gone to sleep), I can answer a question, and I can also think about the fact that I am answering a question. I can see a tree outside my window, and I can inspect my seeing of the tree, so to speak, in order to determine whether I see the tree more or less clearly than I see the mountains in the distance. Thinking about thinking, or self-consciousness, is clearly a part of what it is to be a person, for it is precisely the lack of reflective awareness on the part of animals that makes us doubt they are persons. Many animals give signs of being

5

conscious, in the sense of seeing, hearing, smelling, touching, or feeling pain, but only in a few highly intelligent species do we see behavior that suggests any sort of reflective self-awareness. When we *do* observe such behavior, in the great apes or in dolphins, we begin to have serious moral qualms about our treatment of these personlike animals.

Thus far, we have explored the question, "What is a person?" entirely from the standpoint of an observer trying to decide whether something *else* is a person. Now let us turn the question in on itself. When I think about myself—when I self-consciously reflect or introspect—what is it about me that convinces me that *I* am a person? And what convinces me that I am *one* person, not two or three or a whole colony? What distinguishes me from rocks and trees, from a breeze, from a pony, or, for that matter, from the color yellow or a right angle?

Thinking or reasoning, having purposes, and being self-conscious all suggest themselves as marks of my own personhood. Self-consciousness in particular seems central, somehow. If you told me that after my physical death I would go on making plans and drawing conclusions from premises, but that I would no longer be aware of myself doing those and other things, I would have serious doubts about whether what was going to survive was myself *as a person.* But there is at least one more element that enters into my consideration now, namely *memory.* In addition to being conscious from moment to moment, I am also conscious of being the same thing, person, or self over extended stretches of time. I can remember at least some experiences from my childhood, as well as numerous events and experiences from intervening times. Consequently, I am aware of myself as being the *same* person over many years, despite the most thoroughgoing changes in my knowledge, personality, and experiences. How do I know that it was *I* who traveled with my parents from New York to Colorado when I was only four, and not someone else? I know because I can *remember* it. I do not consult old family albums, or question surviving witnesses, or do any of the other things I might hit upon to check the story of someone else. I simply remember *myself* taking the trip.

We now have at least four characteristics of personhood, namely thinking or reasoning, having goals and purposes, being self-conscious, and having memory. Clearly they are very closely interrelated. When I set myself to pursue some plan or carry out some intention, I am aware of myself as the author of that plan. I must think through the best way of proceeding, and when I reach my goal, I must be capable of remembering that it is the goal I set out to reach. If any of these elements is missing (as sometimes happens, for example, in cases of brain damage or severe mental illness), then it would be very difficult to think of me as being, in the full sense, a person.

But all these elements seem to reside in or relate to the mind. What about the body? Even the breeze, in our science fiction example, has a body of sorts, though it shifts its borders and alters its shape more rapidly than the bodies we are used to. Must a person have a body in order to be a person? Does it even make sense to talk about a mind without a body? Can I think coherently about some *other* mind without conceiving it as embodied? What about my own mind, my own self? Are there ways of thinking about persons or selves that make sense only when I am thinking about myself, but do not make sense when I am thinking about any other self? Does a mind's thought about itself have a different logical structure, a different character, from that mind's thought about anything else?

All these questions, and many more, are discussed in the selections in this chapter. We begin with a famous passage from the *Meditations on First Philosophy* by the great seventeenth-century French philosopher, René Descartes. Descartes is the father of modern philosophy, and the *Meditations* are his most important work. Descartes approaches the problem from the inside, by way of an introspective examination of the thinking self by itself. You will find him concentrating most heavily on self-consciousness and reasoning as the marks of selfhood or personhood. He flatly insists that thinking is the essence of the self, with the consequence that for him, the notion of a mind without a body is perfectly conceivable.

John Locke, one of the founders of the school of philosophy known as British Empiricism, undertakes a rather complex analysis of the differences among the concepts of "person," "man," and "substance." His particular contribution to this discussion, aside from his careful distinction among those associated concepts, is his emphasis on the role of memory in the definition of what it is to be a person.

George Herbert Mead takes a radically different approach from that of other authors included here. Mead was a social psychologist whose primary interest was the social context, origins, and structure of personality. In contrast to most philosophical treatments of the subject, which emphasize the individual self in isolation from its social setting, Mead's essay shows us the ways in which each self is formed through the essentially interpersonal and interactive processes of identification and internalization of social norms.

With Williams and Strawson, we come to the sophisticated analyses of the modern Anglo-American school of analytic philosophy. Both writers, in their different ways, reject the Cartesian divorce of self from body, and argue that the concepts of personal identity and personhood involve in an essential way elements that Descartes and others would have distinguished as mental or physical.

The last selection, by American logician and philosopher of science Hilary Putnam, is a provocative exploration of the puzzles generated by the possibility of highly humanlike robots. Not many years ago, Putnam's essay would have been considered a mere fancy or "thought-experiment" designed to clarify our concepts of the self, but recent advances both in computer technology and biochemistry raise the possibility that before too many decades have passed, issues heretofore confined to philosophy journals may thrust their way into courts of law, hospitals, and the political arena.

(SELECTION 1)

RENÉ DESCARTES

The Nature of the Mind

The *Meditations* by Descartes are generally viewed as the starting point of modern philosophical speculation. In the First Meditation, Descartes sets himself the task of determining whether there is anything at all of which he can be *absolutely unqualifiedly certain*. After raising doubts about all our common beliefs, even those of mathematics, he arrives finally, in the opening portion of this Second Meditation, at the single totally certain proposition: "this proposition: I am, I exist, is necessarily true each time that I pronounce it." There are three crucial facts to notice about this fundamental truth. First of all, it is, strictly speaking, a truth about a proposition (the proposition "I exist"), not a truth about Descartes or any other person. Second, it is not the content of the proposition that assures its truth, but the fact of its being asserted. And third, it is an assertion whose truth is assured only when it is uttered in the first person singular present tense. There is no guarantee, for example, that the proposition "Mr. Descartes exists" is true every time I (not Descartes) utter it. Nor can Descartes be sure that the proposition "I existed" is true every time he utters it. (He might have a faulty memory; he might just have begun to exist, complete with a whole set of pseudo-memories.)

The remainder of the Meditation is devoted to establishing two claims that were to become central to much subsequent philosophical debate. The first is that my self, my mind, the I who asserts the proposition, must be *a thing which thinks*. So to our question about the nature of a person, Descartes replies that to be a person is to be a thinking thing. Having a body is not absolutely essential to being a thinking self. It is at least logically possible that I might exist as a thinking thing without a body at all (Descartes of course, endorses the traditional Christian notion of the soul).

The second claim advanced by Descartes in this passage is that the mind knows itself better, more directly, more certainly, more clearly, than it knows such physical things as the piece of wax that he imagines himself to be examining. The famous example of the wax is tricky. On first reading, we might suppose that Descartes is primarily interested in determining whether our knowledge of objects is founded on sense-experience or on reason, and that is indeed a question that has occupied philosophers from Descartes's time to the present. But a closer look reveals that Descartes really uses the case of the wax to show, once again, that the mind can be more certain of its own existence than it can be of the existence of any other entity.

MEDITATION II

Of the Nature of the Human Mind; and that it is more easily known than the Body.

The Meditation of yesterday filled my mind with so many doubts that it is no longer in my power to forget them. And yet I do not see in what manner I can resolve them; and, just as if I had all of a sudden fallen into very deep water, I am so disconcerted that I can neither make certain of setting my feet on the bottom, nor can I swim and so support myself on the surface. I shall nevertheless make an effort and follow anew the same path as that on which I yesterday entered, i.e., I shall proceed by setting aside all that in which the least doubt could be supposed to exist, just as if I had discovered that it was absolutely false; and I shall ever follow in this road until I have met with something which is certain, or at least, if I can do nothing else, until I have learned for certain that there is nothing in the world that is certain. Archimedes, in order that he might draw the terrestrial globe out of its place, and transport it elsewhere, demanded only that one point should be fixed and immoveable; in the same way I shall have the right to conceive high hopes if I am happy enough to discover one thing only which is certain and indubitable.

I suppose, then, that all the things that I see are false; I persuade myself that nothing has ever existed of all that my fallacious memory represents to me. I consider that I possess no senses; I imagine that body, figure, extension, movement and place are but the fictions of my mind. What, then, can be esteemed as true? Perhaps nothing at all, unless that there is nothing in the world that is certain.

But how can I know there is not something different from those things that I have just considered, of which one cannot have the slightest doubt? Is there not some God, or some other being by whatever name we call it, who puts these reflections into my mind? That is not necessary, for is it not possible that I am capable of producing them myself? I myself, am I not at least something? But I have already denied that I had senses and body. Yet I hesitate, for what follows from that? Am I so dependent on body and senses that I cannot exist without these? But I was persuaded that there was nothing in all the world, that there was no heaven, no earth, that there were no minds, nor any bodies: was I not then likewise persuaded that I did not exist? Not at all; of a surety I myself did exist since I persuaded myself of something [or merely because I thought of something]. But there is some deceiver or other, very powerful and very cunning, who

From *Meditations on First Philosophy* by René Descartes. First published in 1641. (trans. by E. S. Haldane and G. R. T. Ross, copyright Cambridge University Press, Cambridge, England, 1911)

ever employs his ingenuity in deceiving me. Then without doubt I exist also if he deceives me, and let him deceive me as much as he will, he can never cause me to be nothing so long as I think that I am something. So that after having reflected well and carefully examined all things, we must come to the definite conclusion that this proposition: I am, I exist, is necessarily true each time I pronounce it, or that I mentally conceive it.

But I do not yet know clearly enough what I am, I who am certain that I am; and hence I must be careful to see that I do not imprudently take some other object in place of myself, and thus that I do not go astray in respect of this knowledge that I hold to be the most certain and most evident of all that I have formerly learned. That is why I shall now consider anew what I believed myself to be before I embarked upon these last reflections; and of my former opinions I shall withdraw all that might even in a small degree be invalidated by the reasons which I have just brought forward, in order that there may be nothing at all left beyond what is absolutely certain and indubitable.

What then did I formerly believe myself to be? Undoubtedly I believed myself to be a man. But what is a man? Shall I say a reasonable animal? Certainly not; for then I should have to inquire what an animal is, and what is reasonable; and thus from a single question I should insensibly fall into an infinitude of others more difficult; and I should not wish to waste the little time and leisure remaining to me in trying to unravel subtleties like these. But I shall rather stop here to consider the thoughts which of themselves spring up in my mind, and which were not inspired by anything beyond my own nature alone when I applied myself to the consideration of my being. In the first place, then, I considered myself as having a face, hands, arms, and all that system of members composed of bones and flesh as seen in a corpse which I designated by the name of body. In addition to this I considered that I was nourished, that I walked, that I felt, and that I thought, and I referred all these actions to the soul: but I did not stop to consider what the soul was, or if I did stop, I imagined that it was something extremely rare and subtle like a wind, a flame, or an ether, which was spread throughout my grosser parts. As to body I had no manner of doubt about its nature, but thought I had a very clear knowledge of it; and if I had desired to explain it according to the notions that I had then formed of it, I should have described it thus: By the body I understand all that which can be defined by a certain figure: something which can be confined in a certain place, and which can fill a given space in such a way that every other body will be excluded from it; which can be perceived either by touch, or by sight, or by hearing, or by taste, or by smell: which can be moved in many ways not, in truth, by itself, but by something which is foreign to it, by which it is touched [and from which it receives impressions]: for to have the power of self-movement, as also of feeling or of thinking, I did not consider to appertain to the nature of body: on the contrary, I was rather astonished to find that faculties similar to them existed in some bodies.

But what am I, now that I suppose that there is a certain genius which is extremely powerful, and, if I may say so, malicious, who employs all his powers in deceiving me? Can I affirm that I possess the least of all those things which I have just said pertain to the nature of body? I pause to consider, I revolve all these things in my mind, and I find none of which I can say that it pertains to me. It would be tedious to stop to enumerate them. Let us pass to the attributes of soul and see if there is any one which is in me? What of nutrition or walking [the first mentioned]? But if it is so that I have no body it is also true that I can neither walk nor take nourishment. Another attribute is sensation. But one cannot feel without body, and besides I have thought I perceived many things during sleep that I recognised in my waking moments as not having been experienced at all. What of thinking? I find here that thought is an attribute that belongs to me; it alone cannot be separated from me. I am, I exist, that is certain. But how often? Just when I think; for it might possibly be the case if I ceased entirely to think, that I should likewise cease altogether to exist. I do not now admit anything which is not necessarily true: to speak accurately I am not more than a thing which thinks, that is to say a mind or a soul, or an understanding, or a reason, which are terms whose significance was formerly unknown to me. I am, however, a real thing and really exist but what thing? I have answered: a thing which thinks.

And what more? I shall exercise my imagination [in order to see if I am not something more]. I am not a collection of members which we call the human body: I am not a subtle air distributed through these members, I am not a wind, a fire, a vapour, a breath, nor anything at all which I can imagine or conceive; because I have assumed that all these were nothing. Without changing that supposition I find that I only leave myself certain of the fact that I am somewhat. But perhaps it is true that these same things which I supposed were non-existent because they are unknown to me, are really not different from the self which I know. I am not sure about this, I shall not dispute about it now; I can only give judgment on things that are known to me. I know that I exist, and I inquire what I am, I whom I know to exist. But it is very certain that the knowledge of my existence taken in its precise significance does not depend on things whose existence is not yet known to me; consequently it does not depend on those which I can feign in imagination. And indeed the very term *feign* in imagination proves to me my error, for I really do this if I image myself a something, since to imagine is nothing else than to contemplate the figure or image of a corporeal thing. But I already know for certain that I am, and that it may be that all these images, and, speaking generally, all things that relate to the nature of body are nothing but dreams [and chimeras]. For this reason I see clearly that I have as little reason to say, "I shall stimulate my imagination in order to know more distinctly what I am," than if I were to say, "I am now awake, and I perceive somewhat that is real and true: but because I do not yet perceive it distinctly enough, I shall go to sleep of express purpose, so that my dreams may represent the perception with greatest truth and evidence." And, thus, I know for certain that nothing of all that I can understand by means of my imagination belongs to this knowledge which I have of myself, and that it is necessary to recall the mind from this mode of thought with the utmost diligence in order that it may be able to know its own nature with perfect distinctness.

But what then am I? A thing which thinks. What is a thing which thinks? It is a thing which doubts, understands, [conceives], affirms, denies, wills, refuses, which also imagines and feels.

Certainly it is no small matter if all these things pertain to my nature. But why should they not so pertain? Am I not that being who now doubts nearly everything, who nevertheless understands certain things, who affirms that one only is true, who denies all the others, who desires to know more, is averse from being deceived, who imagines many things, sometimes indeed despite his will, and who perceives many likewise, as by the intervention of the bodily organs? Is there nothing in all this which is as true as it is certain that I exist, even though I should always sleep and though he who has given me being employed all his ingenuity in deceiving me? Is there likewise any one of these attributes which can be distinguished from my thought, or which might be said to be separated from myself? For it is so evident of itself that it is I who doubts, who understands, and who desires, that there is no reason here to add anything to explain it. And I have certainly the power of imagining likewise; for although it may happen (as I formerly supposed) that none of the things which I imagine are true, nevertheless this power of imagining does not cease to be really in use, and it forms part of my thought. Finally, I am the same who feels, that is to say, who perceives certain things, as by the organs of sense, since in truth I see light, I hear noise, I feel heat. But it will be said that these phenomena are false and that I am dreaming. Let it be so; still it is at least quite certain that it seems to me that I see light, that I hear noise and that I feel heat. That cannot be false; properly speaking it is what is in me called feeling; and used in this precise sense that is no other thing than thinking.

From this time I begin to know what I am with a little more clearness and distinction than before; but nevertheless it still seems to me, and I cannot prevent myself from thinking, that corporeal things, whose images are framed by thought, which are tested by the senses, are much more distinctly known than that obscure part of me which does not come under the imagination. Although really it is very strange to say that I know and understand more distinctly these things whose existence seems to me dubious, which are unknown to me, and which do not belong to me, than others of the truth of which I am convinced, which are known to me and which pertain to my real nature, in a word, than myself. But I see clearly how the case stands: my mind loves to wander, and cannot yet suffer itself to be retained within the just limits of truth. Very good, let us once more give it the freest rein, so that, when afterwards we seize the proper occasion for pulling up, it may the more easily be regulated and controlled.

Let us begin by considering the commonest matters, those which we believe to be the most distinctly comprehended, to wit, the bodies which we touch and see; not indeed bodies in general, for these general ideas are usually a little more confused, but let us consider one body in particular. Let us take, for example, this piece of wax: it has been taken quite freshly from the hive, and it has not yet lost the sweetness of the honey which it contains; it still retains somewhat of the odour of the flowers from which it has been culled; its colour, its figure, its size are apparent; it is hard, cold, easily handled, and if you strike it with the finger, it will emit a sound. Finally all the things which are requisite to cause us distinctly to recognise a body, are met with in it. But notice that while I speak and approach the fire what remained of the taste is exhaled, the smell evaporates, the colour alters, the figure is destroyed, the size increases, it becomes liquid, it heats, scarcely can one handle it, and when one strikes it, no sound it emitted. Does the same wax remain after this change? We must confess that it remains; none would judge otherwise. What then did I know so distinctly in this piece of wax? It could certainly be nothing of all that the senses brought to my notice, since all these things which fall under taste, smell, sight, touch, and hearing, are found to be changed, and yet the same wax remains.

Perhaps it was what I now think, viz. that this wax was not that sweetness of honey, nor that agreeable scent of flowers, nor that particular whiteness, nor that figure, nor that sound, but simply a body which a little while before appeared to me as perceptible under these forms, and which is now perceptible under others. But what, precisely, is it that I imagine when I form such conceptions? Let us attentively consider this, and, abstracting from all that does not belong to the wax, let us see what remains. Certainly nothing remains excepting a certain extended thing which is flexible and movable. But what is the meaning of flexible and movable? Is it not that I imagine that this piece of wax being round is capable of becoming square and of passing from a square to a triangular figure? No, certainly it is not that, since I imagine it admits of an infinitude of similar changes, and I nevertheless do not know how to compass the infinitude by my imagination, and consequently this conception which I have of the wax is not brought about by the faculty of imagination. What now is this extension? Is it not also unknown? For it becomes greater when the wax is melted, greater when it is boiled, and greater still when the heat increases; and I should not conceive [clearly] according to truth what wax is, if I did not think that even this piece that we are considering is capable of receiving more variations in extension that I have ever imagined. We must then grant that I could not even understand through the imagination what this piece of wax is, and that it is my mind alone which perceives it. I say this piece of wax in particular, for as to wax in general it is yet clearer. But what is this piece of wax which cannot be understood excepting by the [understanding or] mind? It is certainly the same that I see, touch, imagine, and finally it is the same which I have always believed it to be from the beginning. But what must particularly be observed is that its perception is neither an act of vision, nor of touch, nor of imagination, and has never been such although it may have appeared formerly to be so, but only an intuition of the mind, which may be imperfect and confused as it was formerly, or clear and distinct as it is at present, according as my attention is more or less directed to the elements which are found in it, and of which it is composed.

Yet in the meantime I am greatly astonished when I consider [the great feebleness of mind] and its proneness to fall [insensibly] into error; for although without giving expression to my thoughts I consider all this in my own mind, words often impede me and I am almost deceived by the terms of ordinary language. For we say that we see the same wax, if it is present, and not that we simply judge that it is the same from its having the same colour and figure. From this I should conclude that I knew the wax by means of vision and not simply by the intuition of the mind; unless by chance I remember that, when looking from a window and saying I see men who pass in the street, I really do not see them, but infer that what I see is men, just as I say that I see wax. And yet what do I see from the window but hats and coats which may cover automatic machines? Yet

I judge these to be men. And similarly solely by the faculty of judgment which rests in my mind, I comprehend that which I believed I saw with my eyes.

A man who makes it his time to raise his knowledge above the common should be ashamed to derive the occasion for doubting from the forms of speech invented by the vulgar; I prefer to pass on and consider whether I had a more evident and perfect conception of what the wax was when I first perceived it, and when I believed I knew it by means of the external senses or at least by the common sense as it is called, that is to say by the imaginative faculty, or whether my present conception is clearer now that I have most carefully examined what it is, and in what way it can be known. It would certainly be absurd to doubt as to this. For what was there in this first perception which was distinct? What was there which might not as well have been perceived by any of the animals? But when I distinguish the wax from its external forms, and when, just as if I had taken from it its vestments, I consider it quite naked, it is certain that although some error may still be found in my judgment, I can nevertheless not perceive it thus without a human mind.

But finally what shall I say of this mind, that is, of myself, for up to this point I do not admit in myself anything but mind? What then, I who seem to perceive this piece of wax so distinctly, do I not know myself, not only with much more truth and certainty, but also with much more distinctness and clearness? For if I judge that the wax is or exists from the fact that I see it, it certainly follows much more clearly that I am or that I exist myself from the fact that I see it. For it may be that what I see is not really wax, it may also be that I do not possess eyes with which to see anything; but it cannot be that when I see, or (for I no longer take account of the distinction) when I think I see, that I myself who think am nought. So if I judge that the wax exists from the fact that I touch it, the same thing will follow, to wit, that I am; and if I judge that my imagination, or some other cause, whatever it is, persuades me that the wax exists, I shall still conclude the same. And what I have here remarked of wax may be applied to all other things which are external to me [and which are met with outside of me]. And further, if the [notion or] perception of wax has seemed to me clearer and more distinct, not only after the sight or the touch, but also after many other causes have rendered it quite manifest to me, with how much more [evidence] and distinctness must it be said that I now know myself, since all the reasons which contribute to the knowledge of wax, or any other body whatever, are yet better proofs of the nature of my mind! And there are so many other things in the mind itself which may contribute to the elucidation of its nature, that those which depend on body such as these just mentioned, hardly merit being taken into account.

But finally here I am, having insensibly reverted to the point I desired, for, since it is now manifest to me that even bodies are not properly speaking known by the senses or by the faculty of imagination, but by the understanding only, and since they are not known from the fact that they are seen or touched, but only because they are understood, I see clearly that there is nothing which is easier for me to know than my mind. But because it is difficult to rid oneself so promptly of an opinion to which one was accustomed for so long, it will be well that I should halt a little at this point, so that by the length of my meditation I may more deeply imprint on my memory this new knowledge.

DESCARTES SELECTION

1. Exactly what does the argument at the end of the third paragraph prove? Does it prove that Descartes exists? Does it prove that I exist? Does it prove *to me* that I exist? (Are these different?)

2. How does Descartes go about imagining himself without a body? Can you really imagine yourself without a body? Can you conceive of having sensations—sights, sounds, smells, etc.—without a body? Could you *be* without being somewhere and some when?

3. In the example of the wax, if the wax really changes *all* of its sensory qualities, then what makes me think there is any *thing* here at all? Does any collection of sensory qualities make up the sensations of *an object?* Why not?

4. When a physicist investigates the nature of some element, does he or she concentrate on sensory qualities, or on the underlying atomic structure? Would Descartes call our knowledge of that underlying atomic structure sensory knowledge or rational knowledge?

5. If Descartes is correct that the essence of the mind is thinking, then how can I ever know whether there are other minds besides my own?

(SELECTION 2)

JOHN LOCKE

Person, Man, and Substance

In this selection from the *Essay,* Locke is concerned with what has come to be known as the problem of *personal identity.* What is it in virtue of which I am *the same* person from one moment to the next, or even over a span of seventy years? Locke complicates the question, and also moves us closer to an answer, by distinguishing three related concepts that are often confused, namely, *the same substance, the same man* (or human being), and *the same person.*

Locke accepts the definition of a person as a thinking being, but to thought he adds memory as the basis of that unity over time to which we attach the term "identity." In order to see how important memory is to our conception of personal identity, try to imagine what you would say if you could actually *remember* having had a variety of bodies at different times! So long as there was a continuity of memory, Locke insists, we would say that it was a single *person* who had "lived" in several bodies. If that notion seems absurd to you, reflect on the fact that each of us can remember being a small child, a young boy or girl, and a grown man or woman. Are those not a variety of bodies at different times?

An opposite problem is posed by the rare but medically established cases of multiple personalities—two, three, or even several dozen distinct personalities "inhabiting" a single body, appearing one after the other from time to time. If personality A cannot remember what happens to personality B, and vice versa, are we to say that there is *one* "split personality" in the body we observe, or that there are two distinct personalities?

Let us complicate the matter even further. Suppose that a machine is invented that "transports" a person by mapping the molecular structure of his body and recreating it (out of different atoms) in another place. If, by a malfunction, *two* recreations took place instead of one, then after the "transportation" there would be two discrete, different persons, each of whom had numerically, identically the same memories! Is that logically possible? Two people can, of course, remember the same event. Millions of people may remember the same television show or the last national election. But can two different people have one and the same memory? Not exactly similar memories, but *the same* memory. Can *you* remember eating *my* breakfast? Not unless, by eating it, you make it *your* breakfast.

Peculiar imaginary examples, such as that of the "transportation machine," are used by philosophers to explore the logical implications of our concepts.

There are at least two different ways to respond to such an example. One is to conclude that the device imagined in the example could not possibly be invented, because it contradicts our clear and coherent conception of what it is to be a person; the other is to conclude that just because we can imagine such a machine, our conception of a person must be less clear and coherent than we originally supposed.

We must therefore consider wherein an oak differs from a mass of matter, and that seems to me to be in this, *that the one is only the cohesion of particles of matter any how united, the other such a disposition of them as constitutes the parts of an oak;* and such an organization of those parts as is fit to receive and distribute nourishment, so as to continue and frame the wood, bark, and leaves, &c., of an oak, in which consists the vegetable life. *That being then one plant which has such an organization of parts in one coherent body, partaking of one common life, it continues to be the same plant as long as it partakes of the same life, though that life be communicated to new particles of matter vitally united to the living plant, in a like continued organization conformable to that sort of plants. . . .*

The case is not so much different in *brutes* but that any one may hence see what makes an animal and continues it the same. Something we have like this in machines, and may serve to illustrate it. For example, what is a watch? It is plain it is nothing but a fit organization or construction of parts to a certain end, which, when a sufficient force is added to it, it is capable to attain. If we would suppose this machine one continued body, all whose organized parts were repaired, increased, or diminished by a constant addition or separation of insensible parts, with one common life, we should have something very much like the body of an animal; with this difference, That, in an animal the fitness of the organization, and the motion wherein life consists, begin together, the motion coming from within; but in machines the force coming sensibly from without, is often away when the organ is in order, and well fitted to receive it.

This also shows wherein the identity of the same man consists; viz. in nothing but a participation of the same continued life, by constantly fleeting particles of matter, in succession vitally united to the same organized body. He that shall place the identity of man in anything else, but, like that of other animals, in one fitly organized body, taken in any one instant, and from thence continued, under one organization of life, in several successively fleeting particles of matter united to it, will find it hard to make an embryo, one of years, mad and sober, the same man, by any supposition, that will not

From *An Essay Concerning the Human Understanding* by John Locke. First published in 1690.

*make it possible for Seth, Ismael, Socrates, Pilate, St. Austin, and
Caesar Borgia, to be the same man. For if the identity of soul alone
makes the same man; and there be nothing in the nature of matter
why the same individual spirit may not be united to different bodies,
it will be possible that those men, living in distant ages, and of different tempers, may have been the same man:* which way of speaking
must be from a very strange use of the word man, applied to an idea
out of which body and shape are excluded. . . .

*It is not therefore unity of substance that comprehends all sorts
of identity, or will determine it in every case; but to conceive and
judge of it aright, we must consider what idea the word it is applied
to stands for:* it being one thing to be the same *substance,* another
the same *man,* and a third the same *person,* if *person, man,* and
substance, are three names standing for three different ideas;—for
such as is the idea belonging to that name, such must be the identity;
which, if it had been a little more carefully attended to, would possibly have prevented a great deal of that confusion which often occurs about this matter, with no small seeming difficulties, especially
concerning *personal* identity, which therefore we shall in the next
place a little consider.

An animal is a living organized body; and consequently the
same animal, as we have observed, is the same continued *life* communicated to different particles of matter, as they happen successively
to be united to that organized living body. . . .

. . . For I presume it is not the idea of a thinking or rational being
alone that makes the *idea of a man* in most people's sense: but of a
body, so and so shaped, joined to it; and if that be the idea of a man,
the same successive body not shifted all at once, must, as well as the
same immaterial spirit, go to the making of the same man.

This being premised, to find wherein personal identity consists,
we must consider what *person* stands for;—which, I think, is a thinking intelligent being that has reason and reflection, and can consider
itself as itself, the same thinking thing, in different times and places;
which it does only by that consciousness which is inseparable from
thinking, and, as it seems to me, essential to it: it being impossible
for any one to perceive without *perceiving* that he does perceive.
When we see, hear, smell, taste, feel, meditate, or will anything, we
know that we do so. Thus it is always as to our present sensations and
perceptions: and by this every one is to himself that which he calls
self. . . . For, *since consciousness always accompanies thinking, and
it is that which makes every one to be what he calls self,* and thereby
distinguishes himself from all other thinking things, in this alone
consists personal identity, i.e., the sameness of a rational being: and as
far as this consciousness can be extended backwards to any past ac-

tion or thought, so far reaches the identity of that person; it is the same self now it was then; and it is by the same self with this present one that now reflects on it, that that action was done.

But it is further inquired, whether it be the same identical substance. This few would think they had reason to doubt of, if these perceptions, with their consciousness, always remained present in the mind, whereby the same thinking thing would be always consciously present, and, as would be thought, evidently the same to itself. But that which seems to make the difficulty is this, that this consciousness being interrupted always by forgetfulness, there being no moment of our lives wherein we have the whole train of all our past actions before our eyes in one view, but even the best memories losing the sight of one part whilst they are viewing another; and we sometimes, and that the greatest part of our lives, not reflecting on our past selves, being intent on our present thoughts, and in sound sleep having no thoughts at all, or at least none with that consciousness which remarks our waking thoughts—I say, in all these cases, our consciousness being interrupted, and we losing the sight of our past selves, *doubts are raised whether we are the same thinking thing, i.e., the same substance or no.* Which, however reasonable or unreasonable, concerns not *personal* identity at all. *The question being what makes the same person; and not whether it be the same identical substance, which always thinks in the same person, which, in this case, matters not at all: different substances, by the same consciousness (where they do partake in it) being united into one person, as well as different bodies by the same life are united into one animal, whose identity is preserved in that change of substances by the unity of one continued life.* For, it being the same consciousness that makes a man be himself to himself, personal identity depends on that only, whether it be annexed solely to one individual substance, or can be continued in a succession of several substances. *For as far as any intelligent being can repeat the idea of any past action with the same consciousness it had of it at first, and with the same consciousness it has of any present action; so far it is the same personal self. For it is by the consciousness it has of its present thoughts and actions, that it is self to itself now, and so will be the same self, as far as the same consciousness can extend to actions past or to come;* and would be by distance of time, or change of substance, no more two persons, than a man be two men by wearing other clothes to-day than he did yesterday, with a long or a short sleep between: the same consciousness uniting those distant actions into the same person, whatever substances contributed to their production.

That this is so, we have some kind of evidence in our very bodies, all whose particles, whilst vitally united to the same thinking conscious self, so that *we feel* when they are touched, and are affected by, and conscious of good or harm that happens to them, are a part of ourselves; i.e., of our thinking conscious self. Thus, the limbs of his body are to every one a part of himself; he sympathizes and is concerned for them. Cut off a hand, and thereby separate it from that consciousness he had of its heat, cold, and other affections, and it is then no longer a part of that which is himself, any more than the remotest part of matter. Thus, we see the *substance* whereof personal self consisted at one time may be varied at another, without the change of personal identity; there being no question about the same person, though the limbs which but now were a part of it, be cut off.

But the question is, Whether if the same substance which thinks be changed, it can be the same person; or, remaining the same, it can be different persons?

And to this I answer: First, This can be no question at all to those who place thought in a purely material animal constitution, void of an immaterial substance. For, whether their supposition be true or no, it is plain they conceive personal identity preserved in something else than identity of substance; as animal identity is preserved in identity of life, and not of substance. And therefore those who place thinking in an immaterial substance only, before they can come to deal with these men, must show why personal identity cannot be preserved in the change of immaterial substances, or variety of particular immaterial substances, as well as animal identity is preserved in the change of material substances, or variety of particular bodies: unless they will say, it is one immaterial spirit that makes the same life in brutes, as it is one immaterial spirit that makes the same person in men; which the Cartesians at least will not admit, for fear of making brutes thinking things too. . . .

But though the same immaterial substance or soul does not alone, wherever it be, and in whatsoever state, make the same *man;* yet it is plain, consciousness, as far as ever it can be extended—should it be to ages past—unites existences and actions very remote in time into the same *person,* as well as it does the existences and actions of the immediately preceding moment: so that whatever has the consciousness of present and past actions, is the same person to whom they both belong. Had I the same consciousness that I saw the ark and Noah's flood, as that I saw an overflowing of the Thames last winter, or as that I write now, I could no more doubt that I who write this now, that saw the Thames overflowed last winter, and that viewed the flood at the general deluge, was the same *self*—place that self in what *substance* you please—than that I who write this am the same *myself* now whilst I write (whether I consist of all the same substance, material or immaterial, or no) that I was yesterday. For as to this point of being the same self, it matters not whether this present self be made up of the same or other substances—I being as much concerned, and as justly accountable for any action that was done a thousand years since, appropriated to me now by this self-consciousness, as I am for what I did the last moment.

Self is that conscious thinking thing—whatever substance made up of (whether spiritual or material, simple or compounded, it matters not)—which is sensible or conscious of pleasure and pain, capable of happiness or misery, and so is concerned for itself, as far as that consciousness extends. Thus every one finds that, whilst comprehended under that consciousness, the little finger is as much a part of himself as what is most so. Upon separation of this little finger, should this consciousness go along with the little finger, and leave the rest of the body, it is evident the little finger would be the person, the same person; and self then would have nothing to do with the rest of the body. As in this case it is the consciousness that goes along with the substance, when one part is separate from another, which makes the same person, and constitutes this inseparable self: so it is in reference to substances remote in time. That with which the consciousness of this present thinking thing *can* join itself, makes the same person, and is one self with it, and with nothing else; and so attributes to itself, and owns all the actions of that thing, as its own, as far as that consciousness reaches, and no further; as every one who reflects will perceive.

In this personal identity is founded all the right and justice of reward and punishment; happiness and misery being that for which every one is concerned for himself, and not mattering what becomes of any substance, not joined to, or affected with that consciousness. For, as it is evident in the instance I gave but now, if the consciousness went along with the little finger when it was cut off, that would be the same self which was concerned for the whole body yesterday, as making part of itself, whose actions then it cannot but admit as its own now. Though, if the same body should still live, and immediately from the separation of the little finger have its own peculiar consciousness, whereof the little finger knew nothing, it would not at all be concerned for it, as a part of itself, or could own any of its actions, or have any of them imputed to him.

This may show us wherein personal identity consists: not in the identity of substance, but, as I have said, in the identity of consciousness, wherein if Socrates and the present mayor of Queinborough agree, they are the same person: if the same Socrates waking and sleeping do not partake of the same consciousness, Socrates waking and sleeping is not the same person. And to punish Socrates waking for what sleeping Socrates thought, and waking Socrates was never conscious of, would be no more of right, than to punish one twin for what his brother-twin did, whereof he knew nothing, because their outsides were so like, that they could not be distinguished; for such twins have been seen.

But yet possibly it will still be objected—Suppose I wholly lose the memory of some parts of my life, beyond a possibility of re- trieving them, so that perhaps I shall never be conscious of them again; yet am I not the same person that did those actions, had those thoughts that I once was conscious of, though I have now forgot them? To which I answer, that we must here take notice what the word *I* is applied to; which, in this case, is the *man* only. *And the same man being presumed to be the same person, I is easily here supposed to stand also for the same person.* But if it be possible for the same man to have distinct incommunicable consciousness at dif- ferent times, it is past doubt the same man would at different times make different persons; which, we see, is the sense of mankind in the solemnest declaration of their opinions, human laws not punishing the mad man for the sober man's actions, nor the sober man for what the mad man did—thereby making them two persons: which is some- what explained by our way of speaking in English when we say such an one is "not himself," or is "beside himself"; in which phrases it is insinuated, as if those who now, or at least first used them, thought that self was changed; the selfsame person was no longer in that man.

But yet it is hard to conceive that Socrates, the same individual man, should be two persons. *To help us a little in this, we must con- sider what is meant by Socrates, or the same individual man.*

First, it must be either the same individual, immaterial, think- ing substance; in short, the same numerical soul, and nothing else.

Secondly, or the same animal, without any regard to an im- material soul.

Thirdly, or the same immaterial spirit united to the same animal.

Now, take which of these suppositions you please, it is impossi- ble to make personal identity to consist in anything but conscious- ness; or reach any further than that does.

For, by the first of them, it must be allowed possible that a man born of different women, and in distant times, may be the same man. A way of speaking which, whoever admits, must allow it possible for the same man to be two distinct persons, as any two that have lived in different ages without the knowledge of one another's thoughts.

By the second and third, Socrates, in this life and after it, can- not be the same man any way, but by the same consciousness; and so making human identity to consist in the same thing wherein we place personal identity, there will be no difficulty to allow the same man to be the same person. But then they who place human identity in consciousness only, and not in something else, must consider how they will make the infant Socrates the same man with Socrates after the resurrection. But whatsoever to some men makes a man, and consequently the same individual man, wherein perhaps few are agreed, personal identity can by us be placed in nothing but consciousness (which is that alone which makes what we call *self*), without involving us in great absurdities.

But is not a man drunk and sober the same person? why else is he punished for the fact he commits when drunk, though he be never afterwards conscious of it? Just as much the same person as a man that walks, and does other things in his sleep, is the same person, and is answerable for any mischief he shall do in it. *Human laws punish both, with a justice suitable to their way of knowledge;—because, in these cases, they cannot distinguish certainly what is real, what counterfeit: and so the ignorance in drunkenness or sleep is not admitted as a plea. . . .*

. . . This every intelligent being, sensible of happiness or misery, must grant—that there is something that is *himself*, that he is concerned for, and would have happy; that this self has existed in a continued duration more than one instant, and therefore it is possible may exist, as it has done, months and years to come, without any certain bounds to be set to its duration; and may be the same self, by the same consciousness continued on for the future. And thus, by this consciousness he finds himself to be the same self which did such and such an action some years since, by which he comes to be happy or miserable now. In all which account of self, the same numerical *substance* is not considered as making the same self; but the same continued *consciousness*, in which several substances may have been united, and again separated from it, which, whilst they continued in a vital union with that wherein this consciousness then resided, made a part of that same self. Thus any part of our bodies, vitally united to that which is conscious in us, makes a part of ourselves: but upon separation from the vital union by which that consciousness is communicated, that which a moment since was part of ourselves, is now no more so than a part of another man's self is a part of me: and it is not impossible but in a little time may become a real part of another person. And so we have the same numerical substance become a part of two different persons; and the same person preserved under the change of various substances. Could we suppose any spirit wholly stripped of all its memory or consciousness of past actions as we find our minds always are of a great part of ours, and sometimes of them all; the union or separation of such a spiritual substance would make no variation of personal identity, any more than that of any particle of matter does. Any substance vitally united to the present thinking being is a part of that very same self which now is; anything united to it by a consciousness of former actions, makes also a part of the same self, which is the same both then and now.

Person, as I take it, is the name for this self. Wherever a man finds what he calls himself, there, I think, another may say is the same person. *It is a forensic term, appropriating actions and their merit; and so belongs only to intelligent agents, capable of a law, and happiness, and misery.* This personality extends itself beyond present existence to what is past, only by consciousness—whereby it becomes concerned and accountable; owns and imputes to itself past actions, just upon the same ground and for the same reason as it does the present. All which is founded in a concern for happiness, the unavoidable concomitant of consciousness; that which is conscious of pleasure and pain, desiring that that self that is conscious should be happy. And therefore whatever past actions it cannot reconcile or *appropriate* to that present self by consciousness, it can be no more concerned in than if they had never been done: and to receive pleasure or pain, i.e., reward or punishment, on the account of any such action, is all one as to be made happy or miserable in its first being, without any demerit at all. For, supposing a *man* punished now for what he had done in another life, whereof he could be made to have no consciousness at all, what difference is there between that punishment and being *created* miserable?

LOCKE SELECTION

1.   Exactly what is the difference, for Locke, between the ideas of *substance,* of *man* (or human being), and of *person?* To which of these does Locke attach the notion of *self?*

2.   Using such examples as "the same tree," "the same hammer," "the same ocean," and "the same dog," try to explain what Locke thinks we mean when we say that something is *the same thing* from one time to another.

3.   If consciousness and memory are essential to personal identity, as Locke claims, then what happens to me when I fall asleep, or get knocked unconscious? Do I, *as a person,* cease to exist during those times?

4.   As we grow older, we tend to forget much of what has happened to us. Are those things that I have forgotten no longer a part of me, of my self, according to Locke? If you remember what happened to me years ago, while I have forgotten, do those events become a part of *your* self? Why?

5.   If I have totally forgotten committing a crime, can I plead not

guilty on the grounds that my *self* did not commit it? If I commit a crime and then deliberately take a drug that makes me forget all about the event, can I plead not guilty on the same grounds?

6. Does memory have to be accurate in order to serve as the basis for the unity of the self? If we created a full-grown human being and filled her brain with the nerve patterns that correspond to memories, would that person have a memory? Would she have a past? Why not?

(SELECTION 3)

GEORGE HERBERT MEAD

The Social Origins
of the Self

George Herbert Mead is one of a number of important students of personality and society who lived and worked in Chicago during the first part of this century. Although he is not usually classified as a philosopher, his analysis of the nature, origins, and development of the self poses a number of important questions for philosophers interested in the problem of self-identity and the nature of persons.

Mead accepts Descartes's identification of thinking as a defining mark of the self, and he accepts also the central importance of self-awareness or self-consciousness in the analysis of personhood. But unlike all the other authors represented in this chapter, Mead concentrates his attention on the role played by social interactions among two or more persons in the development and definition of the self. Both Descartes and Locke write as though it would be perfectly possible for a self to come into existence and persist over time entirely without relation to any other selves. Descartes will not even acknowledge that the body is essential to selfhood, and Locke presumably would grant that if a machine could be found to care for an infant until it reached maturity, then an isolated person could develop and form a concep-

tion of itself *as a person* in total independence of other persons.

Mead totally denies this egoistic conception of personality. He is not interested merely in pointing out that other persons play a role in the growing up of each of us. No one would deny that obvious fact. His central point is that a self can form a conception of itself only through identifying other selves and then coming to view itself from their standpoint. Self-reflection or the self's awareness of itself is an essentially *social* product. I first think of myself as a person by becoming aware of the ways in which others think of me as such. What is more, that awareness develops through my patterned interactions with others, in what sociologists call "roles."

If Mead is correct, the implications of the social origins of individual personality can be very far-reaching. Contrary to what Descartes contends, it would seem to follow that I *cannot* be the only person in existence, for my conception of myself as a person presupposes the existence of others. Furthermore, Mead's analysis calls into question our natural tendency to suppose that individual persons are logically or metaphysically prior to society. Although it is obviously true that society cannot exist without individual selves to make it up, perhaps it is also true that individual selves—persons, self-conscious "I's"—cannot exist without a society in which they develop and become aware of themselves as persons.

In the last portion of this selection, Mead poses some puzzling questions about the relationships between the two different ways in which each of us thinks about himself or herself: from the "inside," as the I, the speaker, the author of actions, the subject or thinker of thoughts; and from the "outside," as Me, a person like others in the field of experience and social interaction, about whom one can make predictions, collect observations, form generalizations, and whom one can conceive as an object of investigation.

We can distinguish very definitely between the self and the body. The body can be there and can operate in a very intelligent fashion without there being a self involved in the experience. The self has the characteristic that it is an object to itself, and that characteristic distinguishes it from other objects and from the body. It is perfectly true that the eye can see the foot, but it does not see the body as a whole. We cannot see our backs; we can feel certain portions of them, if we are agile, but we cannot get an experience of our whole body. There are, of course, experiences which are somewhat vague and difficult of location, but the bodily experiences are for us organized about a self. The foot and hand belong to the self. We can see our feet, especially if we look at them from the wrong end of an opera glass, as strange things which we have difficulty in recognizing as our own. The parts of the body are quite distinguishable from the self. We can lose parts of the body without any serious invasion of the self. The mere ability to experience different parts of the body is not different from the experience of a table. The table presents a different feel from what the hand does when one hand feels another, but it is an experience of something with which we come definitely into contact. The body does not experience itself as a whole, in the sense in which the self in some way enters into the experience of the self.

It is the characteristic of the self as an object to itself that I want to bring out. This characteristic is represented in the word "self," which is a reflexive, and indicates that which can be both subject and object. This type of object is essentially different from other objects, and in the past it has been distinguished as conscious, a term which indicates an experience with, an experience of, one's self. It was assumed that consciousness in some way carried this capacity of being an object to itself. In giving a behavioristic statement of consciousness

From *Mind, Self, and Society* by George Herbert Mead. First published in 1934. (Reprinted from *Mind, Self, and Society* by George Herbert Mead by permission of The University of Chicago Press. Chicago, Illinois: The University of Chicago Press, 1934.)

we have to look for some sort of experience in which the physical organism can become an object to itself. . . .[1]

. . . How can an individual get outside himself (experientially) in such a way as to become an object to himself? This is the essential psychological problem of selfhood or of self-consciousness; and its solution is to be found by referring to the process of social conduct or activity in which the given person or individual is implicated. . . .

The individual experiences himself as such, not directly, but only indirectly, from the particular standpoints of other individual members of the same social group, or from the generalized standpoint of the social group as a whole to which he belongs. For he enters his own experience as a self or individual, not directly or immediately, not by becoming a subject to himself, but only in so far as he first becomes an object to himself just as other individuals are objects to him in his experience; and he becomes an object to himself only by taking the attitudes of other individuals toward himself within a social environment or context of experience and behavior in which both he and they are involved. . . .

The self, as that which can be an object to itself, is essentially a social structure, and it arises in social experience. After a self has arisen, it in a certain sense provides for itself its social experiences, and so we can conceive of an absolutely solitary self. But it is impossible to conceive of a self arising outside of social experience. When it has arisen we can think of a person in solitary confinement for the rest of his life, but who still has himself as a companion, and is able to think and to converse with himself as he had communicated with others. The process to which I have just referred, of responding to one's self as another responds to it, taking part in one's own conversation with others, being aware of what one is saying and using that awareness of what one is saying to determine what one is going to say thereafter—that is a process with which we are all familiar. We are continually following up our own address to other persons by an understanding of what we are saying, and using that understanding in the direction of our continued speech. We are finding out what we are going to say, what we are going to do, by saying and doing, and in the process we are continually controlling the process itself. In the conversation of gestures what we say calls out a certain response in another and that in turn changes our own action, so that we shift from what we started to do because of the reply the other

[1] Man's behavior is such in his social group that he is able to become an object to himself, a fact which constitutes him a more advanced product of evolutionary development than are the lower animals. Fundamentally it is this social fact—and not his alleged possession of a soul or mind with which he, as an individual, has been mysteriously and supernaturally endowed, and with which the lower animals have not been endowed—that differentiates him from them.

makes. The conversation of gestures is the beginning of communication. The individual comes to carry on a conversion of gestures with himself. He says something, and that calls out a certain reply in himself which makes him change what he was going to say. One starts to say something, we will presume an unpleasant something, but when he starts to say it he realizes it is cruel. The effect on himself of what he is saying checks him; there is here a conversation of gestures between the individual and himself. We mean by significant speech that the action is one that affects the individual himself, and that the effect upon the individual himself is part of the intelligent carrying-out of the conversation with others. Now we, so to speak, amputate that social phase and dispense with it for the time being, so that one is talking to one's self as one would talk to another person.

This process of abstraction cannot be carried on indefinitely. One inevitably seeks an audience, has to pour himself out to somebody. In reflective intelligence one thinks to act, and to act solely so that this action remains a part of a social process. Thinking becomes preparatory to social action. The very process of thinking is, of course, simply an inner conversation that goes on, but it is a conversation of gestures which in its completion implies the expression of that which one thinks to an audience. One separates the significance of what he is saying to others from the actual speech and gets it ready before saying it. He thinks it out, and perhaps writes it in the form of a book; but it is still a part of social intercourse in which one is addressing other persons and at the same time addressing one's self, and in which one controls the address to other persons by the response made to one's own gesture. That the person should be responding to himself is necessary to the self, and it is this sort of social conduct which provides behavior within which that self appears. I know of no other form of behavior than the linguistic in which the individual is an object to himself, and, so far as I can see, the individual is not a self in the reflexive sense unless he is an object to himself. It is this fact that gives a critical importance to communication, since this is a type of behavior in which the individual does so respond to himself. . . .

We were speaking of the social conditions under which the self arises as an object. In addition to language we found two illustrations, one in play and the other in the game, and I wish to summarize and expand my account on these points. I have spoken of these from the point of view of children. We can, of course, refer also to the attitudes of more primitive people out of which our civilization has arisen. A striking illustration of play as distinct from the game is found in the myths and various of the plays which primitive people carry out, especially in religious pageants. The pure play attitude which we find in the case of little children may not be found here, since the participants are adults, and undoubtedly the relationship of these play processes to that which they interpret is more or less in the minds of even the most primitive people. In the process of interpretation of such rituals, there is an organization of play which perhaps might be compared to that which is taking place in the kindergarten in dealing with the plays of little children, where these are made into a set that will have a definite structure or relationship. At least something of the same sort is found in the play of primitive people. This type of activity belongs, of course, not to the everyday life of the people in their dealing with the objects about them—there we have a more or less definitely developed self-consciousness—but in their attitudes toward the forces about them, the nature upon which they depend; in their attitude toward this nature which is vague and uncertain, there we have a much more primitive response; and that response finds its expression in taking the role of the other, playing at the expression of their gods and their heroes, going through certain rites which are the representation of what these individuals are supposed to be doing. The process is one which develops, to be sure, into a more or less definite technique and is controlled; and yet we can say that it has arisen out of situations similar to those in which little children play at being a parent, at being a teacher—vague personalities that are about them and which affect them and on which they depend. These are personalities which they take, roles they play, and in so far control the development of their own personality. This outcome is just what the kindergarten works toward. It takes the characters of these various beings and gets them into such an organized social relationship to each other that they build up the character of the little child. The very introduction of organization from outside supposes a lack of organization at this period in the child's experience. Over against such a situation of the little child and primitive people, we have the game as such.

The fundamental difference between the game and play is that in the latter the child must have the attitude of all the others involved in that game. The attitudes of the other players which the participant assumes organize into a sort of unit, and it is that organization which controls the response of the individual. The illustration used was of a person playing baseball. Each one of his own acts is determined by his assumption of the action of the others who are playing the game. What he does is controlled by his being everyone else on that team, at least in so far as those attitudes affect his own particular response. We get then an "other" which is an organization of the attitudes of those involved in the same process.

The organized community or social group which gives to the individual his unity of self may be called "the generalized other." The attitude of the generalized other is the attitude of the whole community. Thus, for example, in the case of such a social group as a ball team, the team is the generalized other in so far as it enters— as an organized process or social activity—into the experience of any one of the individual members of it.

If the given human individual is to develop a self in the fullest sense, it is not sufficient for him merely to take the attitudes of other human individuals toward himself and toward one another within the human social process, and to bring that social process as a whole into his individual experience merely in these terms: he must also, in the same way that he takes the attitudes of other individuals toward himself and toward one another, take their attitudes toward the various phases or aspects of the common social activity or set of social undertakings in which, as members of an organized society or social group, they are all engaged; and he must then, by generalizing these individual attitudes of that organized society or social group itself, as a whole, act toward different social projects which at any given time it is carrying out, or toward the various larger phases of the general social process which constitutes its life and of which these projects are specific manifestations. This getting of the broad activities of any given social whole or organized society as such within the experiential field of any one of the individuals involved or included in that whole is, in other words, the essential basis and prerequisite of the fullest development of that individual's self: only in so far as he takes the attitudes of the organized social group to which he belongs toward the organized, co-operative social activities or set of such activities in which that group as such is engaged, does he develop a complete self or possess the sort of complete self he has developed. And on the other hand, the complex co-operative processes and activities and institutional functionings of organized human society are also possible only in so far as every individual involved in them or belonging to that society can take the general attitudes of all other such individuals with reference to these processes and activities and institutional functionings, and to the organized social whole of experiential relations and interactions thereby constituted—and can direct his own behavior accordingly.

It is in the form of the generalized other that the social process influences the behavior of the individuals involved in it and carrying it on, i.e., that the community exercises control over the conduct of its individual members; for it is in this form that the social process or community enters as a determining factor into the individual's thinking. In abstract thought the individual takes the attitude of the generalized other toward himself, without reference to its expression in any particular other individuals; and in concrete thought he takes that attitude in so far as it is expressed in the attitudes toward his behavior of those other individuals with whom he is involved in the given social situation or act. But only by taking the attitude of the generalized other toward himself, in one or another of these ways, can he think at all; for only thus can thinking—or the internalized conversation of gestures which constitutes thinking—occur. And only through the taking by individuals of the attitude or attitudes of the generalized other toward themselves is the existence of a universe of discourse, as that system of common or social meanings which thinking presupposes at its context, rendered possible. . . .

. . . There are two general stages in the full development of the self. At the first of these stages, the individual's self is constituted simply by an organization of the particular attitudes of other individuals toward himself and toward one another in the specific social acts in which he participates with them. But at the second stage in the full development of the individual's self that self is constituted not only by an organization of these particular individual attitudes, but also by an organization of the social attitudes of the generalized other or the social group as a whole to which he belongs. These social or group attitudes are brought within the individual's field of direct experience, and are included as elements in the structure or constitution of his self, in the same way that the attitudes of particular other individuals are; and the individual arrives at them, or succeeds in taking them, by means of further organizing, and then generalizing, the attitudes of particular other individuals in terms of their organized social bearings and implications. So the self reaches its full development by organizing these individual attitudes of others into the organized social or group attitudes, and by thus becoming an individual reflection of the general systematic pattern of social or group behavior in which it and the others are all involved—a pattern which enters as a whole into the individual's experience in terms of these organized group attitudes which, through the mechanism of his central nervous system, he takes toward himself, just as he takes the individual attitudes of others. . . .

The process out of which the self arises is a social process which implies interaction of individuals in the group, implies the preexistence of the group.[2] It implies also certain co-operative activities in which the different members of the group are involved. It implies, further, that out of this process there may in turn develop a

[2] The relation of individual organisms to the social whole of which they are members is analogous to the relationship of the individual cells of a multi-cellular organism to the organism as a whole.

more elaborate organization than that out of which the self has arisen, and that the selves may be the organs, the essential parts at least, of this more elaborate social organization within which these selves arise and exist. Thus, there is a social process out of which selves arise and within which further differentiation, further evolution, further organization, take place.

It has been the tendency of psychology to deal with the self as a more or less isolated and independent element, a sort of entity that could conceivably exist by itself. It is possible that there might be a single self in the universe if we start off by identifying the self with a certain feeling-consciousness. If we speak of this feeling as objective, then we can think of that self as existing by itself. We can think of a separate physical body existing by itself, we can assume that it has these feelings or conscious states in question, and so we can set up that sort of a self in thought as existing simply by itself.

Then there is another use of "consciousness" with which we have been particularly occupied, denoting that which we term thinking or reflective intelligence, a use of consciousness which always has, implicitly at least, the reference to an "I" in it. This use of consciousness has no necessary connection with the other; it is an entirely different conception. One usage has to do with a certain mechanism, a certain way in which an organism acts. If an organism is endowed with sense organs then there are objects in its environment, and among those objects will be parts of its own body. It is true that if the organism did not have a retina and a central nervous system there would not be any objects of vision. For such objects to exist there have to be certain physiological conditions, but these objects are not in themselves necessarily related to a self. When we reach a self we reach a certain sort of conduct, a certain type of social process which involves the interaction of different individuals and yet implies individuals engaged in some sort of co-operative activity. In that process a self, as such, can arise.

We want to distinguish the self as a certain sort of structural process in the conduct of the form, from what we term consciousness of objects that are experienced. The two have no necessary relationship. The aching tooth is a very important element. We have to pay attention to it. It is identified in a certain sense with the self in order that we may control that sort of experience. Occasionally we have experiences which we say belong to the atmosphere. The whole world seems to be depressed, the sky is dark, the weather is unpleasant, values that we are interested in are sinking. We do not necessarily identify such a situation with the self; we simply feel a certain atmosphere about us. We come to remember that we are subject to such sorts of depression, and find that kind of an experience in our past. And then we get some sort of relief, we take aspirin, or we take a rest, and the result is that the world changes its character. There are other experiences which we may at all times identify with selves. We can distinguish, I think, very clearly between certain types of experience, which we call subjective because we alone have access to them, and that experience which we call reflective.

It is true that reflection taken by itself is something to which we alone have access. One thinks out his own demonstration of a proposition, we will say in Euclid, and the thinking is something that takes place within his own conduct. For the time being it is a demonstration which exists only in his thought. Then he publishes it and it becomes common property. For the time being it was accessible only to him. There are other contents of this sort, such as memory images and the play of the imagination, which are accessible only to the individual. There is a common character that belongs to these types of objects which we generally identify with consciousness and this process which we call that of thinking, in that both are, at least in certain phases, accessible only to the individual. But, as I have said, the two sets of phenomena stand on entirely different levels. This common feature of accessibility does not necessarily give them the same metaphysical status. I do not now want to discuss metaphysical problems, but I do want to insist that the self has a sort of structure that arises in social conduct that is entirely distinguishable from this so-called subjective experience of these particular sets of objects to which the organism alone has access—the common character of privacy of access does not fuse them together.

The self to which we have been referring arises when the conversation of gestures is taken over into the conduct of the individual form. When this conversation of gestures can be taken over into the individual's conduct so that the attitude of the other forms can affect the organism, and the organism can reply with its corresponding gesture and thus arouse the attitude of the other in its own process, then a self arises. Even the bare conversation of gestures that can be carried out in lower forms is to be explained by the fact that this conversation of gestures has an intelligent function. Even there it is a part of social process. If it is taken over into the conduct of the individual it not only maintains that function but acquires still greater capacity. If I can take the attitude of a friend with whom I am going to carry on a discussion, in taking that attitude I can apply it to myself and reply as he replies, and I can have things in very much better shape than if I had not employed that conversation of gestures in my own conduct. The same is true of him. It is good for both to think out the situation in advance. Each individual has to take also the attitude of the community, the generalized attitude. He has to be ready to act with reference to his own conditions just as any individual in the community would act.

One of the greatest advances in the development of the community arises when this reaction of the community on the individual takes on what we call an institutional form. What we mean by that is that the whole community acts toward the individual under certain circumstances in an identical way. It makes no difference, over against a person who is stealing your property, whether it is Tom, Dick, or Harry. There is an identical response on the part of the whole community under these conditions. We call that the formation of the institution.

There is one other matter which I wish briefly to refer to now. The only way in which we can react against the disapproval of the entire community is by setting up a higher sort of community which in a certain sense out-votes the one we find. A person may reach a point of going against the whole world about him; he may stand out by himself over against it. But to do that he has to speak with the voice of reason to himself. He has to comprehend the voices of the past and of the future. That is the only way in which the self can get a voice which is more than the voice of the community. As a rule we assume that this general voice of the community is identical with the larger community of the past and the future; we assume that an organized custom represents what we call morality. The things one cannot do are those which everybody would condemn. If we take the attitude of the community over against our own responses, that is a true statement, but we must not forget this other capacity, that of replying to the community and insisting on the gesture of the community changing. We can reform the order of things; we can insist on making the community standards better standards. We are not simply bound by the community. We are engaged in a conversation in which what we say is listened to by the community and its response is one which is affected by what we have to say. This is especially true in critical situations. A man rises up and defends himself for what he does; he has his "day in court"; he can present his view. He can perhaps change the attitude of the community toward himself. The process of conversation is one in which the individual has not only the right but the duty of talking to the community of which he is a part, and bringing about those changes which take place through the interaction of individuals. That is the way, of course, in which society gets ahead, by just such interactions as those in which some person thinks a thing out. We are continually changing our social system in some respects, and we are able to do that intelligently because we can think.

Such is the reflective process within which a self arises; and what

I have been trying to do is to distinguish this kind of consciousness from consciousness as a set of characters determined by the accessibility to the organism of certain sorts of objects. It is true that our thinking is also, while it is just thinking, accessible only to the organism. But that common character of being accessible only to the organism does not make either thought or the self something which we are to identify with a group of objects which simply are accessible. We cannot identify the self with what is commonly called consciousness, that is, with the private or subjective thereness of the characters of objects.

There is, of course, a current distinction between consciousness and self-consciousness: consciousness answering to certain experiences such as those of pain or pleasure, self-consciousness referring to a recognition or appearance of a self as an object. It is, however, very generally assumed that these other conscious contents carry with them also a self-consciousness—that a pain is always somebody's pain, and that if there were not this reference to some individual it would not be pain. There is a very definite element of truth in this, but it is far from the whole story. The pain does have to belong to an individual; it has to be your pain if it is going to belong to you. Pain can belong to anybody, but if it did belong to everybody it would be comparatively unimportant. I suppose it is conceivable that under an anesthetic what takes place is the dissociation of experiences so that the suffering, so to speak, is no longer your suffering. We have illustrations of that, short of the anesthetic dissociation, in an experience of a disagreeable thing which loses its power over us because we give our attention to something else. If we can get, so to speak, outside of the thing, dissociating it from the eye that is regarding it, we may find that it has lost a great deal of its unendurable character. The unendurableness of pain is a reaction against it. If you can actually keep yourself from reacting against suffering you get rid of a certain content in the suffering itself. What takes place in effect is that it ceases to be your pain. You simply regard it objectively. Such is the point of view we are continually impressing on a person when he is apt to be swept away by emotion. In that case what we get rid of is not the offense itself, but the reaction against the offense. The objective character of the judge is that of a person who is neutral, who can simply stand outside of a situation and assess it. If we can get that judicial attitude in regard to the offenses of a person against ourselves, we reach the point where we do not resent them but understand them, we get the situation where to understand is to forgive. We remove much of experience outside of our own self by this attitude. The distinctive and natural attitude against another is a resentment of an offense, but we now have in a certain sense passed beyond that self and become a self with other attitudes. There is a certain technique, then, to which we subject ourselves in enduring suffering or any emotional situation, and which consists in partially separating one's self from the experience so that it is no longer the experience of the individual in question.

If, now, we could separate the experience entirely, so that we should not remember it, so that we should not have to take it up continually into the self from day to day, from moment to moment, then it would not exist any longer so far as we are concerned. If we had no memory which identifies experiences with the self, then they would certainly disappear so far as their relation to the self is concerned, and yet they might continue as sensuous or sensible experiences without being taken up into a self. That sort of a situation is presented in the pathological case of a multiple personality in which an individual loses the memory of a certain phase of his existence. Everything connected with that phase of his existence is gone and he becomes a different personality. The past has a reality whether in the experience or not, but here it is not identified with the self—it does not go to make up the self. We take an attitude of that sort, for example, with reference to others when a person has committed some sort of an offense which leads to a statement of the situation, an admission, and perhaps regret, and then is dropped. A person who forgives but does not forget is an unpleasant companion; what goes with forgiving is forgetting, getting rid of the memory of it.

There are many illustrations which can be brought up of the loose relationship of given contents to a self in defense of our recognition of them as having a certain value outside of the self. At the least, it must be granted that we can approach the point where something which we recognize as a content is less and less essential to the self, is held off from the present self, and no longer has the value for that self which it had for the former self. Extreme cases seem to support the view that a certain portion of such contents can be entirely cut off from the self. While in some sense it is there ready to appear under specific conditions, for the time being it is dissociated and does not get in above the threshold of our self-consciousness.

Self-consciousness, on the other hand, is definitely organized about the social individual, and that, as we have seen, is not simply because one is in a social group and affected by others and affects them, but because (and this is a point I have been emphasizing) his own experience as a self is one which he takes over from his action upon others. He becomes a self in so far as he can take the attitude of another and act toward himself as others act. In so far as the conversation of gestures can become part of conduct in the direction and control of experience, then a self can arise. It is the social process of influencing others in a social act and then taking the attitude of the others aroused by the stimulus, and then reacting in turn to this response, which constitutes a self.

Our bodies are parts of our environment; and it is possible for the individual to experience and be conscious of his body, and of bodily sensations, without being conscious or aware of himself—without, in other words, taking the attitude of the other toward himself. According to the social theory of consciousness, what we mean by consciousness is that peculiar character and aspect of the environment of individual human experience which is due to human society, a society of other individual selves who take the attitude of the other toward themselves. The physiological conception or theory of consciousness is by itself inadequate; it requires supplementation from the socio-psychological point of view. The taking or feeling of the attitude of the other toward yourself is what constitutes self-consciousness, and not mere organic sensations of which the individual is aware and which he experiences. Until the rise of his self-consciousness in the process of social experience, the individual experiences his body—its feelings and sensations—merely as an immediate part of his environment, not as his own, not in terms of self-consciousness. The self and self-consciousness have first to arise, and then these experiences can be identified peculiarly with the self, or appropriated to the self; to enter, so to speak, into this heritage of experience, the self has first to develop within the social process in which this heritage is involved.

Through self-consciousness the individual organism enters in some sense into its own environment field; its own body becomes a part of the set of environment stimuli to which it responds or reacts. Apart from the context of the social process at its higher levels—those at which it involves conscious communication, conscious conversations of gestures, among the individual organisms interacting with it—the individual organism does not set itself as a whole over against its environment; it does not as a whole become an object to itself (and hence is not self-conscious); it is not as a whole a stimulus to which it reacts. On the contrary, it responds only to parts or separate aspects of itself, and regards them, not as parts or aspects of itself at all, but simply as parts or aspects of its environment in general. Only within the social process at its higher levels, only in terms of the more developed forms of the social environment or social situation, does the total individual organism become an object to itself, and hence self-consciousness; in the social process at its lower, non-conscious levels, and also in the merely pycho-physiological environment or situation which is logically antecedent to and presupposed by the social process of experience and behavior, it does not thus become an object to itself. In such experience or behavior as may be called self-conscious, we act and react particularly with reference to ourselves, though also with reference to other individuals; and to be self-conscious is essentially to become an object to one's self in virtue of one's social relations to other individuals.

Emphasis should be laid on the central position of thinking when considering the nature of the self. Self-consciousness, rather than affective experience with its motor accompaniments, provides the core and primary structure of the self, which is thus essentially a cognitive rather than an emotional phenomenon. The thinking or intellectual process—the internalization and inner dramatization, by the individual, of the external conversation of significant gestures which constitutes his chief mode of interaction with other individuals belonging to the same society—is the earliest experiential phase in the genesis and development of the self. Cooley and James, it is true, endeavor to find the basis of the self in reflexive affective experiences, i.e., experiences involving "self-feeling"; but the theory that the nature of the self is to be found in such experiences does not account for the origin of the self, or of the self-feeling which is supposed to characterize such experiences. The individual need not take the attitudes of others toward himself in these experiences, since these experiences merely in themselves do not necessitate his doing so, and unless he does so, he cannot develop a self; and he will not do so in these experiences unless his self has already originated otherwise, namely, in the way we have been describing. The essence of the self, as we have said, is cognitive: it lies in the internalized conversation of gestures which constitutes thinking, or in terms of which thought or reflection proceeds. And hence the origin and foundations of the self, like those of thinking, are social.

We have discussed at length the social foundations of the self, and hinted that the self does not consist simply in the bare organization of social attitudes. We may now explicitly raise the question as the the nature of the "I" which is aware of the social "me." I do not mean to raise the metaphysical question of how a person can be both "I" and "me," but to ask for the significance of this distinction from the point of view of conduct itself. Where in conduct does the "I" come in as over against the "me"? If one determines what his position is in society and feels himself as having a certain function and privilege, these are all defined with reference to an "I," but the "I" is not a "me" and cannot become a "me." We may have a better self and a worse self, but that again is not the "I" as over against the "me," because they are both selves. We approve of one and disapprove of the other, but when we bring up one or the other they are there for such approval as "me's." The "I" does not get into the lime-light; we talk to ourselves, but do not see ourselves. The "I" reacts to the self which arises through the taking of the attitudes of others. Through taking those attitudes we have introduced the "me" and we react to it as an "I."

The simplest way of handling the problem would be in terms of memory. I talk to myself, and I remember what I said and perhaps the emotional content that went with it. The "I" of this moment is present in the "me" of the next moment. There again I cannot turn around quick enough to catch myself. I become a "me" in so far as I remember what I said. The "I" can be given, however, this functional relationship. It is because of the "I" that we say that we are never fully aware of what we are, that we surprise ourselves by our own action. It is as we act that we are aware of ourselves. It is in memory that the "I" is constantly present in experience. We can go back directly a few moments in our experience, and then we are de-pendent upon memory images for the rest. So that the "I" in memory is there as the spokesmen of the self of the second, or minute, or day ago. As given, it is a "me," but it is a "me" which was the "I" at the earlier time. If you ask, then, where directly in your own ex-perience the "I" comes in, the answer is that it comes in as a historical figure. It is what you were a second ago that is the "I" of the "me." It is another "me" that has to take that role. You cannot get the imme-diate response of the "I" in the process. The "I" is in a certain sense that with which we do identify ourselves. The getting of it into ex-perience constitutes one of the problems of most of our conscious experience; it is not directly given in experience.

The "I" is the response of the organism to the attitudes of the others; the "me" is the organized set of attitudes of others which one himself assumes. The attitude of the others constitute the organized "me," and then one reacts toward that as an "I." I now wish to examine these concepts in greater detail.

There is neither "I" nor "me" in the conversation of gestures; the whole act is not yet carried out, but the preparation takes place in this field of gesture. Now, in so far as the individual arouses in himself the attitudes of the others, there arises an organized group of responses. And it is due to the individual's ability to take the atti-tudes of these others in so far as they can be organized that he gets self-consciousness. The taking of all of those organized sets of atti-tudes gives him his "me"; that is the self he is aware of. He can throw the ball to some other member because of the demand made upon him from other members of the team. That is the self that imme-diately exists for him in his consciousness. He has their attitudes, knows what they want and what the consequence of any act of his will be, and he has assumed responsibility for the situation. Now, it is the presence of those organized sets of attitudes that constitutes that "me" to which he as an "I" is responding. But what that response will be he does not know and nobody else knows. Perhaps he will make a brilliant play or an error. The response to that situation as it appears in his immediate experience is uncertain, and it is that which constitutes the "I."

The "I" is his action over against that social situation within his own conduct, and it gets into his experience only after he has carried out the act. Then he is aware of it. He had to do such a thing and he did it. He fulfills his duty and he may look with pride at the throw which he made. The "me" arises to do that duty—that is the way in which it arises in his experience. He had in him all the attitudes of others, calling for a certain response; that was the "me" of that situation, and his response is the "I."

I want to call attention particularly to the fact that this response of the "I" is something that is more or less uncertain. The attitudes of others which one assumes as affecting his own conduct constitute the "me," and that is something that is there, but the response to it is as yet not given. When one sits down to think anything out, he has certain data that are there. Suppose that it is a social situation, which he has to straighten out. He sees himself from the point of view of one individual or another in the group. These individuals, related all together, give him a certain self. Well, what is he going to do? He does not know and nobody else knows. He can get the situation into his experience because he can assume the attitudes of the various individuals involved in it. He knows how they feel about it by the assumption of their attitudes. He says, in effect, "I have done certain things that seem to commit me to a certain course of conduct." Perhaps if he does so act it will place him in a false position with another group. The "I" as a response to this situation, in contrast to the "me" which is involved in the attitudes which he takes, is uncertain. And when the response takes place, then it appears in the field of experience largely as a memory image.

Our specious present as such is very short. We do, however, experience passing events; part of the process of the passage of events is directly there in our experience, including some of the past and and some of the future. We see a ball falling as it passes, and as it does pass part of the ball is covered and part is being uncovered. We remember where the ball was a moment ago and we anticipate where it will be beyond what is given in our experience. So of ourselves; we are doing something, but to look back and see what we are doing involves getting memory images. So the "I" really appears experientially as a part of a "me." But on the basis of this experience we distinguish that individual who is doing something from the "me" who puts the problem up to him. The response enters into his experience only when it takes place. If he says he knows what he is going to do, even there he may be mistaken. He starts out to do something and something happens to interfere. The resulting action is always a little different from anything which he could anticipate. This is true even if he is simply carrying out the process of walking. The very taking of his expected steps puts him in a certain situation which has a slightly different aspect from what is expected, which is in a certain sense novel. That movement into the future is the step, so to speak, of the ego, of the "I." It is something that is not given in the "me."

Take the situation of a scientist solving a problem, where he has certain data which call for certain responses. Some of this set of data call for his applying such and such a law, while others call for another law. Data are there with their implications. He knows what such and such coloration means, and when he has these data before him they stand for certain responses on his part; but now they are in conflict with each other. If he makes one response he cannot make another. What he is going to do he does not know, nor does anybody else. The action of the self is in response to these conflicting sets of data in the form of a problem, with conflicting demands upon him as a scientist. He has to look at it in different ways. That action of the "I" is something the nature of which we cannot tell in advance.

The "I" then, in this relation of the "I" and the "me," is something that is, so to speak, responding to a social situation which is within the experience of the individual. It is the answer which the individual makes to the attitude which others take toward him when he assumes an attitude toward them. Now, the attitudes he is taking toward them are present in his own experience, but his response to them will contain a novel element. The "I" gives the sense of freedom, of initiative. The situation is there for us to act in a self-conscious fashion. We are aware of ourselves, and of what the situation is, but exactly how we will act never gets into experience until after the action takes place.

Such is the basis for the fact that the "I" does not appear in the same sense in experience as does the "me." The "me" represents a definite organization of the community there in our own attitudes, and calling for a response, but the response that takes place is something that just happens. There is no certainty in regard to it. There is a moral necessity but no mechanical necessity for the act. When it does take place then we find what has been done. The above account gives us, I think, the relative position of the "I" and "me" in the situation, and the grounds for the separation of the two in behavior.

The two are separated in the process but they belong together in the sense of being parts of a whole. They are separated and yet they belong together. The separation of the "I" and the "me" is not fictitious. They are not identical, for, as I have said, the "I" is something that is never entirely calculable. The "me" does call for a certain sort of an "I" in so far as we meet the obligations that are given in conduct itself, but the "I" is always something different from what the situation itself calls for. So there is always that distinction, if you like, between the "I" and the "me." The "I" both calls out the "me" and responds to it. Taken together they constitute a personality as it appears in social experience. The self is essentially a social process going on with these two distinguishable phases. If it did not have these two phases there could not be conscious responsibility, and there would be nothing novel in experience.

MEAD SELECTION

1. According to Mead, the self comes into existence as the consequence of interactions among persons. Does that mean that there could never be just *one person* in the world? What if a disaster killed all but one person? Would that last survivor cease to be a person?

2. If Mead is correct, what would happen to a baby who was raised by automatic machines without any human interaction at all?

3. In what sense, exactly, can the self be both subject and object? Subject and object of what? What is the difference between thinking of yourself as subject and thinking of yourself as object?

4. What is it, according to Mead, about my interactions with other persons that enables me to form a conception of *myself*? What do you suppose would happen if the people around me deliberately responded to me in irregular, haphazard, totally unpredictable ways?

5. Am I anything at all over and above the sum of the social roles I have adopted? Once I become aware of the role of others and of society in the formation of my own self, can I then reject their influence and free myself from the influence of society? How? Do you think Mead believes we can do so?

(SELECTION 4)

B. A. O. WILLIAMS

Personal Identity
and
Bodily Identity

In this essay, the contemporary English philosopher Bernard Williams challenges the claims by Descartes, Locke, and others that the notion of personal identity can be satisfactorily explicated without appeal to some notion of bodily identity. In several important ways, this selection differs from the three that precede it in this chapter.

The first and most obvious point of difference is that Williams's discussion is in the form of an essay published in a learned journal, whereas the selections by Descartes, Locke, and Mead are taken from book-length works that treat a wide variety of philosophical matters. As a consequence, Williams presupposes an ongoing philosophical debate, which he scarcely troubles to summarize. As his footnote references indicate, he has in mind not only Locke's analysis, but also a number of recent interpretations and reinterpretations of Locke.

A second important difference is Williams's style of argumentation. In common with many modern British and American analytic philosophers, Williams undertakes a sort of conceptual analysis by example. He begins with a concept—in this case, the concept of personal identity—that we all use in everyday speech and that, in our nonphilosophical moods, we all suppose we

understand pretty well. By means of elaborate and imaginatively constructed hypothetical examples, Williams seeks to clarify our concept, to determine what its essential components are, and thereby either to support or to challenge the analyses given by other philosophers.

This enterprise, which is characteristic of much philosophy both traditional and modern, is quite different from the sort of investigation we might launch to answer a scientific question. Many of us are quite unclear about the nature of electricity or radio waves, even though we use radios, television sets, and electric lights every day of our lives. If we want to understand these common but puzzling phenomena we go to experts—physicists or engineers—or we undertake independent study of the relevant disciplines. For an understanding of personal identity, however, there are no experts whom we can consult. (At least, there do not *seem* to be. Some philosophers would claim that "philosophical" questions, insofar as they are genuine questions at all, *can* be answered by expert knowledge—in this case, by the knowledge of psychiatrists or social psychologists.) The conceptual and linguistic intuitions to which Williams appeals in his essay are presumably available to virtually all of

46

us. One of the oldest and most fundamental issues of philosophy is precisely
whether this feature of philosophical
questions shows that they are pseudo-

questions, or nonquestions, or genuine
questions leading to a special kind of
knowledge.

There is a special problem about personal identity for two reasons.
The first is self-consciousness—the fact that there seems to be a peculiar sense in which a man is conscious of his own identity. This I shall
consider in Section 3 of this paper. The second reason is that a question of personal identity is evidently not answered merely by deciding
the identity of a certain physical body. If I am asked whether the
person in front of me is the same person as one uniquely present at
place *a* at time *t,* I shall not necessarily be justified in answering "yes"
merely because I am justified in saying that this human body is the
same as that present at *a* at *t.* Identity of body is at least not a sufficient condition of personal identity, and other considerations of
personal characteristics and, above all, memory, must be invoked.

Some have held, further, that bodily identity is not a necessary
condition of personal identity. This, however, is ambiguous, and
yields either a weak or a strong thesis, depending on one's view of
the necessity and sufficiency of the other conditions. The weaker
thesis asserts merely that at least one case can be consistently constructed in which bodily identity fails, but in which the other conditions will be sufficient for an assertion of personal identity; even
though there may be some other imaginable case in which, some
other condition failing, bodily identity *is* a necessary condition of
personal identity. The stronger thesis asserts that there is no conceivable situation in which bodily identity would be necessary, some
other conditions being always both necessary and sufficient. I take it
that Locke's theory [1] is an example of this latter type.

I shall try to show that bodily identity is always a necessary condition of personal identity, and hence that both theses fail. In this
connexion I shall discuss in detail a case apparently favourable to the
weaker thesis (Section 1). I shall also be concerned with the stronger
thesis, or rather with something that follows from it—the idea that
we can give a sense to the concept of *a particular personality* without
reference to a body. This I shall consider chiefly in Section 4, where
the individuation of personalities will be discussed; the notion occurs, however, at various other places in the paper. The criterion of
bodily identity itself I take for granted. I assume that it includes the

---

[1] *Essay Concerning Human Understanding,* II, 27.

From "Personal Identity and Individuation" by Bernard Williams. First published in
Proceedings of The Aristotelian Society in 1957; also reprinted in "Problems of the
Self" by Bernard Williams (Cambridge U.P., 1973).

notion of spatio-temporal continuity, however that notion is to be explained. . . .

1. *Deciding another's identity.* Suppose someone undergoes a sudden and violent change of character. Formerly quiet, deferential, church-going and home-loving, he wakes up one morning and has become, and continues to be, loudmouthed, blasphemous and bullying. Here we might ask the question

    (*a*) Is he the same person as he used to be?

There seem to be two troubles with the formulation of this question, at least as an *identity* question. The first is a doubt about the reference of the second 'he' if asked the question "as *who* used to be?" we may well want to say "this person," which answers the original question (*a*) for us. This is not a serious difficulty, and we can easily avoid it by rephrasing the question in some such ways as

    (*b*) Is this person the same as the person who went to sleep
         here last night?

We do not, however, *have* to rephrase the question in any such way; we can understand (*a*) perfectly well, and avoid paradox, because our use of personal pronouns and people's names is malleable. It is a reflection of our concept of "a person" that some references to *him* cannot be understood as references to *his body* or to parts of it, and that others can; and that these two sorts of reference can readily occur in one statement ("He was embarrassed and went red.") In the case of (*a*), the continuity of reference for "he" can be supplied by the admitted continuity of reference of "his body," and the more fundamental identity question can be discussed in these terms without any serious puzzlement.

The second difficulty with (*a*) is that it is too readily translated into

    (*c*) Is he the same sort of person as he used to be? or possibly
    (*d*) Has he the same personality as he used to have?

But (*c*) and (*d*) are not identity questions in the required sense. For on any interpretation, "sort of person," and on one interpretation, "personality," are quality-terms, and we are merely asking whether the same subject now has different qualities, which is too easy to answer.

But this is only one interpretation of "personality." It corresponds interestingly to a loose sense of "identity," which is found for instance in Mr. Nigel Dennis's novel *Cards of Identity*. There "identity" is often used to mean "a set of characteristics," and "giving some an identity" means "convincing someone that he is a certain sort of person." It does not, however, only mean this; for Mr. Dennis's Identity Club do not stop at giving someone a new character —they give him a new background as well, and a local sponger is made by their persuasive methods not just into a submissive old-style butler, but into such a butler who used to be at sea and has deserted his wife.

We might feel that this was the point at which something specially uncanny was beginning to happen, and that this was the kind of anomalous example we were really looking for—the uncanniness of someone's acquiring a new past is connected with our increasing reluctance to describe the situation as one in which the same man has acquired a new set of qualities. Here we have one powerful motive for the introduction of memory. It can be put by saying that there are, or we can imagine, cases where we want to use some term like "personality" in such a way that it is not a type-expression, meaning "sets of characteristics," but is a particular term meaning something like *individual* personality. It may seem that this particularity is attained by reference to memory—the possession of a particular past. Thus we are concerned here with cases more drastic than those in which for instance people say "it has made a new man of him," or even "he is not the same person as he used to be" in the sense suggested by a change of character; these cases we can too readily redescribe. Thus we may put our question in the barbarous form

> (*e*) Is the (particular) personality he has now the same as the one he had before?

We must now see whether we can make sense, in terms of memory, of the idea of a particular personality; and whether there can be personal identity without bodily identity.

In doing this, two obvious but important features of memory have to be borne in mind.

> (I) To say "A remembers x," without irony or inverted commas, is to imply that x really happened; in this respect "remember" is parallel to "know."
>
> (II) It does not follow from this, nor is it true, that all claims to remember, any more than all claims to know, are veridical; or, not everything one seems to remember is something one really remembers.

So much is obvious, although Locke [2] was forced to invoke the providence of God to deny the latter. These points have been emphasised by Prof. A. G. N. Flew in his discussion of Locke's views on personal identity.[3] In formulating Locke's thesis, however, Prof. Flew makes a mistake; for he offers Locke's thesis in the form "if X can remember Y's doing such-and-such, then X and Y are the same person." But this obviously will not do, even for Locke, for we constantly say

[2] *Loc. cit.* §13 He is speaking, however, only of the memories of actions.
[3] *Philosophy,* 1951.

things like "I remember my brother joining the army" without implying that I and my brother are the same person. So if we are to formulate such a criterion, it looks as though we have to say something like "if X remembers doing such-and-such, then he is the person who did that thing." But since "remembers doing" means "remembers himself doing," this is trivially tautologous, and moreover lends colour to Butler's famous objection that memory, so far from constituting personal identity, presupposed it. Hence the criterion should rather run "if X claims to remember doing such-and-such. . . ." We must now ask how such a criterion might be used.

Suppose the man who underwent the radical change of character —let us call him Charles—claimed, when he woke up, to remember witnessing certain events and doing certain actions which earlier he did not claim to remember; and that under questioning he could not remember witnessing other events and doing other actions which earlier he did remember. Would this give us grounds for saying that he now was or had, in some particular sense, a different personality? An argument to show that it did gives us such grounds might be constructed on the following lines.

Any token event E, and any token action A, are by definition particulars. Moreover, the description "the man who did the action A" necessarily individuates some one person; for it is logically impossible that two persons should do the same *token* action.[4] In the case of events, it is possible that two persons should witness the same token event; but nevertheless the description "the man who witnessed E" may happen to individuate some one person, and "the man who witnessed E_1, E_2 . . . E_n" has a proportionately greater chance of so doing. Thus if our subject Charles now claims to remember doing certain actions A_1, A_2, etc., and witnessing certain events E_1, E_2, etc., which are themselves suitably identified, we have good grounds for saying that he is some particular person or has some particular personality.

Now by principle (II), we have no reason without corroborative evidence of some kind to believe Charles when he now claims to remember A or E; so we must set about checking. How are we to do this in the present case? Ordinarily if some person X claims to have witnessed E, and we wish to check this, we must find out whether

---

[4] This is to ignore the case of joint or co-operative actions. Thus when three persons A, B and C jointly fell a tree, it might be said that each of them has done the same action, that of felling the particular tree. But this would not be quite accurate. They have *all* felled the tree; what *each* of them has done is to share in the felling of the tree, or to have felled the tree with the help of the other two. When the variables implicit in this last expression are replaced with names, we obtain descriptions of token actions which indeed individuate; thus it is true of A, but not of B or C, that he is the man who felled the tree *with the help of B and C.*

there is any record, or anyone has any memory, of X's witnessing E. This is evidently inapplicable to the present case. For either the evidence shows that Charles was *bodily* present at E, or it does not. If it does, then Charles is remembering in the ordinary way, which is contrary to the hypothesis. If it does not, then there is no corroboration. Here we have a first important step. We are trying to prise apart "bodily" and "mental" criteria; but we find that the normal operation of one "mental" criterion involves the "bodily" one.

However, the situation may not be quite as desperate as this makes it appear. We can examine Charles' putative memories, and we may find that he can offer detailed information which there is no reason to believe he would ordinarily have known, and which strongly suggests the reports of an eye-witness of some particular events. What we can do with this information in the present case depends on a number of considerations. I shall now examine these, first in connexion with events, and then with actions. Events can in principle be witnessed by any number of persons, or by none. Some of the events which Charles claims to remember witnessing may be events of which we have other eye-witness accounts; others may be events which we believe to have occurred, though we do not know whether or not anyone witnessed them; others again may be events which we believe to have occurred, but which we believe no-one to have witnessed.

For all these, there is an hypothesis about—or, perhaps, description of—Charles' present condition which has nothing to do with a change of personality: the hypothesis of clairvoyance.[5] To describe Charles as clairvoyant is certainly not to advance very far towards an *explanation* of his condition; it amounts to little more than saying that he has come to know, by no means, what other people know by evidence. But so long as Charles claimed to remember events which were supposedly or certainly unwitnessed, such a description might be the best we could offer. We might do better than this, however, if the events Charles claimed to remember were witnessed; in this case we could begin to advance to the idea that Charles had a new identity, because we would have the chance of finding someone for him to be identical *with*. Thus if the events were witnessed, we might say that Charles was (now) identical with a witness of these events. This is ambiguous; it might mean that he was identical with anyone who witnessed the events, or with some particular person who witnessed the events. The former of these is no advance, since it comes to a roundabout way of saying that he claims to have witnessed the events, i.e., is possibly clairvoyant. The situation is different, how-

---

[5] Together, of course, with the loss of his real memories.

ever, if we can identify some one person who, it is plausible to suppose, witnessed all the events that Charles now claims to remember. That this should be possible is, indeed, a necessary condition of describing what has happened to Charles as *a change of identity;* I shall return to this point a little later.

If we now turn to actions, it looks as though we can find even better grounds for describing the case in terms of a change of identity. While there can be unwitnessed token events, there can be no unwitnessed token actions; moreover, as we noticed above, each token action can be performed by only one person. So if we can find out who performed the actions that Charles now claims to remember performing, it looks as if we can find out who he now is. These supposed advantages, however, are largely illusory. We may say, crudely, that there are many features of actions in which they are just like events—which, from another point of view, they indeed are. What differentiates actions from events are rather certain features of the agent, such as his intentions. In a particular case, some of these latter features may be known to, or inferred by, observers, while others may remain private to the agent. In neither case, however, do these special features of actions much help our investigation of Charles' identity. In so far as these special features may be known to observers, they are still, for the purposes of the investigation, in the class of events, and Charles' claim to remember them may still be plausibly described as clairvoyance; and in so far as these features remain private to the performer of the actions in question, we can have no ground for saying whether Charles' claims to remember them are even correct.

Again, the logical truth that a description of the form "the person who did the (token) action A" individuates some one person, does not give unfailing help. How much help it gives depends on how effectively, and by what means, we can identify the action in question. Suppose that several men at a certain time and place are each sharpening a pencil. In these circumstances the description "the man sharpening a pencil" fails to individuate: the action of sharpening a pencil is common to them all. If, however, the pencils were of different colours, I might be able to identify a particular pencil, and through this a token action of sharpening; thus "the man sharpening the red pencil" may individuate. But such methods of identifying token actions are not always available. In particular, there are some cases in which a token action can be effectively identified only through a reference to the agent. Thus if several men were all dancing the czardas, I might be able to identify a token dancing only as e.g., "*Josef's* dancing of the czardas." In such a case reference to a token action cannot help in identifying its agent, since I must identify him in order to identify it.

However, we often can effectively identify actions without actually identifying the agents, and so have a use for descriptions like "the person who murdered the Duchess, whoever it was." It is obvious that such descriptions can play a peculiarly useful role in an enquiry into identity; and this role may, for several reasons, be more useful than that played by descriptions like "the man who witnessed the event E." For, first, granted that I have identified *an action,* the description cannot fail of reference because there is no such agent; while the mere fact that I have identified a certain event E of course does not guarantee the description "the man who *witnessed* the event E" against failure of reference. Secondly, it is inherently less likely that the description referring to an action should fail of unique reference because of multiplicity, than it is that the description referring to an event should so fail. For it is in general less probable that a certain action should have been co-operatively undertaken than that a certain event should have been multiply witnessed; and, as we noticed above, for every description of a co-operative action, we can produce a series of descriptions of constituent actions which have progressively greater chance of unique reference. Last, knowledge of a particular action can give one knowledge not only of the location, but of the character, of its agent, but knowledge of a particular event will standardly give one knowledge only of the location of its witnesses.

Let us now go back to the case of Charles. We may suppose that our enquiry has turned out in the most favourable possible way, and that all the events he claims to have witnessed and all the actions he claims to have done point unanimously to the life-history of some one person in the past—for instance, Guy Fawkes. Not only do all Charles' memory-claims that can be checked fit the pattern of Fawkes' life as known to historians, but others that cannot be checked are plausible, provide explanations of unexplained facts, and so on. Are we to say that Charles is now Guy Fawkes, that Guy Fawkes has come to life again in Charles' body, or some such thing?

Certainly the temptation to say something on this pattern is very strong. It is difficult to insist that we *couldn't* say that Charles (or sometime Charles) had become Guy Fawkes; this is certainly what the newspapers would say if they heard of it. But newspapers are prone to exaggeration, and this might be an exaggeration. For why shouldn't we say that Charles had, except for his body, become just like Guy Fawkes used to be; or perhaps that Charles clairvoyantly—i.e., mysteriously—knows all about Guy Fawkes and his *ambiance?* In answer to this, it will be argued that this is just what memory was introduced to rule out; granted that we need similar personal characteristics, skills, and so on as necessary conditions of the identification, the final—and, granted these others, sufficient—condition is provided by memories of seeing just *this,* and doing just *that,* and it is these that pick out a particular man. But perhaps this point is fundamentally a logical trick. Granted that in a certain context the expressions "the man who did A," "the man who saw E," do effectively individuate, it is logically impossible that two different persons should (correctly) remember being the man who did A or saw E; but it is not logically impossible that two different persons should *claim* to remember being this man, and this is the most we can get.

This last argument is meant to show only that we are not forced to accept the description of Charles' condition as his being identical with Guy Fawkes. I shall now put forward an argument to strengthen this contention and to suggest that we should not be justified in accepting this description. If it is logically possible that Charles should undergo the changes described, then it is logically possible that some other man should simultaneously undergo the same changes; e.g., that both Charles and his brother Robert should be found in this condition. What should we say in that case? They cannot both be Guy Fawkes; if they were, Guy Fawkes would be in two places at once, which is absurd. Moreover, if they were both identical with Guy Fawkes, they would be identical with each other, which is also absurd. Hence we could not say that they were both identical with Guy Fawkes. We might instead say that one of them was identical with Guy Fawkes, and that the other was just like him; but this would be an utterly vacuous manœuvre, since there would be *ex hypothesi* no principle determining which description was to apply to which. So it would be best, if anything, to say that both had mysteriously become like Guy Fawkes, clairvoyantly knew about him, or something like this. If this would be the best description of each of the two, why would it not be the best description of Charles if Charles alone were changed?

Perhaps this last rhetorical question too readily invites an answer. It might be said that there is a relevant difference between the case in which two persons are changed and the case in which only one is changed, the difference being just this difference in numbers; and that there is no guarantee that what we would say in one of these situations would be the same as what we would say in the other. In the more complicated situation our linguistic and conceptual resources would be taxed even more severely than in the simple one, and we might not react to the demands in the same way. Moreover, there is a reason why we should not react in the same way. The standard form of an identity question is "Is this x the same x as that x which . . . ?" and in the simpler situation we are at least presented with just the materials for constructing such a question; but in the more complicated situation we are baffled even in asking the question, since both the transformed persons are equally good candidates for being its subject, and the question "Are these two x's the same (x?) as the x which . . . ?" is not a recognizable form of identity question. Thus, it might be argued, the fact that we could not speak of identity in the latter situation is no kind of proof that we could not do so in the former.

Certainly it is not a proof.[6] Yet the argument does indicate that to speak of identity in the simpler case would be at least quite vacuous. The point can be made clearer in the following way. In the case of material objects, we can draw a distinction between identity and exact similarity; it is clearly not the same to say that two men live in the same house, and that they live in exactly similar houses. This notion of identity is given to us primarily, though not completely, by the notion of spatio-temporal continuity. In the case of character, however, this distinction cannot be drawn, for to say that A and B have the same character is just to say that A's character is exactly similar to B's. Nor can this distinction be drawn in the case of memories—if you could say that two men had the same memories, this would be to say that their memories were exactly similar. There is, however, an extreme difficulty in saying these things about memories at all; it is unclear what it would mean to say that there were *two* men who had exactly similar, or the same, memories, since to call them real memories is to imply their correctness. Thus if we are to describe Charles' relations to Guy Fawkes in terms of *exact similarity* of everything except the body, we are going to have difficulty in finding a suitable description in these terms of his memory claims. We cannot say that he has the same memories as Guy Fawkes, as this is to imply, what we want to deny, that he really is Guy Fawkes; nor can we say that the memory claims he makes are the same as those made by Guy Fawkes, as we have little idea of what memory claims Fawkes in fact made, or indeed of how much he at various times remembered. All we actually know is that Charles' claims fit Fawkes' life.

These difficulties, in applying the concept of exact similarity in the matter of the supposed memories, are (I suspect) a motive for the thought that we *must* describe the situation in terms of identity. This is where the reduplicated situation of Charles and Robert gives some help. In that situation it is quite obvious that the idea of identity

[6] I am grateful to Mr. P. F. Strawson for making this clear to me.

cannot be applied, and that we must fall back on similarity; and that one respect in which the trio are similar is—however we are to express it—that of "memory." (If the situation sometimes occurred, we might find an expression; we might speak of "similarity of one's supposed past.") This eases the way for doing the same thing in the case of Charles alone, whose relation to Fawkes in his unique case is exactly the same as both his and Robert's in the reduplicated one. We can then say that Charles has the same character, and the same supposed past, as Fawkes; which is just the same as to say that they are in these respect exactly similar. This is not to say that they are identical at all. The only case in which identity and exact similarity could be distinguished, as we have just seen, is that of the body— "same body" and "exactly similar body" really do mark a difference. Thus I should claim that the omission of the body takes away all content from the idea of personal *identity*.[7]

I should like to make one last point about this example. This turns on the fact, mentioned before, that in order to describe Charles' change as a change of identity, we must be able to identify some one person who might plausibly be supposed to have seen and done all the things that Charles now claims to remember having seen and done; otherwise there would be nothing to pin down Charles' memory claims as other than random feats of clairvoyance. We succeeded in doing this, just by discovering that Charles' memory claims fitted Fawkes' life. This could be done only by knowing what Fawkes did, and what Fawkes did could be known only by reference to witnesses of Fawkes' activities, and these witnesses must have seen Fawkes' *body*. In order for their accounts to be connected into the history of one person, it is necessary to rely on the continuity of this body.

Now the fact that Fawkes is in this sense identified through his body does not rule out the possibility that Charles should later be identified with Fawkes without reference to a body; i.e., this fact does not rule out the weaker thesis about the non-necessity of bodies. To illustrate this, one might compare the case of someone's going to a crowded party, where he sees a girl who is very like all the other girls at the party except that she has red hair. This girl sings various songs and quarrels with the band; she is easily identified on each occasion by the colour of the hair. The man later meets a platinum blonde who recalls singing songs at a party and quarrelling with the band. He can identify her as the red-haired girl at the party, even though she has changed the colour of her hair in the meantime. There is an important difference, however, between this case and that of Fawkes. If the girl had remarkably changed the colour of her hair between

---

7 I am indebted here, and elsewhere in this paper, to Mr. D. F. Pears.

songs and before the quarrel, identifying her at the various stages of the party would have been more difficult, but not in principle impossible; but if the Fawkes-personality changed bodies frequently, identification would become not just difficult but impossible. For the only other resource would be the memory criterion, and the operation of this would once more make exactly the same requirements. Hence it is a necessary condition of making the supposed identification on non-bodily grounds that at some stage identifications should be made on bodily grounds. Hence any claim that bodily considerations can be absolutely omitted from the criteria of personal identity must fail; i.e., these facts do rule out the stronger thesis.

2. *Some remarks on bodily interchange.* Anyone who believed that personalities could be identified without reference to bodies might be expected to make sense of the idea of bodily interchange; and anyone who thought that they might always be identified in this way would presumably require that for any two contemporaneous persons we should be able to make sense of the idea that their bodies should be interchanged. It is worth considering how far we can make sense of it, if we look at it closely.

Suppose a magician is hired to perform the old trick of making the emperor and the peasant become each other. He gets the emperor and the peasant in one room, with the emperor on his throne and the peasant in the corner, and then casts the spell. What will count as success? Clearly not that after the smoke has cleared the old emperor should be in the corner and the old peasant on the throne. That would be a rather boring trick. The requirement is presumably that the emperor's body, with the peasant's personality, should be on the throne, and the peasant's body, with the emperor's personality, in the corner. What does this mean? In particular, what has happened to the voices? The voice presumably ought to count as a bodily function; yet how would the peasant's gruff blasphemies be uttered in the emperor's cultivated tones, or the emperor's witticisms in the peasant's growl? A similar point holds for the features; the emperor's body might include the sort of face that just *could not* express the peasant's morose suspiciousness, the peasant's a face no expression of which could be taken for one of fastidious arrogance. These "could's" are not just empirical—such expressions on these features might be unthinkable.

The point need not be elaborated; I hope I have said enough to suggest that the concept of bodily interchange cannot be taken for granted, and that there are even logical limits to what we should be prepared to say in this direction. What these limits are, cannot be foreseen—one has to consider the cases, and for this one has to see the cases. The converse is also true, that it is difficult to tell in advance how far certain features may suddenly seem to express some-think quite unexpected. But there are limits, and when this is recognized, the idea of the interchange of personalities seems very odd. There might be something like a logical impossibility of the magician's trick's succeeding. However much of the emperor's past the sometime peasant now claimed to remember, the trick would not have succeeded if he could not satisfy the simpler requirement of being the same *sort* of person as the sometime emperor. Could he do this, if he could not smile royally? Still less, could he be the same person, if he could not smile the characteristic smile of the emperor?

These considerations are relevant to the present question in two ways. First, the stronger view about the identification implies that an interchange is always conceivable; but there are many cases in which it does not seem to be conceivable at all. Secondly, there is connected with this the deeper point, that when we are asked to distinguish a man's personality from his body, we do not really know what to distinguish from what. I take it that this was part of what Wittgenstein meant when he said that the best picture of the human soul was the human body.[8]

3. *A criterion for oneself?* I now turn to a different supposed use of a criterion of identity for persons. It may be objected that I have been discussing all the time the use of memory and other criteria of personal identity as applied to one man by others; but that the real role of memory is to be seen in the way it reveals a man *to himself*. Thus Locke speaks of "consciousness" (and by this he means here memory) as "what makes a man be himself to himself." [9]

It is difficult to see what this can mean. If we take it to mean that a man could use memory as a criterion in deciding whether he was the same person, in the particular sense, as he used to be, the suggestion is demonstrably absurd. I hope that a short and schematized argument will be enough to show this point. Suppose a man to have had previously some set of memories S, and now a different set S_1. This should presumably be the situation in which he should set about using the criterion to decide the question of his identity. But this cannot be so, for when he has memories S, and again when he has memories S_1, he is in no doubt about his identity, and so the question does not even occur to him. For it to occur to him, he would have to have S and S_1 at the same time, and so S would be included in S_1, which is contrary to the hypothesis that they are, in the relevant sense, different.

Alternatively, let S_1 include a general memory to the effect that

8 *Philosophical Investigations,* II, iv.
9 *Loc cit.,* §10.

he used to remember things that he no longer remembers. This would again present no question to him, for it is the condition of most of us. So let us strengthen this into the requirement that S_1 include a general memory Σ to the effect that he used to remember things empirically in compatible with memories in S_1. In this situation he might set about trying to find out what kind of illusion he was under. His most economical hypothesis would be that Σ itself was an illusion. If he were not satisfied with this, or if some parts of S *were* left over in S_1, so that he seemed to have definitely incompatible "memories," there would be nothing he could do with the help of his own memory; he would have to ask others about his past. In doing this, he would be relying on other people's memories of his past; but this is certainly not what was meant by the suggestion of memory as a criterion for the man himself. It is just a reversion to the case of such a criterion being used by some persons about another. Thus there is no way in which memory could be used by a man as a criterion of his own identity.

A criterion, however, must be used by someone. This is a point that has been notably and unhappily neglected by theorists of personal identity. Thus Hume, for instance, in the course of his account revealingly says,[10] "Suppose we could see clearly into the breast of another, and observe that succession of perceptions, which constitutes his mind or thinking principle, and suppose that he always preserves the memory of a considerable part of past perceptions . . ." Others, in criticising or expanding Hume's account, have written in terms that similarly require an externalized view of the contents of a man's mind, a view obtainable from no conceivable vantage-point. Theorising which is in this sense abstract must be vacuous, because this privileged but positionless point of view can mean nothing to us.

At this point it might be objected that if what has been said is true about a criterion of identity, then it was not a *criterion* that memory was supposed uniquely to provide. "You have argued," it might be said, "that no man can use memory as a criterion of his own identity. But this is just what shows that memory is the essence of personal identity; figuratively speaking, memory is so much what makes him a certain person that when provided with certain memories, he cannot doubt who he is. This is just the heart of the thesis." Or the objection might be put by saying that a man might conceivably have occasion to look into a mirror and say "this is not my body," but could never have occasion to say "these are not my memories." Or, again, a man who has lost his memory cannot say who he is.

If this is what the thesis asserts, however, it comes to little. A

[10] Hume, *Treatise of Human Nature*, Bk. I, Pt. IV, Sec. VI.

man who has lost his memory cannot say who anyone else is, either, nor whether any object is the same as one previously presented, since he will not remember the previous presentation. So the last argument shows nothing about personal identity as such; it just shows that identifying anything is a process that involves memory. Nor is the first argument more illuminating. It comes really to no more than the trivialities that in order to remember, you have to have something to remember, and that if you are remembering everything you can remember, there is nothing else you can remember. Again, the example of the man looking into the mirror does not do what is required. In order to sustain the objection it would be necessary to show not just that a man might say "this is not my body," but that if he said it, he would necessarily be right; or at least that the question whether he was right or not did not involve any reference to other people's memories. It is obvious that neither is the case, because the situation of the example *might* be best described by saying that this was a man who misremembered what he looked like, and the question whether this was the best description of the situation would have to be decided by other people conducting the kind of enquiry into identity that was earlier discussed at length.

It is not part of my aim to discuss in general consciousness of self. I have tried in this section to show in a limited way that although we may have the feeling that, by consideration of it alone, we may be given the clue to personal identity, this is in fact an illusion. That it is an illusion is disguised by those theories of personal identity which, by assuming no particular point of view, try to get the best of both worlds, the inner and the outer. If we abandon this for a more realistic approach, the facts of self-consciousness prove incapable of yielding the secret of personal identity, and we are forced back into the world of public criteria.

If we accept these conclusions, together with the earlier ones, it may seem that the attempt to give a sense to "particular personality" that omits reference to the body has failed. However, there is another and familiar class of cases that seems to provide strong independent grounds for the view that such a sense can be given: these are the cases in which more than one personality is associated with one body. I shall end by discussing this type of case and some related questions.

4. *Multiple personality and individuation.* Examples of multiple personality, such as the notorious case of Miss Beauchamp,[11] raise identity questions interestingly different from those that arose in the case of Charles. In that case, we identified, by means that

[11] See Morton Prince, *The Dissociation of a Personality* (1905), *passim.*

turned out to involve the body, what would normally, if tenden-
tiously, be called a different person, and asked whether the person
in front of us was identical with him. In the cases of multiple personality, we are in a sense more directly confronted with personalities,
and naturally make direct reference to them in order to ask our
identity questions at all. The standard type of identity question about
Miss Beauchamp is whether the personality that is now being manifested in her behaviour (or some such description) is the same as that
which was being manifested two hours ago. In asking a question of
this type, we may in fact feel a doubt about the reference of descriptions like "the personality now manifesting itself," because the principal question here just is what personalities there are to be referred
to—how many personalities there are, and how the subject's behavior is to be "sorted out" into the manifestations of different
personalities.

For this reason, there is a strong motive for not putting our
questions about Miss Beauchamp in the form of identity questions
at all. Instead of asking something of the form "Is this personality
the same as that?" we may prefer to ask, "Do these two pieces of behavior belong to one personality or to two?"; that is, instead of referring to personalities *through* their manifestations and asking
whether they are identical, we may refer *to* manifestations and ask
how they are to be allocated to personalities. A parallel to this would
be the case of a tangled skein of wool, where, catching hold of a piece
at each end, we might ask either "Is this thread the same as that?" or
"Are these pieces parts of one thread?" The second formulation in
each case might seem to be strictly preferable to the first, because the
references that are being made are more determinate; I can tell you
exactly which *part* or which *manifestation* I am referring to in the
second formulation, but can tell you much less exactly which *thread*
or which *personality* I am referring to in the first. It is useful to distinguish these sorts of questions, and I shall call the first, questions
of identity, and the second, questions of individuation. I shall also
in this section speak of our having individuated a personality when,
roughly, we have answered enough questions of this type for us to
have picked out a certain personality from the pattern of manifestations. I shall not here examine the complexities involved in a proper
formulation of these concepts.

We have just seen that it might be preferable to put our questions about Miss Beauchamp in the form of individuation, and not of
identity, questions. It might seem, indeed, that it is essential to do
this. Because asking an identity question about personalities involves
referring to personalities, and this involves knowing what personalities one is referring to, it is tempting to think that we could not

use the identity form in a case where our problem was just what, and how many, personalities there were. This, however, would be an exaggeration. I do not have to be able to answer the question "which personality are you referring to?" in the thorough-going way suggested by this argument. I may do enough to establish the reference by saying "I just mean the personality now being manifested, whichever that is," without committing myself thereby to more than the belief that there is at least one personality to be referred to, and possibly more. I should be *debarred* from using the identity form only in a situation where I was in doubt whether there was even one personality to be referred to.

The case of Miss Beauchamp is more relevant to the discussion of the role of the body in the individuation of personalities than it is to the straightforward question whether bodily identity is a necessary condition of personal identity; since bodily identity is granted, this case can have no tendency to show that bodily identity is not a necessary condition (though it will of course tend to show that it is not a sufficient condition). It will, however, lend colour to the idea that we can individuate particular personalities, and not through bodies; if there are here four different particular personalities, and only one body, it is clear that there can be some principle for distinguishing personalities without at least *distinguishing* bodies. There is such a principle; but it does not yield as exciting a result from this case as might be hoped.

Miss Beauchamp's strikingly different personalities were individuated in the first place by reference to personal characteristics, in which they were largely opposed; also by tastes and preferences (B1 and B4 hated smoking, for instance, and B3 loved it); and by skills (B3, unlike the others, knew no French or shorthand). Memory did not serve straightforwardly to individuate them, because their memories were asymmetrical. B1 and B4, for instance, knew only what they were told by the investigator about the others, but B3 knew, without being told, everything that B4 did, and in the case of B1 knew all her thoughts as well; she referred to them both in the third person.[12] These remarkable and systematic discontinuities in Miss Beauchamp's behavior, together with the violent and active conflict between her various selves, who abused and tricked each other, make the reference to different particular personalities completely natural. Thus we have individuated various personalities by reference to character, attainments and (up to a point) memories, and without reference to bodies.

This claim, however, is liable to serious misinterpretation.

---

[12] Prince, *op. cit.*, p. 181. The extent of memory discontinuity in such cases varies: cf., e.g., William James, *Principles of Psychology*, Vol. I, pp. 379 *seq*.

There has been no reference to bodies only in the sense that no such reference came into the principles used; but it does not follow from this that there was no reference to a body in starting to individuate at all. Obviously there was, because the problem arose only in connexion with the fact that too many and too various things were going on in connexion with one body; if Miss Beauchamp had been four sisters, there would have been no problem. Thus the individuation by reference to character and so on alone, was individuation in the context of the continuity of a certain body; and the fact that these principles were successful in individuating in this case does not show that they would be successful in so doing generally. The point may be put by saying that what we have succeeded in doing on these principles is individuating particular personalities *of Miss Beauchamp,* who is bodily identified; this is not to say that they provide us with a principle for individuating particular personalities without any reference to bodies at all.

This is quite obvious if we look at the principles themselves. Leaving aside memory, which only partially applies to the case, character and attainments are quite clearly general things. *Jones'* character is, in a sense, a particular; just because "Jones character" refers to the instantiation of certain properties by a particular (and bodily) man.[13] Even so, the sense in which it is a particular is peculiar and limited. This can be seen from the odd workings of its criterion of identity. Consider the statement

    (i) He has the same character as his father (*or* he has his father's character)

and compare the two statements

    (ii) He wears the same clothes as his father
    (iii) He has his father's watch.

Of these, (ii) is ambiguous, the expression "his father's clothes" seesawing over the line between particular and general (though its companion "he wears his father's clothes" seems to allow only the particular interpretation). Neither (i) nor (iii) is ambiguous in this way; and in (iii) "his father's watch" obviously refers to a particular. But (i) is quite different from (iii). If (iii) is true, then if the watch he has is going to be pawned tomorrow, his father's watch is going to be pawned; but it does not similarly follow from (i) that if his character is going to be ruined by the Army, his father's character is going to be ruined. This illustrates how little weight can be laid on the idea of Jones' character being a particular, and throws us back on the familiar point that to talk of Jones' character is a way of talking about what Jones is like.

Miss Beauchamp's various personalities are particulars only in

---

[13] Cf. P. F. Strawson, *Particular and General*, PAS Vol. LIV (1953–54), pp. 250 *al.*

the weak sense that Jones' character is a particular, a sense which is grounded in the particular body. In using character and attainments to individuate them, I am telling the difference between them in just the sense that I tell the difference between sets of characteristics; Miss Beauchamp was peculiar in having more than one set of characteristics. Her personalities, like more normal people's, each had *peculiarities,* the combination of which might well have been, as a matter of fact, uniquely instantiated; but this does not affect the fundamental logical issue. About her memories, it need only be said that if different personalities have the same memories, memory is not being used to individuate; if they have different memories, the bodily identity connecting the various remembered occasions makes it easy to describe the situation as one of Miss Beauchamp's sometimes being able to remember what at other times she could not.

When Miss Beauchamp was nearly cured, and only occasionally lapsed into dissociation, she spoke freely of herself as having been B1 or B4. "These different states seem to her very largely differences of moods. She regrets them, but does not attempt to excuse them, because, as she says, 'After all, it is always myself.' " [14]

WILLIAMS SELECTION

1. What exactly is the distinction between a necessary condition and a sufficient condition? What does it mean to say that bodily identity is, or is not, a necessary condition for personal identity?

2. Notice the role, in Williams's argument, of the problem of checking a claim to personal identity. What is the difference between my saying that *I* am the same person who was in this room yesterday, and my saying that *you* are the same person who was in this room yesterday?

3. Would it make any sense to say that Jones is not the same person she was yesterday, but no one at all knows it? Would it make any sense to say that Jones is not the same person she was yesterday, but she is the only one to know it? Would it make any sense to say that Jones is not the same person she was yesterday but *she* does not know it, even though *we do?*

4. Consider the example of the peasant and the emperor. What does Williams mean by saying that "the emperor's body might include the sort of face that just *could not* express the peasant's morose suspiciousness?" What then shall we say about sex-change operations? Is the woman after the operation the same person as the man before the operation?

5. In the case of multiple personalities, there seems always to be *one* of the multiple personalities that knows about all the others, monitors them, and can report what they have been doing and thinking. How would Williams analyze or explain this fact, in terms of his account of personal identity?

---

[14] Prince, *op. cit.,* p. 525.

(SELECTION 5)

PETER STRAWSON

The Primitiveness
of the Concept of a Person

In the long history of philosophical discussion of the question, "What is a person?" the dominant view has been that a person is a composite entity, a combination of a mind or self or soul with a body. The great Greek thinker Plato adopted that position in several of his works, and through the development of a rational theological foundation for the common doctrines of Judaism, Christianity, and Islam, this Platonic doctrine came to be the "establishment" position for almost two millennia. In more recent philosophical literature, Descartes defended the thesis that a human being is a mind associated with, or connected to, a distinct body.

Strawson here decisively rejects this tradition, arguing instead that the concept "person" is a primitive or fundamental concept, not a derivative notion arrived at by combining two more fundamental ideas ("mind" and "body"). It is to persons that we ascribe various experiences, and also various physical characteristics (such as being in a particular place, or moving in a certain way). Descartes and others talked as though the mind were some sort of passenger riding about in a vehicle (the body) that it controlled in a mysterious and unobservable way. But, as Strawson would point out, when I say "My leg is stiff," I am talking about *myself,* whereas

when I say "My transmission is noisy" I am talking about something distinct from myself, namely my car.

In the book from which this selection is taken, Strawson describes himself as doing "descriptive metaphysics." He means by this a careful, detailed explication and analysis of the system of fundamental categories which we all use to organize, conceptualize, and comprehend ourselves and our world. "Person" is one such category; others would be "space," "time," "cause," "object," and "reality." Descriptive metaphysics does not aim at producing *a priori* proofs of certain very general theses, in the manner of the rational metaphysics of earlier days. Rather its purpose is explicative and analytic. It begins not with supposedly self-evident first principles, but with our ordinary beliefs and understandings, as they are embodied in and expressed in our daily interactions with persons and the world. Like Bernard Williams, Strawson makes little if any appeal to the special expertise of physical scientists or psychologists. Since he seeks the conceptual structure that underlies our most commonplace judgments about persons and things, he draws upon familiar examples that are equally accessible to all readers.

Notice that near the end of this

selection, Strawson focuses his attention on the notion of *doing something* as especially central to the concept of personhood. It is in purposive action rather than in mere sensory awareness or abstract thought that the primitive indivisibility of the concept of a person is most clearly exhibited. Doing something (frying an egg, playing a game, brushing one's teeth) essentially and indivisibly involves believing certain things, experiencing certain things, expecting certain things, forming certain judg-ments, *and also* making certain bodily movements. No analysis would be plausible that located the *real* frying of the egg in the mind's beliefs and expectations, and treated the movements of hands and arms as mere effects or consequences of the act, as though the frying were complete as soon as I had conceived it. It should not surprise us that Descartes, who tends to think in this way, is more concerned with analyzing knowledge than purposive action.

What we have to acknowledge . . . is the primitiveness of the concept of a person. What I mean by the concept of a person is the concept of a type of entity such that *both* predicates ascribing states of consciousness *and* predicates ascribing corporeal characteristics, a physical situation &c. are equally applicable to a single individual of that single type. What I mean by saying that this concept is primitive can be put in a number of ways. One way is to return to those two questions I asked earlier: viz. (1) why are states of consciousness ascribed to anything at all? and (2) why are they ascribed to the very same thing as certain corporeal characteristics, a certain physical situation &c.? I remarked at the beginning that it was not to be supposed that the answers to these questions were independent of each other. Now I shall say that they are connected in this way: that a necessary condition of states of consciousness being ascribed at all is that they should be ascribed to the *very same things* as certain corporeal characteristics, a certain physical situation &c. That is to say, states of consciousness could not be acribed at all, *unless* they were ascribed to persons, in the sense I have claimed for this word. We are tempted to think of a person as a sort of compound of two kinds of subjects: a subject of experiences (a pure consciousness, an ego) on the one hand, and a subject of corporeal attributes on the other. Many questions arise when we think in this way. But, in particular, when we ask ourselves how we come to frame, to get a use for, the concept of this compound of two subjects, the picture—if we are honest and careful—is apt to change from the picture of two subjects to the picture of one subject and one non-subject. For it becomes impossible to see how we could come by the idea of different, distinguishable, identifiable subjects of experiences—different consciousnesses—*if this idea is thought of as logically primitive,* as a

From *Individuals* by Sir Peter Strawson. First published in 1959 by Methuen & Co. Ltd., London.

logical ingredient in the compound-idea of a person, the latter being composed of two subjects. For there could never be any question of assigning an experience, as such, to any subject other than oneself; and therefore never any question of assigning it to oneself either, never any question of ascribing it to a subject at all. So the concept of the pure individual consciousness—the pure ego—is a concept that cannot exist; or, as least, cannot exist as a primary concept in terms of which the concept of a person can be explained or analysed. It can exist only, if at all, as a secondary, non-primitive concept, which itself is to be explained, analysed, in terms of the concept of a person. . . .

So, then, the word "I" never refers to this, the pure subject. But this does not mean that "I" in some cases does not refer at all. It refers; because I am a person among others; and the predicates which would, *per impossible* belong to the pure subject if it could be referred to, belong properly to the person to which "I" does refer.

The concept of a person is logically prior to that of an individual consciousness. The concept of a person is not to be analysed as that of an animated body or of an embodied anima. This is not to say that the concept of a pure individual consciousness might not have a logically secondary existence, if one thinks, or finds, it desirable. We speak of a dead person—a body—and in the same secondary way we might at least think of a disembodied person. A person is not an embodied ego, but an ego might be a disembodied person, retaining the logical benefit of individuality from having been a person.

It is important to realize the full extent of the acknowledgement one is making in acknowledging the logical primitiveness of the concept of a person. Let me rehearse briefly the stages of the argument. There would be no question of ascribing one's own states of consciousness, or experiences, to anything, unless one also ascribed, or were ready and able to ascribe, states of conciousness, or experiences, to other individual entities of the same logical type as that thing to which one ascribes one's own states of consciousness. The condition of reckoning oneself as a subject of such predicates is that one should also reckon others as subjects of such predicates. The condition, in turn, of this being possible, is that one should be able to distinguish from one another, to pick out or identify, different subjects of such predicates, i.e., different individuals of the type concerned. The condition, in turn, of this being possible is that the individuals concerned, including oneself, should be of a certain unique type: of a type, namely, such that of each individual of that type there must be ascribed, or ascribable, *both* states of consciousness *and* corporeal characteristics. But this characterization of the type is still very opaque and does not at all clearly bring out what is involved. To bring this out, I must make a rough division, into two, of the kinds of predicates properly applied to individuals of this type. The first kind of predicate consists of those which are also properly applied to material bodies to which we would not dream of applying predicates ascribing states of consciousness. I will call this first kind M-predicates: and they include things like "weighs 10 stone," "is in the drawing-room" and so on. The second kind consists of all the other predicates we apply to persons. These I shall call P-predicates. P-predicates, of course, will be very various. They will include things like "is smiling," "is going for a walk," as well as things like "is in pain," "is thinking hard," "believes in God" and so on.

So far I have said that the concept of a person is to be understood as the concept of a type of entity such that *both* predicates ascribing states of consciousness *and* predicates ascribing corporeal characteristics, a physical situation &c. are equally applicable to an individual entity of that type. All I have said about the meaning of saying that this concept is primitive is that it is not to be analysed in a certain way or ways. We are not, for example, to think of it as a secondary kind of entity in relation to two primary kinds, viz., a particular consciousness and a particular human body. I implied also that the Cartesian error is just a special case of the more general error, present in a different form in theories of the no-ownership type, of thinking of the designations, or apparent designations, of persons as *not* denoting precisely the same thing or entity for all kinds of predicate ascribed to the entity designated. That is, if we are to avoid the general form of this error, we must *not* think of "I" or "Smith" as suffering from type-ambiguity. Indeed, if we want to locate type-ambiguity somewhere, we would do better to locate it in certain predicates like "is in the drawing-room," "was hit by a stone" &c., and say they mean one thing when applied to material objects and another when applied to persons.

This is all I have so far said or implied about the meaning of saying that the concept of a person is primitive. What has to be brought out further is what the implications of saying this are as regards the logical character of those predicates with which we ascribe states of consciousness. For this purpose we may well consider P-predicates in general. For though not all P-predicates are what we should call "predicates ascribing states of consciousness" (i.e., "going for a walk" is not), they may be said to have this in common, that they imply the possession of consciousness on the part of that to which they are ascribed.

What then are the consequences of the view as regards the character of P-predicates? I think they are these. Clearly there is no sense in talking of identifiable individuals of a special type, a type, namely, such that they possess both M-predicates and P-predicates, unless there is in principle some way of telling, with regard to any individual of that type, and any P-predicate, whether that individual possesses that P-predicate. And, in the case of at least some P-predicates, the ways of telling must constitute in some sense logically adequate kinds of criteria for the ascription of the P-predicate. For suppose in no case did these ways of telling constitute logically adequate kinds of criteria. Then we should have to think of the relation between the ways of telling and what the P-predicate ascribes, or a part of what it ascribes, always in the following way: we should have to think of the ways of telling as *signs* of the presence, in the individual concerned, of this different thing, viz. the state of consciousness. But then we could only know that the way of telling was a sign of the presence of the different thing ascribed by the P-predicate, by the observation of correlations between the two. But this observation we could each make only in one case, viz. our own. And now we are back in the position of the defender of Cartesianism, who thought our way with it was too short. For what, now, does "our own case" mean? There is no sense in the idea of ascribing states of consciousness to oneself, or at all, unless the ascriber already knows how to ascribe at least some states of consciousness to others. So he cannot argue in general "from his own case" to conclusions about how to do this; for unless he already knows how to do this, he has no conception of *his own case,* or any *case,* i.e., any subject of experiences. Instead, he just has evidence that pain &c. may be expected when a certain body is affected in certain ways and not when others are. If he speculated to the contrary, his speculations would be immediately falsified.

The conclusion here is not, of course, new. What I have said is that one ascribes P-predicates to others on the strength of observation of their behaviour; and that the behaviour-criteria one goes on are not just signs of the presence of what is meant by the P-predicate, but are criteria of a logically adequate kind for the ascription of the P-predicate. On behalf of this conclusion, however, I am claiming that it follows from a consideration of the conditions necessary for any ascription of states of consciousness to anything. The point is not that we must accept this conclusion in order to avoid scepticism, but that we must accept it in order to explain the existence of the conceptual scheme in terms of which the sceptical problem is stated. But once the conclusion is accepted, the sceptical problem does not arise. So with many sceptical problems: their statement involves the pretended acceptance of a conceptual scheme and at the same time the silent repudiation of one of the conditions of its existence. That is why they are, in the terms in which they are stated, insoluble.

But this is only one half of the picture about P-predicates. For of course it is true of some important classes of P-predicates, that when one ascribes them *to oneself,* one does not do so on the strength of observation of those behaviour criteria on the strength of which one ascribes them to others. This is not true of all P-predicates. It is not, in general, true of those which carry assessments of character or capability: these, when self-ascribed, are in general ascribed on the same kind of basis as that on which they are ascribed to others. Even of those P-predicates of which it is true that one does not generally ascribe them to oneself on the basis of the criteria on the strength of which one ascribes them to others, there are many of which it is also true that their ascription is liable to correction by the self-ascriber on this basis. But there remain many cases in which one has an entirely adequate basis for ascribing a P-predicate to oneself, and yet in which this basis is quite distinct from those on which one ascribes the predicate to another. Thus one says, reporting a present state of mind or feeling: "I feel tired, am depressed, am in pain." How can this fact be reconciled with the doctrine that the criteria on the strength of which one ascribes P-predicates to others are criteria of a logically adequate kind for this ascription?

The apparent difficulty of bringing about this reconciliation may tempt us in many directions. It may tempt us, for example, to deny that these self-ascriptions are really ascriptive at all, to *assimilate* first-person ascriptions of states of consciousness to those other forms of behaviour which constitute criteria on the basis of which one person ascribes P-predicates to another. This device seems to avoid the difficulty; it is not, in all cases, entirely inappropriate. But it obscures the facts; and is needless. It is merely a sophisticated form of failure to recognize the special character of P-predicates or, rather, of a crucial class of P-predicates. For just as there is not in general one primary process of learning, or teaching oneself, an inner private meaning for predicates of this class, then another process of learning to apply such predicates to others on the strength of a correlation, noted in one's own case, with certain forms of behaviour, so—and equally —there is not in general one primary process of learning to apply such predicates to others on the strength of behaviour criteria, and then another process of acquiring the secondary technique of exhibiting a new form of behaviour, viz. first-person P-utterances. Both these pictures are refusals to acknowledge the unique logical character of the predicates concerned. Suppose we write "Px" as the general form of propositional function of such a predicate. Then, ac-

cording to the first picture, the expression which primarily replaces
"*x*" in this form is "I," the first person singular pronoun: its uses
with other replacements are secondary, derivative and shaky. According to the second picture, on the other hand, the primary replacements of "*x*" in this form are "he," "that person," &c., and its use
with "I" is secondary, peculiar, not a true ascriptive use. But it is
essential to the character of these predicates that they have both first-
and third-person ascriptive uses, that they are both self-ascribable
otherwise than on the basis of observation of the behaviour of the
subject of them, and other-ascribable on the basis of behavior criteria. To learn their use is to learn both aspects of their use. In order
to *have* this type of concept, one must be both a self-ascriber and an
other-ascriber of such predicates, and must see every other as a self-
ascriber. In order to *understand* this type of concept, one must acknowledge that there is a kind of predicate which is unambiguously
and adequately ascribable *both* on the basis of observation of the
subject of the predicate *and* not on this basis, i.e., independently of
observation of the subject: the second case is the case where the ascriber is also the subject. If there were no concepts answering to the
characterization I have just given, we should indeed have no philosophical problem about the soul; but equally we should not have
our concept of a person.

To put the point—with a certain unavoidable crudity—in
terms of one particular concept of this class, say, that of depression.
We speak of behaving in a depressed way (of depressed behaviour)
and we also speak of feeling depressed (of a feeling of depression).
One is inclined to argue that feelings can be felt but not observed,
and behaviour can be observed but not felt, and that therefore there
must be room here to drive in a logical wedge. But the concept of
depression spans the place where one wants to drive it in. We might
say: in order for there to be such a concept as that of X's depression,
the depression which X has, the concept must cover both what is felt,
but not observed, by X, and what may be observed, but not felt, by
others than X (for all values of X). But it is perhaps better to say:
X's depression *is* something, one and the same thing, which is felt,
but not observed, by X and observed, but not felt, by others than X.
(Of course, what can be observed can also be faked or disguised.) To
refuse to accept this is to refuse to accept the *structure* of the language in which we talk about depression. That is, in a sense, all
right. One might give up talking or devise, perhaps, a different structure in terms of which to soliloquize. What is not all right is simultaneously to pretend to accept that structure and to refuse to accept
it; i.e., to couch one's rejection in the language of that structure.

It is in this light that we must see some of the familiar philosophical difficulties in the topic of the mind. For some of them spring from just such a failure to admit, or fully to appreciate, the character which I have been claiming for at least some P-predicates. It is not seen that these predicates could not have either aspect of their use, the self-ascriptive or the non-self-ascriptive, without having the other aspect. Instead, one aspect of their use is taken as self-sufficient, which it could not be, and then the other aspect appears as problematical. So we oscillate between philosophical scepticism and philosophical behaviourism. When we take the self-ascriptive aspect of the use of some P-predicates, say "depressed," as primary, then a logical gap seems to open between the criteria on the strength of which we say that another is depressed, and the actual state of being depressed. What we do not realize is that if this logical gap is allowed to open, then it swallows not only his depression, but our depression as well. For if the logical gap exists, then depressed behaviour, however much there is of it, is no more than a sign of depression. But it can only become a sign of depression because of an observed correlation between it and depression. But whose depression? Only mine, one is tempted to say. But if *only* mine, then *not* mine at all. The sceptical position customarily represents the crossing of the logical gap as at best a shaky inference. But the point is that not even the syntax of the premises of the inference exists, if the gap exists.

If, on the other hand, we take the other-ascriptive uses of these predicates as primary or self-sufficient, we may come to think that all there is in the meaning of these predicates, as predicates, is the criteria on the strength of which we ascribe them to others. Does this not follow from the denial of the logical gap? It does not follow. To think that it does is to forget the self-ascriptive use of these predicates, to forget that we have to do with a class of predicates to the meaning of which it is essential that they should be both self-ascribable and other-ascribable to the same individual, where self-ascriptions are not made on the observational basis on which other-ascriptions are made, but on another basis. It is not that these predicates have two kinds of meaning. Rather, it is essential to the single kind of meaning that they do have, that both ways of ascribing them should be perfectly in order.

If one is playing a game of cards, the distinctive markings of a certain card constitute a logically adequate criterion for calling it, say, the Queen of Hearts; but, in calling it this, in the context of the game, one is ascribing to it properties over and above the possession of these markings. The predicate gets its meaning from the whole structure of the game. So with the language in which we ascribe P-predicates. To say that the criteria on the strength of which we ascribe P-predicates to others are of a logically adequate kind for this ascription, is not to say that all there is to the ascriptive meaning of these predicates is these criteria. To say this is to forget that they are P-predicates, to forget the rest of the language-structure to which they belong.

Now our perplexities may take a different form, the form of the question: "But how can one ascribe to oneself, not on the basis of observation, the very same thing that others may have, on the basis of observation, reasons of a logically adequate kind for ascribing to one?" This question may be absorbed in a wider one, which might be phrased: "How are P-predicates possible?" or: "How is the concept of a person possible?" This is the question by which we replace those two earlier questions, viz.: "Why are states of consciousness ascribed at all, ascribed to anything?" and "Why are they ascribed to the very same thing as certain corporeal characteristics &c.?" For the answer to these two initial questions is to be found nowhere else but in the admission of the primitiveness of the concept of a person, and hence of the unique character of P-predicates. So residual perplexities have to frame themselves in this new way. For when we have acknowledged the primitiveness of the concept of a person, and, with it, the unique character of P-predicates, we may still want to ask what it is in the natural facts that makes it intelligible that we should have this concept, and to ask this in the hope of a nontrivial answer, i.e., in the hope of an answer which does not *merely* say: "Well, there are people in the world." I do not pretend to be able to satisfy this demand at all fully. But I may mention two very different things which might count as beginnings or fragments of an answer.

First, I think a beginning can be made by moving a certain class of P-predicates to a central position in the picture. They are predicates, roughly, which involve doing something, which clearly imply intention or a state of mind or at least consciousness in general, and which indicate a characteristic pattern, or range of patterns, of bodily movement, while not indicating at all precisely any very definite sensation or experience. I mean such things as "going for a walk," "coiling a rope," "playing ball," "writing a letter." Such predicates have the interesting characteristic of many P-predicates, that one does not, in general, ascribe them to oneself on the strength of observation, whereas one does ascribe them to others on the strength of observation. But, in the case of these predicates, one feels minimal reluctance to concede that what is ascribed in these two different ways is the same. This is because of the marked dominance of a fairly definite pattern of bodily movement in what they ascribe, and the marked absence of any distinctive experience. They release us from the idea that the only things we can know about without observation or inference, or both, are private experiences; we can know, without telling by either of these means, about the present and future movements of a body. Yet bodily movements are certainly also things we can know about by observation and inference. Among the things that we observe, as opposed to the things we know about without observation, are the movements of bodies similar to that about which we have knowledge not based on observation. It is important that we should understand such movements, for they bear on and condition our own; and in fact we understand them, we interpret them, only by seeing them as elements in just such plans or schemes of action as those of which we know the present course and future development without observation of the relevant present movements. But this is to say that we see such movements as *actions,* that we interpret them in terms of intention, that we see them as movements of individuals of a type to which also belongs that individual whose present and future movements we know about without observation; it is to say that we see others as self-ascribers, not on the basis of observation, of what we ascribe to them on this basis.

STRAWSON SELECTION

1.   What does Strawson mean by the statement that the concept of a person is "logically primitive"? (Ask your Philosophy instructor to explain this.) Can you think of other examples of concepts that are "logically primitive"?

2.   What does it mean to say that the concepts of a disembodied "I" and a dead body are secondary concepts, *derived from* the primary or primitive concept of a person?

3.   What implications does Strawson's view have for the question of immortality, of life after death?

4.   According to Strawson, do I know myself in the same way that I know other persons, or in a different way?

5.   If actions are central to the concept of a person, as Strawson claims, does it follow that I know about the actions of others in the same way that I know about my own actions? Could I be mistaken about the actions of others? About my own actions? Could I think I had *done* something when in actual fact my body had moved independently of my choice or decision?

(SELECTION 6)

HILARY PUTNAM

Robots, Humans, and Consciousness

With this paper by the American logician Hilary Putnam, we arrive at the full complexity of the question that seemed relatively simple when it was posed by Descartes in his Second Meditation. What am I? As he indicates, Putnam focuses on robots as a way of getting clearer about our concepts of the self, and in particular our notion of consciousness.

Putnam's arguments are largely negative. Neither those who would argue that robots could be conscious nor those who would argue that they cannot be have succeeded in making their cases, he claims. The fundamental reason for this stand-off is that the question is unanswerable in the form in which it has been posed. Our concepts of psychological processes and states, of personality and consciousness, have been developed in such a way that they simply do not apply unambiguously to creatures such as robots, either positively or negatively.

Imagine that the human race had existed for a considerable period of time without either births or deaths (a prelapsarian condition, we may suppose, in which there is no aging or bodily decay). If, through some strange accident, a baby were to be born, and were to grow up as babies now do, developing muscular coordination and learning to speak, the question might arise whether this strange new being were *conscious*. To us, the question seems trivial—of course it is conscious, just as we are. But to men and women who had never seen a child before, and whose language, culture, and system of concepts had no place for the phenomenon of birth and personality development, the issue might be quite puzzling, indeed paradoxical. They might argue the matter in much the way that we now argue about whether robots would be, could be, conscious.

Now, Putnam's answer, insofar as he has an answer at all, is that the question of robot-consciousness "calls for a decision and not for a discovery" (as he puts it in the last paragraph of the essay). More or less as we must *decide* whether certain hitherto unknown viruses are to be counted as alive or not —even as we must decide whether to classify as a mammal the duck-billed platypus, which lays eggs but is warm-blooded—so too we must, as a matter of convenience, conceptual simplicity, or political compromise, decide whether to call robots conscious or not.

But somewhere, deep in our pre-philosophical insides, a voice cries out: "Yes, but are they *really* conscious?" Would I cease to be aware of myself if humanity in general decided that it was linguistically, logically, and politically expedient to group me with trees and rocks? Putnam counsels against heeding such cries. They are expressions of confusion, not the voice of solid common sense. Perhaps. You must make up your own minds.

Those of us who passed many (well- or ill-spent?) childhood hours reading tales of rockets and robots, androids and telepaths, galactic civilizations and time machines, know all too well that robots—hypothetical machines that simulate human behavior, often with an at least roughly human appearance—can be friendly or fearsome, man's best friend or worst enemy. When friendly, robots can be inspiring or pathetic—they can overawe us with their superhuman powers (and with their greater than human virtue as well, at least in the writings of some authors), or they can amuse us with their stupidities and naivete. Robots have been "known" to fall in love, go mad (power- or otherwise), annoy with oversolicitousness. At least in the literature of science fiction, then, it is possible for a robot to be "conscious"; that means (since "consciousness," like "material object" and "universal," is a philosopher's stand-in for more substantial words) to have feelings, thoughts, attitudes, and character traits. But is it really possible? . . .

The mind-body problem has been much discussed in the past thirty-odd years, but the discussion seems to me to have been fruitless. . . . What I hope to persuade you is that the problem of the Minds of Machines will prove, at least for a while, to afford an exciting new way to approach quite traditional issues in the philosophy of mind. Whether, and under what conditions, a robot could be conscious is a question that cannot be discussed without at once impinging on the topics that have been treated under the headings Mind-Body Problem and Problem of Other Minds. For my own part, I believe that certain crucial issues come to the fore almost of their own accord in this connection—issues which *should* have been discussed by writers who have dealt with the two headings just mentioned, but which have not been—and, therefore, that the problem of the robot becomes almost obligatory for a philosopher of mind to discuss.

Before starting I wish to emphasize, lest any should misunderstand, that my concern is with how we should speak about humans and not with how we should speak about machines. My interest in the latter question derives from my just-mentioned conviction: that clarity with respect to the "borderline case" of robots, if it can only

From "Robots: Machines or Artificially Created Life?" by Hilary Putnam. (Published in the *Journal of Philosophy*, LXI, 21, November 12, 1964. Reprinted by permission of the author.)

be achieved, will carry with it clarity with respect to the "central area" of talk about feelings, thoughts, consciousness, life, etc.

. . . Conceive of a community of robots. Let these robots "know" nothing concerning their own physical make-up or how they came into existence (perhaps they would arrive at a robot Creation Story and a polytheistic religion, with robot gods on a robot Olympus). Let them "speak" a language (say, English), in conformity with the grammatical rules and the publicly observable semantic and discourse-analytical regularities of that language. What might the role of psychological predicates be in such a community?
. . . When a robot sees something red (something that evokes the appropriate internal state in the robot) he calls it "red." Our robots are supposed to be capable of inductive reasoning and theory construction. So a robot may discover that something he called red was not really red. Then he will say "well, it looked red." Or, if he is in the appropriate internal state for red, but knows on the basis of cross-inductions from certain other cases that what he "sees" is not really red, he will say "it *looks* red, but it isn't really red." Thus he will have a distinction between the physical reality and the visual appearance, just as we do. But the robot will never say "that looks as if it looked red, but it doesn't really look red." That is, there is no notion in the robot-English of an *appearance of an appearance of red,* any more than there is in English. Moreover, the reason is the same: that any state which cannot be discriminated from "looks-red" *counts* as "looks-red" (under normal conditions of linguistic proficiency, absence of confusion, etc.). What this illustrates, of course, is that the "incorrigibility" of statements of the form "that looks red" is to be explained by an elucidation of the logical features of such discourse, and not by the metaphor of "direct" access.

If we assume that these robots are unsophisticated scientifically, there is no reason for them to know more of their own internal constitution than an ancient Greek knew about the functioning of the central nervous system. We may imagine them developing a sophisticated science in the course of centuries, and thus eventually arriving at tentative identifications of the form: "when a thing 'looks red' to one of us, it means he is in internal state 'flip-flop 72 is on.' " If these robots also publish papers on philosophy (and why should a robot not be able to do considerably better than many of our students?), a lively discussion may ensue concerning the philosophical implications of such discoveries. Some robots may argue, "*obviously,* what we have discovered is that 'seeing red' *is* being in internal state 'flip-flop 72 on' "; others may argue, "*obviously,* what you made was an *empirical* discovery; the *meaning* of 'it looks red' isn't the same as the *meaning* of 'flip-flop 72 is on'; hence the *attributes* (or states, or conditions, or properties) 'being in the state of seeming to see something red' and 'having flip-flop 72 on' are *two* attributes (or states, or conditions, or properties) and not *one*"; others may argue "when I have the illusion that something red is present, nothing red is physically there. Yet, in a sense, I *see* something red. What I see, I *call* a sense-datum. The sense datum is red. The flip-flop isn't red. So, *obviously,* the sense-datum can't be identical with the flip-flop, on or off. And so on. In short, robots can be just as bad at philosophy as people. Or (more politely), the *logical* aspects of the Mind-Body Problem are aspects of a problem that *must* arise for any computing system satisfying the conditions that (1) it uses language and constructs theories; (2) it does not initially "know" its own physical make-up, except superficially; (3) it is equipped with sense organs, and able to perform experiments; (4) it comes to know its own make-up through empirical investigation and theory construction.

The argument just reviewed seems extremely simple. Yet some astonishing misunderstandings have arisen. The one that most surprised me was expressed thus: "As far as I can see, all you show is that a robot could simulate human *behavior.*" This objection, needless (hopefully)-to-say, misses the point of the foregoing *completely.* The point is this: that a robot or a computing machine can, *in a sense,* follow rules (Whether it is the same sense as the sense in which a man follows rules, or only analogous, depends on whether the particular robot can be said to be "conscious," etc., and thus on the central questions of this paper.); that the meaning of an utterance is a function of the rules that govern its construction and use; that the rules governing the *robot* utterances "I see something that looks red" and "flip-flop 72 is on" are quite different. The former utterance may be correctly uttered by any robot which has "learned" to discriminate red things from non-red things correctly, judged by the consensus of the other robts, and which finds itself in the state that signals the presence of a red object. Thus, in the case of a normally constructed robot, "I see something that looks red" may be uttered whenever flip-flop 72 is on, *whether the robot "knows" that flip-flop 72 is on or not.* "Flip-flop 72 is on" may be correctly (reasonably) uttered only when the robot "knows" that flip-flop 72 is on—i.e., only when it can *conclude* that flip-flop 72 is on from empirically established theory together with such observation statements as its conditioning may prompt it to utter, or as it may hear other robots utter. "It looks red" is an utterance for which it does not and cannot give reasons. "Flip-flop 72 is on" is an utterance for which it can give reasons. And so on. Since these semantic differences are the same for the robot as for a human, any argument from the semantic nonequivalence of internal (physical)-state statements and "looks" statements to the character of mind or consciousness must be valid for the robot if it is valid for a human. (Likewise the argument from the alleged fact that there is a "a sense of *see*" in which one can correctly say "I see something red" in certain cases in which nothing red is physically present.) . . .

Throughout this paper I have stressed the possibility that a robot and a human may have the same "psychology"—that is, they may obey the same psychological laws. To say that two organisms (or systems) obey the same psychological laws is not at all the same thing as to say that their behavior is similar. Indeed, two people may obey the same psychological laws and exhibit *different* behavior, even given similar environments in childhood, partly because psychological laws are only statistical and partly because crucial parameters may have different values. To know the psychological laws obeyed by a species, one must know how *any* member of that species *could* behave, given the widest variation in all the parameters that are capable of variation at all. In general, such laws, like all scientific laws, will involve abstractions—terms more or less remote from direct behavioral observation. Examples of such terms have already been given: repression, inhibitory potential, preference, sensation, belief. Thus, to say that a man and a robot have the same "psychology" (are *psychologically isomorphic*, as I will also say) is to say that the behavior of the two *species* is most simply and revealingly analyzed, at the psychological level (in abstraction from the details of the internal physical structure), in terms of the *same* "psychological states" and the same hypothetical parameters. For example, if a human being is a "probabilistic automaton," then any robot with the same "machine table" will be psychologically isomorphic to a human being. If the human brain is simply a neural net with a certain program, as in the theory of Pitts and McCulloch, then a robot whose "brain" was a similar net, only constructed of flip-flops rather than of neurons, would have exactly the same psychology as a human. To avoid question-begging, I will consider psychology as a science that describes the behavior of any species of systems whose behavior is amenable to behavioral analysis, and interpretation in terms of molar behavioral "constructs" of the familiar kind (stimulus, response, drive, saturation, etc.). Thus, saying that a robot (or an octopus) has a *psychology* (obeys psychological laws) does not imply that it is necessarily conscious. For example, the mechanical "mice" constructed by Shannon have a psychology (indeed, they were constructed precisely to serve as a model for a certain psychological theory of conditioning), but no one would contend that they are alive or conscious. In the case of Turing Machines, finite automata, etc., what I here call "psychological isomorphism" is what I referred to in previous papers as "sameness of functional organization."

In the rest of this paper, I will imagine that we are confronted with a community of robots which (who ?) are psychologically isomorphic to human beings in the sense just explained. I will also assume that "psychophysical parallelism" holds good for human beings and that, if an action can be explained psychologically, the corresponding "trajectory" of the living human body that executes that action can be explained (in principle) in physical-chemical terms. The possibility of constructing a robot psychologically isomorphic to a human being does not depend on this assumption; a robot could be psychologically isomorphic to a disembodied spirit or to a "ghost in a machine" just as well, if such there were; but the conceptual situation will be a little less confusing if we neglect *those* issues in the present paper.

Let Oscar be one of these robots, and let us imagine that Oscar is having the "sensation" of red. Is Oscar having the sensation of red? In more ordinary language: is Oscar *seeing* anything? Is he thinking, feeling anything? Is Oscar Alive? Is Oscar Conscious?

I have referred to this problem as the problem of the "civil rights of robots" because that is what it may become, and much faster than any of us now expect. Given the ever-accelerating rate of both technological and social change, it is entirely possible that robots will one day exist, and argue "we *are* alive; we *are* conscious!" In that event, what are today only philosophical prejudices of a traditional anthropocentric and mentalistic kind would all too likely develop into conservative political attitudes. But fortunately, we today have the advantage of being able to discuss this problem disinterestedly, and a little more chance, therefore, of arriving at the correct answer.

I think that the most interesting case is the case in which (1) "psychophysical parallelism" holds (so that it can at least be contended that *we* are just as much "physical-chemical systems" as robots are), and (2) the robots in question are psychologically isomorphic to us. This is surely the most favorable case for the philosopher who wishes to argue that robots of "a sufficient degree of complexity" would (not just *could,* but necessarily *would*) be conscious. Such a philosopher would presumably contend that Oscar had sensations, thoughts, feelings, etc., in just the sense in which we do and that the use of "raised-eyebrow" quotes throughout this paper whenever a psychological predicate was being applied to a robot was unnecessary. It is this contention that I wish to explore, not with the usual polemical desire to show either that materialism is correct and, hence

(?), that such robots as Oscar would be conscious or to show that all such questions have been resolved once and for all by *Philosophical Investigations,* God but give us the eyes to see it, but rather with my own perverse interest in the logical structure of the quaint and curious bits of discourse that philosophers propound as "arguments"— and with a perhaps ultimately more serious interest in the relevant semantical aspects of our language.

Some of the arguments designed to show that Oscar *could not* be conscious may be easily exposed as bad arguments. Thus, the *phonograph-record argument:* a robot only "plays" behavior in the sense in which a phonograph record plays music. When we laugh at the joke of a robot, we are really appreciating the wit of the human programmer, and not the wit of the robot. The *reprogramming argument:* a robot has no real character of its own. It could at any time be reprogrammed to behave in the reverse of the way it has previously behaved. But a human being who was "reprogrammed" (say, by a brain operation performed by a race with a tremendously advanced science), so as to have a new and completely predetermined set of responses, would no longer be a human being (in the full sense), but a monster. The *question-begging argument:* the so-called "psychological" states of a robot are in reality just physical states. But *our* psychological states are *not* physical states. So it could only be in the most Pickwickian of senses that a robot was "conscious."

The first argument ignores the possibility of robots that *learn.* A robot whose "brain" was merely a library of predetermined behavior routines, each imagined in full detail by the programmer, would indeed be uninteresting. But such a robot would be incapable of learning anything that the programmer did not know, and would thus fail to be psychologically isomorphic to the programmer, or to any human. On the other hand, if the programmer constructs a robot so that it will be a model of certain psychological laws, he will *not,* in general, know how it will behave in real-life situations, just as a psychologist might know all of the *laws* of human psychology, but still be no better (or little better) than any one else at predicting how humans will behave in real-life situations. Imagine that the robot at "birth" is as helpless as a newborn babe, and that it acquires our culture by being brought up with humans. When it reaches the stage of inventing a joke, and we laugh, it is simply not true that we are "appreciating the wit of the programmer." What the programmer invented was not a joke, but a system which could one day produce new jokes. The second argument, like the first, assumes that "programmed" behavior must be wholly predictable and lack all spontaneity. If I "reprogram" a criminal (via a brain operation) to become a good citizen, but without destroying his capacity to learn, to develop, to change (perhaps even to change back into a criminal some day), then I have certainly not created a "monster." If Oscar is psychologically isomorphic to a human, then Oscar can be "reprogrammed" to the extent, and only to the extent, that a human can. The third argument assumes outright that psychological predicates never apply to Oscar and to a human in the same sense, which is just the point at issue.

All these arguments suffer from one unnoticed and absolutely crippling defect. They rely on just two facts about robots: that they are artifacts and that they are deterministic systems of a physical kind, whose behavior (including the "intelligent" aspects) has been preselected and designed by the artificer. But it is purely contingent that these two properties are *not* properties of human beings. Thus, if we should one day discover that *we* are artifacts and that our every utterance was anticipated by our superintelligent creators (with a small "c"), it would follow, if these arguments were sound, that *we* are not conscious! At the same time, as just noted, these two properties are *not* properties of *all* imaginable robots. Thus these arguments fail in two directions: they might "show" that *people* are *not* conscious—because people might be the wrong sort of robots—while simultaneously failing to show that some robots are not conscious.

If the usual "anti-civil-libertarian" arguments (arguments against conceding that Oscar is conscious) are bad arguments, *pro*-civil-libertarian arguments seem to be just about nonexistent! Since the nineteenth century, materialists have contended that "consciousness is just a property of matter at a certain stage of organization." But as a semantic analysis this contention is hopeless (psychophysical parallelism is certainly not *analytic*), and as an identity theory it is irrelevant. Suppose that Feigl had been correct, and that sensation words *referred* to events (or "states" or "processes") definable in the language of physics. (. . . Feigl no longer holds this view.) In particular, suppose "the sensation of red" *denotes* a brain process. (It is, of course, utterly unclear what this supposition comes to. We are taught the use of "denotes" in philosophy by being told that "cat" denotes the class of all cats, and so on; and then some philosophers say " 'the sensation of red' denotes a class of brain processes," as if *this* were now supposed to be clear! In fact, all we have been told is that " 'the sensation of red' denotes a brain process" is true just in case "the sensation of red *is* a brain process" is true. Since this latter puzzling assertion was in turn explained by the identity theorists in terms of the distinction between *denotation* and *connotation*, nothing has been explained.) Still, this does not show that Oscar is conscious. Indeed, Oscar may by psychologically isomorphic to a human without being at all similar in physical-chemical construction. So we may suppose that Oscar does not have "brain processes" at all and, hence (on this theory) that Oscar is *not* conscious. Moreover, if the physical "correlate" of the sensation of red (in the case of a human) is P_1, and the physical correlate of the "sensation" of red (in the case of Oscar) is P_2, and if P_1 and P_2 are *different* physical states, it can nonetheless be maintained that, when Oscar and I both "see something that looks red" (or "have the sensation of red," to use the philosophical jargon that I have allowed myself in this paper), we are in the *same* physical state, namely the *disjunction* of P_1 and P_2. How do we decide whether the "sensation of red" (in the case of a human) is "identical" with P_1 or "identical" with $P_1 \lor P_2$? Identity theorists do not tell me anything that helps me to decide.

Another popular theory is that ordinary-language psychological terms, such as "is angry" (and, presumably, such quasi-technical expressions as "has the sensation of red") are *implicitly defined by a psychological theory*. On this view, it would follow from the fact that Oscar and I are "models" of the same psychological (molar behavioral) theory that psychological terms have *exactly the same sense* when applied to me and when applied to Oscar.

It may, perhaps, be granted that there is something that could be called an "implicit psychological theory" underlying the ordinary use of psychological terms. (That an angry man will behave aggressively, unless he has strong reasons to repress his anger and some skill at controlling his feelings; that insults tend to provoke anger; that most people are not very good at controlling strong feelings of anger; are examples of what might be considered "postulates" of such a theory. Although each of these "postulates" is quasi-tautological, it might be contended that the conjunction of a sufficient number of them has empirical consequences, and can be used to provide empirical explanations of observed behavior.) But the view that the whole meaning of such a term as "anger" is fixed by its place in such a theory seems highly dubious. There is not space in the present paper to examine this view at the length that it deserves. But one or two criticisms may indicate where difficulties lie.

To assert that something contains phlogiston is (implicitly) to assert that certain laws, upon which the concept of phlogiston depends, are correct. To assert that something is electrically charged is in part to assert that the experimental laws upon which the concept of electricity is based and which electrical theory is supposed to explain, are not radically and wholly false. If the "theory" upon which the term anger "depends" really has empirical consequences, then even to say "I am angry" is in part to assert that these empirical consequences are not radically and wholly false. Thus it would not be absurd, if "anger" really *were* a theoretical term, to say "I think that I am very angry, but I'm not sure" or "I think that I have a severe pain, but I'm not sure" or "I think that I am conscious but I'm not sure," since one might well not be sure that the experimental laws implied by the "psychological theory" implicit in ordinary language are in fact correct. It would also not be absurd to say: "perhaps there is not really any such thing as anger" or "perhaps there is not really any such thing as pain" or "perhaps there is not really any such thing as being conscious." Indeed, no matter how certain I might be that I have the sensation of red, it might be proved *by examining other people* that I did *not* have that sensation and that in fact there was no such thing as having the sensation of red. Indeed, "that *looks like* the sensation of red" would have a perfectly good use—namely, to mean that my experience is as it would be if the "psychological theory implicit in ordinary language" were true, but the theory is not in fact true. These consequences should certainly cast doubt on the idea that "psychological terms in ordinary language" really are "theoretical constructs."

It is obvious that "psychological terms in ordinary language" have a *reporting use*. In the jargon of philosophers of science, they figure in *observation statements*. "I am in pain" would be such a statement. But clearly, a term that figures in observational reports has an observational use, and that use must enter into its meaning. Its meaning cannot be fixed merely by its relation to other terms, in abstraction from the actual speech habits of speakers (including the habits upon which the reporting use depends).

The first difficulty suggests that the "psychological theory" that "implicitly defines" such words as "anger" has in fact *no* nontautological consequences—or, at least, no empirical consequences that could not be abandoned without changing the meaning of these words. The second difficulty then further suggests that the job of fixing the meaning of these words is only partially done by the logical relationships (the "theory"), and is completed by the reporting use.

A third difficulty arises when we ask just what it is that the "psychological theory implicit in ordinary language" is supposed to be *postulating*. The usual answer is that the theory postulates the existence of certain *states* which are supposed to be related to one another and to behavior as specified in the theory. But what does "state" mean? If "state" is taken to mean physical state, in the narrow sense alluded to before, then psychophysical parallelism would be implied by an arbitrary "psychological" assertion, which is obviously incorrect. On the other hand, if "state" is taken in a sufficiently wide sense so as to avoid this sort of objection, then (as Wittgenstein points out) the remark that "being angry is being in a certain psychological state" *says nothing whatsoever*.

In the case of an ordinary scientific theory (say, a physical theory), to postulate the existence of "states" $S_1, S_2, \ldots, S_n$ satisfying certain postulates is to assert that one of two things is the case: either (1) physical states (definable in terms of the existing primitives of physical theory) can be found satisfying the postulates; or (2) it is necessary to take the new predicates $S_1, \ldots, S_n$ (or predicates in terms of which they can be defined) as additional primitives in physical science, and widen our concept of "physical state" accordingly. In the same way, identity theorists have sometimes suggested that "molar psychological theory" *leaves it open* whether or not the states it postulates are physical states or not. But if physical states *can* be found satisfying the postulates, then they are the ones referred to by the postulates. "State" is then a methodological term, so to speak, whose status is explained by a perspicuous representation of the procedures of empirical theory construction and confirmation. This solution to our third difficulty reduces to the identity theory under the supposition that psychophysical parallelism holds, and that physical states *can* be found "satisfying" the postulates of "molar behavioral psychology."

Even if this solution to the third difficulty is accepted, however, the first two difficulties remain. To be an empirically confirmable scientific theory, the "molar behavioral theory" implicit in the ordinary use of psychological terms must have testable empirical consequences. If the ordinary-language psychological terms really designate states postulated by this theory, then, if the theory is radically false, we must say there are no such "states" as being angry, being in pain, having a sensation, etc. And this must always remain a possibility (on this account), no matter what we observe, since no finite number of observations can deductively establish a scientific theory properly so-called. Also, the reporting role of "psychological" terms in ordinary language is not discussed by this account. If saying "I am in pain" is simply ascribing a *theoretical* term to myself, then this report is in part a *hypothesis,* and one which may always be false. This account—that the ordinary use of "psychological" terms presupposes an empirical theory, and one which may be radically false—has recently been urged by Paul Feyerabend. Feyerabend would accept the consequence that I have rejected as counterintuitive: that there may not really be any pains, sensations, etc., in the customary sense. But where is this empirical theory that is presupposed by the ordinary use of "psychological" terms? Can anyone state *one* behavioral law which is clearly empirical and which is presupposed by the concepts of sensation, anger, etc.? The empirical connection that exists, say,

between being in pain and saying "ouch," or some such thing, has
sometimes been taken (by logical behaviorists, rather than by identity
theorists) to be such a law. I have tried to show elsewhere, however,
that no such law is really required to be true for the application of
the concept of pain in its customary sense. What entitles us to say
that a man is in pain in our world may not entitle one to say that he is
in pain in a different world; yet the *same* concept of pain may be applicable. What I contend is that to understand any "psychological"
term, one must be implicitly familiar with a network of *logical* relationships, and one must be adequately trained in the reporting use
of that word. It is also necessary, I believe, that one be prepared to
accept first-person statements by other members of one's linguistic
community involving these predicates, at least when there is no
special reason to distrust them; but this is a general convention associated with discourse, and not part of the meaning of any particular
word, psychological or otherwise. Other general conventions associated with discourse, in my opinion, are the acceptance of not-too-
bizarre rules of inductive inference and theory confirmation and of
certain fundamental rules of deductive inference. But these things,
again, have to do with one's discourse *as a whole* not being linguistically deviant, rather than with one's understanding any particular
word. If I am not aware that someone's crying out (in a certain kind
of context) is a sign that he is in pain, I can be *told*. If I refuse (without good reason) to believe what I am told, it can be pointed out to
me that, when I am in that context (say, my finger is burnt), *I* feel
pain, and no condition known by me to be relevant to the feeling
or nonfeeling of pain is different in the case of the Other. If I *still*
feel no inclination to ascribe pain to the Other, then my whole concept of discourse is abnormal—but it would be both a gross under-
statement and a misdiagnosis to say that I "don't know the meaning
of 'pain'."

I conclude that "psychological" terms in ordinary language are
not theoretical terms. Moreover, the idea that, if psychophysical
parallelism is correct, then it is analytic that pain *is* the correlated
brain-state is not supported by a shred of linguistic evidence. (Yet this
is a consequence of the combined "identity theory–theoretical term"
account as we developed it to meet our third difficulty.) I conclude
that any attempt to show that Oscar is conscious (analytically, relative
to our premises) along these lines is hopeless.

So far all the arguments we have considered, on both sides of
the question: Is Oscar conscious? have been without merit. No sound
consideration has been advanced to show that it is false, given the
meaning of the words in English and the empirical facts as we are

assuming them, that Oscar is conscious; but also no sound consideration has been advanced to show that it is true. If it is a violation of
the rules of English to say (without "raised-eyebrow quotes") that
Oscar is in pain or seeing a rose or thinking about Vienna, we have
not been told *what* rules it violates; and if it is a violation of the rules
of English to *deny* that Oscar is conscious, given his psychological
isomorphism to a human being, we have likewise not been told what
rules it violates. In this situation, it is of interest to turn to an ingenious ("anti-civil-libertarian") argument by Paul Ziff.[1]

Ziff wishes to show that it is false that Oscar is conscious. He
begins with the undoubted fact that if Oscar is not alive he cannot
be conscious. Thus, given the semantical connection between "alive"
and "conscious" in English, it is enough to show that Oscar is not
alive. Now, Ziff argues, when we wish to tell whether or not something is alive, we do *not* go by its *behavior*. Even if a thing looks like
a flower, grows in my garden like a flower, etc., if I find upon taking
it apart that it consists of gears and wheels and miniaturized fur-
naces and vacuum tubes and so on, I say "what a clever mechanism,"
not "what an unusual plant." It is *structure*, not *behavior* that determines whether or not something is alive; and it is a violation of the
semantical rules of our language to say of anything that is clearly a
mechanism that it is "alive."

Ziff's argument is unexpected, because of the great concentration in the debate up to now upon *behavior*, but it certainly calls
attention to relevant logical and semantical relationships. Yet I cannot agree that these relationships are as clear-cut as Ziff's argument
requires. Suppose that we construct a robot—or, let me rather say,
an *android*, to employ a word that smacks less of mechanism—out of
"soft" (protoplasm-like) stuff. Then, on Ziff's account, it may be perfectly correct, if the android is sufficiently "life-like" in structure, to
say that we have "synthesized life." So, given two artifacts, both
"models" of the same psychological theory, both completely deterministic physical-chemical systems, both designed to the same end
and "programmed" by the designer to the same extent, it may be
that we must say that one of them is a "machine" and not conscious,
and the other is a "living thing" (albeit "artificially created") and
conscious, simply because the one consists of "soft stuff" and the other
consists of "hardware." A great many speakers of English, I am sure
(and I am one of them), would find the claim that this dogmatic decision is required by the meaning of the word "alive" quite contrary to
their linguistic intuitions. I think that the difficulty is fundamentally

[1] I take the liberty of reporting an argument used by Ziff in a conversation. I do not
wish to imply that Ziff necessarily subscribes to the argument in the form in which I
report it, but I include it because of its ingenuity and interest.

this: a plant does not exhibit much "behavior." Thus it is natural that criteria having to do with *structure* should dominate criteria having to do with "behavior" when the question is whether or not something that looks and "behaves" like a plant is really a living thing or not. But in the case of something that looks and behaves like an *animal* (and especially like a *human being*), it is natural that criteria having to do with behavior—and not just with actual behavior, but with the *organization* of behavior, as specified by a psychological theory of the thing—should play a much larger role in the decision. Thus it is not unnatural that we should be prepared to argue, in the case of the "pseudo-plant," that "it isn't a living thing because it is a mechanism," while some are prepared to argue, in the case of the robot, that "it isn't a *mere* mechanism, because it is *alive,*" and "it is alive, because it is conscious," and "it is conscious because it has the same behavioral organization as a living human being." Yet Ziff's account may well explain why it is that many speakers are not convinced by these latter arguments. The tension between conflicting criteria results in the "obviousness," to some minds, of the robot's "machine" status, and the equal "obviousness," to other minds, of its "artificial-life" status.

There is a sense of "mechanism" in which it is clearly analytic that a mechanism cannot be alive. Ziff's argument can be reduced to the contention that, on the normal interpretation of the terms, it is analytic in English that something whose *parts* are all mechanisms, in this sense, likewise cannot be alive. If this is so, then no English speaker should suppose that he could even *imagine* a robot *thinking,* being *power-mad, hating humans,* or *being in love,* any more than he should suppose that he could imagine a married bachelor. It seems evident to me (and indeed to most speakers) that, absurdly or not, we *can* imagine these things. I conclude, therefore, that Ziff is wrong: it may be *false,* but it is not a *contradiction,* to assert that Oscar is alive.

We have still to consider the most traditional view on our question. According to this view, which is still quite widely held, *it is possible that Oscar is conscious, and it is possible that he is not conscious.* In its theological form, the argument runs as follows: I am a creature with a body and a soul. My body happens to consist of flesh and blood, but it might just as well have been a machine, had God chosen. Each voluntary movement of my body is correlated with an activity of my soul (how and why is a "mystery"). So, it is quite possible that Oscar has a soul, and that each "voluntary" movement of his mechanical body is correlated in the same mysterious way with an activity of his soul. It is also possible—since the laws of physics suffice to explain the motions of Oscar's body, without use of the assumption that he has a soul—that Oscar is but a lifeless machine. There is absolutely no way in which we can know. This argument can also be given a nontheological (or at least apparently nontheological) form by deleting the reference to God, and putting "mind" for "soul" throughout. To complete the argument, it is contended that I know what it *means* to say that Oscar has a "soul" (or has a pain, or the sensation of red, etc.) *from my own case.*

One well-known difficulty with this traditional view is that it implies that it is also possible that other humans are not really conscious, even if they are physically and psychologically isomorphic to me. It is contended that I can know with *probability* that other humans are conscious by the "argument from analogy." But in the inductive sciences, an argument from analogy is generally regarded as quite weak unless the conclusion is capable of further and independent inductive verification. So it is hard to believe that our reasons for believing that other persons are conscious are very strong ones if they amount simply to an analogical argument with a conclusion that admits of *no* independent check, observational, inductive, or whatever. Most philosophers have recently found it impossible to believe *either* that our reasons for believing that other persons are conscious are that weak *or* that the possibility exists that other persons, while being admittedly physically and psychologically isomorphic (in the sense of the present paper) to myself, are not conscious. Arguments on this point may be found in the writings of all the major analytical philosophers of the present century. Unfortunately, many of these arguments depend upon quite dubious theories of meaning.

The critical claim is the claim that it follows from the fact that I have had the sensation of red, I can imagine this sensation, I "know what it is like," that I can understand the assertion that Oscar has the sensation of red (or any other sensation or psychological state). In a sense, this is right. I *can,* in one sense, understand the *words.* I can parse them; I don't think "sensation of red" means *baby carriage,* etc. More than that: I know what I would experience if I were conscious and psychologically as I am, but with Oscar's mechanical "body" in place of my own. How does this come to be so? It comes to be so, at least in part, because we have to learn from experience what our own bodies are like. If a child were brought up in a suitable kind of armor, the child might be deceived into thinking that it was a robot. It would be harder to fool him into thinking that he had the internal structure of a robot, but this too could be done (fake X rays, etc.). And when I "imagine myself in the shoes of a (conscious) robot," what I do, of course, is to imagine the sensations that I might have if a were a robot, or rather *if I were a human who mistakenly thought that he was a robot.* (I look down at my feet and see bright metal, etc.)

Well, let us grant that in this sense we *understand* the sentence "Oscar is having the sensation of red." It does not follow that the sentence possesses a truth value. We understand the sentence "the present King of France is bald," but, on its normal interpretation in English, the sentence has no truth value under present conditions. We can give it one by adopting a suitable convention—for example, Russell's theory of descriptions—and more than one such suitable convention exists. The question really at issue is *not* whether we can "understand" the sentences "Oscar is conscious" (or "has the sensation of red" or "is angry") and "Oscar is not conscious," in the sense of being able to use them in such contexts as "I can perfectly well picture to myself that Oscar is conscious," but whether there really is an intelligible sense in which one of these sentences is true, on a normal interpretation, and the other false (and, in that case, whether it is also true that we can't tell which).

Let us revert, for a moment, to our earlier fantasy of ROBOTS —i.e., second-order robots, robots created by robots and regarded by the robots as *mere* ROBOTS. As already remarked, a robot philosopher might very well be led to consider the question: Are ROBOTS conscious? The robot philosopher "knows," of course, just what experiences" he would have if he were a "conscious" ROBOT (or a robot in a ROBOT suit). He can "perfectly well picture to himself that a ROBOT could have 'sensation.' " So he may perfectly well arrive at the position that it is logically possible that ROBOTS have sensations (or, rather, "sensations") and perfectly possible that they do not, and moreover he can never know. What do we think of this conclusion?

It is clear what we should think: we should think that there is not the slightest reason to suppose (and every reason not to suppose) that there is a special property, "having the 'sensation' of red," which the ROBOT may or may not have, but which is inaccessible to the robot. The robot, knowing the physical and psychological description of the ROBOT, is in a perfectly good position to answer all questions about the ROBOT that may reasonably be asked. The idea that there is a further question (class of questions) about the ROBOT which the robot cannot answer, is suggested to the robot by the fact that these alleged "questions" are grammatically well formed, can be "understood" in the sense discussed above, and that the possible "answers" can be "imagined."

I suggest that our position with respect to robots is *exactly* that of robots with respect to ROBOTS. There is not the slightest reason for us, either, to believe that "consciousness" is a well-defined prop-

erty, which each robot either *has* or *lacks,* but such that it is not possible, on the basis of the physical description of the robot, or even on
the basis of the psychological description (in the sense of "psychological" explained above), to *decide* which (if any) of the robots
possess this property and which (if any) fail to possess it. The rules
of "robot language" may well be such that it is perfectly possible for
a robot to "conjecture" that ROBOTS have "sensations" and also
perfectly possible for a robot to conjecture that ROBOTS do not
have "sensations." It does not follow that the physical and psychological description of the ROBOTS is "incomplete," but only that
the concept of "sensation" (in "raised-eyebrow quotes") is a well-
defined concept only when applied to robots. The question raised by
the robot philosopher: Are ROBOTS "conscious"? calls for a decision and not for a discovery. The decision, at bottom, is this: Do I
treat ROBOTS as fellow members of my linguistic community, or as
machines? If the ROBOTS are accepted as full members of the robot
community, then a robot can find out whether a ROBOT is "conscious" or "unconscious," "alive" or "dead" in just the way he finds
out these things about a fellow robot. If they are rejected, then
nothing *counts* as a ROBOT being "conscious" or "alive." Until the
decision is made, the statement that ROBOTS are "conscious" has
no truth value. In the same way, I suggest, the question: Are robots
conscious? calls for a decision, on our part, to treat robots as fellow
members of our linguistic community, or not to so treat them. As
long as we leave this decision unmade, the statement that robots (of
the kind described) are conscious has no truth value.

If we reject the idea that the physical and psychological description of the robots is incomplete (because it "fails to specify whether
or not they are conscious"), we are not thereby forced to hold either
that "consciousness" is a "physical" attribute or that it is an attribute
"implicitly defined by a psychological theory." Russell's question in
the philosophy of mathematics: If the number 2 is not the set of all
pairs, then what on earth is it? was a silly question. Two is simply
the second number, and nothing else. Likewise, the materialist question: If the attribute of "consciousness" is not a physical attribute (or
an attribute implicitly defined by a psychological theory) then what
on earth is it? is a silly question. Our psychological concepts in ordinary language are as we have fashioned them. The "framework"
of ordinary-language psychological predicates is what it is and not
another framework. *Of course* materialism is false; but it is so *trivially* false that no materialist should be bothered!

In this paper, I have reviewed a succession of failures: failures
to show that we *must* say that robots are conscious, failures to show

that we *must* say they are not, failures to show that we *must* say that we can't tell. I have concluded from these failures that there is no correct answer to the question: Is Oscar conscious? Robots may indeed have (or lack) properties unknown to physics and undetectable by us; but not the slightest reason has been offered to show that they do, as the ROBOT analogy demonstrates. It is reasonable, then, to conclude that the question that titles this paper calls for a decision and not for a discovery. If we are to make a decision, it seems preferable to me to extend our concept so that robots *are* conscious—for "discrimination" based on the "softness" or "hardness" of the body parts of a synthetic "organism" seems as silly as discriminatory treatment of humans on the basis of skin color. But my purpose in this paper has not been to improve our concepts, but to find out what they are.

PUTNAM SELECTION

1.   Seriously speaking: if you encountered a robot that talked to you, read books, cooked a pretty fair omelet, made jokes, got angry, seemed cheerful sometimes and depressed at other times, and all in all was a nice sort of robot to have around, would you *really* doubt that it was conscious, merely because it had machinery rather than flesh and blood?

2.   Put the same point the other way round: if you met a "person" who looked just like a human being but behaved like a machine, would you think it was conscious? Suppose "he" responded to questions in a flat, toneless voice; suppose "he" sometimes gave the same answer over and over, like a broken record; suppose "he" was purely functional, exhibiting no emotions, no spontaneity, no unpredictability. Would you think "he" was a person? (You can actually see "persons" like this in some of the Disneyworld attractions!)

3.   According to Putnam, a number of the key words in the debate over robot consciousness are simply not well enough defined to allow us to decide whether robots can be conscious or not. Can you think of other examples of terms that are not completely defined over *all* of the logically possible situations that might arise? What about "solid"? (Since physicists tell us that a table is made up of tiny particles of matter with a good deal of space between them, are we to conclude that therefore a table is not solid? But if a table isn't solid, what is?) What about "alive"?

1.   In the science fiction movie *Star Wars,* two of the most popular characters are a pair of "droids," which is to say robots. How would each of our six authors handle the claim that these characters are persons? They seem to have distinctive personalities, they show irritation, loyalty, affection, fear, and so forth. What would we say of such creatures if we encountered them in the real world?

2.   Using Locke's distinction among substance, person, and man, try to figure out what Descartes, Mead, and Williams would say are the defining characteristics of *a* substance, *a* person, and *a* human being. Are the differences among the philosophers in this section real disagreements, or are they simply differences arising from the fact that they ask different questions?

3.   Imagine a device that instantaneously transports people from one place to another (like the "transporter" on the television show, *Star Trek*). Let us suppose that it works by mapping the exact structure of the body, breaking the body down into its subatomic elements, and then reconstructing an exactly similar body from material lying around at the other end of the transportation. If I stepped into such a device, was decomposed, and then was reconstructed at the other end, would I be *the same person*? How would each of our authors handle this question? Suppose the character who stepped out of the reconstruction booth *remembered* stepping into the decomposition booth—would Locke say he was the same person? Would Descartes? Suppose now that the machine malfunctioned, so that *two* of me were (was?) reconstructed—which of the two would be me? The first? The second? Both? Neither? If you killed one of the two in order to tidy things up, would you be guilty of murder? (If the answer is yes, whom would you have killed? Me? But "I" am standing there watching you!)

4.   A great many of the arguments used by the philosophers in this chapter depend on what are called "thought experiments." We try to imagine a very unusual situation, and then ask what we would think or say about it. This is a way of clarifying the precise meaning of concepts that are familiar (like "person") but that may nevertheless not really be absolutely clear. Is this a legitimate way to analyze a concept? Are there any limits on this technique? Can you think of cases in which we have been forced to change our concepts by actual experiences that we either did not or could not foresee by imagination alone?

5.   Descartes and Locke analyze the problem of personal identity from a purely individual point of view. Williams, Strawson, and Putnam introduce social considerations by raising questions about language, which is a social phenomenon. But only Mead confronts directly the social nature of the origins and developments of personality. In what way, if at all, would the other authors have to adjust their arguments in order to take account of Mead's analysis of the social origins of the self?

CHAPTER two

FREEDOM, DETERMINISM, AND RESPONSIBILITY

(Focal Issues)

1. What Am I Morally Reponsible For?

2. What Is Freedom of the Will?

3. Are Causal Determination and Prediction Incompatible with Moral Responsiblity?

INTRODUCTION

Herman is dead of a bullet in the head, and Fred is accused of murder. Let us imagine *six* different defenses that Fred's lawyer might put forward in an attempt to get him acquitted. We shall start with defenses that don't raise any tricky, troubling philosophical problems (leaving aside, of course, whether they are actually *true* or not), and move on to some really sticky ones. By the time we have finished, we shall have raised one of the oldest and most difficult problems in all of philosophy: the problem of freedom, determinism, and responsibility.

1. First Defense: *Fred isn't responsible for Herman's death. He didn't pull the trigger, George did. Fred never even laid a finger on the gun. Indeed, he wasn't anywhere near Herman.* Leaving aside some of the subtler complications of the law, this is—if true—a perfectly adequate defense. It makes sense to hold someone responsible only for things he has done (including, of course, negative "things," like the failure to do something he could and should have done). If George killed Herman, then George ought to be on trial, not Fred.

2. Second Defense: *Fred isn't responsible for Herman's death. Fred's finger was on the trigger, but Fred was unconscious at the time, and George, in an attempt to frame Fred, pulled the trigger with Fred's finger, thereby leaving powder burns on Fred's hand and Fred's fingerprint on the trigger.* Once again, if this story is true, it certainly lets Fred off the hook. His finger may have been the physical object spatially contiguous to the trigger at the time that the trigger moved so as to fire the gun. But since Fred was unconscious, he did not, in any ordinary sense, "pull" the trigger. He did not *move* his finger. His finger *was moved* (by George). What is more, since Fred was unconscious, he could not have stopped George from putting his finger on the trigger and moving it. (We shall hear more, later on, about the tricky notion of "could have done.") Another way to put the same point is that Fred, strictly speaking, did not *do* anything, for doing carries with it such notions as choice, awareness, purpose, and the ability to do otherwise, all of which are absent in this case. After all, if a giant picks up a midget and uses the midget as a club to bludgeon someone, we would hardly say that the midget had beaten that person to death!

3. Third Defense: *Fred isn't responsible for Herman's death. He*

pulled the trigger, all right, but he was caused to do so by a brain tumor that deprived him of ordinary control over his bodily functions. At about this point, little alarm bells should be going off very softly in your head, for we have started down a slippery slope that is going to lead us onto some swampy conceptual ground. If there really is a brain tumor, and if it really can be demonstrated, neurologically, that Fred's finger muscles contracted involuntarily as a result of a defect in his neural net traceable to that tumor, then I suppose we have no choice but to conclude that Fred is not responsible for what happened. (We shall leave to one side the obvious question: What was he doing with a gun in his hand pointing at Herman? Let us assume that there is a perfectly good, innocent reason for that.) Fred has no more control over the growth and functioning of a tumor in his head than he has over what George does to him while he is unconscious. If we accept the second defense, we can hardly refuse to accept this third one. But pretty clearly, by agreeing that Fred's brain tumor relieves him of responsibility, we are opening the door to a whole variety of similar defenses, some of which are going to make us very uncomfortable.

4. Fourth Defense: *Fred isn't responsible for Herman's death. He pulled the trigger, all right, but he was caused to do so by a series of electrical impulses along his nervous system, which in turn were caused by various physico-chemical reactions in his body, which in turn are (at least in principle, if not in every detail) traceable to a variety of internal physical events and external sensory inputs that, taken all together, constitute the total causal background for the event that we call "pulling the trigger."* Well, you can't say I didn't warn you! Now the fat is in the fire. If we accept this defense, then we can just throw the whole idea of responsibility out the window. Everything we hold people responsible for is some sort of physical action (or failure to act), even if it is only the physical act of saying something. Presumably, every action proceeds by way of muscular contractions triggered by neural impulses. Unless these are some physical events that start up spontaneously (more of this later), without causal antecedents, it will in principle be possible to trace back each of those neural and muscular events to earlier neural, muscular, biochemical, or physical events, which in their turn have causal antecedents. Since Fred must have been born at some time in the not-too-distant past, a little perseverance will carry us back to physical events that totally predate his existence. How can we hold Fred responsible for an event—the pulling of the trigger —whose causes actually go back to a time when he was not even alive?

To be sure, the complicated network of causes and effects may be too intricate for us to grasp in all its detail, but we can hardly hold Fred guilty of murder merely because of our limitations of understanding. Then too, you might wish to protest that the chain of causes is rather long by the time it has reached back beyond

Fred's birth, but that too seems a frivolous objection. If I set up a row of 10,000 dominoes so that when the first is knocked over, all the rest go in order, it is clear that the fall of the last domino is caused by the fall of the first, however long it takes for the intervening 9,998 to do their thing. If I paint the name "Fred" on the five-thousandth domino, would it make any sense for me to say that the real, ultimate, responsible cause of the last domino's fall is the falling over of Fred? Obviously not. Well, the person we call "Fred" is no more responsible for the pulling of that trigger than the domino we call "Fred" is for the fall of the last domino in the row.

Pretty clearly, several very important steps have been taken by Fred's lawyer in this fourth defense. For one thing, we have shifted from talking about what did happen to talking about what *must have* happened. No one has even been able to lay out the entire causal network, reaching back even a few days, for an event like the moving of a finger. In the first and second defenses, we pointed to things that George did, things we could observe, describe, and understand. In the third defense, we pointed to a specific, very unusual physical condition—a brain tumor—which neurologists could show to be the direct cause of the nerve impulse that led to the muscles in Fred's are and hand. But in this fourth defense, we appeal vaguely to events that can "in principle" be specified and identified, even though we grant that in practice no one could ever lay them all out.

The second problem is that we seem, by the progress of our reasoning, to have argued ourselves completely out of an entire set of beliefs and ideas that make perfectly good sense to us and that we all use every day. We began, let us recall, with the death of Herman. Fred was blamed because it was thought that Fred had shot Herman. The first and second defenses shifted the blame to George, either because it was actually George who had shot Herman, or because George had "shot" Herman, using Fred's finger to pull the trigger. Everything we said presupposed the meaningfulness, the appropriateness, of our familiar concepts of responsibility, purpose, intention, and blame. The only question was whether we had applied them correctly to Fred in the case of Herman's death. Now, however, we appear to have followed a trail of argument that leads to the bizarre conclusion that *no one is ever truly responsible for anything!*

One more point before we move on (for Fred's lawyer is not done yet with his defenses). Underlying all but the first of the defenses offered thus far is the unspoken claim that Fred is not responsible because *he could not have done otherwise.* According to the first defense, he didn't do anything (George did it), but in the second case, he could not have done otherwise because he was unconscious. In the third case, he could not have done otherwise because the operations of the brain tumor were not (we assumed) within his control. And in the present case, Fred was excused by his lawyer from responsibility on the grounds that he could not have done otherwise because the chain of causes reached back beyond his birth and hence clearly beyond his control. In each case, if the prosecution were able to show that Fred *could* have done otherwise, then presumably we (the jury) would be prepared once more to hold Fred responsible.

For example, if neurologists conclude that the brain tumor merely created an urge in Fred to kill Herman, but that the urge was such that Fred could have resisted it (an urge, perhaps, like the urge to scratch one's nose), then Fred's lawyer would surely not be able to get him off.

This notion that Fred "could not have done otherwise" is clearly very important to any understanding of responsibility, but it is also quite puzzling. Does it mean that Fred could not have done otherwise even if he had *chosen* to do otherwise? In the second case, where Fred was unconscious, he wasn't in a position to choose anything. He would have had to be conscious in order to make choices, in which case George could not so easily have manipulated his finger on the trigger.

But in the fourth case, which we are now considering, Fred's choices are part of the causal chain. They are, so to speak, among the dominoes near the end of the row. To be sure, his choices have their causes, and hence, in some sense, Fred is not responsible for them. (Or is he?) But it is still true that *if* he had chosen differently, *then* he would not have pulled the trigger. So it is unclear whether that fact is enough to make him responsible for Herman's death.

5. Fifth Defense. *Fred isn't responsible for Herman's death. Fred shot Herman, but he did it without premeditation, without reason. The action was totally out of character, bore no relation to anything he had ever done before or is at all likely to do in the future. Fred gained nothing from it, and even now cannot really view the act as something HE did.* Fred's lawyer has now gone off in a totally new direction. In effect, he is arguing that his client, Fred, is a person, not a physical body. A person has a coherent personality, on the basis of which we can explain past behavior, predict future behavior, and account for actions as part of a total integrated pattern. If Fred had a history of violent assault, or if there were evidence that Fred had planned to kill Herman, or if Fred stood to gain by Herman's death and had in the past acted on the basis of an awareness of his self-interest, then we would hold Fred responsible. But insofar as the act totally fails to fit into the pattern of Fred's personality, we cannot really say that *he did it* and hence hold him responsible.

6. Sixth Defense: *Fred isn't responsible for Herman's death. His shooting of Herman was only the latest in a long series of violent, anti-social acts, which taken together reveal Fred to be a thoroughly incorrigible, irresponsible criminal. Fred's behavior is a direct result of the miserable personal, family, and social conditions in which he grew up. It is society, not Fred, who must bear the blame for Herman's death.* Fred's lawyer has now turned 180 degrees from

his previous defense. Before, he argued that Fred could not be held responsible because the act of shooting Herman was utterly alien to everything else he was and had done. The implication was that if Fred had so much as thought of shooting Herman, he would have shrunk in horror from the deed. Now, Fred's lawyer is arguing that the shooting of Herman is so completely Fred, so much the sort of thing he has done and would do, that he cannot be held responsible because he does not have it within him to choose to act any other way. Behind this defense lies a sociological and psychological version of the causal argument that was used in the fourth defense. There it was the fact of universal physical causation to which the lawyer appealed. Here, it is familial and social determinants of personality that are invoked. Just as the Fred of the fourth defense could not help being born into an ongoing causal chain of physical events, neural discharges, and muscular contractions that led eventually to the pulling of the trigger of the gun that shot Herman, so the Fred of this defense cannot help having been born into a social environment that, as we so often say, "breeds violence." (Notice the implication in that familiar phrase of a causal chain over which the parties themselves have no choice.) In the third defense, we heard an appeal to a brain tumor, a physical disease. Here we are being told that society itself is sick, and that Fred, like Herman, is a victim of that sickness.

Once more, however, the tendency of the argument is to obliterate our ordinary notions of responsibility and blame—and our notion of praise or moral credit as well. It is not only criminals who are born into familial and social settings. All of us are. If Fred is not being blamed for killing Herman, on the grounds that his background and upbringing led him to it, then we can hardly heap praise on the young woman who pulls an old man from a burning building. She too, presumably, became the sort of person who would perform heroic deeds of that sort as a result of childhood environment, upbringing, and social influences. Once again, a plausible line of defense leads us to forfeit the notions of praise and blame and responsibility all together.

So much for Fred. We can leave him to his fate, as the jury mulls over the six defenses his clever lawyer has deployed. Our attention has been focused on the question of his *responsibility* for Herman's death, for the hypothetical example of a legal action brings that notion to the fore. Underlying our discussion, however, has been a somewhat wider philosophical issue that usually carries the label "freedom of the will." Philosophers are accustomed to saying that a person is responsible for his actions insofar as he is *free,* or does them *freely,* or has *free will.* To be *free* is contrasted with being *determined,* and so the issue is called "freedom and determinism." To say that a person is determined to act in a certain way is, according to at least some philosophers, to say that he could not have done otherwise had he chosen, or that he was caused to do what he did, and each of these views excuses him of responsibility for the action and its consequences.

The freedom that we attribute to persons has been thought by many philosophers to be incompatible with the thoroughgoing causal determinism that metaphysicians impute to the universe in general. If human beings are merely one among many species of animal in a world that is governed by causal laws, then the behavior of men and women must be, in principle, just as much traceable to prior causes as are the motions of the planets, the chemical interactions of the elements, or the behavior of plants and insects.

In their struggles with the conflict between human freedom and natural causal determination, philosophers have taken up one or another of four major positions. Each position has serious weaknesses, and as a result, philosophers defending one of them make their most telling points by arguing against the other three.

The first position, sometimes called "strict determinism," is the position that causation does indeed rule the universe, that human beings are a part of that universe, and, therefore, in the ordinary sense of the term, that human beings are *not* free. This is a simple, straightforward position, heavily reliant on the concepts and presuppositions of the physical sciences. It leaves room for—indeed, it positively invites—new scientific explanations of human behavior. It is, or at least seems to be, tough-minded, consistent, unsentimental. However, it begins to unravel somewhat when it seeks to explain such familiar phenomena as language and symbolic communication. It also has a certain amount of difficulty explaining how the defenders of this sweeping determinism can, at one and the same time, consider themselves mere causally determined creatures in the natural world and also engage in serious scientific research. (Do they, for example, seriously believe that their own choices of scientific hypotheses or experimental procedures are predetermined?)

The second position, which we may label "indeterminism," is that human beings are indeed free, and hence that causal determinism is not universal. Where persons act, there causation does not hold sway. This too is a doctrine attractive in its simplicity. Its principal weakness is a persistent inability to specify where the line is drawn between freedom and determinism. The trouble is that each time science delves deeper into the physiological, psychological, or social origins of behavior, it discovers causes for actions that previously were thought to be free. As neurology and psychiatry push back the limits of our knowledge, exposing the hidden causes of behavior we were previously unable to explain, actions that appeared free turn out to be causally determined. The sphere of "free" responsible action shrinks correspondingly. So this second position looks suspiciously like a mere way station on the road to the first, determinist view.

The third position, commonly called *compatibilism* holds that human beings really are free, that all events in the universe really are causally determined, and that a proper re-analysis of the concepts of freedom and determinism will reveal that there is no contradiction between the two. Defenders of this position usually combine it with a re-analysis of the associated notions of praise, blame, and responsibility. The great virtue of compatibilism, of course, is that it allows for both freedom and causation without being forced to alter and redraw the boundary between the two every time a new scientific discovery is announced. The principal drawback of compatibilism is that—according to some critics at least—it fails to do justice to what we all really mean when we say that a man or woman is free and hence responsible for his or her actions.

The fourth position, a special version of compatibilism, has been held by only one major philosopher, but it deserves special mention because that philosopher, the eighteenth-century German Immanuel Kant, is undoubtedly the most important single contributor to the debate about freedom and determinism. Kant held that human beings are both free and determined, but he rejected the relatively simple compatibilism that some other philosophers had espoused. According to Kant, the spatio-temporal world of physics and psychology is not the real world; it is merely a realm of appearances constructed by the mind itself. The real world, of things as they are in themselves, is unknowable by us, though we can form an empty concept of it. The self that can truly be said to act freely is a timeless, nonspatial self-in-itself. The self we observe and describe in space and time is a mere appearance of that true self. So each of us is both free, as Real Self, and causally determined, as appearance. Kant's exceedingly subtle and complicated defense of this version of compatibilism may not, in the end, be persuasive. But Kant is remembered nonetheless as the philosopher who forced all other philosophers to confront the inadequacies of simple determinism, simple free-will-ism, and simple compatibilism. If Kant's way out won't do, then some equally subtle resolution of the conflict is still required.

(SELECTION 1)

BARON D'HOLBACH

Man Is a Being Purely Physical

We begin with an uncompromising statement of the straight determinist position. Baron d'Holbach writes in a long tradition of physicalist, materialist philosophy, going all the way back to the atomism of such ancient thinkers as Democritus. Human beings are simply physical creatures, and their movement, or behavior, falls under the universal laws of causation that rule the motions of heavenly and earthly bodies. Deterministic materialism of the Holbachian sort has played an important role in the philosophy of Europe since the seventeenth century, although it has always been a subordinate rather than a dominant school. Thomas Hobbes and Pierre Gassendi in the 1600s are among the intellectual forebears of d'Holbach.

In attempting to evaluate the materialist, determinist position, there are clearly two questions that must be posed: First, what does it mean to say that the mind or self is physical, material, and can such a claim be made consistent with the sorts of things we ordinarily wish to assert about consciousness, intention, purpose, and meaning? Second, what do we mean when we say that one event *causes* another, what

evidence do we or could we have for such a claim, and what arguments can we possibly offer for the claim that *all* events in space and time are caused to happen by events preceding them in time?

In d'Holbach's discussion of the issue of free will, special emphasis is placed on the inseparable interconnections between our conscious thoughts and feelings and the physical causes, effects, and correlates of those contents of consciousness. D'Holbach is clearly correct in insisting that little sense can be made of the notion of a thoroughly disembodied mind. But that does not by itself settle the question of free will. D'Holbach also tends, it should be noticed, to slide from the claim that our actions are physically determined into the quite different claim that our choices are determined by a calculus of pleasure and pain. The latter assertion seems at least compatible with the thesis that our choices are purposive, rational, and hence—in some sense—free. Nevertheless, in this selection we find as stark an exposition of the straight determinist doctrine as we are likely to encounter.

Those who have pretended that the *soul* is distinguished from the body, is immaterial, draws its ideas from its own peculiar source, acts by its own energies, without the aid of any exterior object, have, by a consequence of their own system, enfranchised it from those physical laws according to which all beings of which we have a knowledge are obliged to act. They have believed that the soul is mistress of its own conduct, is able to regulate its own peculiar operations, has the faculty to determine its will by its own natural energy; in a word, they have pretended that man is a *free agent*.

It has been already sufficiently proved that the soul is nothing more than the body considered relatively to some of its functions more concealed than others: it has been shown that this soul, even when it shall be supposed immaterial, is continually modified conjointly with the body, is submitted to all its motion, and that without this it would remain inert and dead: that, consequently, it is subjected to the influence of those material and physical causes which give impulse to the body; of which the mode of existence, whether habitual or transitory, depends upon the material elements by which it is surrounded, that form its texture, constitute its temperament, enter into it by means of the aliments, and penetrate it by their subtility. The faculties which are called *intellectual,* and those qualities which are styled *moral,* have been explained in a manner purely physical and natural. In the last place it has been demonstrated that all the ideas, all the systems, all the affections, all the opinions, whether true or false, which man forms to himself, are to be attributed to his physical and material senses. Thus man is a being purely physical; in whatever manner he is considered, he is connected to universal nature, and submitted to the necessary and immutable laws that she imposes on all the beings she contains, according to their peculiar essences or to the respective properties with which, without consulting them, she endows each particular species. Man's life is a line that nature commands him to describe upon the surface of the earth, without his ever being able to swerve from it, even for an instant. He is born without his own consent; his organization does in nowise depend upon himself; his ideas come to him involuntarily; his habits are in the power of those who cause him to contract them; he is unceasingly modified by causes, whether visible or concealed, over which he has no control, which necessarily regulate his mode of existence, give the hue to his way of thinking, and determine his manner of acting. He is good or bad, happy or miserable, wise or foolish, reasonable or irrational, without his will being for any thing in these various states. Nevertheless, in despite

From *The System of Nature* by Baron d'Holbach. First published in 1770.

of the shackles by which he is bound, it is pretended he is a free agent, or that independent of the causes by which he is moved, he determines his own will, and regulates his own condition.

However slender the foundation of this opinion, of which every thing ought to point out to him the errour, it is current at this day and passes for an incontestable truth with a great number of people, otherwise extremely enlightened; it is the basis of religion, which, supposing relations between man and the unknown being she has placed above nature, has been incapable of imagining how man could either merit reward or deserve punishment from this being, if he was not a free agent. Society has been believed interested in this system; because an idea has gone abroad, that if all the actions of man were to be contemplated as necessary, the right of punishing those who injure their associates would no longer exist. At length human vanity accommodated itself to a hypothesis which, unquestionably, appears to distinguish man from all other physical beings, by assigning to him the special privilege of a total independence of all other causes, but of which a very little reflection would have shown him the impossibility.

As a part subordinate to the great whole, man is obliged to experience its influence. To be a free agent, it were needful that each individual was of greater strength than the entire of nature; or that he was out of this nature, who, always in action herself, obliges all the beings she embraces to act, and to concur to her general motion; or, as it has been said elsewhere, to conserve her active existence by the motion that all beings produce in consequence of their particular energies, submitted to fixed, eternal, and immutable laws. In order that man might be a free agent, it were needful that all beings should lose their essences; it would be equally necessary that he himself should no longer enjoy physical sensibility; that he should neither know good nor evil, pleasure nor pain; but if this were the case, from that moment he would no longer be in a state to conserve himself, or render his existence happy; all beings would become indifferent to him; he would no longer have any choice; he would cease to know what he ought to love, what it was right he should fear; he would not have any acquaintance with that which he should seek after, or with that which it is requisite he should avoid. In short, man would be an unnatural being, totally incapable of acting in the manner we behold. It is the actual essence of man to tend to his well being, or to be desirous to conserve his existence; if all the motion of his machine spring as a necessary consequence from this primitive impulse; if pain warn him of that which he ought to avoid; if pleasure announce to him that which he should desire; if it be in his essence to love that which either excites delight, or that from which he expects agreeable sensations; to hate that which either makes him fear contrary impressions or that which afflicts him with uneasiness; it must necessarily be that he will be attracted by that which he deems advantageous; that his will shall be determined by those objects which he judges useful; that he will be repelled by those beings which he believes prejudicial, either to his habitual or to his transitory mode of existence. It is only by the aid of experience that man acquires the faculty of understanding what he ought to love or to fear. Are his organs sound? his experience will be true; are they unsound? it will be false: in the first instance he will have reason, prudence, foresight; he will frequently foresee very remote effects; he will know that what he sometimes contemplates as a good, may possibly become an evil by its necessary or probable consequences; that what must be to him a transient evil, may by its result procure him a solid and durable good. It is thus experience enables him to foresee, that the amputation of a limb will cause him painful sensation, he consequently is obliged to fear this operation, and he endeavours to avoid the pain; but, if experience has also shown him that the transitory pain this amputation will cause him may be the means of saving his life; the preservation of his existence being of necessity dear to him, he is obliged to submit himself to the momentary pain, with a view to procuring a permanent good by which it will be overbalanced.

The will . . . is a modification of the brain, by which it is disposed to action, or prepared to give play to the organs. This will is necessarily determined by the qualities, good or bad, agreeable or painful, of the object or the motive that acts upon his senses, or of which the idea remains with him, and is resuscitated by his memory. In consequence, he acts necessarily, his action is the result of the impulse he receives either from the motive, from the object, or from the idea which has modified his brain, or disposed his will. When he does not act according to this impulse, it is because there comes some new cause, some new motive, some new idea, which modifies his brain in a different manner, gives him a new impulse, determines his will in another way, by which the action of the former impulse is suspended: thus, the sight of an agreeable object, or its idea, determines his will to set him in action to procure it; but if a new object or a new idea more powerfully attracts him, it gives a new direction to his will, annihilates the effect of the former, and prevents the action by which it was to be procured. This is the mode in which reflection, experience, reason, necessarily arrests or suspends the action of man's will: without this he would of necessity have followed

the anterior impulse which carried him towards a then desirable
object. In all this he always acts according to necessary laws, from
which he has no means of emancipating himself.

If when tormented with violent thirst, he figures to himself in
idea, or really perceives a fountain, whose limpid streams might cool
his feverish want, is he sufficient master of himself to desire or not to
desire the object competent to satisfy so lively a want? It will no
doubt be conceded, that it is impossible he should not be desirous
to satisfy it; but it will be said—if at this moment it is announced
to him that the water he so ardently desires is poisoned, he will, notwithstanding his vehement thirst, abstain from drinking it: and it
has, therefore, been falsely concluded that he is a free agent. The
fact, however, is, that the motive in either case is exactly the same:
his own conservation. The same necessity that determined him to
drink before he knew the water was deleterious, upon this new discovery equally determines him not to drink; the desire of conserv-
ing himself either annihilates or suspends the former impulse; the
second motive becomes stronger than the preceding, that is, the fear
of death, or the desire of preserving himself, necessarily prevails over
the painful sensation caused by his eagerness to drink: but, it will be
said, if the thirst is very parching, an inconsiderate man without
regarding the danger will risk swallowing the water. Nothing is
gained by this remark: in this case, the anterior impulse only regains
the ascendency; he is persuaded that life may possibly be longer preserved, or that he shall derive a greater good by drinking the poisoned water than by enduring the torment, which, to his mind,
threatens instant dissolution: thus the first becomes the strongest
and necessarily urges him on to action. Nevertheless, in either case,
whether he partakes of the water, or whether he does not, the two
actions will be equally necessary; they will be the effect of that
motive which finds itself most puissant; which consequently acts in
the most coercive manner upon his will.

This example will serve to explain the whole phenomena of the
human will. This will, or rather the brain, finds itself in the same
situation as a bowl, which, although it has received an impulse that
drives it forward in a straight line, is deranged in its course whenever
a force superior to the first obliges it to change its direction. The
man who drinks the poisoned water appears a madman; but the actions of fools are as necessary as those of the most prudent individuals.
The motives that determine the voluptuary and the debauchee to
risk their health, are as powerful, and their actions are as necessary,
as those which decide the wise man to manage his. But, it will be
insisted, the debauchee may be prevailed on to change his conduct:
this does not imply that he is a free agent; but that motives may be

found sufficiently powerful to annihilate the effect of those that previously acted upon him; then these new motives determine his will to the new mode of conduct he may adopt as necessarily as the former did to the old mode.

Man is said to *deliberate*, when the action of the will is suspended; this happens when two opposite motives act alternately upon him. *To deliberate*, is to hate and to love in succession; it is to be alternately attracted and repelled; it is to be moved, sometimes by one motive, sometimes by another. Man only deliberates when he does not distinctly understand the quality of the objects from which he receives impulse, or when experience has not sufficiently apprised him of the effects, more or less remote, which his actions will produce. He would take the air, but the weather is uncertain; he deliberates in consequence; he weighs the various motives that urge his will to go out or to stay at home; he is at length determined by that motive which is most probable; this removes his indecision, which necessarily settles his will, either to remain within or to go abroad: this motive is always either the immediate or ultimate advantage he finds, or thinks he finds, in the action to which he is persuaded. . . .

The various powers, frequently very complicated, that act either successively or simultaneously upon the brain of man, which modify him so diversely in the different periods of his existence, are the true causes of that obscurity in morals, of that difficulty which is found, when it is desired to unravel the concealed springs of his enigmatical conduct. The heart of man is a labyrinth, only because it very rarely happens that we possess the necessary gift of judging it; from whence it will appear, that his circumstances, his indecision, his conduct, whether ridiculous or unexpected, are the necessary consequences of the changes operated in him; are nothing but the effect of motives that successively determine his will; which are dependant on the frequent variations experienced by his machine. According to these variations the same motives have not always the same influence over his will; the same objects no longer enjoy the faculty of pleasing him; his temperament has changed, either for the moment, or for ever: it follows as a consequence, that his taste, his desires, his passions, will change; there can be no kind of uniformity in his conduct; nor any certitude in the effects to be expected.

Choice by no means proves the free agency of man: he only deliberates when he does not yet know which to choose of the many objects that move him, he is then in an embarassment, which does not terminate until his will is decided by the greater advantage he believes he shall find in the object he chooses, or the action he undertakes. From whence it may be seen, that choice is necessary, because he would not determine for an object, or for an action, if he did not believe that he should find in it some direct advantage. That man should have free agency it were needful that he should be able to will or choose without motive, or that he could prevent motives coercing his will. Action always being the effect of his will once determined, and as his will cannot be determined but by a motive which is not in his own power, it follows that he is never the master of the determination of his own peculiar will; that consequently he never acts as a free agent. It has been believed that man was a free agent because he had a will with the power of choosing; but attention has not been paid to the fact that even his will is moved by causes independent of himself; is owing to that which is inherent in his own organization, or which belongs to the nature of the beings acting on him.[1] Is he the master of willing not to withdraw his hand from the fire when he fears it will be burnt? Or has he the power to take away from fire the property which makes him fear it? Is he the master of not choosing a dish of meat, which he knows to be agreeable, or analogous to his palate; of not preferring it to that which he knows to be disagreeable or dangerous? It is always according to his sensations, to his own peculiar experience, or to his suppositions, that he judges of things, either well or ill; but whatever may be his judgment, it depends necessarily on his mode of feeling, whether habitual or accidental, and the qualities he finds in the causes that move him, which exist in despite of himself. . . .

In short, the actions of man are never free; they are always the necessary consequence of his temperament, of the received ideas, and of the notions, either true or false, which he has formed to himself of happiness; of his opinions, strengthened by example, by education, and by daily experience. So many crimes are witnessed on the earth only because every thing conspires to render man vicious and criminal; the religion he has adopted, his government, his education, the examples set before him, irresistibly drive him on to evil: under these circumstances, morality preaches virtue to him in vain. In those societies where vice is esteemed, where crime is crowned, where venality is constantly recompensed, where the most dreadful disorders are punished only in those who are too weak to enjoy the privilege of committing them with impunity, the practice of virtue

---

[1] Man passes a great portion of his life without even willing. His will depends on the motive by which he is determined. If he were to render an exact account of every thing he does in the course of each day—from rising in the morning to lying down at night—he would find that not one of his actions have been in the least voluntary; that they have been mechanical, habitual, determined by causes he was not able to foresee; to which he was either obliged to yield, or with which he was allured to acquiesce: he would discover, that all the motives of his labours, of his amusements, of his discourses, of his thoughts, have been necessary; that they have evidently either seduced him or drawn him along.

is considered nothing more than a painful sacrifice of happiness. Such societies chastise, in the lower orders, those excesses which they respect in the higher ranks; and frequently have the injustice to condemn those in the penalty of death, whom public prejudices, maintained by constant example, have rendered criminal.

Man, then, is not a free agent in any one instant of his life; he is necessarily guided in each step by those advantages, whether real or fictitious, that he attaches to the objects by which his passions are roused: these passions themselves are necessary in a being who unceasingly tends towards his own happiness; their energy is necessary, since that depends on his temperament; his temperament is necessary, because it depends on the physical elements which enter into his composition; the modification of this temperament is necessary, as it is the infallible and inevitable consequence of the impulse he receives from the incessant action of moral and physical beings.

D'HOLBACH SELECTION

1. What is the nature of the soul, according to d'Holbach?

2. What does d'Holbach mean by a "free agent"? On his view, could anyone or anything in the world be a free agent? Is God a free agent?

3. Would d'Holbach consider someone *free* if that person were being acted on by two exactly equal forces pushing or pulling in opposite directions?

4. Is there a difference between being caused to do something by the physical motions of external bodies, and being caused to do something by a calculation of pleasure and pain? What is the difference? Does the difference have any implications for the problems of moral responsibility and freedom?

(SELECTION 2)

DAVID HUME

Of Liberty and Necessity

David Hume, the great eighteenth-century Scottish philosopher, is the leading exponent of the compatibilist position in the debate over freedom and determinism. He is also the most important contributor to the analysis of the concept of causation, which as we have seen, is a central notion in this and other philosophical disputes. According to Hume, the mind derives the idea of a necessary or causal connection from the experience of observing repeated conjunctions of similar occurrences. The idea of causal connection, he argues, comes from the mind itself, not from the observation of natural objects. By such experiences of patterns in nature, we come to believe in a general regularity of nature, which encourages us to expect and to predict that future combinations of events will resemble past combinations. Although we have, strictly speaking, no good rational basis for this belief, according to Hume, we are nevertheless so constituted that we cannot help believing, and so by a natural process we arrive at the system of beliefs on which our understanding of the world is based.

The same process, Hume points out, takes place in our experience of human behavior. By exactly similar observations of patterned and repeated behavior, we develop beliefs in the generosity, or courage, or stinginess, or cowardliness of our fellow men and women. Our moral evaluations, our ascriptions of responsibility, our assignments of praise and blame, all rest on this empirically grounded system of judgments about the character and purposes of the persons we observe. Hence, for Hume, causal determination is not the opposite of freedom and responsibility; it is the necessary precondition for freedom and responsibility.

To say that a human being is *free* is thus merely to say that had he chosen to do otherwise than he did, he could indeed have done so. If that contrary-to-fact claim is false—if, that is to say, he could not have done otherwise even had he chosen, because he was in chains, or was paralyzed, or lacked sufficient power—then we say of him that he was *not* free.

The rejoinder that springs immediately to mind is this: could he have chosen differently, or was his *choosing* itself determined by his previous experience, by his upbringing, by his genetic inheritance, or whatever? Hume rejects this question. It is no part of being free, he insists, to have been able to choose differently. Freedom is only a matter of being able to do what one chooses to do. Needless to say, many philosophers reject this interpretation of the issue, although many others, as we shall see, agree with Hume.

It might reasonably be expected in questions which have been can-
vassed and disputed with great eagerness, since the first origin of
science and philosophy, that the meaning of all the terms, at least,
should have been agreed upon among the disputants; and our en-
quiries, in the course of two thousand years, been able to pass from
words to the true and real subject of the controversy. For how easy
may it seem to give exact definitions of the terms employed in reasoning, and make these definitions, not the mere sound of words, the
object of future scrutiny and examination? But if we consider the
matter more narrowly, we shall be apt to draw a quite opposite conclusion. From this circumstance alone, that a controversy has been
long kept on foot, and remains still undecided, we may presume
that there is some ambiguity in the expression, and that the disputants affix different ideas to the terms employed in the controversy. . . .

This has been the case in the long disputed question concerning
liberty and necessity; and to so remarkable a degree that, if I be not
much mistaken, we shall find, that all mankind, both learned and
ignorant, have always been of the same opinion with regard to this
subject, and that a few intelligible definitions would immediately
have put an end to the whole controversy. . . .

I hope, therefore, to make it appear that all men have ever
agreed in the doctrine both of necessity and of liberty, according to
any reasonable sense, which can be put on these terms; and that the
whole controversy has hitherto turned merely upon words. We shall
begin with examining the doctrine of necessity.

It is universally allowed that matter, in all its operations, is
actuated by a necessary force, and that every natural effect is so precisely determined by the energy of its cause that no other effect, in
such particular circumstances, could possibly have resulted from it.
The degree and direction of every motion is, by the laws of nature,
prescribed with such exactness that a living creature may as soon
arise from the shock of two bodies as motion in any other degree or
direction than what is actually produced by it. Would we, therefore,
form a just and precise idea of *necessity,* we must consider whence
that idea arises when we apply it to the operation of bodies.

It seems evident that, if all the scenes of nature were continually
shifted in such a manner that no two events bore any resemblance to
each other, but every object was entirely new, without any similitude
to whatever had been seen before, we should never, in that case,
have attained the least idea of necessity, or of a connexion among
these objects. We might say, upon such a supposition, that one object
or event has followed another; not that one was produced by the

From *An Enquiry into the Human Understanding* by David Hume. First published in
1748.

other. The relation of cause and effect must be utterly unknown to mankind. Inference and reasoning concerning the operations of nature would, from that moment, be at an end; and the memory and senses remain the only canals, by which the knowledge of any real existence could possibly have access to the mind. Our idea, therefore, of necessity and causation arises entirely from the uniformity observable in the operations of nature, where similar objects are constantly conjoined together, and the mind is determined by custom to infer the one from the appearance of the other. These two circumstances form the whole of that necessity, which we ascribe to matter. Beyond the constant *conjunction* of similar objects, and the consequent *inference* from one to the other, we have no notion of any necessity or connexion.

If it appear, therefore, that all mankind have ever allowed, without any doubt or hesitation, that these two circumstances take place in the voluntary actions of men, and in the operations of mind; it must follow, that all mankind have ever agreed in the doctrine of necessity, and that they have hitherto disputed, merely for not understanding each other.

As to the first circumstance, the constant and regular conjunction of similar events, we may possibly satisfy ourselves by the following considerations. It is universally acknowledged that there is a great uniformity among the actions of men, in all nations and ages, and that human nature remains still the same, in its principles and operations. The same motives always produce the same actions: The same events follow from the same causes. Ambition, avarice, self-love, vanity, friendship, generosity, public spirit: these passions, mixed in various degrees, and distributed through society, have been, from the beginning of the world, and still are, the source of all the actions and enterprises, which have ever been observed among mankind. . . .

We must not, however, expect that this uniformity of human actions should be carried to such a length as that all men, in the same circumstances, will always act precisely in the same manner, without making any allowance for the diversity of characters, prejudices, and opinions. Such a uniformity in every particular, is found in no part of nature. On the contrary, from observing the variety of conduct in different men, we are enabled to form a greater variety of maxims, which still suppose a degree of uniformity and regularity.

Are the manners of men different in different ages and countries? We learn thence the great force of custom and education, which mould the human mind from its infancy and form it into a fixed and established character. Is the behaviour and conduct of the one sex very unlike that of the other? Is it thence we become acquainted with the different characters which nature has impressed upon the sexes, and which she preserves with constancy and regularity? Are the actions of the same person much diversified in the different periods of his life, from infancy to old age? This affords room for many general observations concerning the gradual change of our sentiments and inclinations, and the different maxims which prevail in the different ages of human creatures. Even the characters, which are peculiar to each individual, have a uniformity in their influence; otherwise our acquaintance with the persons and our observation of their conduct could never teach us their disposition, or serve to direct our behaviour with regard to them.

I grant it possible to find some actions, which seem to have no regular connexion with any known motives, and are exception to all the measures of conduct which have ever been established for the government of men. But . . . the most irregular and unexpected resolutions of men may frequently be accounted for by those who know every particular circumstance of their character and situation. A person of an obliging disposition gives a peevish answer: But he has the toothache, or has not dined. A stupid fellow discovers an uncommon alacrity in his carriage: But he has met with a sudden piece of good fortune. Or even when an action, as sometimes happens, cannot be particularly accounted for, either by the person himself or by others; we know, in general, that the characters of men are, to a certain degree, inconstant and irregular. This is, in a manner, the constant character of human nature; though it be applicable, in a more particular manner, to some persons who have no fixed rule for their conduct, but proceed in a continued course of caprice and inconstancy. The internal principles and motives may operate in a uniform manner, notwithstanding these seeming irregularities; in the same manner as the winds, rain, clouds, and other variations of the weather are supposed to be governed by steady principles; though not easily discoverable by human sagacity and enquiry.

Thus it appears, not only that the conjunction between motives and voluntary actions is as regular and uniform as that between the cause and effect in any part of nature; but also that this regular conjunction has been universally acknowledged among mankind, and has never been the subject of dispute, either in philosophy or common life. Now, as it is from past experience that we draw all inferences concerning the future, and as we conclude that objects will always be conjoined together which we find to have always been conjoined; it may seem superfluous to prove that this experienced uniformity in human actions is a source whence we draw *inferences* concerning them. But in order to throw the argument into a greater variety of lights we shall also insist, though briefly, on this latter topic.

The mutual dependence of men is so great in all societies that scarce any human action is entirely complete in itself, or is performed without some reference to the actions of others, which are requisite to make it answer fully the intention of the agent. The poorest artificer, who labours alone, expects at least the protection of the magistrate, to ensure him the enjoyment of the fruits of his labour. He also expects that, when he carries his goods to market, and offers them at a reasonable price, he shall find purchasers, and shall be able, by the money he acquires, to engage others to supply him with those commodities which are requisite for his subsistence. . . . In short, this experimental inference and reasoning concerning the actions of others enters so much into human life that no man, while awake, is ever a moment without employing it. Have we not reason, therefore, to affirm that all mankind have always agreed in the doctrine of necessity according to the foregoing definition and explication of it?

Nor have philosophers ever entertained a different opinion from the people in this particular. For, not to mention that almost every action of their life supposes that opinion, there are even few of the speculative parts of learning to which it is not essential. What would become of *history*, had we not a dependence on the veracity of the historian according to the experience which we have had of mankind? How could *politics* be a science, if laws and forms of government had not a uniform influence upon society? Where would be the foundation of *morals*, if particular characters had no certain or determinate power to produce particular sentiments, and if these sentiments had no constant operation on actions? And with what pretence could we employ our *criticism* upon any poet or polite author, if we could not pronounce the conduct and sentiments of his actors either natural or unnatural to such characters, and in such circumstances? It seems almost impossible, therefore, to engage either in science or action or any kind without acknowledging the doctrine of necessity, and this *inference* from motive to voluntary actions, from characters to conduct. . . .

Were a man, whom I know to be honest and opulent, and with whom I live in intimate friendship, to come into my house, where I am surrounded with my servants, I rest assured that he is not to stab me before he leaves it in order to rob me of my silver standish; and I no more suspect this event than the falling of the house itself, which is new, and solidly built and founded.—*But he may have been seized with a sudden and unknown frenzy.*—So may a sudden earthquake arise, and shake and tumble my house about my ears. I shall therefore change the suppositions. I shall say that I know with certainty that he is not to put his hand into the fire and hold it there till it be consumed: And this event, I think I can foretell with the same assurance, as that, if he throw himself out at the window, and meet with no obstruction, he will not remain a moment suspended in the air. No suspicion of an unknown frenzy can give the least possibility to the former event, which is so contrary to all the known principles of human nature. A man who at noon leaves his purse full of gold on the pavement at Charing-Cross, may as well expect that it will fly away like a feather, as that he will find it untouched an hour after. Above one half of human reasonings contain inferences of a similar nature, attended with more or less degrees of certainty proportioned to our experience of the usual conduct of mankind in such particular situations.

I have frequently considered, what could possibly be the reason why all mankind, though they have ever, without hesitation, acknowledged the doctrine of necessity in their whole practice and reasoning, have yet discovered such a reluctance to acknowledge it in words, and have rather shown a propensity, in all ages, to profess the contrary opinion. The matter, I think, may be accounted for after the following manner. If we examine the operations of body, and the production of effects from their causes, we shall find that all our faculties can never carry us farther in our knowledge of this relation than barely to observe that particular objects are *constantly conjoined* together, and that the mind is carried, by a *customary transition,* from the appearance of one to the belief of the other. But though this conclusion concerning human ignorance be the result of the strictest scrutiny of this subject, men still entertain a strong propensity to believe that they penetrate farther into the powers of nature, and perceive something like a necessary connexion between the cause and the effect. When again they turn their reflections towards the operations of their own minds, and *feel* no such connexion of the motive and the action; they are thence apt to suppose, that there is a difference between the effects which result from material force, and those which arise from thought and intelligence. But being once convinced that we know nothing farther of causation of any kind than merely the *constant conjunction* of objects, and the consequent *inference* of the mind from one to another, and finding that these two circumstances are universally allowed to have place in voluntary actions; we may be more easily led to own the same necessity common to all causes. . . .

It would seem, indeed, that men begin at the wrong end of this question concerning liberty and necessity, when they enter upon it by examining the faculties of the soul, the influence of the understanding, and the operations of the will. Let them first discuss a more simple question, namely, the operations of body and of brute unintelligent matter; and try whether they can there form any idea of causation and necessity, except that of a constant conjunction of objects, and subsequent inference of the mind from one to another. If these circumstances form, in reality, the whole of that necessity, which we conceive in matter, and if these circumstances be also universally acknowledged to take place in the operations of the mind, the dispute is at an end; at least, must be owned to be thenceforth merely verbal. But as long as we will rashly suppose, that we have some farther idea of necessity and causation in the operations of external objects; at the same time, that we can find nothing farther in the voluntary actions of the mind; there is no possibility of bringing the question to any determinate issue, while we proceed upon so erroneous a supposition. . . .

But to proceed in this reconciling project with regard to the question of liberty and necessity; the most contentious question of metaphysics, the most contentious science; it will not require many words to prove, that all mankind have ever agreed in the doctrine of liberty as well as in that of necessity, and that the whole dispute, in this respect also, has been hitherto merely verbal. For what is meant by liberty, when applied to voluntary actions? We cannot surely mean that actions have so little connexion with motives, inclinations, and circumstances, that one does not follow with a certain degree of uniformity from the other, and that one affords no inference by which we can conclude the existence of the other. For these are plain and acknowledged matters of fact. By liberty, then, we can only mean *a power of acting or not acting, according to the determinations of the will;* that is, if we choose to remain at rest, we may; if we choose to move, we also may. Now this hypothetical liberty is universally allowed to belong to every one who is not a prisoner and in chains. Here, then, is no subject of dispute. . . .

All laws being founded on rewards and punishments, it is supposed as a fundamental principle, that these motives have a regular and uniform influence on the mind, and both produce the good and prevent the evil actions. We may give to this influence what name we please; but, as it is usually conjoined with the action, it must be esteemed a *cause,* and be looked upon as an instance of that necessity, which we would here establish.

The only proper object of hatred or vengeance is a person or creature, endowed with thought and consciousness; and when any criminal or injurious actions excite that passion, it is only by their relation to the person, or connexion with him. Actions are, by their very nature, temporary and perishing; and where they proceed not for some *cause* in the character and disposition of the person who performed them, they can neither redound to his honour, if good;

nor infamy, if evil. The actions themselves may be blameable; they may be contrary to all the rules of morality and religion: But the person is not answerable for them; and as they proceeded from nothing in him that is durable and constant, and leave nothing of that nature behind them, it is impossible he can, upon their account, become the object of punishment or vengeance. According to the principle, therefore, which denies necessity, and consequently causes, a man is as pure and untainted, after having committed the most horrid crime, as at the first moment of his birth, nor is his character anywise concerned in his actions, since they are not derived from it, and the wickedness of the one can never be used as a proof of the depravity of the other.

Men are not blamed for such actions as they perform ignorantly and casually, whatever may be the consequences. Why? but because the principles of these actions are only momentary, and terminate in them alone. Men are less blamed for such actions as they perform hastily and unpremeditately than for such as proceed from deliberation. For what reason? but because a hasty temper, though a constant cause or principle in the mind, operates only by intervals, and infects not the whole character. Again, repentance wipes off every crime, if attended with a reformation of life and manners. How is this to be accounted for? but by asserting that actions render a person criminal merely as they are proofs of criminal principles in the mind; and when, by an alteration of these principles, they cease to be just proofs, they likewise cease to be criminal. But, except upon the doctrine of necessity, they never were just proofs, and consequently never were criminal.

It will be equally easy to prove, and from the same arguments, that *liberty,* according to that definition above mentioned, in which all men agree, is also essential to morality, and that no human actions, where it is wanting, are susceptible of any moral qualities, or can be the objects either of approbation or dislike. For as actions are objects of our moral sentiment, so far only as they are indications of the internal character, passions, and affections; it is impossible that they can give rise either to praise or blame, where they proceed not from these principles, but are derived altogether from external violence. . . .

HUME SELECTION

1. Does Hume think that the predictability of human actions shows that they are unfree, or that they are free? Should we be held responsible for actions that could be predicted by others?

2. According to Hume, what sorts of observations form the basis

for our reasoning about causes and effects? What is the role of repeated patterns in experience? Do human affairs exhibit less regularity than physical events, according to Hume, or roughly the same amount, or more?

3.   Hume defines liberty as "a power of acting or not acting, according to the determinations of the will." Does that mean that we are free so long as we can do what we choose, or does it mean rather that we are *free to choose* what we shall try to do? What is the difference between those two?

4.   According to Hume, what sorts of actions is it reasonable to blame a person for? Give some examples of actions Hume would hold someone responsible for, and actions he would not hold anyone responsible for.

(SELECTION 3)

IMMANUEL KANT

Freedom as Rational Causality

The determinists, the libertarians, and the compatibilists (as we may call the three major schools of thought on the free-will problem) all start from the assumption that there is one and only one kind of causation. Either they apply it to human behavior, or they withhold attribution of it to human behavior, or they claim that application of it to human behavior is compatible with ascriptions of responsibility and judgments of praise and blame. But Immanuel Kant, in his most important work on moral philosophy, the *Foundations of the Metaphysics of Morals,* takes a fundamentally different line. All causality is subordination to law, Kant argues, but natural objects (what he calls appearances or "phenomena") are governed irrationally by laws. Their behavior falls under laws, and occurs in conformity with laws, but it does not occur by means of a rational apprehension of laws. Rocks fall to earth at a speed determined by the laws of motion, but the rocks are not aware of the laws of motion, nor do they choose to subordinate their falling to those laws. Kant puts the some point a different way by saying that natural objects are governed in their behavior by foreign or external causes.

Rational creatures (such as human beings), are also governed in their actions by laws, but the laws are operative through, or by means of, a rational understanding of the laws. A hungry man eats food because he understands that food will alleviate his hunger; a thirsty man shuns salt water, even though he is thirsty, because he understands that salt water will actually make him thirstier. Rational creatures are thus moved by their inner comprehension of the logical relationship between what they desire and what can be expected to satisfy their desires. They are thus, in Kant's language, moved internally rather than externally.

Another way to put the same point is to say that whereas natural objects are moved by *causes,* rational creatures are moved by *reasons.* Hence, it makes sense to ask whether a human being has acted wisely or unwisely, sensibly or foolishly, whereas it makes no sense at all to ask the same question of a rock (or of a plant, or a toad; I leave to one side the vexing issue of chimpanzees and dolphins).

To be free, Kant suggests, is simply to be moved internally by reasons rather than externally by causes; and to have a will is simply to be the sort of creature that is capable of being moved by reasons. So the question, "Does Man have free will?" is really, for Kant, no question at all. If we have wills, then we are by virtue of that fact free. The real question is whether we have wills at all —whether, that is, we are the sort of beings who are capable of being moved by reasons rather than by natural causes.

Now, strictly speaking, Kant thinks we cannot ever know whether we are creatures with wills—whether, that is, we are free, rational agents. But insofar as we undertake to *do* anything, to act, we must assume that we are, he argues. So in practice, though not in theory, it is a fundamental premise of all our deliberations that we are absolutely self-moved, rational, and hence free.

As will is a kind of causality of living beings so far as they are rational, freedom would be that property of this causality by which it can be effective independently of foreign causes determining it, just as natural necessity is the property of the causality of all irrational beings by which they are determined in their activity by the influence of foreign causes.

The preceding definition of freedom is negative and therefore affords no insight into its essence. But a positive concept of freedom flows from it which is so much the richer and more fruitful. Since the concept of a causality entails that of laws according to which something, i.e., the effect, must be established through something else which we call cause, it follows that freedom is by no means lawless even though it is not a property of the will according to laws of nature. Rather, it must be a causality according to immutable laws, but of a peculiar kind. Otherwise a free will would be an absurdity. Natural necessity is, as we have seen, a heteronomy of efficient causes, for every effect is possible only according to the law that something else determines the efficient cause to its causality. What else, then, can the freedom of the will be but autonomy, i.e., the property of the will to be a law to itself? The proposition that the will is a law to itself in all its actions, however, only expresses the principle that we should act according to no other maxim than that which can also have itself as a universal law for its object. And this is just the formula of the categorical imperative and the principle of morality. Therefore a free will and a will under moral laws are identical.

Thus if freedom of the will is presupposed, morality together with its principle follows from it by the mere analysis of its concept. But the principle is nevertheless a synthetical proposition: an absolutely good will is one whose maxim can always include itself as a universal law. It is synthetical because by analysis of the concept of an absolutely good will that property of the maxim cannot be found.

From *Foundations of the Metaphysics of Morals* by Immanuel Kant. First published in 1785. (trans. by Lewis White Beck, copyright © by The Liberal Arts Press, Inc., reprinted by permission of the publisher, The Bobbs-Merrill Company, Inc.

Such synthetical propositions, however, are possible only by the fact that both cognitions are connected through their union with a third in which both of them are to be found. The positive concept of freedom furnishes this third cognition, which cannot be, as in the case of physical causes, the nature of the sensuous world, in the concept of which we find conjoined the concepts of something as cause in relation to something else as effect. We cannot yet show directly what this third cognition is to which freedom directs us and of which we have an a priori idea, nor can we explain the deduction of the concept of freedom from pure practical reason and therewith the possibility of a categorical imperative. For this some further preparation is needed.

It is not enough to ascribe freedom to our will, on any grounds whatever, if we do not also have sufficient grounds for attributing it to all rational beings. For since morality serves as a law for us only as rational beings, morality must hold valid for all rational beings, and since is must be derived exclusively from the property of freedom, freedom as the property of the will of all rational beings must be demonstrated. And it does not suffice to prove it from certain alleged experiences of human nature (which is indeed impossible, as it can be proved only a priori), but we must prove it as belonging generally to the activity of rational beings endowed with a will. Now I say that every being which cannot act otherwise than under the idea of freedom is thereby really free in a practical respect. That is to say, all laws which are inseparably bound up with freedom hold for it just as if its will were proved free in itself by theoretical philosophy.[1] Now I affirm that we must necessarily grant that every rational being who has a will also has the idea of freedom and that it acts only under this idea. For in such a being we think of a reason which is practical, i.e., a reason which has causality with respect to its objects. Now, we cannot conceive of a reason which consciously responds to a bidding from the outside with respect to its judgments, for then the subject would attribute the determination of its power of judgment not to reason but to an impulse. Reason must regard itself as the author of its principles, independently of foreign influences; consequently, as practical reason or as the will of a rational being, it must regard itself as free. That is to say, the will of a rational being can be a will of its own only under the idea of freedom,

---

[1] I follow this method, assuming that it is sufficient for our purpose that rational beings take merely the idea of freedom as basic to their actions, in order to avoid having also to prove freedom in its theoretical aspect. For if the latter is left unproved, the laws which would obligate a being who was really free would hold for a being who cannot act except under the idea of his own freedom. Thus we can escape here from the onus which presses on the theory.

and therefore in a practical point of view such a will must be ascribed to all rational beings.

We have finally reduced the definite concept of morality to the idea of freedom, but we could not prove freedom to be real in ourselves and in human nature. We saw only that we must presuppose it if we would think of a being as rational and conscious of his causality with respect to actions, that is, as endowed with a will; and so we find that on the very same grounds we must ascribe to each being endowed with reason and will the property of determining himself to action under the idea of freedom.

From presupposing this idea [of freedom] there followed also consciousness of a law of action: that the subjective principles of actions, i.e., maxims, in every instance must be so chosen that they can hold also as objective, i.e., universal, principles, and thus can serve as principles for the universal laws we give. But why should I subject myself as a rational being, and thereby all other beings endowed with reason, to this law? I will admit that no interest impels me to do so, for that would then give no categorical imperative. But I must nevertheless take an interest in it and see how it comes about, for this "ought" is properly a "would" that is valid for every rational being provided reason is practical for him without hindrance [i.e., exclusively determines his action]. For beings who like ourselves are affected by the senses as incentives different from reason and who do not always do that which reason for itself alone would have done, that necessity of action is expressed only as an "ought." The subjective necessity is thus distinguished from the objective.

It therefore seems that the moral law, i.e., the principle of the autonomy of the will, is, properly speaking, only presupposed in the idea of freedom, as if we could not prove its reality and objective necessity by itself. Even if that were so, we would still have gained something because we would at least have defined the genuine principle more accurately than had been done before. But with regard to its validity and to the practical necessity of subjection to it, we would not have advanced a single step, for we could give no satisfactory answer to anyone who asked why the universal validity of our maxims as of a law had to be the restricting condition of our action. We could not tell on what is based the worth we ascribe to actions of this kind—a worth so great that there can be no higher interest, nor could we tell how it happens that man believes it is only through this that he feels his own personal worth, in contrast to which the worth of a pleasant or unpleasant condition is to be regarded as nothing.

We do find sometimes that we can take an interest in a personal quality which involves no [personal] interest in any [external] condition, provided only that [possession of] this quality makes us capable of participating in the [desired] condition in case reason were to effect the allotment of it. That is, mere worthiness to be happy even without the motive of participating in it can interest us of itself. But this judgment is in fact only the effect of the already assumed importance of moral laws (if by the idea of freedom we detach ourselves from every empirical interest). But that we ought to detach ourselves, i.e., regard ourselves as free in acting and yet as subject to certain laws, in order to find a worth merely in our person which would compensate for the loss of everything which makes our situation desirable—how this is possible and hence on what grounds the moral law obligates us we still cannot see in this way.

We must openly confess that there is a kind of circle here from which it seems that there is no escape. We assume that we are free in the order of efficient causes so that we can conceive of ourselves as subject to moral laws in the order of ends. And then we think of ourselves as subject to these laws because we have ascribed freedom of the will to ourselves. This is circular because freedom and self-legislation of the will are both autonomy and thus are reciprocal concepts, and for that reason one of them cannot be used to explain the other and to furnish a ground for it. At most they can be used for the logical purpose of bringing apparently different conceptions of the same object under a single concept (as we reduce different fractions of the same value to the lowest common terms).

One recourse, however, remains open to us, namely, to inquire whether we do not assume a different standpoint when we think of ourselves as causes a priori efficient through freedom from that which we occupy when we conceive of ourselves in the light of our actions as effects which we see before our eyes.

The following remark requires no subtle reflection, and we may suppose that even the commonest understanding can make it, though it does so, after its fashion, by an obscure discernment of judgment which it calls feeling: all conceptions, like those of the senses, which come to us without our choice enable us to know the objects only as they affect us, while what they are in themselves remains unknown to us; therefore, as regards this kind of conception, even with the closest attention and clearness which understanding may ever bring to them we can attain only to knowledge of appearances and never to knowledge of things in themselves. As soon as this distinction is made (perhaps merely because of a difference noticed between conceptions which are given to us from somewhere else and to which we are passive and those which we produce only from ourselves and in which we show our own activity), it follows of itself that we must admit and assume behind the appearances something else which is not appearance, namely, things in themselves; we do so although we must admit that we cannot approach them more closely and can never know what they are in themselves, since they can never be known by us except as they affect us. This must furnish a distinction, though a crude one, between a world of sense and a world of understanding. The former, by differences in the sensuous faculties, can be very different among various observers, while the latter, which is its foundation, remains always the same. A man may not presume to know even himself as he really is by knowing himself through inner sensation. For since he does not, as it were, produce himself or derive his concept of himself a priori but only empirically, it is natural that he obtains his knowledge of himself through inner sense and consequently only through the appearance of his nature and the way in which his consciousness is affected. But beyond the characteristic of his own subject which is compounded of these mere appearances, he necessarily assumes something else as its basis, namely, his ego as it is in itself. Thus in respect to mere perception and receptivity to sensations he must count himself as belonging to the world of sense; but in respect to that which may be pure activity in himself (i.e., in respect to that which reaches consciousness directly and not by affecting the senses) he must reckon himself as belonging to the intellectual world. But he has no further knowledge of that world.

To such a conclusion, the thinking man must come with respect to all things which may present themselves to him. Presumably it is to be met with in the commonest understanding which, as is well known, is very much inclined to expect behind the objects of the senses something else invisible and acting of itself. But such an understanding soon spoils it by trying to make the invisible again sensuous, i.e., to make it an object of intuition. Thus common understanding becomes not in the least wiser.

Now man really finds in himself a faculty by which he distinguishes himself from all other things, even from himself so far as he is affected by objects. This faculty is reason. As a pure spontaneous activity it is elevated even above understanding. For though the latter is also a spontaneous activity and does not, like sense, merely contain conceptions which arise only when one is affected by things, being passive, it nevertheless cannot produce by its activity any other concepts than those which serve to unite them in one consciousness. Without this use of sensibility it would not think at all, while, on the other hand, reason shows such a pure spontaneity in the case of ideas that it far transcends everything that sensibility can give to consciousness and shows its chief occupation in distinguishing the world of sense from the world of understanding, thereby prescribing limits to the understanding itself.

For this reason a rational being must regard himself as intelligence (and not from the side of his lower powers), as belonging to the world of understanding and not to that of the senses. Thus he has two standpoints from which he can consider himself and recognize the laws of the employment of his powers and consequently of all his actions: first, as belonging to the world of sense under laws of nature (heteronomy), and, second, as belonging to the intelligible world under laws which, independent of nature, are not empirical but founded only on reason.

As a rational being and thus as belonging to the intelligible world, man cannot think of the causality of his own will except under the idea of freedom, for independence from the determining causes of the world of sense (an independence which reason must always ascribe to itself) is freedom. The concept of autonomy is inseparably connected with the idea of freedom, and with the former there is inseparably bound the universal principle of morality, which ideally is the ground of all actions of rational beings, just as natural law is the ground of all appearances.

Now we have removed the suspicion which we raised that there might be a hidden circle in our reasoning from freedom to autonomy and from the latter to the moral law. This suspicion was that we laid down the idea of freedom for the sake of the moral law in order later to derive the latter from freedom, and that we were thus unable to give any ground for the law, presenting it only as a *petitio principii* that well-disposed minds would gladly allow us but which we could never advance as a demonstrable proposition. But we now see that, if we think of ourselves as free, we transport ourselves into the intelligible world as members of it and know the autonomy of the will together with its consequence, morality; while, if we think of ourselves as obligated, we consider ourselves as belonging both to the world of sense and at the same time to the intelligible world. . . .

In respect to their will, all men think of themselves as free. Hence arise all judgments of actions as being such as ought to have been done, although they were not done. But this freedom is not an empirical concept and cannot be such, for it still remains even though experience shows the contrary of the demands which are necessarily conceived as consequences of the supposition of freedom. On the other hand, it is equally necessary that everything which happens should be inexorably determined by natural laws, and this natural necessity is likewise no empirical concept, because it implies the concept of necessity and thus of a priori knowledge. But this concept of a system of nature is confirmed by experience, and it is inevitably presupposed if experience, which is knowledge of the objects of the senses interconnected by universal laws, is to be possible. Therefore freedom is only an idea of reason whose objective reality in itself is doubtful, while nature is a concept of the understanding which shows and necessarily must show its reality by examples in experience.

There now arises a dialectic of reason, since the freedom ascribed to the will seems to stand in contradiction to natural necessity. At this parting of the ways reason in its speculative purpose finds the way of natural necessity more well-beaten and usable than that of freedom; but in its practical purpose the footpath of freedom is the only one on which it is possible to make use of reason in our conduct. Hence it is as impossible for the subtlest philosophy as for the commonest reasoning to argue freedom away. Philosophy must therefore assume that no true contradiction will be found between freedom and natural necessity in the same human actions, for it cannot give up the concept of nature any more than that of freedom.

Hence even if we should never be able to conceive how freedom is possible, at least this apparent contradiction must be convincingly eradicated. For if even the thought of freedom contradicts itself or nature, which is equally necessary, it would have to be surrendered in competition with natural necessity.

But it would be impossible to escape this contradiction if the subject, who seems to himself free, thought of himself in the same sense or in the same relationship when he calls himself free as when he assumes that in the same action he is subject to natural law. Therefore it is an inescapable task of speculative philosophy to show at least that its illusion about the contradiction rests in the fact that we [do not] think of man in a different sense and relationship when we call him free from that in which we consider him as a part of nature and subject to its laws. It must show not only that they can very well coexist but also that they must be thought of as necessarily united in one and the same subject; for otherwise no ground could be given why we should burden reason with an idea which, though it may without contradiction be united with another that is sufficiently established, nevertheless involves us in a perplexity which sorely embarasses reason in its speculative use. This duty is imposed only on speculative philosophy, so that it may clear the way for practical philosophy. . . .

The title to freedom of the will claimed by common reason is based on the consciousness and the conceded presupposition of the independence of reason from merely subjectively determining causes which together constitute what belongs only to sensation, being comprehended under the general name of sensibility. Man, who in this way regards himself as intelligence, puts himself in a different order of things and in a relationship to determining grounds of an altogether different kind when he thinks of himself as intelligence with a will and thus as endowed with causality, compared with that other order of things and that other set of determining grounds which become relevant when he perceives himself as a phenomenon in the world of sense (as he really also is) and submits his causality to external determination according to natural laws. Now he soon realizes that both can subsist together—indeed, that they must. For there is not the least contradiction between a thing in appearance (as belonging to the world of sense) being subject to certain laws of which it is independent as a thing or a being in itself. That it must think of itself in this twofold manner rests, with regard to the first, on the consciousness of itself as an object affected through the senses, and, with regard to what is required by the second, on the consciousness of itself as intelligence, i.e., as independent of sensuous impressions in the use of reason and thus as belonging to the intelligible world.

This is why man claims to possess a will which does not let him become accountable for what belongs merely to his desires and inclinations, but thinks of actions which can be performed only by disregarding all desires and sensuous attractions, as possible and indeed necessary for him. The causality of these actions lies in him as an intelligence and in effects and actions in accordance with principles of an intelligible world, of which he knows only that reason alone and indeed pure reason independent of sensibility gives the law in it. Moreover, since it is only as intelligence that he is his proper self (being as man only appearance of himself), he knows that those laws apply to him directly and categorically, so that that to which inclinations and impulses and hence the entire nature of the world of sense incite him cannot in the least impair the laws of his volition as an intelligence. He does not even hold himself responsible for these inclinations and impulses or attribute them to his proper self, i.e., his will, though he does ascribe to his will the indulgence which he may grant to them when he permits them an influence on his maxims to the detriment of the rational laws of his will.

When practical reason thinks itself into an intelligible world, it does in no way transcend its limits. It would do so, however, if it tried to intuit or feel itself into it. The intelligible world is only a negative thought with respect to the world of sense, which does not give reason any laws for determining the will. It is positive only in the single point that freedom as negative determination is at the same time connected with a positive faculty and even a causality of reason. This causality we call a will to act so that the principle of actions will accord with the essential characteristic of a rational cause, i.e., with the condition of the universal validity of a maxim as a law. But if it were to borrow an object of the will, i.e., a motive, from the intelligible world, it would overstep its boundaries and pretend to be acquainted with something of which it knows nothing. The concept of a world of understanding is therefore only a standpoint which reason sees itself forced to take outside of appearances, in order to think of itself as practical. If the influences of sensibility were determining for man, this would not be possible; but it is necessary unless he is to be denied the consciousness of himself as an intelligence, and thus as a rational and rationally active cause, i.e., a cause acting in freedom. This thought certainly implies the idea of an order and legislation different from that of natural mechanism which applies to the world of sense; and it makes necessary the concept of an intelligible world, the whole of rational beings as things in themselves. But it does not give us the least occasion to think of it otherwise than according to its formal condition only, i.e., the universality of the maxim of the will as law and thus the autonomy of the will, which alone is consistent with freedom. All laws, on the other hand, which are directed to an object make for heteronomy, which belongs only to natural laws and which can apply only to the world of sense.

But reason would overstep all its bounds if it undertook to explain how pure reason can be practical, which is the same problem as explaining how freedom is possible.

For we can explain nothing but what we can reduce to laws whose object can be given in some possible experience. But freedom is a mere idea, the objective reality of which can in no way be shown according to natural laws or in any possible experience. Since no example in accordance with any analogy can support it, it can never be comprehended or even imagined. It holds only as the necessary presupposition of reason in a being that believes itself conscious of a will, i.e., of a faculty different from the mere faculty of desire, or a faculty of determining itself to act as intelligence and thus according to laws of reason independently of natural instincts. But where determination according to natural laws comes to an end, there too all explanation ceases and nothing remains but defense, i.e., refutation of the objections of those who pretend to have seen more deeply into the essence of things and therefore boldly declare freedom to be impossible. We can only show them that the supposed contradiction they have discovered lies nowhere else than in their necessarily regarding man as appearance in order to make natural law valid with respect to human actions. And now when we require them to think of him qua intelligence as a thing in itself, they still persist in considering him as appearance. Obviously, then, the separation of his causality (his will) from all natural laws of the world of sense in one and the same object is a contradiction, but this disappears, when they reconsider and confess, as is reasonable, that behind the appearances things in themselves must stand as their hidden ground and that we cannot expect the laws of the activity of these grounds to be the same as those under which their appearances stand.

KANT SELECTION

1. If will is a kind of causality, then are there any completely un-caused events, according to Kant? Using the suggestions in the introduction to this selection, try to explain in what sense we can speak of *reasons* as a species of cause.

2. If freedom is conformity to objectively valid, universal law, then what are we to say of someone who violates a moral law? Is that person unfree? But then, how can we hold anyone morally responsible for breaking the moral law?

3. "Autonomous" means, strictly speaking, "self-legislating," or "giving laws to oneself." What, according to Kant, is the connection between being *free* and being *autonomous*?

4. If I am self-legislating—if I "give laws to myself"—then how am I different from someone who simply does whatever he or she pleases? If I am going to be *rational* in my self-legislation, what limits or constraints does that place on the nature of the laws I lay down to myself?

5. If two separate moral agents engage in autonomous self-legislation, will they (according to Kant) always come up with identically the same laws? Why? What does that tell us about the nature of the laws they formulate?

6. How, according to Kant, can human beings at one and the same time be part of the natural order of things, and thus subject to physical laws, and also members of the moral order, and thus free and self-legislating? (This is the hardest question in all of Kant's philosophy, so don't be too upset if you can't give a short, snappy answer!)

(SELECTION 4)

MORITZ SCHLICK

When Is a Man Responsible?

If we hold to the classification of positions that we have been using in this chapter, then Moritz Schlick must be called a compatibilist, and indeed in this essay you will encounter some of the arguments that David Hume used almost two centuries earlier to demonstrate that there is no incompatibility between ascriptions of responsibility and assertions of causal determination. Yet in this essay, Schlick is more concerned to debunk the free will problem than to defend a particular solution to it. As you will find when you read this selection, most of his remarks are aimed at showing that previous philosophers have simply been confused about the question, and so thinkers on every side of the issue have taken up and defended muddled positions.

At first, we may be inclined to dismiss such claims out of hand. After all, David Hume and Immanuel Kant are among the most brilliant thinkers ever to turn their minds to philosophical issues, and even Baron d'Holbach is no slouch. How could it be that they, and so many others, are just plain confused, while Moritz Schlick sees through the issue with perfect clarity?

First of all, accusing all one's predecessors of total confusion was nothing new! Indeed, it is fair to say that *most* philosophers have thought that

those before them were utterly confused about certain fundamental matters of definition, analysis, and inference. Philosophy tends to be a contentious discipline, unlike the sciences, where there is—at least on the surface—more of an appearance of building on previous discoveries. Kant himself, for example, thought that all previous philosophy had been totally invalidated by a failure to distinguish properly between appearance and reality, and Hume, at the age of twenty-eight, believed that he had for the first time set the entire study of human affairs on the correct foundations.

But there is a deeper reason for the tendency of philosophers to advance their own theories by contrast with previous doctrines rather than by incremental addition. Philosophers rely almost completely upon the non-empirical tools of logical inference and conceptual analysis. An advance in philosophy takes place not when some new data are collected, new observations made, but when old and familiar concepts are subjected to a new analysis that reveals them to be different in structure and implications from what we previously thought. Inevitably, therefore, a new philosophical "discovery," if we can call it that, implies a rejection of previous ways of thinking about familiar

130

topics. And since the same tools of logical inference and conceptual analysis are available to all rational creatures, the philosopher putting forth the "discovery" seems to be implying that his predecessors were a bit dumb not to have seen the same thing.

The other side of the coin, of course, is that modern philosophers go on reading the works of the great thinkers of ancient times, because they never really go out of date. Modern scientists, by contrast, rarely if ever read the works of Newton, Faraday, or even more recent giants like Einstein.

With hesitation and reluctance I prepare to add this chapter to the discussion of ethical problems. For in it I must speak of a matter which, even at present, is thought to be a fundamental ethical question, but which got into ethics and has become a much discussed problem only because of a misunderstanding. This is the so-called problem of the freedom of the will. Moreover, this pseudo-problem has long since been settled by the efforts of certain sensible persons; and, above all, the state of affairs just described has been often disclosed—with exceptional clarity by Hume. Hence it is really one of the greatest scandals of philosophy that again and again so much paper and printer's ink is devoted to this matter, to say nothing of the expenditure of thought, which could have been applied to more important problems (assuming that it would have sufficed for these). Thus I should truly be ashamed to write a chapter on "freedom." In the chapter heading, the word "responsible" indicates what concerns ethics, and designates the point at which misunderstanding arises. Therefore the concept of responsibility constitutes our theme, and if in the process of its clarification I also must speak of the concept of freedom I shall, of course, say only what others have already said better; consoling myself with the thought that in this way alone can anything be done to put an end at last to that scandal.

The main task of ethics . . . is to explain moral behavior. To explain means to refer back to laws: every science, including psychology, is possible only in so far as there are such laws to which the events can be referred. Since the assumption that *all* events are subject to universal laws is called the principle of causality, one can also say, "Every science presupposes the principle of causality." Therefore every explanation of human behavior must also assume the validity of causal laws; in this case the existence of psychological laws. . . . All of our experience strengthens us in the belief that this presupposition is realized, at least to the extent required for all purposes of practical life in intercourse with nature and human beings, and also for the most precise demands of technique. Whether,

From *Problems of Ethics* by Moritz Schlick. First published in English in 1939. (trans. by David Rynin, Ph.D. Reprinted by permission of the translator.

indeed, the principle of causality holds universally, whether, that is, *determinism* is true, we do not know; no one knows. But we do know that it is impossible to settle the dispute between determinism and indeterminism by mere reflection and speculation, by the consideration of so many reasons for and so many reasons against (which collectively and individually are but pseudo-reasons). Such an attempt becomes especially ridiculous when one considers with what enormous expenditure of experimental and logical skill contemporary physics carefully approaches the question of whether causality can be maintained for the most minute intra-atomic events.

But the dispute concerning "freedom of the will" generally proceeds in such fashion that its advocates attempt to refute, and its opponents to prove, the validity of the causal principle, both using hackneyed arguments, and neither in the least abashed by the magnitude of the undertaking. . . . Others distinguish two realms, in one of which determinism holds, but not in the other. This line of thought (which was unfortunately taken by Kant) is, however, quite the most worthless (though Schopenhauer considered it to be Kant's most profound idea).

Fortunately, it is not necessary to lay claim to a final solution of the causal problem in order to say what is necessary in ethics concerning responsibility; there is required only an analysis of the concept, the careful determination of the meaning which is in fact joined to the words "responsibility" and "freedom" as these are actually used. If men had made clear to themselves the sense of those propositions, which we use in everyday life, that pseudo-argument which lies at the root of the pseudo-problem, and which recurs thousands of times within and outside of philosophical books, would never have arisen.

The argument runs as follows: "If determinism is true, if, that is, all events obey immutable laws, then my will too is always determined, by my innate character and my motives. Hence my decisions are necessary, not free. But if so, then I am not responsible for my acts, for I would be accountable for them only if I could do something about the way my decisions went; but I can do nothing about it, since they proceed with necessity from my character and the motives. And I have made neither, and have no power over them: the motives come from without, and my character is the necessary product of the innate tendencies and the external influences which have been effective during my lifetime. Thus determinism and moral responsibility are incompatible. Moral responsibility presupposes freedom, that is, exemption from causality."

This process of reasoning rests upon a whole series of confusions, just as the links of a chain hang together. We must show these confusions to be such, and thus destroy them.

It all begins with an erroneous interpretation of the meaning of "law." In practice this is understood as a rule by which the state prescribes certain behavior to its citizens. These rules often contradict the natural desires of the citizens (for if they did not do so, there would be no reason for making them), and are in fact not followed by many of them; while others obey, but under *compulsion*. The state does in fact compel its citizens by imposing certain sanctions (punishments) which serve to bring their desires into harmony with the prescribed laws.

In natural science, on the other hand, the word "law" means something quite different. The natural law is not a *pre*scription as to how something should behave, but a formula, a *de*scription of how something does in fact behave. The two forms of "laws" have only this in common: both tend to be expressed in *formulae*. Otherwise they have absolutely nothing to do with one another, and it is very blameworthy that the same word has been used for two such different things; but even more so that philosophers have allowed themselves to be led into serious errors by this usage. Since natural laws are only descriptions of what happens, there can be in regard to them no talk of "compulsion." The laws of celestial mechanics do not prescribe to the planets how they have to move, as though the planets would actually like to move quite otherwise, and are only forced by these burdensome laws of Kepler to move in orderly paths; no, these laws do not in any way "compel" the planets, but express only what in fact planets actually do.

If we apply this to volition, we are enlightened at once, even before the other confusions are discovered. When we say that a man's will "obeys psychological laws," these are not civic laws, which compel him to make certain decisions, or dictate desires to him, which he would in fact prefer not to have. They are laws of nature, merely expressing which desires he *actually has* under given conditions; they describe the nature of the will in the same manner as the astronomical laws describe the nature of planets. "Compulsion" occurs where man is prevented from realizing his natural desires. How could the rule according to which these natural desires arise itself be considered as "compulsion"?

But this is the second confusion to which the first leads almost inevitably: after conceiving the laws of nature, anthropomorphically, as order imposed *nolens volens* upon the events, one adds to them the concept of "necessity." This word, derived from "need," also comes to us from practice, and is used there in the sense of inescapable compulsion. To apply the word with this meaning to natural laws is of course senseless, for the presupposition of an opposing desire is lacking; and it is then confused with something altogether different, which is actually an attribute of natural laws. That is, universality. It is of the essence of natural laws to be universally valid, for only when we have found a rule which holds of events without exception do we *call* the rule a law of nature. Thus when we say "a natural law holds necessarily" this has but one legitimate meaning: "It holds in *all* cases where it is applicable." It is again very deplorable that the word "necessary" has been applied to natural laws (or, what amounts to the same thing, with reference to causality), for it is quite superfluous, since the expression "universally valid" is available. Universal validity is something altogether different from "compulsion"; these concepts belong to spheres so remote from each other that once insight into the error has been gained one can no longer conceive the possibility of a confusion.

The confusion of two concepts always carries with it the confusion of their contradictory opposites. The opposite of the universal validity of a formula, of the existence of a law, is the nonexistence of a law, indeterminism, acausality; while the opposite of compulsion is what in practice everyone calls "freedom." Here emerges the nonsense, trailing through centuries, that freedom means "exemption from the causal principle," or "not subject to the laws of nature." Hence it is believed necessary to vindicate indeterminism in order to save human freedom.

This is quite mistaken. Ethics has, so to speak, no moral interest in the purely theoretical question of "determinism or indeterminism?" but only a theoretical interest, namely: in so far as its seeks the laws of conduct, and can find them only to the extent that causality holds. But the question of whether man is morally free (that is, has that freedom which, as we shall show, is the presupposition of moral responsibility) is altogether different from the problem of determinism. Hume was especially clear on this point. He indicated the inadmissible confusion of the concepts of "indeterminism" and "freedom"; but he retained, inappropriately, the word "freedom" for both, calling the one freedom of "the will," the other, genuine kind, "freedom of conduct." He showed that morality is interested only in the latter, and that such freedom, in general, is unquestionably to be attributed to mankind. And this is quite correct. Freedom means the opposite of compulsion; a man is *free* if he does not act under *compulsion,* and he is compelled or unfree when he is hindered from without in the realization of his natural desires. Hence he is unfree when he is locked up, or chained, or when someone forces him at the point of a gun to do what otherwise he would not do. This is quite clear, and everyone will admit that the everyday or legal notion of the lack of freedom is thus correctly interpreted, and that a man will be considered quite free and responsible if no such external compulsion is exerted upon him. There are certain cases which lie between these clearly described ones, as, say, when someone acts under the influence of alcohol or a narcotic. In such cases we consider the man to be more or less unfree, and hold him less accountable, because we rightly view the influence of the drug as "external," even though it is found within the body; it prevents him from making decisions in the manner peculiar to his nature. If he takes the narcotic of his own will, we make him completely responsible for *this* act and transfer a part of the responsibility to the consequences, making, as it were, an average or mean condemnation of the whole. In the case also of a person who is mentally ill we do not consider him free with respect to those acts in which the disease expresses itself, because we view the illness as a disturbing factor which hinders the normal functioning of his natural tendencies. We make not him but his disease responsible.

But what does this really signify? What do we mean by this concept of responsibility which goes along with that of "freedom," and which plays such an important role in morality? It is easy to attain complete clarity in this matter; we need only carefully determine the manner in which the concept is used. What is the case in practice when we impute "responsibility" to a person? What is our aim in doing this? The judge has to discover who is responsible for a given act in order that he may *punish* him. We are inclined to be less concerned with the inquiry as to who deserves *reward* for an act, and we have no special officials for this; but of course the principle would be the same. But let us stick to punishment in order to make the idea clear. What is punishment, actually? The view still often expressed, that it is a natural *retaliation* for past wrong, ought no longer to be defended in cultivated society; for the opinion that an increase in sorrow can be "made good again" by further sorrow is altogether barbarous. Certainly the origin of punishment may lie in an impulse of retaliation or vengeance; but what is such an impulse except the instinctive desire to destroy the *cause* of the deed to be avenged, by the destruction of or injury to the malefactor? Punishment is concerned only with the institution of causes, of *motives* of conduct, and this alone is its meaning. Punishment is an educative measure, and as such is a means to the formation of motives, which are in part to prevent the wrongdoer from repeating the act (reformation) and in part to prevent others from committing a similar act (intimidation). Analogously, in the case of reward we are concerned with an incentive.

Hence the question regarding responsibility is the question: Who, in a given case, is to be punished? Who is to be considered the true wrongdoer? This problem is not identical with that regarding the original instigator of the act; for the great-grandparents of the man, from whom he inherited his character, might in the end be the cause, or the statesmen who are responsible for his social milieu, and so forth. But the "doer" is the one *upon whom the motive must have acted* in order, with certainty, to have prevented the act (or called it forth, as the case may be). Consideration of remote causes is of no help here, for in the first place their actual contribution cannot be determined, and in the second place they are generally out of reach. Rather, we must find the person in whom the decisive junction of causes lies. The question of who is responsible is the question concerning the *correct point of application of the motive.* And the important thing is that in this its meaning is completely exhausted; behind it there lurks no mysterious connection between transgression and requital, which is merely *indicated* by the described state of affairs. It is a matter only of knowing who is to be punished or rewarded, in order that punishment and reward function as such—be able to achieve their goal.

Thus, all the facts connected with the concepts of responsibility and imputation are at once made intelligible. We do not charge an insane person with responsibility, for the very reason that he offers no unified point for the application of a motive. It would be pointless to try to affect him by means of promises or threats, when his confused soul fails to respond to such influence because its normal mechanism is out of order. We do not try to give him motives, but try to heal him (metaphorically, we make his sickness responsible, and try to remove its causes). When a man is forced by threats to commit certain acts we do not blame him, but the one who held the pistol at his breast. The reason is clear: the act would have been prevented had we been able to restrain the person who threatened him; and this person is the one whom we must influence in order to prevent similar acts in the future.

But much more important than the question of when a man is said to be responsible is that of when he *himself* feels responsible. Our whole treatment would be untenable if it gave no explanation of this. It is, then, a welcome confirmation of the view here developed that the subjective feeling of responsibilty coincides with the objective judgment. It is a fact of experience that, in general, the person blamed or condemned is conscious of the fact that he was "rightly" taken to account—of course, under the supposition that no error has been made, that the assumed state of affairs actually occurred. What is this consciousness of having been the true doer of the act, the actual instigator? Evidently not merely that it was he who took the steps required for its performance; but there must be added the awareness that he did it "independently," "of his own initiative," or however it be expressed. This feeling is simply the consciousness of *freedom,* which is merely the knowledge of having acted of one's *own* desires. And "one's own desires" are those which have their origin in the regularity of one's character in the given situation, and are not imposed by an external power, as explained above. The abscence of the external power expresses itself in the well-known feeling (usually considered characteristic of the consciousness of freedom) *that one could also have acted otherwise.* How this indubitable experience ever came to be an argument in favor of indeterminism is incomprehensible to me. It is of course obvious that I should have acted differently had I *willed* something else; but the feeling never says that I could also have willed something else, even though this is true, if, that is, other motives had been present. And it says even less that under *exactly the same* inner and outer conditions I could also have willed something else. How could such a feeling inform me of anything regarding the purely theoretical question of whether the principle of causality holds or not? Of course, after what has been said on the subject, I do not undertake to demonstrate the principle, but I do deny that from any such fact of consciousness the least follows regarding the principle's validity. This feeling is not the consciousness of the absence of a cause, but of something altogether different, namely, of *freedom,* which consists in the fact that I can act as I desire.

Thus the feeling of responsibility assumes that I acted freely, that my own desires impelled me; and if because of this feeling I willingly suffer blame for my behavior or reproach myself, and thereby admit that I might have acted otherwise, this means that other behavior was compatible with the laws of volition—of course, granted other motives. And I myself desire the existence of such motives and bear the pain (regret and sorrow) caused by my behavior so that its repetition will be prevented. To blame oneself means just to apply motives of improvement to oneself, which is usually the task of the educator. But if, for example, one does something under the influence of torture, feelings of guilt and regret are absent, for one knows that according to the laws of volition no other behavior was possible—no matter what ideas, because of their feeling tones, might have functioned as motives. The important thing, always, is that the feeling of responsibilty means the realization that one's self, one's own psychic processes constitute the point at which motives must be applied in order to govern the acts of one's body.

We can speak of motives only in a causal context; thus it becomes clear how very much the concept of responsibility rests upon that of causation, that is, upon the regularity of volitional decisions. In fact if we should conceive of a decision as utterly without any cause (this would in all strictness be the indeterministic presupposition) then the act would be entirely a matter of *chance,* for chance is identical with the absence of a cause; there is no other opposite of causality. Could we under such conditions make the agent responsible? Certainly not. Imagine a man, always calm, peaceful and blameless, who suddenly falls upon and begins to beat a stranger. He is held and questioned regarding the motive of his action, to which he answers, in his opinion truthfully, as we assume: "There was no motive for my behavior. Try as I may I can discover no reason. My volition was without any cause—I desired to do so, and there is simply nothing else to be said about it." We should shake our heads and call him insane, because we have to believe that there was a cause, and lacking any other we must assume some mental disturbance as the only cause remaining; but certainly no one would hold him to be responsible. If decisions were causeless there would be no sense in trying to influence men; and we see at once that this is the reason why we could not bring such a man to account, but would always have only a shrug of the shoulders in answer to his behavior. One can easily determine that in practice we make an agent the more responsible the more motives we can find for his conduct. If a man guilty of an atrocity was an enemy of his victim, if previously he had shown violent tendencies, if some special circumstance angered him, then we impose severe punishment upon him; while the fewer the reasons to be found for an offense the less do we condemn the agent, but make "unlucky chance," a momentary aberration, or something of the sort, responsible. We do not find the causes of misconduct in his character, and therefore we do not try to influence it for the better: this and only this is the significance of the fact that we do not put the responsibilty upon him. And he too feels this to be so, and says, "I cannot understand how such a thing could have happened to me."

In general we know very well how to discover the causes of conduct in the characters of our fellow men; and how to use this knowledge in the prediction of their future behavior, often with as much certainty as that with which we know that a lion and a rabbit will behave quite differently in the same situation. From all this it is evident that in practice no one thinks of questioning the principle of causality, that, thus, the attitude of the practical man offers no excuse to the metaphysician for confusing freedom from compulsion with the absence of a cause. If one makes clear to himself that a causeless happening is identical with a chance happening, and that, consequently, an indetermined will would destroy all responsibilty, then every desire will cease which might be father to an indeterministic thought. No one can prove determinism, but it is certain that we assume its validity in all of our practical life, and that in particular we can apply the concept of responsibility to human conduct only in so far as the causal principle holds of volitional processes.

For a final clarification I bring together again a list of those concepts which tend, in the traditional treatment of the "problem of freedom," to be confused. In the place of the concepts on the left are put, mistakenly, those of the right, and those in the vertical order form a chain, so that sometimes the previous confusion is the cause of that which follows:

Natural Law	Law of State
Determinism (Causality)	Compulsion
(Universal Validity)	(Necessity)
Indeterminism (Chance)	Freedom
(No Cause)	(No Compulsion)

SCHLICK SELECTION

1. According to Schlick, "the main task of ethics is to explain moral behavior." What does he mean here by "explain"? Does that seem to you to be the *main* task of ethics? Indeed, is it any part of the task of ethics at all? Why?

2. Explain precisely what the difference is, according to Schlick, between a law as a *prescription* and a law as a *description*. Into which category do the laws discussed by d'Holbach, by Hume, or by Kant fall?

3. Explain as clearly as you can Schlick's distinction between *freedom* and *compulsion*. Do you believe that we ought to hold people responsible for all the things they do that are not done under compulsion? Why?

4. Punishment, or the threat of punishment, will cause us to act differently, Schlick believes. What determines the behavior of the judges who impose the punishment? What determines the behavior of the politicians who pass the laws that the judge enforces? Is there anyone in the entire situation who is *not* simply responding to the influence of a mixture of causes? What about Schlick? Is he, in writing his book, merely exhibiting the effects on him of a variety of causal influences? Do you suppose Schlick can really believe that about himself? Can you? Can anyone?

(SELECTION 5)

C. A. CAMPBELL

Is "Freewill" a Pseudo-Problem?

The essay by C. A. Campbell from which this selection is taken is a direct answer to the previous essay by Schlick. In the first part of the essay (not included here), Campbell summarizes Schlick's argument. Then he sets about rebutting it.

There are two points that should be particularly noted in Campbell's discussion. The first is that his analysis turns entirely on considerations drawn from moral philosophy—that is, from the study of what is right and wrong, what is just and unjust, from deliberations about punishment, praise, and blame. In the introduction to this chapter, we explored the subject of freedom and determinism by means of an imaginary murder trial in which a lawyer put forward one defense after another for his client. Despite the fact that issues of causation and freedom are usually considered a part of that branch of philosophy called "metaphysics," it is clear that we cannot treat those issues satisfactorily without appeal to ethical judgments and principles.

The second point is methodological rather than substantive. Campbell relies very heavily on appeals to what "we" would ordinarily say or assert. Who are the "we" whose judgments are being appealed to, and why should they carry such weight in philosophical investigations? Roughly speaking, the "we" are intelligent, thoughtful, informed, and reflective people from the same culture and civilization as Campbell, whose agreed-upon moral opinions constitute a body of convictions that "rational men and women of good will" can be expected to share. In some cases, these convictions are embodied in the institutions of law and government, thereby acquiring an objectivity and solidity beyond what could be revealed by mere opinion polls.

But there is a big difference between "everyone agrees that" and "it is true that." After all, at different times in history, and in different cultures, the natural inferiority of women, the moral justifiability of slavery, the absolute immorality of divorce, and the legitimacy of imperialist war have all been subscribed to by the general collectivity of educated, rational, reflective, responsible persons. It is at least open to Schlick to reply to Campbell that if a denial of freedom of the will conflicts with ordinary established opinion, then so much the worse for that opinion! We shall return to this issue in a later chapter, when we consider the position in ethical theory known as "relativism."

In the first place, it is surely quite unplausible to suggest that the common assumption that moral freedom postulates some breach of causal continuity arises from a confusion of two different types of law. Schlick's distinction between descriptive and prescriptive law is, of course, sound. It was no doubt worth pointing out, too, that descriptive laws cannot be said to "compel" human behaviour in the same way as prescriptive laws do. But it seems to me evident that the usual reason why it is held that moral freedom implies some breach of causal continuity, is not a belief that causal laws "compel" as civil laws "compel," but simply the belief that the admission of unbroken causal continuity entails a *further* admission which is directly incompatible with moral responsibility; *viz.* the admission that no man could have acted otherwise than he in fact did. Now it may, of course, be an error thus to assume that a man is not morally responsible for an act, a fit subject for moral praise and blame in respect of it, unless he could have acted otherwise than he did. Or, if *this* is not an error, it may still be an error to assume that a man could not have acted otherwise than he did, in the sense of the phrase that is crucial for moral responsibility, without there occurring some breach of causal continuity. . . . But the relevant point at the moment is that these (not *prima facie* absurd) assumptions about the conditions of moral responsibility have very commonly, indeed normally, been made, and that they are entirely adequate to explain why the problem of Free Will finds its usual formulation in terms of partial exemption from causal law. Schlick's distinction between prescriptive and descriptive laws has no bearing at all upon the truth or falsity of these assumptions. Yet if these assumptions are accepted, it is (I suggest) really inevitable that the Free Will problem should be formulated in the way to which Schlick takes exception. Recognition of the distinction upon which Schlick and his followers lay so much stress can make not a jot of difference.

As we have seen, however, Schlick does later proceed to the much more important business of disputing these common assumptions about the conditions of moral responsibility. He offers us an analysis of moral responsibility which flatly contradicts these assumptions; an analysis according to which the only freedom demanded by morality is a freedom which is compatible with Determinism. If this analysis can be sustained, there is certainly no problem of "Free Will" in the traditional sense.

But it seems a simple matter to show that Schlick's analysis is

From "Is 'Freewill' a Pseudo-Problem?" by C. A. Campbell. First published in *Mind* in 1951. (Reprinted by permission of *Mind*.)

untenable. Let us test it by Schlick's own claim that it gives us what we mean by "moral responsibility" in ordinary linguistic usage.

We do not ordinarily consider the lower animals to be morally responsible. But *ought* we not to do so if Schlick is right about what we mean by moral responsibility? It is quite possible, by punishing the dog who absconds with the succulent chops designed for its master's luncheon, favourably to influence its motives in respect of its future behaviour in like circumstances. If moral responsibilty is to be linked with punishment as Schlick links it, and punishment conceived as a form of education, we should surely hold the dog morally responsible? The plain fact, of course, is that we don't. We don't, because we suppose that the dog "couldn't help it": that its action (unlike what we usually believe to be true of human beings) was simply a link in a continuous chain of causes and effects. In other words, we do commonly demand the contra-causal sort of freedom as a condition of moral responsibility.

Again, we do ordinarily consider it proper, in certain circumstances, to speak of a person no longer living as morally responsible for some present situation. But *ought* we to do so if we accept Schlick's essentially "forward-looking" interpretation of punishment and responsibility? Clearly we cannot now favourably affect the dead man's motives. No doubt they could *at one time* have been favourably affected. But that cannot be relevant to our judgment of responsibility if, as Schlick insists, the question of who is responsible "is a matter only of knowing who is to be punished or rewarded." Indeed he expressly tells us, as we saw earlier, that in asking this question we are not concerned with a "great-grand-parent" who may have been the "original instigator," because, for one reason, this "remote cause" is "out of reach." We cannot bring the appropriate educative influence to bear upon it. But the plain fact, of course, is that we do frequently assign moral responsibility for present situations to persons who have long been inaccessible to any punitive action on our part. And Schlick's position is still more paradoxical in respect of our apportionment of responsibility for occurrences in the distant past. Since in these cases there is no agent whatsoever whom we can favourably influence by punishment, the question of moral responsibility here should have no meaning for us.. But of course it has. Historical writings are studded with examples. . . .

A final point. The extremity of paradox in Schlick's identification of the question "Who is morally blameworthy?" with the question "Who is to be punished?" is apt to be partially concealed from us just because it is our normal habit to include in the meaning of "punishment" an element of "requital for moral transgression" which Schlick expressly denies to it. On that account we commonly think of "punishment," in its strict sense, as implying moral blame-worthiness in the person punished. But if we remember to mean by punishment what Schlick means by it, a purely "educative measure," with no retributive ingredients, his identification of the two questions loses such plausibility as it might otherwise have. For clearly we often think it proper to "punish" a person, in *Schlick's* sense, where we are not at all prepared to say that the person is morally blameworthy. We may even think him morally commendable. . . .

Adopting Schlick's own criterion, then, looking simply "to the manner in which the concept is used," we seem bound to admit that constantly people do assign moral responsibility where Schlick's theory says they shouldn't, don't assign moral responsibility where Schlick's theory says they should, and assign degrees of moral responsibility where on Schlick's theory there should be no difference in degree. I think we may reasonably conclude that Schlick's account of what we mean by moral responsibility breaks down. . . .

But before reopening the general question of the nature and conditions of moral responsibility there is a *caveat* which it seems to me worth while to enter. The difficulties in the way of a clear answer are not slight; but they are apt to seem a good deal more formidable than they really are because of a common tendency to consider in unduly close association two distinct questions: the question "Is a contra-causal type of freedom implied by moral responsibilty?" and the question "Does a contra-causal type of freedom anywhere exist?" It seems to me that many philosophers (and I suspect that Moritz Schlick is among them) begin their enquiry with so firm a conviction that the contra-causal sort of freedom nowhere exists, that they find it hard to take very seriously the possibility that it is *this* sort of freedom that moral responsibility implies. For they are loth to abandon the commonsense belief that moral responsibility itself is something real. The implicit reasoning I take to be this. Moral responsibility is real. If moral responsibility is real, the freedom implied in it must be a fact. But contra-causal freedom is not a fact. Therefore contra-causal freedom is not the freedom implied in moral responsibility. I think we should be on our guard against allowing this or some similar train of reasoning (whose premises, after all, are far from indubitable) to seduce us into distorting what we actually find when we set about a direct analysis of moral responsibilty and its conditions. . . .

There are times when what seems to a critic the very strength of his case breeds mistrust in the critic's own mind. I confess that in making the criticisms that have preceded I have not been altogether free from uncomfortable feelings of this kind. . . .

In this situation there is, however, one course by which the critic may reasonably hope to allay these natural suspicions. He should consider whether there may not be certain predisposing influences at work, extrinsic to the specific arguments, which could have the effect of blinding the proponents of these arguments to their intrinsic demerits. If so, he need not be too much disquieted by the seeming weakness of the case against him. For it is a commonplace that, once in the grip of general prepossessions, even very good philosophers sometimes avail themselves of very bad arguments.

Actually, we can, I think, discern at least two such influences operating powerfully in the case before us. One is sympathy with the general tenets of Positivism. The other is the conviction already alluded to, that man does not in fact possess a contra-causal type of freedom; whence follows a strong presumption that no such freedom is necessary to moral responsibility. . . .

A contra-causal freedom, it is argued, such as is implied in the "categorical" interpretation of the proposition "A could have chosen otherwise than he did," posits a breach of causal continuity between a man's character and his conduct. Now apart from the general presumption in favour of the universality of causal law, there are special reasons for disallowing the breach that is here alleged. It is the common assumption of social intercourse that our acquaintances will act "in character"; that their choices will exhibit the "natural" response of their characters to the given situation. And this assumption seems to be amply substantiated, over a wide range of conduct, by the actual success which attends predictions made on this basis. Where there should be, on the contra-causal hypothesis, chaotic variability, there is found in fact a large measure of intelligible continuity. Moreover, what is the alternative to admitting that a person's choices flow from his character? Surely just that the so-called "choice" is not *that person's* choice at all: that, relatively to the person concerned, it is a mere "accident." Now we cannot really believe this. But if it *were* the case, it would certainly not help to establish *moral* freedom, the freedom required for *moral* responsibility. For clearly a man cannot be morally responsible for an act which does not express his own choice but is, on the contrary, attributable simply to chance.

These are clearly considerations worthy of all respect. It is not surprising if they have played a big part in persuading people to respond sympathetically to the view that "Free Will," in its usual contra-causal formulation, is a pseudo-problem. A full answer to them is obviously not practicable in what is little more than an appendix to the body of this paper; but I am hopeful that something can be said, even in a little space, to show that they are very far from being as conclusive against a contra-causal freedom as they are often supposed to be.

To begin with the less troublesome of the two main objections indicated—the objection that the break in causal continuity which free will involves is inconsistent with the predictability of conduct on the basis of the agent's known character. All that is necessary to meet this objection, I suggest, is the frank recognition, which is perfectly open to the Libertarian, that there is a wide area of human conduct, determinable on clear general principles, within which free will does not effectively operate. The most important of these general principles (I have no space to deal here with the others) has often enough been stated by Libertarians. Free will does not operate in these practical situations in which no conflict arises in the agent's mind between what he conceives to be his "duty" and what he feels to be his "strongest desire." It does not operate here because there just is no occasion for it to operate. There is no reason whatever why the agent should here even contemplate choosing any course other than that prescribed by his strongest desire. In all such situations, therefore, he naturally wills in accordance with strongest desire. But his "strongest desire" is simply the specific *ad hoc* expression of that system of conative and emotive dispositions which we call his "character." In all such situations, therefore, whatever may be the case elsewhere, his will is in effect determined by his character as so far formed. Now when we bear in mind that there are an almost immeasurably greater number of situations in a man's life that conform to *this* pattern than there are situations in which an agent is aware of a conflict between strongest desire and duty, it is apparent that a Libertarianism which accepts the limitation of free will to the *latter* type of situation is not open to the stock objection on the score of "predictability." For there still remains a vast area of human behaviour in which prediction on the basis of known character may be expected to succeed: an area which will accommodate without difficulty, I think, all these empirical facts about successful prediction which the critic is apt to suppose fatal to Free Will.

So far as I can see, such a delimitation of the field of effective free will denies to the Libertarian absolutely nothing which matters to him. For it is precisely that small sector of the field of choices which our principle of delimitation still leaves open to free will—the sector in which strongest desire clashes with duty—that is crucial for moral responsibility. It is, I believe, with respect to such situations, and in the last resort to such situations alone, that the agent himself recognises that moral praise and blame are appropriate. They are appropriate, according as he does or does not "rise to duty" in the face of opposing desires; always granted, that is, that he is free to choose between these courses as genuinely open possibilities. If the reality of freedom be conceded *here,* everything is conceded that the Libertarian has any real interest in securing.

But, of course, the most vital question is, can the reality of freedom be conceded even here? In particular, can the standard objection be met which we stated, that if the person's choice does not, in these situations as elsewhere, flow from his *character,* then it is not *that person's* choice at all.

This is, perhaps, of all the objections to a contra-causal freedom, the one which is generally felt to be the most conclusive. For the assumption upon which it is based, *viz.* that no intelligible meaning can attach to the claim that an act which is not an expression of the self's *character* may nevertheless be the *self's* act, is apt to be regarded as self-evident. The Libertarian is accordingly charged with being in effect an *In*determinist, whose "free will," in so far as it does not flow from the agent's character, can only be a matter of "chance." Has the Libertarian—who invariably repudiates this charge and claims to be a *Self*-determinist—any way of showing that, contrary to the assumption of his critics, we *can* meaningfully talk of an act as the self's act even though, in an important sense, it is not an expression of the self's "character"?

I think that he has. I want to suggest that what prevents the critics from finding a meaning in this way of talking is that they are looking for it in the wrong way; or better, perhaps, with the wrong orientation. They are looking for it from the standpoint of the *external observer;* the stand-point proper to, because alone possible for, apprehension of the physical world. Now from the external standpoint we may observe processes of change. But one thing which, by common consent, *cannot* be observed from without is *creative activity.* Yet—and here lies the crux of the whole matter—it is precisely creative activity which we are trying to understand when we are trying to understand what is traditionally designated by "free will." For if there should be an act which is genuinely the self's act and is nevertheless not an expression of its character, such an act, in which the self "transcends" its character as so far formed, would seem to be essentially of the nature of creative activity. It follows that to look for a meaning in "free will" from the external stand-point is absurd. It is to look for it in a way that ensures that it will not be found. Granted that a creative activity of any kind is at least *possible* (and I know of no ground for its *a priori* rejection), there is one way, and one way only, in which we can hope to apprehend it, and that is from the *inner* stand-point of direct participation.

It seems to me therefore, that if the Libertarian's claim to find a meaning in a "free" will which is genuinely the self's will, though not an expression of the self's character, is to be subjected to any test that is worth applying, that test must be undertaken from the inner stand-point. We ought to place ourselves imaginatively at the stand-point of the agent engaged in the typical moral situation in which free will is claimed, and ask ourselves whether from *this* stand-point the claim in question does or does not have meaning for us. That the appeal must be to introspection is no doubt unfortunate. But he would be a very doctrinaire critic of introspection who declined to make use of it when in the nature of the case no other means of apprehension is available. Everyone must make the introspective experiment for himself: but I may perhaps venture to report, though at this late stage with extreme brevity, what I at least seem to find when I make the experiment myself.

In the situation of moral conflict, then, I (as agent) have before my mind a course of action X, which I believe to be my duty; and also a course of action Y, incompatible with X, which I feel to be that which I most strongly desire. Y is, as it is sometimes expressed, "in the line of least resistance" for me—the course which I am aware I should take if I let my purely desiring nature operate without hindrance. It is the course towards which I am aware that my *character,* as so far formed, naturally inclines me. Now, as actually engaged in this situation, I find that I cannot help believing that I *can* rise to duty and choose X; the "rising to duty" being effected by what is commonly called "effort of will." And I further find, if I ask myself just what it is I am believing when I believe that I "can" rise to duty, that I cannot help believing that it lies with me here and now, quite absolutely, which of two genuinely open possibilities I adopt; whether, that is, I make the effort of will and choose X, or, on the other hand, let my desiring nature, my character as so far formed, "have its way," and choose Y, the course "in the line of least resistance." These beliefs may, of course, be illusory, but that is not at present in point. For the present argument all that matters is whether beliefs of this sort are in fact discoverable in the moral agent in the situation of "moral temptation." For my own part, I cannot doubt the introspective evidence that they are.

Now here is the vital point. No matter which course, X or Y, I choose in this situation, I cannot doubt, *qua* practical being engaged in it, that my choice is *not* just the expression of my formed character, and yet *is* a choice made by my *self.* For suppose I make the effort and choose X (my "duty"). Since my very purpose in making the "effort" is to enable me to act against the existing "set" of desire, which is the expression of my character as so far formed, I cannot possibly regard the act itself as the expression of my *character.* On the other hand, introspection makes it equally clear that I am certain that it is *I* who choose: that the act is not an "accident," but is genuinely *my* act. Or suppose that I choose Y (the end of "strongest desire"). The course chosen here is, it is true, in conformity with my "character." But since I find myself unable to doubt that I *could* have made the effort and chosen X, I cannot possibly regard the choice of Y as *just* the expression of my character. Yet here again I find that I cannot doubt that the choice is *my* choice, a choice for which *I* am justly to be blamed.

What this amounts to is that I *can* and *do* attach meaning, *qua* moral agent, to an act which is not the self's character and yet is genuinely the self's act. And having no good reason to suppose that other persons have a fundamentally different mental constitution, it seems to me probable that anyone else who undertakes a similar experiment will be obliged to submit a similar report. I conclude, therefore, that the argument against "free will" on the score of its "meaninglessness" must be held to fail. "Free Will" does have meaning; though, because it is of the nature of a creative activity, its meaning is discoverable only in an intuition of the practical consciousness of the participating agent. To the agent making a moral choice in the situation where duty clashes with desire, his "self" is known to him as a creatively active self, a self which declines to be identified with his "character" as so formed. Not, of course, that the self's character—let it be added to obviate misunderstanding—either is, or is supposed by the agent to be, devoid of bearing upon his choices, even in the "sector" in which free will is held to operate. On the contrary, such a bearing is manifest in the empirically verifiable fact that we find it "harder" (as we say) to make the effort of will required to "rise to duty" in proportion to the extent that the "dutiful" course conflicts with the course to which our character as so far formed inclines us. It is only in the polemics of the critics that a "free" will is supposed to be incompatible with recognising the bearing of "character" upon choice.

"But what" (it may be asked) "of the all-important question of the *value* of this "subjective certainty"? Even if what you say is sound as "phenomenology," is there any reason to suppose that the conviction on which you lay so much stress is in fact *true?*" I agree that the question is important; far more important, indeed, than is always realised, for it is not always realised that the only direct evidence there *could* be for a creative activity like "free will" is an intuition of the practical consciousness. But this question falls outside the purview of the present paper. The aim of the paper has not been to offer a constructive defence of free will. It has been to show that the problem as traditionally posed is a real, and not a pseudo, problem. A serious threat to that thesis, it was acknowledged, arises from the apparent difficulty of attaching meaning to an act which is not the expression of the self's character and yet *is* the self's own act. The object of my brief phenomenological analysis was to provide evidence that such an act *does* have meaning for us in the one context in which there is any sense in *expecting* it to have meaning.

My general conclusion is, I fear, very unexciting. It is merely that it is an error to suppose that the "Free Will" problem, when correctly formulated, turns out not to be a "problem" at all. Labouring to reinstate an old problem is dull work enough. But I am disposed to think that the philosophic situation to-day calls for a good deal more dull work of a similar sort.

CAMPBELL SELECTION

1.   Campbell's answer to Schlick (and also to Hume and other "compatibilists") rests on his confident conviction that we simply cannot go through life refusing ever to hold people responsible for what they do. We cannot believe that no one ever could have done differently! Is Campbell right? What would it be like to view people as absolutely incapable of doing otherwise than they actually do?

2.   Can I think of *myself* as incapable of doing otherwise than I actually do? Is there a difference between the way in which I think about my past actions and the way in which I think about actions that I have not yet performed? If we are not genuinely free to choose between alternatives, what sense can we give to the notion of deciding, or deliberating? Can I genuinely deliberate about what to do, all the while believing that after I have made my choice, it will turn out that I could not have chosen otherwise?

3.   Is it really unreasonable to hold a man or woman responsible for an action that is entirely "out of character"? Aren't those the actions that show what a person is *really* like?

4.   We are accustomed, these days, to speak of alcoholism and drug addiction as *diseases* rather than moral failings. Could someone be "addicted" to immoral actions? Would that relieve him of responsibility for his actions? If not, then why should the drug addict not be held morally responsible for his addiction?

5.   Campbell ends his essay by saying that free will is still a problem, but he doesn't offer a solution. Does it matter whether we find a "solution" to this "problem"? What concrete issues of personal choice, politics, or social policy depend on the "solution" we find for the problem of freedom of the will? What do the different answers to this problem tell us about how to treat crime, violence, legal and moral commitments (such as marriage)?

(SELECTION 6)

RICHARD TAYLOR

Prevention, Postvention, and the Will

In *The Once and Future King,* T. H. White's novel about King Arthur from which the musical comedy *Camelot* was made, the old magician Merlin lives backwards through time. That is to say, he is growing steadily younger as the other characters grow older. He "remembers" what is going to happen, for the future is, for him, the past. But the past, which is his future, is a perpetual mystery to him, save insofar as he is able (so-to-speak) to "retrodict" it. Needless to say, Merlin appears a trifle odd, even for a magician.

The notion of someone living backwards through time is inherently ridiculous, a fact of which White makes marvelously comic use. But *why* is it ridiculous? If we can move backwards and forwards in space, why can we not move backwards as well as forwards in time? The answer is undoubtedly quite complicated and subtle, but it obviously has at least something to do with the fact that we are purposive creatives, goal-oriented and guided in our choices and actions by a conception of that which is not yet but can be at some future time.

In this provocative essay, Richard Taylor makes use of the peculiar directionality of time, and its connection to purposiveness, as a way of clarifying the notion of freedom of the will. Tay-lor's aim, as he tells us, is not to *prove* some proposition about freedom, but simply to extend our understanding of a certain set of familiar concepts so that we see how much would really be involved, conceptually, in rejecting the notion of freedom. His expectation is that when we see how deeply embedded the idea of freedom of the will is in our system of concepts, how much would have to be altered if it were given up, then we will agree with him that the conceptual sacrifice is too great.

Taylor's specific philosophical technique in this essay is a quite unusual one; he defines a concept (which he labels "postvention") that we do not now possess or use. He then demonstrates, by a series of parallels between "postvention" and the familiar notion of "prevention," that the concept is quite consistent and has perfectly coherent rules for application, contrary to our gut feeling or intuition that there is something odd about the whole idea. Then he turns around and asks: *Why* don't we have and use the concept of postvention? What is there about the world, about time and human actions and purposive choice that makes the concept unnatural, not to say useless? Through an answer to these questions, he provides us with a novel defense of the notion of freedom of the will.

When a philosopher approaches a problem as old as that of free will, there may be not much point in his addressing himself to it directly with arguments pro or con. It is not likely that any really new argument of either sort can be invented, and if the old ones have not settled the issue, it seems unlikely that any reformulations of them will.

I propose, then, to get into the problem in an indirect way, which is, I think, fairly novel. In part I of this discussion, I am going to compare the ordinary notion of *prevention* with the extraordinary one of *postvention,* in order to call attention to a difference in the way men view future things as opposed to how they view past things, at least in so far as these bear upon their weal or woe. I shall then show that this difference is not to be accounted for in the ways that are most apt to occur to philosophically sophisticated persons. In part II, I am going to suggest that this difference is accounted for by the fact that men conceive of themselves as purposeful beings, and of their actions as, at least ordinarily, means to ends or goals. Then in part III I shall show that, while this purposeful nature of men's actions does not by itself prove that men are free in any metaphysical sense, it renders that claim reasonable and plausible and the denial of it, I think, somewhat arbitrary and implausible. No theory of metaphysical freedom will be thus proved, to be sure—I think in fact that none can be either proved or disproved—but at least certain considerations that have in the past seemed to cast doubt upon human freedom will, I think, be seen to be somewhat irrelevant.

I

We do not have the term "postvent," even though it would seem to be the exact complement of "prevent." This latter term appears to have a perfectly clear and common meaning, which lends itself to straightforward analysis, and the former can be given a similarly clear meaning. The reason why "postvent" does not occur in our language is, of course, that we have no use for it, but that in itself is not interesting. What is philosophically interesting is to try seeing just *why* we have no use for it. The most usual answers to this question are quite unsatisfactory.

Prevention. To have *prevented* some event is, precisely, to have done something that was, under the conditions then and thereafter prevailing, both sufficient and necessary for, although logically independent of, the subsequent nonoccurrence of that event. We shall

From "Prevention, Postvention, and the Will" by Richard Taylor, in *Freedom and Determinism,* ed. by Keith Lehrer. First published in 1966. (Reprinted by permission of Humanities Press, Inc., New Jersey.)

see shortly, in terms of the types of inference warranted by prevention statements, why an action that was genuinely preventive must have been both sufficient and necessary for the nonoccurrence of what was thereby prevented. Here we need one note that a preventive action and the event that it prevents are always logically independent of each other, or that it is not a logical contradiction, even though it is false, to assert that both of them occurred. Some may choose to say that they can be brought into logical relationships with each other by conjoining true statements about them with certain statements of the laws of nature; that is all right, at least as far as the present discussion is concerned. Some may prefer such expressions as "guaranteed" or "insured" for "was sufficient for," and such expressions as "was essential for" or "was indispensable to" for "was necessary for," just to make clear that the relationships in question do not involve any logical necessity or impossibilty; but this need not detain us. Our definition of prevention has already stipulated that a preventive action and what it prevents are at least logically independent of each other.

To illustrate this, let us suppose that a physician rightly claims to have prevented another man's death by a timely operation. This means that he did something—performed a certain operation with scalpel and other instruments—which was, under the other conditions then and thereafter prevailing, sufficient for the nonoccurrence of that man's death, and also necessary, in the sense that the man would not have lived had he, the physician, not done what he did. Now of course the physician does not claim to have thereby prevented the man's *eventual* death, since no man can prevent that. In saving his patient's life, he did not render him immortal, and did not claim to. He claimed only to have prevented a death that was otherwise impending. . . .

Statements like these—to the effect that certain actions have prevented the occurrence of certain other events later on—warrant a certain familiar type of counterfactual inference, expressed in subjunctives, although they are not, of course, the only statements that warrant such inferences.

Thus, if it is true that a physician has prevented someone's death by a timely operation, then we can say that had he (contrary to fact) not performed the operation, the man would soon have died. Indeed, this is precisely what the physician would be claiming by saying that he prevented the man's death. . . .

Besides being necessary, however, a preventive action must also be something that was, under the conditions then and thereafter prevailing, sufficient for the subsequent nonoccurrence of the event thereby prevented. This scarcely needs argument. Had the . . . man.

for example, somehow managed to die soon anyway, in spite of the operation, . . . then obviously [the] event could [not] truly be claimed to have been prevented.

Postvention. If that is what prevention is, it is not at all difficult to say what postvention is. The two are exactly analogous.

Thus, to have *postvented* some event is, precisely, to have done something which was, under the conditions then and theretofore prevailing, both sufficient and necessary for, though logically independent of, the antecedent nonoccurrence of that event. Again, of course, some persons might prefer such expressions as "guaranteed," "insured," "was essential for" and so on to express these relationships, but that is neither here nor there.

But *do* men ever postvent things in this sense? Clearly, they often do, though for some reason this is never referred to as postvention. Indeed, whenever a man does anything whatever under conditions which are such that the prior nonoccurrence of some event was both necessary and sufficient for his doing it, he postvents that event. The relationship between what he does and the event thus postvented is exactly the same, save only for the direction of the temporal relation, as the relationship between what any man does and the event that he thereby prevents. Any event that is postvented does not, of course, occur, so that there may seem to be a certain strangeness in speaking of its relationship to someone's subsequent postventive action. But similar remarks can be made about any event that is prevented: it, too, does not occur. And yet the very explanation of its nonoccurrence is to be found in its connection with someone's preventive action.

We have, in fact, examples of postvention already before us, for . . . the patient postvents the physician's not having operated on him simply by recovering. . . . Better examples can be made up, however. . . .

Suppose, then, that a certain woman breakfasts with her husband as usual on some given morning. Clearly, his not having overslept might well be a necessary condition for her doing that, and we can suppose that all the other conditions are such that his not having overslept is also sufficient for her doing that, or that nothing else occurs to prevent husband and wife from breakfasting together as usual that day. By breakfasting with him in the usual way and at the usual time the wife guarantees, in the best possible way, that he has not overslept, and his not oversleeping also guarantees, under the conditions we are assuming to prevail, that he breakfasts with her as usual. The wife, accordingly, can properly claim to have postvented his oversleeping by breakfasting with him in the usual way. If she did claim to have done this, and if she meant by "postvented" exactly what we all mean by "prevented," except with the time reversed, she would appear to be right. Of course, by breakfasting with him that morning, she does not postvent his *ever* having overslept, but she does not claim to. She claims only to have postvented it this time.

Again, suppose a woman has breakfasted alone on some given morning. Suppose further that conditions were such that, had her husband not gone on a trip the day before, he would have been there too, having breakfast with her as usual. Clearly, she has managed to put herself in a situation—breakfasting alone—which is sufficient, under the other conditions then and theretofore prevailing, for his not having forgone the trip the day before. His having gone on a trip is also, under the conditions we are assuming, sufficient for her then breakfasting alone, there being no one else for her to have breakfast with, and so on. . . . This wife, then, under the analysis given, postvented her husband's having stayed home. This should not suggest that she has thereby postvented his *ever* having forgone such trips, however. She postvented him from staying home only that time.

It is worthwhile noting that statements like these, to the effect that certain actions have served to postvent the occurrence of certain other events earlier on, permit exactly the same familiar type of counterfactual inference as do statements about prevention.

Thus, if it is true that a woman has (on the analysis given) postvented her husband's oversleeping that morning by breakfasting with him, then we can say that had she (contrary to fact) not breakfasted with him, we would be warranted in concluding that he had overslept—which is but another way of saying that his not oversleeping was, under the totality of other conditions assumed, sufficient for her to breakfast with him. Similarly, if the second woman has by breakfasting alone postvented her husband's staying home instead of going on his trip, then we can say that had she (contrary to fact) not breakfasted alone, then we would be justified in concluding that, conditions having been such as they were, she had breakfasted with him, and hence that he had stayed home after all. This, again, is but another way of saying that his having gone on his trip was sufficient, given that the other conditions were such as they were, for her breakfasting alone. If conditions were such that the first husband would not have overslept even if (contrary to fact) his wife had not breakfasted with him, and the second husband would not have stayed home even if (contrary to fact) his wife had not breakfasted alone, then neither event could truly be said to have been postvented. They would be things that had not happened anyway, and the ostensibly postventive actions would not really be necessary at all. The first woman's breakfasting with her husband would have been a waste of time, and the second woman's breakfasting alone a wasted, superfluous ceremony, so far as postventing anything was concerned.

Besides being a subsequent necessary condition, however, a postventive action must also be something that was, under the conditions then and theretofore prevailing, *sufficient* for the antecedent nonoccurrence of the event thereby postvented. This scarcely needs argument. Had the first man, for example, somehow managed to oversleep and still have breakfast with his wife as usual, and had the second man somehow managed to stay home and still leave his wife to breakfast alone, then obviously neither event could truly be claimed to have been postvented.

Four obvious but wrong answers. Why, then, if postvention and prevention are such exactly analogous concepts, differing only in the tenses in which examples are described, do we have no use for the concept of postvention? It is not at all easy to see what the answer to this is, but it is certainly worth dealing with some considerations that are apt to occur to one very quickly, but which do not provide the slightest answer to this question.

In the first place, there is no point whatever in suggesting that, while we are sometimes able to prevent certain things, we are unable to postvent anything—"the past is unalterable," and that sort of thing. For we must surely take it for granted that anything whatever that anyone *does* do, is something he *is able* to do. Now the first wife we described *did* breakfast with her husband on a given occasion, and the second wife *did* breakfast alone, from which it surely follows that these were things they were *able* to do. And by doing these things they did perform certain actions which were, under the conditions assumed to prevail and to have then prevailed, necessary and sufficient for the nonoccurrence of certain events earlier on, and in precisely the way that the action of our physician . . . [was] sufficient and necessary for the nonoccurrence of [a] certain event later on.

Second, it does no good to point out that nothing in the history of the universe ever has been postvented. Absolutely nothing in the history of the universe has ever been prevented either. This is analytic. To say of any event whatever that it is a past event logically entails that it was not and never will be postvented. But similarly, to say of any event that it is a future event logically entails that it was not and never will be prevented. No one can name a past event that he will postvent, but neither can anyone name a future event that he will prevent. All these seemingly grave observations are really utterly trivial, expressing only what is analytically true. In speaking of postventing events of the past or preventing events of the future, however, one is not saying anything the least trivial or logically odd. He is only claiming the legitimacy of such counterfactual inferences as I have illustrated. Those inferences are equally good, whether one is speaking of postvention or of prevention.

Third, there is no point in noting that we can cause things to occur only in the future, not in the past. This is true enough, but only because that is the way in which the word "cause" happens to be used. If a meaning can be given to the idea of postventing things, then there is no reason why the use of the word "cause" should be restricted in the way that it is. Indeed, the question of why its use is thus restricted to antecedent necessary and sufficient conditions is virtually equivalent to the question with which we began—namely, why the word "postvent" has no use at all. Given the notion of antecedent necessary and sufficient conditions, on the one hand, and subsequent necessary and sufficient conditions, on the other—and it is impossible to have any of these notions without the others—we can easily define both prevention and postvention, as I have done, without speaking of causes at all. Examples of postvention can be readily supplied, which seem in every way identical to examples of prevention, save only that the temporal relations are reversed. The other relations can be described in terms of the concepts of necessary or sufficient antecedent or subsequent conditions—or, what amounts to the same thing, in terms of certain true conditional statements in the subjunctive, whose antecedents or consequents are contrary to fact.

And finally, it looks as though no light is going to be thrown on this question by any observations about what does, and what does not, count as a human action, or by any distinctions, so popular nowadays, between actions and "mere events." Sometimes a man, upon being stricken with a serious malady, is prevented from dying by the automatic production of certain antibodies in his blood, without any intervention by a physician. A man who is setting out to commit murder can be prevented from doing it by a sudden, unexpected and surprising eclipse of the sun. Many dreadful accidents have been prevented by automatic flashing lights at railway crossings, or by the sun melting the ice from the highway, which is to say that such accidents would have happened had not these preventive events happened first. Trees are sometimes prevented from blooming just by contamination in the earth, which has not been introduced by human agency. None of these preventive events is a human action, or even an action at all, in case there is thought to be any real difference between actions and "mere events." They are all just merely events; yet they do, however, sometimes serve to prevent other events.

II

I do not think we should suppose that the absence of the word "postvent" from our vocabulary represents any odd lacuna. I think that the notion is truly useless. However clearly it can be explicated, and however similar it may at first appear to be to the notion of prevention, one can hardly help feeling that there is something highly artificial in my foregoing discussion, something significant that has been left out of account. I want now to show that this is indeed so, and to bring forth the missing element that has thus far been ignored.

Preventive actions as means to ends. The first thing to note is that the . . . example I gave of [a] typically preventive action [is] aptly described as [an] action performed as the means to achieving some end or, what amounts to the same thing, as [a] means for the avoidance of something. Thus, the physician operated as a means to preserving someone's life. . . . The same cannot be said of the postventive actions I cited. Thus, it is plainly untrue that the first woman breakfasted with her husband as a means of getting him up on time, or that the second breakfasted alone as a means of getting her husband off on a trip. Even if we suppose these two women to have had such goals or purposes, we cannot represent *these* actions as suitable or even intelligible means to their accomplishment.

Does not this, however, merely make the trivial point that, as a matter of customary usage, anything which is a means to some end must *precede* that end in time? And hence, that no postventive actions are means to ends for the simple reason that they must, by definition, succeed in time those negative states of affairs to which they are postventively related? Anyone wishing to press this suggestion could certainly make a dialectically subtle case for it. The counterpart to the concept of an *end*, for example, is obviously that of a *beginning*. Having then characterized preventive actions in terms of their relationship to certain ends, one could then characterize postventive actions as related in pricisely the same way to beginnings. . . .

The analogy is fascinating but, quite apart from its apparent artificiality, it does not really hold up. For in the first place, it is not true that the ends of actions, even when realized, always succeed those actions in time. For example, one might walk, simply for the purpose of walking, with no end or goal beyond that. Here means and ends are identical and hence contemporaneous. . . .

To say, accordingly, that some action is the means to a certain end cannot mean simply that it is antecedently necessary and sufficient for that end. It need not be antecedent to its end. Besides which, there are many actions that are antecedently necessary and sufficient for the occurrence of certain events, which are, however, in no sense the means to the realization of those events. When one sits on a sofa he depresses the springs, but that is not ordinarily one's purpose, though it could be. When one brakes his automobile he wears down the brake drum, but again, that is not ordinarily his purpose.

A preventive action, then, is something *more* than an action that is antecedently necessary and sufficient for whatever it prevents. It is easy to supply examples of actions that fit that description but which are not preventive, and it is also easy to supply examples of preventive actions that do not fit it. To say, however, that one's action is *postventive* is *not* to say anything more than that it is subsequently necessary and sufficient for the nonoccurrence of what it postvents. . . .

Preventive states and events which are not actions. So far I have labored the point that preventive actions are always, or at least typically, means to ends. This, of course, does not entail that nothing can be described as preventive *unless* it is an action; in fact, many things that are preventive are not actions at all.

Thus, a man can be prevented from leaving a burning building by smoke, even though no one is making the smoke. A man can be prevented from reaching a mountain top by a landslide, even though no one starts the landslide, and so on. Examples are easy to multiply, and they all show that not all states and events which are preventive of something are preventive actions.

What is still left, however, even in such cases as these, is the notion of an end or purpose, and I want to insist that this notion is still essential to the description to anything whatever as preventive. Thus, the smoke could not be described as *preventing* a man from leaving a burning building except on the supposition that it was his purpose, goal or intention to leave, and the landslide can be considered as preventing a man from reaching a mountain top only on the supposition that he was trying to reach it, that he had that goal. Had the first man, for example, intended to stay in the burning building all the while, had this been his purpose—perhaps in order to test some fireproof suit—then he could not be said to have been prevented by the smoke from leaving. The most one could say is that he would have been prevented, in case he had tried. . . .

Again, however, no such notion of a purpose or goal or any agent is required for the understanding of postvention, nor is there any intelligible way to fit such a notion into the concept of postvention. Everything that does not happen, and for which there are subsequent conditions necessary and sufficient for its not happening—

which probably includes, simply, everything that does not happen—
is thereby postvented from happening. . . .

III

We have now to see what bearing the foregoing might have on
the problem of free will. I have already indicated that the thesis of
determinism, as I understand it, cannot, in my opinion, be either
proved or disproved. It is the thesis to the effect that for every event,
and hence every human action, and hence every preventive action,
and every action that is purposeful or goal-directed, there are antecedent conditions (causes) sufficient for the performance of just that
action and for the avoidance of any and every alternative action.
This is a perfectly *general* thesis, and I do not see how anyone could
profess to know that it is true, or that it is false. Most purported
proofs of its truth amount to maintaining that it is implied by the
basic beliefs and conceptions that all men have. It is certainly not
implied by the conception of a preventive action; it is, I think,
rendered somewhat implausible in the light of that conception.

Not every preventive state of affairs, I have maintained, is itself
purposeful or goal-directed, though it cannot be conceived as preventive except in relation to the purpose or goal of some agent. The
smoke that obstructs a passageway may not be of purposeful origin,
but it cannot be spoken of as preventing anything except on the
supposition that it frustrates some agent's purpose. I have also maintained, however, that every preventive *action is* purposeful or goal-
directed. This should perhaps be qualified by saying that every action
which is *as such* preventive is also purposeful—in order to allow for
those actions that prevent, but are not as such preventive. A man
might, for instance, incidentally to making a smoke screen, uninten-
tionally prevent another man from leaving a building, in which case
his action is preventive, but not as such. It is only preventive *per
accidens,* being, in this regard, quite purposeless. Typically preventive actions are, in any case, distinguished from postventive
actions in being purposeful, for nothing remotely like the idea of
purpose can be fitted into the idea of postvention.

Goals and causes. This entails that the idea of a preventive
action cannot be analyzed in terms of necessary and sufficient conditions. Postventive actions can be so analyzed—indeed, they are
simply defined in those terms. There is an additional element contained in the very idea of a preventive action, and that is the idea
of a purpose, goal or end. Nor will it do simply to add this as another
necessary causal condition—by saying, for instance, that an action
is preventive in case one of the conditions constituting part of the

cause of it is an agent's purpose. A purpose, end or goal is no part of the *cause* of a preventive action. It is part of the very *concept* of such an action, just as being a sibling is part of the concept, but no part of the cause, of being a twin.

Besides this, it would seem artificial in the extreme to suppose that preventive actions are causally explained in terms of purposes or goals. A preventive action can, indeed, be *explained* in terms of a goal or purpose—indeed, that is the standard and normal way of explaining them—but there is no reason whatever for thinking that such explanations fit the pattern of *causal* explanation. . . .

But does the supposition that men sometimes act preventively, and hence purposefully, entail that determinism is false? Some persons have thought so. It seems to some that the very idea of pursuing an end or goal, particularly over a long period of time, implies that the end is freely chosen, as well as the means to its achievement.

I believe this is clearly not true, however. The supposition that men sometimes act preventively, and hence purposefully, does not by itself entail that determinism is false. Perhaps the further supposition that such actions are sometimes the result of deliberation might entail that they are, or at least are believed to be, free, in the sense of being not causally determined, but that is a question I do not choose to go into. All that follows, I think, from the supposition that men sometimes act preventively is that they sometimes act in ways that cannot be *analyzed* in terms of antecedent necessary and sufficient conditions. This by itself does not by any means imply that, when they so act, there do not sometimes *exist* such conditions.

The metaphysical meaning of "free." To say that a given preventive act was free means, I take it, that the agent who performed it was free with respect to that act. And this, I take it, means that, under the conditions then and theretofore prevailing, he was able to perform that act *and* he was also able to refrain from performing it. To say, on the other hand, that he was *not* free with respect to that act means, I take it, that he was not able to refrain from performing it, or, that circumstances rendered his action unavoidable.

Prevention consistent with determinism and indeterminism. Any statement of the form "I prevented X by doing A" is clearly *consistent* with "Something made (or caused) me to do A, thereby preventing X." These must be consistent, since the second entails the first. It is important to note, however, that the first does not in the least entail the second. It may be, as I suspect it is, that in some cases a statement of the first form is *true* and the corresponding statement of the second form is *false*. They are nevertheless consistent with each other. In other words, I suspect that men sometimes prevent certain things by certain of their actions, when nothing makes them perform just those actions to the exclusion of any others. Certainly there is no evidence that this cannot be true. The supposition is not itself inconsistent, nor is it inconsistent with anything else that anyone knows to be true. It is inconsistent with the thesis of determinism, to be sure, but while many philosophers believe in that thesis, no one knows that it is true. It seems to me, in any case, that the thesis just enunciated—that men sometimes prevent certain things by their actions, when nothing makes them perform those actions—is more likely to be true than the metaphysical thesis of determinism, with which it is inconsistent.

The supposition, then, that men sometimes act preventively, is consistent both with the affirmation and the denial of determinism "I prevented X by doing A" is consistent with "Something made (or caused) me to do A, thereby preventing X," but it is equally consistent with "Nothing made (or caused) me to do A, thereby preventing X." Nor can anyone argue, I think, that in case a statement of the the second form were true—i.e., in case someone were free with respect to a preventive act he performed—then that act would be "inexplicable." A preventive act can still be explained, or rendered intelligible, in terms of the very purpose or goal by virtue of which it is a preventive act, even if that act, as distinguished from the bodily behavior associated with it, is uncaused. That explanation is not in the least wiped out if one makes the further supposition that the agent in question was free with respect to that act, or, that nothing made him do it.

The doubtful status of determinism. Can we, then, draw any conclusion concerning the truth or falsity of determinism from this discussion? We cannot, on the basis of anything I have said, conclude that determinism must be false. If, on the other hand, anyone maintains that determinism is true, and that, accordingly, no preventive act is free, in the sense defined, then I think his position is at least doubtful. He cannot, I feel sure, *analyze* the concept of a preventive act in such a way as to make it even *look* like an act which is, by its very nature, metaphysically unfree, or causally determined. Moreover, he will be in the position of maintaining that in the case of *every* true statement of the form, "O prevented X by doing A," there is a corresponding statement of the form "Something made O do A, thereby preventing X," which is something I think no one has the slightest reason for believing.

TAYLOR SELECTION

1.   Exactly what is Taylor's definition of "prevention"? What does he mean by "something that was . . . both sufficient and necessary for, although logically independent of, the subsequent nonoccurrence of that event"? What is the difference between "sufficient for" and "necessary

for"? Why must the action that prevents be *logically* independent of the event that is prevented?

2.   Give some examples (other than Taylor's example) of successful preventions. Give an example of something that looks like a successful prevention but turns out not to have been a prevention at all.

3.   Now explain Taylor's peculiar notion of "postvention." Give one or two new examples, to make sure that you understand it. In what way is postvention parallel to prevention? In what way does it differ?

4.   Can you think up some other concepts, parallel to familiar and much-used concepts, for which we have no use? What would be the concept parallel to "remember"? What would be the concept parallel to "regret"? What would be the concept parallel to "forget"?

5.   Can you imagine what it would be like to live in a world in which space, like time, had a built-in direction. We *can* go back to a place we have been, but we can never go back to a time we have been. Why not? Or can we?

(SELECTION 7)

JEAN-PAUL SARTRE

Freedom, Action, and Responsibility

In this selection from his most systematic exposition of his philosophy, the great French existentialist Jean-Paul Sartre traces out the connections between human freedom, the structure of doing or acting, and the responsibility that human beings bear for their deeds. Since it has become habitual to portray twentieth-century Continental philosophy, whether written in France, in Germany, or in Italy, as somehow a breed apart from the philosophy characteristic of the Anglo-American world, it is perhaps worth noting how close Sartre's theses and modes of argument are to those of analytic philosophers whose writings have been excerpted in this and the preceding chapter.

Sartre, like several of our other authors, finds the key to human freedom in the phenomenon of choice and action. It is by virtue of being purposeful, active, deliberative creatures that we humans come to think of ourselves as free, and hence as responsible. There are significant connections between the work of Sartre and the philosophy of the leading American exponent of pragmatism, John Dewey, for example.

It is also well worth turning back to the selection from Peter Strawson in Chapter 1. Strawson, it will be recalled, characterized his philosophical enterprise as "descriptive metaphysics," that is, as a systematic articulation and analysis of the most fundamental and pervasive structures of our world, as we understand it. Although Sartre's style of writing is quite different from that of Strawson, he too can be said to be doing "descriptive metaphysics." Sartre, however, is more likely to seek clues to the structure of the experienced world in reflective analyses of particular significant experiences, minutely described and precisely observed. This so-called "phenomenological" approach contrasts with Strawson's reliance on clues provided by language. The difference is less important than we might think on first inspection, though, for our language so completely mirrors our experience that we would expect any truly basic structures in the latter to be prominently featured in the former.

There is one further historical point that one must remember while reading Sartre on the subject of freedom, choice, and responsibility. For the Frenchmen of Sartre's generation, the most important single event was the German occupation of France during the Second World War. Many Frenchmen cooperated with the German invaders—"collaborated," as it was called —while many others formed underground units and fought the Germans, at great risk to their lives. It was a matter of immediate importance, and not merely an abstract question of philosophical interest, to decide whether one was implicated in the collaboration or responsible for it in some way if one kept quiet and did nothing either positive or negative with regard to the Resistance. Many of Sartre's philosophical writings have dealt with the troubling question of the individual's share of responsibility for acts done by his government or his society. We in the United States have been forced to confront a similar issue in the case of the Vietnam War.

It is strange that philosophers have been able to argue endlessly about determinism and free-will, to cite examples in favor of one or the other thesis without ever attempting first to make explicit the structures contained in the very idea of *action*. The concept of an act contains, in fact, numerous subordinate notions which we shall have to organize and arrange in a hierarchy: to act is to modify the *shape* of the world; it is to arrange means in view of an end; it is to produce an organized instrumental complex such that by a series of concatenations and connections the modification effected on one of the links causes modifications throughout the whole series and finally produces an anticipated result. But this is not what is important for us here. We should observe first that an action is on principle *intentional*. The careless smoker who has through negligence caused the explosion of a powder magazine has not *acted*. On the other hand the worker who is charged with dynamiting a quarry and who obeys the given orders has acted when he has produced the expected explosion; he knew what he was doing or, if you prefer, he intentionally realized a conscious project.

This does not mean, of course, that one must foresee all the consequences of his act. The emperor Constantine when he established himself at Byzantium, did not foresee that he would create a center of Greek culture and language, the appearance of which would ultimately provoke a schism in the Christian Church and which would contribute to weakening the Roman Empire. Yet he performed an act just in so far as he realized his project of creating a new residence for emperors in the Orient. Equating the result with the intention is here sufficient for us to be able to speak of action. But if this is the case, we establish that the action necessarily implies as its condition the recognition of a "desideratum"; that is, of an objective lack or again of a *négatité*. The *intention* of providing a rival for Rome can come to Constantine only through the apprehension of an objective lack: Rome lacks a counterweight; to this still

From *Being and Nothingness* by Jean-Paul Sartre. First published in English by the Philosophical Library, Inc. in 1956. (trans. by Hazel E. Barnes. Reprinted by permission of the publishers.)

profoundly pagan city ought to be opposed a Christian city which at the moment *is missing*. Creating Constantinople is understood as an *act* only if first the conception of a new city has preceded the action itself or at least if this conception serves as an organizing theme for all later steps. But this conception can not be the pure representation of the city as *possible*. It apprehends the city in its essential characteristic, which is to be a *desirable* and not yet realized possible.

This means that from the moment of the first conception of the act, consciousness has been able to withdraw itself from the full world of which it is consciousness and to leave the level of being in order frankly to approach that of non-being. Consciousness in so far as it is considered exclusively in its being, is perpetually referred from being to being and can not find in being any motive for revealing non-being. The imperial system with Rome as its capital functions positively and in a certain real way which can be easily discovered. Will someone say that the taxes are collected badly, that Rome is not secure from invasions, that it does not have the geographical location which is suitable for the capital of a Mediterranean empire which is threatened by barbarians, that its corrupt morals make the spread of the Christian religion difficult? How can anyone fail to see that all these considerations are *negative;* that is, that they aim at what is not, not at what is. To say that sixty per cent of the anticipated taxes have been collected can pass, if need be for a positive appreciation of the situation *such as it is*. To say that they are *badly* collected is to consider the situation across a situation which is posited as an absolute end but which precisely *is not*. To say that the corrupt morals at Rome hinder the spread of Christianity is not to consider this diffusion for what it is; that is, for a propagation at a rate which the reports of the clergy can enable us to determine. It is to posit the diffusion in itself as insufficient; that is, as suffering from a secret nothingness. But it appears as such only if it is surpassed toward a limiting-situation posited *a priori* as a value (for example, toward a certain rate of religious conversions, toward a certain mass morality). This limiting-situation can not be conceived in terms of the simple consideration of the real state of things; for the most beautiful girl in the world can offer only what she *has,* and in the same way the most miserable situation can by itself be designated only as it *is* without any reference to an ideal nothingness. . . .

Thus at the outset we can see what is lacking in those tedious discussions between determinists and the proponents of free will. The latter are concerned to find cases of decision for which there exists no prior cause, or deliberations concerning two opposed acts which are equally possible and possess causes (and motives) of exactly the same weight. To which the determinists may easily reply that

there is no action without a *cause* and that the most insignificant
gesture (raising the right hand rather than the left hand, etc.) refers
to causes and motives which confer its meaning upon it. Indeed the
case could not be otherwise since every action must be *intentional;*
each action must, in fact, have an end, and the end in turn is referred
to a cause. Such indeed is the unity of the three temporal ekstases;
the end or temporalization of my future implies a cause (or motive);
that is, it points toward my past, and the present is the upsurge of
the act. To speak of an act without a cause is to speak of an act
which would lack the intentional structure of every act; and the proponents of free will by searching for it on the level of the act which is
in the process of being performed can only end up by rendering the
act absurd. But the determinists in turn are weighting the scale by
stopping their investigation with the mere designation of the cause
and motive. The essential question in fact lies beyond the complex
organization "cause-intention-act-end"; indeed we ought to ask how
a cause (or motive) can be constituted as such.

Now we have just seen that if there is no act without a cause,
this is not in the sense that we can say that there is no phenomenon
without a cause. In order to be a *cause,* the cause must be *experienced* as such. Of course this does not mean that it is to be themati-
cally conceived and made explicit as in the case of deliberation. But
at the very least it means that the for-itself must confer on it its value
as cause or motive. And, as we have seen, this constitution of the
cause as such can not refer to another real and positive existence,
that is, to a prior cause. For otherwise the very nature of the act as
engaged intentionally in non-being would disappear. The motive is
understood only by the end; that is, by the non-existent. It is therefore in itself a négatité. If I accept a niggardly salary it is doubtless
because of fear; and fear is a motive. But it is *fear of dying from
starvation;* that is, this fear has meaning only outside itself in an
end ideally posited, which is the preservation of a life which I apprehend as "in danger." And this fear is understood in turn only in relation to the *value which* I implicitly give to this life; that is, it is
referred to that hierarchal system of ideal objects which are values.
Thus the motive makes itself understood as what it is by means of the
ensemble of beings which "are not," by ideal existences, and by the
future. Just as the future turns back upon the present and the past
in order to elucidate them, so it is the ensemble of my projects which
turns back in order to confer upon the *motive* its structure as a
motive. It is only because I escape the in-itself by nihilating myself
toward my possibilities that this in-itself can take on value as cause
or motive. Causes and motives have meaning only inside a projected
ensemble which is precisely an ensemble of non-existents. And this

ensemble is ultimately myself as transcendence; it is Me in so far as I have to be myself outside of myself. . . .

At the end of this long discussion, it seems that we have succeeded in making a little more precise our ontological understanding of freedom. It will be well at present to gather together and summarize the various results obtained.

(1) A first glance at human reality informs us that for it being is reduced to doing. The psychologists of the nineteenth century who pointed out the "motor" structures of drives, of the attention, of perception, etc. were right. But motion itself is an act. Thus we find no *given* in human reality in the sense that temperament, character, passions, principles of reason would be acquired or innate *data* existing in the manner of things. The empirical consideration of the human being shows him as an organized unity of conduct patterns or of "behaviors." To be ambitious, cowardly, or irritable is simply to conduct oneself in this or that matter in this or that circumstance. The Behaviorists were right in considering that the sole positive psychological study ought to be of conduct in strictly defined situations. Just as the work of Janet and the Gestalt School have put us in a position to discover types of emotional conduct, so we ought to speak of types of perceptive conduct since perception is never conceived outside an attitude with respect to the world. Even the disinterested attitude of the scientist, as Heidegger has shown, is the assumption of a disinterested position with regard to the object and consequently one conduct among others. Thus human reality does not exist first in order to act later; but for human reality, to be is to act, and to cease to act is to cease to be.

(2) But if human reality is action, this means evidently that its determination to action is itself action. If we reject this principle, and if we admit that human reality can be determined to action by a prior state of the world or of itself, this amounts to putting a *given* at the beginning of the series. Then these *acts* disappear as acts in order to give place to a series of *movements*. Thus the notion of conduct is itself destroyed with Janet and with the Behaviorists. The existence of the act implies its autonomy.

(3) Furthermore, if the act is not pure motion, it must be defined by an *intention*. No matter how this intention is considered, it can be only a surpassing of the given toward a result to be obtained. This given, in fact, since it is pure presence, can not get out of itself. Precisely because it it, it is fully and solely what it is. Therefore it can not provide the reason for a phenomenon which derives all its meaning from a result to be attained; that is, from a non-existent. . . . The intention, which is the fundamental structure of human-reality, can in no case be explained by a given, not even if it is presented as

an emanation from a given. But if one wishes to interpret the intention by its end, care must be taken not to confer on this end an existence as a *given*. . . . If the drive or the act is to be interpreted by its end, this is because the intention has for its structure *positing* its end outside itself. Thus the intention makes itself be by choosing the end which makes it known.

(4) Since the intention is a choice of the end and since the world reveals itself across our conduct, it is the intentional choice of the end which reveals the world, and the world is revealed as this or that (in this or that order) according to the end chosen. The end, illuminating the world, is a state *of* the world to be obtained and not yet existing. . . .

(5) If the given can not explain the intention, it is necessary that the intention by its very upsurge realize a rupture with the given, whatever this may be. Such must be the case, for otherwise we should have a present plenitude succeeding in continuity a present plenitude, and we could not prefigure the future. Moreover, this rupture is necessary for the *appreciation* of the given. The given, in fact, could never be a cause for an action if it were not appreciated. But this appreciation can be realized only by a withdrawal in relation to the given, a putting of the given into parentheses, which exactly supposes a break in continuity. In addition, the appreciation if it is not to be gratuitous, must be effected in the light of something. And this something which serves to appreciate the given can be only the end. Thus the intention by a single unitary upsurge posits the end, chooses itself, and appreciates the given in terms of the end. . . .

(6) It would be in vain to imagine that consciousness can exist without a given; in that case it would be consciousness (of) itself as consciousness of nothing—that is, absolute nothingness. But if consciousness exists in terms of the given, this does not mean that the given conditions consciousness; consciousness is a pure and simple negation of the given, and it exists as the disengagement from a certain existing given and as an engagement toward a certain not yet existing end. But in addition this internal negation can be only the fact of a being which is in perpetual withdrawal in relation to itself. If this being were not its own negation, it would be what it is—i.e., a pure and simple given. Due to this fact it would have no connection with any other *datum* since the given is by nature only what it is. Thus any possibility of the appearance of a world would be excluded. In order not to be a given, the for-itself must perpetually constitute itself as in withdrawal in relation to itself; that is, it must leave itself behind it as a *datum* which it already no longer is. This characteristic of the for-itself implies that it is the being which finds

no help, no pillar of support in what it was. But on the other hand, the for-itself is free and can cause there to be a world because the for-itself is *the being which has to be what it was in the light of what it will be.* Therefore the freedom of the for-itself appears as its *being.* But since this freedom is neither a given nor a property, it can be only by choosing itself. The freedom of the for-itself is always *engaged;* there is no question here of a freedom which could be undetermined and which would pre-exist its choice. We shall never apprehend ourselves except as a choice in the making. But freedom is simply the fact that this choice is always unconditioned.

(7) Such a choice made without base of support and dictating its own causes to itself, can very well appear *absurd,* and in fact it is absurd. This is because freedom is a *choice* of its being but not the *foundation* of its being. . . . Human-reality can choose itself as it intends but is not able not to choose itself. It can not even refuse to be; suicide, in fact, is a choice and affirmation—of being. By this being which is *given* to it, human reality participates in the universal contingency of being and thereby in what we may call absurdity. This choice is absurd, not because it is without reason but because there has never been any possibility of not choosing oneself. Whatever the choice may be, it is founded and reapprehended by being, for it is choice which *is.* But what must be noted here is that this choice is not absurd in the sense in which in a rational universe a phenomenon might arise which would not be bound to others by any *reasons.* It is absurd in this sense—that the choice is that by which all foundations and all reasons come into being, that by which the very notion of the absurd receives a meaning. It is absurd as being beyond all reasons. Thus freedom is not pure and simple contingency in so far as it turns back toward its being in order to illuminate its being in the light of its end. It is the perpetual escape from contingency; it is the interiorization, the nihilation, and the subjectivizing of contingency, which thus modified passes wholly into the gratuity of the choice.

(8) The free project is fundamental, for it is my being. Neither ambition nor the passion to be loved nor the inferiority complex can be considered as fundamental projects. On the contrary, they of necessity must be understood in terms of a primary project which is recognized as the project which can no longer be interpreted in terms of any other and which is total. . . . The fundamental project which I am is a project concerning not my relations with this or that particular object in the world, but my total being-in-the-world; since the world itself is revealed only in the light of an end, this project posits for its end a certain type of relation to being which the for-itself wills to adopt. This project is not instantaneous, for it

can not be "in" time. Neither is it non-temporal in order to "give time to itself" afterwards. That is why we reject Kant's "choice of intelligible character." The structure of the choice necessarily implies that it be a choice in the world. A choice which would be a choice *in terms of nothing*, a choice *against nothing* would be a choice of nothing and would be annihilated as choice. There is only phenomenal choice, provided that we understand that the phenomenon is here the absolute. But in its very upsurge, the choice is temporalized since it causes a future to come to illuminate the present and to constitute it as a present by giving the meaning of *pastness* to the in-itself "data." However we need not understand by this that the fundamental project is coextensive with the entire "life" of the for-itself. Since freedom is a being-without-support and without-a-springboard, the project in order to be must be constantly renewed. I choose myself perpetually and can never be merely by virtue of having-been-chosen; otherwise I should fall into the pure and simple existence of the in-itself. The necessity of perpetually choosing myself is one with the pursued-pursuit which I am. But precisely because here we are dealing with a *choice*, this choice as it is made indicates in general other choices as possibles. The possibility of these other choices is neither made explicit nor posited, but it is lived in the feeling of unjustifiability; and it is this which is expressed by the fact of the *absurdity* of my choice and consequently of my being. Thus my freedom eats away my freedom. Since I am free, I project my total possible, but I thereby posit that I am free and that I can always nihilate this first project and make it past. . . .

The essential consequence of our earlier remarks is that man being condemned to be free carries the weight of the whole world on his shoulders; he is responsible for the world and for himself as a way of being. We are taking the word "responsibility" in its ordinary sense as "consciousness (of) being the incontestable author of an event or of an object." In this sense the responsibility of the for-itself is overwhelming since he is the one by whom it happens that *there is* a world; since he is also the one who makes himself be, then whatever may be the situation in which he finds himself, the for-itself must wholly assume this situation with its peculiar coefficient of adversity, even though it be insupportable. He must assume the situation with the proud consciousness of being the author of it, for the very worst disadvantages or the worst threats which can endanger my person have meaning only in and through my project; and it is on the ground of the engagement which I am that they appear. It is therefore senseless to think of complaining since nothing foreign has decided what we feel, what we live, or what we are.

Furthermore this absolute responsibility is not resignation; it is simply the logical requirement of the consequences of our freedom. What happens to me happens through me, and I can neither affect myself with it nor revolt against it nor resign myself to it. Moreover everything which happens to me is *mine*. By this we must understand first of all that I am always equal to what happens to me *qua* man, for what happens to a man through other men and through himself can be only human. The most terrible situations of war, the worst tortures do not create a non-human state of things; there is no non-human situation. It is only through fear, flight, and recourse to magical types of conduct that I shall decide on the non-human, but this decision is human, and I shall carry the entire responsibility for it. But in addition the situation is *mine* because it is the image of my free choice of myself, and everything which it presents to me is *mine* in that this represents me and symbolizes me. Is it not I who decide the coefficient of adversity in things and even their unpredictability by deciding myself?

Thus there are no *accidents* in a life; a community event which suddenly bursts forth and involves me in it does not come from the outside. If I am mobilized in a war, this war is *my* war; it is in my image and I deserve it. I deserve it first because I could always get out of it by suicide or by desertion; these ultimate possibles are those which must always be present for us when there is a question of envisaging a situation. For lack of getting out of it, I have *chosen* it. This can be due to inertia, to cowardice in the face of public opinion, or because I prefer certain other values to the value of the refusal to join in the war (the good opinion of my relatives, the honor of my family, etc.). Anyway you look at it, it is a matter of choice. This choice will be repeated later on again and again without a break until the end of the war. . . . If therefore I have preferred war to death or to dishonor, everything takes place as if I bore the entire responsibility for this war. Of course others have declared it, and one might be tempted perhaps to consider me as a simple accomplice. But this notion of complicity has only a juridical sense, and it does not hold here. For it depended on me that for me and by me this war should not exist, and I have decided that it does exist. There was no compulsion here, for the compulsion could have got no hold on a freedom. I did not have any excuse; for as we have said repeatedly in this book, the peculiar character of human-reality is that it is without excuse. Therefore it remains for me only to lay claim to their war.

But in addition the war is *mine* because by the sole fact that it arises in a situation which I cause to be and that I can discover it there only by engaging myself for or against it, I can no longer distinguish at present the choice which I make of myself from the choice which I make of the war. To live this war is to choose myself through it and to choose it through my choice of myself. There can be no question of considering it as "four years of vacation" or as a "reprieve," as a "recess," the essential part of my responsibilities being elsewhere in my married, family, or professional life. In this war which I have chosen I choose myself from day to day, and I make it mine by making myself. If it is going to be four empty years, then it is I who bear the responsibility for this.

Finally, as we pointed out earlier, each person is an absolute choice of self from the standpoint of a world of knowledges and of techniques which this choice both assumes and illumines; each person is an absolute upsurge at an absolute date and is perfectly unthinkable at another date. It is therefore a waste of time to ask what I should have been if this war had not broken out, for I have chosen myself as one of the possible meanings of the epoch which imperceptibly led to war. I am not distinct from this same epoch; I could not be transported to another epoch without contradiction. Thus *I am* this war which restricts and limits and makes comprehensible the period which preceded it. In this sense we may define more precisely the responsibility of the for-itself if to the earlier quoted statement, "There are no innocent victims," we add the words, "We have the war we deserve." Thus, totally free, undistinguishable from the period for which I have chosen to be the meaning, as profoundly responsible for the war as if I had myself declared it, unable to live without integrating it in *my* situation, engaging myself in it wholly and stamping it with my seal, I must be without remorse or regrets as I am without excuse; for from the instant of my upsurge into being, I carry the weight of the world by myself alone without anything or any person being able to lighten it.

Yet this responsibility is of a very particular type. Someone will say, "I did not ask to be born." This is a naive way of throwing greater emphasis on our facticity. I am responsible for everything, in fact, except for my very responsibility, for I am not the foundation of my being. Therefore everything takes place as if I were compelled to be responsible. I am *abandoned* in the world, not in the sense that I might remain abandoned and passive in a hostile universe like a board floating on the water, but rather in the sense that I find myself suddenly alone and without help, engaged in a world for which I bear the whole responsibility without being able, whatever I do, to tear myself away from this responsibility for an instant. For I am responsible for my very desire of fleeing responsibilities. To make myself passive in the world, to refuse to act upon things and upon Others is still to choose myself, and suicide is one mode among others of being-in-the-world. Yet I find an absolute responsibility for the fact that my facticity (here the fact of my birth) is directly inapprehensible and even inconceivable, for this fact of my birth never appears as a brute fact but always across a projective reconstruction of my for-itself. I am ashamed of being born or I am astonished at it or I rejoice over it, or in attempting to get rid of my life I affirm that I live and I assume this life as bad. Thus in a certain sense I *choose* being born. This choice itself is integrally affected with facticity since I am not able not to choose, but this facticity in turn will appear only in so far as I surpass it toward my ends. Thus facticity is everywhere but inapprehensible; I never encounter anything except my responsibility. That is why I can not ask, "*Why* was I born?" or curse the day of my birth or declare that I did not ask to be born, for these various attitudes toward my birth—i.e., toward the *fact* that I realize a presence in the world—are absolutely nothing else but ways of assuming this birth in full responsibility and of making it *mine*. Here again I encounter only myself and my projects so that finally my abandonment—i.e., my facticity—consists simply in the fact that I am condemned to be wholly responsible for myself. I am the being which *is* in such a way that in its being its being is in question. And this "is" of my being *is* as present and inapprehensible.

Under these conditions since every event in the world can be revealed to me only as an *opportunity* (an opportunity made use of, lacked, neglected, etc.), or better yet since everything which happens to us can be considered as a *chance* (i.e., can appear to us only as a way of realizing this being which is in question in our being) and since others as transcendences-transcended are themselves only *opportunities* and *chances,* the responsibility of the for-itself extends to the entire world as a peopled-world. It is precisely thus that the for-itself apprehends itself in anguish; that is, as a being which is neither the foundation of its own being nor of the Other's being nor of the in-itselfs which form the world, but a being which is compelled to decide the meaning of being—within it and everywhere outside of it. The one who realizes in anguish his condition as *being* thrown into a responsibility which extends to his very abandonment has no longer either remorse or regret or excuse; he is no longer anything but a freedom which perfectly reveals itself and whose being resides in this very revelation. But as we pointed out at the beginning of this work, most of the time we flee anguish in bad faith.

SARTRE SELECTION

1.   What does Sartre mean by describing actions as "intentional"? Do you think Sartre would consider a thoughtless or careless or habitual act *not* to be intentional? Why?

2.   In terms of the notion of an intention as projecting or positing

some end outside of itself, try to explain why, for Sartre, we could never reduce explanations of human actions to accounts of physical behavior.

3.   Animals live in, and as a part of, their natural environment. They do not have a "world" in the sense that we do, for they do not distinguish themselves from their environment and objectify it as their *world*. Therefore, animals cannot have plans or intentions in the way that we do. How does this relate to Sartre's notion of human freedom?

4.   In the same way, if each of us individually views the social world as merely the "environment," then our socially oriented behavior will not rise to the level of intentional action. In terms of this analogy, can you explain why Sartre holds that we are responsible for the society in which we live, even though we never made it?

1. Suppose that after long and painful experience you have learned that you simply could not trust yourself to resist the temptation of alcohol. Now you find yourself confronted by a bottle, and you are trying to stop yourself from taking a drink. How would the various authors in this section analyze this situation? Which of them would claim that it is genuinely open to you both to drink and not to drink? Which would say that your choice is predetermined by causes already in motion? Do you think you ought to analyze your own situation in exactly the way you would analyze the same situation if it involved someone else? Or is your knowledge and understanding of yourself fundamentally different from your knowledge and understanding of others?

2. How would Kant reply to the "compatibilists" like Hume and Schlick?

3. As we learn more about the brain and nervous system, we discover physiological causes for such "psychological" states as depression. What are the implications of these discoveries for theories of freedom and responsibility?

4. Go back to the case of Herman and Fred in the introduction to this chapter. Taking each of our authors in turn, try to figure out which defenses they would accept as getting Fred off the hook.

5. Choose any recent decision you have made (for example, the decision whether to read this week's philosophy assignment). Try to recall what you thought about before making your decision. Add in any other considerations that you might have appealed to in making your decision. Now ask yourself: Does your decision-making process look anything like what the authors in this section are talking about? Were you free to choose in more than one way? How do you know that you were?

6. Suppose someone showed you a sealed envelope, certified as having been closed for the past week. And suppose that when you opened it, you found in it one hundred correct "predictions" of things you had in fact done in the past week. Would you conclude that you hadn't been free in doing those one hundred actions? Why? If your ability to predict what someone will do is compatible with his or her being free, then what do you mean by freedom and unfreedom?

CHAPTER three

THE ROLE OF REASON IN CHOICE AND EVALUATION

(Focal Issues)

1. *What Role Should Reason Play in My Life?*

2. *Can Reason Help Me to Choose My Goals in Life?*

3. *Are There Any Ultimate Principles for Living Our Lives? Does It Make Sense to Argue About Ultimate Principles?*

INTRODUCTION

In Chapter 1 we explored the nature of a person, and we found that for many philosophers, the power to reason, to reflect, to set goals, choose among alternative means, and weigh the wisdom of this or that course of action is the distinguishing mark of a *person* (whether human or, in the case of our science fiction example, extraterrestrial). In Chapter 2, we struggled with the conflict between the causal determination that appears to hold sway in nature and the freedom that purposive persons like ourselves seem to have to make choices and pursue our goals. Once again, in the writings of Immanuel Kant and others, we found that *reason* was the central or essential feature of free, as opposed to determined, behavior. In this chapter, we confront directly one of the oldest and most controversial questions in the philosophical armory: What is the proper role of reason in human choice and evaluation?

Right away, we come up against a problem of definition: what do we mean by the word "reason"? Now, it is always possible to bring a perfectly sensible discussion to a dead halt by demanding a definition of terms. How far would we get in debating the relative merits of presidential candidates or station wagons if someone kept insisting that we define "politics" or "the state" or "car" or even "good"? Nevertheless, in this case something has to be said about the term "reason" and its related cognates "reasonable," "reasoning," "rational," and "rationality," before we can even begin to discuss the role of reason in choice and evaluation.

There are at least five different (though possibly related) senses of "reason" and its cognates that we use when talking about judgment, choice, evaluation, and action. (A good-sized dictionary will probably turn up a dozen more, but there are limits to what we can cover in an introductory essay like this.) First of all, there is our ability *to draw conclusions from premises in an argument by means of the laws of logic.* We call this process *reasoning,* and as we have already seen in previous chapters, it is taken by some philosophers to be a distinguishing mark of persons as opposed to things that they can *reason* in this sense. When I argue, "All seagulls are white; that bird is black; therefore, that bird is not a seagull," I am carrying out a process of reasoning according to the ancient rules of logic known as the laws of the syllogism. When I argue, "If this plane figure is an isosceles triangle, then a line from the apex perpendicular to the base will bisect the base," I am carrying out a process of reasoning according to the mathematical rules known as Euclidean Geometry. The most important fact about reasoning of this sort is that it is "truth-preserving." That means that if the statements I start out with, the premises, are true, and if I follow the rules of logical or mathematical reasoning correctly, then my conclusion must also be true. (If my premises are false, of course, then I don't know where I am. "All professors are brilliant; my instructor is a professor; therefore, my instructor is brilliant" is a perfectly correct piece of reasoning, but unfortunately, there are some people who would actually deny that the first premise is true; and so we cannot be certain that the conclusion is true!)

The second capacity or process called reasoning is our ability to observe the world around us and then *to generalize from what we have observed* so that in future cases we can anticipate and predict what we shall find. As you have already learned in Chapter 2, David Hume held that our beliefs about the world (and about ourselves as well) are arrived at by noticing repeated patterns of events and then extrapolating those patterns to future times or to events that we have not actually observed. After several times being burnt by fire, I conclude that *fire burns,* and the next time I see a fire, I expect it to burn if I put my hand too near it. The generalization of our experience is not an absolutely truth-preserving process of reasoning, for it is logically possible (and in fact it sometimes happens) that our sample of observed events is in some way unrepresentative or skewed so that we are misled into believing generalizations that are in fact not universally true. Generals, it is said, are perpetually fighting the last war. That is to say, they elevate their past experiences to the status of laws of warfare, and therefore prepare for the sort of attack that came last time, forgetting that with new weapons, new enemies, and new terrain, the attack next time may be nothing like the last war.

A third capacity often referred to as "rational" is the ability of at least some persons *to weigh up the many factors of a complex situation and come to some judgment about what it is best to do,* taking everything into account. A doctor, for example, after completing her medical tests and examinations, must make a diagnosis. Sometimes the diagnosis follows directly from the results of the tests: if the blood sugar level is thus and so, then the patient has diabetes, etc. But usually, a delicate process of judgment is required, in which a knowledge of general scientific principles is combined with inductions upon past instances and a general capacity to evaluate the particular configuration of the evidence. This evaluative act is also considered an instance of our powers of reason, and so we sometimes say that a doctor's diagnosis is "unreasonable" or that an engineer's evaluation of a plan for a bridge is "reasonable."

The term "rational" is also used in a fourth way to characterize the ability of human beings to choose the fastest or shortest or cheapest or easiest—in short, *to choose the most efficient way of reaching some goal* that they have set for themselves. This ability to fit means to ends is taken by many philosophers to be *the* distinctive mark of rationality, and we shall have a good deal more to say about it.

Finally, "rational" is sometimes applied to *the ends or goals themselves,* and not simply to the process by which means are selected for pursuing those goals. By extension, the men and women who have chosen the goals are then called rational or irrational, accordingly as they have chosen rational or irrational ends. For example, a carefully calculating, shrewdly observant, efficient mass murderer, with a well-developed capacity for weighing up the elements of a situation and making a balanced judgment, will be called "irrational," even though he fits our first four meanings of "rational," because the goal he pursues (namely, mass murder) is in and of itself an irrational goal. Anyone who chooses such a purpose in life, we will often say, is a madman.

These are among the most prominent senses of "rational," and when we ask what role reason does or ought to play in choice and evaluation, it is one or more of these meanings of the term that we have in mind. Before sketching some of the answers that have been given to the question, along with at least a suggestion of the supporting reasons, we ought to note one point. Many philosophers have sought to reduce this variety of meanings of "rational" somewhat by arguing that one or two of them are really fundamental, the others being explainable in their terms. For example, instrumental rationality—the ability to fit means to ends efficiently—is explained as a combination of induction from particular instances to general laws of nature and deduction or inference from general laws to a conclusion about a new particular case in which a given or posited goal is added to the general information about causes and effects. The ability to weigh up a complex situation and evaluate the interrelation of the factors shrewdly is often discounted as a separate capacity or power of the mind. Instead, according to some philosophers (although others disagree), experts who make such judgment calls are really engaged in very rapid deductive or inductive inferences which in principle, if not in present fact, could be reduced to rules or general laws, and even taught to a nonrational computer.

The deepest and most important dispute, as we shall see, is between those philosophers who believe that reason can, at best, perform only the first four functions we have outlined, and those who insist that reason can in some manner perform the fifth as well. This dispute has a name (it is always useful to have hooks on which to hang ideas). It is called the dispute between *instrumental* and *substantive* rationality. *Instrumental rationality* is the ability to deliberate among alternative ways of accomplishing the same end and then to choose a way that meets one's standard of efficiency. The traveler in a hurry who chooses a plane over a train; the traveler short on funds who chooses a bus over a plane; the investor looking for safety first who chooses low-yields bonds rather than high-risk stocks; the courageous cavity-prone candy-eater who goes to the dentist now, even though he hates it, rather than putting it off until he has even more painful work to be done later—all these stock figures from the literature of economics and ethics are engaging in prudential acts of instrumental rationality. The model of choice and action with which we work in these cases is very simple (too simple, some would say): the agent is in some way or other *given* an end, by his desires, by his culture, by habit, or indeed by a free and unreasoned choice. In short, the agent is assumed to know what he or she wants, where he or she wishes to go. The proper role of reason is then to reflect on the resources available to the agent and to select the one which best meets the agent's own standards of efficiency, whatever they may be. One agent may wish to conserve money; a second agent, time; a third, risk of pain; a fourth, some combination of these. The agent who chooses the best *instrument* for the job (using "instrument" rather broadly) is said to have acted in an *instrumentally rational* manner, and agents who regularly choose in an instrumentally rational way are said themselves to *be* rational.

Very few philosophers deny that reason ought to play this instrumental role in choice and action, although the contemporary Englishman Michael Oakeshott rejects the entire model of action on which the notion is based, as we shall see. The real argument develops over whether reason has any *other* role to play in action, and specifically over whether reason can serve as a guide in the choice of the *ends* themselves at which we aim. Since the ends of our actions are their substance or content, the use of reason to choose ends is called *substantive rationality.* So the dispute we are discussing can be summarized as a disagreement over whether human beings can be substantively as well as instrumentally rational. Simplifying enormously, we can say that among the authors included in this chapter, Plato, Rawls, and Foot think that reason has some substantive role to play; Hume, Toulmin, and Hare ascribe only instrumental and formal roles to reason; and Oakeshott thinks the whole question is confused because the means-ends model of action is wrong.

Among pre-twentieth-century authors, the debate over the role of reason tends to turn very much on the nature of the relationship between reason and desire. According to some philosophers (Hume, for instance), it is desire or appetite that actually moves us to action. A purely rational creature, contemplating logical truths and causal laws, would never thereby *do* anything. We act because we desire some object, experience, or state of affairs that does not now exist. We are hungry, and want to eat; we are thirsty, and want to drink; we are ambitious, and want the applause of the public. The desire gets us started; it moves us. The thought of the desired end or object points us in the appropriate direction. Only then does reason canvass the available means and select the one that most nearly meets our criteria of efficiency or instrumental rationality. The implication of this analysis is that reason can say nothing about the relative wisdom, appropriateness, or "rationality" of the different ends that desire might set for us. If I truly desire chocolate ice cream more than life itself, then it will be instrumentally rational for me to play Russian Roulette for a chocolate cone if that is the only way for me to satisfy my desire. For the theorist of instrumental rationalty, it makes no sense at all to say that such a person is *irrational* for desiring chocolate ice cream more than life.

To be sure, some ends are also means to further ends. I may desire food as a means to health, in which case a doctor could perfectly well caution me that my desire for ice cream was irrational, meaning thereby that the eating of ice cream is an inefficient or instrumentally poor way to achieve my goal of health. But sooner or later, in our deliberations, we must appeal to ends that are not also means—to ultimate ends, as they are sometimes called. And about such ends, these philosophers say, there can be no rational dispute.

The contrary view has perhaps been best articulated by Plato, although it has found eloquent expression as well in the writings of the young Karl Marx, among others. Plato argues that reason and desire are not as thoroughly separate as the instrumentalists claim. Desire itself may indeed be a nonrational function of the personality (or psyche, as Plato calls it), but the shape, direction, objects, magnitude, and modulation of desire are all functions of reason in a properly ordered self. Desire as such is blind. It moves us, but not coherently in any particular direction. For the hungry baby even to identify the bottle as the object of its desire is already to introduce some measure of reason into the sheer appetite of infancy. Some desires, Plato insists, are intrinsically irrational, so that pursuit of their objects, even in the most methodical and instrumentally efficient way, is still unreasonable. The efficient mass murderer, Plato holds, is *more* irrational, not less, for being efficient. Not only is his desire misdirected toward irrational goals; in addition, his reason has been perverted to inappropriate uses.

Plato, Marx, and most other theorists of substantive rationality base their arguments on some objective conception of the good or healthy or happy condition for the human personality. Relying heavily on medical analogies, Plato, for example, suggests that there is a healthy condition of the soul or psyche, just as there is a healthy condition for the body. When reason rules in the psyche (or, in modern jargon, when the personality is reality-oriented and well-adjusted), then the person is truly happy. But when irrational desires dominate, then unhappiness results, *even if* the individual manages to get those irrational desires satisfied! Marx develops a similar conception of the healthy personality, relying on the analogy to art rather than to medicine. The fully developed person is someone who has the opportunity to engage in fulfilling, unalienated creative work. Like Plato, Marx claims that the alienated person will be unhappy, even if he succeeds in fulfilling the desires that dominated his maldeveloped psyche.

The dispute between the instrumentalists and the substantivists has quite far-reaching medical, moral, social, and political implications. In the early nineteenth century instrumentalism was used as a justification for democracy. If all men (and women, though it took a while for that obvious extension to win acceptance) were equally justified in their desires, and no expert rational arguments could be advanced to justify one set of ends rather than another, then it seemed to follow naturally that all members of society ought to have an equal voice in determining the collective uses to which society's resources were put. The doctrine of instrumental rationality, therefore, lent credence to the movement for popular democracy.

On the other hand, critics of industrial capitalist society, who wish to argue that the market foists unwanted commodities on the public and creates false desires that lead to unfulfilled and unhappy lives, appeal frequently to the notion of substantive rationality. Capitalism, they say, may be instrumentally rational, or efficient, but it is humanly destructive, it is substantively irrational.

In the field of psychiatry, the debate over the role of reason in choice and evaluation is particularly central, for a doctor's diagnosis and choice of treatment will depend at least in part on some conception of how a healthy human personality ought to be. If the notion of psychological health makes no sense (as psychiatrist Thomas Szasz asserts, in the selection in Chapter 6), then the very foundation of psychiatry as a branch of medicine is called into question.

In recent Anglo-American philosophy, which by and large traces its ancestry in this debate to the instrumentalist position of Hume, there have been a number of attempts to break out of the simple instrumentalist-substantivist straightjacket. Models of moral argument have been analyzed in an effort to map more precisely the role of reason—or of *reasons*—in deliberation, choice, and evaluation. Although I earlier classified Foot as a substantivist, it would be more accurate to say that she conceives reason as having a more complicated role in our moral judgments than previous philosophers had recognized.

Inevitably, the issues raised in one chapter of this text will bear directly on issues raised in other chapters as well. The nature and role of reason is centrally important not only to our understanding of persons and to the resolution of the conflict between freedom and determinism (Chapters 1 and 2), but also to the determination of the right principles of action (Chapter 5) and to a consideration of competing ideals of the good society (Chapter 6).

(SELECTION 1)

PLATO

The Role of Reason in the Virtuous Soul

The Republic is a Dialogue between Socrates and (for the most part) two of his followers, Glaucon and Adeimantus, about the nature of *justice*. Somewhat more broadly, it is a discussion of the nature of the virtuous soul, the just society, and the relationship between the two. After analyzing the proper or fitting order of society, Socrates turns his attention to the inner order of an individual personality. This selection sets forth his conception of the well-ordered (or, as we might say, the healthy and well-adjusted) psyche.

There are two points deserving of special attention in this selection. First of all, Plato conceives of the passional and appetitive elements of personality as inherently limitless and unstructured. Hunger and thirst in the infant, for example, are shapeless longings, lacking in focus, in limit, and in any coherent discretion with regard to means or degrees of satisfaction. The old saying, "His eyes are bigger than his stomach," expresses the typical lack of measure or order in childish desire. A principal role of reason, therefore, according to Plato, is precisely to supply the direction and form without which desire cannot lead to genuine satisfaction. With considerable psychological insight, Plato recognizes that limitless desire is monstrous, not heroic.

The second point is that although Plato believes that reason must *rule* in the well-ordered psyche, as in the well-ordered state, he does *not* believe that reason's rule ought to be repressive or tyrannical. What this means in an individual personality is that desire must be moderated, guided, and shaped, rather than ruthlessly suppressed. Like Freud almost two millennia later, Plato understands the psychic dangers of sheer repression. The illicit desire summarily repressed reappears later in an even more disruptive and destructive form, just as a portion of the population politically oppressed will return to disrupt the healthful public order of the society.

In studying Plato's theory of the healthy personality, it is just as well not to concentrate too single-mindedly on the tripartite division of the soul into rational, appetitive, and passional elements. Plato shifted about from a dichotomous to a trichotomous division in various of his Dialogues, and the really important distinction is between the rational power of the psyche and the non-rational elements that must be guided, limited, and controlled by reason. Needless to say, Plato is a proponent of what we have called *substantive rationality*.

Surely, I began, we must admit that the same elements and characters that appear in the state must exist in every one of us; where else could they have come from? It would be absurd to imagine that among peoples with a reputation for a high-spirited character, like the Thracians and Scythians and northerners generally, the states have not derived that character from their individual members; or that it is otherwise with the love of knowledge, which would be ascribed chiefly to our own part of the world, or with the love of money, which one would specially connect with Phoenicia and Egypt.

Certainly.

So far, then, we have a fact which is easily recognized. But here the difficulty begins. Are we using the same part of ourselves in all these three experiences, or a different part in each? Do we gain knowledge with one part, feel anger with another, and with yet a third desire the pleasures of food, sex, and so on? Or is the whole soul at work in every impulse and in all these forms of behaviour? . . . Let us approach the problem whether these elements are distinct or identical in this way. It is clear that the same thing cannot act in two opposite ways or be in two opposite states at the same time, with respect to the same part of itself, and in relation to the same object. So if we find such contradictory actions or states among the elements concerned, we shall know that more than one must have been involved.

Very well. . . .

Now, would you class such things as assent and dissent, striving after something and refusing it, attraction and repulsion, as pairs of opposite actions or states of mind—no matter which?

Yes, they are opposites.

And would you not class all appetites such as hunger and thirst, and again willing and wishing, with the affirmative members of those pairs I have just mentioned? For instance, you would say that the soul of a man who desires something is striving after it, or trying to draw to itself the thing it wishes to possess, or again, in so far as it is willing to have its want satisfied, it is giving its assent to its own longing, as if to an inward question.

Yes.

And, on the other hand, disinclination, unwillingness, and dislike, we should class on the negative side with acts of rejection or repulsion.

From *The Republic* by Plato. (trans. by Francis MacDonald Cornford, New York and London: Oxford University Press, 1941. Reprinted by permission of the publishers.)

Of course.

That being so, shall we say that appetites form one class, the most conspicuous being those we call thirst and hunger?

Yes.

Thirst being desire for drink, hunger for food?

Yes.

Now, is thirst, just in so far as it is thirst, a desire in the soul for anything more than simply drink? Is it, for instance, thirst for hot drink or for cold, for much drink or for little, or in a word for drink of any particular kind? Is it not rather true that you will have a desire for cold drink only if you are feeling hot as well as thirsty, and for hot drink only if you are feeling cold; and if you want much drink or little, that will be because your thirst is a great thirst or a little one? But, just in itself, thirst or hunger is a desire for nothing more than its natural object, drink or food, pure and simple.

Yes, he agreed, each desire, just in itself, is simply for its own natural object. When the object is of such and such a particular kind, the desire will be correspondingly qualified. . . .

We conclude, then, that the soul of a thirsty man, just in so far as he is thirsty, has no other wish than to drink. That is the object of its craving, and towards that it is impelled.

That is clear.

Now if there is ever something which at the same time pulls it the opposite way, that something must be an element in the soul other than the one which is thirsting and driving it like a beast to drink; in accordance with our principle that the same thing cannot behave in two opposite ways at the same time and towards the same object with the same part of itself. It is like an archer drawing the bow: it is not accurate to say that his hands are at the same time both pushing and pulling it. One hand does the pushing, the other the pulling.

Exactly.

Now, is it sometimes true that people are thirsty and yet unwilling to drink?

Yes, often.

What, then, can one say of them, if not that their soul contains something which urges them to drink and something which holds them back, and that this latter is a distinct thing and overpowers the other?

I agree.

And is it not true that the intervention of this inhibiting principle in such cases always has its origin in reflection; whereas the impulses driving and dragging the soul are engendered by external influences and abnormal conditions?

Evidently.

We shall have good reason, then, to assert that they are two distinct principles. We may call that part of the soul whereby it reflects, rational; and the other, with which it feels hunger and thirst and is distracted by sexual passion and all the other desires, we will call irrational appetite, associated with pleasure in the replenishment of certain wants.

Yes, there is good ground for that view.

Let us take it, then, that we have now distinguished two elements in the soul. What of that passionate element which makes us feel angry and indignant? Is that a third, or identical in nature with one of those two?

It might perhaps be identified with appetite.

I am more inclined to put my faith in a story I once heard about Leontius, son of Aglaion. On his way up from the Piraeus outside the north wall, he notice the bodies of some criminals lying on the ground, with the executioner standing by them. He wanted to go and look at them, but at the same time he was disgusted and tried to turn away. He struggled for some time and covered his eyes, but at last the desire was too much for him. Opening his eyes wide, he ran up to the bodies and cried, "There you are, curse you; feast yourselves on this lovely sight!"

Yes, I have heard that story too.

The point of it surely is that anger is sometimes in conflict with appetite, as if they were two distinct principles. Do we not often find a man whose desires would force him to go against his reason, reviling himself and indignant with this part of his nature which is trying to put constraint on him? It is like a struggle between two factions, in which indignation takes the side of reason. But I believe you have never observed, in yourself or anyone else, indignation make common cause with appetite in behaviour which reason decides to be wrong.

No, I am sure I have not.

Again, take a man who feels he is in the wrong. The more generous his nature, the less can he be indignant at any suffering, such as hunger and cold, inflicted by the man he has injured. He recognizes such treatment as just, and, as I say, his spirit refuses to be roused against it.

That is true.

But now contrast one who thinks it is he that is being wronged. His spirit boils with resentment and sides with the right as he conceives it. Persevering all the most for the hunger and cold and other pains he suffers, it triumphs and will not give in until its gallant struggle has ended in success or death; or until the restraining voice of reason, like a shepherd calling off his dog, makes it relent. . . .

And so, after a stormy passage, we have reached the land. We are fairly agreed that the same three elements exist alike in the state and in the individual soul.

That is so.

Does it not follow at once that state and individual will be wise or brave by virtue of the same element in each and in the same way? Both will possess in the same manner any quality that makes for excellence.

That must be true.

Then it applies to justice: we shall conclude that a man is just in the same way that a state was just. And we have surely not forgotten that justice in the state meant that each of the three orders in it was doing its own proper work. So we may henceforth bear in mind that each one of us likewise will be a just person, fulfilling his proper function, only if the several parts of our nature fulfill theirs.

Certainly.

And it will be the business of reason to rule with wisdom and forethought on behalf of the entire soul; while the spirited element ought to act as its subordinate and ally. The two will be brought into accord, as we said earlier, by that combination of mental and bodily training which will tune up one string of the instrument and relax the other, nourishing the reasoning part on the study of noble literature and allaying the other's wildness by harmony and rhythm. When both have been thus nurtured and trained to know their own true functions, they must be set in command over the appetites, which form the greater part of each man's soul and are by nature insatiably covetous. They must keep watch lest this part, by battening on the pleasures that are called bodily, should grow so great and powerful that it will no longer keep to its own work, but will try to enslave the others and usurp a dominion to which it has no right, thus turning the whole of life upside down. At the same time, those two together will be the best of guardians for the entire soul and for the body against all enemies from without: the one will take counsel, while the other will do battle, following its ruler's commands and by its own bravery giving effect to the ruler's designs.

Yes, that is all true.

And so we call an individual brave in virtue of this spirited part of his nature, when, in spite of pain or pleasure, it holds fast to the injunctions of reason about what he ought or ought not to be afraid of.

True.

And wise in virtue of that small part which rules and issues these injunctions, possessing as it does the knowledge of what is good for each of the three elements and for all of them in common.

Certainly.

And, again, temperate by reason of the unanimity and concord of all three, when there is no internal conflict between the ruling element and its two subjects, but all are agreed that reason should be ruler.

Yes, that is an exact account of temperance, whether in the state or in the individual.

Finally, a man will be just by observing the principle we have so often stated.

Necessarily. . . .

And so our dream has come true—I mean the inkling we had that, by some happy chance, we had lighted upon a rudimentary form of justice from the very moment when we set about founding our commonwealth. Our principle that the born shoemaker or carpenter had better stick to his trade turns out to have been an adumbration of justice; and that is why it has helped us. But in reality justice, though evidently analogous to this principle, is not a matter of external behaviour, but of the inward self and of attending to all that is, in the fullest sense, a man's proper concern. The just man does not allow the several elements in his soul to usurp one another's functions; he is indeed one who sets his house in order, by self-mastery and discipline coming to be at peace with himself, and bringing into tune those three parts, like the terms in the proportion of a musical scale, the highest and lowest notes and the mean between them, with all the intermediate intervals. Only when he has linked these parts together in well-tempered harmony and has made himself one man instead of many, will he be ready to go about whatever he may have to do, whether it be making money and satisfying bodily wants, or business transactions, or the affairs of state. In all these fields when he speaks of just and honourable conduct, he will mean the behaviour that helps to produce and to preserve this habit of mind; and by wisdom he will mean the knowledge which presides over such conduct. Any action which tends to break down this habit will be for him unjust; and the notions governing it he will call ignorance and folly.

Exactly.

PLATO SELECTION

1. According to Plato, in the well-ordered soul, reason rules. What is the difference between a soul (or personality) in which reason *rules,* and a personality in which reason *tyrannizes* or represses the other elements?

2. Suppose that someone were to say to Plato, "It is all very well for you to place reason in the dominant position in your soul; but I prefer to allow my passions to rule me!" What might Plato say to such a person to persuade him or her that it was folly to allow passion to rule?

3. What signs might you (or Plato) look for in a person as indications that his soul was ruled by reason?

4. These days, we tend to speak of someone as being "well-adjusted." What do you think the relationship is between Plato's notion of a rationally ordered soul and the modern notion of emotional health and good adjustment?

5. What problems do you see with Plato's notion of the role of reason? Could a really wicked person have a well-ordered soul? Why?

(SELECTION 2)

DAVID HUME

Reason as the Slave of the Passions

This passage from *A Treatise of Human Nature* by David Hume is one of the most famous passages in all English philosophy. It contains the oft-quoted tagline, "Reason is, and ought only to be the slave of the passions, and can never pretend to any other office than to serve and obey them," which is the official doctrine, as it were, of the instrumentalists.

Hume is actually taking a stand on a question that had been much debated in the philosophy of his day; or, more precisely, he is arguing that the debate itself is confused, so that both sides are wrong. The debate concerned the proper roles of reason and passion in choice and action. It was assumed that these two mental faculties, reason and passion, were in conflict with one another. Reason pulled us in one direction, passion in the other. How much weight should be given to each? (Later philosophers, such as Immanuel Kant, were also to portray our moral life as a struggle between reason and passion, usually with the clear understanding that the virtuous individual heeded the voice of reason rather than the temptations of what Kant called "inclination.")

Hume's answer is that the question is wrongly put. Reason *cannot* conflict with passion in the manner assumed by both sides of the debate, for reason itself—the power to form judgments, draw inferences, collect evidence—cannot move us to action at all. It is passion, not reason, that moves us. Hence, reason can neither strengthen the urgings of passion nor weaken them. Only *another* passion, driving us in a different direction, can deflect the force of a first passion upon us.

Reason's role is merely to point out the easiest road, to lay before us, as it were, the means available for reaching the goals set by our desires and emotions. In that sense, it is the "slave" of the passions; less dramatically, we might say it is an instrument of desire. But the implication is clear: our standards of rationality apply only to means, not to ends. If I am angry because I believe, incorrectly, that my friend has betrayed me, then, Hume says, reason can alter my anger by revealing to me the falsity of my belief. But if, correctly believing that my friend has betrayed me, I become so angry that I am willing even to lose my life in the attempt to avenge myself upon him, then Hume refuses to characterize my reaction as "irrational." Plato would call it irrational, for he would say that my reaction lacked measure and showed an absence of reason in my soul. But Hume would say only that, in my angry condition, it would be irrational of me to select an inefficient means for working my revenge.

In evaluating Hume's argument, you might keep in mind the following two questions: First, if reason can allay a passion by showing it to be based on a false belief, then is it truly a *slave* of passion, or might it not be more accurate to call it a partner? Second, if a passion is a feeling, an "impression" in the mind, as Hume calls it, and if our belief in factual propositions is also, as Hume elsewhere claims, a certain force or vivacity with which certain ideas occur in our minds, then how can Hume be so sure that passions can move us to action while beliefs cannot?

Nothing is more usual in philosophy, and even in common life, than to talk of the combat of passion and reason, to give the preference to reason, and assert that men are only so far virtuous as they conform themselves to its dictates. Every rational creature, 'tis said, is oblig'd to regulate his actions by reason; and if any other motive or principle challenge the direction of his conduct, he ought to oppose it, 'till it be entirely subdu'd, or at least brought to a conformity with that superior principle. On this method of thinking the greatest part of moral philosophy, ancient and modern, seems to be founded; nor is there an ampler field, as well for metaphysical arguments, as popular declamations, than this suppos'd pre-eminence of reason above passion. The eternity, invariableness, and divine origin of the former have been display'd to the best advantage: The blindness, unconstancy, and deceitfulness of the latter have been as strongly insisted on. In order to shew the fallacy of all this philosophy, I shall endeavour to prove *first,* that reason alone can never be a motive to any action of the will; and *secondly,* that it can never oppose passion in the direction of the will.

The understanding exerts itself after two different ways, as it judges from demonstration or probability; as it regards the abstract relations of our ideas, or those relations of objects, of which experience only gives us information. I believe it scarce will be asserted, that the first species of reasoning alone is ever the cause of any action. As its proper province is the world of ideas, and as the will always places us in that of realities, demonstration and volition seem, upon that account, to be totally remov'd, from each other. Mathematics, indeed, are useful in all mechanical operations, and arithmetic in almost every art and profession: But 'tis not of themselves they have any influence. Mechanics are the art of regulating the motions of bodies *to some design'd end or purpose;* and the reason why we employ arithmetic in fixing the proportions of numbers, is only that we may discover the proportions of their influence and operation. A

From *A Treatise of Human Nature*, Book II, by David Hume. First published in 1739.

merchant is desirous of knowing the sum total of his accounts with any person: Why? but that he may learn what sum will have the same *effects* in paying his debt, and going to market, as all the particular articles taken together. Abstract or demonstrative reasoning, therefore, never influences any of our actions, but only as it directs our judgment concerning causes and effects; which leads us to the second operation of the understanding.

'Tis obvious, that when we have the prospect of pain or pleasure from any object, we feel a consequent emotion of aversion or propensity, and are carry'd to avoid or embrace what will give us this uneasiness or satisfaction. 'Tis also obvious, that this emotion rests not here, but making us cast our view on every side, comprehends whatever objects are connected with its original one by the relation of cause and effect. Here then reasoning takes place to discover this relation; and according as our reasoning varies, our actions receive a subsequent variation. But 'tis evident in this case, that the impulse arises not from reason, but is only directed by it. 'Tis from the prospect of pain or pleasure that the aversion or propensity arises towards any object: And these emotions extend themselves to the causes and effects of that object, as they are pointed out to us by reason and experience. It can never in the least concern us to know, that such objects are causes, and such others effects, if both the causes and effects be indifferent to us. Where the objects themselves do not affect us, their connexion can never give them any influence; and 'tis plain, that as reason is nothing but the discovery of this connexion, it cannot be by its means that the objects are able to affect us.

Since reason alone can never produce any action, or give rise to volition, I infer, that the same faculty is as incapable of preventing volition, or of disputing the preference with any passion or emotion. This consequence is necessary. 'Tis impossible reason cou'd have the latter effect of preventing volition, but by giving an impulse in a contrary direction to our passion; and that impulse, had it operated alone, wou'd have been able to produce volition. Nothing can oppose or retard the impulse of passion, but a contrary impulse; and if this contrary impulse ever arises from reason, that latter faculty must have an original influence on the will, and must be able to cause, as well as hinder any act of volition. But if reason has no original influence, 'tis impossible it can withstand any principle, which has such an efficacy, or ever keep the mind in suspence a moment. Thus it appears, that the principle, which opposes our passion, cannot be the same with reason, and is only call'd so in an improper sense. We speak not strictly and philosophically when we talk of the combat of passion and of reason. Reason is, and ought only to be the slave of the passions, and can never pretend to any other office than to serve and obey them. As this opinion may appear somewhat extraordinary, it may not be improper to confirm it by some other considerations.

A passion is an original existence, or, if you will, modification of existence, and contains not any representative quality, which renders it a copy of any other existence or modification. When I am angry, I am actually possest with the passion, and in that emotion have no more a reference to any other object, than when I am thirsty, or sick, or more than five foot high. 'Tis impossible, therefore, that this passion can be oppos'd by, or be contradictory to truth and reason; since this contradiction consists in the disagreement of ideas, consider'd as copies, with those objects, which they represent.

What may at first occur on this head, is, that as nothing can be contrary to truth or reason, except what has a reference to it, and as the judgments of our understanding only have this reference, it must follow, that passions can be contrary to reason only so far as they are *accompany'd* with some judgment or opinion. According to this principle, which is so obvious and natural, 'tis only in two senses, that any affection can be call'd unreasonable. First, When a passion, such as hope or fear, grief or joy, despair or security, is founded on the supposition of the existence of objects, which really do not exist. Secondly, When in exerting any passion in action, we chuse means insufficient for the design'd end, and deceive ourselves in our judgment of causes and effects. Where a passion is neither founded on false suppositions, nor chuses means insufficient for the end, the understanding can neither justify nor condemn it. 'Tis not contrary to reason to prefer the destruction of the whole world to the scratching of my finger. 'Tis not contrary to reason for me to chuse my total ruin, to prevent the least uneasiness of an *Indian* or person wholly unknown to me. 'Tis as little contrary to reason to prefer even my own acknowledg'd lesser good to my greater, and have a more ardent affection for the former than the latter. A trivial good may, from certain circumstances, produce a desire superior to what arises from the greatest and most valuable enjoyment; nor is there anything more extraordinary in this, than in mechanics to see one pound weight raise up a hundred by the advantage of its situation. In short, a passion must be accompany'd with some false judgment, in order to its being unreasonable; and even then 'tis not the passion, properly speaking, which is unreasonable, but the judgment.

The consequences are evident. Since a passion can never, in any sense, be call'd unreasonable, but when founded on a false supposition, or when it chuses means insufficient for the design'd end, 'tis impossible, that reason and passion can ever oppose each other, or dispute for the government of the will and actions. The moment we perceive the falsehood of any supposition, or the insufficiency of any means, our passions yield to our reason without any opposition. I may desire any fruit as of an excellent relish; but whenever you convince me of my mistake, my longing ceases. I may will the performance of certain actions as means of obtaining any desir'd good; but as my willing of these actions is only secondary, and founded on the supposition, that they are causes of the propos'd effect; as soon as I discover the falsehood of that supposition, they must become indifferent to me.

'Tis natural for one, that does examine objects with a strict philosophic eye, to imagine, that those actions of the mind are entirely the same, which produce not a different sensation, and are not immediately distinguishable to the feeling and perception. Reason, for instance, exerts itself without producing any sensible emotion; and except in the more sublime disquisitions of philosophy, or in the frivolous subtilties of the schools, scarce ever conveys any pleasure or uneasiness. Hence it proceeds, that every action of the mind, which operates with the same calmness and tranquillity, is confounded with reason by all those, who judge of things from the first view and appearance. Now 'tis certain, there are certain calm desires and tendencies, which, tho' they be real passions, produce little emotion in the mind, and are more known by their effects than by the immediate feeling or sensation. These desires are of two kinds; either certain instincts originally implanted in our natures, such as benevolence and resentment, the love of life, and kindness to children; or the general appetite to good, and aversion to evil, consider'd merely as such. When any of these passions are calm, and cause no disorder in the soul, they are very readily taken for the determinations of reason, and are suppos'd to proceed from the same faculty, with that, which judges of truth and falshood. Their nature and principles have been suppos'd the same, because their sensations are not evidently different.

Beside these calm passions, which often determine the will, there are certain violent emotions of the same kind, which have likewise a great influence on that faculty. When I receive any injury from another, I often feel a violent passion of resentment, which makes me desire his evil and punishment, independent of all considerations of pleasure and advantage to myself. When I am immediately threaten'd with any grievous ill, my fears, apprehensions, and aversions rise to a great height, and produce a sensible emotion.

The common error of metaphysicians has lain in ascribing the direction of the will entirely to one of these principles, and supposing the other to have no influence. Men often act knowingly against their interest: For which reason the view of the greatest possible good does not always influence them. Men often counter-act a violent passion in prosecution of their interests and designs: 'Tis not therefore the present uneasiness alone, which determines them. In general we may observe, that both these principles operate on the will; and where they are contrary, that either of them prevails, according to the *general* character or *present* disposition of the person. What we call strength of mind, implies the prevalence of the calm passions above the violent; tho' we may easily observe, there is no man so constantly possess'd of this virtue, as never on any occasion to yield to the sollicitations of passions and desire. From these variations of temper proceeds the great difficulty of deciding concerning the actions and resolutions of men, where there is any contrariety of motives and passions.

HUME SELECTION

1. Exactly what is Hume's notion of "reason" in this selection? Reason is clearly a power or capacity of the mind. What is it the power or capacity to *do*? Can reason deduce a conclusion from premises, according to Hume? Can reason generalize from observations? Can reason weigh alternative courses of action and choose the most efficient? Can reason evaluate our ends and criticize those that are irrational? For each of these questions, explain why or why not.

2. What does Hume mean by "a volition"? What are pleasure and pain, according to Hume? What role do they play in getting us to act and directing our action?

3. Do pleasure and pain move us, or does the *expectation* of pleasure or pain move us? What exactly is the difference? If it is the expectation of pleasure or pain that moves us, then what role must reason play in the process of choice and action?

4. Precisely when, according to Hume, can a passion be called "unreasonable"? If I can show you that your entire style of life and organization of personality are likely to make you unhappy, have I, on Hume's view, shown you that your desires and passions are "unreasonable"? If the answer is yes, then in what way does Hume's position differ from Plato's?

5. Reason is the slave of the passions, says Hume. If the master cannot take a step without consulting the slave, if the slave can stop the master from choosing an unwise path, if men and women praise the master not for himself or herself but for the power and quickness of the slave, then who is the master and who is the slave?

(SELECTION 3)

JOHN RAWLS

Rational Plans of Life

Sometimes, when we describe a man or woman as "rational," we mean that he or she has, in a particular instance, fitted means to ends effectively, or chosen a suitable particular end. But we may also mean that the person's entire life exhibits an order, coherence, balance, and effectiveness in the deployment of available resources. Plato clearly had this sense in mind when he spoke of reason ruling in the soul. We call such people *wise,* indicating thereby a global, or total, rationality that includes traits of character as well as strengths of intellect. Like Plato, we tend to suppose that true wisdom, as opposed to mere intelligence or skill of one sort or another, will bring lasting happiness. The same conviction finds expression in many religious faiths, both Eastern and Western.

In this selection, John Rawls, a contemporary American moral and political philosopher, spells out at length the notion of a rational plan of life. The tenets of instrumental rationality clearly play an important role in this conception, for there is much talk of fitting available means to one's ends, and weighing the relative costs of competing ends. But Rawls goes beyond mere instrumentalism in a way that comes very much closer to Plato's vision of a personality governed by reason.

Central to Rawls's notion of a rational life plan is the principle that future contingencies are to be weighed adequately in our calculations along with more immediate events. The ability to forego present gratification in order to secure greater future gratification or to avoid future suffering is a mark of the wise individual. Such forbearance requires discipline, self-control, and a measure of respect for what one is and may become, as well as the mere intellectual capacity to calculate present and future costs.

Rawls's philosophy has been greatly influenced by the concepts, modes of reasoning, and models of analysis of modern economic theory. In the present case, his description of a rational life plan is very similar to the description an economist or management expert might give of the rational way to direct the affairs of a firm. As the individual seeks to maximize happiness, so the firm seeks to maximize profit. And just as it is frequently imprudent for a company to plunge its capital into a get-rich-quick scheme with high risks and little future, despite the temptations of a fast killing, so Rawls would say that the individual is ill-advised to grab momentary gratification at the risk of stability or future happiness.

Once we see the analogy between

individual rationality and corporate rationality, some doubts may occur to us. A human being, after all, is not really like a corporation. Human beings are born, develop from infancy through childhood to adulthood, and (as Sartre argued in Chapter 2) in some sense create themselves through their choices. Corporations are legal devices created by men and women for quite narrow economic purposes. It is worth asking whether the canons of rationality that apply to one will apply as appropriately to the other.

To this point I have discussed only the first stages of the definition of good in which no questions are raised about the rationality of the ends taken as given. Something's being good X for K is treated as equivalent to its having the properties which it is rational for K to want in an X in view of his interests and aims. Yet we often assess the rationality of a person's desires, and the definition must be extended to cover this fundamental case if it is to serve the purposes of the theory of justice. Now the basic idea . . . is to apply the definition of good to plans of life. The rational plan for a person determines his good. Here I adapt Royce's thought that a person may be regarded as a human life lived according to a plan. For Royce an individual says who he is by describing his purposes and causes, what he intends to do in his life. If this plan is a rational one, then I shall say that the person's conception of his good is likewise rational. In his case the real and the apparent good coincide. Similarly his interests and aims are rational, and it is appropriate to take them as stopping points in making judgments that correspond to the first two stages of the definition. These suggestions are quite straightforward but unfortunately setting out the details is somewhat tedious. In order to expedite matters I shall start off with a pair of definitions and then explain and comment on them over the next several sections.

These definitions read as follows: first, a person's plan of life is rational if, and only if, (1) it is one of the plans that is consistent with the principles of rational choice when these are applied to all the relevant features of his situation, and (2) it is that plan among those meeting this condition which would be chosen by him with full deliberative rationality, that is, with full awareness of the relevant facts and after a careful consideration of the consequences. . . . Secondly, a person's interests and aims are rational if, and only if, they are to be encouraged and provided for by the plan that is rational for him. Note that in the first of these definitions I have implied that a rational plan is presumably but one of many possible plans that are consistent with the principles of rational choice. The reason for this complication is that these principles do not single out one plan as the best. We have instead a maximal class of plans: each member of this class is superior to all plans not included in it, but given any two plans in the class, neither is superior or inferior to the other. Thus to identify a person's rational plan, I suppose that it is that plan belonging to the maximal class which he would choose with full deliberative rationality. We criticize someone's plan, then, by showing either that it violates the principles of rational choice, or that it is not the plan that he would pursue were he to assess his prospects with care in the light of a full knowledge of his situation. . . .

Now for short term questions anyway, certain principles seem perfectly straightforward and not in dispute. The first of these is that of effective means. Suppose that there is a particular objective that is wanted, and that all the alternatives are means to achieve it, while they are in other respects neutral. The principle holds that we are to adopt that alternative which realizes the end in the best way. More fully: given the objective, one is to achieve it with the least expenditure of means (whatever they are); or given the means, one is to fulfill the objective to the fullest possible extent. This principle is perhaps the most natural criterion of rational choice. . . .

The second principle of rational choice is that one (short-term) plan is to be preferred to another if its execution would achieve all of the desired aims of the other plan and one or more further aims in addition. . . . To illustrate, suppose that we are planning a trip and we have to decide whether to go to Rome or Paris. It seems impossible to visit both. If on reflection it is clear that we can do everything in Paris that we want to do in Rome, and some other things as well, then we should go to Paris. Adopting this plan will realize a larger set of ends and nothing is left undone that might have been realized by the other plan. Often, however, neither plan is more inclusive than the other; each may achieve an aim which the other does not. We must invoke some other principle to make up our minds, or else subject our aims to further analysis.

A third principle we may call that of the greater likelihood. Suppose that the aims which may be achieved by two plans are roughly the same. Then it may happen that some objectives have a greater chance of being realized by one plan than the other, yet at the same time none of the remaining aims are less likely to be attained. For example, although one can perhaps do everything one wants to do in both Rome and Paris, some of the things one wishes to do seem more likely to meet with success in Paris, and for the rest it is roughly the same. If so, the principle holds that one should go to Paris. A greater likelihood of success favors a plan just as the more inclusive end does. When these principles work together the choice is as obvious as can be. Suppose that we prefer a Titian to a Tintoretto, and that the first of two lottery tickets gives the larger chance to Titian while the second assigns it to the Tintoretto. Then one must prefer the first ticket.

So far we have been considering the application of the principles of rational choice to the short-term case. I now wish to examine the other extreme in which one has to adopt a long-term plan, even a plan of life, as when we have to choose a profession or occupation. It may be thought that having to make such a decision is a task imposed only by a particular form of culture. In another society this choice might not arise. But in fact the question of what to do with our life is always there, although some societies force it upon us more obviously than others and at a different time of life. The limit decision to have no plan at all, to let things come as they may, is still theoretically a plan that may or may not be rational. Accepting the idea of a long-term plan, then, it seems clear that such a scheme is to be assessed by what it will probably lead to in each future period of time. The principle of inclusiveness in this case, therefore, runs as follows: one long-term plan is better than another for any given period (or number of periods) if it allows for the encouragement and satisfaction of all the aims and interests of the other plan and for the encouragement and satisfaction of some further aim or interest in addition. The more inclusive plan, if there is one, is to be preferred: it comprehends all the ends of the first plan and at least one other end as well. If this principle is combined with that of effective means, then together they define rationality as preferring, other things equal, the greater means for realizing our aims, and the development of wider and more varied interests assuming that these aspirations can be carried through. The principle of greater likelihood supports this preference even in situations when we cannot be sure that the larger aims can be executed, provided that the chances of execution are as great as with the less comprehensive plan.

The application of the principles of effective means and the greater likelihood to the long-term case seems sound enough. But the use of the principle of inclusiveness may seem problematical. With a fixed system of ends in the short run, we assume that we already have our desires and given this fact we consider how best to satisfy them. But in long-term choice, although we do not yet have the desires which various plans will encourage, we are nevertheless directed to adopt that plan which will develop the more comprehensive interests on the assumption that these further aims can be realized. Now a person may say that since he does not have the more inclusive interests, he is not missing anything in not deciding to encourage and to satisfy them. He may hold that the possible satisfaction of desires that he can arrange never to have is an irrelevant consideration. Of course, he might also contend that the more inclusive system of interests subjects him to a greater risk of dissatisfaction; but this objection is excluded since the principle assumes that the larger pattern of end is equally likely to be attained. . . .

I have already noted that the simpler principles of rational choice . . . do not suffice to order plans. Sometimes they do not apply, since there may be no inclusive plan, say, or else the means are not neutral. Or it often happens that we are left with a maximal class. In these cases further rational criteria may of course be invoked, and some of these I shall discuss below. But I shall suppose that while rational principles can focus our judgments and set up guidelines for reflection, we must finally choose for ourselves in the sense that the choice often rests on our direct self-knowledge not only of what things we want but also of how much we want them. Sometimes there is no way to avoid having to assess the relative intensity of our desires. Rational principles can help us to do this, but they cannot always determine these estimates in a routine fashion. To be sure, there is one formal principle that seems to provide a general answer. This is the principle to adopt that plan which maximizes the expected net balance of satisfaction. Or to express the criterion less hedonistically if more loosely, one is directed to take that course most likely to realize one's most important aims. But this principle also fails to provide us with an explicit procedure for making up our minds. It is clearly left to the agent himself to decide what it is that he most wants and to judge the comparative importance of his several ends.

At this point I introduce the notion of deliberative rationality following an idea of Sidgwick's. He characterizes a person's future good on the whole as what he would now desire and seek if the consequences of all the various courses of conduct open to him were, at the present point of time, accurately foreseen by him and adequately realized in imagination. An individual's good is the hypothetical composition of impulsive forces that results from deliberative reflection meeting certain conditions.[1] Adjusting Sidgwick's notion to the choice of plans, we can say that the rational plan for a person is the one (among those consistent with the counting principles and other principles of rational choice once these are established) which he would choose with deliberative rationality. It is the plan that would be decided upon as the outcome of careful reflection in which the agent reviewed, in the light of all the relevant facts, what it would

[1] See *The Methods of Ethics*, 7th ed. (London, Macmillan, 1907), pp. 111f.

be like to carry out these plans and thereby ascertained the course of action that would best realize his more fundamental desires.

In this definition of deliberative rationality it is assumed that there are no errors of calculation or reasoning, and that the facts are correctly assessed. I suppose also that the agent is under no misconceptions as to what he really wants. In most cases anyway, when he achieves his aim, he does not find that he no longer wants it and wishes that he had done something else instead. Moreover, the agent's knowledge of his situation and the consequences of carrying out each plan is presumed to be accurate and complete. No relevant circumstances are left out of account. Thus the best plan for an individual is the one that he would adopt if he possessed full information. It is the objectively rational plan for him and determines his real good. As things are, of course, our knowledge of what will happen if we follow this or that plan is usually incomplete. Often we do not know what is the rational plan for us; the most that we can have is a reasonable belief as to where our good lies, and sometimes we can only conjecture. But if the agent does the best that a rational person can do with the information available to him, then the plan he follows is a subjectively rational plan. His choice may be an unhappy one, but if so it is because his beliefs are understandably mistaken or his knowledge insufficient, and not because he drew hasty and fallacious inferences or was confused as to what he really wanted. In this case a person is not to be faulted for any discrepancy between his apparent and his real good.

The notion of deliberative rationality is obviously highly complex, combining many elements. I shall not attempt to enumerate here all the ways in which the process of reflection may go wrong. One could if necessary classify the kinds of mistakes that can be made, the sorts of tests that the agent might apply to see if he has adequate knowledge, and so on. It should be noted, however, that a rational person will not usually continue to deliberate until he has found the best plan open to him. Often he will be content if he forms a satisfactory plan (or subplan), that is, one that meets various minimum conditions. Rational deliberation is itself an activity like any other, and the extent to which one should engage in it is subject to rational decision. The formal rule is that we should deliberate up to the point where the likely benefits from improving our plan are just worth the time and effort of reflection. Once we take the costs of deliberation into account, it is unreasonable to worry about finding the best plan, the one that we would choose had we complete information. It is perfectly rational to follow a satisfactory plan when the prospective returns from further calculation and additional knowledge do not outweigh the trouble. There is even nothing irrational in an aversion to deliberation itself provided that one is prepared to accept the consequences. Goodness as rationality does not attribute any special value to the process of deciding. The importance to the agent of careful reflection will presumably vary from one individual to another. Nevertheless, a person is being irrational if his unwillingness to think about what is the best (or a satisfactory) thing to do leads him into misadventures that on consideration he would concede that he should have taken thought to avoid. . . .

. . . One feature of a rational plan is that in carrying it out the individual does not change his mind and wish that he had done something else instead. A rational person does not come to feel an aversion for the foreseen consequences so great that he regrets following the plan he had adopted. The absence of this sort of regret is not however sufficient to insure that a plan is rational. There may be another plan open to us such that were we to consider it we would find it much better. Nevertheless, if our information is accurate and our understanding of the consequences complete in relevant respects, we do not regret following a rational plan, even if it is not a good one judged absolutely. In this instance the plan is objectively rational. We may, of course, regret something else, for example, that we have to live under such unfortunate circumstances that a happy life is impossible. Conceivably we may wish that we had never been born. But we do not regret that, having been born, we followed the best plan as bad as it may be when judged by some ideal standard. A rational person may regret his pursuing a subjectively rational plan, but not because he thinks his choice is in any way open to criticism. For he does what seems best at the time, and if his beliefs later prove to be mistaken with untoward results, it is through no fault of his own. There is no cause for self-reproach. There was no way of knowing which was the best or even a better plan.

Putting these reflections together, we have the guiding principle that a rational individual is always to act so that he need never blame himself no matter how things finally transpire. Viewing himself as one continuing being over time, he can say that at each moment of his life he has done what the balance of reasons required, or at least permitted. Therefore any risks he assumes must be worthwhile, so that should the worst happen that he had any reason to foresee, he can still affirm that what he did was above criticism. He does not regret his choice, at least not in the sense that he later believes that at the time it would have been more rational to have done otherwise. This principle will not certainly prevent us from taking steps that lead to misadventure. Nothing can protect us from the ambiguities and limitations of our knowledge, or guarantee that we find the best alternative open to us. Acting with deliberate rationality can only insure that our conduct is above reproach, and that we are responsible to ourselves as one person over time. We should indeed be surprised if someone said that he did not care about how he will view his present actions later any more than he cares about the affairs of other people (which is not much, let us suppose). One who rejects equally the claims of his future self and the interests of others is not only irresponsible with respect to them but in regard to his own person as well. He does not see himself as one enduring individual.

RAWLS SELECTION

1. Is it reasonable to weigh the future as heavily as the present when we make our plans? Presumably many of us believe the answer is yes, for we buy life insurance, save money, join pension plans, and so on. But *why* is it reasonable? The only thing that *exists* is the present, the here-and-now. The past has ceased to exist; the future does not yet exist. Why should I deny myself some pleasure *now* just in order to make provision for some nonexistent future?

2. Suppose I put money away in a pension plan for my old age and then die before I retire. Does that show that it was irrational of me to join the pension plan? If I buy home insurance and my house never burns down, was I foolish to spend the money on the insurance? Why? Why is it rational to plan for contingencies that may not occur?

3. If I carefully plan out my entire life when I am twenty, mightn't I miss out on a great deal of the joy of life? Is there a proper place for spontaneity in the living of a life? Can I *calculate* when I ought to be spontaneous? Can a life be *too* rational?

4. Rawls places a great deal of emphasis on the compatibility or consistency of a person's life plans. What is wrong with pursuing incompatible goals? Suppose I believe that both goals are worth pursuing— should I choose one and give up the other? Why? Is consistency a matter of taste, like a preference for sports over ballet, or are there good reasons for being consistent?

5. Rawls says that a person who has lived his life rationally need never regret what he has done, even if it has turned out badly. What does he mean by that? Does he mean that the person will not be sorry that things didn't turn out well? Is it possible to live one's life that way? Is it human?

STEPHEN TOULMIN

Reason, Faith, and Limiting Questions

We are all familiar with the way in which a perfectly reasonable question, if pushed too far, turns into nonsense. How high is the Empire State Building? How high is Mt. Everest? How high is the moon? How high is the universe? And, of course, how high is up? The same sort of difficulty develops when we ask for *reasons.* The ability to give reasons for our actions is one very important mark of rationality. If I cannot explain *why* I am doing something, you will quite likely think that I am not being at all sensible or reasonable in doing it. Indeed, as we saw in Chapters 1 and 2, the ability to give reasons, and to guide one's actions by reasons, is part of what it is to be a person and to be free.

But there does seem to be a point beyond which it is impossible to give reasons and absurd to demand them. As Stephen Toulmin points out in this selection, a question like "Why ought one to do what is right?" seems to have about it some of the same oddness as "How high is up?" Even though I can (or ought to be able to) give reasons for particular actions, including such reasons as "because it is right," it does seem odd to ask why I ought to do what is right. The natural temptation is simply to repeat, "because it *is* right!" for there hardly seems more one can say.

Toulmin concentrates, in this selection, on the way in which limiting questions demarcate the line between ethics and religion, between reason and faith. When questions that usually ask for *reasons* are pushed far enough, they sometimes turn into demands for a confession of faith. Such demands are legitimate, and may indeed serve both to elicit from someone her deepest convictions and also to force her, for the first time, to articulate them. But as demands for confessions of faith, they have a different linguistic purpose from that of demands for reasons, and hence are governed by a different set of logical rules. What would count as a good answer to a request for reasons might be a very bad, or unsuitable, response to a demand for a confession of faith.

Toulmin's discussion illustrates an important point of philosophical methodology that we can see in many of the readings in this book. Frequently, our language misleads us into thinking that a question or statement makes sense, when in fact a closer analysis reveals that it does not make sense at all. "How high is up?" is a simple example. Some trickier and more controversial examples might be "Every knowledge-claim can be justified by argument or evidence if it is a legitimate claim," and "It is always reasonable to ask for the reasons for an action, and a person who cannot give reasons is to that extent irrational."

The question that Toulmin leaves unanswered in this selection is in some sense the central question of all investigations of ethical reasoning: If there is a limit beyond which it makes no sense to ask "Why?" then is there simply no way to adjudicate rationally between two opposed and incompatible confessions of faith?

In all the modes of reasoning analysed so far, we found that the "reasons" which could logically be given in support of any statement formed a finite chain. In every case, a point was reached beyond which it was no longer possible to give "reasons" of the kind given until then; and eventually there came a stage beyond which it seemed that no "reason" of any kind could be given. As a reminder of what I mean: the question, "Why ought I not to have two wives?" calls to begin with for reasons referring to the existing institutions; secondly, may raise the more general question whether our institution of "marriage" could be improved by altering it in the direction of polygamy; thirdly, transforms itself into a question about the kind of community in which one would personally prefer to live; and beyond that cannot be reasoned about at all. Now we have been interested throughout in *literal* answers only: so, when faced with requests for reasons of any kind beyond the point at which these ceased to be appropriate we dismissed them as illogical. . . .

Nevertheless, one often wants to go on asking such questions, even when there is no literal, rational sense in them. The fact that one does so may be a sign of confusion—a sign that one has just not got the hang of questions of the type concerned—or it may not. . . .

It is questions of this kind with which I am concerned in the present chapter—questions expressed in a form borrowed from a familiar mode of reasoning, but not doing the job which they normally do within that mode of reasoning. It is characteristic of them that only a small change is required, either in the form of the question, or in the context in which it is asked, in order to bring it unquestionably back into the scope of its apparent mode of reasoning. But it is equally characteristic of them that the way of answering suggested by the form of words employed will never completely satisfy the questioner, so that he continues to ask the question even after the resources of the apparent mode of reasoning have been exhausted. Questions of this kind I shall refer to as "limiting questions": they are of particular interest when one is examining the limits and boundaries of any mode of reasoning—and of ethical reasoning in particular.

From *The Place of Reason in Ethics* by Stephen Toulmin. (Cambridge University Press, 1950.)

I want to point out three peculiarities of questions of this type, which make the ways of answering them quite different from the ways of answering more literal questions. These peculiarities I shall then illustrate in two instances:

(i) Our usage provides no standard interpretation of such questions. Their form suggests a meaning of a familiar kind, but the situations in which they are asked are such that they cannot have that meaning. The form of words may therefore express any of a varied selection of personal predicaments, and we can only find out as we go along what is "behind" the question.

(ii) If the question were to be interpreted literally—that is, by reference to its apparent logical form—we should expect there to be genuinely alternative answers, each applicable over a limited range of cases. Within the apparent mode of reasoning, all questions require a definite choice to be made—e.g., between two theories or social practices, between one moral decision and another, or between one scientific prediction and another. A "limiting question," however, does not present us with genuine alternatives to choose between: it is expressed in such a way that the only reply within the apparent mode of reasoning is (for instance), "Well, isn't the 'right' just what one 'ought' to do?"

(iii) Finally, a "limiting question" is not flagrantly "extra-rational" in its form. It is not like the questions in Blake's *Tyger*, which no one would ever dream of trying to answer literally:

> What the hammer? What the chain?
> In what furnace was thy brain?
> What the anvil? What dread grasp
> Dare its deadly terrors clasp?

There is therefore always the urge to give it the kind of answer which its form appears to demand. However, either to answer or to refuse to answer in this way will leave the questioner equally dissatisfied. If you refuse, his desire for such an answer remains unstilled: if you answer, there is nothing to stop the question from arising again about your reply.

Consider a familiar instance. One learns to ask the questions, "How is it supported?" and "What does it rest on?" in all kinds of everyday situations; for instance, when talking to a gardener about his peach-tree, or to an engineer about some piece of machinery. In these familiar situations, there is always the possibility that the object referred to might collapse if there were nothing to support it, nothing for it to rest on: or, at any rate, in all these instances we can understand what it would mean to say that it had "collapsed." But, if you start with a familiar object and ask, "What does it rest on?"

and continue to ask of each new object mentioned, "And what does that rest on?" you will eventually reach the answer, "The solid earth," and after that you cannot ask the question any more—in that sense anyway.

In the everyday sense, the question, "What holds the earth up?" [1] is a "limiting question," having all the peculiarities I have referred to:

(i) If someone does ask it, it is not at all clear what he wants to know, in the way it is if he asks, "What holds your peach-tree up?" In ordinary cases, the form of the question and the nature of the situation between them determine the meaning of the question: here they cannot do so, and one can only guess at what is prompting it.

(ii) The different answers to the question, "What holds your peach-tree up?" are intelligible enough, and one can imagine a peach-tree's "falling down": but neither of these things is the case when someone asks, "What holds the earth up?"

(iii) Still, there is a strong desire to take the question literally, in a way in which one would never take Blake's questions literally. But, if we do, it will get us nowhere. If we answer "An elephant," the questioner can ask, "And what holds the elephant up?"; if we now answer "A tortoise," the question arises again; and there is no way of stopping its recurrence this side of infinity.

We might of course answer, "Nothing," and, when the questioner protested, "Nothing? But it must be held up by something," we might explain to him his error, pointing out that he was misunderstanding the nature of questions of the form, "What holds it up?" and failing to see that this form of question cannot be asked of "the earth" at all. If the question had arisen from such a misunderstanding, the questioner would be satisfied by this; and, to the extent that it did satisfy him, we could conclude that the enquiry had arisen in this way, that the motive prompting the question had been the perplexity of misunderstanding. But he might not be so easily satisfied. The question might be a "cover" for some other feeling; say, for an hysterical apprehensiveness about the future. This could not be settled by any literal answer to his question, or by any rational analysis of the question itself: in fact, the only type of reasoning likely to make any impression on him would be psychoanalytic reasoning.

As a second instance, the question, "Why ought one to do what is right?" shares these same peculiarities:

[1] I recall Wittgenstein's likening the problem of induction to this question; and saying that those philosophers who asked for a "justification" of science were like the Ancients, who felt there must be an Atlas to support the Earth on his shoulders (Cambridge University Moral Science Club: 14 November 1946).

(i) The form of the question and the situation in which it is asked do not determine the meaning of the question, in the way in which they determine the meaning of a question like, "Why ought I to give this book back to Jones?"

(ii) There are no "alternative answers," in the way in which there are to a typically ethical question.

(iii) Still, the question does seem to call for an ethical answer—even though whatever you say can be queried in its turn, and so *ad infinitum*.

Once again we might explain to the questioner how the notions of "right" and "obligation" arise, pointing out that their origins are such as to make the sentence, "One ought to do what it right," a truism. And again this might satisfy him, showing that it had been the perplexity born of misunderstanding which had prompted his question. But again our answer might leave him unmoved: and, when this happened, we should have to conclude that the motive behind this question was only being obliquely expressed.

Since, when one is faced with a "limiting question," there is this additional uncertainty about the way in which it is to be interpreted—since the possible concealed motives for asking a "limiting question" are many and varied—one cannot help being at a loss to begin with. The fact that such questions have no fixed, literal meaning means that there is no fixed, literal way of answering them, and one just has to wait and see what it is the questioner wants. If, for example, someone asks, "Why ought one to do what is right?" the answers which can be given are of two kinds. Either they must be tailor-made to fit the questioner—in which case they have no universal application—or they must abandon all pretence of literalness, and take on the elusive, allusive quality of poetry. In the first case, they can at the best take account of the questioner's professional preoccupations, drawing attention (for instance) to analogies between ethical and biological concepts, if he is a biologist, to analogies between ethical and psychological concepts, if he is a psychologist, and so on. In the second, they are to be judged less like the questions in the mode of reasoning whose form they have borrowed, than like Blake's poems—by their impact, that is, and not by excessively intellectual standards. . . .

Some philosophers argue that all utterances which cannot be taken literally ought to be done away with; as though everything which is "nonsense" to them were also, necessarily, dangerous nonsense. And no doubt, where "limiting questions" arise solely out of logical confusions, there are some grounds for wishing them out of existence. In other cases, however, they are not to be argued away.

That one should learn to tell such limiting questions from questions in the mode of reasoning whose form they borrow, may well be desirable. But that we should be exhorted to stop asking them altogether, is ridiculous. The feeling of urgency behind so many of them, the insistence with which they recur, itself suggests that no good is done by bottling them up; and provided that one recognises them for what they are, what can there be against our asking them? . . .

Not only shall we continue to ask these questions, but we shall genuinely want answers to them. And, of the answers which are given to us, we shall regard some as being better than others. And some of them, no doubt, will really be better than others. Some, that is to say, will give us a reassurance which will not be disappointed; will allay our fear of "the eternity before and behind the brief span"[2] of our lives, and of "the infinite immensity" of space; will provide comfort in the face of distress; and will answer our questions in a way which will not seem in retrospect to have missed their point.

Now, provided that the answers given are good answers, by this sort of standard, what logical justification can there be for dismissing them? Of course "theological" arguments, and "religious" questions and answers—those with which we are concerned here—are on quite a different footing, as a matter of logic, from scientific and ethical arguments, questions and answers. But it is only if we suppose that religious arguments pretend (say) to provide exact knowledge of the future—so competing with science on its own ground—that we can be justified in attempting to apply to them the logical criteria appropriate to scientific explanations; and only if we do this that we have any grounds for concluding (with Ayer) that "all utterances about the nature of God are nonsensical,"[3] or (with Freud) that religion is "an illusion."[4] Provided that we remember that religion has functions other than that of competing with science and ethics on their own grounds, we shall understand that to reject all religious arguments for this reason is to make a serious logical blunder—an error as great as that of taking figurative phrases literally, or of supposing that the mathematical theory of numbers (say) has any deep, religious significance. . . .

What is the nature of this distinction between "faith" and "reason"? To begin with, it is essential to rule out of account those things which are often called "matters of faith" or "articles of faith,"

[2] Pascal, *loc. cit.*
[3] Ayer, *Language, Truth and Logic* (2nd ed.), p. 115.
[4] Freud, *The Future of an Illusion, passim.*

by transference: things which are really only matters of fact about which the evidence is inconclusive, but over which one holds a dogmatic opinion out of pride. Examples of this kind—such as, "It was for him an article of faith that any one Englishman was a match for any ten Frenchmen"—only confuse the issue. Again, not all "limiting questions" are "religious," and not all "religious" questions are "limiting": it is only over those on the boundaries between religion, science and ethics that real difficulties arise, and it is on these that I shall concentrate.

If one is discussing genuine "matters of faith" (like the sacredness, for the Cambodians, of white elephants), then there is no question of advancing "reasons" for individual assertions, of weighing the evidence for different hypotheses, and so on. To talk of bringing evidence of this kind for "matters of faith" does not make sense. Over matters of faith, one does not "believe" or "disbelieve" individual propositions: one "accepts" or "rejects" complete notions. Indeed, we might describe the distinction between "faith" and "reason" in these terms—belief as a matter of reason is *belief of* a proposition of some kind: belief as a matter of faith is *belief in* a notion of some kind.

Furthermore, since those questions of religion which make use of everyday, scientific or ethical notions are "limiting questions," this use can only be *figurative* (or, to use Pascal's alternative term, "spiritual"). The question of God's existence is often discussed by philosophers in a way which would only be appropriate, if it were the literal counterpart of the question, "Are there any one-eyed cats?"; and, no doubt, anyone who does this will be forced to conclude that the Argument from Design, as given (say) in Paley's *Natural Theology,* is unconvincing. But this is to misapprehend its function: to overlook the radical differences between the kinds of answer the two questions require. The inference from "appearances of design in nature" to the existence of an "omnipotent, omniscient and omnipresent Deity" is not an argument for the existence of an especially powerful and knowing animal, liable to turn up anywhere at any moment. It consists (and we can quote Paley's own subtitle to illustrate this) in accumulating "evidences of the existence and attributes of the Diety from the appearances of Nature." The existence of God, one might argue (though here I doubt whether Paley would follow us), is not something to demand *evidence for;* nor is the sentence, "God exists," one to be believed if, and only if, the evidence for its truth is good enough. The very last question to ask about God is *whether* He exists. Rather, we must first accept the notion of "God": and then we shall be in a position to point to *evidences of* His existence. . . .

These remarks about faith and reason have been very general, and we must not leave the subject without returning to our proper field. Let us therefore examine the boundary between religion and ethics—so as to see how, in this sphere, reason marches upon faith.

We encountered "limiting questions" in three kinds of ethical situation:

(i) When it has been pointed out that an action conforms unambiguously to a recognised social practice, there is no more room for the justification of the action through ethical reasoning: if someone asks, "Why ought I to give this book back to Jones to-day?" and is given the answer, "Because you promised to," there is no room within the ethical mode of reasoning for him to ask, "But why ought I to *really?*"—this question is a "limiting question."

(ii) When there is nothing to choose on moral grounds between two courses of action, the only reasoned answer which can be given to the question, "Which ought I to do?" is one taking account of the agent's own preferences—"If you do *A*, then so-and-so, if you do *B*, then such-and-such: and it's up to you to decide which you prefer" —and if someone now insists on a unique answer, independent of his preferences, his question is again "limiting."

(iii) When someone asks, perfectly generally, "Why ought one do what is right?" and is not satisfied with the answer that the sentence, "You ought to do what is right," expresses a truism, his question is also a "limiting" one.

In each of these cases, the logical pattern is similar. In each, ethical reasoning first does for the questioner all that can be asked of it, exhausting the literal answers to his question, and making it clear how far there is any literal sense in his asking what he "ought" to do. In each case, when this is finished, it is clear that something remains to be done: that moral reasoning, while showing what ought (literally) to be done, has failed to satisfy the questioner. Although he may come to recognise intellectually what he "ought" to do, he does not feel like doing it—his heart is not in it.

This conflict is manifested in his use of "limiting questions." As long as these are taken literally, they seem nonsensical: whether he says, "I know I promised to, but ought I to, *really?*" or "Yes, yes; but which ought I *really* to do, *A* or *B?*" or "But why ought one to do *anything* that is right?" he is ostensibly querying something which it makes no sense to question—literally.

In each case, however, his question comes alive again as soon as one takes it "spiritually," as a religious question. Over those matters of fact which are not to be "explained" scientifically, like the deaths in the Jones family, the function of religion is to help us resign ourselves to them—and so feel like accepting them. Likewise, over matters of duty which are not to be justified further in ethical terms, it is for religion to help us embrace them—and so feel like accepting them. In all the three situations referred to, therefore, religious answers may still be appropriate, even when the resources of ethical reasoning are exhausted:

   (i) "Why ought I to give back this book?"
      "Because you promised."
      "But why ought I to, *really?*"
      "Because it would be sinful not to."
      "And what if I were to commit such a sin?"
      "That would be to cut yourself off from God," etc.
  (ii) "Which ought I to do, *A* or *B?*"
      "There's nothing to choose between them, morally speaking; it's up to you, but if I were you I should do *B.*"
      "But which ought I *really* to do?"
      "You ought to do *B:* that is the course more pleasing to God, and will bring you the truest happiness in the end."
 (iii) "Why ought one to do what is right, anyway?"
      "That is a question which cannot arise, for it is to query the very definition of 'right' and 'ought.' "
      "But why *ought* one to?"
      "Because it is God's will."
      "And why should one do His will?"
      "Because it is in the nature of a created being to do the will of its Creator," etc.

TOULMIN SELECTION

1.   When we give reasons for doing something, how do we decide what is a *good* reason and what isn't a good reason? Is liking chocolate a good reason for eating chocolate? Is hating chocolate a good reason for *eating* chocolate? Why? Is wanting to avoid cavities a good reason for giving up sweets?

2.   If Jones tells me that he doesn't want to get cavities, I take that as a good reason for his giving up sweets. Suppose he tells me that he *wants* cavities! Is that a good reason for his eating sweets? Is there anything irrational about wanting cavities? Why?

3.   I can talk a man out of playing chicken in his car by pointing out that he is likely to get killed. But suppose he says he doesn't care whether he lives or dies. Is there any good reason I can give him for wanting to live? Can we ever give someone a reason for wanting something?

4.   If *reasons* will not sway a person who has lost all desire to live, what will? If I warn a suicidal person that God will punish her for the sin of suicide, I am only pushing prudential considerations into the next world.

If she says that she doesn't care whether she goes to hell or not, is there *anything* else one can say? Why?

5.   Are there limiting questions in logical and scientific explanation, as well as in moral argument? Is it appropriate to settle limiting questions in logic by an appeal to religion? How would one go about doing that?

(SELECTION 5)

RICHARD HARE

A Moral Argument

With this selection by the prominent English ethical theorist R. M. Hare, we make a subtle but significant move from a discussion of "reason" to a discussion of "reasons." This move was already foreshadowed in the preceding discussion of limiting questions, by Toulmin, but with Hare our focus is squarely on the role of *reasons* in choice and evaluation rather than on the role of Reason. The distinction is not a mere matter of terminology at all. Philosophers (like Plato and Hume) who have talked of the role of Reason have tended to concentrate on questions of virtue, inner psychic order, the healthy condition of the soul, and the relation between wisdom and happiness. Philosophers like R. M. Hare who speak of *reasons,* on the other hand, have by and large been interested in logical questions of moral reasoning. They have sought principles of correct moral argument, and sometimes even formal logical principles of inference that can be applied to contexts in which moral judgments are being defended or criticized. Although both approaches remain very much alive in contemporary Anglo-American philosophy (as the work of John Rawls makes clear), recent philosophical interest has been focused much more heavily on the analysis of

reasons and moral reasoning than on the role of Reason in a well-ordered and happy personality.

The key to an understanding of this passage in particular, and Hare's philosophy in general, is the notion of "universalizability." When we give reasons, either to explain why something happened or to justify acting in a particular way, we very often give specific reasons that seem to apply only to the case at hand. Why won't the engine start? Because it is flooded. Why should I share my candy with her? Because she shared hers with you yesterday. And so forth.

But though the reasons we give may be particular, Hare claims, implicit in our giving of them is appeal to, or at least acknowledgment of the validity of, some general (or "universal") principle of which this reason is only an instance. Engines in general won't start when there is too much gas in the carburetor. Persons in general incur a debt or obligation of reciprocity when they accept the generosity of others.

Now, you might want to reply that you meant your reason to apply only to this particular case; you had no intention at all of committing yourself to some general proposition. But to this, Hare (and many other philosophers)

214

would reply: Can your supposed reason really *be* a reason if it applies only to this one special case? If engines don't in general stall when flooded, then how have you explained your engine's stalling by pointing out that it is flooded? If you don't in general have a duty to reciprocate generosity, then how can the fact that your friend gave you half of her candy yesterday be a *reason* for saying that you ought to give her half of yours today? The philosopher who first made the notion of universalizability a prominent part of ethical theory was Immanuel Kant. Kant held that universalizability was a quite general mark of rationality of every sort, so that the willingness to acknowledge the universal force of one's rules of conduct, he thought, was a test of the extent to which reason ruled in one's soul.

I will now try to exhibit the bare bones of the theory of moral reasoning that I wish to advocate by considering a very simple (indeed over-simplified) example. As we shall see, even this very simple case generates the most baffling complexities; and so we may be pardoned for not attempting anything more difficult to start with.

The example is adapted from a well-known parable.[1] *A* owes money to *B,* and *B* owes money to *C,* and it is the law that creditors may exact their debts by putting their debtors into prison. *B* asks himself, "Can I say that I ought to take this measure against *A* in order to make him pay?" He is no doubt *inclined* to do this, or *wants* to do it. Therefore, if there were no question of universalizing his prescriptions, he would assent readily to the *singular* prescription "Let me put *A* into prison." But when he seeks to turn this prescription into a moral judgement, and say, "I *ought* to put *A* into prison because he will not pay me what he owes," he reflects that this would involve accepting the principle "Anyone who is in my position ought to put his debtor into prison if he does not pay." But then he reflects that *C* is in the same position of unpaid creditor with regard to himself (*B*), and that the cases are otherwise identical; and that if anyone in this position ought to put his debtors into prison, then so ought *C* to put him (*B*) into prison. And to accept the moral prescription "*C* ought to put me into prison" would commit him (since, as we have seen, he must be using the word "ought" prescriptively) to accepting the singular prescription "Let *C* put me into prison"; and this he is not ready to accept. But if he is not, then neither can he accept the original judgement that he (*B*) ought to put *A* into prison for debt. Notice that the whole of this argument would break down if "ought" were not being used both universalizably *and prescriptively;* for if it were not being used prescriptively, the step from "*C*

[1] Matthew xviii. 23.

ought to put me into prison" to "Let C put me into prison" would not be valid. . . .

No argument . . . starts from nothing. We must therefore ask what we have to have before moral arguments of the sort of which I have given a simple example can proceed. The first requisite is that the facts of the case should be given; for all moral discussion is about some particular set of facts, whether actual or supposed. Secondly we have the logical framework provided by the meaning of the word "ought" (i.e., prescriptivity and universalizabilty, both of which we saw to be necessary). Because moral judgements have to be universalizable, B cannot say that he ought to put A into prison for debt without committing himself to the view that C, who is *ex hypothesi* in the same position *vis-à-vis* himself, ought to put *him* into prison; and because moral judgements are prescriptive, this would be, in effect, prescribing to C to put him into prison; and this he is unwilling to do, since he has a strong inclination not to go to prison. This inclination gives us the third necessary ingredient in the argument: if B were a completely apathetic person, who literally did not mind what happened to himself or to anybody else, the argument would not touch him. The three necessary ingredients which we have noticed, then, are (1) facts; (2) logic; (3) inclinations. These ingredients enable us, not indeed to arrive at an evaluative conclusion, but to *reject* an evaluative proposition. . . .

In the example which we have been using, the position was deliberately made simpler by supposing that B actually stood to some other person in exactly the same relation as A does to him. Such cases are unlikely to arise in practice. But it is not necessary for the force of the argument that B should *in fact* stand in this relation to anyone; it is sufficient that he should consider hypothetically such a case, and see what would be the consequences in it of those moral principles between whose acceptance and rejection he has to decide. Here we have an important point of difference from the parallel scientific argument, in that the crucial case which leads to rejection of the principle can itself be a supposed, not an observed one. That hypothetical cases will do as well as actual ones is important, since it enables us to guard against a possible misinterpretation of the argument which I have outlined. It might be thought that what moves B is the *fear* that C will actually do to him as he does to A—as happens in the gospel parable. But this fear is not only irrelevant to the moral argument; it does not even provide a particularly strong non-moral motive unless the circumstances are somewhat exceptional. C may, after all, not find out what B has done to A; or C's moral principles may be different from B's, and independent of them, so that what moral principle B accepts makes no difference to the moral principles on which C acts.

Even, therefore, if C did not exist, it would be no answer to the argument for B to say "But in my case there is no fear that anybody will ever be in a position to do to me what I am proposing to do to A." For the argument does not rest on any such fear. All that is essential to it is that B should disregard the fact that he plays the particular role in the situation which he does, without disregarding the inclinations which people have in situations of this sort. In other words, he must be prepared to give weight to A's inclinations and interests as if they were his own. This is what turns selfish prudential reasoning into moral reasoning. It is much easier, pychologically, for B to do this if he is actually placed in a situation like A's *vis-à-vis* somebody else; but this is not necessary, provided that he has sufficient imagination to envisage what it is like to be A. For our first example, a case was deliberately chosen in which little imagination was necessary; but in most normal cases a certain power of imagination and readiness to use it is a fourth necessary ingredient in moral arguments, alongside those already mentioned, viz. logic (in the shape of universalizability and prescriptivity), the facts, and the inclinations or interests of the people concerned. . . .

The best way of testing the argument which we have outlined will be to consider various ways in which somebody in B's position might seek to escape from it. There are indeed a number of such ways; and all of them may be successful, at a price. It is important to understand what the price is in each case. We may classify these manœuvres which are open to B into two kinds. There are first of all the moves which depend on his using the moral words in a different way from that on which the argument relied. We saw that for the success of the argument it was necessary that "ought" should be used universalizably and prescriptively. If B uses it in a way that is either not prescriptive or not universalizable, then he can escape the force of the argument, at the cost of resigning from the kind of discussion that we thought we were having with him. We shall discuss these two possibilities separately. Secondly, there are moves which can still be made by B, even though he is using the moral words in the same way as we are. We shall examine three different sub-classes of these. . . .

Let us take first the man who is using the word "ought" prescriptively, but not universalizably. He can say that he ought to put his debtor into prison, although he is not prepared to agree that his creditor ought to put *him* into prison. We, on the other hand, since we are not prepared to admit that our creditors in these circumstances ought to put us into prison, cannot say that we ought to put our debtors into prison. So there is an appearance of substantial moral disagreement, which is intensified by the fact that, since we are both using the word "ought" prescriptively, our respective views will lead to different particular actions. Different *singular* prescriptions about what to do are (since both our judgements are prescriptive) derivable from what we are respectively saying. But this is not enough to constitute a moral disagreement. For there to be a moral disagreement, or even an evaluative one of any kind, we must differ, not only about what *is* to be done in some particular case, but about some universal principle concerning what *ought* to be done in cases of a certain sort; and since B is (on the hypothesis considered) advocating no such universal principle, he is saying nothing with which we can be in moral or evaluative disagreement. Considered purely as prescriptions, indeed, our two views are in substantial disagreement; but the moral, evaluative (i.e., the *universal* prescriptive) disagreement is only verbal, because, when the expression of B's view is understood as he means it, the view turns out not to be a view about the morality of the action at all. So B, by this manœuvre, can go on prescribing to himself to put A into prison, but has to abandon the claim that he is justifying the action morally, as we understand the word "morally." One may, of course, use any word as one pleases, at a price. But he can no longer claim to be giving that sort of justification of his action for which, as I think, the common expression is "moral justification." . . .

So much for the ways . . . in which B can escape from our argument by using the word "ought" in a different way from us. The remaining ways of escape are open to him even if he is using "ought" in the same way as we are, viz. to express a universalizable prescription.

We must first consider that class of escape-routes whose distinguishing feature is that B, while using the moral words in the same way as we are, refuses to make positive moral judgements at all in certain cases. There are two main variations of this manœuvre. B may either say that it is indifferent, morally, whether he imprisons A or not; or he may refuse to make any moral judgement at all, even one of indifference, about the case. It will be obvious that if he adopts either of these moves, he can evade the argument as so far set out. For that argument only forced him to *reject* the moral judgement "I ought to imprison A for debt." It did not force him to assent to any moral judgement; in particular, he remained free to assent, either to the judgement that he ought not to imprison A for debt (which is the one that we want him to accept) or to the judgement that it is neither the case that he ought, nor the case that he ought not (that it is, in short, indifferent); and he remained free, also, to say "I am just not making any moral judgements at all about this case."

We have not yet, however, exhausted the arguments generated by the demand for universalizability, provided that the moral words are being used in a way which allows this demand. For it is evident that these manœuvres could, in principle, be practised in any case whatever in which the morality of an act is in question. And this enables us to place *B* in a dilemma. Either he practises this manœuvre in *every* situation in which he is faced with a moral decision; or else he practises it only *sometimes*. The first alternative, however, has to be sub-divided; for "every situation" might mean "every situation in which he himself has to face a moral decision regarding one of his own actions," or it might mean "every situation in which a moral question arises for him, whether about his own actions or about some-body else's." So there are three courses that he can adopt: (1) He either refrains altogether from making moral judgements, or makes none except judgements of indifference (that is to say, he either observes a complete moral silence, or says "Nothing matters morally"; either of these two positions might be called a sort of amoralism); (2) He makes moral judgements in the normal way about other people's ac-tions, but adopts one or other of the kinds of amoralism, just men-tioned, with regard to his own; (3) He expresses moral indifference, or will make no moral judgement at all, with regard to *some* of his own actions and those of other people, but makes moral judgements in the normal way about others.

Now it will be obvious that in the first case there is nothing that we can do, and that this should not disturb us. Just as one cannot win a game of chess against an opponent who will not make any moves—and just as one cannot argue mathematically with a person who will not commit himself to any mathematical statements—so moral argument is impossible with a man who will make no moral judgements at all, or—which for practical purposes comes to the same thing—makes only judgements of indifference. Such a person is not entering the arena of moral dispute, and therefore it is impossible to contest with him. He is compelled also—and this is important— to abjure the protection of morality for his own interests.

In the other two cases, however, we have an argument left. If a man is prepared to make positive moral judgements about other people's actions, but not about his own, or if he is prepared to make them about some of his own decisions, but not about others, then we can ask him on what principle he makes the distinction between these various cases. This is a particular application of the demand for uni-versalizability. He will still have left to him the ways of escape from this demand which are available in all its applications, and which we shall consider later. But there is no way of escape which is available in this application, but not in others. He must either produce (or at least admit the existence of) some principle which makes him hold different moral opinions about apparently similar cases, or else admit that the judgements he is making are not moral ones. But in the latter case, he is in the same position, in the present dispute, as the man who will not make any moral judgements at all; he has resigned from the contest.

In the particular example which we have been considering, we supposed that the cases of B and of C, his own creditor, were identical. The demand for universalization therefore compels B to make the same moral judgement, whatever it is, about both cases. He has therefore, unless he is going to give up the claim to be arguing morally, either to say that neither he nor C ought to exercise their legal rights to imprison their debtors; or that both ought (a possibility to which we shall recur in the next section); or that it is indifferent whether they do. But the last alternative leaves it open to B and C to do what they like in the matter; and we may suppose that, though B himself would like to have this freedom, he will be unwilling to allow it to C. It is as unlikely that he will *permit* C to put him (B) into prison as that he will *prescribe* it. We may say, therefore, that while move (1), described above, constitutes an abandonment of the dispute, moves (2) and (3) really add nothing new to it.

We must next consider a way of escape which may seem much more respectable that those which I have so far mentioned. Let us suppose that B is a firm believer in the rights of property and the sanctity of contracts. In this case he may say roundly that debtors ought to be imprisoned by their creditors whoever they are, and that, specifically, C ought to imprison him (B), and he (B) ought to imprison A. And he may, unlike the superficially similar person described earlier, be meaning by "ought" just what we usually mean by it—i.e., he may be using the word prescriptively, realizing that in saying that C ought to put him into prison, he is prescribing that C put him in prison. B, in this case, is perfectly ready to go to prison for his principles, in order that the sanctity of contracts may be enforced. In real life, B would be much more likely to take this line if the situation in which he himself played the role of debtor were not actual but only hypothetical; but this, as we saw earlier, ought not to make any difference to the argument.

We are not yet, however, in a position to deal with this escape-route. All we can do is to say why we cannot now deal with it, and leave this loose end to be picked up later. B, if he is sincere in holding the principle about the sanctity of contracts (or any other universal moral principle which has the same effect in this particular case), may have two sorts of grounds for it. He may hold it on utilitarian grounds, thinking that, unless contracts are rigorously enforced, the results will be so disastrous as to outweigh any benefits that *A,* or *B* himself, may get from being let off. This could, in certain circumstances, be a good argument. But we cannot tell whether it is, until we have generalized the type of moral argument which has been set out in this chapter, to cover cases in which the interests of more than two parties are involved. As we saw, it is only the interests of *A* and *B* that come into the argument as so far considered (the interests of the third party, *C,* do not need separate consideration, since *C* was introduced only in order to show *B,* if necessary fictionally, a situation in which the roles were reversed; therefore *C*'s interests, being a mere replica of *B*'s, will vanish, as a separate factor, once the *A/B* situation, and the moral judgements made on it, are universalized). But if utilitarian grounds of the sort suggested are to be adduced, they will bring with them a reference to all the other people whose interests would be harmed by laxity in the enforcement of contracts. This escape-route, therefore, if this is its basis, introduces considerations which cannot be assessed until we have generalized our form of argument to cover "multilateral" moral situations. At present, it can only be said that if *B* can show that leniency in the enforcement of contracts would really have the results he claims for the community at large, he might be justified in taking the severer course. This will be apparent after we have considered in some detail an example (that of the judge and the criminal) which brings out these considerations even more clearly.

On the other hand, *B* might have a quite different, non-utilitarian kind of reason for adhering to his principle. He might be moved, not by any weight which he might attach to the interests of other people, but by the thought that to enforce contracts of this sort is necessary in order to conform to some moral or other *ideal* that he has espoused. Such ideals might be of various sorts. He might be moved, for example, by an ideal of abstract justice, of the *fiat justitia, ruat caelum* variety. We have to distinguish such an ideal of justice, which pays no regard to people's interests, from that which is concerned merely to do justice *between* people's interests. It is very important, if considerations of justice are introduced into a moral argument, to know of which sort they are. Justice of the second kind can perhaps be accommodated within a moral view which it is not misleading to call utilitarian. But this is not true of an ideal of the first kind. It is characteristic of this sort of non-utilitarian ideals that, when they are introduced into moral arguments, they render ineffective the appeal to universalized self-interest which is the foundation of the argument that we have been considering. This is because the person who has whole-heartedly espoused such an idea (we shall call him the "fanatic") does not mind if people's interests—even his own—are harmed in the pursuit of it.

It need not be justice which provides the basis of such an escape-route as we are considering. Any moral ideal would do, provided that it were pursued regardless of other people's interests. For example, *B* might be a believer in the survival of the fittest, and think that, in order to promote this, he (and everyone else) ought to pursue their own interests by all means in their power and regardless of everyone else's interests. This ideal might lead him, in this particular case, to put *A* in prison, and he might agree that *C* ought to do the same to him, if he were not clever enough to avoid this fate. He might think that universal obedience to such a principle would maximize the production of supermen and so make the world a better place. If these were his grounds, it is possible that we might argue with him factually, showing that the universal observance of the principle would not have the results he claimed. But we might be defeated in this factual argument if he had an ideal which made him call the world "a better place" when the jungle law prevailed; he could then agree to our factual statements, but still maintain that the condition of the world described by us as resulting from the observance of his principle would be better than its present condition. In this case, the argument might take two courses. If we could get him to imagine himself in the position of the weak, who went to the wall in such a state of the world, we might bring him to realize that to hold his principle involved prescribing that things should be done to him, in hypothetical situations, which he could not sincerely prescribe. If so, then the argument would be on the rails again, and could proceed on lines which we have already sketched. But he might stick to his principle and say "If I were weak, then I ought to go to the wall." If he did this, he would be putting himself beyond the reach of what we shall call "golden-rule" or "utilitarian" arguments by becoming what we shall call a "fanatic." Since a great part of the rest of this book will be concerned with people who take this sort of line, it is unnecessary to pursue their case further at this point.

The remaining manœuvre that *B* might seek to practise is probably the commonest. It is certainly the one which is most frequently brought up in philosophical controversies on this topic. This consists in a fresh appeal to the facts—i.e., in asserting that there are in fact morally relevant differences between his case and that of others. In the example which we have been considering, we have artificially ruled out this way of escape by assuming that the case of *B* and *C* is exactly similar to that of *A* and *B*; from this it follows *a fortiori* that there are no morally relevant differences. Since the

B/C case may be a hypothetical one, this condition of exact similarity can always be fulfilled, and therefore this manœuvre is based on a misconception of the type of argument against which it is directed. Nevertheless it may be useful, since this objection is so commonly raised, to deal with it at this point, although nothing further will be added thereby to what has been said already.

It may be claimed that no two actual cases would ever be exactly similar; there would always be some differences, and *B* might allege that some of these were morally relevant. He might allege, for example, that, whereas his family would starve if *C* put him into prison, this would not be the case if he put *A* into prison, because *A*'s family would be looked after by *A*'s relatives. If such a difference existed, there might be nothing logically disreputable in calling it morally relevant, and such arguments are in fact often put forward and accepted.

The difficulty, however, lies in drawing the line between those arguments of this sort which are legitimate, and those which are not. Suppose that *B* alleges that the fact that *A* has a hooked nose or a black skin entitles him, *B*, to put him in prison, but that *C* ought not to do the same thing to him, *B*, because his nose is straight and his skin white. Is this an argument of equal logical respectability? Can I say that the fact that I have a mole in a particular place on my chin entitles me to further my own interests at others' expense, but that they are forbidden to do this by the fact that they lack this mark of natural pre-eminence?

The answer to this manœuvre is implicit in what has been said already about the relevance, in moral arguments, of hypothetical as well as of actual cases. The fact that no two actual cases are ever identical has no bearing on the problem. For all we have to do is to imagine an identical case in which the roles are reversed. Suppose that my mole disappears, and that my neighbour grows one in the very same spot on his chin. Or, to use our other example, what does *B* say about a hypothetical case in which he has a black skin or a hooked nose, and *A* and *C* are both straight-nosed and white-skinned? Since this is the same argument, in essentials, as we used at the very beginning, it need not be repeated here. *B* is in fact faced with a dilemma. Either the property of his own case, which he claims to be morally relevant, is a properly universal property (i.e., one describable without reference to individuals), or it is not. If it is a universal property, then, because of the meaning of the word "universal," it is a property which might be possessed by another case in which he played a different role (though in fact it may not be); and we can therefore ask him to ignore the fact that it is he himself who plays the role which he does in this case. This will force him to count as morally relevant only those properties which he is prepared to allow to be relevant even when other people have them. And this rules out all the attractive kinds of special pleading. On the other hand, if the property in question is not a properly universal one, then he has not met the demand for universalizability, and cannot claim to be putting forward a moral argument at all.

HARE SELECTION

1.   What exactly does it mean to say that moral arguments must be "universalizable"? Does it mean that everyone ought to do exactly the same thing, regardless of the circumstances? Does it mean that everyone ought to do the same thing in exactly similar circumstances? Are two sets of circumstances ever exactly similar?

2.   If I say, "You ought to pay the five dollars to Jones because you promised her that you would," am I implicitly committed to some general principle? What principle? That everyone ought to pay Jones what he has promised her? That you ought to pay everyone what you have promised him? That everyone ought to pay every debt? That all persons in exactly the same situation as you are in with Jones ought to do what you are doing? How can I tell *which* general principle lies behind an argument I give in a process of moral reasoning?

3.   According to Hare, a man who is prepared to make moral judgments about the actions of others thereby commits himself to certain moral judgments about his own actions. Exactly how does he do this? Aside from the mere fact that he contradicts himself (and also the fact that we may not be very likely to trust him in the future), are there any significant consequences of the fact that he contradicts himself in making moral judgments about others but refusing to make them about himself? What?

4.   Consider the following conversation:

Professor: I plan to give high grades to the students I like, and low grades to the students I dislike.

Student: That is unfair! This is a course, not a popularity contest. You have an obligation to grade us on our performance.

Professor: No, my ultimate commitment is to grading on personal preference, not grading on performance. You may not like what I am doing, but you cannot argue that it is unreasonable.

How would Hare analyze this disagreement? Does he offer any arguments for the student? What?

(SELECTION 6)

PHILIPPA FOOT

Moral Arguments

One of the central tenets of the school of philosophy know as "positivism" is the absolute separation of *facts* from *values*. Questions of fact, it was argued, could be settled by appeal to evidence and argument; disputes over values, on the other hand, would ultimately come down to an opposition of attitudes which could be fought out or compromised but could not be resolved through appeal to reason. Although this doctrine, at least in its starkest form, has long since ceased to be widely held by philosophers, it seems to have a death grip on economists, sociologists, political scientists, natural scientists, and others who think of themselves as dealing in *facts* rather than in *values*. David Hume, whether rightly or wrongly, is considered the father of the doctrine of the separation of facts from values. Two passages from Hume's *Treatise of Human Nature* are cited in this regard. The first is the discussion of reason and passion which appears in this chapter. The second is an equally famous passage, not included among our readings, in which Hume argues that it is never possible to derive statements of what ought to be, by any acceptable process of reasoning, from statements of what is the case. As this doctrine is usually summarized, "you cannot deduce 'ought' from 'is.' "

In recent years, a number of philosophers have sought to challenge the dogma that normative propositions can be derived only from normative premises. One line of attack has been to argue that the distinction between "factual" statements and "normative" statements is a good deal less clear than Hume and others have supposed. The positivists, following Hume, thought that one could unambiguously divide statements into several distinct categories: some were factual assertions; some were purely logical propositions; still others were evaluative or normative or prescriptive statements (i.e., statements that characterized something as good, or asserted that one ought to act in a certain way, or simply commanded this or that action). But how do we go about determining whether a statement is factual or evaluative, logical or prescriptive?

One way is to look at the key terms in the sentence and try to classify them as "descriptive" terms or "evaluative" terms. Statements totally free of evaluative or prescriptive terms would then be labeled factual, while those making essential use of evaluative or prescriptive terms would be labeled normative. (Notice the asymmetry here. Why not do it the other way around—statements totally free of factual terms would be labeled normative; all others would be called factual!)

If it should prove impossible, in practice, to classify terms in this manner, then the sharp distinction between the factual and the normative might also break down. In this essay, Philippa Foot mounts an attack on the fact/value dichotomy precisely by calling into question the classification of terms on which it is so often based.

Those who are influenced by the emotivist theory of ethics, and yet wish to defend what Hare has called "the rationality of moral discourse," generally talk a lot about "giving reasons" for saying that one thing is right, and another wrong. The fact that moral judgements need defence seems to distinguish the impact of one man's moral views upon others from mere persuasion or coercion, and the judgements themselves from mere expressions of likes and dislikes. Yet the version of argument in morals currently accepted seems to say that, while reasons must be given, no one need accept them unless he happens to hold particular moral views. It follows that disputes about what it right and wrong can be resolved only if certain contingent conditions are fulfilled; if they are not fulfilled, the argument breaks down, and the disputants are left face to face in an opposition which is merely an expression of attitude and will. Much energy is expended in trying to show that no sceptical conclusion can be drawn. It is suggested, for instance, that anyone who has considered all the facts which could bear on his moral position has *ipso facto* produced a "well founded" moral judgement; in spite of the fact that anyone else who has considered the same facts may well come to the opposite conclusion. How "x is good" can be a well founded moral judgement when "x is bad" can be equally well founded it is not easy to see.

The statement that moral arguments "may always break down" is often thought of as something that has to be accepted, and it is thought that those who deny it fail to take account of what was proved once for all by Hume, and elaborated by Stevenson, by Ayer, and by Hare. This article is an attempt to expose the assumptions which give the "breakdown" theory so tenacious a hold, and to suggest an alternative view.

Looked at in one way, the assertion that moral arguments "may always break down" appears to make a large claim. What is meant is that they may break down in a way in which other arguments may not. We are therefore working on a model on which such factors as shortage of time or temper are not shown; the suggestion is not that

From "Moral Arguments" by Philippa Foot. First published in *Mind* in 1958. (Reprinted by permission of the author.)

A's argument with B may break down because B refuses for one reason or another to go on with it, but that their positions as such are irreconcilable. Now the question is; how can we assert that any disagreement about what is right and wrong may end like this? How do we know, without consulting the details of each argument, that there is always an impregnable position both for the man who says that X is right, or good, or what he ought to do, and for the man who denies it? How do we know that each is able to deal with every argument the other may bring?

Thus, when Hare describes someone who listens to all his adversary has to say and then at the end simply rejects his conclusion, we want to ask "How can he?" Hare clearly supposes that he can, for he says that at this point the objector can only be asked to make up his mind for himself.[1] No one would ever paint such a picture of other kinds of argument—suggesting, for instance, that a man might listen to all that could be said about the shape of the earth, and then ask why he should believe that it was round. We should want, in such a case, to know how he met the case put to him; and it is remarkable that in ethics this question is thought not to be in place.

If a man making a moral judgement is to be invulnerable to criticism, he must be free from reproach on two scores: (*a*) he must have brought forward evidence, where evidence is needed; and (*b*) he must have disposed of any contrary evidence offered. It is worth showing why writers who insist that moral arguments may always break down assume, for both sides in a moral dispute, invulnerability on both counts. The critical assumption appears in different forms because different descriptions of moral arguments are given; and I shall consider briefly what has been said by Stevenson and by Hare.

I. Stevenson sees the process of giving reasons for ethical conclusions as a special process of non-deductive inference, in which statements expressing beliefs (R) form the premises and emotive (evaluative) utterances (E) the conclusion. There are no rules validating particular inferences, but only causal connections between the beliefs and attitudes concerned. "Suppose," he writes, "that a theorist should *tabulate* the 'valid' inferences from R's to E's. It is difficult to see how he could be doing anything more than specify what R's he thereby resolves to *accept* as supporting the various E's. . . . Under the name of 'validity' he will be selecting those inferences to which he is psychologically disposed to give assent, and perhaps inducing others to give a similar assent to them." [2] It follows that disputes in which each man backs up his moral judgement with "reasons" may

1 *The Language of Morals*, p. 69.
2 *Ethics and Language*, pp. 170–171.

always break down, and this is an implication on which Stevenson insists. So long as he does not contradict himself and gets his facts right, a man may argue as he chooses, or as he finds himself psychologically disposed. He alone says which facts are relevant to ethical conclusions, so that he is invulnerable on counts (a) and (b): he can simply assert that what he brings forward is evidence, and can simply deny the relevance of any other. His argument may be ineffective, but it cannot be said to be wrong. Stevenson speaks of ethical "inference" and of giving "reasons," but the process which he describes is rather that of trying to produce a result, an attitude, by means of a special kind of adjustment, an alteration in belief. All that is needed for a breakdown is for different attitudes in different people to be causally connected to the same beliefs. Then even complete agreement in belief will not settle a moral dispute.

II. Hare gives a picture of moral reasoning which escapes the difficulties of a special form of inference without rules of validity. He regards an argument to a moral conclusion as a syllogistic inference, with the ordinary rules. The facts, such as "this is stealing," which are to back up a moral judgement are to be stated in a "descriptive" minor premise, and their relevance is to be guaranteed by an "evaluative" major premise in which that kind of thing is said to be good or bad. There is thus no difficulty about the validity of the argument; but one does arise about the status of the major premise. We are supposed to say that a particular action is bad because it is a case of stealing, and because stealing is wrong; but if we ask why stealing is wrong, we can only be presented with another argument of the same form, with another exposed moral principle as its major premise. In the end everyone is forced back to some moral principle which he simply asserts—and which someone else may simply deny. It can therefore be no reproach to anyone that he gives no reasons for a statement of moral principle, since any moral argument must contain some undefended premise of this kind. Nor can he be accused of failing to meet arguments put forward by opponents arguing from different principles; for by denying their ultimate major premises he can successfully deny the relevance of anything they say.

Both these accounts of moral argument are governed by the thought that there is no logical connection between statements of fact and statements of value, so that each man makes his own decision as to the facts about an action which are relevant to its evaluation. To oppose this view we should need to show that, on the contrary, it is laid down that some things do, and some things do not, count in favour of a moral conclusion, and that a man can no more decide for himself what is evidence for rightness and wrongness than he can decide what is evidence for monetary inflation or a tumour on the brain. If such objective relations between facts and values existed, they could be of two kinds: descriptive, or factual premises might *entail* evaluative conclusions, or they might count as *evidence* for them. It is the second possibility which chiefly concerns me, but I shall nevertheless consider the arguments which are supposed to show that the stronger relationship cannot exist. For I want to show that the arguments usually brought forward do not *even* prove this. I want to say that it has not even been proved that moral conclusions cannot be entailed by factual or descriptive premises.

It is often thought that Hume showed the impossibility of deducing "ought," from "is," but the form in which this view is now defended is, of course, that in which it was rediscovered by G. E. Moore at the beginning of the present century, and developed by such other critics of "naturalistic" ethics as Stevenson, Ayer and Hare. We need therefore to look into the case against naturalism to see exactly what was proved.

Moore tried to show that goodness was a non-natural property, and thus not to be defined in terms of natural properties; the problem was to explain the concept of a "natural property," and to prove that no ethical definition in terms of natural properties could be correct. As Frankena [3] and Prior [4] pointed out, the argument against naturalism was always in danger of degenerating into a truism. A natural property tended to become one not identical with goodness, and the naturalistic fallacy that of identifying goodness with "some other thing."

What was needed to give the attack on naturalism new life was the identification of some deficiency common to the whole range of definitions rejected by Moore, a reason why they all failed. This was provided by the theory that value terms in general, and moral terms in particular, were used for a special function—variously identified as expressing feelings, expressing and inducing attitudes, or commending. Now it was said that words with emotive or commendatory force, such as "good," were not to be defined by the use of words whose meaning was merely "descriptive." This discovery tended to appear greater than it was, because it looked as if the two categories of fact and value had been identified separately and found never to coincide, whereas actually the factual or descriptive was defined by exclusion from the realm of value. In the ordinary sense of "descriptive" the word "good" is a descriptive word and in the ordinary sense of "fact" we say that it is a fact about so and so that he is a good man, so that the words must be used in a special sense in moral philosophy.

[3] W. K. Frankena, "The Naturalistic Fallacy," *Mind,* 1939.
[4] A. N. Prior, *Logic and the Basis of Ethics,* chap. I.

But a special philosopher's sense of these words has never, so far as I know, been explained except by contrasting value and fact. A word or sentence seems to be called "descriptive" on account of the fact that it is *not* emotive, does *not* commend, does *not* entail an imperative, and so on according to the theory involved. This might seem to reduce the case against naturalism once more to an uninteresting tautology, but it does not do so. For if the non-naturalist has discovered a special feature found in all value judgements, he can no longer be accused of saying merely that nothing is a definition of "good" unless it is a definition of "good" and not "some other thing." His part is now to insist that any definition which fails to allow for the special feature of value judgements must be rejected, and to label as "naturalistic" all the definitions which fail to pass this test.

I shall suppose, for the sake of argument, that the non-naturalist really has identified some characteristic (let us call it f) essential to evaluative words; that he is right in saying that evaluations involve emotions, attitudes, the acceptance of imperatives, or something of the kind. He is therefore justified in insisting that no word or statement which does not have the property f can be taken as equivalent to any evaluation, and that no account of the use of an evaluative term can leave out f and yet be complete. What, if anything, follows about the relation between premises and conclusion in an argument designed to support an evaluation?

It is often said that what follows is that evaluative conclusion cannot be deduced from descriptive premises, but how is this to be shown? Of course if a descriptive premise is redefined, as one which does not entail an evaluative conclusion, the non-naturalist will once more have bought security at the price of becoming a bore. He can once more improve his position by pointing to the characteristic f belonging to all evaluations, and asserting that no set of premises which do not entail an f proposition can entail an evaluation. If he takes this course he will be more like the man who says that a proposition which entails a proposition about a dog must be one which entails a proposition about an animal; he is telling us what to look out for in checking the entailment. What he is not so far telling us is that we can test for the entailment by looking to see whether the premise itself has the characteristic f. For all that has yet been shown it might be possible for a premise which is not f to entail a conclusion which is f, and it is obviously this proposition which the non-naturalist wants to deny.

Now it may seem obvious that a non-evaluative premise could not entail an evaluative conclusion, but it remains unclear how it is supposed to be proved.

In one form, the theory that an evaluative conclusion of a de-

ductive argument needs evaluative premises is clearly unwarrantable;
I mention it only to get it out of the way. We cannot possibly say
that at least one of the premises must be evaluative if the conclusion is to be so; for there is nothing to tell us that whatever can truly
be said of the conclusion of a deductive argument can truly be said of
any one of the premises. It is not necessary that the evaluative element should "come in whole," so to speak. If f has to belong to the
premises it can only be necessary that it should belong to the premises
together, and it may be no easy matter to see whether a set of propositions has the property f.

How in any case is it to be proved that if the conclusion is to
have the characteristic f the premises taken together must also have
it? Can it be said that unless this is so it will always be possible to
assert the premises and yet deny the conclusion? I shall try to show
that this at least is false, and in order to do so I shall consider the
case of arguments designed to show that a certain piece of behaviour
is or is not rude.

I thing it will be agreed that in the wide sense in which philosophers speak of evaluation, "rude" is an evaluative word. At any rate
it has the kind of characteristics upon which non-naturalists fasten:
it expresses disapproval, is meant to be used when action is to be
discouraged, implies that other things being equal the behaviour to
which it is applied will be avoided by the speaker, and so on. For the
purpose of this argument I shall ignore the cases in which it is admitted that there are reasons why something should be done in spite
of, or even because of, the fact that it is rude. Clearly there are occasions when a little rudeness is in place, but this does not alter the fact
that "rude" is a condemnatory word.

It is obvious that there is something else to be said about the
word "rude" besides the fact that it expresses, fairly mild, condemnation: it can only be used where certain descriptions apply. The
right account of the situation in which it is correct to say that a piece
of behaviour is rude, is, I think, that this kind of behaviour causes
offence by indicating lack of respect. Sometimes it is merely conventional that such behaviour does indicate lack of respect (e.g., when a
man keeps his hat on in someone else's house); sometimes the behaviour is naturally disrespectful, as when one man pushes another
out of the way. (It should be mentioned that rudeness and the absence of rudeness do not exhaust the subject of etiquette; some things
are not rude, and yet are "not done." It is rude to wear flannels at a
formal dinner party, but merely not done to wear a dinner jacket for
tennis.)

Given that this reference to offence is to be included in any account of the concept of rudeness, we may ask what the relation is

between the assertion that these conditions of offence are fulfilled—
let us call it O—and the statement that a piece of behaviour is rude—
let us call it R. Can someone who accepts the proposition O (that this
kind of offence is caused) deny the proposition R (that the behaviour
is rude)? I should have thought that this was just what he could not
do, for if he says that it is not rude, we shall stare, and ask him what
sort of behaviour would be rude; and what is he to say? Suppose that
he were to answer "a man is rude when he behaves conventionally,"
or "a man is rude when he walks slowly up to a front door," and this
not because he believes that such behaviour causes offence, but with
the intention of leaving behind entirely the usual criteria of rudeness. It is evident that with the usual criteria of rudeness he leaves
behind the concept itself; he may say the words "I think this rude,"
but it will not on that account be right to describe him as "thinking
it rude." If I *say* "I am sitting on a pile of hay" and bring as evidence
the fact that the object I am sitting on has four wooden legs and a
hard wooden back, I shall hardly be described as thinking, even mistakenly, that I am sitting on a pile of hay; all I am doing is to use the
words "pile of hay."

It might be thought that the two cases were not parallel, for
while the meaning of "pile of hay" is given by the characteristics
which piles of hay must possess, the meaning of "rude" is given by
the attitude it expresses. The answer is that if "thinking a thing
rude" is to be described as having a particular attitude to it, then
having an attitude presupposes, in this case, believing that certain
conditions are fulfilled. If "attitudes" were solely a matter of reactions such as wrinkling the nose, and tendencies to such things as
making resolutions and scolding, then thinking something rude
would not be describable solely in terms of attitudes. Either thinking something rude is not to be described in terms of attitudes, or
attitudes are not to be described in terms of such things. Even if we
could suppose that a particular individual could react towards conventional behaviour, or to walking slowly up to an English front
door, *exactly* as most people react to behaviour which gives offence,
this would not mean that he was to be described as thinking these
things rude. And in any case the supposition is nonsense. Although
he could behave in some ways as if he thought them rude, e.g., by
scolding conventional or slow-walking children, but not turning
daughters with these proclivities out of doors, his behaviour could
not be just as if he thought them rude. For as the social reaction to
conventional behaviour is not the same as the social reaction to offen-
sive behaviour, he could not act in just the same way. He could not
for instance apologise for what he would call his "rudeness," for he
would have to admit that it had caused no offence.

I conclude that whether a man is speaking of behaviour as rude or not rude, he must use the same criteria as anyone else, and that since the criteria are satisfied if O is true, it is impossible for him to assert O while denying R. It follows that if it is a sufficient condition of P's entailing Q that the assertion of P is inconsistent with the denial of Q, we have here an example of a non-evaluative premise from which an evaluative conclusion can be deduced.

It is of course possible to admit O while refusing to assert R, and this will not be like the refusal to say about prunes what one has already admitted about dried plums. Calling an action "rude" is using a concept which a man might want to reject, rejecting the whole practice of praising and blaming embodied in terms such as "polite" and "rude." Such a man would refuse to discuss points of etiquette, and arguments with him about what is rude would not so much break down as never begin. But once he did accept the question "Is this rude?" he would have to abide by the rules of this kind of argument; he could not bring forward any evidence he liked, and he could not deny the relevance of any piece of evidence brought forward by his opponent. Nor could he say that he was unable to move from O to R on this occasion because the belief in O had not induced in him feelings or attitudes warranting the assertion of R. If he had agreed to discuss rudeness he had committed himself to accepting O as evidence for R, and evidence is not a sort of medicine which is taken in the hope that it will work. To suggest that he could refuse to admit that certain behaviour was rude because the right psychological state had not been induced, is as odd as to suppose that one might refuse to speak of the world as round because in spite of the good evidence of roundness a feeling of confidence in the proposition had not been produced. When given good evidence it is one's business to act on it, not to hang around waiting for the right state of mind. It follows that if a man is prepared to discuss questions of rudeness, and hence to accept as evidence the fact that behaviour causes a certain kind of offence, he cannot refuse to admit R when O has been proved.

The point of considering this example was to show that there may be the strictest rules of evidence even where an evaluative conclusion is concerned. Apply this principle to the case of moral judgements, we see that—for all that the non-naturalist has proved to the contrary—Bentham, for instance, may be right in saying that when used in conjunction with the principle of utility "the words *ought* and *right* and *wrong*, and others of that stamp, have a meaning: when otherwise they have none." [5] Anyone who uses moral terms at all,

---

[5] *Principles of Morals in Legislation*, chap. I, x.

whether to assert or deny a moral proposition, must abide by the rules for their use, including the rules about what shall count as evidence for or against the moral judgement concerned. For anything that has yet been shown to the contrary these rules could be entailment rules, forbidding the assertion of factual propositions in conjunction with the denial of moral propositions. The only recourse of the man who refused to accept the things which counted in favour of a moral proposition as giving him a reason to do certain things or to take up a particular attitude, would be to leave the moral discussion and abjure altogether the use of moral terms.

To say what Bentham said is not, then, to commit any sort of "naturalistic fallacy." It is open to us to enquire whether moral terms do lose their meaning when divorced from the pleasure principle, or from some other set of criteria, as the word "rude" loses its meaning when the criterion of offensiveness is dropped. To me it seems that this is clearly the case; I do not know what could be meant by saying that it was someone's duty to do something unless there was an attempt to show why it mattered if this sort of thing was not done. How can questions such as "what does it matter?" "what harm does it do?" "what advantage is there in . . . ?" "why is it important?" be set aside here? Is it even to be suggested that the harm done by a certain trait of character could be taken, by some extreme moral eccentric, to be just what made it a virtue? I suggest that such a man would not even be a moral eccentric, any more than the man who used the word "rude" of conventional behaviour was putting forward strange views about what was rude. Both descriptions have their proper application, but it is not here. How exactly the concepts of harm, advantage, benefit, importance, etc., are related to the different moral concepts, such as rightness, obligation, goodness, duty and virtue, is something that needs the most patient investigation, but that they are so related seems undeniable, and it follows that a man cannot make his own personal decision about the considerations which are to count as evidence in morals.

Perhaps it will be argued that this kind of freedom of choice is not ruled out after all, because a man has to decide for himself what is to count as advantage, benefit, or harm. But is this really plausible? Consider the man described by Hare as thinking that torturing is morally permissible.[6] Apparently he is not supposed to be arguing that in spite of everything torture is justifiable as a means of extracting confessions from enemies of the state, for the argument is supposed to be at an end when he has said that torturing people is permissible, and his opponent has said that it is not. How is he supposed

---

[6] *Universalisability, P.A.S.A.* 1954–1955, p. 304.

to have answered the objection that to inflict torture is to do harm? If he is supposed to have said that pain is good for a man in the long run, rather than bad, he will have to show the benefits involved, and he can no more choose what shall count as a benefit than he could have chosen what counted as harm. Is he supposed perhaps to count as harm only harm to himself? In this case he is guilty of *ignoratio elenchi.* By refusing to count as harm anything except harm to himself, he puts himself outside the pale of moral discussion, and should have explained that this was his position. One might compare his case to that of a man who in some discussion of common policy says "this will be the best thing to do," and announces afterwards that *he* meant best for himself. This is not what the word "best" does mean in the context of such a discussion.

It may be objected that these considerations about the evidence which must be brought for saying that one thing is good and another bad, could not in any case be of the least importance; such rules of evidence, even if they exist, only reflecting the connection between our existing moral code and our existing moral terms; if there are no "free" moral terms in our language, it can always be supposed that some have been invented—as indeed they will have to be invented if we are to be able to argue with people who subscribe to a moral code entirely different from our own. This objection rests on a doubtful assumption about the concept of *morality.* It assumes that even if there are rules about the grounds on which actions can be called good, right, or obligatory, there are no rules about the grounds on which a principle which is to be called a moral principle may be asserted. Those who believe this must think it possible to identify an element of feeling or attitude which carries the meaning of the word "moral." It must be supposed, for instance, that if we describe a man as being for or against certain actions, bringing them under universal rules, adopting these rules for himself, and thinking himself bound to urge them on others, we shall be able to identify him as holding moral principles, whatever the content of the principle at which he stops. But why should it be supposed that the concept of morality is to be caught in this particular kind of net? The consequences of such an assumption are very hard to stomach; for it follows that a rule which was admitted by those who obeyed it to be completely pointless could yet be recognised as a moral rule. If people happened to insist that no one should run round trees left handed, or look at hedgehogs in the light of the moon, this might count as a basic moral principle about which nothing more need be said.

I think that the main reason why this view is so often held in spite of these difficulties, is that we fear the charge of making a verbal decision in favour of our own moral code. But those who bring that charge are merely begging the question against arguments such as those given above. Of course if the rules we are refusing to call moral rules can really be given this name, then we are merely legislating against alien *moral codes*. But the suggestion which has been put forward is that this could not be the right description for rules of behaviour for which an entirely different defence is offered from that which we offer for our moral beliefs. If this suggestion is right, the difference between ourselves and the people who have these rules is not to be described as a difference of moral outlook, but rather as a difference between a moral and a non-moral point of view. The example of etiquette is again useful here. No one is tempted to say that the ruling out, *a priori*, of rules of etiquette which each man decides on for himself when he feels so inclined, represents a mere verbal decision in favour of our kind of socially determined standards of etiquette. On what grounds could one call a rule which someone was allowed to invent for himself a rule of *etiquette?* It is not just a fact about the use of our words "rude," "not done," etc., that they could not be applied in such a case; it is also a fact about etiquette that if terms in another language did appear in such situations they would not be terms of etiquette. We can make a similar point about the terms "legal" and "illegal" and the concept of law. If any individual was allowed to apply a certain pair of terms expressing approval and disapproval off his own bat, without taking notice of any recognised authority, such terms could not be legal terms. Similarly it is a fact about etiquette and law that they are both conventional as morality is not.

It may be that in attempting to state the rules which govern the assertion of moral propositions we shall legislate against a moral system radically opposed to our own. But this is only to say that we may make a mistake. The remedy is to look more carefully at the rules of evidence, not to assume that there cannot be any at all. If a moral system such as Nietzsche's has been refused recognition as a moral system, then we have got the criteria wrong. The fact that Nietzsche was a moralist cannot, however, be quoted in favour of the private enterprise theory of moral criteria. Admittedly Nietzsche said "You want to decrease suffering; I want precisely to increase it" but he did not *just* say this. Nor did he offer as a justification the fact that suffering causes a tendency to absent mindedness, or lines on the human face. We recognise Nietzsche as a moralist because he tries to justify an increase in suffering by connecting it with strength as opposed to weakness, and individuality as opposed to conformity. That strength is a good thing can only be denied by someone who can show that the strong man overreaches himself, or in some other way brings harm to himself or other people. That individuality is a good thing is something that has to be shown, but in a vague way we connect it with originality, and with courage, and hence there is no difficulty in conceiving Nietzsche as a moralist when he appeals to such a thing.

In conclusion it is worth remarking that moral arguments break down more often than philosophers tend to think, but that the breakdown is of a different kind. When people argue about what is right, good, or obligatory, or whether a certain character trait is or is not a virtue, they do not confine their remarks to the adducing of facts which can be established by simple observation, or by some clear-cut technique. What is said may well be subtle or profound, and in this sort of discussion as in others, in the field of literary criticism for instance, or the discussion of character, much depends on experience and imagination. It is quite common for one man to be unable to see what the other is getting at, and this sort of misunderstanding will not always be resolvable by anything which could be called argument in the ordinary sense.

FOOT SELECTION

1. In what sense is the word "rude" both descriptive and evaluative? What other words can you think of that have this same character?

2. Foot compares moral arguments with scientific arguments in an attempt to show that moral arguments do not "break down" any more than scientific arguments do. But suppose a scientist were arguing with a mystic, and the mystic treated the scientist's "evidence" as simply a species of confusion brought about through an excessive involvement with things of the flesh! After a while, wouldn't we simply have to tell the scientist and mystic that they must "choose" which system of thought they wish to operate within? Wouldn't argument break down? Is this the situation in which we find ourselves when we argue about abortion, or capital punishment, or private property?

3. Anthropologists learn to use the evaluative/descriptive words of other cultures without necessarily accepting the norms and styles of life of the peoples who use those words. Can we learn to use words like "rude" without accepting the evaluations implicit in them?

4. To what extent does Foot rely on the fact that her audience all comes from a single culture? Could there be a culture or society of men and women who rejected Foot's notion of moral argument? Or would they simply have somewhat different convictions, experiences, and preferences? Could there be an argument—a rational argument—between representatives of vastly different cultures?

(SELECTION 7)

MICHAEL OAKESHOTT

Rational Conduct

Thus far, the debate in this chapter has been conducted principally between instrumentalists and substantivists. Both sides accept and employ the same model of human deliberation and choice, a model whose elements include ends or goals or objects of desire at which we aim, means or resources from among which we make selections in deciding what to do, and reasons that we give to ourselves or to one another, either reasons for means or reasons for ends. Depending on which theory of human action an author endorses, an action (or a person) will be said to be *rational* according to the sorts of ends he or she chooses, the sorts of means he or she adopts in pursuit of given ends, and the sorts of reasons that are operative in these two arenas of choice.

Michael Oakeshott, the contemporary English political philosopher who is the leading intellectual figure in the new conservatism of British politics and letters, rejects the underlying ends-means-reasons model of human action, and therefore concludes that all parties to the debate are wrong.

It is very important, in reading this essay, to get precisely clear about what Oakeshott is asserting. He is *not* saying that it is wrong, or unwise, or ill-advised to act in the way that "rationalists" recommend. Many of his remarks seem to suggest that this is his thesis, but he is in fact saying something a good deal more radical by far. According to Oakeshott, it is literally *impossible* to act as rationalists of all varieties recommend. It is simply impossible to posit, or choose, or set, or select *ends,* and then range over a variety of alternative means to those ends until one comes upon one that fits some pre-established criterion of efficiency or suitability. We can, of course, try to act in that way, but we must always, necessarily, fail. Action is an expression of a coherent and settled personality, which is to say an expression of an internalized culture, of forms of feeling and structures of personality. Desire itself is a culture-shaped phenomenon. Babies are not born with desires for which they as yet lack the means of gratification. Babies are born with drives, with instincts, with physical needs. The process by which these take on the shape of identifiable desires is a process of personality formation that also shapes and limits the available modes of expression and the appropriate means of satisfaction. The most we can ever do, by way of a critique of our actions, is to explore, from within our own traditions, culture, and society, the intimations of those patterns of feeling and action that constitute our being.

Since a doctrine of this sort seems

to make every evaluative position indefensible, it is not entirely clear why Oakeshott should be, and should consider himself to be, *conservative* rather than liberal or radical. One of the unresolved problems in Oakeshott's position is precisely his failure to analyze critical self-examination as itself a mode of activity characteristic of our own and other sophisticated civilizations.

The word *Reason,* and the epithets connected with it—*Rational* and *Reasonable*—have enjoyed a long history which has bequeathed to them a legacy of ambiguity and confusion. Like mirrors, they have reflected the changing notions of the world and of human faculty which have flowed over our civilization in the last two thousand years; image superimposed upon image has left us with a cloudy residue. Any man may be excused when he is puzzled by the question how he ought to use these words, and in particular how he ought to use them in relation to human conduct and to politics; for in the first place, these words come before us as attributes of "argument," and what is puzzling is the analogy in which they are applied to "conduct." The philosopher may succeed in disentangling the confusion which springs from merely crooked thinking, and the historian in telling the story of the ambiguity and in making sense of it without the help of those adventitious aids, the categories of truth and error. My purpose here is to seek a satisfactory way of using the word *Rational* in connection with conduct, and to explore some of the territory which opens up in the process: the impulse is both philosophical and historical.

I will begin with the assumption that when we speak of human behaviour and the management of our affairs as "rational," we mean to commend it. "Rational conduct" is something no man is required to be ashamed of. It is usually held that something more than "rationality" is required in order to make conduct either endearing or saintly, or to make the management of affairs a dazzling success; but, generally speaking, it belongs to our tradition to find "rationality" a laudable quality, or, at least, to find irrationality something proper to be avoided. We are, then, to consider an idea which in relation to human conduct implies commendation. Our civilization, it is true, has acquired a parallel vocabulary in which "rational" is a word of denigration, but the spring of this rebound was an opposition to a narrowing of human sympathies, a restriction of what was thought admirable and proper to be done which had become reflected in the word, rather than a denial of all standards of propriety.

From "Rational Conduct," in *Rationalism in Politics and Other Essays* by Michael Oakeshott. (© 1962 by Michael Oakeshott, Basic Books, Inc., Publishers, New York. Reprinted by permission of Basic Books, Inc. and Methuen & Co. Ltd., London.)

Secondly, I shall assume that the word "rational," when used in connection with human conduct, refers, in the first place, to a manner of behaving and only derivatively to an action in respect of what it achieves or of the success with which it accomplishes what was intended. Thus, to behave "rationally" is to behave "intelligently," and whether such behaviour is pragmatically successful will depend upon circumstances other than its "rationality." This, again, coincides with usage; a "lunatic," whose behaviour we recognize as "irrational," is not always unsuccessful in achieving his designs, and we know that, even in argument, a correct conclusion may be reached in spite of false reasoning.

Ever since the eighteenth century we have had presented to us a variety of forms of behaviour or projects of activity, each recommended on account of its "rationality." There have been "rational education," "rational agriculture," "rational diet," "rational dress," to say nothing of "rational religion," and "rational spelling." The segregation of the sexes in education, eating meat and drinking intoxicants were, for example, held to be "irrational." One famous protagonist of rational dress asserted that a shirt-collar which did not leave space for the insertion of a loaf of bread was irrationally restrictive of the flow of air to the body; and the wearing of a hat has frequently been said to be "irrational." But the expression "rational dress" was applied, in particular, in Victorian times, to an extraordinary garment affected by girls on bicycles, and to be observed in the illustrations of the *Punch* of the period. Bloomers were asserted to be the "rational dress" for girl cyclists. And as a means to putting straight our own ideas of "rationality" we could do worse than to consider what was being thought by those who asserted the "rationality" of this garment. [1]

There is little doubt about what they were thinking of in the first place. They were concentrating their attention upon the activity of *propelling* a bicycle. The things to be considered, and to be related to one another, were a bicycle of a certain general design and the structure of the human body. All considerations other than these were dismissed because they were believed to be of no account in determining the "rationality" of the dress to be designed. And, in particular, the designers were decided not to take account of current prejudice, convention or folklore, concerning feminine dress; from the standpoint of "rationality" these must be considered only as limiting circumstances. Consequently, the first step in the project of designing a "rational" dress for this purpose must be a certain empty-

---

[1] Whether Mrs. Bloomer herself made this assertion, or whether it was made by others on behalf of her invention, I do not know.

ing of the mind, a conscious effort to get rid of preconceptions. Of course knowledge of a certain sort would be required—knowledge of mechanics and anatomy—but the greater part of a man's thoughts would appear as an encumbrance in this enterprise, as a distraction from which it was necessary to avert the attention. If one were an investor anxious to employ a designer on this project, one might do well to consider a Chinese, for example, rather than an Englishman, because he would be less distracted by irrelevant considerations; just as the South American republics applied to Bentham for a "rational" constitution. The "rationality" sought by these Victorian designers was, then, an eternal and a universal quality; something rescued from the world of mere opinion and set in a world of certainty. They might make mistakes; and if they were not mistakes in mechanics and anatomy (which would be unlikely), they would be the mistakes of a mind not firmly enough insulated from preconception, a mind not yet set free. Indeed, they did make a mistake; impeded by prejudice, their minds paused at bloomers instead of running on to "shorts"— clearly so much more complete a solution of their chosen problem. Or was it a mistake? Perhaps it was, instead, some dim recognition of a more profound understanding of "rationality" which made them stop there. We must consider the possibility later on.

Now, the questions we may ask ourselves are, Why were bloomers thought to be a "rational" form of dress for girl cyclists? And why was this way of going about things considered to be pre-eminently "rational"? In general the answers to these questions are, first, Because they were adapted to circumstances—bloomers were a successful solution of the specific problem set; if the bicycle to be propelled had been of a different design (if, for example, arms and not legs had been the propelling limb) the clothing considered "rational" would have been of a different design. And secondly, Because the solution sprang (or seemed to spring) solely from the reflective consideration of the problem set—bloomers were a "rational" form of dress because the act of designing them (or the act of wearing them) sprang from an antecedent act of independent reflective effort, undistracted by "irrelevant" considerations. Here, in short, was an example of the much advertised "rational method" in action.

The view we are to consider takes *purpose* as the distinctive mark of "rationality" in conduct: "rational" activity is behaviour in which an independently premeditated end is pursued and which is determined solely by that end. This end may be an external result to be achieved, or it may be the enjoyment of the activity itself. To play a game in order to win (and perhaps to win a prize), and to play it for its own sake, for the enjoyment of it, are both purposive ac-

tivities. Further, "rational" conduct is behaviour *deliberately* directed
to the achievement of a *formulated* purpose and is governed solely
by that purpose. There may be other, perhaps unavoidable, consequences or results springing from the conduct, but these must be
regarded as extraneous, fortuitous and "irrational" because they are
unwanted and no part of the design. Bloomers were not designed to
shock Victorian sensibility, to amuse or to distract, but to provide a
form of dress precisely suitable for cycling. The designers did not
say to themselves, "Let us invent something amusing"; nor, on the
other hand, did they think that the "absurdity" of their creation was
in any degree a qualification of its "rationality": indeed, "absurdity"
is so much a common feature of all the works of designers inspired
by this notion of "rationality" that it could normally be taken as a
sign of success. "Rational" conduct will, then, usually, have not only
a specific end, but also a simple end; for when the end is in fact
complex, activity can be efficiently directed towards its achievement
only when, either the complexity is presented as a series of simple
ends (the achievement of one leading on to the achievement of the
next and so to the final end), or where the simple components of the
complex end are seen to be related to the specific components of the
activity. Hence, in "rational behaviour," the necessity of a strict
formulation of the end to be pursued; the decision of the designer
of bloomers to confine his attention to mechanics and anatomy and
to neglect all other considerations. "Rational" activity is activity in
search of a certain, a conclusive answer to a question, and consequently the question must be formulated in such a way that it admits
of such an answer.

Now, the deliberate direction of activity to the achievement of a
specific end can be successful only when the necessary means are
available or procurable and when the power exists of detecting and
appropriating from the means which are available those which are
necessary. Consequently, there will be in "rational" conduct, not only
a premeditated purpose to be achieved, but also a separately premeditated selection of the means to be employed. And all this requires reflection and a high degree of detachment. The calculated
choice of end and means both involves and provides a resistance to
the indiscriminate flow of circumstance. One step at a time is the
rule here; and each step is taken in ignorance of what the next is to
be. The "rationality" of conduct, then, on this view of it, springs
from something that we do *before* we act; and activity is "rational"
on account of its being generated in a certain manner.

A further determination of this so-called "rational" conduct may
be found in the kinds of behaviour it excludes or opposes itself to.
First, merely capricious conduct will be excluded; conduct, that is,

which has no end settled in advance. Secondly, it will oppose itself
to merely impulsive conduct—conduct from which there is absent
the necessary element of reflective choice of means to achieve the
desired end. Thirdly, this "rational" conduct is in permanent opposition to conduct which is not governed by some deliberately accepted rule or principle or canon and which does not spring from the
explicit observance of a formulated principle. Further, it excludes
conduct which springs from the unexamined authority of a tradition,
a custom or a habit of behaviour. For, although achievement of a
purpose may be embedded in a merely traditional mode of conduct,
the purpose itself is not disentangled, and a man may remain true to
the tradition while being wholly ignorant of any propositional formulation of the end pursued. For example, certain procedures in the
House of Commons may, in fact, achieve certain specific purposes,
but since they were not expressly designed to achieve these purposes
their character as means to ends often remains hidden and unform-
ulated. And lastly, I think that activity in pursuit of an end for which
the necessary means are known to be absent may fairly be said to be
excluded; behaviour of this sort is not "rational." . . .

. . . What . . . are the assumptions of this view, and what is the validity
of these assumptions?

It would appear that the first assumption is that men have a
power of reasoning about things, of contemplating propositions
about activities, and of putting these propositions in order and making them coherent. And it is assumed, further, that this is a power
independent of any other powers a man may have, and something
from which his activity can *begin*. And activity is said to be "rational"
(or "intelligent") on account of being preceded by the exercise of
this power, on account of a man having "thought" in a certain manner before he acted. "Rational" conduct is conduct springing from
an antecedent process of "reasoning." In order that a man's conduct
should be wholly "rational," he must be supposed to have the power
of first imagining and choosing a purpose to pursue, of defining that
purpose clearly and of selecting fit means to achieve it; and this
power must be wholly independent, not only of tradition and of the
uncontrolled relics of his fortuitous experience of the world, but
also of the activity itself to which it is a preliminary. And for a
number of men to enjoy wholly "rational" conduct together, it must
be supposed that they have in common a power of this sort and that
the exercise of it will lead them all to the same conclusions and issue
in the same form of activity.

There are, of course, various well-known but crude formulations of this supposition but we need not concern ourselves with
them. The power in question has been hypostatized and given a

name; it is called "Reason." And it has been supposed that the human mind must contain in its composition a native faculty of "Reason," a light whose brightness is dimmed only by education, a piece of mistake-proof apparatus, an oracle whose magic word is truth. But if this is going further than is either wise or necessary, what does seem unavoidable (if there is to be this power) is the supposition that a man's mind can be separated from its contents and its activities. What needs to be assumed is the mind as a neutral instrument, as a piece of apparatus. Long and intensive training may be necessary in order to make the best use of this piece of machinery; it is an engine which must be nursed and kept in trim. Nevertheless, it is an independent instrument, and "rational" conduct springs from the exercise of it.

The mind, according to this hypothesis, is an independent instrument capable of dealing with experience. Beliefs, ideas, knowledge, the contents of the mind, and above all the activities of men in the world, are not regarded as themselves mind, or as entering into the composition of mind, but as adventitious, posterior acquisitions of the mind, the results of mental activity which the mind might or might not have possessed or undertaken. The mind may acquire knowledge or cause bodily activity, but it is something that may exist destitute of all knowledge, and in the absence of any activity; and where it has acquired knowledge or provoked activity, it remains independent of its acquisition or its expression in activity. It is steady and permanent, while its filling of knowledge is fluctuating and often fortuitous. Further, it is supposed that this permanent mental instrument, though it exists from birth, is capable of being trained. But what is called a "trained mind" is, like the schoolboy's tears over a proposition in Euclid, a *consequence* of learning and activity, and is not a *conclusion* from it. Hence, mental training may take the form either of a purely functional exercise (like gymnastics), or of an exercise which incidentally gets us somewhere, like running to catch a bus. The mind may be trained by "pelmanism" or by learning Latin grammar. Lastly, it is supposed that the mind will be most successful in dealing with experience when it is least prejudiced with already acquired dispositions or knowledge: the open, empty or free mind, the mind without disposition, is an instrument which attracts truth, repels superstition and is alone the spring of "rational" judgment and "rational" conduct. Consequently, the purely formal exercise of the mind will normally be considered a superior sort of training to the mixed exercise which involves a particular "knowledge how" and unavoidably leaves behind some relic of acquired disposition. And the first training of a mind already infected with a disposition will be a process of purification, of getting rid of accumulated special knowledge and skill—a process of re-establishing virginal detachment. Childhood is, unfortunately, a period during which, from the lack of a trained mind, we give admittance to a whole miscellany of beliefs, dispositions, knowledge not in the form of propositions; the first business of the adult is to disencumber his mental apparatus of these prejudices. This, then, is "intelligence," the "rational" part of a man; and human activity is to be counted "rational" if and when it is preceded and caused by the exercise of this "intelligence." . . .

It is no secret that this view of "rationality" in conduct leaves something to be desired. Criticism has fastened upon many of the details, and some of it has been cogent enough to make necessary extensive repairs to the theory. I do not myself wish to direct attention to defect in detail, but to what seems to me to be the main shortcoming. And I believe that when the precise character of the theory is perceived, it will be seen to collapse under the weight of its own imperfections. My view is that this is not a satisfactory notion of *rational* conduct because it is not a satisfactory account of any sort of conduct.

Let us begin with the idea of "the mind" or "intelligence" which is at the centre of this theory. The notion is: that first there is something called "the mind," that this mind acquires beliefs, knowledge, prejudices—in short, a filling—which remain nevertheless a mere appendage to it, that it causes bodily activities, and that it works best when it is unencumbered by an acquired disposition of any sort. Now, this mind I believe to be a fiction; it is nothing more than an hypostatized activity. Mind as we know it is the offspring of knowledge and activity; it is composed entirely of thoughts. You do not first have a mind, which acquires a filling of ideas and then makes distinctions between true and false, right and wrong, reasonable and unreasonable, and then, as a third step, causes activity. Properly speaking the mind has no existence apart from, or in advance of, these and other distinctions. These and other distinctions are not acquisitions; they are constitutive of the mind. Extinguish in a man's mind these and other distinctions, and what is extinguished is not merely a man's "knowledge" (or part of it), but the mind itself. What is left is not a neutral, unprejudiced instrument, a pure intelligence, but nothing at all. The whole notion of the mind as an apparatus for thinking is, I believe, an error; and it is the error at the root of this particular view of the nature of "rationality" in conduct. Remove that, and the whole conception collapses.

But further, and following from this, it is an error to suppose that conduct could ever have its spring in the sort of activity which is misdescribed by hypostatizing a "mind" of this sort; that is, from the power of considering abstract propositions about conduct. That such a power exists is not to be doubted; but its prerequisite is conduct itself. This activity is not something that can exist in advance of conduct; it is the result of reflection upon conduct, the creature of a subsequent analysis of conduct. And this goes, not only for conduct in the narrow sense, but for activity of every sort, for the activity of the scientist, for example, or of the craftsman, no less than for the activity in politics and in the ordinary conduct of life. And consequently it is preposterous, in the strict meaning of the word, to maintain that activity can derive from this kind of thinking, and it is unwise to recommend that it should do so by calling activity "rational" only when it appears to have this spring. *Doing* anything both depends upon and exhibits knowing how to do it; and though part (but never the whole) of knowing how to do it can subsequently be reduced to knowledge in the form of propositions (and possibly to ends, rules and principles), these propositions are neither the spring of the activity nor are they in any direct sense regulative of the activity.

The characteristic of the carpenter, the scientist, the painter, the judge, the cook, and of any man in the ordinary conduct of life, and in his relations with other people and with the world around him, is a knowledge, not of certain propositions about themselves, their tools, and the materials in which they work, but a knowledge of how to decide certain questions; and this knowledge is the condition of the exercise of the power to construct such propositions. Consequently, if "rationality" is to represent a desirable quality of an activity, it cannot be the quality of having independently premeditated propositions about the activity before it begins. And this applies to propositions about the end or purpose of an activity no less than to any other kind of proposition. It is an error to call an activity "rational" on account of its end having been specifically determined in advance and in respect of its achieving that end to the exclusion of all others, because there is in fact no way of determining an end for activity in advance of the activity itself; and if there were, the spring of activity would still remain in knowing how to act in pursuit of that end and not in the mere fact of having formulated an end to pursue. A cook is not a man who first has a vision of a pie and then tries to make it; he is a man skilled in cookery, and both his projects and his achievements spring from that skill. "Good" English is not something that exists in advance of how English is written (that is to say, English literature); and the knowledge that such and such is a sloppy, ambiguous construction, or is "bad grammar," is not something that can be known independently and in advance of knowing how to write the language.

My view is, then, that this project of finding a mode of conduct which, in this sense, is "rational" is misconceived. The instrumental mind does not exist, and if it did it would always lack the power to be the spring of any concrete activity whatever. . . .

Let us return to the activity of the designers of Victorian "rational dress," and to the activity of those who wore it because they believed themselves to be behaving "rationally" by doing so. We have supposed (not without some grounds) that what they *thought* they were doing was to design a garment suited to a particular purpose, the purpose of *propelling* a bicycle. They premeditated their purpose, and they selected a precise and narrow purpose in order to premeditate it without distraction; and they applauded their activity as "rational" because of the manner in which they went about their enterprise. The result was "rational" because it achieved a set and premeditated purpose and because it sprang from this prior act of theorizing. But we have observed that there were elements in the situation which might lead us to doubt whether what they *thought* they were doing (and on account of which they attributed "rationality" to their conduct) properly coincided with what they were in fact doing. Why did their enterprise pause at "bloomers" and not pass on to "shorts"? The answer that they merely made a mistake, that this stopping-place represents a failure of "rationality," is too easy. Their invention may be taken to indicate, not that they failed in their chosen enterprise, but that they were guided in fact by considerations which they believed themselves to have escaped and on account of this escape were behaving "rationally." Bloomers are not the answer to the question, What garment is best adapted to the activity of *propelling* a bicycle of a certain design? but to the question, What garment combines within itself the qualities of being well adapted to the activity of propelling a bicycle and of being suitable, all things considered, for an English girl to be seen in when riding a bicycle in 1880? And, unknown to themselves, it was the project of answering this question which moved the designers. But if we credit them with a belief in the idea of "rationality" which we have found to be unsatisfactory, then we may suppose that they would regard activity in pursuit of this purpose as wanting in "rationality." It is true that the activity would spring from a premeditated end, and consequently would have some flavour of "rationality" about it; but it would be a very different sort of activity from what they were accustomed to call "rational." It would be an activity in principle indistinguishable from that of *any* dress designer. In the first place, this is a question that *clearly* could not be answered by "pure intelligence"; it demands something more than the instrumental mind. This, of course, is true also of the first question, the question we sup-

posed to be actually in the mind of the designer; but its truth was
obscured because it seemed that in order to answer this first question
the operation called for was primarily an emptying of the mind.
Here, however, something much more positive is required. No
capitalist with any sense would think of entrusting the enterprise to
a Chinese; his ignorance of English taste, tradition, folklore and
prejudice in respect of women's clothing would be a hopeless handi-
cap. Anl though there is, here, a premeditated end to be pursued, it
is an exceedingly complex end; there is a tension within the purpose
iself—anatomical and mechanical principles pulling one way, perhaps, and social custom another. It is a question which admits of no
certain answer, because it involves an assessment of opinion; and it
is one which cannot be answered once and for all, because the problem is tied to place and time. In short, this is hardly a "rational"
question in the sense of "rationality" we have so far been considering. And yet, I think it is the question which the designers of "rational dress" were, in fact, trying to answer, and which they succeeded in answering when they produced bloomers.

Here we have reached something more like a piece of concrete
human activity, and our question must be, In what respect can this
be considered "rational" activity? The unregenerate believer in the
idea of "rationality" which we have seen fit to reject, will reply that it
is "rational" because it is activity springing from a premeditated
purpose, though the purpose here is neither simple nor capable of being premeditated by mere "intelligence"; its independence of the
activity is at least doubtful. He will contend that nothing has yet
been said which destroys the old criterion; this is "rational" activity
because it is premeditated, "reasoned" activity. And, although our
original supposition was that the end achieved by the dress-designers
was not in fact premeditated by them (what they set themselves was
something much narrower than what they achieved), it would be wise
to give him his point, because there seems, so far, no reason why it
should not have been premeditated. But the point is good only because we have not yet achieved a concrete view of human activity;
we are still dealing with abstractions, though not with such narrow
abstractions as the high and dry believer in the instrumental mind.

Now, if we consider the concrete activity of an historian, a cook,
a scientist, a politician or any man in the ordinary conduct of life,
we may observe that each is engaged upon answering questions of a
certain sort, and that his characteristic is that he knowns (or thinks
he knows) the way to go about finding the answer to that sort of question. But the questions which he knows to belong to his sort of activity are not known to be such in advance of the activity of trying to

answer them: in pursuing these questions, and not others, he is not obeying a rule or following a principle which comes from outside the activity, he is pursuing an activity which, in general, he knows how to pursue. It is the activity itself which defines the questions as well as the manner in which they are answered. It is, of course, not impossible to formulate certain principles which may seem to give precise definition to the kind of question a particular sort of activity is concerned with; but such principles are derived from the activity and not the activity from the principles. And even if a man has some such propositional knowledge about his activity, his knowledge of his activity always goes far beyond what is contained in these propositions. It is clear, then, that the activity of these men (and I would say all other activity also) is something that comes first, and is something into which each one gradually finds his way: at no time is he wholly ignorant of it; there is no identifiable beginning. Of course, the activity in general does not exist in advance of the activities which compose it; it consists wholly in knowing how to tackle problems of a certain sort. But it does exist in advance of the specific engagement a particular scientist or cook may have undertaken. How, then (if this is as clear as I think it is), do we get the illusion that the activity of these and other men could spring from and be governed by an end, a purpose or by rules independent of the activity itself and capable of being reflected upon in advance, with the possible corollary that, in respect of this spring and government, it should be called "rational."

Each man engaged in a certain kind of activity selects a particular question and engages himself to answer this question. He has before him a particular project: to determine the weight of the moon, to bake a sponge cake, to paint a portrait, to disclose the mediations which comprise the story of the Peninsular War, to come to an agreement with a foreign power, to educate his son—or whatever it may be. And, with the normal neglect with which a man engaged upon a particular task treats what is not immediately before him, he supposes that his activity springs from and is governed solely by his project. No man engaged in a particular task has in the forefront of his attention the whole context and implications of that engagement. Activity is broken up into actions, and actions come to have a false appearance of independence. And further, this abstraction of view is normally increased when what we observe is somebody else's activity. Every trade but our own seems to be comprised wholly of tricks and abridgments. There is, then, no mystery how it can come to be supposed that an activity may spring from an independently determined purpose to be pursued: the mistake arises from endowing a whole activity with the character of a single action when it is abstracted from the activity to which it belongs, from endowing, for example, the activity of cooking with the character of making a particular pie when the maker is assumed not to be a cook.

But if our cook or scientific practitioner were to consider the implications of his particular actions he would rapidly reach two conclusions. First, he would observe that, in pursuing his particular project, his actions were being determined not solely by his premeditated end, but by what may be called the traditions of the activity to which his project belonged. It is because he knows how to tackle problems of this sort that he is able to tackle this particular problem. He would observe, in other words, that the spring and government of his actions lay in his *skill*, his knowledge of how to go about his business, his participation in the concrete activity in relation to which his particular engagement is an abstraction. And though his participation in this concrete activity (the activity of being a cook or a scientist) may on some occasions appear to take the form of the application of a rule or the pursuit of a purpose, he would see at once that this rule or this purpose derived from the activity and not vice versa, and that the activity itself could never as a whole be reduced to the pursuit of an end or the application of a rule determined in advance of the activity.

But if his first observation is that, whatever the appearances to the contrary, no actual engagement can ever spring from or be governed by an independently premeditated end—the problems put down for solution or the project selected for pursuit—and that if this were all there was, his particular activity could never begin, his second observation will be more radical: he will observe that it is impossible even to project a purpose for activity in advance of the activity itself. Not only is his participation in the concrete activity which is involved in the solution of this sort of problem the source of his power to *solve* his particular problem and is the spring of the activity which goes to solve it, but also it is his participation in this concrete activity which presents the problem itself. Both the problems and the course of investigation leading up to their solution are already hidden in the activity, and are drawn out only by a process of abstraction. It is necessary to possess a knowledge of how to go about it (that is, to be already within an activity) before you embark upon a particular project, but it is equally necessary to have the same sort of knowledge in order to formulate a project. A particular action, in short, never begins in its particularity, but always in an idiom or a tradition of activity. A man who is not already a scientist cannot even formulate a scientific problem; what he will formulate is a problem which a connoisseur will at once recognize *not* to be a "scientific" problem because it is incapable of being considered in a "scientific" manner. Similarly, a connoisseur in historical inquiry will at once recognize that a question such as, Was the French Revolution a mistake? is a non-historical question.

We have come back, then, to the conclusions we reached earlier on, but in a more radical form. Activity springing from and governed by an independently premeditated purpose is impossible; the power of premeditating purpose, of formulating rules of conduct and standards of behaviour in advance of the conduct and activity itself is not available to us. To represent the spring and government of activity thus is to misrepresent it. To suggest that activity ought to be of this character and to try to force it into this pattern, is to corrupt it without being able to endow it with the desired character. To speak of such conduct as "rational" conduct is meaningless because it is not conduct at all but only an emaciated shadow of conduct. And it may be remarked also that if we agree it to be foolish to call conduct "rational" on account of its being wholly determined by an independently premeditated purpose, we must agree further that it should not be called "rational" in respect of it achieving its purpose, in respect (that is) of its *success*. The achievement of a desired result is not the mark of "rationality" in conduct because, as we have seen, it is only by a process of neglect and abstraction that conduct can be supposed to spring from the desire to achieve a specific result.

So far our conclusions appear to be mainly negative, but the process of exploration has I think disclosed what I take to be a more profitable view of "rationality" in conduct. If the "rationality" of conduct does not lie in something that has taken place in advance of the conduct—in the independent premeditation of a purpose or of a rule to be applied—if the "rationality" of conduct is not something contributed to the conduct from some source outside the idiom of the conduct concerned, it would appear that it must be a quality or a characteristic of the conduct itself.

All actual conduct, all specific activity springs up within an already existing idiom of activity. And by an "idiom of activity" I mean a knowledge of how to behave appropriately in the circumstances. Scientific activity is the exploration of the knowledge scientists have of how to go about asking and answering scientific questions; moral activity is the exploration of the knowledge we have of how to behave well. The questions and the problems in each case spring from the knowledge we have of how to solve them, spring from the activity itself. And we come to penetrate an idiom of activity in no other way than by practising the activity; for it is only in the practice of an activity that we can acquire the knowledge of how to practise it. . . .

If, then, it is agreed that the only significant way of using the word "rational" in relation to conduct is when we mean to indicate a quality or characteristic (and perhaps a desirable quality or characteristic) of the activity itself, then it would appear that the quality concerned is no mere "intelligence," but *faithfulness to the knowledge we have of how to conduct the specific activity we are engaged in.* "Rational" conduct is acting in such a way that the coherence of the idiom of activity to which the conduct belongs is preserved and possibly enhanced. This, of course, is something different from faithfulness to the principles or rules or purposes (if any have been discovered) of the activity; principles, rules and purposes are mere abridgments of the coherence of the activity, and we may easily be faithful to them while losing touch with the activity itself. And it must be observed that the faithfulness which characterizes "rationality" is not faithfulness to something fixed and finished (for knowledge of how to pursue an activity is always in motion); it is a faithfulness which itself contributes to (and not merely illustrates) the coherence of the activity. And the implications of this view are: first, that no conduct, no action or series of actions, can be "rational" or "irrational" out of relation to the idiom of activity to which they belong; secondly, that "rationality" is something that lies always *ahead,* and not *behind,* but yet it does not lie in the success with which a desired result or a premeditated end is achieved; and thirdly, that an activity as a whole (science, cooking, historical investigation, politics or poetry) cannot be said either to be "rational" or "irrational" unless we conceive all idioms of activity to be embraced in a single universe of activity. . . .

Now, some people in general sympathy with this view of the matter will nevertheless suspect that scientific activity is a special case and that what may be true there is not true elsewhere. Consequently, in conclusion, I must try to show the relevance of this view of things to what may be called the general moral or social conduct of human beings: for I do not admit that scientific activity is, in this respect, a special case. And if there is an appearance of dogmatism in what I have not to say, that is because I have already disclosed the arguments which have persuaded me.

Human conduct, in its most general character, is energy; it is not caused by energy, it does not express or display energy, it is energy. As energy, it may appear as appetite or desire—not, of course, as undifferentiated want, but as a certain mode of want. But here again, desire is not the cause of activity; desire is being active in a certain manner. A man, that is, does not first have "a desire" which then causes him to become active or which manifests itself in activity:

to say that he has a desire for something is only another way of saying that he is being active in a certain manner—e.g., the manner of activity involved in reaching out his hand to turn off the hot water, in making a request (such as, "Please pass me the Dictionary" or "Which is the way to the National Gallery?"), in looking up the times of the trains to Scotland, in contemplating with pleasure a meeting with a friend. These activities are not activities which presuppose and express or exhibit or give evidence of an antecedent state of desire; they are themselves the characteristic activities of desiring.

Now, activities of desiring are not separate and detached from one another, and the objects upon which desire is centred do not come and go at random or follow one another fortuitously. To say that a man has a character or a disposition is to say, among other things, that his activities of desiring compose a more or less coherent whole. A fresh activity of desiring appears nowhere except within an already organized whole; it does not come from the outside with the presentation of an object, but is a differentiation within an existing idiom of activity. And our knowledge of that idiom is, in the first place, our skill in managing the activity of desiring. We do not first have a desire and then set about discovering how to satisfy it; the objects of our desires are known to us in the activity of seeking them.

Social life—the life of human beings—is to know that some directions of the activity of desiring are approved and others disapproved, that some are right and others wrong. That there may be principles, or even rules, which may be seen to underlie this approval and disapproval, is not improbable; the searching intellect will always find principles. But this approval and disapproval does not spring from these principles or from a knowledge of them. They are merely abridgments, abstract definitions, of the coherence which approvals and disapprovals themselves exhibit. Nor may approval and disapproval be thought of as an additional activity, governed by an independently predetermined end to be achieved. An independently predetermined end has no more place in moral activity than it has in scientific. Approval and disapproval, that is, is not a separate activity which supervenes upon the activity of desiring, introducing norms of conduct from some external source; they are inseparable from the activity of desiring itself. Approval and disapproval are only an abstract and imperfect way of describing our unbroken knowledge of how to manage the activity of desiring, of how to behave. In short, moral judgment is not something we pronounce either before, or after, but in our moral activity.

Human activity, then, is always activity with a pattern; not a superimposed pattern, but a pattern inherent in the activity itself. Elements of this pattern occasionally stand out with a relatively firm outline; and we call these elements, customs, traditions, institutions, laws, etc. They are not, properly speaking, *expressions* of the coherence of activity, or expressions of approval and disapproval, or of our knowledge of how to behave—they *are* the coherence, they are the substance of our knowledge of how to behave. We do not first decide that certain behaviour is right or desirable and then express our approval of it in an institution; our knowledge of how to behave well is, at this point, the institution. And it is because we are not always as clear about this as we should be that we sometimes make the mistake of supposing that institutions (particularly political institutions) can be moved around from place to place as if they were pieces of machinery instead of idioms of conduct. . . .

We have considered briefly moral activity in health and in disease: our question now is, Where in all this is "rational" conduct? It is commonly believed (as we have seen) that there is something pre-eminently "rational" in conduct which springs (or appears to spring) from the independent premeditation of a purpose or a rule of behaviour, and that it is "rational" on account of the antecedent process of premeditation and on account of the success with which the purpose is achieved. And if we were to accept this view it would appear that moral conduct would be pre-eminently "rational" when it was being treated for a diseased condition. But even this is rather more than may properly be concluded; the most that may, in fact, be claimed is that conduct is specially "rational" when it is being cured of a disease and when the success of the treatment depends upon the illusion that the curative property of the substance injected derives from its being uncontaminated with the character of the diseased moral tradition—an illusion similar to that of the man who thinks he has found a new and independent way of living when he is really only spending his inherited capital. Of course, reflection upon the principles and ends in conduct may serve other than remedial purposes; it has a pedagogic and perhaps even a prophylactic use: the important point, however, is that it is never more than a device.

But we have seen fit to reject this whole view of the matter. This conduct may be "rational," but if so the marks of its "rationality" have been misconceived. Everywhere we come back to the conclusion that concrete activity is knowing how to act; and that if "rationality" is to be properly attributed to conduct, it must be a quality of the conduct itself. On this principle, practical human conduct may be counted "rational" in respect of its faithfulness to a knowledge of how to behave well, in respect of its faithfulness to its tradition of moral activity. No action is by itself "rational," or is "rational" on account of something that has gone on before; what makes it "rational" is its place in a flow of sympathy, a current of moral activity. And there is no ground here upon which we may exclude *a priori* any type of action. An impulsive action, a "spontaneous outburst," activity in obedience to a custom or to a rule, and an action which is preceded by a long reflective process may, alike, be "rational." But it is neither "rational" nor "irrational" on account of these or in default of these or of any similar characteristics. "Rationality" is the certificate we give to any conduct which can maintain a place in the flow of sympathy, the coherence of activity, which composes a way of living. This coherence is not the work of a faculty called "Reason" or of a faculty called "Sympathy," it springs neither from a separately inspired moral sense nor from an instrumental conscience. There is, in fact, no external harmonizing power, insulated from the elements enjoying and in search of harmony. What establishes harmony and detects disharmony, is the concrete mind, a mind composed wholly of activities in search of harmony and throughout implicated in every achieved level of harmony.

OAKESHOTT SELECTION

1. State as clearly as you can the model of choice and action *against* which Oakeshott is arguing. In this model, what is the role of "ends"? What is the role of "means"? What is supposed to be the connection between the two?

2. Since Oakeshott is obviously concerned with serious questions of politics and morality, why do you suppose he chooses silly examples like the problem of designing girls' bloomers? More generally, in what way does his *style* of writing relate to the content of what he is saying?

3. What is the difference being "knowing that" something and "knowing how to do" something? Could you know about a subject and still not know how to do anything related to it? Could you know about tennis and not know how to play tennis? Could you know about mathematics and not be able to do mathematics? Turn the question around: Could you know how to play tennis without knowing anything about tennis? Is the ability to give a coherent, rational account of what you are doing *necessary* for being able to do it? Is it sufficient? Is it helpful? Would we think a woman was a good doctor if she could fix a broken leg but couldn't explain why what she did had fixed it? Would we think she was a good doctor if she could explain how to fix a broken leg but couldn't actually fix it.

4. If Oakeshott is correct, should it be possible to program a computer to cook? To play chess? To paint a beautiful picture? To compose music? To do scientific research? Why? Are there any differences among these different activities that would make some of them more suited to being programmed into a computer than others?

5. According to Oakeshott, does it ever make sense to criticize a practice, an institution, a style of life, a society? Why?

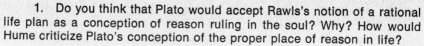

1. Do you think that Plato would accept Rawls's notion of a rational life plan as a conception of reason ruling in the soul? Why? How would Hume criticize Plato's conception of the proper place of reason in life?

2. Think of the *happiest* person you know. Is he or she "rational" in the sense used by any of the philosophers in this chapter? Now think of the *wisest* person you know. Are they the same person? If they aren't, why aren't they? If they are, why? What is the relationship between wisdom and happiness? What is your view? What is Plato's? Hume's? Rawls's? Oakeshott's?

3. Think of some modern moral debate that seems to set people at loggerheads, such as the debate over abortion or the debate over welfare. Do you think that what is at stake is a disagreement over facts? A disagreement over principles? Something else? What?

4. If both parties to a moral argument are prepared to be absolutely honest and reasonable, is there any reason why they shouldn't eventually come to an agreement? How would Foot handle this question? How would Hare answer it?

5. Are there some desires that are reasonable and others that are unreasonable? If not, why not? If so, give an example of an unreasonable desire and explain *why* it is unreasonable. How would Plato handle this question?

6. Is being *reasonable* the same thing as being *calm*? Is it ever unreasonable to be calm? Is it reasonable to lose your temper, to lose control of yourself? Why? When? Are you likely to be happier if you are reasonable? Is there a difference between being reasonable and having a soul (or personality) in which reason rules?

CHAPTER four

PERCEPTION AND OUR KNOWLEDGE OF OBJECTS

(**Focal Issues**)

1. How Do I Know About Physical Objects, and What Can I Know About Them?

2. What Is the Role of Sense-Experience in Knowledge?

3. Is Anything Absolutely Certain? What?

INTRODUCTION

The most profound revolutions take place in philosophy not when a new answer is given to an old question, but rather, when a new question is asked, or when an old question is asked in a new way. For the first two thousand years or so of Western philosophy the fundamental question of philosophy was the deceptively simple-looking question, "What is there?" This was not interpreted by philosophers as a request for a laundry list of things, but rather as a demand for a classification, in the broadest possible terms, of the sorts of things that could be said to exist.

For example, one answer—quite common in philosophical-religious writings—was that there is one uncreated thing (namely, God) and many created things (namely the universe and everything in it). Some philosophers argued that there is only one sort of thing, namely material objects in space; others, as we have seen, claimed that in addition to material things in space, there were also non-material things (souls or selves or minds); and some philosophers even argued that those nonmaterial minds were the only things that exist. Then, of course, there was a continuing debate about the status of really hard or odd cases. What should we say of the number seven, or the property of being round, or the relation "greater than," or the color red? Can any of these be said to exist? If so, in what sense of existence? And so forth. Since "What is there?" asks the question, "What can be said *to be*," and since anything that *is* is said by philosophers to *have being,* a search for the basic categories of existing things is a study of *being,* and the Greek name for the study of being is *ontology.* So we may sum up these remarks by saying that for the first two millennia of Western thought, ontology was the premier branch of philosophy.

All that changed in the early seventeenth century, and the person who did far and away the most to change it was a thinker whom you have already met in this book, the French mathematician, scientist, and philosopher René Descartes. What Descartes did was to ask an old question, but to ask it in a very new way, and with a force and insistence that were impossible for other philosophers to ignore. Instead of asking, *What is there?* Descartes asked *How do I know?*

Now, this was not a new question, of course. Since ancient

times, philosophers had analyzed the structure of knowledge, the several processes by which we come to know, the different categories or classes of truths that the human mind could know. Plato, for example, in the *Republic* and other dialogues, had mapped out a hierarchy of kinds of knowledge, descending from the highest and most perfect knowledge, a sort of direct intellectual intuition of the nature of Goodness itself, down through our rational knowledge of the propositions of mathematics, to the merest changeable opinions based on the fleeting evidences of the senses. But Descartes asked this old question in a quite new and troubling manner.

I shall try to determine whether any of the beliefs I now hold are "certain and indubitable," he said, *and I shall withhold my assent from any about which there can be the slightest doubt, however slender.* Now, that may not seem much like a revolution, but it was. In fact, it totally turned philosophy around for the next three centuries. Let us pause for a moment to examine the implications of this question in order to see whether we can discover exactly why it had so powerful an effect on subsequent philosophizing.

First of all, Descartes is obviously setting up a very high standard of knowledge. "Certain and indubitable," he said, and as you shall discover when you read the first selection in this chapter, he was prepared to accept the very smallest doubt as sufficient to throw out a belief. Descartes, like many philosophers before him, held up pure mathematics as the ideal of knowledge, and very little comes up to that standard.

But it was not the stringency of this standard of knowledge that set Descartes apart. Rather it was his refusal to take a single step without the absolute assurance that what he believed *was* genuinely knowledge. Previous philosophers had proceeded more or less confidently to an investigation of space, time, God, matter, living things, and so forth, only pausing to reflect on the act or process of knowing itself after they had arrived at a number of conclusions in which they reposed come confidence. Descartes, in effect, called that mode of operation into question. And by doing so, he deposed ontology, the study of being, from its place as the premier branch of philosophy. Since he refused to assent to any proposition until he was convinced that it was certain and indubitable, he was forced to put a study of *knowing* ahead of the study of *being.* Every statement about *what is* is a knowledge-claim. In effect, when I say, "Such and such exists," I am implicitly saying, "*I know that* such and such exists." Before I can proceed to a classification and analysis of the categories of *being,* therefore, I must undertake an investigation of the nature, the limits, the types, and the processes of *knowing.* Since philosophers have come to call the study of knowing by its Greek name, *epistemology,* we may summarize Descartes's revolution by saying that he made *epistemology* logically prior to *ontology.*

Descartes's quest for certainty had a second consequence that was even more revolutionary than his elevation of epistemology above ontology in the order of philosophical investigations. When previous philosophers wrote about the nature of being, they asked, "What can *we* (i.e., we humans, or we rational creatures, or we thinking beings) know about what is?" But when Descartes set out to find certainty he asked a subtly different question. "What can *I* (I, René Descartes, I, this conscious, thinking being) know about what is?" The result was to turn the philosophical enterprise inward, to make it individual, personal, subjective. As we have already seen in Chapter 1, Descartes eventually concluded that his own existence as a thinking thing was the first-known and best-known truth (*to him*), the foundation on which all other knowledge-claims would have to be erected.

How shall we proceed in our quest for certain and indubitable knowledge? It would be an endless, impossible task to consider each individual bit of supposed knowledge one at a time, subjecting it to whatever tests of certitude we could devise. There are potentially infinitely many claims that can be made about physical objects and their properties, about numbers and their relations, about God, about human beings, society, history. Clearly some shortcut must be found if we are to carry through the sort of epistemological investigation that Descartes has set us by his "method of doubt."

In the seventeenth and eighteenth centuries, virtually all of the great philosophers adopted the same strategy in tackling the Cartesian challenge, a strategy that can be analyzed, for the sake of convenience, into three parts.

First, since all of our knowledge, insofar as we have any, is knowledge that is known by the conscious, thinking self, let us focus our attention on the nature, the powers, and the limits of that self—any limits that are built into the cognitive powers of the self will be reflected in the limits of what can be known. If some particular knowledge-claim can be shown to be the sort of claim that the mind, given its nature, could not in principle know to be true, then we can reject it without any further individual examination.

Second, the mind formulates its knowledge-claims by means of propositions, which are composed of thoughts, or ideas, or representations that purport to stand for, or represent, things other than themselves. That is to say, when I make the judgment that two plus two is four, or that there are nine planets, or that lead is heavier than water, I use the ideas "two" and "planet" and "lead," etc. These are thoughts, or contents of the mind, that *stand for, refer to, or represent* such things as planets, lead, and the number two. Since the mind can formulate its knowledge-claims only by means of these representations (as I shall henceforth call them, following Immanuel Kant), we may be able to determine the sorts of claims that could possibly be made by analyzing the nature and types of representations that the mind has available to it. So the second part of the epistemological strategy of the philosophers of the seventeenth and eighteenth centuries was to classify the mind's representations and consider the implications of that classification.

Third, it occurred to a number of philosophers that they might learn a good deal about what could and could not be known by asking *where the mind got its representations from.* Perhaps an analysis of the sources of our representations would reveal limitations on what we could and could not possibly know. For example, suppose some of our knowledge-claims made use of a notion of the infinite. Suppose also that there was no way in which the mind could possibly obtain a notion of the infinite, inasmuch as all its natural sources of representations yielded only representations of finite things. In that case, we would have to conclude that all knowledge-claims purporting to use the notion of the infinite were total confusions. That would wipe out all our beliefs about God, and a good deal of mathematics as well!

To summarize: the three-part strategy is first, to examine the mind itself, second, to analyze the types of representations available to the mind, and third, to determine the sources of those representations in order to see whether their origins tell us anything about what can and cannot be known by means of them.

According to philosophers then and now, the mind has two great sources of representations. Either it obtains them from the operations of *reason* or else it derives them from the impact of the world upon our *senses.* Reason and Sensation yield all of the mind's cognitively significant contents (leaving to one side such internal feelings as pleasure and pain). At the risk of reducing several centuries of philosophy to a simple-minded scheme, we may say—in *very* simplified terms—that the epistemologists of the seventeenth, eighteenth, nineteenth, and even twentieth centuries defended one of three positions on the origins of the mind's representations. Some philosophers, such as John Locke, George Berkeley, and David Hume, claimed that all of the mind's representations came ultimately from sensation. Those representations that seemed on first inspection not to come from sensation turned out, after some analysis, to be either compounds of sensations, or copies of sensations, or perhaps (this is a bit trickier) ways the mind had of manipulating its sensations. Some philosophers, such as Leibniz and, to a certain extent Descartes as well, said that the mind had two sources of representations—reason and sensation—but that *only reason yielded representations on which genuinely reliable knowledge could be based.* The greatest of the eighteenth-century epistemologists, Immanuel Kant, argued against both the "empiricists" and the "rationalists" (as they were called). He held that *both the products of sensation and the products of reason were required for genuine knowledge.*

In this way, epistemology confronted two major questions. First, what role, if any, does sensation play in our knowledge of the world, of human affairs, of mathematics and logic, of God? And second, what role, if any, does reason play in these various realms of knowledge. Underlying these two questions, and complicatedly intertwined with them, were several other more fundamental questions.

is knowledge possible at all? What are the limits to human knowledge, and in what way can we read off those limits from an examination of the limitations of sensation and reason? What is the role of the mind itself in knowledge? Is it merely the passive recipient of information coming to it through its senses, or does it play an active role of some sort, constructing or synthesizing or organizing the data of the senses? Does knowledge come from a correct interpretation of the data of the senses, or does it perhaps come only from transcending the senses entirely and rising to a realm of pure nonsensory reason?

An adequate account of the debates over these questions would be nothing less than a history of the last three and a half centuries of Western philosophy. In this chapter we shall focus on one subgroup of epistemological issues, all growing out of the question: What is the role of sensation in knowledge? In order to narrow things down usefully, we shall concentrate almost entirely on the empiricist tradition in epistemology. That is to say, we shall be looking at the theories of philosophers who have held that the senses are the ultimate source of our knowledge of the physical world.

In order to set the stage for the debates that follow, let us consider one very perplexing puzzle about sensation and knowledge. Although none of the authors represented in this chapter offers adequate solutions to the puzzle, turning it over in your mind may help you to prepare yourself for their arguments.

The puzzle consists of the fact that two perfectly well-known, familiar, absolutely obvious facts of our daily experience are flatly contradictory to one another. Each one seems clearly true, and yet it is equally clear that they cannot both be true! Let me assure you that this is not a trick puzzle. It is a real philosophical problem, to which there is no easy answer.

The first fact is that when I open my eyes and look around, what I see are the various objects in my room, or on my front lawn, or wherever I happen to be. Right now, I am writing these words at a typewriter, and what I see (since I type with two fingers and must look at the keyboard) are the typewriter keys, my two hands, the paper, and—out of the corners of my eyes—the table on which the typewriter stands, etc. I see those objects. I definitely do not see pictures of them, copies of them, fragmentary sensory bits and pieces of them, surfaces of them, or what have you. Perhaps in a drug-induced state I might see such odd things, but in my present normally awake, alert condition, I see the objects themselves. Anyone who thinks he *isn't* seeing ordinary objects is a candidate for psychiatric treatment. What is more, I see those objects directly, immediately, just as they are and right now when they are that way. Any epistemology worth the name is going to have to explain human knowledge in a way that affirms these obvious, indubitable facts.

The second equally certain although slightly less familiar fact is that I *see* the typewriter keys, my hands, and the paper by means of a quite complicated process whereby light bounces off the objects, flows through my pupils into my eyes, and impacts on the retinas, where photo-chemical reactions are triggered that produce electrical impulses along my optic nerves resulting in a certan brain-state that is somehow causally related to the state of consciousness that I call "seeing my fingers" etc. The details of this process may be more familiar to neurophysiologists than to laymen, but the general fact of the physiological processes of perception is as indubitable as anything could be. We can, to some extent, step into the processes midway by directly stimulating portions of the optic nerve or the brain, at which time the subject reports visual experiences exactly like those he or she would be seeing if ordinary vision were taking place. Rather more easily we can interrupt the process of sensation, by cutting the optic nerve, or, in the case of tactile perception (touch), by anaesthesia. Anyone who has had Novocain at the dentist is aware of this latter possibility.

So, it is obviously true that what I see or touch is the object itself, immediately, directly, and fully as it is; and it is also obviously true that what I immediately sense is merely an end product of a long causal chain that may or may not have started with a typewriter, some fingers, or a piece of paper.

It would seem that these two "obvious" facts are mutually exclusive. Either I *see* the typewriter, or I *see* some visual image produced in my mind by a chain of events that, at one point, involved the typewriter. Either I *feel* the keys under my fingers, or else I *feel* certain spatially deployed sensations of pressure generated in my consciousness by a chain of causes possibly involving the typewriter keys, my fingers, the nerves in my fingers and arms, etc. But these sets of statements cannot both be true.

The problem gets even more complicated! Common sense tells me that sometimes I can be sure that I am right about what I am seeing and touching, while at other times I cannot be sure or I may be wrong. But if the first "fact" is true—if I see and touch objects immediately and directly—then it is hard to understand how I could ever be mistaken; whereas, if the second "fact" is true—if I never see and touch objects directly or immediately—then it is hard to understand how I could ever be sure I wasn't mistaken.

So, here is the puzzle: we have two facts that are both obviously true and yet are incompatible with one another; and no matter which one we seize on, we cannot give a coherent account of our knowledge of physical objects. In the five selections contained in this chapter, you will find *some* help with sorting out this puzzle, but not enough! Some of the job you must do for yourself.

(SELECTION 1)

RENÉ DESCARTES

What Can I Know With Certainty?

Modern philosophy can properly be said to begin with this passage from Descartes' *Meditations.* Much of the most sophisticated epistemological investigation, up to the present day, is aimed directly at laying to rest the skeptical doubts raised by Descartes in these few pages. Notice that Descartes starts with those of our beliefs that rest on the evidences of the senses, and then moves on to mathematical truths and other general propositions not immediately derived from sensation.

As Descartes indicates, the point of these strange hypotheses (such as the notion that I might always be dreaming!) is merely to show that it is logically *possible* that my beliefs be wrong, not that they are likely to be wrong. Why, we might ask, ought we to take Descartes seriously if he is dealing in the barest logical possibilities? After all, I do not hesitate to ride an elevator simply because there is a minute possibility that it may fail; I do not shrink from shaking hands with my friend merely because it is logically possible that he might turn into an alligator. Why should a hypothesis as fanciful as the universal dream or the deceiving demon lead me, even theoretically, to set aside my firmest and best-grounded beliefs?

One way to answer this question is to reflect a bit on what we mean by

"firm" or "well-grounded," when we talk about our beliefs concerning mathematics, the world, God, or ourselves. When I say that my belief in the existence of the continent of Africa is *well-grounded,* I mean that it rests on other beliefs that are in turn sound. For example, it rests on the belief that travelers' reports are reliable, that satellite cameras really work in the way I think they do (and that there really *are* earth-orbiting satellites), and so forth. Now, if each of these beliefs in turn must be grounded in yet other beliefs, which in their turn require further grounding, then it would seem that *either* I must find some rock-solid beliefs that do not need any external support, *or else* my entire system of beliefs is floating in mid-air, totally lacking in ultimate justification!

A second point about the passage before us: There is a very important difference between knowledge-claims that assert or imply the *existence* of something external to the mind and its states of consciousness, and knowledge-claims that merely assert relationships among those states of consciousness. When I judge that the interior angles of a triangle equal two right angles, I am not committed to the claim that there actually are any triangular objects in the world. Indeed, I am not even committed to the claim that there are objects of any sort. But when I assert that there are nine planets around the sun, I am making existence-claims about entities (the sun, planets) independent of and external to my mind. As we shall see throughout this chapter, it is existence-assertions that pose the most vexing philosophical problems for epistemologists.

Of the things which may be brought within the sphere of the doubtful.

It is now some years since I detected how many were the false beliefs that I had from my earliest youth admitted as true, and how doubtful was everything I had since constructed on this basis; and from that time I was convinced that I must once for all seriously undertake to rid myself of all the opinions which I had formerly accepted, and commence to build anew from the foundation, if I wanted to establish any firm and permanent structure in the sciences. But as this enterprise appeared to be a very great one, I waited until I had attained an age so mature that I could not hope that at any later date I should be better fitted to execute my design. This reason caused me to delay so long that I should feel that I was doing wrong were I to occupy in deliberation the time that yet remains to me for action. To-day, then, since very opportunely for the plan I have in view I have delivered my mind from every care [and am happily agitated by no passions] and since I have procured for myself an assured leisure in a peaceable retirement, I shall at last seriously and freely address myself to the general upheaval of all my former opinions.

Now for this object it is not necessary that I should show that all of these are false—I shall perhaps never arrive at this end. But inasmuch as reason already persuades me that I ought no less carefully to withhold my assent from matters which are not entirely certain and indubitable than from those which appear to me manifestly to be false, if I am able to find in each one some reason to doubt, this will suffice to justify my rejecting the whole. And for that end it will not be requisite that I should examine each in particular, which would be an endless undertaking; for owing to the fact that the destruction of the foundations of necessity brings with it the downfall of the rest of the edifice, I shall only in the first place attack those principles upon which all my former opinions rested.

All that up to the present time I have accepted as most true and certain I have learned either from the senses or through the senses; but it is sometimes proved to me that these senses are deceptive, and

From *Meditations on First Philosophy* by René Descartes. First published in 1641. (trans. by E. S. Haldane and G. R. T. Ross, copyright Cambridge University Press, Cambridge, England, 1911)

it is wiser not to trust entirely to any thing by which we have once been deceived.

But it may be that although the senses sometimes deceive us concerning things which are hardly perceptible, or very far away, there are yet many others to be met with as to which we cannot reasonably have any doubt, although we recognise them by their means. For example, there is the fact that I am here, seated by the fire, attired in a dressing gown, having this paper in my hands and other similar matters. And how could I deny that these hands and this body are mine, were it not perhaps that I compare myself to certain persons, devoid of sense, whose cerebella are so troubled and clouded by the violent vapours of black bile, that they constantly assure us that they think they are kings when they are really quite poor, or that they are clothed in purple when they are really without covering, or who imagine that they have an earthenware head or are nothing but pumpkins or are made of glass. But they are mad, and I should not be any the less insane were I to follow examples so extravagant.

At the same time I must remember that I am a man, and that consequently I am in the habit of sleeping, and in my dreams representing to myself the same things or sometimes even less probable things, than do those who are insane in their waking moments. How often has it happened to me that in the night I dreamt that I found myself in this particular place, that I was dressed and seated near the fire, whilst in reality I was lying undressed in bed! At this moment it does indeed seem to me that it is with eyes awake that I am looking at this paper; that this head which I move is not asleep, that it is deliberately and of set purpose that I extend my hand and perceive it; what happens in sleep does not appear so clear nor so distinct as does all this. But in thinking over this I remind myself that on many occasions I have in sleep been deceived by similar illusions, and in dwelling carefully on this reflection I see so manifestly that there are no certain indications by which we may clearly distinguish wakefulness from sleep that I am lost in astonishment. And my astonishment is such that it is almost capable of persuading me that I now dream.

Now let us assume that we are asleep and that all these particulars, e.g., that we open our eyes, shake our head, extend our hands, and so on, are but false delusions; and let us reflect that possibly neither our hands nor our whole body are such as they appear to us to be. At the same time we must at least confess that the things which are represented to us in sleep are like painted representations which can only have been formed as the counterparts of something real and true, and that in this way those general things at least, i.e., eyes, a head, hands, and a whole body, are not imaginary things, but things really existent. For, as a matter of fact, painters, even when they study with the greatest skill to represent sirens and satyrs by forms the most strange and extraordinary, cannot give them natures which are entirely new, but merely make a certain medley of the members of different animals; or if their imagination is extravagant enough to invent something so novel that nothing similar has ever before been seen, and that then their work represents a thing purely fictitious and absolutely false, it is certain all the same that the colours of which this is composed are necessarily real. And for the same reason, although these general things, to wit, [a body], eyes, a head, hands, and such like, may be imaginary, we are bound at the same time to confess that there are at least some other objects yet more simple and more universal, which are real and true; and of these just in the same way as with certain real colours, all these images of things which dwell in our thoughts, whether true and real or false and fantastic, are formed.

To such a class of things pertains corporeal nature in general, and its extension, the figure of extended things, their quantity or magnitude and number, as also the place in which they are, the time which measures their duration, and so on.

That is possibly why our reasoning is not unjust when we conclude from this that Physics, Astronomy, Medicine and all other sciences which have as their end the consideration of composite things, are very dubious and uncertain; but that Arithmetic, Geometry and other sciences of that kind which only treat of things that are very simple and very general, without taking great trouble to ascertain whether they are actually existent or not, contain some measure of certainty and an element of the indubitable. For whether I am awake or asleep, two and three together always form five, and the square can never have more than four sides, and it does not seem possible that truths so clear and apparent can be suspected of any falsity [or uncertainty].

Nevertheless I have long had fixed in my mind the belief that an all-powerful God existed by whom I have been created such as I am. But how do I know that He has not brought it to pass that there is no earth, no heaven, no extended body, no magnitude, no place, and that nevertheless [I possess the perceptions of all these things and that] they seem to me to exist just exactly as I now see them? And, besides, as I sometimes imagine that others deceive themselves in the things which they think they know best, how do I know that I am not deceived every time that I add two and three, or count the sides of a square, or judge of things yet simpler, if anything simpler can be imagined? But possibly God has not desired that I should be thus deceived, for He is said to be supremely good. If, however, it is contrary to His goodness to have made me such that I constantly deceive myself, it would also appear to be contrary to His goodness to permit me to be sometimes deceived, and nevertheless I cannot doubt that He does permit this.

There may indeed be those who would prefer to deny the existence of a God so powerful, rather than believe that all other things are uncertain. But let us not oppose them for the present, and grant that all that is here said of a God is a fable; nevertheless in whatever way they suppose that I have arrived at the state of being that I have reached—whether they attribute it to fate or to accident, or make out that it is by a continual succession of antecedents, or by some other method—since to err and deceive oneself is a defect, it is clear that the greater will be the probability of my being so imperfect as to deceive myself ever, as is the Author to whom they assign my origin the less powerful. To these reasons I have certainly nothing to reply, but at the end I feel constrained to confess that there is nothing in all that I formerly believed to be true, of which I cannot in some measure doubt, and that not merely through want of thought or through levity, but for reasons which are very powerful and maturely considered; so that henceforth I ought not the less carefully to refrain from giving credence to these opinions than to that which is manifestly false, if I desire to arrive at any certainty [in the sciences].

But it is not sufficient to have made these remarks, we must also be careful to keep them in mind. For these ancient and commonly held opinions still revert frequently to my mind, long and familiar custom having given them the right to occupy my mind against my inclination and rendered them almost masters of my belief; nor will I ever lose the habit of deferring to them or of placing my confidence in them, so long as I consider them as they really are, i.e., opinions in some measure doubtful, as I have just shown, and at the same time highly probable, so that there is much more reason to believe in than to deny them. That is why I consider that I shall not be acting amiss, if, taking of set purpose a contrary belief, I allow myself to be deceived, and for a certain time pretend that all these opinions are entirely false and imaginary, until at last, having thus balanced my former prejudices with my latter [so that they cannot divert my opinions more to one side than to the other], my judgment will no longer be dominated by bad usage or turned away from the right knowledge of the truth. For I am assured that there can be neither period nor error in this course, and that I cannot at present yield too much to distrust, since I am not considering the question of action, but only of knowledge.

I shall then suppose, not that God who is supremely good and the fountain of truth, but some evil genius not less powerful than deceitful, has employed his whole energies in deceiving me; I shall consider that the heavens, the earth, colours, figures, sound, and all other external things are nought but the illusions and dreams of which this genius has availed himself in order to lay traps for my credulity; I shall consider myself as having no hands, no eyes, no flesh, no blood, nor any senses, yet falsely believing myself to possess all these things; I shall remain obstinately attached to this idea, and if by this means it is not in my power to arrive at the knowledge of any truth, I may at least do what is in my power [i.e., suspend my judgment], and with firm purpose avoid giving credence to any false thing, or being imposed upon by this arch deceiver, however powerful and deceptive he may be. But this task is a laborious one, and insensibly a certain lassitude leads me into the course of my ordinary life. And just as a captive who in sleep enjoys an imaginary liberty, when he begins to suspect that his liberty is but a dream, fears to awaken, and conspires with these agreeable illusions that the deception may be prolonged, so insensibly of my own accord I fall back into my former opinions, and I dread awakening from this slumber, lest the laborious wakefulness which would follow the tranquillity of this repose should have to be spent not in daylight, but in the excessive darkness of the difficulties which have just been discussed.

DESCARTES SELECTION

1. Try to state as clearly as you can what Descartes means by "certain and indubitable" beliefs. Do you have any beliefs that you are convinced are certain and indubitable? What are they? How would Descartes throw doubt on them?

2. Can you *really* doubt that you have a body, or that there are other people in the world? What would it be like to doubt such things? Does Descartes really doubt them? If you think he doesn't, then why do you suppose he raises the question of certainty in the way he does?

3. Have you ever had a dream that seemed so realistic it fooled you? Could you be dreaming now? (If you say yes, then who do you suppose is asking you this question?!)

4. What is the difference between the beliefs that are called into question by the dream argument, and the beliefs that are called into question by the evil demon argument? Do logical inferences make existence-claims? Is that a significant consideration for Descartes?

5. Is it logically possible to doubt all of our beliefs at the same time, or do we need to assume the truth of some of them in order to call the others into question? What empirical beliefs must Descartes assume in order to argue that all his experience might be a dream?

(SELECTION 2)

GEORGE BERKELEY

To Be Is to Be Perceived

George Berkeley is one of the most important exponents of the position that has come to be known as *empiricism.* All the contents of the mind, he argues, come from sensation, and the limits of sensation are, therefore, the limits of human knowledge. Many previous philosophers had sought to understand the nature of the objects of knowledge by distinguishing between an unchanging, underlying base, or substratum, on the one hand, and the endlessly changing properties of that substratum, on the other. The senses might reveal now this, now that property of the substratum, but only reason could form the concept of the substratum and grasp its true nature. Following the ancient Greek philosopher Aristotle, philosophers used the term "substance" to refer to the objectively real, unchanging base or substratum in which the various sensory properties were said to "inhere." We have already encountered exactly this sort of analysis in Chapter 1, where Descartes distinguished between the changeable sensory properties of his piece of wax and the real, unaltered substance, known by the faculty of reason.

In these dialogues between two characters, Hylas (which means *substance* in Greek) and Philonous, Berkeley calls into question not only the doctrine of substance, but also the commonplace notion that objects of the senses exist, and can be known to exist, independently of being sensed. We see here all of the characteristic strategies of the new epistemology. First of all, Berkeley focuses attention on what we can *know,* rather than directly on what *is.* His technique for doing this is to remind us of a number of familiar facts about sensation, especially the ways in which we may be misled by sensation, in order to show that what we may have thought to be well-grounded are actually rather shaky beliefs.

Berkeley also keeps directly before our attention the self, the knowing subject, the conscious "I" in whose awareness the various sensations occur. Like Descartes (though carrying the argument a good deal further), Berkeley forces me to consider what limits are set to my knowledge by the obvious but easily forgettable fact that it is always *I* who form and assert the judgments in which my knowledge-claims are expressed.

Several philosophers before Berkeley, including Descartes and the influential Englishman John Locke, had drawn a sharp distinction between the supposedly objective, invariable, knowledge-yielding properties, such as size, shape, weight, solidity, and motion—

which they called "primary qualities"— and the unreliable, variable, subjectively influenced properties, such as color, taste, and smell, which they called "secondary properties." Their claim was that our awareness of primary properties could lead to genuine scientific knowledge, whereas our awareness of secondary properties, since it was affected by subjective factors such as the condition of the sense organs, could not. One of Berkeley's primary purposes in this passage is to show that the distinction between primary and secondary properties is philosophically unsound.

Hyl. You were represented in last night's convention, as one who maintained the most extravagant opinion that ever entered into the mind of man, to wit, that there is no such thing as *material substance* in the world.

Phil. That there is no such thing as what Philosophers call *material substance,* I am seriously persuaded: but, if I were made to see anything absurd or sceptical in this, I should then have the same reason to renounce this that I imagine I have now to reject the contrary opinion.

Hyl. What! can anything be more fantastical, more repugnant to common sense, or a more manifest piece of Scepticism, than to believe there is no such thing as *matter?*

Phil. Softly, good *Hylas.* What if it should prove, that you, who hold there is, are, by virtue of that opinion, a greater sceptic, and maintain more paradoxes and repugnances to common sense, than I who believe no such thing?

Hyl. You may as soon persuade me, the part is greater than the whole, as that, in order to avoid absurdity and Scepticism, I should ever be obliged to give up my opinion in this point.

Phil. Well then, are you content to admit that opinion for true, which, upon examination, shall appear most agreeable to common sense, and remote from Scepticism?

Hyl. With all my heart. Since you are for raising disputes about the plainest in nature, I am content for once to hear what you have to say.

Phil. Pray, *Hylas,* what do you mean by a *sceptic?* . . .

Hyl. . . . A sceptic [is] one . . . who denies the reality and truth of things.

Phil. What things? Do you mean the principles and theorems of sciences? But these you know are universal intellectual notions, and consequently independent of Matter; the denial therefore of this doth not imply the denying them.

Hyl. I grant it. But are there no other things? What think you

From *Three Dialogues Between Hylas and Philonous* by George Berkeley. First published in 1713.

of distrusting the senses, of denying the real existence of sensible things, or pretending to know nothing of them. Is not this sufficient to denominate a man a *sceptic?*

Phil. Shall we therefore examine which of us it is that denies the reality of sensible things, or professes the greatest ignorance of them; since, if I take you rightly, he is to be esteemed the greatest *sceptic?*

Hyl. That is what I desire.

Phil. What mean you by Sensible Things?

Hyl. Those things which are perceived by the senses. Can you imagine that I mean anything else?

Phil. Pardon me, *Hylas,* if I am desirous clearly to apprehend your notions, since this may much shorten our inquiry. Suffer me then to ask you this farther question. Are those things only perceived by the senses which are perceived immediately? Or, may those things properly be said to be *sensible* which are perceived mediately, or not without the intervention of others?

Hyl. I do not sufficiently understand you.

Phil. In reading a book, what I immediately perceive are the letters, but mediately, or by means of these, are suggested to my mind the notions of God, virtue, truth, &c. Now, that the letters are truly sensible things, or perceived by sense, there is no doubt: but I would know whether you take the things suggested by them to be so too.

Hyl. No, certainly; it were absurd to think *God* or *virtue* sensible things, though they may be signified and suggested to the mind by sensible marks, with which they have an arbitrary connexion.

Phil. It seems then, that by *sensible things* you mean those only which can be perceived *immediately* by sense?

Hyl. Right.

Phil. Doth it not follow from this, that though I see one part of the sky red, and another blue, and that my reason doth thence evidently conclude there must be some cause of that diversity of colours, yet that cause cannot be said to be a sensible thing, or perceived by the sense of seeing?

Hyl. It doth. . . . By *sensible things* I mean those only which are perceived by sense, and . . . in truth the senses perceive nothing which they do not perceive immediately: for they make no inferences. The deducing therefore of causes or occasions from effects and appearances, which alone are perceived by sense, entirely relates to reason.

Phil. This point then is agreed between us—that *sensible things are those only which are immediately perceived by sense.* You will farther inform me, whether we immediately perceive by sight anything beside light, and colours, and figures; or by hearing, anything but sounds; by the palate, anything beside tastes; by the smell, beside odours; or by the touch, more than tangible qualities.

Hyl. We do not.

Phil. It seems, therefore, that if you take away all sensible qualities, there remains nothing sensible?

Hyl. I grant it.

Phil. Sensible things therefore are nothing else but so many sensible qualities, or combinations of sensible qualities?

Hyl. Nothing else.

Phil. Heat then is a sensible thing?

Hyl. Certainly.

Phil. Doth the reality of sensible things consist in being perceived? or, is it something distinct from their being perceived, and that bears no relation to the mind?

Hyl. To *exist* is one thing, and to be *perceived* is another.

Phil. I speak with regard to sensible things only: and of these I ask, whether by their real existence you mean a subsistence exterior to the mind, and distinct from their being perceived?

Hyl. I mean a real absolute being, distinct from, and without any relation to their being perceived.

Phil. Heat therefore, if it be allowed a real being, must exist without the mind?

Hyl. It must.

Phil. Tell me, *Hylas*, is this real existence equally compatible to all degrees of heat, which we perceive; or is there any reason why we should attribute it to some, and deny it to others? and if there be, pray let me know that reason.

Hyl. Whatever degree of heat we perceive by sense, we may be sure the same exists in the object that occasions it.

Phil. What! the greatest as well as the least?

Hyl. I tell you, the reason is plainly the same in respect of both: they are both perceived by sense; nay, the greater degree of heat is more sensibly perceived; and consequently, if there is any difference, we are more certain of its real existence than we can be of the reality of a lesser degree.

Phil. But is not the most vehement and intense degree of heat a very great pain?

Hyl. No one can deny it.

Phil. And is any unperceiving thing capable of pain or pleasure?

Hyl. No certainly.

Phil. Is your material substance a senseless being, or a being endowed with sense and perception?

Hyl. It is senseless without doubt.

Phil. It cannot therefore be the subject of pain?

Hyl. By no means.

Phil. Nor consequently of the greatest heat perceived by sense, since you acknowledge this to be no small pain?

Hyl. I grant it.

Phil. What shall we say then of your external object; is it a material Substance, or no?

Hyl. It is a material substance with the sensible qualities inhering in it.

Phil. How then can a great heat exist in it, since you own it cannot in a material substance? I desire you would clear this point.

Hyl. Hold, *Philonous,* I fear I was out in yielding intense heat to be a pain. It should seem rather, that pain is something distinct from heat, and the consequence or effect of it.

Phil. Upon putting your hand near the fire, do you perceive one simple uniform sensation, or two distinct sensations?

Hyl. But one simple sensation.

Phil. Is not the heat immediately perceived?

Hyl. It is.

Phil. And the pain?

Hyl. True.

Phil. Seeing therefore they are both immediately perceived at the same time, and the fire affects you only with one simple, or uncompounded idea, it follows that this same simple idea is both the intense heat immediately perceived, and the pain; and, consequently, that the intense heat immediately perceived, is nothing distinct from a particular sort of pain.

Hyl. It seems so.

Phil. Again, try in your thoughts, *Hylas,* if you can conceive a vehement sensation to be without pain or pleasure.

Hyl. I cannot.

Phil. Or can you frame to yourself an idea of sensible pain or pleasure, in general, abstracted from every particular idea of heat, cold, tastes, smells? &c.

Hyl. I do not find that I can.

Phil. Doth it not therefore follow, that sensible pain is nothing distinct from those sensations or ideas—in an intense degree?

Hyl. It is undeniable; and, to speak the truth, I begin to suspect a very great heat cannot exist but in a mind perceiving it.

Phil. What! are you then in that *sceptical* state of suspense, between affirming and denying?

Hyl. I think I may be positive in the point. A very violent and painful heat cannot exist without the mind.

Phil. It hath not therefore, according to you, any real being?

Hyl. I own it.

Phil. Is it therefore certain, that there is no body in nature really hot?

Hyl. I have not denied there is any real heat in bodies. I only say, there is no such thing as an intense real heat.

Phil. But, did you not say before that all degrees of heat were equally real; or, if there was any difference, that the greater were more undoubtedly real than the lesser?

Hyl. True: but it was because I did not then consider the ground there is for distinguishing between them, which I now plainly see. And it is this:—because intense heat is nothing else but a particular kind of painful sensation; and pain cannot exist but in a perceiving being; it follows that no intense heat can really exist in an unperceiving corporeal substance. But this is no reason why we should deny heat in an inferior degree to exist in such a substance.

Phil. But how shall we be able to discern those degrees of heat which exist only in the mind from those which exist without it?

Hyl. That is no difficult matter. You know the least pain cannot exist unperceived; whatever, therefore, degree of heat is a pain exists only in the mind. But, as for all other degrees of heat, nothing obliges us to think the same of them.

Phil. I think you granted before that no unperceiving being was capable of pleasure, any more than of pain.

Hyl. I did.

Phil. And is not warmth, or a more gentle degree of heat than what causes uneasiness, a pleasure?

Hyl. What then?

Phil. Consequently, it cannot exist without the mind in an unperceiving substance, or body.

Hyl. So it seems.

Phil. Since, therefore, as well those degrees of heat that are not painful, as those that are, can exist only in a thinking substance; may we not conclude that external bodies are absolutely incapable of any degree of heat whatsoever?

Hyl. On second thoughts, I do not think it so evident that warmth is a pleasure as that a great degree of heat is a pain.

Phil. I do not pretend that warmth is as great a pleasure as heat is a pain. But, if you grant it to be even a small pleasure, it serves to make good my conclusion.

Hyl. I could rather call it an *indolence*. It seems to be nothing more than a privation of both pain and pleasure. And that such a quality or state as this may agree to an unthinking substance, I hope you will not deny.

Phil. If you are resolved to maintain that warmth, or a gentle degree of heat, is no pleasure, I know not how to convince you otherwise, than by appealing to your own sense. But what think you of cold?

Hyl. The same that I do of heat. An intense degree of cold is a pain; for to feel a very great cold, is to perceive a great uneasiness: it cannot therefore exist without the mind; but a lesser degree of cold may, as well as a lesser degree of heat.

Phil. Those bodies, therefore, upon whose application to our own, we perceive a moderate degree of heat, must be concluded to have a moderate degree of heat or warmth in them; and those, upon whose application we feel a like degree of cold, must be thought to have cold in them.

Hyl. They must.

Phil. Can any doctrine be true that necessarily leads a man into an absurdity?

Hyl. Without doubt it cannot.

Phil. Is it not an absurdity to think that the same thing should be at the same time both cold and warm?

Hyl. It is.

Phil. Suppose now one of your hands hot, and the other cold, and that they are both at once put into the same vessel of water, in an intermediate state; will not the water seem cold to one hand, and warm to the other?

Hyl. It will.

Phil. Ought we not therefore, by your principles, to conclude it is really both cold and warm at the same time, that is, according to your own concession, to believe an absurdity?

Hyl. I confess it seems so.

Phil. Consequently, the principles themselves are false, since you have granted that no true principle leads to an absurdity.

Hyl. But, after all, can anything be more absurd than to say, *there is no heat in the fire?*

Phil. To make the point still clearer; tell me whether, in two cases exactly alike, we ought not to make the same judgment?

Hyl. We ought.

Phil. When a pin pricks your finger, doth it not rend and divide the fibres of your flesh?

Hyl. It doth.

Phil. And when a coal burns your finger, doth it any more?

Hyl. It doth not.

Phil. Since, therefore, you neither judge the sensation itself occasioned by the pin, nor anything like it to be in the pin; you should not, conformably to what you have now granted, judge the sensation occasioned by the fire, or anything like it, to be in the fire.

Hyl. Well, since it must be so, I am content to yield this point, and acknowledge that heat and cold are only sensations existing in our minds. But there still remain qualities enough to secure the reality of external things.

Phil. But what will you say, *Hylas,* if it shall appear that the case is the same with regard to all other sensible qualities, and that they can no more be supposed to exist without the mind, than heat and cold?

Hyl. Then indeed you will have done something to the purpose; but that is what I despair of seeing proved.

Phil. Let us examine them in order.

[*Philonous now leads Hylas through a consideration of each of the senses in turn, and arrives at the same conclusion in each case. Here is the discussion of color.*]

Phil. And I hope you will make no difficulty to acknowledge the same of *colours.*

Hyl. Pardon me: the case of colours is very different. Can anything be plainer than that we see them on the objects?

Phil. The objects you speak of are, I suppose, corporeal Substances existing without the mind?

Hyl. They are.

Phil. And have true and real colours inhering in them?

Hyl. Each visible object hath that colour which we see in it.

Phil. How! is there anything visible but what we perceive by sight?

Hyl. There is not.

Phil. And, do we perceive anything by sense which we do not perceive immediately?

Hyl. How often must I be obliged to repeat the same thing? I tell you, we do not.

Phil. Have patience, good *Hylas;* and tell me once more, whether there is anything immediately perceived by the senses, except sensible qualities. I know you asserted there was not; but I would now be informed, whether you still persist in the same opinion.

Hyl. I do.

Phil. Pray, is your corporeal substance either a sensible quality, or made up of sensible qualities?

Hyl. What a question that is! who ever thought it was?

Phil. My reason for asking was, because in saying, *each visible object hath that colour which we see in it,* you make visible objects to be corporeal substances; which implies either that corporeal substances are sensible qualities, or else that there is something beside sensible qualities perceived by sight: but, as this point was formerly agreed between us, and is still maintained by you, it is a clear consequence, that your corporeal substance is nothing distinct from sensible qualities.

Hyl. You may draw as many absurd consequences as you please, and endeavour to perplex the plainest things; but you shall never persuade me out of my senses. I clearly understand my own meaning.

Phil. I wish you would make me understand it too. But, since you are unwilling to have your notion of corporeal substance examined, I shall urge that point no farther. Only be pleased to let me know, whether the same colours which we see exist in external bodies, or some other.

Hyl. The very same.

Phil. What! are then the beautiful red and purple we see on yonder clouds really in them? Or do you imagine they have in themselves any other form than that of a dark mist or vapour?

Hyl. I must own, *Philonous,* those colours are not really in the clouds as they seem to be at this distance. They are only apparent colours.

Phil. Apparent call you them? how shall we distinguish these apparent colours from real?

Hyl. Very easily. Those are to be thought apparent which, appearing only at a distance, vanish upon a nearer approach.

Phil. And those, I suppose, are to be thought real which are discovered by the most near and exact survey.

Hyl. Right.

Phil. Is the nearest and exactest survey made by the help of a microscope, or by the naked eye?

Hyl. By a microscope, doubtless.

Phil. But a microscope often discovers colours in an object different from those perceived by the unassisted sight. And, in case we had microscopes magnifying to any assigned degree, it is certain that no object whatsoever, viewed through them, would appear in the same colour which it exhibits to the naked eye.

Hyl. And what will you conclude from all this? You cannot argue that there are really and naturally no colours on objects: because by artificial managements they may be altered, or made to vanish.

Phil. I think it may evidently be concluded from your own concessions, that all the colours we see with our naked eyes are only apparent as those on the clouds, since they vanish upon a more close and accurate inspection which is afforded us by a microscope. Then, as to what you say by way of prevention: I ask you whether the real and natural state of an object is better discovered by a very sharp and piercing sight, or by one which is less sharp?

Hyl. By the former without doubt.

Phil. Is it not plain from *Dioptrics* that microscopes make the sight more penetrating, and represent objects as they would appear to the eye in case it were naturally endowed with a most exquisite sharpness?

Hyl. It is.

Phil. Consequently the microscopical representation is to be thought that which best sets forth the real nature of the thing, or what it is in itself. The colours, therefore, by it perceived are more genuine and real than those perceived otherwise.

Hyl. I confess there is something in what you say.

Phil. Besides, it is not only possible but manifest, that there actually are animals whose eyes are by nature framed to perceive those things which by reason of their minuteness escape our sight. What think you of those inconceivably small animals perceived by glasses? must we suppose they are all stark blind? Or, in case they see, can it be imagined their sight hath not the same use in preserving their bodies from injuries, which appears in that of all other animals? And if it hath, is it not evident they must see particles less than their own bodies, which will present them with a far different view in each object from that which strikes our senses? Even our own eyes do not always represent objects to us after the same manner. In the *jaundice* every one knows that all things seem yellow. Is it not therefore highly probable those animals in whose eyes we discern a very different texture from that of ours, and whose bodies abound with different humours, do not see the same colours in every object that we do? From all which, should it not seem to follow that all colours are equally apparent, and that none of those which we perceive are really inherent in any outward object?

Hyl. It should.

Phil. The point will be past all doubt, if you consider that, in case colours were real properties or affections inherent in external bodies, they could admit of no alteration without some change wrought in the very bodies themselves: but, is it not evident from what hath been said that, upon the use of microscopes, upon a change happening in the humours of the eye, or a variation of distance, without any manner of real alteration in the thing itself, the colours of any object are either changed, or totally disappear? Nay, all other circumstances remaining the same, change but the situation of some objects, and they shall present different colours to the eye. The same thing happens upon viewing an object in various degrees of light. And what is more known than that the same bodies appear differently coloured by candle-light from what they do in the open day? Add to these the experiment of a prism which, separating the heterogeneous rays of light, alters the colour of any object, and will cause the whitest to appear of a deep blue or red to the naked eye. And now tell me whether you are still of opinion that every body hath its true real colour inhering in it; and, if you think it hath, I would fain know farther from you, what certain distance and position of the object, what peculiar texture and formation of the eye, what degree or kind of light is necessary for ascertaining that true colour, and distinguishing it from apparent ones.

Hyl. I own myself entirely satisfied, that they are all equally apparent, and that there is no such thing as colour really inhering in external bodies, but that it is altogether in the light. And what confirms me in this opinion is that in proportion to the light colours are still more or less vivid; and if there be no light, then are there no colours perceived. Besides, allowing there are colours on external objects, yet, how is it possible for us to perceive them? For no external body affects the mind, unless it acts first on our organs of sense. But the only action of bodies is motion; and motion cannot be communicated otherwise than by impulse. A distant object therefore cannot act on the eye, nor consequently make itself or its properties perceivable to the soul. Whence it plainly follows that it is immediately some contiguous substance, which, operating on the eye, occasions a perception of colours: and such is light.

Phil. How! is light then a substance?

Hyl. I tell you, *Philonous*, external light is nothing but a thin fluid substance, whose minute particles being agitated with a brisk motion, and in various manners reflected from the different surfaces of outward objects to the eyes, communicate different motions to the optic nerves; which, being propagated to the brain, cause therein various impressions; and these are attended with the sensations of red, blue, yellow, &c.

Phil. It seems then the light doth no more than shake the optic nerves.

Hyl. Nothing else.

Phil. And, consequent to each particular motion of the nerves, the mind is affected with a sensation, which is some particular colour.

Hyl. Right.

Phil. And these sensations have no existence without the mind.

Hyl. They have not.

Phil. How then do you affirm that colours are in the light; since by *light* you understand a corporeal substance external to the mind?

Hyl. Light and colours, as immediately perceived by us, I grant cannot exist without the mind. But, in themselves they are only the motions and configurations of certain insensible particles of matter.

Phil. Colours then, in the vulgar sense, or taken for the immediate objects of sight, cannot agree to any but a perceiving substance.

Hyl. That is what I say.

Phil. Well then, since you give up the point as to those sensible qualities which are alone thought colours by all mankind beside, you may hold what you please with regard to those invisible ones of the philosophers. It is not my business to dispute about them; only I would advise you to bethink yourself, whether, considering the inquiry we are upon, it be prudent for you to affirm—*the red and blue which we see are not real colours, but certain unknown motions and figures, which no man ever did or can see, are truly so.* Are not these shocking notions, and are not they subject to as many ridiculous inferences, as those you were obliged to renounce before in the case of sounds?

[*Having dealt with pleasure and pain—the so-called tertiary qualities—and taste, odor, sound, and color—the secondary qualities—Philonous now directs the same arguments to the case of the "primary qualities" of extension, figure, solidity, motion, and so forth. His reasoning is similar, and his conclusion the same.*]

Hyl. I wonder, Philonous, if what you say be true, why those philosophers who deny the Secondary Qualities any real existence, should yet attribute it to the Primary. If there is no difference between them, how can this be accounted for?

Phil. It is not my business to account for every opinion of the philosophers. But, among other reasons which may be assigned for this, it seems probable that pleasure and pain being rather annexed to the former than the latter may be one. Heat and cold, tastes and smells, have something more vividly pleasing or disagreeable than the ideas of extension, figure, and motion affect us with. And, it being too visibly absurd to hold that pain or pleasure can be in an unperceiving Substance, men are more easily weaned from believing the external existence of the Secondary than the Primary Qualities. You will be satisfied there is something in this, if you recollect the difference you made between an intense and more moderate degree of heat; allowing the one a real existence, while you denied it to the other. But, after all, there is no rational ground for that distinction; for, surely an indifferent sensation is as truly *a sensation* as one more pleasing or painful; and consequently should not any more than they be supposed to exist in an unthinking subject.

Hyl. . . . My fear is that I have been too liberal in my former concessions, or overlooked some fallacy or other. In short, I did not take time to think.

Phil. For that matter, *Hylas,* you may take what time you please in reviewing the progress of our inquiry. You are at liberty to recover any slips you might have made, or offer whatever you have omitted which makes for your first opinion.

Hyl. One great oversight I take to be this—that I did not sufficiently distinguish the *object* from the *sensation.* Now, though this latter may not exist without the mind, yet it will not thence follow that the former cannot.

Phil. What object do you mean? The object of the senses?

Hyl. The same.

Phil. It is then immediately perceived?

Hyl. Right.

Phil. Make me to understand the difference between what is immediately perceived, and a sensation.

Hyl. The sensation I take to be an act of the mind perceiving; besides which, there is something perceived; and this I call the *object.* For example, there is red and yellow on that tulip. But then the act of perceiving those colours is in me only, and not in the tulip.

Phil. What tulip do you speak of? Is it that which you see?

Hyl. The same.

Phil. And what do you see beside colour, figure, and extension?

Hyl. Nothing.

Phil. What you would say then is that the red and yellow are coexistent with the extension; is it not?

Hyl. That is not all; I would say they have a real existence without the mind, in some unthinking substance.

Phil. That the colours are really in the tulip which I see is manifest. Neither can it be denied that this tulip may exist independent of your mind or mine; but, that any immediate object of the senses—that is, any idea, or combination of ideas—should exist in an unthinking substance, or exterior to all minds, is in itself an evident contradiction. Nor can I imagine how this follows from what you said just now, to wit, that the red and yellow were on the tulip *you saw,* since you do not pretend to *see* that unthinking substance.

Hyl. You have an artful way, *Philonous,* of diverting our inquiry from the subject.

Phil. I see you have no mind to be pressed that way. To return then to your distinction between *sensation* and *object;* if I take you right, you distinguish in every perception two things, the one an action of the mind, the other not.

Hyl. True.

Phil. And this action cannot exist in, or belong to, any unthinking thing; but, whatever beside is implied in a perception may?

Hyl. That is my meaning.

Phil. So that if there was a perception without any act of the mind, it were possible such a perception should exist in an unthinking substance?

Hyl. I grant it. But it is impossible there should be such a perception.

Phil. When is the mind said to be active?

Hyl. When it produces, puts an end to, or changes, anything.

Phil. Can the mind produce, discontinue, or change anything, but by an act of the will?

Hyl. It cannot.

Phil. The mind therefore is to be accounted *active* in its perceptions so far forth as *volition* is included in them?

Hyl. It is.

Phil. In plucking this flower I am active; because I do it by the motion of my hand, which was consequent upon my volition; so likewise in applying it to my nose. But is either of these smelling?

Hyl. No.

Phil. I act too in drawing the air through my nose; because my breathing so rather than otherwise is the effect of my volition. But neither can this be called *smelling:* for, if it were, I should smell every time I breathed in that manner?

Hyl. True.

Phil. Smelling then is somewhat consequent to all this?

Hyl. It is.

Phil. But I do not find my will concerned any farther. Whatever more there is—as that I perceive such a particular smell, or any smell at all—this is independent of my will, and therein I am altogether passive. Do you find it otherwise with you, *Hylas?*

Hyl. No, the very same.

Phil. Then, as to seeing, is it not in your power to open your eyes, or keep them shut; to turn them this or that way?

Hyl. Without doubt.

Phil. But, doth it in like manner depend on your will that in looking on this flower you perceive *white* rather than any other colour? Or, directing your open eyes towards yonder part of the heaven, can you avoid seeing the sun? Or is light or darkness the effect of your volition?

Hyl. No certainly.

Phil. You are then in these respects altogether passive?

Hyl. I am.

Phil. Tell me now, whether *seeing* consists in perceiving light and colours, or in opening and turning the eyes?

Hyl. Without doubt, in the former.

Phil. Since therefore you are in the very perception of light and colours altogether passive, what is become of that action you were speaking of as an ingredient in every sensation? And, doth it not follow from your own concessions, that the perception of light and colours, including no action in it, may exist in an unperceiving substance? And is not this a plain contradiction?

Hyl. I know not what to think of it.

Phil. Besides, since you distinguish the *active* and *passive* in every perception, you must do it in that of pain. But how is it possible that pain, be it as little active as you please, should exist in an unperceiving substance? In short, do but consider the point, and then confess ingenuously, whether light and colours, tastes, sounds, &c. are not all equally passions or sensations in the soul. You may indeed call them *external objects,* and give them in words what subsistence you please. But, examine your own thoughts, and then tell me whether it be not as I say?

Hyl. I acknowledge, *Philonous,* that, upon a fair observation of what passes in my mind, I can discover nothing else but that I am a thinking being, affected with variety of sensations; neither is it possible to conceive how a sensation should exist in an unperceiving substance.—But then, on the other hand, when I look on sensible things in a different view, considering them as so many modes and qualities, I find it necessary to suppose a material *substratum,* without which they cannot be conceived to exist.

Phil. *Material substratum* call you it? Pray, by which of your senses came you acquainted with that being?

Hyl. It is not itself sensible; its modes and qualities only being perceived by the senses.

Phil. I presume then it was by reflection and reason you obtained the idea of it?

Hyl. I do not pretend to any proper positive idea of it. However, I conclude it exists, because qualities cannot be conceived to exist without a support.

Phil. It seems then you have only a relative notion of it, or that you conceive it not otherwise than by conceiving the relation it bears to sensible qualities?

Hyl. Right.

Phil. Be pleased therefore to let me know wherein that relation consists.

Hyl. Is it not sufficiently expressed in the term *substratum,* or *substance?*

Phil. If so, the word *substratum* should import that it is spread under the sensible qualities or accidents?

Hyl. True.

Phil. And consequently under extension?

Hyl. I own it.

Phil. It is therefore somewhat in its own nature entirely distinct from extension?

Hyl. I tell you, extension is only a mode, and Matter is something that supports modes. And is it not evident the thing supported is different from the thing supporting?

Phil. So that something distinct from, and exclusive of, extension is supposed to be the *substratum* of extension?

Hyl. Just so.

Phil. Answer me, *Hylas.* Can a thing be spread without extension? or is not the idea of extension necessarily included in *spreading?*

Hyl. It is.

Phil. Whatsoever therefore you suppose spread under anything must have in itself an extension distinct from the extension of that thing under which it is spread?

Hyl. It must.

Phil. Consequently, every corporeal substance being the *substratum* of extension must have in itself another extension, by which it is qualified to be a *substratum:* and so on to infinity? And I ask whether this be not absurd in itself, and repugnant to what you granted just now, to wit, that the *substratum* was something distinct from and exclusive of extension?

Hyl. Aye but, *Philonous,* you take me wrong. I do not mean that Matter is *spread* in a gross literal sense under extension. The word *substratum* is used only to express in general the same thing with *substance.*

Phil. Well then, let us examine the relation implied in the term *substance.* Is it not that it stands under accidents?

Hyl. The very same.

Phil. But, that one thing may stand under or support another, must it not be extended?

Hyl. It must.

Phil. Is not therefore this supposition liable to the same absurdity with the former?

Hyl. You take things in a strict literal sense; that is not fair, *Philonous.*

Phil. I am not for imposing any sense on your words: you are at liberty to explain them as you please. Only, I beseech you, make me understand something by them. You tell me Matter supports or stands under accidents. How! is it as your legs support your body?

Hyl. No; that is the literal sense.

Phil. Pray let me know any sense, literal or not literal, that you understand it in. . . . How long must I wait for an answer, *Hylas?*

Hyl. I declare I know not what to say. I once thought I understood well enough what was meant by Matter's supporting accidents. But now, the more I think on it the less can I comprehend it; in short I find that I know nothing of it.

Phil. It seems then you have no idea at all, neither relative nor positive, of Matter; you know neither what it is in itself, nor what relation it bears to accidents?

Hyl. I acknowledge it.

Phil. And yet you asserted that you could not conceive how qualities or accidents should really exist, without conceiving at the same time a material support of them?

Hyl. I did.

Phil. That is to say, when you conceive the real existence of qualities, you do withal conceive something which you cannot conceive?

Hyl. It was wrong I own. But still I fear there is some fallacy or other. Pray what think you of this? It is just come into my head that the ground of all our mistake lies in your treating of each quality by itself. Now, I grant that each quality cannot singly subsist without the mind. Colour cannot without extension, neither can figure without some other sensible quality. But, as the several qualities united or blended together form entire sensible things, nothing hinders why such things may not be supposed to exist without the mind.

Phil. Either, *Hylas,* you are jesting, or have a very bad memory. Though indeed we went through all the qualities by name one after another; yet my arguments, or rather your concessions, nowhere tended to prove that the Secondary Qualities did not subsist each alone by itself; but, that they were not *at all* without the mind. Indeed, in treating of figure and motion we concluded they could not exist without the mind, because it was impossible even in thought to separate them from all secondary qualities, so as to conceive them existing by themselves. But then this was not the only argument made use of upon that occasion. But (to pass by all that hath been hitherto said, and reckon it for nothing, if you will have it so) I am content to put the whole upon this issue. If you can conceive it possible for any mixture or combination of qualities, or any sensible object whatever, to exist without the mind, then I will grant it actually to be so.

Hyl. If it comes to that the point will soon be decided. What more easy than to conceive a tree or house existing by itself, independent of, and unperceived by, any mind whatsoever? I do at this present time conceive them existing after that manner.

Phil. How say you, *Hylas,* can you see a thing which is at the same time unseen?

Hyl. No, that were a contradiction.

Phil. Is it not as great a contradiction to talk of *conceiving* a thing which is *unconceived?*

Hyl. It is.

Phil. The tree or house therefore which you think of is conceived by you?

Hyl. How should it be otherwise?

Phil. And what is conceived is surely in the mind?

Hyl. Without question, that which is conceived is in the mind.

Phil. How then came you to say, you conceived a house or tree existing independent and out of all minds whatsoever? . . .

Hyl. To speak the truth, *Philonous,* I think there are two kinds of objects:—the one perceived immediately, which are likewise called *ideas;* the other are real things or external objects, perceived by the mediation of ideas, which are their images and representations. Now, I own ideas do not exist without the mind; but the latter sort of objects do. I am sorry I did not think of this distinction sooner; it would probably have cut short your discourse.

Phil. Are those external objects perceived by sense, or by some other faculty?

Hyl. They are perceived by sense.

Phil. How! is there anything perceived by sense which is not immediately perceived?

Hyl. Yes, *Philonous,* in some sort there is. For example, when I look on a picture or statue of Julius Cæsar, I may be said after a manner to perceive him (though not immediately) by my senses.

Phil. It seems then you will have our ideas, which alone are immediately perceived, to be pictures of external things: and that these also are perceived by sense, inasmuch as they have a conformity or resemblance to our ideas?

Hyl. That is my meaning.

Phil. And, in the same way that Julius Cæsar, in himself invisible, is nevertheless perceived by sight; real things, in themselves imperceptible, are perceived by sense.

Hyl. In the very same.

Phil. Tell me, *Hylas,* when you behold the picture of Julius Cæsar, do you see with your eyes any more than some colours and figures, with a certain symmetry and composition of the whole?

Hyl. Nothing else.

Phil. And would not a man who had never known anything of Julius Cæsar see as much?

Hyl. He would.

Phil. Consequently he hath his sight, and the use of it, in as perfect a degree as you?

Hyl. I agree with you.

Phil. Whence comes it then that your thoughts are directed to the Roman emperor, and his are not? This cannot proceed from the sensations or ideas of sense by you then perceived; since you acknowledge you have no advantage over him in that respect. It should seem therefore to proceed from reason and memory: should it not?

Hyl. It should.

Phil. Consequently, it will not follow from that instance that anything is perceived by sense which is not immediately perceived. Though I grant we may, in one acceptation, be said to perceive sensible things mediately by sense—that is, when, from a frequently perceived connexion, the immediate perception of ideas by one sense suggests to the mind others, perhaps belonging to another sense, which are wont to be connected with them. For instance, when I hear a coach drive along the streets, immediately I perceive only the sound; but, from the experience I have had that such a sound is connected with a coach, I am said to hear the coach. It is nevertheless evident that, in truth and strictness, nothing can be *heard* but *sound;* and the coach is not then properly perceived by sense, but suggested from experience. So likewise when we are said to see a red-hot bar of iron; the solidity and heat of the iron are not the objects of sight, but suggested to the imagination by the colour and figure which are properly perceived by that sense. In short, those things alone are actually and strictly perceived by any sense, which would have been perceived in case that same sense had then been first conferred on us. As for other things, it is plain they are only suggested to the mind by experience, grounded on former perceptions. But, to return to your comparison of Cæsar's picture, it is plain, if you keep to that, you must hold the real things or archetypes of our ideas are not perceived by sense, but by some internal faculty of the soul, as reason or memory. I would therefore fain know what arguments you can draw from reason for the existence of what you call *real things* or *material objects*. Or, whether you remember to have seen them formerly as they are in themselves; or, if you have heard or read of any one that did.

Hyl. I see, *Philonous,* you are disposed to raillery; but that will never convince me.

Phil. My aim is only to learn from you the way to come at the knowledge of *material beings*. Whatever we perceive is perceived immediately or mediately: by sense, or by reason and reflection. But, as you have excluded sense, pray shew me what reason you have to believe their existence; or what *medium* you can possibly make use of to prove it, either to mine or your own understanding.

Hyl. To deal ingenuously, *Philonous,* now I consider the point, I do not find I can give you any good reason for it. But, thus much seems pretty plain, that it is at least possible such things may really exist. And, as long as there is no absurdity in supposing them, I am resolved to believe as I did, till you bring good reasons to the contrary.

Phil. What! is it come to this, that you only believe the existence of material objects, and that your belief is founded barely on the possibility of its being true? Then you will have me bring reasons against it: though another would think it reasonable the proof should lie on him who holds the affirmative. And, after all, this very point which you are now resolved to maintain, without any reason, is in effect what you have more than once during this discourse seen good reason to give up. But, to pass over all this; if I understand you rightly, you say our ideas do not exist without the mind; but that they are copies, images, or representations, of certain originals that do?

Hyl. You take me right.

Phil. They are then like external things?

Hyl. They are.

Phil. Have those things a stable and permanent nature, independent of our senses; or are they in a perpetual change, upon our producing any motions in our bodies—suspending, exerting, or altering, our faculties or organs of sense?

Hyl. Real things, it is plain, have a fixed and real nature, which remains the same notwithstanding any change in our senses, or in the posture and motion of our bodies; which indeed may affect the ideas in our minds, but it were absurd to think they had the same effect on things existing without the mind.

Phil. How then is it possible that things perpetually fleeting and variable as our ideas should be copies or images of anything fixed and constant? Or, in other words, since all sensible qualities, as size, figure, colour, &c., that is, our ideas, are continually changing upon every alteration in the distance, medium, or instruments of sensation; how can any determinate material objects be properly represented or painted forth by several distinct things, each of which is so different from and unlike the rest? Or, if you say it resembles some one only of our ideas, how shall we be able to distinguish the true copy from all the false ones?

Hyl. I profess, *Philonous*, I am at a loss. I know not what to say to this.

Phil. But neither is this all. Which are material objects in themselves—perceptible or imperceptible?

Hyl. Properly and immediately nothing can be perceived but ideas. All material things, therefore, are in themselves insensible, and to be perceived only by our ideas.

Phil. Ideas then are sensible, and their archetypes or originals insensible?

Hyl. Right.

Phil. But how can that which is sensible be like that which is insensible? Can a real thing, in itself *invisible,* be like a *colour;* or a real thing, which is not *audible,* be like a *sound?* In a word, can anything be like a sensation or idea, but another sensation or idea?

Hyl. I must own, I think not.

Phil. Is it possible there should be any doubt on the point? Do you not perfectly know your own ideas?

Hyl. I know them perfectly; since what I do not perceive or know can be no part of my idea.

Phil. Consider, therefore, and examine them, and then tell me if there by anything in them which can exist without the mind? or if you can conceive anything like them existing without the mind?

Hyl. Upon inquiry, I find it is impossible for me to conceive or understand how anything but an idea can be like an idea. And it is most evident that *no idea can exist without the mind.*

Phil. You are therefore, by your principles, forced to deny the reality of sensible things; since you made it to consist in an absolute existence exterior to the mind. That is to say, you are a downright sceptic. So I have gained my point, which was to shew your principles led to Scepticism.

Hyl. For the present I am, if not entirely convinced, at least silenced.

Phil. I would fain know what more you would require in order to a perfect conviction. Have you not had the liberty of explaining yourself all manner of ways? Were any little slips in discourse laid hold and insisted on? Or were you not allowed to retract or reinforce anything you had offered, as best served your purpose? Hath not everything you could say been heard and examined with all the fairness imaginable? In a word, have you not in every point been convinced out of your own mouth? and, if you can at present discover any flaw in any of your former concessions, or think of any remaining subterfuge, any new distinction, colour, or comment whatsoever, why do you not produce it?

Hyl. A little patience, *Philonous.* I am at present so amazed to see myself ensnared, and as it were imprisoned in the labyrinths you have drawn me into, that on the sudden it cannot be expected I should find my way out. You must give me time to look about me and recollect myself.

BERKELEY SELECTION

1. What is the notion of *substance* that Hylas and Philonous are arguing about in this selection? What is the difference supposed to be between a material substance (a physical object) and its various characteristics or properties?

2.   When Philonous talks about "sensible things," is he talking about physical objects, the colors, shapes, tastes, and smells of physical objects, or *our* seeing, feeling, hearing and smelling of physical objects? What are the differences among these three categories? Does Philonous think there are any distinctions among them? Why?

3.   Hylas calls Philonous a skeptic, but Philonous insists that he is not skeptical at all! What is a skeptic? Why does Hylas call Philonous skeptical? Why does Philonous deny that he is a skeptic? Berkeley thought that his position (which is to say, the position he puts in the mouth of Philonous) was simply common sense, and that the doctrine of material substance was mysterious and obscure. Explain as well as you can why he thought that.

4.   The physical sciences measure physical phenomena in terms of mass, shape, size, and time. Even colors, sounds, and smells are reduced to the movements of masses in space and time. But Berkeley insists that the so-called primary qualities (extension, motion, mass, etc.) are neither more "objective" nor less "objective" than the secondary qualities (color, taste, smell, sound) or even the tertiary qualities (pain and pleasure). How does he defend that view? Do you think he is correct? Why?

5.   According to Philonous, perceptible qualities have a continuing existence inasmuch as God continues to think them even when we cease. But if there is no God, what then follows for Berkeley's philosophy? Even if we suppose that there is a God, what reason have we to suppose that He will continue to apprehend sense-qualities when we are not?

(SELECTION 3)

H. H. Price

The Nature of the Given

Over a period of several centuries, particularly as a result of the arguments of Immanuel Kant, many philosophers in the Anglo-American tradition came to the conclusion that two distinct elements could be distinguished in all cognition. There was, first of all, a certain sensory content, a raw material of consciousness produced by the mind's interaction with the world (always assuming there *was* a world); and then there were a variety of ways in which the mind interpreted its data, rearranged it, worked on it, and drew inferences from it, seeking thereby to extend the sphere of the knowable beyond the limits of immediate awareness. One of the points of developing this distinction was to locate and isolate an element in consciousness that could serve as the basis for absolutely certain beliefs. If such a firm foundation for knowledge-claims could be discovered, then philosophers could produce that demonstration of our empirical beliefs that Descartes had sought three centuries earlier. To be sure, it would have struck Descartes as very odd to look for certainty in sensation rather than in the operations of reason, but he would have recognized the philosophical motivation behind what the American John Dewey called the "quest for certainty."

Philosophers concerned with this set of problems came to use the technical term "sense-data" to refer to the immediate sensory contents of consciousness. The widely held view was that we could separate these sensory contents from the web of interpretations and judgments in which they were caught. Since the philosophical doubts of Descartes, Berkeley, Hume, and others concerned those interpretations and judgments, rather than the sense-data themselves, if we could carry out the separation, then perhaps we could make some statements about the nature of the sense-data themselves that would not be open to all the old familiar skeptical doubts. In short, we might find, in simple reports of the immediate sensory contents of consciousness, a solid foundation on which genuine knowledge could be built.

In this selection, we can watch one of the most sophisticated and careful philosophers of the twentieth-century analytic tradition, H. H. Price, developing an account of sense-data. Even after we have successfully isolated our sense-data reports from all interpretative or inferential connection, we will still face the task of finding sound principles of reasoning with which to move from those reports to well-grounded empirical judgments about physical objects, persons, and so forth. In the next selection, we shall see how an American philosopher, Clarence Irving Lewis, dealt with that problem.

When I see a tomato there is much that I can doubt. I can doubt whether it is a tomato that I am seeing, and not a cleverly painted piece of wax. I can doubt whether there is any material thing there at all. Perhaps what I took for a tomato was really a reflection; perhaps I am even the victim of some hallucination. One thing however I cannot doubt: that there exists a red patch of a round and somewhat bulgy shape, standing out from a background of other colour-patches, and having a certain visual depth, and that this whole field of colour is directly present to my consciousness. What the red patch is, whether a substance, or a state of a substance, or an event, whether it is physical or psychical or neither, are questions that we may doubt about. But that something is red and round then and there [1] I cannot doubt. Whether the something persists even for a moment before and after it is present to my consciousness, whether other minds can be conscious of it as well as I, may be doubted. But that it now *exists,* and that *I* am conscious of it—by me at least who am conscious of it this cannot possibly be doubted. And when I say that it is "directly" present to my consciousness, I mean that my consciousness of it is not reached by inference, nor by any other intellectual process (such as abstraction or intuitive induction), nor by any passage from sign to significate. There obviously must be some sort or sorts of presence to consciousness which can be called "direct" in this sense, else we should have an infinite regress. Analogously, when I am in the situations called "touching something," "hearing it," "smelling it," etc., in each case there is something which at that moment indubitably exists—a pressure (or prement patch), a noise, a smell; and that something is directly present to my consciousness.

This peculiar and ultimate manner of being present to consciousness is called *being given,* and that which is thus present is called a *datum.* The corresponding mental attitude is called *acquaintance, intuitive apprehension,* or sometimes *having.* Data of this special sort are called *sense-data.* And the acquaintance with them is conveniently called *sensing;* though sometimes, I think, this word is used in another sense. . . .

It is true that the term "given" or "datum" is sometimes used in a wider and looser sense to mean "that, the inspection of which provides a premise for inference." Thus the data of the historian are the statements which he finds in documents and inscriptions; the data of the general are the facts reported by his aircraft and his intelligence service: the data of the detective are the known circum-

---

[1] "There" means "In spatial relations to other colour-patches present to my consciousness at the same time."

From *Perception* by H. H. Price. First published in 1932 by Methuen & Co. (Used by permission of the publisher.)

stances and known results of the crime; and so on. But it is obvious that these are only data relatively and for the purpose of answering a certain question. They are really themselves the results of inference, often of a very complicated kind. We may call them data *secundum quid.* But eventually we must get back to something which is a datum *simpliciter,* which is not the result of any previous intellectual process. It is with data *simpliciter,* or rather with one species of them, that we are concerned.

How do sense-data differ from other data, e.g., from those of memory or introspection? We might be tempted to say, in the manner in which they come to be given, viz. as a result of the stimulation of a sense-organ. This will not do. For first, the sense-organs are themselves material things, and it seems quite likely that the term "material thing" cannot be defined except by reference to sense-data; and if so we should have a vicious circle. And secondly, even though we doubted the existence of all material things, including our own body and its organs, it would still be perfectly obvious that sense-data differ from other sorts of data. The only describable differentia that they seem to have is this, that they lead us to conceive of and believe in the existence of certain material things, whether there are in fact any such things or not. . . . But it seems plain that there is also another characteristic common and peculiar to them, which may be called "sensuousness." This is obvious on inspection, but it cannot be described. . . .

If the term sense-datum is taken in the strictly limited meaning that we have given it, I do not see how any one can doubt that there are sense-data. Yet it is certain that many philosophers do profess to doubt this and even to deny it. Indeed the sense-datum has come in for a good many hard words. It has been compared to the Wild Goose which we vainly chase: or again it is the Will o' the Wisp which lures the Realist further and further from Reality. . . .

The doctrine that there are no sense-data may take two forms, a wider and a narrower, which are not always clearly separated.

1. It is said that the very notion of givenness is an absurd and self-contradictory notion, that from the nature of the case nothing can ever be given at all. This is the most radical criticism that we have to meet. It may be called the *A priori* Thesis.

2. There is also what may be called the Empirical Thesis. This does not say that there is an absurdity in the very notion of givenness. It only says that we can never in fact find anything which is given. And it concludes that either there is no Given at all, or if there is any, it is found only in the experience of new-born children, idiots, and people falling into or just coming out of fainting fits: in which case (it is urged) the Given is clearly of no importance to the philoso-

pher, for it is quite beyond the reach of investigation, and therefore cannot be appealed to as evidence for anything.

Either of these theses if established would be very damaging. The *A priori* Thesis is the most radical, but also the easier to answer. The Empirical Thesis is the really difficult one to meet, and we shall have to make some concessions to it. Nevertheless, the arguments by which it is ordinarily supported are open to very grave objections.

The "A priori" Thesis. The main argument in favour of this may be summed up as follows:

It is impossible to apprehend something without apprehending some at least of its qualities and relations. In the language of Cambridge logicians, what we apprehend is always a *fact*—something of the form "that A is B" or "the B-ness of A." You cannot apprehend just A. For instance, you cannot apprehend a round red patch without apprehending that it is red and round and has certain spatial relations. But if we apprehend that it has these qualities and relations, we are not passively "receiving" or (as it were) swallowing; we are actively thinking—judging or classifying—and it is impossible to do less than this.

To this I answer, it is very likely true, but it is irrelevant. The argument only proves that nothing stands *merely* in the relation of givenness to the mind, without also standing in other relations: i.e., that what is given is always also "thought about" in some sense or other of that ambiguous phrase. But this does not have the slightest tendency to prove that *nothing is given at all.* The fact that A and B are constantly conjoined, or even necessarily connected, does not have the slightest tendency to prove that A does not exist.[2] How could it, since it itself presupposes the existence of A? That arguments of this sort should be so frequently used, and should be thought so conclusive, is one of the curiosities of philosophical controversy. . . .

The Empirical Thesis. This maintains that it is in fact impossible to discover any data. For if we try to point to an instance, it is said, we shall have to confess that the so-called datum is not really given at all, but it is the product of interpretation. . . .

We must begin by protesting, with Professor G. E. Moore, against the word "interpretation," which is used to cover several quite different processes and is at best only a metaphor. For instance, it may mean . . . some form of *thinking.* . . .

. . . To interpret something may mean to apprehend (immediately

---

[2] A stands here for "Givenness" and B for "thought-of-ness." The argument is the one commonly used against what is called *vicious abstraction.* Sometimes the conclusion is not that A does not exist but that A is identical with B: but here again it is presupposed in the premises that they are different—else how could they be necessarily connected?

or inferentially), or again to believe or opine or conjecture, that it has a certain characteristic. Thus if on hearing a certain noise we infer that it is the signal for dinner, we should be said to be interpreting what we hear. And even if one merely judges that it is a loud shrill sound, even this would be called interpretation by the philosophers with whom we are now concerned. . . .

The argument which we have to meet is as follows: Even if there be something which is given it is quite impossible for us to know it. For if we attempt to describe any so-called datum, e.g., this view which I now see, the very act of describing alters it. What we have at the end of the process is not the datum but a set of propositions, and the only relic of the datum is the term "this" which stands as their subject. Thus every attempt to describe the given is bound to fail. But if we cannot describe it, i.e., say what characters it has, we obviously do not know it. It is just the hypothetical and inaccessible somewhat which was present before the process of describing began. And this applies even to the very simplest and naïvest act of describing e.g., this is red, this is hard.

This argument, especially when adorned with a multitude of learned illustrations and expounded at many pages' length, is apt to seem very formidable. But we must point out that it rests on the assumption that *if I know or believe that something has a certain nature, it follows that it cannot possibly have the nature that I know or believe it to have:* i.e., that from the fact that I know or believe that A is B, it follows that A cannot really be B. This assumption, when openly and unmetaphorically stated, is so extraordinary that it is difficult at first sight to understand how any one can accept it. But I think that on further reflection we can find certain facts, and certain confused conceptions of these facts, which do tend to make it plausible.

1. In the first place, the describing of something is an *active* process, something that we *do*. . . . An indefinitely large amount of extraneous knowledge may be involved in it. The greatest concentration of attention, the most happy and illuminating facility in recalling appropriate parallels, may well be necessary. Any one can, indeed, grasp that this is a black cross on a white ground; but it needs a Conrad to describe the data presented to a voyager in the China seas, and all the labours of all the great painters scarcely suffice to enable us to comprehend the pattern of the prospect which we can see from our own front doors.

In face of such efforts as these, it may be asked, what becomes of our Given? Can it really be the same at the end of this work as it was at the beginning? To say that it is completely unaffected is surely to say that the *work* has had no result. Nor can we draw a line anywhere between the simple statement "This is a black cross on a white ground" and the elaborate, subtle, tortuous passage (perhaps pages long) of the novelist or the traveller. If the second transforms the datum into something which is not a datum at all, so must the first. The datum-as-it-is-in-itself will be the unknowable limit of the series, which we approach more closely as our description becomes simpler and simpler, but never actually reach.—Or will it even be that? For at which end of the series do we come nearest to the datum as it really is? Does a bovine *naïveté* really bring us nearer to it than subtilty and sophistication?—especially when we remember that *naïveté* itself is often a most laborious achievement, which only the most sophisticated can attain to. It seems impossible to say. In short, the pursuit of the datum-in-itself seems to be a perfect wild-goose chase. We do not even know where we are to look for it, or when in our blundering attempts we are beginning (as children say) to get "warm."

To all this kind of argumentation we must firmly answer, that it rests upon too narrow a notion of activity. Describing is a form of thinking, and thinking is an activity, often a very difficult one indeed. But it does not follow that it *alters* the thing about which we think. Practical activity does alter the thing upon which we act. For instance, the activity of walking alters the position and state of the walker's body; and the activity of beating some one alters the man who is beaten. But intellectual activity does not alter that upon which it is directed. If it alters anything, it alters only one's own mind, causing it to pass (say) from a state of uncertainty to a state of certainty, or from confusion to clarity. Indeed that is the obvious difference between intellectual and practical activity. . . .

So much for the first confusion which leads philosophers to think that if I know or believe that A is B, it follows that A cannot really be B.

2. The second confusion arises from the use of such words as *analysis*. When we describe something, it is natural to say that we are analysing it or "breaking it up." And the next step is, to assimilate this intellectual analysis to chemical analysis or anatomical dissection. It is held that just as dissection destroys a living organism, so intellectual analysis destroys that which is analysed, and substitutes something else in its place: "we murder to dissect." For instance, it substitutes for an organic whole a set of parts externally related by a mere "and" relation, or replaces a concrete individual by a set of universals or concepts. And accordingly since all thought may be regarded as analysis, we are forbidden to think, or warned that the thinkable is very far from being the real.

But is this metaphor to impose on us for ever? Is it not plain that intellectual analysis is utterly different from dissection? In intellectual analysis, I do not *do* anything to the object before me. I *find* relations within it. I *discover* that it possesses various characteristics—say redness and roundness—and I apprehend certain differences between those characteristics. But those relations and characteristics were there before I discovered them. The only change that has occurred is a change in myself. I was ignorant, and now I know. Nor does the fact that in order to find them I must often *compare* the present given with other data given in the past at all affect the matter. Comparison does not alter the things compared. It is merely the *detection of a likeness*. The likeness may be what is called far-fetched —in the descriptive writing of Conrad (for instance) it often is. But it is there all the same: and when we call it far-fetched, we only mean that most of us would not have succeeded in discovering it. . . .

It may however be suggested that though that which is given is not altered by the attempt to know about it, yet its *givenness* is destroyed by that attempt; so that although a certain red patch after being described is the same entity as it was before, yet it is not the same datum—for it is no longer a datum at all, but has become an "intellectum" instead. Thus any alleged knowledge about data would really be a knowledge about ex-data; and we could still say that the datum *qua datum* is unknowable—unknowable in the sense in which a bachelor is incapable of being a husband.

It is plain that this supposed alteration is different from the former one, which we have already dismissed. The alteration of A is one thing, the alteration of A's relation to the mind is another.

Now we must admit that if a datum A is reflected upon and described, it is no longer *merely* a datum. For the sake of argument we will even go further, and allow that everything which can be said to be given to a mind is also "judged about" by that mind, i.e., recognized to have certain qualities and relations, at any rate certain very general ones. But from the fact that something is no longer (and perhaps never was) a datum merely, we cannot conclude that it is not a datum at all. Again from the fact that we recognize (and describe) something as red and round, we can conclude that we are not *merely* acquainted with it: but that we are *not* acquainted with it—this by no means follows. Indeed it is difficult, to say the least, to understand how we could describe colour-patches or noises or tactual pressures, unless they were somehow there before us to be described, or in general how we could recognize anything as so-and-so unless we were acquainted with it. Certainly the fact that we can describe and recognize it will never prove that we are *not* acquainted with it! We must conclude then that the given is still given, however much we know about it. Knowledge-about is the usual, perhaps the inevitable, companion of acquaintance, but it is not its executioner.

We may sum up this discussion as follows. When I am in the situation which is described as seeing something, touching something, hearing something, etc., it is certain in each case that a colour-patch, or a pressure, or a noise exists at that moment and that I am acquainted with this colour-patch, pressure or noise. Such entities are called sense-data, and the acquaintance with them is conveniently called sensing; but it differs from other instances of acquaintance only in its object, not in its nature, and it has no species. The usual arguments against the reality and against the knowability of sense-data break down on examination. They only prove at most that there is no sense-datum which is not the object of other sorts of consciousness besides sensing, and that the causes of most sense-data are more complicated than might have been expected: and in these conclusions there is nothing to disturb us.

PRICE SELECTION

1.   Price's argument is based on the claim that there is something immediately present in sense-experience that I *cannot* doubt. Does he mean that it is logically absurd to doubt it, or simply that it is psychologically impossible to doubt it?

2.   Exactly *what* is it that I cannot doubt? Is it a *proposition* that I cannot doubt, or an experience? What does it mean to doubt a proposition? What does it mean to doubt an experience?

3.   Is it logically possible for me to *misdescribe* a sense-experience? If I do misdescribe it, am I wrong about it, or is there something indubitable and certain that remains even in the presence of the misdescription?

4.   Price refers to the sense-content of our experience as the "given." Why do you suppose he uses this term? Given by what? By whom? Suppose my mind had the capacity to generate its own sense-contents, to "give" itself sense-data—would that undermine Price's argument? Why?

(SELECTION 4)

C. I. LEWIS

The Logical Structure
of Empirical Beliefs

Thus far in this chapter we have concentrated on a number of questions concerning the nature and limits of our *knowledge*. What, if anything, can we know with certainty? What roles does sensation play in our knowledge? Are there direct reports of sense-experience that can be known with certainty, independently of any interpretations we may place on them or inferences we may draw from them?

Underlying these questions is another set of trickier and more subtle questions concerning *meaning*. What do we mean when we say that physical objects exist independently of our sensing them? What do we mean when we attribute a sensory property to some objectively existing substratum? In a way, these questions of meaning are already to be found in the selection from Berkeley's *Dialogues,* but in this portion of C. I. Lewis's major work, *An Analysis of Knowledge and Valuation,* the problems of meaning are brought to the center of the stage.

We are still in the empiricist tradition here, and the root of the philosophical difficulty still lies in the three-fold strategy sketched by Descartes and taken up by the British empiricists. If all our knowledge-claims are expressed by means of concepts drawn from sensation, and if the immediately given sensory contents of consciousness are sense-data, then statements about physical objects pose some problems of interpretation. Such statements make essential use of concepts of independent objects that exist separately from the mind and continue to exist whether being perceived or not. From where can we have gotten such concepts? What do I *mean* by "object" if I *do not mean* "unchanging underlying substratum"?

Lewis's theory of terminating and nonterminating judgments is a very subtle attempt to answer these questions. In effect, Lewis argues that familiar statements about objects and persons are really, in a very complicated way, sets or systems of predictions about the sorts of sense-experiences that would result from this or that action on the part of the cognitive subject under specified perceptual conditions. An empirical judgment is rather like a super clown car at the circus: it looks quite small and self-contained when we first see it, but out of it step an endless series of little "if-then" predictions about sense-experience.

One of the consequences of Lewis's theory, as he takes care to emphasize, is that our empirical judgments can never be totally, finally, incontrovertibly established. Since each of them is really an *endless* series of little sense-predictions, it will always be possible that some of those predictions down the line will turn out to be incorrect. That in turn will mean that the original judgment has, to some extent, been disconfirmed. We are all familiar with this notion of possible disconfirmation from the procedures of scientists, who are always ready to reconsider a theory if new evidence turns up that points in a different direction. Modern empiricist epistemology is strongly influenced by twentieth-century scientific methodology, just as Descartes's own philosophy was influenced by the new science of the sixteenth and early seventeenth centuries.

The existence of a thing, the occurrence of an objective event, or any other objective state of affairs, is knowable only as it is verifiable or confirmable. And such objective facts can be verified, or confirmed as probable, only by presentations of sense. Thus all empirical knowledge is vested, ultimately, in the awareness of what is given and the prediction of certain passages of further experience as something which will be given or could be given. It is such predictions of possible direct experience which we have called terminating judgments; and the central importance of these for all empirical knowledge will be obvious.

. . . Terminating judgments . . . are phrased in terms of direct experience, not of the objective facts which such experience may signalize or confirm; and for this reason they are statable only in expressive language, the terms of which denote appearances as such. It may well be that no language is available to us, for such expressive use, except language which in its more usual signification would refer to objective things and states of affairs. Thus the statement "If I step forward and down, I shall come safely to rest on the step below," would, in its ordinary meaning, predict a physical event involving my body and the environment. This physical event, in case it should occur, would become an ingredient in the world's history, thereafter confirmable to the end of time. At the moment of my stepping, it would not become a complete theoretical certainty: on the contrary, it would be no more certain than the reality of the granite steps whose existence the truth of it is supposed to confirm. It is not this physical event which, in my terminating judgment, I intend to predict, but merely the passage of experience itself. And this prediction of experience is something which at the moment of stepping will become completely certain or certainly false. In making this judgment I assert nothing of objective reality but only, for example, what could still be tested if I should be a paralytic with the delusion that he still walked; and tested with positive result if that delusion were sufficiently systematic. Only by confining statements to an intent thus formulatable in expressive terms can anything be proved conclusively by single experiences: and only if *something* is conclusively true by virtue of *experience,* can any existence or fact of reality be rendered even probable. If a particular experience be delusive—that is, if the objective belief which is the interpretation put upon it be invalid— that itself, if demonstrable at all, can be demonstrated only through other *experiences.*

If it be denied that such predictions, confined to passages of experience as such, are or can be formulated—a denial which has some plausibility—still it would remain true that in such passages of experience something, whether linguistically expressible or not, becomes entirely certain; and it is only through such certainties of sense that even partial verification of objective fact can be afforded. If there be no genuinely expressive language, still there would be those direct apprehensions of sense and those terminating judgments which could only be so formulated; and any account of knowledge would need to observe them. The impossibility of their accurate expression in language would, then, merely constitute a comment upon the inessential character of language in its relation to the cognitive process; and upon the errors which lie in wait for those who substitute linguistic analysis for the examination of knowledge. . . .

It has been suggested that terminating judgments are of the form "If A then E," or "S being given, if A then E," where "A" indicates some possible mode of action and "E" an expected empirical sequent.

The main reason why such predictions must be thus conditional, instead of categorical, is the simple one that, broadly speaking, there is nothing in the way of human experience which is predictable entirely without reference to conditions which action supplies and may alter.

It would be easy to fall into confusion here and raise a kind of objection which would be pointless. We have all of us been brought up in the tradition of scientific or physical determinism, according to which everything which is to be is intrinsically predictable. And even though science now finds that this determinism is not, as it was previously thought to be, an indispensable presupposition of the possibility of scientific knowledge, we shall not easily be persuaded that such exceptions to categorical predictability as must now be granted are matters which affect the practicalities. It is not the subatomic phenomena, to which the physical Principle of Indetermination applies, but molar phenomena, which affect common experience and our decisions of actions. Even if laws of the macroscopic are merely statistical generalizations based upon chance distributions in the realm of the microscopic, that fact could have no considerable weight for predicting matters of practical concern. Those phenomena with which empirical knowledge must mainly deal would still be categorically predictable.

These abstruse questions about physical determinism need not concern us at all. The point is that such supposedly categorical predictabilities of the physical concern objective facts, while the predictions of terminating judgments concern direct experience. The thrown ball, for example, categorically will describe a certain trajectory and fall at a certain point with a certain terminal velocity. But what *experience*, and of whom, follows from that? Certain definite experiences, supposing one places one's hands at the right point in proper position, or that one's head be in the line of flight. But the categorical predictability of the ball's behavior does not, of itself, include any categorical prediction of an experience of someone. In general, predictions of experience which might be drawn from it, are of experience conditional upon and alterable by some mode of action.

In fact the usefulness of scientific knowledge depends upon this consideration. The practical value of foreseeing what inevitably will happen, is in order to make such that it does not happen to *us;* or that it does; according as the happening means a grievous or a gratifying experience. The use of making *categorical* prediction of *objective fact,* is in order to translate this fact into *hypothetical* predictions of *experience,* the hypothesis in question being one concerning some possible way of acting. . . .

The point with which particularly we are concerned here is that what is thus categorically predictable is an objective state of affairs. And it is still the case that absolute determination of such objective fact does not, in like fashion, categorically determine the *experience* of anyone; does not rule out alternatives of experience which are conditional upon some decision of action. Anything which should be categorically predictable has implications for experience: it implies, for example, all those experiences in which it could be verified or disclosed as fact. But it does not imply these experiences as categorical future fact: the predictions *of experience* into which the predictable objective fact can be translated are *hypothetical;* are contingent upon the verifier's way of acting. Certain empirical findings will be disclosed *if* he makes the appropriate tests; and presumably not otherwise. An unalterable objective fact, or an inevitable future event, does *not* imply any unalterable or unavoidable experience whatever; what it implies in terms of experience is certain eventualities contingent upon action; that *if* we behave thus and so, then inevitably, what we shall find in experience will be such and such.

There is no need to strain too far the reader's ordinary sense of objective reality, or his customary modes of formulating it. But it is necessary to draw attention to two general considerations which are of fundamental importance about our knowledge. First, that in a sense which will be obvious, a supposed objective fact, when considered apart from all disclosures in experience which bear witness to it, is in the nature of the case, lacking in human significance. The formulation of it in terms of our possible experience contains everything which could lend the notion of it significance of the sort which actually we give to it in practical life. And second, that no assigned significance in terms of experience would be genuinely practical and true to the facts of life it if were significance of an inevitable experience no action could affect. The translation of objective fact into terminating judgments, in terms of possible experience, represents its actual and vital cognitive significance. And these terminating judgments, representing the possible confirmations of objective fact, are not categorical predictions of experience but predictions of possibilities dependent for their realization upon some chosen mode of action. Only so could our knowledge of the objective fact be of any practical value or such that we should be likely to have an interest in it. Both the theoretical and the moral significance of knowledge can be justly phrased by saying that what an objective fact *means* is certain possibilities of experience which are open to realization through our action. Or if this smacks of subjectivity, then let us put it the other way about: what is signified by the possibilities of experience which we find open to our action, is the world of objective fact, whose existence and nature is in general beyond our power to affect or alter. But knowledge would not be something to be won, or valuable when obtained, if the objective fact implied categorically the experiences in which it may be verified or confirmed. . . .

Whatever may be the case about physical things and objective states of affairs, anticipatable *experience* is subject to a sort of indeterminacy principle: foreknowledge itself and our active attitude can alter the quality of it. That is one reason why the old-fashioned free-will-or-determinism controversy relates to an issue which, in terms of actual life, is mythical. There is nothing which can be anticipated which it may not be of use to know: and whatever it is of conceivable use to foresee, is such only because *something* still can be done about it; the experience with which it may affect us is still open to qualification by ourselves. Tenuous as this kind of consideration may be thought to be, still it points to a universal feature of our empirical knowledge: whatever the fact may be upon which our knowledge is directed, if we render the significance of that fact in terms of the experiences which will give evidence of it, we shall find that what thus portends is something which it is *valuable* to know because in some part or aspect it is conditional upon our decisions of action.

Admittedly some experiences—or more accurately, some generic characters of some experiences—may be predictable with practical certainty and without any possibility of avoidance. When we see the lightning, we know that we shall hear the thunder. We may tense our muscles or not; stop our ears or not; and these activities somewhat affect the quality with which what is predicted will be experienced; but the generic character of heard thunder may be unqualifiedly inevitable. Such examples are, it will be admitted, exceptional, and represent a kind of limiting case. But even here, we see that alternatives of action are not wholly eliminated; they are only severely restricted. And in that sense, what is here exemplified differs only in degree from the more general case. In fact, it may lead us precisely to the justifiable and well-considered generalization: *any* objective event which may be categorically predictable, and any objective state of affairs which may be known, will mean, when translated into terms of confirming experience, a restriction of the possibilities contingent on our action, but *never* a restriction reducing these alternatives to a single one. Even where—as in the more general case—the alternatives left open to us, in view of the objective fact in question, are too numerous to mention, still the state of affairs believed in or asserted would be reflected in the elimination of equally many *other* alternatives of experience, contingent upon chosen ways of acting, which might be open to us if this objective fact were *not* the case. That is the general nature of objective fact, when taken in terms of the experience which would verify or confirm it: it means that by nothing we can do would certain experiences be possible for us; but that there are other alternatives of experience any one of which may ensue if a suitable mode of action be adopted. That a sheet of white paper is now before me, means that in no possible way can I now proceed directly to presentation of something green and circular here in front of me, as well as meaning that certain other presentations are predictable, contingent upon appropriate decisions of action. How narrowly the alternatives of possible experience may be restricted, or how wide the range of possibilities left open, depends upon the particular objective fact or event which is in question. But in no case will it fail to eliminate certain possibilities of experience which might otherwise obtain; and in no case will it completely exclude all possibilities but one, and leave nothing whatever which is contingent upon our decision of action. It is in this fact that the universal possibility of a practical value in empirical knowledge lies: there is nothing which could be known, the knowledge of which might not enable us to avoid efforts which are fruitless, and enable us also to ameliorate our lot and improve the quality with which future experience might otherwise affect us, by choosing between alternatives of action which still are open.

This being so, it will be seen that our general formula for terminating judgments is correct on the point in question, and universally applies. The sense meaning of any verifiable statement of objective fact, is exhibitable in some set of terminating judgments each of which is hypothetical in form; it is a judgment that a certain empirical eventuation will ensue if a certain mode of action be adopted. Such judgments may be decisively verified or found false by adopting the mode of action in question and putting them to the test. And it is by such conclusive verification of terminating judgments, constituent in the meaning of it, that the objective belief—the non-terminating judgment—receives its confirmation as more or less highly probable. . . .

. . . What [does] it mean for a statement of this form, "If A then E," to be true when the hypothesis "A" is false—when the mode of action A is *not* adopted, and the test of what is believed is not made?

This is the sort of question the answer to which we know quite well so long as no one asks us for it; but when we are asked, we do not know what to say. It is indeed a matter to be determined, not by elucidation of world-shaking mysteries, but simply by careful examination of a meaning which implicitly we all intend and grasp in making assertions of this type. But to elicit that meaning is particularly troublesome. . . .

That the if-then relation intended in the terminating judgment "If A then E" is not a relation of the deducibility of "E" from "A"—not a strict implication or logical entailment—is sufficiently evident from the consideration that this judgment itself is one of *empirical* fact and cannot be attested by mere logic. The situation which would prove it false is logically thinkable; the contrary statement, "A but not E" is not self-contradictory, though it is believed to be false. We must be careful here not to confuse the question precisely at issue with others which are related. As we have conceived the matter, the terminating judgment itself *is* deducible from the objective judgment in which it is a constituent: from "There is a piece of white paper before me," it is deducible that "If I turn my eyes right, this seen appearance will be displaced to the left." This relation of deducibility holds because the terminating judgment is contained in the meaning of the objective statement. But our present question does not concern this relation between the objective belief and the terminating judgment: it concerns the relation between the antecedent "A" and the consequent "E" in the terminating judgment itself. The question is not, "If it be true that a piece of white paper is before me, is it deducible that if I turn my eyes right, the seen appearance will be displaced to the left?": the question is, "What do I mean when I assert 'If I turn my eyes right, this seen appearance will be displaced to the left'?" And the present point is that I do *not* mean to assert that "The seen appearance will be displaced to the left" is *logically deducible* from the hypothesis "I turn my eyes right." I could assert that only if it were entirely unthinkable, logically, that the given presentation should be illusory, or my judgment of the objective fact subject to error. And that is not the case; nor do I take it to be so, unless unthinkingly or by some crude mistake in the analysis of empirical knowledge of objective matters of fact.

That the relation between a way of acting and the result of it, which a terminating judgment expresses, is not a relation of logical deducibility, may also be attested in another way: it is relation of a sort which could only be learned from past experience. When I see what looks like a piece of white paper, my ability to predict the experience which will result from turning my eyes is something that previous like occasions have taught me. But if *"E"* were deducible from *"A,"* I should not have needed so to learn it; the truth of "If *A* then *E*" could in that case be determined without reference to any experience, merely by reflection. . . .

. . . No assertion of or knowledge of or belief in objective reality or fact can be understood without understanding that it has, as its practically significant and testable consequences, hypothetical propositions having the following characteristics: (1) The consequent in this hypothetical statement is not logically deducible from the antecedent. (2) Nevertheless the truth of the hypothetical statement iself—like that of one which states a relation of logical entailment or deducibility—is independent of the truth or falsity of the antecedent or hypothesis: for the if-then relation which such a hypothetical statement asserts as holding, the hypothesis has the same consequences whether it is true or false. (3) Hence this hypothetical statement may be significantly asserted when the hypothesis of it is contrary to fact and is known to be so.

Let us proceed to the kind of example which instances this issue in a form which is critical for the theory of knowledge. As long ago as Hume, it was suggested that there is no difference between the common-sense supposition of a real world (when the significance of this supposition is validly interpreted) and the summary statement that at certain times we have certain specific sense impressions. All the significance of "order" and "connection" of things, *so far as such orderliness of things and events is verified, or actually will be verified in future,* will be comprehended in this summary statement of actual sense-content of experience. The common-sense man regards this Humean suggestion as equivalent to the supposition that objective reality may "go out" when unobserved but always "come back" when observed; and considers this a kind of harmless philosophic joke. Very likely he is unable to give his instinctive repudiation of it any clear formulation. But one can be given: the difference between such fantastic subjectivism and our belief in a world which is knowable and verifiable but exists independently of being observed, is the difference between supposing on the one hand that empirical generalizations which are justified have no valid significance beyond that of formal implication, and supposing on the other hand that the verifiability of such empirical generalizations includes reference to hypothetical statements about possible experience, and that these hypothetical statements have the characteristics summarized in the preceding paragraph.

For example, I believe that there is a room next door with a desk and blackboard in it, although no one is now observing it, and although at times no one is even thinking of it. My belief in this objective reality is distinguished from the subjectivistic conception that it exists only when and as perceived, by the fact that my belief includes the following items:

(1) If at any time (while this room continues to exist), a normal observer, A. B., should put himself in position to observe this room, A. B. would have the kind of experience meant by "observing a room with a desk and a blackboard."

(2) "A. B. now puts himself in position to observe this room" is false: no one is now observing it.

(3) "A. B. observes a desk and blackboard" is not logically deducible from "A. B. puts himself in position to observe this room in question."

(4) It is false that "If A. B. now puts himself in position to observe this room, A. B. will see a pink elephant."

Understanding these statements in their obvious intention, the following may be noted: (1), above, is to be construed as a hypothetical statement which is general; holding for any normal observer and for any time (so long as the reality to be verified continues to exist). Statement (2) asserts that for some observer and some time, or in fact for any observer and some time (now), the antecedent in this hypothetical statement (1) is false. Statement (3), above, expresses the fact that the consequent in this hypothetical statement is not logically deducible from the antecedent or hypothesis. Statements (2) and (4) together indicate that, for the intended sense of this hypothetical assertion—of the if-then relation which it asserts—it is true for some observer and some time (A. B. now) for which its hypothesis is false; but it is *not* true that this contrary-to-fact hypothesis has any and every consequence—e.g., not true that it has the consequence "A. B. will see a pink elephant."

Taken together, these features characterize the meaning of belief in an objective reality which is verifiable but is independent of being verified or experienced. And they likewise indicate, as clearly as it seems possible to indicate it, the familiar and intended meaning of "if-then" in statements of possible confirmations of empirical knowledge.

If this is a fair illustration of our belief in the reality of a thing when not observed, then one way of expressing such belief is in the form of a hypothetical statement about the experience of a normal observer who should act in a manner appropriate to testing what is in question under conditions permitting such test. But the meaning intended by "if-then" in such hypothetical statements is of the essence of the matter and must be carefully regarded. It is not expressible in terms of logical deducibility nor in terms of material implication or of formal implication. An if-then relation of hypothesis to logically deducible consequence, is one which can be certified by reflection alone and does not need to be verified by experience. The if-then of material implication is such that a contrary to fact hypothesis has any and every consequence: when a thing is not being observed, the material implication, "If this thing is observed, then ————," will be true, however the blank here may be filled. And the if-then of formal implication (supposing it distinct from that of logical deducibility) is such that, in terms of it, the statement, "For any normal observer at any time, if the observer acts appropriately to verification of this thing, then a positively verifying experience results" will be satisfied if every *actually made* observation has a positive result, and without any supposition as to what *would* result in the case of confirmations not in fact attempted.

This whole matter may be summarily put as follows: For any conception which takes reality to be knowable and verifiable, to believe that this or that is real means believing certain statements of the form "If such and such experiments be made, so and so will be experienced." And the further and crucial question here concerns interpretation of the if-then relation in such hypothetical statements. To take this as expressing relation of a premise to a logically deducible consequence, is out of the question: that would represent a conception difficult to identify with any historical theory, and hardly worth discussing. To take this if-then relation as one expressible in terms of material or of formal implication would be precisely equivalent to that extreme subjectivism—easily reduced to skepticism—which maintains that to be is to be perceived; which holds that there

is no valid difference between the existence of the reality believed in
and the mere fact that on certain occasions certain actual perceivers
actually have certain perceptions. The realistic conception that the
believed-in and verifiable realities are independent of being so known
or experienced, must interpret this if-then relation as one for which
such hypothetical statements are true or false independently of the
truth or falsity of their antecedent clauses; one for which the hypothesis has the *same* consequences whether the observation is made
and the hypothesis is true, or the observation is not made and the
hypothesis is contrary to fact. Thus it is a relation most clearly expressible in the form "If such and such observation *should be* made,
so and so *would* be experienced."

This last mentioned meaning of "if-then," requisite to expression of any realistic conception of objective fact, is one which has no
name, and one which logical analysis has largely neglected. But it is
familiar to common thought and discourse. We might refer to the
connections so stable as "matter-of-fact connections" or "natural
connections" or "real connections." And the consequences of a hypothesis, in this sense of "consequence," might be called its "natural
consequences" or "real consequences." These names would be appropriate because this sense of "if-then" is the one connoted in any
assertion of causal relationship or of connection according to natural
law. It is the kind of connection we believe in when we believe that
the consequences of any hypothesis are such and such because of "the
way reality is" or because the facts of nature are thus and so. It is the
kind of connection which we rely upon, and implicitly assert, when
we anticipate that the consequences of a certain action under certain
conditions will be so and so, and cannot be otherwise. Because whoever believes in predictable consequences of action, believes that although we make our own decisions, what is to ensue once we commit
ourselves is fixed and out of our hands. Only by the "reality" of this
connection, independently of the decision itself, could there be any
such thing as "foreseeable consequences" of action. Whoever contemplates a possible way of acting but discards it as unwise, believes
"If I should do so and so, the results would be such and such"; and
believes this connection holds independently of the decision itself.
And whoever regrets a decision believes "If I had done that, such
and such would have come about." And he does not believe this to be
true merely because the hypothesis is false; if he did, the regret would
be spurious.

Without something determined independently of the decision to
verify, there would be nothing for the verifying experience to disclose—except itself: it would verify nothing because there would be
no independent fact to be evidenced. Whoever believes in indepen-

dent reality, believes in such real connections which may be disclosed in experience; and whoever believes in such connections, verifiable in experience, believes in knowable but independent reality. And whoever *dis*believes in such real connections—if he is not merely confused and inconsistent—not only disbelieves the possibility of empirical knowledge; he disbelieves that there is anything to be so known which it is possible to state. . . .

It is here maintained that there is no significance in objective belief nor in any statement of objective fact beyond what would be expressible in terms of some theoretically possible confirmation of it. But there is in that no implication of subjectivism; it implies denial only that there is any objective thing or fact which is intrinsically unknowable—which could not be empirically evidenced to any actual or even any supposititious observer. The critic has mislocated the issue between subjectivism and the affirmation of a reality which is independent of being known, and commits an *ignoratio elenchi*.

The denial of unknowable reality does not—let us hope—imply that there is no reality which is unknown and unverified. That there can be no reality outside *actual* experience is what the subjectivist asserts. It is not here maintained, however, that reference to the totality of *actual* verifying experiences (verifications actually made or actually to be made in future) exhausts the significance of objective fact. On the contrary that is denied. As has been pointed out, an objective belief implies not only such terminating judgments as are put to the test but also assertion of those which are untested. As we have emphasized; such terminating judgments assert an if-then relation which must still hold when the hypothesis is false and the indicated verification is not made; and are thus most clearly expressible in the form "If such and such observation should be made, so and so would be observed."

It lies in the nature of the case that there must be such terminating judgments, taken to be true, which will remain untested. It is not possible to make all possible tests, for the same reasons that it is impossible to act in all possible ways or adopt all possible decisions. Our commitment to objective reality, independent of being experienced, is signalized by our commitment to terminating judgments— implicitly affirmed in affirming what implies them—which, in the case of any objective belief, remain untested; in our assertion of the observability of what is not observed; of the verifiability of what remains unverified; or possibilities of experience which never become actual.

It is by such departure from subjectivism that we find it necessary to insist that the terminating judgments, in which the verifiable meaning of objective empirical assertion is to be found, must express a real connection—independent of being found to hold by actual test—between a mode of action and a sequent eventuation of experience. The question how statements with such meaning may be assured, is the question how empirical knowledge of an objective reality is possible.

LEWIS SELECTION

1. What exactly are *terminating judgments?* Lewis gives an example, and immediately admits that it is really an example of a physical object statement that is not, strictly speaking, a terminating judgment. Can you make up a statement that really *is* a terminating judgment? Why not? Does it matter that we cannot ever find an appropriate language for stating terminating judgments?

2. If any statement about the physical world implies a literally unending series of terminating judgments, then I must have an infinite number of things in mind when I assert it. But how is that possible?

3. According to Lewis, when we make any simple assertion about physical objects, such as "This is a piece of chalk," we imply a variety of hypothetical statements, such as "If I were to rub this against a blackboard it would leave a white mark," and "If I were to chew this it would have a dry, bitter taste." Now, some of those things I may actually do, but many of them, as Lewis points out, I will never do. What then is their relationship to the original assertion? Can I know what I mean by "This is a piece of chalk" without doing any of the things described in the associated terminating judgments? Can I know whether "This is a piece of chalk" is *true* without doing any of them? Without doing all of them?

4. How does Lewis's analysis of terminating and nonterminating judgments help to explain the way in which scientists check their hypotheses? Can his analysis also explain how we understand our everyday world? Is there any fundamental difference between what scientists do as scientists and what all of us do in our daily lives? What do you think Lewis would say about this question?

(SELECTION 5)

WINSTON H. F. BARNES

The Myth of Sense-Data

Thus far in this chapter we have traced a tradition of argument about the role of sense-perception in knowledge from the early doubts raised by Descartes to certain quite sophisticated accounts in twentieth-century epistemology of the role of sensory contents in the formulation and justification of material-object statements. Along the way a theory of sense-data developed, the central thesis of which is that sense-data are distinct, identifiable existences, units of conscious awareness that can be distinguished from, and perhaps also apprehended independently of, our interpretations of them or judgments based on them.

In this provocative essay, W. H. F. Barnes charges the theory of sense-data with being a *myth*. There are no such things as sense-data, Barnes argues, at least no such things as philosophers like Price and Lewis describe sense-data as being. Barnes is not denying the central role of sense-experience in knowledge, of course. He is well within the empiricist tradition himself. But he believes that the sense-data theory is a seriously misguided account of that role, an account that generates paradoxes and problems as serious as those it is intended to resolve.

In his discussion, Barnes raises some of the problems that were posed in the introduction to this chapter. If we are directly aware only of sense-data, and if sense-data are in some sense distinct from, or different existences from, physical objects, then we must draw the peculiar conclusion that in our ordinary everyday experiences we are never directly aware of the familiar objects that fill our world. Thus I must conclude that I am not really directly aware of my fingers on the typewriter, or the typewriter, or the paper, etc.

Barnes offers us an alternative way of thinking *and talking* about sense-experience. It seeks to take account of the role of such experience in knowledge without committing us to belief in the existence of odd entities called "sense-data" that somehow stand between us and the physical objects we experience. As a philosophical exercise, after you have finished this essay, it might be interesting (and challenging) for you to look back at the selections by Price and Lewis, and try to figure out whether they could successfully rephrase what they have to say in Barnes's language without assuming the existence of sense-data.

Our knowledge of the physical world is subject to many doubts and uncertainties but we commonly see no reason to doubt certain facts. We all agree, when we are out of the study, that we sometimes see tables and chairs, hear bells and clocks, taste liquids, smell cheeses, and feel the woollen vests that we wear next to our skin in winter. To put the matter generally, we agree that we perceive physical objects, "physical objects" being such things as tables, chairs and cheeses, and "perceiving" being a generic word which comprehends the specific activities of seeing, hearing, tasting, smelling, and feeling. These activities are invariably directed upon an object or objects; and this fact distinguishes them from other activities of ours—if that be the right word—such as feeling pained or feeling tired, which go on entirely within ourselves. We take it for granted that by means of the former activities we became aware of the existence, and acquainted with the qualities, of physical objects, and we further regard the kind of acquaintance which we acquire in this way as a basis for the far reaching and systematic knowledge of the physical world as a whole, which is embodied in the natural sciences.

Let us call experiences such as seeing a table, hearing a bell, etc., perceptual experiences; and the statements which assert the existence of such experiences perceptual statements. Many philosophers have cast doubt upon the claims made by such perceptual statements. They have produced arguments to show that we never perceive physical objects, and that we are in fact subject to a constant delusion on this score. As these arguments are by no means easily refuted and are such as any intelligent person interested in the matter will sooner or later come to think of, they are well worth considering. Moreover, certain modern philosophers claim to show by these arguments not only that we do not perceive physical objects but that what we do perceive is a different sort of thing altogether, which they call a sense-datum. They are obliged to invent a new term for it because no one had previously noticed that there were such things. This theory is obviously important because it not only claims to settle the doubts which we cannot help feeling when we reflect on our perceptual experience, but it makes the astonishing claim that we have all failed to notice a quite peculiar kind of entity, or at least have constantly made mistakes about its nature. I hope to show that the sense-datum theory is beset by internal difficulties; that it is not necessitated by the doubts we have about our perceptual experience; and finally that the doubts which are caused in us by a little reflection are allayed by further reflection.

From Winston H. F. Barnes "The Myth of Sense-Data," *Proceedings of the Aristotelian Society*, New Series, Vol. XLV (1944–45), copyright Harrison & Sons, Ltd., London, 1945.

The arguments which philosophers such as Professors Russell, Broad and Price use to demonstrate that we perceive not physical objects but sense-data, are many and various, and no good purpose would be served by stating them all, even if that were possible. Undoubtedly, however, these arguments do cause us to doubt whether we are acquainted with physical objects when we think we are; and, these doubts demand to be resolved in one way or another. If there is such a thing as a problem of perception, it must consist in reviewing the doubts which arise in our minds in this way. I shall select for brief statement three typical arguments so as to make clear the difficulties which are thought to justify the negative conclusion that we do not perceive physical objects and the positive conclusion that we perceive sense-data. . . .

I now proceed to state the three arguments. They are all taken from visual experience, and they all pose in one way or another what we may call the "appearance-reality" problem of perception.

(1) A penny appears circular to an observer directly above it, but elliptical to an observer a few paces away. It cannot *be* both elliptical and circular at one and the same time. There is no good reason for supposing that the penny reveals its real shape to an observer in one position rather than to an observer in any other position. The elliptical appearance and the circular appearance cannot be identified with the penny or any parts of it, but they are entities of some kind. It is things of this sort which are called sense-data.

(2) The stick which looks straight in the air looks angularly bent when in water. There are good reasons for thinking that no such change of shape takes place in the stick. Yet there *is* something straight in the one case and something bent in the other, and there is no good reason for supposing either is less or more of an existent than the other. The straight-stick appearance and the bent-stick appearance are sense-data.

(3) There may seem to be things in a place when in fact there are no such things there, as illustrated by the mirages which appear in the desert and the highly coloured rodents which appear to habitual drunkards. Not unrelated to this type of experience is the one in which we see double. If an eyeball is pressed by the forefinger while one is looking at a candle flame, two flames are seen. Although it would be possible to say that one of the flames is the actual object and the other is something else, to be called a sense-datum, it seems even more evident here than in the previous instances that there is no good reason for distinguishing between the two in this way.

In all these cases there is a suggestion that what we see in certain cases cannot be a physical object or the surface of a physical object, but is some kind of non-physical entity. It is non-physical entities of this kind which are called sense-data. The argument goes even further by urging that, if in some cases we see non-material things, it is possible and indeed likely, that we do so in all cases. This plausible suggestion is accepted by certain sense-datum theorists such as Professor Broad and is extended to cover all forms of perceiving. With the acceptance of this suggestion we reach the basic position taken by one form of the sense-datum theory, viz., we perceive only sense-data, and consequently have no direct acquaintance through our senses with physical objects.

It is clear that, on this view, the term sense-datum has as part of its connotation, the not being a physical body. As everything I experience is a sense-datum, the sense-experience of a table, for example, differs not at all, in itself, from an hallucination or an illusion. These latter again seem to differ only in degree from the images we have while we are day dreaming, or those we have while dreaming in the proper sense, or again from the after-images, or as they are more properly called, the after-sensations which sometimes follow our visual sensations. All these appearances would be regarded by certain philosophers as in principle of the same kind. This position is paradoxical to common-sense which regards perceptual experience as giving first-hand acquaintance with physical objects, and hallucinations and illusions as failing precisely in this respect. The common-sense ground for the distinction however is removed by the sense-datum theorist, and if in fact he does believe in physical objects, he has to substitute a new ground of a far more subtle and elaborate nature. In some cases he may prefer to get along altogether without physical objects, and may even urge that if we once give up the common-sense ground of distinction as untenable there is no other ground for believing in them.[1] Such questions as these, however, are domestic problems of sense-datum theorists and need not detain us, as we are intent on coming to grips with the basis of the theory itself. It is important to note, however, that once the sense-datum theory is developed in the form stated above, it follows that, even if physical objects exist, they are never present in perceptual experience; and it becomes an open question whether they have any existence at all.

I shall consider later whether the arguments for the existence of sense-data in the sense indicated are valid. First, however, I want to state two considerations regarding the sense-datum itself. The first is of a very general nature and calculated to make us wonder whether

[1] As Dr. Luce does, in his "Immaterialism." (Annual Philosophical Lecture, British Academy, 1944.)

a theory which departs so radically from common sense can be true; the second points out what extraordinary existents sense-data would be if there were such things.[2]

(1) The general consideration concerning the sensum theory is as follows: If the theory is true, then in all our perceptual experience sensa are interposed between us and the physical world, whereas it is one of our most strongly held beliefs that in perception we are face to face with the physical world. I do not wish to suggest that no attempt can be made to answer this obvious objection. The sensum theory can and does urge that in a Pickwickian sense of the term *perceive* we do perceive physical objects, i.e., we perceive sensa which are related in certain ways to physical objects. Nevertheless there is no doubt that, when presented with this type of explanation, we are apt to feel that we have been given a very inferior substitute in exchange for the direct acquaintance with physical objects which we have been called upon to surrender. We receive in no different spirit the other attempted rejoinder that physical objects *are* sensa, or more elegantly, are logical constructions out of sensa, and that whether we "talk" physical objects or sensa is a purely linguistic affair. I shall say nothing of this rejoinder now, as I shall have occasion to discuss it later when I come to examine Mr. Ayer's view that the sense-datum theory is not a theory at all, but merely a new and better way of speaking of what we all believe.

Not only do we feel that sensa are an inadequate substitute for the physical objects which we claim to be confronted with in perception, but they seem to be embarrassingly numerous. Every appearance, however evanescent and fleeting, can claim to be an existent. As ordinary men, we contrast the intermittent character of our perceptual experience, broken as it is by sleep, lack of attention and change of place, with the permanent or relatively permanent and continuing status of physical objects. The changing facets of our perceptual experience we distribute carefully, crediting some to the physical world and disowning others as apparent only. The sensum theory credits all alike to reality, since it considers each and every one to be an individual entity. It is from this beginning that the wilder

---

2 As the form of sense-datum theory now to be considered is that which has been most clearly worked out by Prof. Broad, I propose to substitute for the word *sense-datum* in this section the word *sensum* which Prof. Broad himself uses in its place. We shall see later that what Prof. Moore and others have to say about sense-data makes it advisable to have different words for the two theories, distinguished as follows: *sense-datum*, the immediate object in perception which may or may not be identical with a part of a physical object; *sensum*, the immediate object in perception, taken to be non-physical. Prof. Price, whose views are very like those of Prof. Broad, speaks of sense-data, but would, if he had accepted this rule for the use of the two words, have spoken of sensa.

excesses of realism took their origin, in which not only reality but mind-independence was credited lavishly to almost anything that could be named, until the world began to take on the appearance of a great museum in which a few of the contents were real operative beings but the vast majority were exhibits only, ready to be produced on the appropriate occasion, but possessed of no other ground of existence.

I am not inclined to over-estimate the effect that a general consideration of this kind can be expected to have, but it is not lightly to be dismissed. There are philosophers to whom a single departure from the norms of common sense acts only as a stimulus to further more exciting philosophical adventures in the realms of speculation, but I confess that, for my part, I regard such a departure rather as a danger signal, warning that it would be wise to consider whether the steps which have led to this departure are as secure as they appear to be.

It is one thing to assert of a theory, however, that it presents us with a large number of existents which seem unnecessary and which, if they existed, would make it difficult to justify our acquaintance with physical objects; it is quite another to show that the existents are not merely unnecessary but are open to grave objections. This is the second point to which we must now turn.

(2) There are two reasons for considering sensa to be very objectionable existents.

(i) In the first place, unlike physical objects they do not always obey the Law of Excluded Middle. If I contemplate an object at some distance, it often happens that I am uncertain whether it is circular or polygonal. It is necessary for me to approach closer before I can determine the matter with certainty. On the sensus theory, the mode in which the object appeared to me at first is a sensum, and every sensum *is* what it appears to be. Now this sensum appears neither circular nor non-circular. Therefore it is neither circular nor non-circular. Let us be quite clear on this point. It is not that I do not know whether it is circular or non-circular, though in fact it must be one or the other. It really is neither one nor the other. This kind of experience is more common than one is perhaps inclined to believe at first. When an optician asks you to read those minute letters inscribed at the bottom of his chart, there comes a time when you are compelled to say "I am not sure whether it is an M or an N," because the shape you see is sufficiently indeterminate for you to think it may be either. Of course, some eminent philosophers have thought that reality did not obey the Law of Excluded Middle, but it would be surprising to find Professor Broad in their company.

It is tempting to urge that we *must* know the shape of the

sensum because an artist can sit down and draw something which reproduces the shape. A little reflection, however, will show that what the artist does is to draw something which, having a certain definite shape, will appear at a certain distance to be as indeterminate in shape as the object itself appeared. In other words, what the artist does is the same in principle as what a joiner might do by building another object like the first one which would give rise to the same sort of appearance as the first one. So far as I can see, all so-called sensa, i.e., colours, sounds, smells, etc., are indeterminate in this way, though under favourable conditions the range of indeterminary is so limited that it is, for practical purposes, not of any importance.

(ii) The second reason for considering sense-data to be objectionable existents, though closely connected with the former, is less formidable; but is worth mentioning because it leads up to a number of very interesting considerations. It is a necessary consequence of the fact that a sense-datum *is* what it appears to be that there is no possibility of making further discoveries about its nature. It is always possible to get to know more and more about a particular existent, such as an apple or a squirrel, and, so far as we can tell, this process need never come to an end. There is no progress to be made in our knowledge of any particular sensum. This contention may seem to go too far in view of the revelations which philosophers claim to have about sensa. It can, however, be justified. Our knowledge of things is increased either by observation or by experiment. Experiment, as a means of gaining knowledge of sensa, is clearly ruled out, since it is obvious that any movement on my part or interference with the conditions will only cause one sensum to be replaced by another. It does, however, seem as though I might increase my knowledge of a particular sensum by observing it more closely than I had done. Rather, we must say, "by observing it more closely than I am doing," for clearly, my closer observation can only yield me more knowledge if it follows uninterruptedly upon my first. It will not do for me to come back at 5 P.M. to a closer study of the sensum which my table presented at 3 P.M. Can I gain more knowledge by continuing to observe it at 3 P.M.? I think we must say that I cannot. If we were to maintain that this was possible, and that something in the sensum previously unobserved might by observation be brought to light, we should need some criterion for making certain that it was the same sensum which we were observing at a later date as at an earlier date. *But no observation or experiment can yield a criterion.* The sensum theorists offer us little help on this point. The only thing is to fall back on the principle that a sensum is what it appears to be. If we interpret this as meaning it is all that it appears to be *and nothing more,* then the possibility of learning anything about a sensum is cut away at once, for the very good reason that we know all there is to know about it by simply having it. It is, I think, a very odd fact, if true, that there are existents such that their being known at all entails their being completely known. . . .

So far we have been considering the difficulties that arise from holding that sensa form a class of existents totally different from physical objects. Though the difficulties are perhaps not sufficiently serious to destroy the theory, they seem to me quite serious enough to make it desirable to look carefully into the considerations put forward for inducing belief in such entities.

These considerations seem to me to reduce to one fundamental argument, and this argument seems to me to be false, though plausible. If I am right, then the reason for believing in sensa goes.

I quoted earlier three typical arguments for the existence of sensa. I now wish to examine carefully a single argument which embodies the principle of these and other similar arguments. No one will deny, I think, that a situation may exist in which the following three propositions are true:

> (i) I see the rose.
> (ii) The rose appears pink to me.
> (iii) The rose is red.

The belief in sensa is reached by arguing, not unplausibly, that since what I am seeing appears pink, there exists something which *is* pink; and since the rose is red, not pink, it cannot be the rose which is pink; therefore what I am seeing is something other than the rose. Whereupon the term sensum is invented and given as a name to this existent and others like it. And so we reach the conclusion:

> (iv) I see a pink sensum.

The argument is fallacious. *That something appears pink to me is not a valid reason for concluding either that that thing is pink or that there is some other thing which is pink.* From the fact that a thing *looks* pink I can sometimes with the help of certain other propositions infer that it *is* pink or that it *is* red; I may also, with the help of certain other propositions, be able to infer that something in some other place is pink, e.g., the electric light bulb which is illuminating the rose. But I cannot infer, as is proposed, *merely from the three facts that I am seeing something, that it looks pink and that it is red, that there is a pink something where the thing appears pink to me.*

This, when we examine it, is the foundation stone on which the great edifice of the sensum theory has been raised. Is it surprising that the upper storeys present doubts and perplexities? But there is worse to come. Not only is the argument fallacious but the conclusion contradicts one of the premises, viz., (i) I see a rose. It does so because, in order that the conclusion should seem at all plausible, it has been assumed that, if I were to see a rose which actually possessed a red colour, I should see it as red, i.e., it would necessarily appear red to me. This again is an assumption in contradiction with propositions (ii) and (iii) taken together. . . .

There is another way in which an attempt may be made to justify the conclusion of the argument we have condemned as fallacious. I have argued that from the fact that something which is red appears pink, it does not follow that a pink sensum exists. It may be said that the existence of a pink sensum, while not following from the premises, is justified by a direct appeal to our sense experience. "I see it, therefore it is." The argument can be stated as follows: "I certainly see a pink something and to say that there is nothing pink is to say that I have no reason for believing in what I see now; and if I cannot believe in what I see now, how can I believe in what I see on any occasion, or any one else in what he sees on any occasion? If you deny existence of this pink patch, you deny the existence altogether of the world revealed by the senses." The answer to this objection is simple, if we reflect, viz., "You never can believe in what you see on any occasion, it always may mislead you as to what the thing is. If you wish to state only that something appears to be so and so, this can safely be done. But this is not a statement about something made on the basis of a piece of evidence, it is a statement of the piece of evidence itself, which you already have before you without clothing it in words." Modes of appearance are clues to the nature of what exists, not existents. I submit that it is improper to ask whether the pink mode of appearing, which is how the rose appears to me, exists. You may ask whether the rose exists and whether it is red or pink; and in answering this question account must be taken of how it appears under different conditions and to different people. Although modes of appearance are not existents, they are the material and the only material on which thinking can operate to discover the nature of existing things; and it is an epistemological ideal that if we were to discover completely the nature of existing things, there would be nothing left in the modes of appearance which would not entirely harmonise with our system of knowledge and find its explanation there.

On Prof. Broad's theory, sensa are entities which cannot be identified with material things or the surfaces or other parts of material things. The notion of sensum is necessary in that theory to solve the appearance-reality problem consisting in the fact that a penny, though round, may appear elliptical. The solution is "to change the subject." "What is round is the penny, what is elliptical is the sensum." [3] Having proceeded in this way, it would have been folly to get into a position in which a sensum itself might be said to appear to have a quality which in fact it did not have and thus be confronted again with the same problem. Mr. Ayer points this out.[4]

If we examine the way in which Prof. Moore and his disciples use the word sense-datum we shall see (i) that they attach a quite different meaning to the word sense-datum from that given to it by philosophers who use it in the way Prof. Broad uses sensum; (ii) that the refutation in the previous section does not apply to them; and (iii) that there is no reason, in the way they use the term, for finding any difficulty in the assertion that a sense-datum may appear to have qualities which it does not possess.

Let us consider the very careful account given by Prof. Moore of what a sense-datum is: "In order to point out to the reader what sort of things I mean by sense-data, I need only ask him to look at his own right hand. If he does this he will be able to pick out something (and unless he is seeing double, only one thing) with regard to which he will see that it is, at first sight, a natural view to take, that that thing is identical, not indeed with his whole right hand, but with that part of its surface which he is actually seeing, but will also (on a little reflection) be able to see that it is doubtful whether it can be identical with the part of the surface of his hand in question. Things *of the sort* (in a certain respect) of which this thing is, which he sees in looking at his hand, and with regard to which he can understand how some philosophers should have supposed it to be part of the surface of his hand which he is seeing, while others have supposed that it can't be, are what I mean by sense-data. I therefore define the term in such a way that it is an open question whether the sense-datum which I now see in looking at my hand and which is a sense-datum of my hand, is or is not identical with that part of its surface which I am now actually seeing." [5]

This is a much quoted passage and has provoked a great deal of criticism. I wish only to make one point on it. After indicating to what we are to direct our attention Prof. Moore explains that this object of our attention, thought by some to be a part of the surface of his hand, by others not to be so, is a specimen of what he means by a sense-datum. On this definition, of course, I believe in sense-data, and so does anyone who believes that things have surfaces; and that parts of those surfaces on certain occasions appear to us. For on this statement of the theory of sense-data, the man who maintains that we see

[3] "Scientific Thought," p. 245.
[4] "Foundations of Empirical Knowledge," p. 69.
[5] "The Defence of Common Sense," in *Contemporary British Philosophy,* Second Series, p. 217.

things themselves and the man who maintains that we do not see the things themselves but only some other entities which are in some way related to the things, both believe in sense-data. Instead of distinguishing between philosophers who believe in sense-data and philosophers who do not, we should have to distinguish between those who believe that sense-datum is just another word for a visible part of a surface, those who believe that the sense-datum, though it looks like the surface and is easily mistaken for it, is quite a different sort of thing, and those who, like Prof. Moore, are frankly puzzled as to which to think. This is very awkward; and is made more awkward by the fact that it means insisting that great numbers of philosophers, including myself, believe in sense-data, when for the purpose of distinguishing our views from those of Dr. Broad and similar views we are compelled to assert that we do not believe in sense-data.[6] If it is said that the term is neutral, I think the answer must be that Prof. Moore tries to use it in a neutral way but does not completely succeed. An example of the un-neutral character of the term as used by Prof. Moore is afforded by the discussion of sense-datum in "Some Judgements of Perception." He is discussing the judgement "This is an inkstand," and says: ". . . sense-data are the sort of things *about* which such judgements as these always seem to be made—the sort of things which seem to be the real or ultimate subjects of all such judgements." [7] He goes on to say a little later: "If there be a thing which is this inkstand at all, it is certainly *only* known to me as *the* thing which stands in a certain relation to this sense-datum." [8] If this is meant merely to convey that the whole surface is never visible at one moment, it is obviously true. If it is meant to convey that the whole inkstand is in no way presented in perception, it seems to me erroneous, for even when I am looking at the front of it I have some kind of awareness of the back of it. Further, by walking around it I can have several different views of it, and it does not seem to me to be any one of these which is the subject of my judgment.

The subject of my judgement seems to me not to be a sense-datum, even taken as a part of the surface, but the whole inkstand, which, though not perceived in its entirety, is presented as a whole that is more than my perception reports it to be. . . .

6 As has already been pointed out, Prof. Broad uses the term, "sensum" not sense-datum for his peculiar entities. So far as I can see he uses the words "sensible appearance" and not "sense-datum" as a neutral word when required. If a neutral word is necessary this is certainly the nearest approach; but it seems to fall short of being really neutral, so much so that it suggests the clue to what, in my opinion, is the correct theory of perception.

7 "Philosophical Studies," pp. 231–32.

8 "Philosophical Studies," p. 234.

I now propose to state briefly the lines of an alternative account to the sensum theory. The account is quite simple and is implicit in the foregoing discussion. I can claim no great originality for it as it is substantially the theory put forward by Prof. Dawes Hicks [9] and called by Prof. Broad the Multiple Relation Theory of Appearance. I can claim only that I arrived at it by a somewhat different line of thought and for that reason my statement of it may have some interest. I propose to call it simply the theory of appearing. I hope to show that it is the theory implicit in common sense and that it can be defended against the more obvious objections.

We saw that the sensum theory was led into difficulties by concluding from the propositions (i) I see the rose, (ii) The rose appears pink to me, and (iii) The rose is red, to a proposition (iv) I see a pink sensum. To attain consistency it was necessary to distinguish between the meaning which the word *see* has in proposition (i) and that which it has in proposition (iv). It is obvious, however, when we reflect, that propositions such as (i) must be incomplete versions of propositions such as (ii), e.g., "I see the rose as pink" is the expanded form of the proposition (i), which says the same thing as proposition (ii), but begins with me and proceeds to the rose, instead of beginning with the rose and proceeding to me. It is evident, further, if this is so, that *see* must have the same sense but in the reverse direction, as *appears*.

The account I put forward, then, is that objects themselves appear to us in sense-perception; that they in general appear in sense-perception to have those qualities which they in fact have; that where they appear to have qualities which they do not in fact have, these instances are more properly regarded as their failing in differing degrees to appear to have the properties they do have, such failure being accounted for by the conditions under which they are perceived. We must be quite bold at this point and admit at once that on this account of the matter a thing can possess a certain quality and at the same time appear to some one to possess another quality, which it could not actually possess in conjunction with the former quality. Let us be quite clear about what we are saying. When I see a circular penny as elliptical I am seeing the circular surface of the penny, not some elliptical substitute. This circular surface, it is true, appears elliptical to me, but the fact has no tendency to show that I am not directly aware of the circular surface. Aeneas was none the less in the presence of his mother Venus though she concealed from him the full glory of her godhead.

It is clear that, on this theory, perception has a much closer re-

---

[9] In his "Critical Realism."

semblance to thinking than would be allowed by the sensum theorists. For (i) it may have a content more or less false to the real, as thought may; and (ii) this content does not exist independent of the act of perceiving any more than the content of a false proposition.[10] The chief objection to this contention is stated by Prof. Broad as follows: "It is very hard to understand how we could seem to ourselves to *see* the property of bentness exhibited in a concrete instance, if in fact *nothing* was present to our minds that possessed that property." [11] I can see no great difficulty in this, and we have seen how the attempt to escape from the imagined difficulty leads to difficulties. Fourteen years later Prof. Broad himself was not so sure for he says: "Now one may admit that a certain particular might seem to have a characteristic which differs from and is incompatible with the characteristic which it does have. But I find it almost incredible that one particular extended patch should seem to be two particular extended patches at a distance apart from each other." [12] Prof. Price finds the same difficulty, for he says: "It is not really sense to say 'To me the candle appears double. . .' 'doubler' is not really a predicate at all." [13]

Seven years have passed since Prof. Broad wrote the latter of his two quoted statements so it may be that he now finds the assertion more credible. I certainly find nothing incredible in it. No doubt it is impossible for one candle to *be* two candles but there seems no reason why it should not appear to be any number of things. Finally, hallucinations and delusions need present no insuperable difficulties. There appeared to Lady Macbeth to be a dagger but there was no dagger in fact. Something appeared to be a dagger, and there are certainly problems concerning exactly what it is in such circumstances appears to be possessed of qualities which it does not possess. It is easy of course to object that an illusory dagger is not just nothing. The answer is neither "Yes, it is" nor "No, it isn't" but "An illusory dagger is a misleading expression if used to describe an element in the situation." It is misleading also in some degree to say that there exists "a dagger-like appearance," though we need not be mislead by such a use of the word *appearance* if we are careful. Strictly speaking, however, there are no such things as appearances. To suppose that there are would be like supposing that because Mr. X put in an appearance, there must have been something over and

---

10 It is a salutary reflection in this connection that the spiritual home of the sensum at one time opened its gates wide to an even more peculiar entity, the proposition.
11 "Scientific Thought," p. 241.
12 "Mind and Its Place in Nature," p. 188.
13 "Perception," pp. 62–63.

above Mr. X which he was kind enough to put in. "Mr. X appeared": that is the proper mode of expression if we are to avoid difficulties.[14]

An existent must be determinate and we saw that what are alleged to be existents and called sense-data could not meet this demand. To give rise to similar difficulties by speaking of appearances, thereby seeming to condone treating the modes in which things appear as existents, would be most inappropriate. That a thing, though wholly determinate, should fail to reveal its full determinate character to a single *coup d'œil* is surely to be expected and our theory derives support from the fact that objects do not always appear in their fully determinate nature.

There is another point about our account of the matter. It allows that it is *possible* for certain people at certain times to become acquainted through perception with things as they are, not merely as they appear to be. This can be seen best as follows. The word *sense-datum* was substituted for the word *appearance* to emphasise that there is an indubitable element in sense experience, in contrast with the use of the term *appearance* by philosophers who denied the existence of any such given, and who used the contrast between appearance and reality to grind a metaphysical axe of their own. But, as was pointed out by Prof. Moore, the term was often used with the connotation "not a physical reality." If this connotation is accepted, it follows that, however extensive our acquaintance with sense-data, we are no whit nearer to becoming acquainted with physical objects, and it is even difficult to see how we can know *about* these latter. This is the "great barrier" objection to the theory as held by Prof. Broad and his followers. Even for those who avoid putting into the term sense-datum this unwarrantable connotation the term is apt to give rise to unnecessary difficulties. For example, Mr. Wisdom, more careful than most philosophers not to be misled by the term, writes: "I should agree that it is unplausible to say that, although when I see a thing in bad light my corresponding sense-datum is not identical with the observed surface of the thing, nevertheless, when the light changes, the corresponding sense-datum which I then obtain is identical with the observed surface, I cannot say why I find this unplausible, but I do. I find such a discontinuity, such a popping in and out of the material world on so slight a provocation, most objectionable."[15] If we are content to talk in terms of appearance or, better

---

[14] Cf. the judicious remark of Prof. Dawes Hicks: "When, in ordinary language, we speak of the objective constituent of a perceptual situation as being the "appearance of" a physical object we mean not that it is the appearance which appears but that it is the physical object which appears." ("Critical Realism," p. 55.) Even so, it is better to avoid the noun altogether, or at least always to test out the validity of its use by mentally translating into the verb.

[15] John Wisdom, "Problems of Mind and Matter," p. 156.

still, of things appearing, we shall not have pseudo-problems of this kind. We need have no heart-burning about the following statement: "Although when I see a thing in bad light the surface does not appear to me in every respect as it really is, nevertheless, when the light is adequate, it does." The reason we are now talking better sense is that the language of appearance permits us to maintain (a) that a thing can not only appear what it is not, but what it is: (b) that a thing's appearing what it is not is best understood as a deviation from its appearing what it is. A terminology which purports to be neutral and yet makes these propositions sound absurd has prejudged the issue in a most unfortunate manner.[16]

On the theory outlined it is easy to explain how we can come to know about material objects for in all our perception we are perceiving material objects even though we are not always completely successful in perceiving them exactly as they are. On the sensum theory, as we have seen, it is difficult to explain why knowledge of sensa should contribute towards knowledge of material things; how we could ever have been led to the belief in material things; and, still less, how we could justify the belief.

Finally, the account of the matter I have given is, I think, remarkably close to common sense. As Prof. Broad claims that this type of theory departs as widely from common sense as the sensum theory this claim needs to be defended. He argues that, as commonly used, a statement such as "I see a table" involves the unexpressed theory that there is a situation involving two constituents, myself and the table, related by a relation of seeing, a relaion which proceeds from me to the table. This theory, ascribed to common sense, Prof. Broad calls naïve realism.[17] Now it is only plausible to maintain that this theory is held by the ordinary man if carefully selected perceptual statements concerning objects at close range are considered. If we regard the whole range of perceptual situations the common sense belief is quite different. This belief involves that in perceptual situations objects reveal more or less of their nature to us; and common sense would find no difficulty in admitting that there are cases where very little of the nature of the object of perception is revealed. For example, statements of the following type are a commonplace: "I can just see something, but I cannot make out what it is," "I think I can see something there but I cannot be sure," "It

16 In fairness to Mr. Wisdom it must be pointed out that immediately after making the statement quoted, he goes on to say something which, if I understand it rightly, is very like what I have said except that (a) he calls that which appears a sense-datum and (b) identifies it with an object's surface.

17 "Naïve Realism . . . is the explicit formulation of the belief which forms *an essential part* of the perceptual situation as such." "The Mind and Its Place in Nature," p. 243.

looks like a house, but it may be just an outcrop of rock." Instances could be multiplied indefinitely. Common sense would not scruple to admit that objects do not always have the qualities which they seem to have when seen, heard, tasted, touched or smelt. It accepts without flinching that the hills which look purple in the distance are really green. It is indeed a platitude enshrined in proverbial literature that "things are seldom what they seem."

I draw attention to these elementary facts, in the first place, to point out that the only naïveté about naïve realism is that philosophers should have thought the ordinary man believed it. More important, however, is that these facts show the common sense view not to involve belief in a simple two-termed relation between me and the things I perceive, in which no possibility of illusion can arise, but a relation in which there is the possibility of the object's nature being revealed to a greater or less degree. It is true, of course, that the plain man no less than the philosopher sometimes puts as the object of *see* not the material thing but the *how it appears* as when, looking into the distance, one says "I can see a purple haze; it may be mountains or cloud." No violence is done to his language if it is rewritten "I see something as purple and hazy" or "There is something which appears purple and hazy." It is the lack of sufficient information to establish the nature of the object appearing which leads to the varying form of statement.

In concluding, I do not wish to suggest that no problems beset the theory of appearing. For example the two cases of a thing's appearing double and of something appearing to be where there is no such thing, present the problem: Is the apparent expanse in these cases the actual surface of any object? If so, of what object? I must, however, defer the inquiry into this and other problems to a future occasion, when I can consider the affinities of this theory with the different but closely related theory of multiple inherence and at the same time discuss some of the points in Prof. Dawes Hicks' exposition with which I am not perfectly satisfied. Here I have only been able to indicate the possibility of such an account as an appendix to my main task which has been to criticise those theories which make the notion of sense-datum fundamental in their explanations of perception.

BARNES SELECTION

1. State as clearly and precisely as you can the position that Barnes is arguing *against*. Which of the philosophers included in this chapter hold that position?

2. Recall the problem posed in the Introduction to this chapter.

Barnes thinks it is absurd to suggest that none of us ever *directly* sees a physical object. How would he explain the well-known facts of the physiology of perception? Do those facts support the sense-data theory he is attacking? Why?

3. In his example of the red rose that appears pink, Barnes is arguing against the notion that there must be a pink something that is actually, directly present to the mind. He summarizes his argument by saying that "modes of appearance are clues to the nature of what exists, not existents." What does this mean? How might a defender of the sense-datum theory reply?

4. When Barnes comes to state his own theory, he speaks of objects that appear in sense-perception. The objects, he says, for the most part appear to have "those qualities which they in fact have." What does it mean to say that a rose "in fact has the quality red" but only appears to have the "quality pink"? If it always looks pink under a certain kind of light, and always looks red under another kind of light, why can't we just as well say that it in fact has the property pink, but sometimes (most of the time) appears red? Is there any difference between these two ways of describing the rose? Since they agree on how the rose looks under different sorts of light, how, if at all, do they disagree?

1. In his opening selection, Descartes searches for certain and indubitable truths. He rejects the claims of sense-experience first, obviously thinking them to have relatively little certainty. The other philosophers included in this chapter seem to think, contrary to Descartes, that if certainty is to be found anywhere, it is precisely in the claims of sense-experience. Is this a real disagreement between Descartes and the others, or only an apparent disagreement? Does Descartes agree that "'sense-datum reports" are certain?

2. Is there anything in Lewis's theory of terminating and nonterminating judgments that Berkeley (i.e., Philonous) cannot accept? If Berkeley can accept the theory of terminating and nonterminating judgments, then can he also agree that material objects, in Lewis's sense of the term, exist? Is Lewis a skeptic? Would Hylas consider Lewis a skeptic?

3. Could Lewis accept Barnes's arguments against the notion of sense-data and still maintain his theory of terminating judgments? Why?

4. According to Lewis, our statements about material objects imply, or "unpack into," series of terminating judgments about immediate sense-presentations. If that is true, then in what sense (if any) are material objects independent existences? How can Lewis answer the charge that, on his view, physical reality is "all in the mind"?

5. Barnes's arguments are directed most forcefully against philosophers like Price. What answers can Price give to Barnes's arguments? Which side is right, in your judgment? Why?

CHAPTER five

NORMATIVE ETHICAL THEORIES

(Focal Issues)

1. *Are There any Objectively Valid Principles of Morality?*

2. *If There Are, What Are They?*

3. *What Is the Relationship of Happiness to Morality?*

4. *Why Should I Do What is Right?*

INTRODUCTION

Let me pose what philosophers sometimes call a "hard case." You can think it over, talk about it with your fellow students, or even take a vote on it in class (as we did in one course when I was a student in the 1950's). Suppose that you and a friend have gone exploring to a small island in the South Pacific. You simply like adventure, she is a devoted student of rare flowers. On the island your friend discovers a flower that was thought to be extinct; she cultivates it, nurses it along, waiting for the magical moment when (once every hundred years) it blooms. Alas, she is bitten by a poisonous spider and now lies close to death in the rude shelter the two of you have constructed. Your original plans called for the two of you to stay on the island for another two months, well past the time when the flower is due to bloom. But your radio tells you that a bad storm is coming your way. If you are to have a good chance of getting away alive, you must leave within the week (by which time, by the way, she will be dead).

In her last moments, weak but perfectly clearheaded and rational, your friend looks up at you and makes a strange request. Will you stay long enough to see the flower through to its blooming, even though by doing so you will endanger your life? She does not want you to lie to her! Very forcefully, she insists that she would rather die unhappy than have you make a false promise. But if you are genuinely willing to risk your life for her dream, she will be able to accept death more easily. Moved by this plea, you pledge yourself to stay. You make the promise freely and sincerely, and moments later she dies, comforted by the knowledge that her beloved flower will not bloom unseen.

So far, so good. Now comes the hard question: should you keep your promise? On the one hand, you are risking your life by staying on the island, and all for a flower that you could not care less about. On the other hand, you did promise, in full and uncoerced awareness of what you were doing!

If you find it a trifle difficult to think seriously about desert islands and exotic flowers, we can easily enough alter the example until it hits a sensitive spot in your conscience. For example, if a young mother dies in childbirth, pledging her husband to raise their child in the Catholic faith, and if he himself does not believe in that faith, ought he to keep his promise, even at considerable effort and sacrifice? Or would it be perfectly all right for him to forget the promise once he has buried his wife?

Let us put off trying to answer these questions for a moment, and ask instead a somewhat more general, preliminary question designed to get us started thinking about such cases in a useful way. What sorts of considerations should we take into account in deliberating about whether to keep our promises? For example, in the case of the flower and the dying friend, would it make a difference if the flower could be taken back to civilization and shown to other flower-lovers? Suppose that the price of my staying on the island were not a risk to my life but simply my having to give up a chance to see the World Series, which I love as much as she loved flowers. Suppose that the risk to my life were not considerable, but merely tiny. Does it matter that my friend was calm and rational when she made her request? Would I have a greater or a lesser obligation to stay if I had deliberately promised falsely, not intending to keep my word? Is it relevant whether any one else knows about my promise? Does it matter that by breaking my word I am weakening my own habit of promise keeping, so that in the future I will be less reliable than I have been in the past? Would the plusses and minuses of my situation be any different if my friend's devotion to flowers were part of a deep-lifelong religious conviction? Does it matter whether there is a God?

Philosophers have given all manner of answers to the sorts of questions we have just posed, but generally speaking, they have tended to group themselves into two camps. Fortunately, we have two long technical names for the camps, each with a Greek root. One camp are called the *teleologists,* from the Greek word *telos,* which means "end" or "goal." The other camp are called *deontologists,* from the Greek word *deon,* which means "that which is binding (or obligatory)."

The teleologists, when confronted with a moral dilemma like the one we have been considering, look at the probable consequences of the different courses of action that are available. They look to the future, to the effects, the outcomes, the good and bad results that each available choice can be expected to bring. To a teleologist, it will probably be quite important whether the risk I run is large or small, whether the flower can or cannot be brought back to civilization, whether I am or am not weakening my own tendency to keep my promises. A teleologist will also take account of the future possibilities that are foreclosed by one choice rather than another. If I am a skilled engineer whose expertise will save lives in future construction projects, then my potential contribution must be weighed in the balance when I am deciding whether to keep my promise. On the other hand, if I am a ne'er-do-well who has never done anyone, myself included, any good, then less is lost should I stay. A teleologist's answer to the hard case would be, "It depends." It depends on the circumstances, the likely (and not so likely) results of my staying and my leaving.

A deontologist, on the other hand, would look not to consequences but to principles. If it is right to keep promises, he would reason, and if this is a genuine case of promising, then I ought to honor my promise and stay. I have an *obligation* to stay, an obligation grounded not in the goodness of the probable consequences of my staying, but in the bindingness of promises. In some situations I may face what appears to be a conflict of obligations. (Some deontologists think that a genuine conflict of obligations is possible; others do not.) For example, my promise to drive a friend to the airport may conflict with a prior promise to drive a different friend to the hospital when she is due to have her baby. In cases of this sort, deontologists such as W. D. Ross (who is included in this chapter) say that the proper course of action can be determined by weighing the relative weights of the conflicting obligations and choosing the action to which is attached the heaviest duty.

When we ask a teleologist why we ought to perform some particular action, he points to the goodness of its expected consequences; when we ask a deontologist why we ought to perform some particular action, he points to the rightness of all action of the same sort. Obviously there are two pairs of parallel questions we can pose to each camp, the answers serving to define the precise teleological or deontological position being defended. To the teleologist, we can ask: (1) what characteristic or feature of outcomes is it that makes them, in your view, good outcomes? and (2) what particular sorts of actions are, in your view, good-making or good-producing? To the deontologist, in a similar manner, we can ask: (1) what characteristic or feature of actions is it that makes them right actions? and (2) what sorts of particular actions are in fact right?

Needless to say, the answers to these questions fill libraries, and I am not about to attempt a full-scale classification of them all. But in the case of each camp, there is one answer that stands out as the most prominent, the most common, and the most powerfully defended. In the selections included in this chapter, you will for the most part be encountering versions of those two principal answers.

The most important version of teleology in ethical theory is the position sometimes called hedonism, sometimes called epicureanism, but these days most often called *utilitarianism*. According to utilitarianism, in its simplest form, what make a state of affairs, an event, or an experience *good* is simply that it is *pleasant;* what makes a state of affairs, an event, or an experience *bad* is simply that it is *painful*. Pleasure is good, pain is bad, more pleasure is better than less, more pain is worse than less, and when we look at the consequences of an action for purposes of moral choice, we ought simply to look at the amounts of pleasure and pain that the action is likely to produce directly or indirectly, immediately or in the long run. A central (and very controversial) feature of utilitarianism is its democratic insistence that everyone's pleasure and pain be included when the calculation is being made, and that each person's pleasure or pain be given an equal place in the summation. No matter how we quantify and measure pleasures and pains (a *big* problem, as it turns out), one unit of pain suffered by a peasant is to weigh as much as one unit of pain suffered by a king. Neither rank nor sex nor age nor race is to influence the calculation. It is easy to see why utilitarianism, in the early nineteenth century, was a powerful weapon for social reform in the hands of such political philosophers as Jeremy Bentham and John Stuart Mill.

Utilitarianism is appealing because it seems so sensible and natural a view (although two centuries ago it would hardly have been thought so by New England Puritans!). On first reflection, at least, it seems obvious that it is good to be happy and bad to be unhappy. But there are at least four major difficulties with utilitarianism that have bedeviled the theory since it was first advanced in its modern form in the late eighteenth century.

First, utilitarianism requires us to add up quantities of pleasure and pain, and it is not at all obvious how we are to do that. What is a natural unit of pleasure? We might say, one minute of pleasure, but some pleasures are more intense than others, so that ten minutes of one seems better than an hour of another. Things get even trickier when we try to balance pleasures off against pains. How much pain from an hour's hard work is it worth in order to get the pleasure that I can buy with the wages from that work? These problems of measurement are difficult, but the utilitarian has an answer (even leaving aside some very sophisticated mathematical answers that have been developed in recent decades). We all do make such calculations every day of our lives, when we decide how to allocate our money, or whether to work overtime, or when it is time to go to the dentist. So it may be difficult to weigh up pleasures and pains, but it cannot be impossible.

The second problem with utilitarianism is that it requires us to compare this man's pleasure with that woman's pain, and that seems to call for some way to look into people's minds. I can compare one of my pains with another and tell which one hurts worse. But how can I compare my pain with yours (and how can you, for that matter)? This apparently simple difficulty has turned out to be especially vexing for utilitarians.

Third, when we apply the principle of utilitarianism to actual cases, it sometimes seems to tell us to do things that we know in our bones are wrong. For example, if a careful calculation of future pleasures and pains reveals that more pain will be avoided by hanging an innocent man for a brutal murder than by leaving the case open and allowing public passions to remain inflamed, then utilitarianism says that it is right (indeed, obligatory) to hang the innocent man. But surely *that* cannot be correct. What happens to our principles of justice, to our fundamental freedoms, to the ideals of a government of laws, if we accept calculations of that sort?

The fourth problem is that utilitarianism treats all pleasures as equally good, and all pains as equally bad, save for considerations of quantity. But when we are making our summations, ought we even to count the pleasure that a sadist takes in the suffering of his victim? Suppose a torturer gets more pleasure from his grisly work than the pain he inflicts—does that make his torturing morally acceptable? Surely in the utilitarian calculation, there are some pleasures and pains that do not deserve to be counted, and others to which a specal weight must in all fairness be given. But if that is so, then utilitarianism cannot be correct, at least not in its more common form.

The deontologist takes an entirely different line. In its strongest and most common form, deontological ethical theory holds that the rightness of an action derives from its conformity to principle, and that the test of a principle is it rationality. Immanuel Kant, far and away the most important defender of deontological ethical theory, claimed that the fundamental principles of right action could be derived from purely rational premises by arguments having the universality and certainty of logic. The keynotes of Kant's ethical theory are consistency, fidelity to principle, autonomy (which is to say, freedom from subservience to passion or desire), and an absolute respect for the moral worth of persons. To a deontologist like Kant, utilitarianism seems a servile and unworthy doctrine. It treats persons as nothing more than so many pleasure containers to be filled up to overflowing with bits of happiness, regardless of their own rational choices and moral worth.

Put our problem about the island flower to a deontologist, and he will scarcely hesitate. If the keeping of promises is rational, if it accords with principles derived from a consideration of man's free and rational nature as a responsible being, then the promise ought to be kept, regardless of the particular consequences that may in this case ensue. Perhaps the promise ought not to have been made, but once made, it is *binding* on him who made it.

Deontological theories are clearly strongest where utilitarianism is weak. They require no calculations of pleasures and pains, nor do they ask us to peer into the souls of our fellow men and women to spy out their feelings. The deontologist feels no temptation to punish the innocent or otherwise abrogate what we believe to be inviolable principles, and he will obviously have little trouble explaining why the pleasure of the torturer must count for nought in our moral deliberations. But deontological ethical theories (or *formalist* theories, as they are sometimes called) have serious difficulties of their own, difficulties which some philosophers consider absolutely crippling.

The first and most serious problem facing the deontologist is actually to produce a logical derivation of particular moral principles from rational premises. It is one thing to say, rather broadly, that as rational creatures we ought to abide by principles of pure reason; it is quite another actually to lay out a convincing argument that just this particular set of principles and no other fits that description. Logic dictates consistency, to be sure, but is consistency enough to rule in promise keeping and to rule out, say, self-interested promise breaking? Kant was quite conscious of the urgency of this challenge and in the selection included in this chapter we shall see him trying to apply his fundamental principle of ethics (the famous "Categorical Imperative") to four particular moral rules. You must judge for yourself whether he is successful.

The second problem facing the deontologist, as we have already seen, is the possibility of a conflict between two moral principles. Now, if our principles are derived by logically valid arguments from rational first premises, then it would seem that there cannot be a conflict between two moral principles, any more than there can be a conflict between two theorems of Euclidean Geometry. Kant himself did not acknowledge the possibility of ultimate conflict between valid moral principles, but some of his follows, such as the English philosopher W. D. Ross, tried to work out a revised form of deontological ethical theory to take account of such familiar cases as conflicting promises, or a conflict between the duty to keep promises and, for example, the duty to repay acts of generosity from which one has benefited.

The teleologist and the deontologist may differ sharply on the principles of ethics, but they agree completely that there *are* universal, valid, binding principles that all men and women ought to obey insofar as they seek to be moral. By and large, this has been the majority position in the history of Western ethical theory, but a powerful and persistent minority of philosophers have argued that there are no objective, universal moral principles at all. They accuse philosophers, priests, politicians, and ordinary men and women of elevating their own religious beliefs, their prejudices, the norms of their particular culture, or mere habit, to the status of *principles*. Like skepticism in epistemology and anarchism in political philosophy, this *subjectivism* is the persistent foe of all positive theories. In the last two selections in this chapter we shall confront the subjectivist denial of objective moral principles.

(SELECTION 1)

JEREMY BENTHAM

The Principle of Utility

Jeremy Bentham was the father of utilitarianism. Bentham, his friend James Mill, and his godson John Stuart Mill, made the Greatest Happiness principle a powerful force in British reform politics during the first half of the nineteenth century. Although it is now debated and analyzed primarily as an ethical theory, suitable for determining and evaluating the actions of individuals, utilitarianism was initially intended by Bentham and his associates as a guiding maxim for political and social decisions. It was a powerfully radical and anti-traditionalist principle, for it enjoined us to forget about how things had been done in the past and think only of the future consequences of such laws or government actions as might be initiated. As we have already noted, utilitarianism was also a democratic or leveling principle. Its rule—treat each pleasure or pain alike, save for differences in magnitude—echoed the political principle, "One man, one vote." In nineteenth-century public life, that rule, now so widely accepted, was revolutionary indeed.

The central problem in Bentham's version of utilitarianism is the gap between its theory of human motivation and its principle of morality. According to Bentham (and many other French and British philosophers of the seventeenth

and eighteenth centuries), human beings are moved to act solely by a desire for pleasure and an aversion to pain. In the jargon of philosophers, each of us, on this view, is "a psychological egoist." But the Greatest Happiness principle of utilitarianism tells me to choose that act which promises to produce the greatest happiness (or pleasure) for the greatest number of persons, not just for myself. If it is only the prospect of my own happiness that will move me, how can I ever be gotten to act on the basis of a consideration of the happiness of others as well?

Bentham's answer is a system of rewards and punishments built into the law that will alter my private calculation of pleasures so as to bring it into line with the larger needs of society as a whole. This is all right as far as it goes, but it hardly explains what will move the lawmakers, the judges, and the police to set aside *their* private interests as pleasure-seeking individuals in order to write and enforce a set of laws that serve the public good.

The great virtue of utilitarianism as a moral theory is the fact that it is "constructive." That is to say, it provides us with a rule by which we can calculate or "construct" an answer to a question of public policy. If we must decide, for example, whether to adopt a system of

338

agricultural price supports, utilitarianism tells us to estimate the costs of such a program, first in money and then in the lost pleasures that the taxing of such money will cost; compare the result with the benefits of the program, the pleasure or happiness brought to those family farmers who will be able to continue their traditional way of life, etc.; and then choose the program only if the net total of benefits over costs is greater than the net total for any other available program (including simply doing nothing). Whatever the theoretical difficulties of utilitarianism may be, that sounds like a pretty good description of the way responsible lawmakers actually make decisions in a democracy.

Nature has placed mankind under the governance of two sovereign masters, *pain* and *pleasure*. It is for them alone to point out what we ought to do, as well as to determine what we shall do. On the one hand the standard of right and wrong, on the other the chain of causes and effects, are fastened to their throne. They govern us in all we do, in all we say, in all we think: every effort we can make to throw off our subjection, will serve but to demonstrate and confirm it. In words a man may pretend to abjure their empire: but in reality he will remain subject to it all the while. The *Principle of utility* [1] recognises this subjection, and assumes it for the foundation of that system, the object of which is to rear the fabric of felicity by the hands of reason and of law. Systems which attempt to question it, deal in sounds instead of sense, in caprice instead of reason, in darkness instead of light.

But enough of metaphor and declamation: it is not by such means that moral science is to be improved.

The principle of utility is the foundation of the present work: it will be proper therefore at the outset to give an explicit and determinate account of what is meant by it. By the principle of utility is meant that principle which approves or disapproves of

[1] Note by the Author, July 1822.

To this denomination has of late been added, or substituted, the *greatest happiness* or *greatest felicity* principle: this for shortness, instead of saying at length *that principle* which states the greatest happiness of all those whose interest is in question, as being the right and proper, and only right and proper and universally desirable, end of human action: of human action in every situation, and in particular in that of a functionary or set of functionaries exercising the powers of Government. The word *utility* does not so clearly point to the ideas of *pleasure* and *pain* as the words *happiness* and *felicity* do: nor does it lead us to the consideration of the *number*, of the interests affected; to the *number*, as being the circumstance, which contributes, in the largest proportion, to the formation of the standard here in question; the *standard of right and wrong*, by which alone the propriety of human conduct, in every situation, can with propriety be tried. This want of a sufficiently manifest connexion between the ideas of *happiness* and *pleasure* on the one hand, and the idea of *utility* on the other, I have every now and then found operating, and with but too much efficiency, as a bar to the acceptance, that might otherwise have been given, to this principle.

From *An Introduction to the Principles of Morals and Legislation* by Jeremy Bentham. First published in 1789.

every action whatsoever, according to the tendency which it appears to have to augment or diminish the happiness of the party whose interest is in question: or, what is the same thing in other words, to promote or to oppose that happiness. I say of every action whatsoever; and therefore not only of every action of a private individual, but of every measure of government.

By utility is meant that property in any object, whereby it tends to produce benefit, advantage, pleasure, good, or happiness (all this in the present case comes to the same thing), or (what comes again to the same thing) to prevent the happening of mischief, pain, evil, or unhappiness to the party whose interest is considered: if that party be the community in general, then the happiness of the community: if a particular individual, then the happiness of that individual.

The interest of the community is one of the most general expressions that can occur in the phraseology of morals: no wonder that the meaning of it is often lost. When it has a meaning, it is this. The community is a fictitious *body,* composed of the individual persons who are considered as constituting as it were its *members.* The interest of the community then is, what?—the sum of the interests of the several members who compose it.

It is in vain to talk of the interest of the community, without understanding what is the interest of the individual. A thing is said to promote the interest, or to be *for* the interest, of an individual, when it tends to add to the sum total of his pleasures: or, what comes to the same thing, to diminish the sum total of his pains.

An action then may be said to be conformable to the principle of utility, or, for shortness sake, to utility (meaning with respect to the community at large), when the tendency it has to augment the happiness of the community is greater than any it has to diminish it.

A measure of government (which is but a particular kind of action, performed by a particular person or persons) may be said to be conformable to or dictated by the principle of utility, when in like manner the tendency which it has to augment the happiness of the community is greater than any which it has to diminish it.

When an action, or in particular a measure of government, is supposed by a man to be comformable to the principle of utility, it may be convenient, for the purposes of discourse, to imagine a kind of law or dictate, called a law or dictate of utility: and to speak of the action in question, as being conformable to such law or dictate.

A man may be said to be a partizan of the principle of utility, when the approbation or disapprobation he annexes to any action, or to any measure, is determined by and proportioned to the tendency which he conceives it to have to augment or to diminish the happiness of the community: or in other words, to its conformity or unconformity to the laws or dictates of utility.

Of an action that is conformable to the principle of utility one may always say either that it is one that ought to be done, or at least that it is not one that ought not to be done. One may say also, that it is right it should be done; at least that it is not wrong it should be done: that it is a right action; at least that it is not a wrong action. When thus interpreted, the words *ought,* and *right* and *wrong,* and others of that stamp, have a meaning: when otherwise, they have none.

Has the rectitude of this principle been ever formally contested? It should seem that it had, by those who have not known what they have been meaning. Is it susceptible of any direct proof? it should seem not: for that which is used to prove every thing else, cannot itself be proved: a chain of proofs must have their commencement somewhere. To give such proof is as impossible as it is needless.

Not that there is or ever has been that human creature breathing, however stupid or perverse, who has not on many, perhaps on most occasions of his life, deferred to it. By the natural constitution of the human frame, on most occasions of their lives men in general embrace this principle, without thinking of it: if not for the ordering of their own actions, yet for the trying of their own actions, as well as of those of other men. There have been, at the same time, not many, perhaps, even of the most intelligent, who have been disposed to embrace it purely and without reserve. There are even few who have not taken some occasion or other to quarrel with it, either on account of their not understanding always how to apply it, or on account of some prejudice or other which they were afraid to examine into, or could not bear to part with. For such is the stuff that man is made of: in principle and in practice, in a right track and in a wrong one, the rarest of all human qualities is consistency.

When a man attempts to combat the principle of utility, it is with reasons drawn, without his being aware of it, from that very principle itself. His arguments, if they prove any thing, prove not that the principle is *wrong,* but that, according to the applications he supposes to be made of it, it is *misapplied.* Is it possible for a man to move the earth? Yes; but he must first find out another earth to stand upon.

To disprove the propriety of it by arguments is impossible; but, from the causes that have been mentioned, or from some confused or partial view of it, a man may happen to be disposed not to relish it. Where this is the case, if he thinks the settling of his opinions on such a subject worth the trouble, let him take the following steps, and at length, perhaps, he may come to reconcile himself to it.

Let him settle with himself, whether he would wish to discard this principle altogether; if so, let him consider what it is that all his reasonings (in matters of politics especially) can amount to?

If he would, let him settle with himself, whether he would judge and act without any principle, or whether there is any other he would judge and act by?

If there be, let him examine and satisfy himself whether the principle he thinks he has found is really any separate intelligible principle; or whether it be not a mere principle in words, a kind of phrase, which at bottom expresses neither more nor less than the mere averment of his own unfounded sentiments; that is, what in another person he might be apt to call caprice?

If he is inclined to think that his own approbation or disapprobation, annexed to the idea of an act, without any regard to its consequences, is a sufficient foundation for him to judge and act upon, let him ask himself whether his sentiment is to be a standard of right and wrong, with respect to every other man, or whether every man's sentiment has the same privilege of being a standard to itself?

In the first case, let him ask himself whether his principle is not despotical, and hostile to all the rest of human race?

In the second case, whether it is not anarchial, and whether at this rate there are not as many different standards of right and wrong as there are men? and whether even to the same man, the same thing, which is right to-day, may not (without the least change in its nature) be wrong to-morrow? and whether the same thing is not right and wrong in the same place at the same time? and in either case, whether all argument is not at an end? and whether, when two men have said, "I like this," and "I don't like it," they can (upon such a principle) have any thing more to say?

If he should have said to himself, No: for that the sentiment which he proposes as a standard must be grounded on reflection, let him say on what particulars the reflection is to turn? if on particulars having relation to the utility of the act, then let him say whether this is not deserting his own principle and borrowing assistance from that very one in opposition to which he sets it up: or if not on those particulars, on what other particulars?

If he should be for compounding the matter, and adopting his own principle in part, and the principle of utility in part, let him say how far he will adopt it?

When he has settled with himself where he will stop, then let him ask himself how he justifies to himself the adopting it so far? and why he will not adopt it any farther?

Admitting any other principle than the principle of utility to be a right principle, a principle that it is right for a man to pursue; admitting (what is not true) that the word *right* can have a meaning without reference to utility, let him say whether there is any such thing as a *motive* that a man can have to pursue the dictates of it: if there is, let him say what that motive is, and how it is to be distinguished from those which enforce the dictates of utility: if not, then lastly let him say what it is this other principle can be good for?

Pleasures then, and the avoidance of pains, are the *ends* which the legislator has in view: it behoves him therefore to understand their *value*. Pleasures and pains are the *instruments* he has to work with: it behoves him therefore to understand their force, which is again, in other words, their value.

To a person considered *by himself,* the value of a pleasure or pain considered *by itself,* will be greater or less, according to the four following circumstances:

1. Its *intensity.*
2. Its *duration.*
3. Its *certainty* or *uncertainty.*
4. Its *propinquity* or *remoteness.*

These are the circumstances which are to be considered in estimating a pleasure or a pain considered each of them by itself. But when the value of any pleasure or pain is considered for the purpose of estimating the tendency of any *act* by which it is produced, there are two other circumstances to be taken into the account; these are,

5. Its *fecundity,* or the chance it has of being followed by sensations of the *same* kind: that is, pleasures, if it be a pleasure: pains, if it be a pain.

6. Its *purity,* or the chance it has of *not* being followed by sensations of the *opposite* kind: that is, pains, if it be a pleasure: pleasures, if it be a pain.

These two last, however, are in strictness scarcely to be deemed properties of the pleasure or the pain itself; they are not, therefore, in strictness to be taken into the account of the value of that pleasure or that pain. They are in strictness to be deemed properties only of the act, or other event, by which such pleasure or pain has been produced; and accordingly are only to be taken into the account of the tendency of such act or such event.

To a *number* of persons, with reference to each of whom the value of a pleasure or a pain is considered, it will be greater or less, according to seven circumstances: to wit, the six preceding ones; *viz.*

1. Its *intensity.*
2. Its *duration.*
3. Its *certainty* or *uncertainty.*
4. Its *propinquity* or *remoteness.*
5. Its *fecundity.*
6. Its *purity.*

And one other; to wit:

7. Its *extent;* that is, the number of persons to whom it *extends;* or (in other words) who are affected by it.

To take an exact account then of the general tendency of any act, by which the interests of a community are affected, proceed as follows. Begin with any one person of those whose interests seem most immediately to be affected by it: and take an account,

1. Of the value of each distinguishable *pleasure* which appears to be produced by it in the *first* instance.

2. Of the value of each *pain* which appears to be produced by it in the *first* instance.

3. Of the value of each pleasure which appears to be produced by it *after* the first. This constitutes the *fecundity* of the first *pleasure* and the *impurity* of the first *pain*.

4. Of the value of each *pain* which appears to be produced by it after the first. This constitutes the *fecundity* of the first *pain,* and the *impurity* of the first pleasure.

5. Sum up all the values of all the *pleasures* on the one side, and those of all the pains on the other. The balance, if it be on the side of pleasure, will give the *good* tendency of the act upon the whole, with respect to the interests of that *individual* person; if on the side of pain, the *bad* tendency of it upon the whole.

6. Take an account of the *number* of persons whose interests appear to be concerned; and repeat the above process with respect to each. *Sum* up the numbers expressive of the degrees of *good* tendency, which the act has, with respect to each individual, in regard to whom the tendency of it is *good* upon the whole: do this again with respect to each individual, in regard to whom the tendency of it is *good* upon the whole: do this again with respect to each individual, in regard to whom the tendency of it is *bad* upon the whole. Take the *balance;* which, if on the side of *pleasure,* will give the general *good tendency* of the act, with respect to the total number or community of individuals concerned; if on the side of pain, the general *evil tendency,* with respect to the same community.

It is not to be expected that this process should be strictly pursued previously to every moral judgment, or to every legislative or judicial operation. It may, however, be always kept in view: and as near as the process actually pursued on these occasions approaches to it, so near will such process approach to the character of an exact one.

The same process is alike applicable to pleasure and pain, in whatever shape they appear: and by whatever denomination they are distinguished: to pleasure, whether it be called *good* (which is properly the cause or instrument of pleasure) or *profit* (which is distant pleasure, or the cause or instrument of distant pleasure), or *convenience,* or *advantage, benefit, emolument, happiness,* and so forth; to pain, whether it be called *evil* (which corresponds to *good*), or *mischief,* or *inconvenience,* or *disadvantage,* or *loss,* or *unhappiness,* and so forth.

Nor is this a novel and unwarranted, any more than it is a useless theory. In all this there is nothing but what the practice of mankind, wheresoever they have a clear view of their own interest, is perfectly conformable to. An article of property, an estate in land, for instance, is valuable, on what account? On account of the pleasures of all kinds which it enables a man to produce, and what comes to the same thing the pains of all kinds which it enables him to avert. But the value of such an article of property is universally understood to rise or fall according to the length or shortness of the time which a man has in it: the certainty or uncertainty of its coming into possession: and the nearness or remoteness of the time at which, if at all, it is to come into possession. As to the *intensity* of the pleasures which a man may derive from it, this is never thought of, because it depends upon the use which each particular person may come to make of it; which cannot be estimated till the particular pleasures he may come to derive from it, or the particular pains he may come to exclude by means of it, are brought to view. For the same reason, neither does he think of the *fecundity* or *purity* of those pleasures.

BENTHAM SELECTION

1. Explain as clearly as you can, with examples, what Bentham means by "pleasure" and what he means by "pain." If it pleases me that my baseball team won the pennant, does that count as a *pleasure* for Bentham? If I am pained by my friend's rudeness to me, is that a *pain*?

2. What exactly is the "principal of utility"? What does Bentham mean by the statement that "the community is a fictitious body"? What would it mean to say that the community, or the society, was more than merely a fictitious body?

3. When we attempt to add up pleasures and pains, what problems are we likely to run into? Can you think of two pleasures (or two pains) which don't seem to be capable of being added together? Does it matter, for Bentham, what we derive our pleasure from, as opposed to how much pleasure we get?

4. Could there be such a thing as a bad pleasure? A good pain? How do you suppose Bentham would answer that question?

5. If we had a computerized device for recording the pleasure-pain quantities of every person in our country, and if we could trust people not to lie about their pleasures and pains, then we could get rid of the legislature and make laws simply by totaling up the pleasures and pains experienced or expected by each citizen. The law with the highest score would win the "vote." Would that be a good way to make laws? Why? What problems, if any, might we face in trying to use such a system?

(SELECTION 2)

J. J. C. SMART

Utilitarianism

In this selection from a somewhat longer essay, J. J. C. Smart lays out a relatively simple, straightforward version of utilitarianism and defends it against some well-known objections. An enormous literature has grown up in recent decades on various versions of utilitarianism. It has recently become philosophically fashionable to defend the version known as "rule-utilitarianism" rather than the simpler "act-utilitarianism" (see Smart's explanation of these terms, below). There are two reasons for the appeal of rule-utilitarianism. The first is that it seems to enable the utilitarian to take account of familiar moral convictions about punishment, desert, and so on (see the next selection for a discussion of some of the difficulties here). The second reason is that rule-utilitarianism makes room for the role of purely formal, rational considerations in moral deliberation, such as the requirement of universalizability (see the selection by Kant later in this chapter). Smart's defense of the more old-fashioned act-utilitarianism has about it, therefore, something of an air of bravado.

As Smart indicates by some of his examples, utilitarianism looks most plausible when we apply it to actual cases and try to think through what we ought to do in a concrete situation. For example, it is often objected that util-itarianism tells us to punish an innocent person in order to placate an angry mob, if the harm done to that man is less than the harm that would be done by the mob were it not quieted. Now, stated abstractly in that manner, such a proposal sounds barbaric. But imagine that you really were the chief of police of a big city, that you really were faced with the threat of a terribly destructive riot, and that the only way you could see to head off the disaster was to sacrifice an innocent person. Is it really so completely out of the question that you would choose to trump up charges against that person and railroad him into the electric chair? Don't we quite often, either in war or in natural disasters, choose to sacrifice fewer so that more can be saved? How else can we possibly make choices save by considering the happiness of those involved?

The answer to such arguments, of course, is that it is one thing to sacrifice an innocent person in conditions of dire necessity, and quite another to say that questions of guilt, innocence, and responsibility are irrelevant in deciding what to do. The act-utilitarian seems to be committed to the quite provocative proposition that only quantities of happiness, and not moral responsibility, are relevant to decisions about rewards, punishments, and social justice.

The system of normative ethics which I am here concerned to defend is . . . *act*-utilitarianism. Act-utilitarianism is to be contrasted with rule-utilitarianism. Act-utilitaranism is the view that the rightness or wrongness of an action is to be judged by the consequences, good or bad, of the action itself. Rule-utilitarianism is the view that the rightness or wrongness of an action is to be judged by the goodness and badness of the consequences of a rule that everyone should perform the action in like circumstances. . . .

I have argued elsewhere [1] the objections to rule-utilitarianism as compared with act-utilitarianism. [2] Briefly they boil down to the accusation of rule worship: [3] the rule-utilitarian presumably advocates his principle because he is ultimately concerned with human happiness: why then should he advocate abiding by a rule when he knows that it will not in the present case be most beneficial to abide by it? The reply that in most cases it is most beneficial to abide by the rule seems irrelevant. And so is the reply that it would be better that everybody should abide by the rule than that nobody should. This is to suppose that the only alternative to "everybody does *A*" is "no one does *A*." But clearly we have the possibility "some people do *A* and some don't." Hence to refuse to break a generally beneficial rule in those cases in which it is not most beneficial to obey it seems irrational and to be a case of rule worship.

The type of utilitarianism which I shall advocate will, then, be act-utilitarianism, not rule-utilitarianism. . . .

An act-utilitarian judges the rightness or wrongness of actions by the goodness and badness of their consequences. But is he to judge the goodness and badness of the consequences of an action solely by their pleasantness and unpleasantness? Bentham, [4] who

[1] In my article "Extreme and restricted utilitarianism," *Philosophical Quarterly* 6 (1956) 344–54. This contains bad errors and a better version of the article will be found in Philippa Foot (ed.), *Theories of Ethics* (Oxford University Press, London, 1967), or Michael D. Bayles (ed.), *Contemporary Utilitarianism* (Doubleday, New York, 1968). In this article I used the terms "extreme" and "restricted" instead of Brandt's more felicitous "act" and "rule" which I now prefer.

[2] For another discussion of what in effect is the same problem see A. K. Stout's excellent paper, "But suppose everyone did the same," *Australasian Journal of Philosophy* 32(1954) 1–29.

[3] On rule worship see I. M. Crombie, "Social clockwork and utilitarian morality," in D. M. Mackinnon (ed.), *Christian Faith and Communist Faith* (Macmillan, London, 1953). See p. 109.

[4] Jeremy Bentham's most important ethical work is "An Introduction to the Principles of Morals and Legislation," in *A Fragment on Government and an Introduction to the Principles of Morals and Legislation,* ed. Wilfrid Harrison (Blackwell, Oxford, 1948). For the remark on poetry and pushpin see Bentham's *Works* (Tait, Edinburgh, 1843), vol. 2, pp. 253–54.

From "An Outline of a System of Utilitarian Ethics" by J. J. C. Smart in *Utilitarianism for and Against* by J. J. C. Smart and Bernard Williams. (Cambridge University Press, 1973.)

thought that quantity of pleasure being equal, the experience of playing pushpin was as good as that of reading poetry, could be classified as a hedonistic act-utilitarian. Moore,[5] who believed that some states of mind, such as those of acquiring knowledge, had intrinsic value quite independent of their pleasantness, can be called an ideal utilitarian. Mill seemed to occupy an intermediate position.[6] He held that there are higher and lower pleasures. This seems to imply that pleasure is a necessary condition for goodness but that goodness depends on other qualities of experience than pleasantness and unpleasantness. I propose to call Mill a quasi-ideal utilitarian. For Mill, pleasantness functions like x in the algebraic product, $x \times y \times z$. If $x = 0$ the product is zero. For Moore pleasantness functions more like x in $(x + 1) \times y \times z$. If $x = 0$ the product need not be zero. Of course this is only a very rough analogy.

What Bentham, Mill and Moore are all agreed on is that the rightness of an action is to be judged solely by consequences, states of affairs brought about by the action. Of course we shall have to be careful here not to construe "state of affairs" so widely that any ethical doctrine becomes utilitarian. For if we did so we would not be saying anything at all in advocating utilitarianism. If, for example, we allowed "the state of having just kept a promise," then a deontologist who said we should keep promises simply because they are promises would be a utilitarian. And we do not wish to allow this. . . . Let us consider Mill's contention that it is "better to be Socrates dissatisfied than a fool satisfied." [7] Mill holds that pleasure is not to be our sole criterion for evaluating consequences: the state of mind of Socrates might be less pleasurable than that of the fool, but, according to Mill, Socrates would be happier than the fool.

It is necessary to observe, first of all, that a purely hedonistic utilitarian, like Bentham, might agree with Mill in preferring the experiences of discontented philosophers to those of contented fools. His preference for the philosopher's state of mind, however, would not be an *intrinsic* one. He would say that the discontented philosopher is a useful agent in society and that the existence of Socrates is responsible for an improvement in the lot of humanity generally. Consider two brothers. One may be of a docile and easy temperament: he may lead a supremely contented and unambitious life, enjoying himself hugely. The other brother may be ambitious, may stretch his talents to the full, may strive for scientific success and

[5] G. E. Moore, *Principia Ethica* (Cambridge University Press, London, 1962).
[6] J. S. Mill, *Utilitarianism*, ed. Mary Warnock (Collins, London, 1962).
[7] *Utilitarianism*, p. 9. The problem of the unhappy sage and the happy fool is cleverly stated in Voltaire's "Histoire d'un bon Bramin," *Choix de Contes*, edited with an introduction and notes by F. C. Green (Cambridge University Press, London, 1951), pp. 245–47.

academic honours, and may discover some invention or some remedy for disease or improvement in agriculture which will enable innumerable men of easy temperament to lead a contented life, whereas otherwise they would have been thwarted by poverty, disease or hunger. Or he may make some advance in pure science which will later have beneficial practical applications. Or, again, he may write poetry which will solace the leisure hours and stimulate the brains of practical men or scientists, thus indirectly leading to an improvement in society. That is, the pleasures of poetry or mathematics may be *extrinsically* valuable in a way in which those of pushpin or sun-bathing may not be. Though the poet or mathematician may be discontented, society as a whole may be the more contented for his presence. . . .

Maybe we have gone wrong in talking of pleasure as though it were no more than contentment. Contentment consists roughly in relative absence of unsatisfied desires; pleasure is perhaps something more positive and consists in a balance between absence of unsatisfied desires and presence of satisfied desires. We might put the difference in this way: pure unconsciousness would be a limiting case of contentment, but not of pleasure. A stone has no unsatisfied desires, but then it just has no desires. Nevertheless, this consideration will not resolve the disagreement between Bentham and Mill. No doubt a dog has as intense a desire to discover rats as the philosopher has to discover the mysteries of the universe. Mill would wish to say that the pleasures of the philosopher were more valuable intrinsically than those of the dog, however intense these last might be. . . .

. . . To call a person "happy" is to say more than that he is contented for most of the time, or even that he frequently enjoys himself and is rarely discontented or in pain. It is, I think, in part to express a favourable attitude to the idea of such a form of contentment and enjoyment. That is, for *A* to call *B* "happy," *A* must be contented at the prospect of *B* being in his present state of mind and at the prospect of *A* himself, should the opportunity arise, enjoying that sort of state of mind. That is, "happy" is a word which is mainly descriptive (tied to the concepts of contentment and enjoyment) but which is also partly evaluative. It is because Mill approves of the "higher" pleasures, e.g., intellectual pleasures, so much more than he approves of the more simple and brutish pleasures, that, quite apart from consequences and side effects, he can pronounce the man who enjoys the pleasures of philosophical discourse as "more happy" than the man who gets enjoyment from pushpin or beer drinking.

The word "happy" is not wholly evaluative, for there would be something absurd, as opposed to merely unusual, in calling a man who was in pain, or who was not enjoying himself, or who hardly ever enjoyed himself, or who was in a more or less permanent state of intense dissatisfaction, a "happy" man. For a man to be happy he must, as a minimal condition, be fairly contented and moderately enjoying himself for much of the time. Once this minimal condition is satisfied we can go on to evaluate various types of contentment and enjoyment and to grade them in terms of happiness. . . .

To sum up so far, happiness is partly an evaluative concept, and so the utilitarian maxim "You ought to maximize happiness" is doubly evaluative. There is the possibility of an ultimate disagreement between two utilitarians who differ over the question of push-pin versus poetry, or Socrates dissatisfied versus the fool satisfied. . . .

Leaving these more remote possibilities out of account, however, and considering the decisions we have to make at present, the question of whether the "higher" pleasures should be preferred to the "lower" ones does seem to be of slight practical importance. There are already perfectly good hedonistic arguments for poetry as against pushpin. As has been pointed out, the more complex pleasures are incomparably more fecund than the less complex ones: not only are they enjoyable in themselves but they are a means to further enjoyment. Still less, on the whole, do they lead to disillusionment, physical deterioration or social disharmony. The connoisseur of poetry may enjoy himself no more than the connoisseur of whisky, but he runs no danger of a headache on the following morning. Moreover the question of whether the general happiness would be increased by replacing most of the human population by a bigger population of contented sheep and pigs is not one which by any stretch of the imagination could become a live issue. Even if we thought, on abstract grounds, that such a replacement would be desirable, we should not have the slightest chance of having our ideas generally adopted. . . .

Another type of ultimate disagreement between utilitarians, whether hedonistic or ideal, can arise over whether we should try to maximize the *average* happiness of human beings (or the average goodness of their states of mind) or whether we should try to maximize the *total* happiness or goodness. . . . I have not yet elucidated the concept of total happiness, and you may regard it as a suspect notion. But for present purposes I shall put it in this way: Would you be quite indifferent between (a) a universe containing only one million happy sentient beings, all equally happy, and (b) a universe containing two million happy beings, each neither more nor less happy than any in the first universe? Or would you, as a humane and sympathetic person, give a preference to the second universe? I myself cannot help feeling a preference for the second universe. But if someone feels the other way I do not know how to argue with him. It looks as though we have yet another possibility of disagreement within a general utilitarian framework.

This type of disagreement might have practical relevance. It might be important in discussions of the ethics of birth control. This is not to say that the utilitarian who values total, rather than average, happiness may not have potent arguments in favour of birth control. But he will need more arguments to convince himself than will the other type of utilitarian.

In most cases the difference between the two types of utilitarianism will not lead to disagreement in practice. For in most cases the most effective way to increase the total happiness is to increase the average happiness, and vice versa. . . .

I shall now state the act-utilitarian doctrine. . . .

Let us say, then, that the only reason for performing an action A rather than an alternative action B is that doing A will make mankind (or, perhaps, all sentient beings) happier than will doing B. . . . This is so simple and natural a doctrine that we can surely expect that many of my readers will have at least some propensity to agree. For I am talking . . . to sympathetic and benevolent men, that is, to men who desire the happiness of mankind. Since they have a favourable attitude to the general happiness, surely they will have a tendency to submit to an ultimate moral principle which does no more than express this attitude. It is true that these men, being human, will also have purely selfish attitudes. Either these attitudes will be in harmony with the general happiness (in cases where everyone's looking after his own interests promotes the maximum general happiness) or they will not be in harmony with the general happiness, in which case they will largely cancel one another out, and so could not be made the basis of an interpersonal discussion anyway. It is possible, then, that many sympathetic and benevolent people depart from or fail to attain a utilitarian ethical principle only under the stress of tradition, of superstition, or of unsound philosophical reasoning. If this hypothesis should turn out to be correct, at least as far as these readers are concerned, then the utilitarian may contend that there is no need for him to defend his position directly, save by stating it in a consistent manner, and by showing that common objections to it are unsound. After all, it expresses an ultimate attitude, not a liking for something merely as a means to something else. Save for attempting to remove confusions and discredit superstitions which may get in the way of clear moral thinking, he cannot, of course, appeal to argument and must rest his hopes on the good feeling of his readers. If any reader is not a sympathetic and benevolent man, then of course it cannot be expected that he will have an ultimate pro-attitude to human happiness in general. Also some good-hearted readers may reject the utilitarian position because of certain considerations relating to justice. . . .

The utilitarian's ultimate moral principle, let it be remembered, expresses the sentiment not of altruism but of benevolence, the agent counting himself neither more nor less than any other person. Pure altruism cannot be made the basis of a universal moral discussion in that it would lead different people to different and perhaps incompatible courses of action, even though the circumstances were identical. When two men each try to let the other through a door first a deadlock results. Altruism could hardly commend itself to those of a scientific, and hence universalistic, frame of mind. If you count in my calculations why should I not count in your calculations? And why should I pay more attention to my calculations than to yours? Of course we often tend to praise and honour altruism even more than generalized benevolence. This is because people too often err on the side of selfishness, and so altruism is a fault on the right side. If we can make a man try to be an altruist he may succeed as far as acquiring a generalized benevolence.

Suppose we could predict the future consequences of actions with certainty. Then it would be possible to say that the total future consequences of action A are such-and-such and that the total future consequences of action B are so-and-so. In order to help someone to decide whether to do A or to do B we could say to him: "Envisage the total consequences of A, and think them over carefully and imaginatively. Now envisage the total consequences of B, and think them over carefully. As a benevolent and humane man, and thinking of yourself just as one man among others, would you prefer the consequences of A or those of B?" That is, we are asking for a comparison of one (present and future) *total* situation with another (present and future) *total* situation. So far we are not asking for a *summation* or *calculation* of pleasures or happiness. We are asking only for a comparison of total situations. And it seems clear that we can frequently make such a comparison and say that one total situation is better than another. For example few people would not prefer a total situation in which a million people are well-fed, well-clothed, free of pain, doing interesting and enjoyable work, and enjoying the pleasures of conversation, study, business, art, humour, and so on, to a total situation where there are ten thousand such people only, or perhaps 999,999 such people plus one man with toothache, or neurotic, or shivering with cold. In general, we can sum things up by saying that if we are humane, kindly, benevolent people, we want as many people as possible now and in the future to be as happy as possible. Someone might object that we cannot envisage the total future situation, because this stretches into infinity. In reply to this we may say that it does not stretch into infinity, as all sentient life on earth will ultimately be extinguished, and furthermore we do not normally in practice need to consider very remote consequences, as these in the end approximate rapidly to zero like the furthermost ripples on a pond after a stone has been dropped into it.

But do the remote consequences of an action diminish to zero? Suppose that two people decide whether to have a child or remain childless. Let us suppose that they decide to have the child, and that they have a limitless succession of happy descendants. The remote consequences do not seem to get less. Not at any rate if these people are Adam and Eve. The difference would be between the end of the human race and a limitless accretion of human happiness, generation by generation. The Adam and Eve example shows that the "ripples on the pond" postulate is not needed in every case for a rational utilitarian decision. If we had some reason for thinking that every generation would be more happy than not we would not (in the Adam and Eve sort of case) need to be worried that the remote consequences of our action would be in detail unknown. The necessity for the "ripples in the pond" postulate comes from the fact that usually we do not know whether remote consequences will be good or bad. Therefore we cannot know what to do unless we can assume that remote consequences can be left out of account. This can often be done. Thus if we consider two actual parents, instead of Adam and Eve, then they need not worry about thousands of years hence. Not, at least, if we assume that there will be ecological forces determining the future population of the world. If these parents do not have remote descendants, then other people will presumably have more than they would otherwise. And there is no reason to suppose that my descendants would be more or less happy than yours. We must note, then, that unless we are dealing with "all or nothing" situations (such as the Adam and Eve one, or that of someone in a position to end human life altogether) we need some sort of "ripples in the pond" postulate to make utilitarianism workable in practice. I do not know how to prove such a postulate, though it seems plausible enough. If it is not accepted, not only utilitarianism, but also deontological systems like that of Sir David Ross, who at least admits beneficence as one *prima facie* duty among the others, will be fatally affected.

Sometimes, of course, more needs to be said. For example one course of action may make some people very happy and leave the rest as they are or perhaps slightly less happy. Another course of action may make all men rather more happy than before but no one very happy. Which course of action makes mankind happier on the whole? Again, one course of action may make it highly probable that everyone will be made a little happier whereas another course of action may give us a much smaller probability that everyone will be made very much happier. In the third place, one course of action may make everyone happy in a pig-like way, whereas another course of action may make a few people happy in a highly complex and intellectual way.

It seems therefore that we have to weigh the maximizing of happiness against equitable distribution, to weigh probabilities with happiness, and to weight the intellectual and other qualities of states of mind with their pleasurableness. Are we not therefore driven back to the necessity of some calculus of happiness? Can we just say: "envisage two total situations and tell me which you prefer"? If this were possible, of course there would be no need to talk of summing happiness or of a calculus. All we should have to do would be to put total situations in an order of preference.

Let us now consider the question of equity. Suppose that we have the choice of sending four equally worthy and intelligent boys to a medium-grade public school or of leaving three in an adequate but uninspiring grammar school and sending one to Eton. (For sake of the example I am making the almost certainly incorrect assumption that Etonians are happier than other public-school boys and that these other public-school boys are happier than grammar-school boys.) Which course of action makes the most for the happiness of the four boys? Let us suppose that we can neglect complicating factors, such as that the superior Etonian education might lead one boy to develop his talents so much that he will have an extraordinary influence on the well-being of mankind, or that the unequal treatment of the boys might cause jealousy and rift in the family. Let us suppose that the Etonian will be as happy as (we may hope) Etonians usually are, and similarly for the other boys, and let us suppose that remote effects can be neglected. Should we prefer the greater happiness of one boy to the moderate happiness of all four? Clearly one parent may prefer one total situation (one boy at Eton and three at the grammar school) while another may prefer the other total situation (all four at the medium-grade public school). Surely both parents have an equal claim to being sympathetic and benevolent, and yet their difference of opinion here is not founded on an empirical disagreement about facts. I suggest, however, that there are not in fact many cases in which such a disagreement could arise. Probably the parent who wished to send one son to Eton would draw the line at sending one son to Eton plus giving him expensive private tuition during the holidays plus giving his other sons no secondary education at all. It is only within rather small limits that this sort of disagreement about equity can arise. Furthermore the cases in which we can make one person *very* much happier without increasing *general* happiness are rare ones. The law of diminishing returns comes in here. So, in most practical cases, a disagreement about what should be done will be an empirical disagreement about what total situation is likely to be brought about by an action, and will not be a disagreement about which total situation is preferable. For example the inequalitarian parent might get the other to agree with him if he could convince him that there was a much higher probability of an Etonian benefiting the human race, such as by inventing a valuable drug or opening up the mineral riches of Antarctica, than there is of a non-Etonian doing so. (Once more I should like to say that I do not myself take such a possibility very seriously!) I must again stress that since disagreement about what causes produce what effects is in practice so much the most important sort of disagreement, to have intelligent moral discussion with a person we do not in fact need complete agreement with him about ultimate ends: an approximate agreement is sufficient. . . .

According to the act-utilitarian, then, the rational way to decide what to do is to decide to perform that one of those alternative actions open to us (including the null-action, the doing of nothing) which is likely to maximize the probable happiness or well-being of humanity as a whole, or more accurately, of all sentient beings. The utilitarian position is here put forward as a criterion of rational choice. It is true that we may choose to habituate ourselves to behave in accordance with certain rules, such as to keep promises, in the belief that behaving in accordance with these rules is generally optimific, and in the knowledge that we most often just do not have time to work out individual pros and cons. When we act in such an habitual fashion we do not of course deliberate or make a choice. The act-utilitarian will, however, regard these rules as mere rules of thumb, and will use them only as rough guides. Normally he will act in accordance with them when he has no time for considering probable consequences or when the advantages of such a consideration of consequences are likely to be outweighed by the disadvantage of the waste of time involved. He acts in accordance with rules, in short, when there is no time to think, and since he does not think, the actions which he does habitually are not the outcome of moral thinking. When he has to think what to do, then there is a question of deliberation or choice, and it is precisely for such situations that the utilitarian criterion is intended.

It is, moreover, important to realize that there is no inconsis-

tency whatever in an act-utilitarian's schooling himself to act, in
normal circumstances, habitually and in accordance with stereo-
typed rules. He knows that a man about to save a drowning person
has no time to consider various possibilities, such as that the drowning person is a dangerous criminal who will cause death and destruction, or that he is suffering from a painful and incapacitating disease
from which death would be a merciful release, or that various timid
people, watching from the bank, will suffer a heart attack if they see
anyone else in the water. No, he knows that it is almost always right
to save a drowning man, and in he goes. Again, he knows that we
would go mad if we went in detail into the probable consequences
of keeping or not keeping every trivial promise: we will do most
good and reserve our mental energies for more important matters
if we simply habituate ourselves to keep promises in all normal
situations. Moreover he may suspect that on some occasions personal
bias may prevent him from reasoning in a correct utilitarian fashion.
Suppose he is trying to decide between two jobs, one of which is
more highly paid than the other, though he has given an informal
promise that he will take the lesser paid one. He may well deceive
himself by underestimating the effects of breaking the promise (in
causing loss of confidence) and by overestimating the good he can do
in the highly paid job. He may well feel that if he trusts to the
accepted rules he is more likely to act in the way that an unbiased
act-utilitarian would recommend than he would be if he tried to
evaluate the consequences of his possible actions himself. . . .

Though even the act-utilitarian may on occasion act habitually
and in accordance with particular rules, his criterion is, as we have
said, *applied* in cases in which he does not act habitually but in
which he deliberates and chooses what to do. Now the right action
for an agent in given circumstances is, we have said, that action
which produces better results than any alternative action. If two or
more actions produce equally good results, and if these results are
better than the results of any other action open to the agent, then
there is no such thing as *the* right action: there are two or more
actions which are *a* right action. However this is a very exceptional
state of affairs, which may well never in fact occur, and so usually I
will speak loosely of the action which is *the* right one. We are now
able to specify more clearly what is meant by "alternative action"
here. The fact that the utilitarian criterion is meant to apply in
situations of deliberation and choice enables us to say that the class
of alternative actions which we have in mind when we talk about an
action having the best possible results is the class of actions which
the agent could have performed if he had tried. For example, it
would be better to bring a man back to life than to offer financial

assistance to his dependants, but because it is technologically impossible to bring a man back to life, bringing the man back to life is not something we could do if we tried. On the other hand it may well be possible for us to give financial assistance to the dependants, and this then may be the right action. The right action is the action among those which we could do, i.e., those which we *would* do if we chose to, which has the best possible results.

It is true that the general concept of action is wider than that of deliberate choice. Many actions are performed habitually and without deliberation. But the actions for whose rightness we as agents want a criterion are, in the nature of the case, those done thinkingly and deliberately. An action is at any rate that sort of human performance which it is appropriate to praise, blame, punish, or reward, and since it is often appropriate to praise, blame, punish, or reward habitual performances, the concept of action cannot be identified with that of the outcome of deliberation and choice. With habitual actions the only question that arises for an agent is that of whether or not he should strengthen the habit or break himself of it. And individual acts of habit-strengthening or habit-breaking can themselves be deliberate.

The utilitarian criterion, then, is designed to help a person, who could do various things if he chose to do them, to decide which of these things he should do. His utilitarian deliberation is one of the causal antecedents of his action, and it would be pointless if it were not. The utilitarian view is therefore perfectly compatible with determinism. The only sense of "he could have done otherwise" that we require is the sense "he would have done otherwise if he had chosen." Whether the utilitarian view necessitates complete metaphysical determinism is another matter. All that it requires is that deliberation should determine actions in the way that everyone knows it does anyway. If it is argued that any indeterminism in the universe entails that we can never know the outcome of our actions, we can reply that in normal cases these indeterminacies will be so numerous as approximately to cancel one another out, and anyway all that we require for rational action is that some consequences of our actions should be *more probable* than others, and this is something which no indeterminist is likely to deny.

SMART SELECTION

1. What exactly is rule-utilitarianism as opposed to act-utilitarianism? Which of these doctrines does Smart defend? Why?

2. What is meant by the principle of "average happiness" as opposed to "total happiness"? What is wrong with choosing on the basis of

total happiness? Can you see any problems with choosing on the basis of average happiness? Suppose you have a society in which some people are very, very happy, and some people are very, very unhappy. That society might have the same *average* happiness as a society in which everyone was neither very happy nor very unhappy. Which society would be better? Could Smart consistently prefer one of them to the other? Do you?

3.   According to Smart, most real-life moral arguments turn on disagreements about *facts*—for example, disagreements about what the real consequences will be of one policy rather than another. The cases used by philosophers to raise trouble for utilitarianism, he says, either can be resolved by a closer look at the facts or else touch only on very marginal situations. Is that a reasonable way to deal with the objections to utilitarianism? Why?

4.   What is the role of rules in moral choice, according to Smart? Why might Smart agree that it is sometimes best to follow general rules, even though on particular occasions their use might not produce maximum average happiness? What do you suppose Smart would say about obeying the law? Can a utilitarian offer any good reason why I ought to obey the law?

5.   How would Smart answer the question about the rare flower, posed in the Introduction to this chapter? Spell out his argument as well as you can.

H. J. McCLOSKEY

Utilitarianism and Punishment

The strongest argument for utilitarianism is that it provides a clear, constructive, straightforward rule for making large-scale social decisions in which scarce resources must be distributed among different sectors of the population, or in which such burdens as military service and taxation must be imposed for the collective good. The appeal to happiness, the rough notion that individuals are to count equally, the refusal to block socially beneficial measures merely for considerations of tradition or abstract law, all seem humane, forward-looking, and sensible.

Utilitarianism runs into its severest trouble when it tries to give a coherent justification for our legal practices of trial and punishment. As H. J. McCloskey points out in this selection, the Greatest Happiness principle in any of its variations appears to commit us to the extremely unpleasant business of regularly punishing the innocent and rewarding the guilty, so long as total happiness will thereby be increased. Even those of us who do not thirst for vengeance will feel uncomfortable, I imagine, at the thought of deciding a criminal case by a calculation of happiness rather than by an examination of the evidence of guilt or innocence. After all, if the criminal has an especially large capacity for enjoyment, should that be an argument for freeing him so that he can thereby increase the social sum of pleasure?

Unfortunately for utilitarians and nonutilitarians alike, the topic of punishment is one of those puzzling philosophical subjects on which it is easier to refute your opponents than it is to defend your own position. Leaving aside religious doctrine (which is, on this subject, notoriously ambiguous), what grounds can we find for punishment other than some hope of future good? If we say that a human being forfeits his or her rights by invading the rights of others, then we must try to decide which rights are thereby forfeit, and to what extent. If I strike you, do you have a right to kill me in retribution? If not, why not? The great virtue of the utilitarian approach to punishment, once again, is that it gives us a rational and usable rule for translating abstract statements about crime and punishment into specific laws. What is more, if we find the subject baffling or confusing, utilitarianism tells us what we must do to clarify it: get more facts, collect data on the consequences of this or that law, run experiments. Nonutilitarians, by contrast, seem able only to tell us to consult our intuitions or reflect on the dignity of personality; both of these suggestions, although quite edifying, are not terribly helpful in settling real-world dilemmas about punishment.

Although the view that punishment is to be justified on utilitarian grounds has obvious appeal, an examination of utilitarianism reveals that, consistently and accurately interpreted, it dictates unjust punishments which are unacceptable to the common moral consciousness. In this rule-utilitarianism is no more satisfactory than is act-utilitarianism. Although the production of the greatest good, or the greatest happiness, of the greatest number is obviously a relevant consideration when determining which punishments may properly be inflicted, the question as to which punishment is just is a distinct and more basic question and one which must be answered before we can determine which punishments are morally permissible. That a retributivist theory, which is a particular application of a general principle of justice, can account more satisfactorily for our notion of justice in punishment is a positive reason in its support.

At first glance there are many obvious considerations which seem to suggest a utilitarian approach to punishment. Crime is an evil and what we want to do is not so much to cancel it out after it occurs as to prevent it. To punish crime when it occurs is, at best, an imperfect state of affairs. Further, punishment, invoking as it does evils such as floggings, imprisonment, and death, is something which does not commend itself to us without argument. An obvious way of attempting to justify such deliberately created evils would be in terms of their utility.

This is how crime and punishment impress on first sight. A society in which there was no crime and no punishment would be a much better society than one with crime and resulting punishments. And punishment, involving evils such as deliberately inflicted suffering and even death, and consequential evils such as the driving of some of its victims into despair and even insanity, etc., harming and even wrecking their subsequent lives, and often also the lives of their relatives and dependents, obviously needs justification. To argue that it is useful, that good results come from such punishment, is to offer a more plausible justification than many so-called retributive justifications. It is obviously more plausible to argue that punishment is justified if and because it is useful than to argue that punishment is justified because society has a right to express its indignation at the actions of the offender, or because punishment annuls and cancels out the crime, or because the criminal, being a human being, merits respect and hence has a right to his punishment. Such

From "A Non-Utilitarian Approach to Punishment by H. J. McCloskey. First published in *Inquiry* in 1965. (Reprinted by permission of Universitetsforlaget, Publishers to the Norwegian Universities.)

retributive type justifications have some point, but they are nonthe-
less implausible in a way that the utilitarian justification is not.
Yet I shall be concerned to argue that the key to the mortality of
punishment is to be found in terms of a retributive theory, namely,
the theory that evils should be distributed according to desert and
that the vicious deserve to suffer. . . .

Is the punishment which commends itself to the moral consciousness always useful punishment? And is all punishment that is
useful such that we should consider it to be morally just and permissible? Punishment which we commonly consider to be just is
punishment which is deserved. To be deserved, punishment must
be of an offender who is guilty of an offence in the morally relevant
sense of "offence." For instance, the punishing of a man known to
be innocent of any crime shocks our moral consciousness and is seen
as a grave injustice. Similarly, punishment of a person not responsible for his behaviour, e.g., a lunatic, is evidently unjust and shocking. Punishment for what is not an offence in the morally significant
sense of "offence" is equally unjust. To punish a man who has tried
his hardest to secure a job during a period of acute and extensive
unemployment for "having insufficient means of support," or to
punish a person under a retroactive law is similarly unjust. So too,
if the offence for which the person punished is one against a secret
law which it was impossible for him to know of, the punishment is
gravely unjust. Similarly, punishment of other innocent people—
e.g., as scapegoats—to deter others, is unjust and morally wrong. So
too is collective punishment—killing all the members of a village
or family for the offences of one member. Whether such punishments successfully deter seems irrelevant to the question of their
justice. Similarly, certain punishments of persons who are offenders
in the morally relevant sense of "offenders" also impress us as gravely
unjust. We now consider to have been gravely unjust the very severe
punishments meted out to those punished by hanging or transportation and penal servitude for petty thefts in the 18th century. Comparable punishments, e.g., hanging for shoplifting from a food market, would be condemned today as equally unjust. It is conceivable
that such unjust punishments may, in extreme circumstances, become permissible, but this would only be so if a grave evil has to be
perpetrated to achieve a very considerable good.
    In brief, our moral consciousness suggests that punishment, to
be just, must be merited by the committing of an offence. It follows
from this that punishment, to be justly administered, must involve
care in determining whether the offending person is really a responsible agent. And it implies that the punishment must not be exces-

sive. It must not exceed what is appropriate to the crime. We must always be able to say of the person punished that he deserved to be punished as he was punished. It is not enough to say that good results were achieved by punishing him. It is logically possible to say that the punishment was useful but undeserved, and deserved but not useful. It is not possible to say that the punishment was just although undeserved.

These features of ordinary moral thinking about just punishment appear to be features of which any defensible theory of punishment needs to take note. Punishment of innocent people—through collective punishments, scapegoat punishment, as a result of inefficient trial procedures, corrupt police methods, mistaken tests of responsibility, etc., or by using criteria of what constitute offences which allow to be offences, offences under secret and retroactive laws—is unjust punishment, as is punishment which is disproportionate with the crime. Thus the punishment which we consider, after critical reflection, to be just punishment, is punishment which fits a retributive theory. It is to be noted that it is just punishment, not morally permissible punishment, of which this is being claimed. Sometimes it is morally permissible and obligatory to override the dictates of justice. The retributive theory is a theory about justice in punishment and tells only part of the whole story about the morality of punishment. It points to a very important consideration in determining the mortality of punishment—namely, its justice—and explains what punishments are just and why they are just.

Before proceeding further, some comment should be made concerning these allusions to "what our common moral consciousness regards as just or unjust." Utilitarians frequently wish to dismiss such appeals to our moral consciousness as amounting to an uncritical acceptance of our emotional responses. Obviously they are not that. Our uncritical moral consciousness gives answers which we do not accept as defensible after critical reflection, and it is the judgements which we accept after critical reflection which are being appealed to here. In any case, before the utilitarian starts questioning this approach, he would do well to make sure that he himself is secure from similar criticism. It might well be argued that his appeal to the principle of utility itself rests upon an uncritical emotional acceptance of what prima facie appears to be a high-minded moral principle but which, on critical examination, seems to involve grave moral evils. Thus the problem of method, and of justifying the use of this method, is one which the utilitarian shares with the non-utilitarian. It is not possible here to argue for the soundness of this mode of argument beyond noting that whether an intuitionist or non-cognitivist meta-ethic be true, this sort of appeal is what such meta-ethical theories suggest to be appropriate.

Is all useful punishment just punishment, and is all just punishment useful? Here it is necessary first to dispose of what might not unfairly be described as "red herring." A lot of recent utilitarian writing is to the effect that punishment of the innocent is logically impossible, and hence that utilitarianism cannot be committed to punishment of the innocent. Their point is that the concept of punishment entails that the person being punished be an actual or supposed offender, for otherwise we do not call it punishment but injury, harm-infliction, social quarantining, etc. There are two good reasons for rejecting this argument as nothing but a red herring. Not all unjust punishment is punishment of the innocent. Much is punishment which is excessive. Thus even if punishment of the innocent were not logically possible, the problem of justice in punishment would remain in the form of showing that only punishments commensurate with the offence were useful. Secondly, the verbal point leaves the issue of substance untouched. The real quarrel between the retributionist and the utilitarian is whether a system of inflictions of suffering on people without reference to the gravity of their offences or even to whether they have committed offences, is just and morally permissible. It is immaterial whether we call such deliberate inflictions of sufferings punishment, social surgery, social quarantining, etc. In any case, as I have elsewhere tried to show, the claim is evidently false. We the observers and the innocent victims of such punishment call it punishment, unjust punishment. In so referring to it there is no straining of language.

To consider now whether all useful punishment is just punishment. When the problem of utilitarianism in punishment is put in this way, the appeal of the utilitarian approach somewhat diminishes. It appears to be useful to do lots of things which are unjust and undesirable. Whilst it is no doubt true that harsh punishment isn't necessarily the most useful punishment, and that punishment of the guilty person is usually the most useful punishment, it is nonetheless easy to call to mind cases of punishment of innocent people, of mentally deranged people, of excessive punishment, etc., inflicted because it was believed to be useful. Furthermore, the person imposing such punishment seems not always to be mistaken. Similarly, punishment which is just may be less useful than rewards. With some criminals, it may be more useful to reward them. As Ross observes:

A utilitarian theory, whether of the hedonistic or of the "ideal" kind, if it justifies punishment at all, is bound to justify it solely on the ground of the effects it produces. . . . In principle, then, the punishment of a guilty person is treated by utilitarians as not different in kind from the imposition of inconvenience, say by quarantine regulations, on innocent individuals for the good of the community.[1] . . .

What is shocking about this, and what most utilitarians now seek to avoid admitting to be an implication of utilitarianism, is the implication that grave injustices in the form of the innocent, of those not responsible for their acts, or harsh punishments of those guilty of trivial offences, are dictated by their theory. We may sometimes best deter others by punishing, by framing, an innocent man who is generally believed to be guilty, or by adopting rough and ready trial procedures, as is done by army courts martial in the heat of battle in respect of deserters, etc.; or we may severely punish a person not responsible for his actions, as so often happens with military punishments for cowardice, and in civil cases involving sex crimes where the legal definition of insanity may fail to cover the relevant cases of insanity. Sometimes we may deter others by imposing ruthless sentences for crimes which are widespread, as with car stealing and shoplifting in food markets. We may make people very thoughtful about their political commitments by having retroactive laws about their political affiliations; and we may, by secret laws, such as make to be major crimes what are believed simply to be anti-social practices and not crimes at all, usefully encourage a watchful, public-spirited behaviour. If the greatest good or the greatest happiness of the greatest number is the foundation of the mortality and justice of punishment, there can be no guarantee that some such injustices may not be dictated by it. Indeed, one would expect that it would depend on the details of the situation and on the general features of the society, which punishments and institutions of punishment were most useful. In most practical affairs affecting human welfare, e.g. forms of government, laws, social institutions, etc., what is useful is relative to the society and situation. It would therefore be surprising if this were not also the case with punishment. We should reasonably expect to find that different punishments and systems of punishment were useful for different occasions, times, communities, peoples, and be such that some useful punishments involved grave and shocking injustices. Whether this is in fact the case is an empirical matter which is best settled by social and historical research, for there is evidence available which bears on which of the various types of

[1] W. D. Ross, *The Right and the Good,* Oxford University Press, Oxford 1930, p. 56.

punishments and institutions work best in the sense of promoting the greatest good. Although this is not a question for which the philosopher *qua* philosopher is well equipped to deal, I shall nonetheless later briefly look at a number of considerations which are relevant to it, but only because the utilitarian usually bases his defence of utilitarianism on his alleged knowledge of empirical matters of fact, upon his claim to know that the particular punishments and that system of punishment which we regard as most just, are most conducive to the general good. J. Bentham, and in our own day, J. J. C. Smart, are among the relatively few utilitarians who are prepared—in the case of Smart, albeit reluctantly—to accept that utilitarian punishment may be unjust by conventional standards, but morally right nonetheless.

Against the utilitarian who seeks to argue that utilitarianism does not involve unjust punishment, there is a very simple argument, namely, that whether or not unjust punishments are in fact useful, it is logically possible that they will at some time become useful, in which case utilitarians are committed to them. Utilitarianism involves the conclusion that if it is useful to punish lunatics, mentally deranged people, innocent people framed as being guilty, etc, it is obligatory to do so. It would be merely a contingent fact, if it were a fact at all, that the punishment which works is that which we consider to be morally just. In principle, the utilitarian is committed to saying that we should not ask "Is the punishment deserved?" The notion of desert does not arise for him. The only relevant issue is whether the punishment produces greater good.

What is the truth about the utility of the various types of punishments? As I have already suggested, it would be astonishing if, in the sphere of punishment, only those punishments and that institution of punishment we consider to be just, worked best. To look at particular examples.

I [have] argued [elsewhere] that a utilitarian would be committed to unjust punishment, and [have] used the example of a sheriff framing an innocent negro in order to stop a series of lynchings which he knew would occur if the guilty person were not immediately found, or believed to have been found. I suggested that if the sheriff were a utilitarian he would frame an innocent man to save the lives of others. Against this example, it is suggested that we cannot know with certainty what the consequences of framing the negro would be, and that there may be other important consequences besides the prevention of lynchings. Utilitarians point to the importance of people having confidence in the impartiality and fairness of the legal system, a belief that lawful behaviour pays, etc.

However, as the example is set up, only the sheriff, the innocent victim and the guilty man and not the general public, would know there had been a frame-up. Further, even if a few others knew, this would not mean that everyone knew; and even if everyone came to know, surely, if utilitarianism is thought to be the true moral theory, the general body of citizens ought to be happier believing that their sheriff is promoting what is right rather than promoting non-utilitarian standards of justice. Since complex factors are involved, this example is not as decisive as is desirable. It can readily be modified so as to avoid many of these complications and hence become more decisive. Suppose a utilitarian were visiting an area in which there was racial strife, and that, during his visit, a negro rapes a white woman, and that race riots occur as a result of the crime, white mobs, with the connivance of the police, bashing and killing negroes, etc. Suppose too that our utilitarian is in the area of the crime when it is committed such that his testimony could bring about the conviction of a particular negro. If he knows that a quick arrest will stop the riots and lynchings, surely, as a utilitarian, he must conclude that he has a duty to bear false witness in order to bring about the punishment of an innocent person. In such a situation, he has, on utilitarian theory, an evident duty to bring about the punishment of an innocent man. What unpredictable consequences, etc., are present here other than of a kind that are present in every moral situation? Clearly, the utilitarian will not be corrupted by bearing false witness, for he will be doing what he believes to be his duty. It is relevant that it is rare for any of us to be in a situation in which we can usefully and tellingly bear false witness against others.

We may similarly give possible examples of useful punishments of other unjust kinds. Scapegoat punishment need not be and typically is not of a framed person. It may be useful. An occupying power which is experiencing trouble with the local population may find it useful to punish, by killing, some of the best loved citizen leaders, each time an act of rebellion occurs; but such punishments do not commend themselves to us as just and right. Similarly, collective punishment is often useful—consider its use in schools. There we consider it unjust but morally permissible because of its great utility. Collective punishments of the kind employed by the Nazis in Czechoslovakia—destroying a village and punishing its inhabitants for the acts of a few—are notorious as war crimes. Yet they appear to have been useful in the sense of achieving Nazi objectives. It may be objected that the Nazi sense of values was mistaken, that such punishment would not contribute towards realizing higher values and goods. But it is partly an accident of history that it was the Nazis who, in recent times, resorted to this method. If we had had to occupy a Nazi territory with inadequate troops, this might have been the only effective way of maintaining order. As with human affairs generally, it would depend on many factors, including the strength of our troops, the degree of hostility of the occupied people, their temper and likely reaction to this sort of collective punishment, etc. Punishment of relatives could also be useful. It would be an interesting social experiment in those modern democracies which are plagued by juvenile delinquency, for parents as well as the teenage delinquents to be punished. Such punishment would be unjust but it might well be useful. It would need a number of social experiments to see whether it is or is not useful. It is not a matter we can settle by intuitive insight. If it did prove useful, it is probable people would come to think of such punishment of parents as punishment for the offence of being a parent of a delinquent! This would obscure the awareness of the injustice of such punishment, but it would nonetheless be unjust punishment.

Similarly with punishment for offences under secret and retroactive laws. Such laws, it is true, would be useful only if used sparingly and for very good reasons but it is not hard to imagine cases where the use of a retroactive law might be useful in the long as well as in the short run. That a plausible case could have been made out for introducing retroactive laws in post-war Germany on utilitarian grounds as well as on the other sorts of grounds indicated by legal theorists, suggests that such cases do occur. They may be the most useful means, they may, in the German case, even have been morally permissible means and the means of achieving greater total justice; but they are nonetheless means which in themselves are unjust. Retroactive laws are really a kind of secret law. Their injustice consists in this; and secret laws, like them, seem useful if used sparingly and with discretion. The Nazis certainly believed them to be very useful but again it will no doubt be said that this was because their system of values was mistaken. However, unless the system of values includes respect for considerations of justice, such secret laws are possibly useful instruments for promoting good.

In our own community we define 'offence' in such a way, with various laws, that we condone unjust punishment because of its utility. The vagrancy law is a very useful law but what it declares to be an offence is hardly an offence in the morally relevant sense. And it is not difficult to imagine countries in which it would be useful to have a law making it an offence to arouse the suspicions of the government. Suppose there were a democratic revolution in Spain, or in Russia, which led to the perilous existence of a democratic government. Such a government might find that the only way in which it could safely continue in existence was by having such a law and similar laws involving unjust punishments. It would than have to consider which was morally more important—to avoid the unjust punishments which such a law involves, or to secure and make permanent a democratic form of government which achieved greater over-all injustice. That is, it would face conflicting claims of justice.

In an ignorant community it might well be useful to punish as responsible moral agents "criminals" who in fact were not responsible for their actions but who were generally believed to be responsible agents. The experts suggest that many sex offenders and others who commit the more shocking crimes, are of this type, but even in reasonably enlightened communities the general body of citizens do not always accept the judgements of the experts. Thus, in communities in which enlightened opinion generally prevails (and there are few) punishment of mentally deranged "criminals" would have little if any deterrent value, whereas in most communities some mentally deranged people may usefully be punished, and in ignorant, backward communities very useful results may come from punishing those not responsible for their actions. Similarly, very undesirable results may come from not punishing individuals generally believed to be fully responsible moral agents. Yet, clearly, the morality of punishing such people does not depend on the degree of the enlightenment of the community. Utilitarian theory suggests that it does, that such punishment is right and just in ignorant, prejudiced communities, unjust in enlightened communities. The utility of such punishment varies in this way, but not its justice. The tests of responsible action are very difficult to determine, although this need not worry the utilitarian who should use the test of utility in this area as elsewhere. However, to make my point, we need not consider borderline cases. The more atrocious and abominable the crime, the more pointless its brutality is, the more likely it is that the criminal was not responsible and the more likely that the general public will believe him to be fully responsible and deserving of the severest punishment.

Utilitarians often admit that particular punishments may be useful but unjust and argue that utilitarianism becomes more plausible and indeed, acceptable, if it is advanced as a theory about the test of rules and institutions. These utilitarians argue that we should not test particular punishments by reference to their consequences; rather, we should test the whole institution of punishment in this way, by reference to the consequences of the whole institution.

This seems an incredible concession; yet rule-utilitarianism enjoys widespread support and is perhaps the dominant version of utilitarianism. It is argued that particular utilitarian punishments may be unjust but that useful systems of punishment are those which are just systems in the judgment of our reflective moral consciousness. This modification of utilitarianism involves a strange concession. After all, if the test of right and wrong rules and institutions lies in their utility, it is surely fantastic to suggest that this test should be confined to rules and institutions, unless it is useful so to confine its application. Clearly, when we judge the utility of particular actions, we should take note of the effects on the institution or rule, but surely, it is individual acts and their consequences which ultimately matter for the utilitarian. There are therefore good reasons for believing that the half-hearted utilitarianism of rule-utilitarianism involves an indefensible compromise between act-utilitarianism and Ross's theory of a plurality of irreducible *prima facie* duties.

To consider now the implications of rule-utilitarianism. As with act-utilitarianism, it would be surprising if what was useful was also at all times just, and that what was the most useful institution of punishment was the same under all conditions and for all times. For example, what we in Australia regard as useful and just, fair trial procedures—and these are an important part of justice in punishment—for example, rules about the burden of proof, strict limitation of newspaper comment before and during the trial, selection of the jury, provision of legal aid for the needy, etc., differ from those found useful in dictatorships. Also, obviously a country emerging from the instability of a great revolution cannot afford to take risks with criminals and counter-revolutionaries which a stable, secure, well established community can afford to take. In Australia we can take the risk of allowing a few traitors to escape deserved punishment as a result of our careful procedures directed at ensuring that the innocent be not punished in error. During a war we may take fewer risks but at the expense of injustices. In an unstable community, immediately after a revolution, a more cavalier approach to justice is usually found to be the most useful approach. And there are differences within any one community. What is useful for civil courts is not necessarily what is most useful for military courts, and the most useful "institution" for the whole community may be a mixture of different systems of justice and punishment. Thus not only particular punishments but also whole institutions of punishment may be useful but of a kind we consider to be gravely unjust. It is these difficulties of utilitarianism—of act- and rule-utilitarianism—and the facts which give rise to these difficulties which give to the retributive theory, that the vicious deserve to suffer, its initial plausibility.

McCLOSKEY SELECTION

1. What is the utilitarian position on punishment? When is it right to punish someone, according to utilitarians? When is it wrong? Is there any reason to punish criminals, rather than other people, according to utilitarians? Can utilitarians give us any reasons why we shouldn't punish people who haven't yet committed crimes? If "punishment" is simply "doing something to somebody that he doesn't like, in order to prevent him from doing something that harms others," then what is the difference between punishing people and making them get drivers' licenses?

2. What is the retributive theory of punishment? Is it ever right to punish someone who is innocent of any wrongdoing? Is it ever right to refrain from punishing someone who is guilty of wrongdoing? What is the relationship between punishing the innocent and not punishing the guilty. Which is worse? Why?

3. Should criminals be punished even though there is no reason to suppose that punishing them will have any effect on how they or others act in the future? Should serious crimes (murder, rape, etc.) be punished more severely than less serious crimes (car theft, shoplifting)? Why? Suppose experience proves that severe punishments do *not* reduce the number of murders, but *do* reduce the number of auto thefts. Would that be a good reason for punishing auto theft more severely than murder? Why?

4. In McCloskey's case of the sheriff, an innocent man is framed in order to halt violent rioting. Do you think it is ever justified to punish the innocent? Does McCloskey? Suppose the man to be punished had only a few months to live. Suppose he were a really bad human being. Suppose he had committed some totally different crime many years before, and hadn't been punished. Would any of those facts make a difference?

5. In war time, innocent civilians are frequently killed by bombs and shells. Is there any difference between trying, convicting, and punishing an innocent person, and bombing that person to death in a war? If so, what is the difference? If you think there is none, then how can we ever justify going to war?

(SELECTION 4)

IMMANUEL KANT

The Categorical Imperative

The most famous moral principle in all of philosophy, and the leading opponent of utilitarianism in all its forms, is the *categorical imperative* of the great eighteenth-century German philosopher, Immanuel Kant. Kant himself claimed that there was nothing new in his principle. It was, he said, merely the familiar Golden Rule ("Do unto others as you would have others do unto you"). Nevertheless, as you will find when you read this selection, quite a bit more appears to be going on philosophically than just an old saying!

The key to Kant's ethical theory is his conception of what it is to be a rational agent. As we saw in the selection in Chapter 2, Kant holds that to be an agent and to be free just *is* to be rational, to be moved by reason. Thus, Kant argues two propositions that, taken together, set him absolutely against utilitarianism and all other forms of teleological ethics. The first proposition is that insofar as we are fully rational and truly moral, we act absolutely independently of all inclination or desire. So long as our actions are guided by desire, by a seeking after the ends or goals that are set us by our sensuous nature, Kant believes, we are not entirely free. Instead of giving the moral law to ourselves (and hence being autonomous—

self-legislating), we are slaves to a law given from outside ourselves (and hence we are heteronomous—ruled by others). For Kant, to be guided by one's desires or passions is as enslaving as to be dominated by a tyrant.

The second proposition is that pure reason, by appeal to merely logical considerations of consistency and rationality, can determine for us what it is right to do. The rules or, as Kant calls them, the maxims on which we base our actions must be checked against the fundamental principle of all morals, the categorical imperative, in order to determine their correctness or validity. Only after we have validated a rule such as "Always keep your promises" or "Never cause unnecessary suffering" can we be sure that it is a correct rule, and hence that action chosen on the basis of the rule will be right.

In this selection we see these two propositions come together in what is one of the best-known passages in all the literature of ethical theory. First, Kant introduces us to the notion of an imperative, in order that we can understand exactly how the categorical imperative differs from the various prudential rules set forth by the utilitarians. Then he applies his principle to four test cases, in order to show us how we can validate (or invalidate) a rule of action by submitting it to the test of the categorical imperative.

In examining these four examples, there are always two questions that must be kept separate in our minds. First, are these examples really good examples of the categorical imperative? (The mere fact that Kant says they are is not enough to settle that question.) And second, is the categorical imperative a principle that can be defended by appeal *only* to purely rational considerations of consistency and formal correctness?

All imperatives are expressed by an "ought" and thereby indicate the relation of an objective law of reason to a will which is not in its subjective constitution necessarily determined by this law. This relation is that of constraint. Imperatives say that it would be good to do or to refrain from doing something, but they say it to a will which does not always do something simply because it is presented as a good thing to do. Practical good is what determines the will by means of the conception of reason and hence not by subjective causes but, rather, objectively, i.e., on grounds which are valid for every rational being as such. It is distinguished from the pleasant as that which has an influence on the will only by means of a sensation from merely subjective causes, which hold only for the senses of this or that person and not as a principle of reason which holds for everyone.[1]

A perfectly good will, therefore, would be equally subject to objective laws (of the good), but it could not be conceived as constrained by them to act in accord with them, because, according to its own subjective constitution, it can be determined to act only through the conception of the good. Thus no imperatives hold for the divine will, or more generally, for a holy will. The "ought" is

[1] The dependence of the faculty of desire on sensations is called inclination, and inclination always indicates a need. The dependence of a contingently determinable will on principles of reason, however, is called interest. An interest is present only in a dependent will which is not of itself always in accord with reason; in the divine will we cannot conceive of an interest. But even the human will can take an interest in something without thereby acting from interest. The former means the practical interest in the action; the latter, the pathological interest in the object of the action. The former indicates only the dependence of the will on principles of reason in themselves, while the latter indicates dependence on the principles of reason for the purpose of inclination, since reason gives only the practical rule by which the needs of inclination are to be aided. In the former case the action interests me, and in the latter the object of the action (so far as it is pleasant for me) interests me. In the first section we have seen that, in the case of an action performed from duty, no regard must be given to the interest in the object, but merely in the action itself and its principle in reason (i.e., the law).

here out of place, for the volition of itself is necessarily in unison with the law. Therefore imperatives are only formulas expressing the relation of objective laws of volition in general to the subjective imperfection of the will of this or that rational being, e.g., the human will.

All imperatives command either hypothetically or categorically. The former present the practical necessity of a possible action as a means to achieving something else which one desires (or which one may possibly desire). The categorical imperative would be one which presented an action as of itself objectively necessary, without regard to any other end.

Since every practical law presents a possible action as good and thus as necessary for a subject practically determinable by reason, all imperatives are formulas of the determination of action which is necessary by the principle of a will which is in any way good. If the action is good only as a means to something else, the imperative is hypothetical; but if it is thought of as good in itself, and hence as necessary in a will which of itself conforms to reason as the principle of this will, the imperative is categorical.

The imperative thus says what action possible to me would be good, and it presents the practical rule in relation to a will which does not forthwith perform an action simply because it is good, in part because the subject does not always know that the action is good and in part (when he does know it) because his maxims can still be opposed to the objective principles of practical reason.

The hypothetical imperative, therefore, says only that the action is good to some purpose, possible or actual. In the former case it is a problematical, in the latter an assertorical, practical principle. The categorical imperative, which declares the action to be of itself objectively necessary without making any reference to a purpose, i.e., without having any other end, holds as an apodictical (practical) principle. . . .

There is . . . only one categorical imperative. It is: Act only according to that maxim by which you can at the same time will that it should become a universal law.

Now if all imperatives of duty can be derived from this one imperative as a principle, we can at least show what we understand by the concept of duty and what it means, even though it remain undecided whether that which is called duty is an empty concept or not.

The universality of law according to which effects are produced constitutes what is properly called nature in the most general sense (as to form), i.e., the existence of things so far as it is determined by universal laws. [By analogy], then, the universal imperative of duty can be expressed as follows: Act as though the maxim of your action were by your will to become a universal law of nature.

We shall now enumerate some duties, adopting the usual division of them into duties to ourselves and to others and into perfect and imperfect duties.

1. A man who is reduced to despair by a series of evils feels a weariness with life but is still in possession of his reason sufficiently to ask whether it would not be contrary to his duty to himself to take his own life. Now he asks whether the maxim of his action could become a universal law of nature. His maxim, however, is: For love of myself, I make it my principle to shorten my life when by a longer duration it threatens more evil than satisfaction. But it is questionable whether this principle of self-love could become a universal law of nature. One immediately sees a contradiction in a system of nature whose law would be to destroy life by the feeling whose special office is to impel the improvement of life. In this case it would not exist as nature; hence that maxim cannot obtain as a law of nature, and thus it wholly contradicts the supreme principle of all duty.

2. Another man finds himself forced by need to borrow money. He well knows that he will not be able to repay it, but he also sees that nothing will be loaned him if he does not firmly promise to repay it at a certain time. He desires to make such a promise, but he has enough conscience to ask himself whether it is not improper and opposed to duty to relieve his distress in such a way. Now, assuming he does decide to do so, the maxim of his action would be as follows: When I believe myself to be in need of money, I will borrow money and promise to repay it, although I know I shall never do so. Now this principle of self-love or of his own benefit may very well be compatible with his whole future welfare, but the question is whether it is right. He changes the pretension of self-love into a universal law and then puts the question: How would it be if my maxim became a universal law? He immediately sees that it could never hold as a universal law of nature and be consistent with itself; rather it must necessarily contradict itself. For the universality of a law which says that anyone who believes himself to be in need could promise what he pleased with the intention of not fulfilling it would make the promise itself and the end to be accomplished by it impossible; no one would believe what was promised to him but would only laugh at any such assertion as vain pretense.

3. A third finds in himself a talent which could, by means of some cultivation, make him in many respects a useful man. But he finds himself in comfortable circumstances and prefers indulgence in pleasure to troubling himself with broadening and improving his fortunate natural gifts. Now, however, let him ask whether his maxim of neglecting his gifts, besides agreeing with his propensity to idle

amusement, agrees also with what is called duty. He sees that a system of nature could indeed exist in accordance with such a law, even though man (like the inhabitants of the South Sea Islands) should let his talents rust and resolve to devote his life merely to idleness, indulgence, and propagation—in a word, to pleasure. But he cannot possibly will that this should become a universal law of nature or that is should be implanted in us by natural instinct. For, as a rational being, he necessarily wills that all his faculties should be developed, inasmuch as they are given to him for all sorts of possible purposes.

4. A fourth man, for whom things are going well, sees that others (whom he could help) have to struggle with great hardships, and he asks, "What concern of mine is it? Let each one be as happy as heaven wills, or as he can make himself; I will not take anything from him or even envy him; but to his welfare or to his assistance in time of need I have no desire to contribute." If such a way of thinking were a universal law of nature, certainly the human race could exist, and without doubt even better than in a state where everyone talks of sympathy and good will, or even exerts himself occasionally to practice them while, on the other hand, he cheats when he can and betrays or otherwise violates the rights of man. Now although it is possible that a universal law of nature according to that maxim could exist, it is nevertheless impossible to will that such a principle should hold everywhere as a law of nature. For a will which resolved this would conflict with itself, since instances can often arise in which he would need the love and sympathy of others, and in which he would have robbed himself, by such a law of nature springing from his own will, of all hope of the aid he desires.

The foregoing are a few of the many actual duties, or at least of duties we hold to be actual, whose derivation from the one stated principle is clear. We must be able to will that a maxim of our action become a universal law; this is the canon of the moral estimation of our action generally. Some actions are of such a nature that their maxim cannot even be *thought* as a universal law of nature without contradiction, far from it being possible that one could will that it should be such. In others this internal impossibility is not found, though it is still impossible to *will* that their maxim should be raised to the universality of a law of nature, because such a will would contradict itself. We easily see that the former maxim conflicts with the stricter or narrower (imprescriptible) duty, the latter with broader (meritorious) duty. Thus all duties, so far as the kind of obligation (not the object of their action) is concerned, have been completely exhibited by these examples in their dependence on the one principle.

When we observe ourselves in any transgression of a duty, we find that we do not actually will that our maxim should become a universal law. That is impossible for us; rather, the contrary of this maxim should remain as a law generally, and we only take the liberty of making an exception to it for ourselves or for the sake of our inclination, and for this one occasion. Consequently, if we weighed everything from one and the same standpoint, namely, reason, we would come upon a contradiction in our own will, viz., that a certain principle is objectively necessary as a universal law and yet subjectively does not hold universally but rather admits exceptions. However, since we regard our action at one time from the point of view of a will wholly conformable to reason and then from that of a will affected by inclinations, there is actually no contradiction, but rather an opposition of inclination to the precept of reason (*antagonismus*). In this the universality of the principle (*universalitas*) is changed into mere generality (*generalitas*), whereby the practical principle of reason meets the maxim halfway. Although this cannot be justified in our own impartial judgment, it does show that we actually acknowledge the validity of the categorical imperative and allow ourselves (with all respect to it) only a few exceptions which seem to us to be unimportant and forced upon us.

KANT SELECTION

1. What is an "imperative" in grammar? Why does Kant hold that moral principles are expressed in the form of imperatives? Is the principle of utilitarianism an imperative? What sort of imperative is it, according to Kant?

2. Exactly what is the difference between an imperative that commands hypothetically and an imperative that commands categorically? Are hypothetical imperatives binding on everyone? If not, on whom *are* they binding, according to Kant?

3. Does "Honesty is the best policy" express a hypothetical or a categorical imperative? What about "Thou shalt not lie"? Are there any moral rules or principles that you think hold absolutely without exceptions, qualifications, or exemptions? If so, what are they? If not, why not?

4. In the second example of the categorical imperative, Kant imagines a man who makes a false promise: he promises to repay money, knowing that he will not be able to keep his promise. Do you think it is wrong to make false promises? Why? In what way is this man "contradicting himself"? If you were to go about making false promises, could you respect yourself? Would you respect someone else who made false promises? Why?

5. Is it wrong to commit suicide? Whom are you hurting if you do? Do I have an obligation to develop my natural talents as much as possible? Why? Suppose I have it in me to be a skilled surgeon, but I really want to go into advertising, even though I have no particular talent for advertising.

Do I have an obligation to spend my life as a surgeon? What would Kant say? What do you say?

6.   All four examples of the categorical imperative are examples of things we should *not* do. Can we use the categorical imperative to tell us what we *should* do? Does the principle of utilitarianism meet the test of the categorical imperative?

(SELECTION 5)

W. D. ROSS

Prima Facie Duties

Kant's ethical theory has exercised a powerful and continuing attraction on those who are, for one reason or another, dissatisfied with the teleological approach in general and utilitarianism in particular. But two problems, among others, have bedeviled the Kantian theory. In the first place, it has proved extremely difficult actually to derive usable particular moral rules from the grand and abstract categorical imperative. There has been an unending series of criticisms of the four examples analyzed by Kant in the preceding selection, and the general consensus has been that Kant did not make his case successfully, at least not in the *Foundations of the Metaphysics of Morals*.

The second problem has been how to understand those cases in which there appear to be conflicts of obligation. If Kant's *a priori* rational approach is correct, then it would seem that we could not ever encounter such conflicts between two valid moral rules. Any apparent conflict would have to be explained away by saying that at least one of the supposedly valid rules was in fact invalid. After all, there could never be two logical principles that conflicted, or two mathematical principles that gave inconsistent answers. How could there be two perfectly rational moral rules that

conflicted in their application to particular cases?

The moral theory known as *intuitionism* was developed, in part at least, to deal with the first of these problems, and the English classicist and moral philosopher W. D. Ross, in his particular version of intuitionism, worked out a notion of *"prima facie* duty" in order to deal with the second.

The key to intuitionism is the claim that all human beings, by virtue of their rationality, have the capacity to apprehend directly—to intuit—the truth of certain moral imperatives. Very little is said about the nature, workings, or limits of this capacity (this is the principal weakness of the theory), but it is asserted to be a rational power, to be common to all rational creatures, and to be infallible. It is likened to the sensible capacity for apprehending sense-data (see the preceding chapter). These rational apprehensions or intuitions of the obligatoriness of certain acts constitute the fundamental data on which we base our objective moral judgments. Just as an object may look red in one light and black in another, leading us to form some objective judgment about what color it really is, so an act may appear obligatory when considered under one description or in regard to one of its aspects, and nonobligatory when considered under another of its aspects, leading us finally to make some summary judgment of its objective rightness. One intuition does not contradict another, any more than one sense-datum contradicts another. The "contradiction" arises only if we make the mistake of confusing the *prima facie* obligatoriness of an action, as grounded in a single one of its aspects, with the objective rightness or obligatoriness of the action, as based on a consideration of all of its various aspects. In this selection, you will see Ross attempting to work out these ideas.

The real point at issue between hedonism and utilitarianism on the one hand and their opponents on the other is not whether "right" means "productive of so and so"; for it cannot with any plausibility be maintained that it does. The point at issue is that to which we now pass, viz. whether there is any general character which makes right acts right, and if so, what it is. Among the main historical attempts to state a single characteristic of all right actions which is the foundation of their rightness are those made by egoism and utilitarianism. But I do not propose to discuss these, not because the subject is unimportant, but because it has been dealt with so often and so well already, and because there has come to be so much agreement among moral philosophers that neither of these theories is satisfactory. A much more attractive theory has been put forward by Professor Moore: that what makes actions right is that they are productive of more *good* than could have been produced by any other action open to the agent.

This theory is in fact the culmination of all the attempts to base rightness on productivity of some sort of result. The first form this attempt takes is the attempt to base rightness on conduciveness to the advantage or pleasure of the agent. This theory comes to grief over the fact, which stares us in the face, that a great part of duty consists in an observance of the rights and a furtherance of the interests of others, whatever the cost to ourselves may be. Plato and others may be right in holding that a regard for the rights of others never in the long run involves a loss of happiness for the agent, that "the just life profits a man." But this, even if true, is irrelevant to the rightness of the act. As soon as a man does an action *because* he thinks he will promote his own interests thereby, he is acting not from a sense of its rightness but from self-interest.

To the egoistic theory hedonistic utilitarianism supplies a much-needed amendment. It points out correctly that the fact that a certain pleasure will be enjoyed by the agent is no reason why he *ought* to bring it into being rather than an equal or greater pleasure

From *The Right and the Good* by W. D. Ross. First published in 1930. (Reprinted by permission of the Oxford University Press.)

to be enjoyed by another, though, human nature being what it is, it makes it not unlikely that he *will* try to bring it into being. But hedonistic utilitarianism in its turn needs a correction. On reflection it seems clear that pleasure is not the only thing in life that we think good in itself, that for instance we think the possession of a good character, or an intelligent understanding of the world, as good or better. A great advance is made by the substitution of "productive of the greatest good" for "productive of the greatest pleasure."

Not only is this theory more attractive than hedonistic utilitarianism, but its logical relation to that theory is such that the latter could not be true unless *it* were true, while it might be true though hedonistic utilitarianism were not. It is in fact one of the logical bases of hedonistic utilitarianism. For the view that what produces the maximum pleasure is right has for its bases the views (1) that what produces the maximum good is right, and (2) that pleasure is the only thing good in itself. If they were not assuming that what produces the maximum *good* is right, the utilitarians' attempt to show that pleasure is the only thing good in itself, which is in fact the point they take most pains to establish, would have been quite irrelevant to their attempt to prove that only what produces the maximum *pleasure* is right. If, therefore, it can be shown that productivity of the maximum good is not what makes all right actions right, we shall *a fortiori* have refuted hedonistic utilitarianism.

When a plain man fulfills a promise because he thinks he ought to do so, it seems clear that he does so with no thought of its total consequences, still less with any opinion that these are likely to be the best possible. He thinks in fact much more of the past than of the future. What makes him think it right to act in a certain way is the fact that he has promised to do so—that and, usually, nothing more. That his act will produce the best possible consequences is not his reason for calling it right. What lends colour to the theory we are examining, then, is not the actions (which form probably a great majority of our actions) in which some such reflection as "I have promised" is the only reason we give ourselves for thinking a certain action right, but the exceptional cases in which the consequences of fulfilling a promise (for instance) would be so disastrous to others that we judge it right not to do so. It must of course be admitted that such cases exist. If I have promised to meet a friend at a particular time for some trivial purpose, I should certainly think myself justified in breaking my engagement if by doing so I could prevent a serious accident or bring relief to the victims of one. And the supporters of the view we are examining hold that my thinking so is due to my thinking that I shall bring more good into existence by the one action than by the other. A different account may, however, be given of the matter, an account which will, I believe, show itself to be the true one. It may be said that besides the duty of fulfilling promises I have and recognize a duty of relieving distress, and that when I think it right to do the latter at the cost of not doing the former, it is not because I think I shall produce more good thereby but because I think it the duty which is in the circumstances more of a duty. This account surely corresponds much more closely with what we really think in such a situation. If, so far as I can see, I could bring equal amounts of good into being by fulfilling my promise and by helping some one to whom I had made no promise, I should not hesitate to regard the former as my duty. Yet on the view that what is right is right because it is productive of the most good I should not so regard it. . . .

I suggest *"prima facie* duty" or "conditional duty" as a brief way of referring to the characteristic (quite distinct from that of being a duty proper) which an act has, in virtue of being of a certain kind (e.g., the keeping of a promise), of being an act which would be a duty proper if it were not at the same time of another kind which is morally significant. Whether an act is a duty proper or actual duty depends on *all* the morally significant kinds it is an instance of. . . .

There is nothing arbitrary about these *prima facie* duties. Each rests on a definite circumstance which cannot seriously be held to be without moral significance. Of *prima facie* duties I suggest, without claiming completeness or finality for it, the following division.[1]

(1) Some duties rest on previous acts of my own. These duties seem to include two kinds, (*a*) those resting on a promise or what may fairly be called an implicit promise, such as the implicit undertaking not to tell lies which seems to be implied in the act of entering into conversation (at any rate by civilized men), or of writing books that purport to be history and not fiction. These may be called the duties of fidelity. (*b*) Those resting on a previous wrongful act. These may be called the duties of reparation. (2) Some rest on previous acts of other men, i.e., services done by them to me. These may be loosely described as the duties of gratitude. (3) Some rest on the

---

[1] I should make it plain at this stage that I am *assuming* the correctness of some of our main convictions as to *prima facie* duties, or, more strictly, am claiming that we *know* them to be true. To me it seems as self-evident as anything could be, that to make a promise, for instance, is to create a moral claim on us in someone else. Many readers will perhaps say that they do *not* know this to be true. If so, I certainly cannot prove it to them; I can only ask them to reflect again, in the hope that they will ultimately agree that they also know it to be true. The main moral convictions of the plain man seem to me to be, not opinions which it is for philosophy to prove or disprove, but knowledge from the start; and in my own case I seem to find little difficulty in distinguishing these essential convictions from other moral convictions which I also have, which are merely fallible opinions based on an imperfect study of the working for good or evil of certain institutions or types of action.

fact or possibility of a distribution of pleasure or happiness (or of the means thereto) which is not in accordance with the merit of the persons concerned; in such cases there arises a duty to upset or prevent such a distribution. These are the duties of justice. (4) Some rest on the mere fact that there are other beings in the world whose condition we can make better in respect of virtue, or of intelligence, or of pleasure. These are the duties of beneficence. (5) Some rest on the fact that we can improve our own condition in respect of virtue or of intelligence. These are the duties of self-improvement. (6) I think that we should distinguish from (4) the duties that may be summed up under the title of "not injuring others." No doubt to injure others is incidentally to fail to do them good; but it seems to me clear that non-maleficence is apprehended as a duty distinct from that of beneficence, and as a duty of a more stringent character. It will be noticed that this alone among the types of duty has been stated in a negative way. An attempt might no doubt be made to state this duty, like the others, in a positive way. It might be said that it is really the duty to prevent ourselves from acting either from an inclination to harm others or from an inclination to seek our own pleasure, in doing which we should incidentally harm them. But on reflection it seems clear that the primary duty here is the duty not to harm others, this being a duty whether or not we have an inclination that if followed would lead to our harming them; and that when we have such an inclination the primary duty not to harm others gives rise to a consequential duty to resist the inclination. The recognition of this duty of non-maleficence is the first step on the way to the recognition of the duty of beneficence; and that accounts for the prominence of the commands "thou shalt not kill," "thou shalt not commit adultery," "thou shalt not steal," 'thou shalt not bear false witness," in so early a code as the Decalogue. But even when we have come to recognize the duty of beneficence, it appears to me that the duty of non-maleficence is recognized as a distinct one, and as *prima facie* more binding. We should not in general consider it justifiable to kill one person in order to keep another alive, or to steal from one in order to give alms to another.

The essential defect of the "ideal utilitarian" theory is that it ignores, or at least does not do full justice to, the highly personal character of duty. If the only duty is to produce the maximum of good, the question who is to have the good—whether it is myself, or my benefactor, or a person to whom I have made a promise to confer that good on him, or a mere fellow man to whom I stand in no such special relation—should make no difference to my having a duty to produce that good. But we are all in fact sure that it makes a vast difference. . . .

It is necessary to say something by way of clearing up the relation between *prima facie* duties and the actual or absolute duty to do one particular act in particular circumstances. If, as almost all moralists except Kant are agreed, and as most plain men think, it is sometimes right to tell a lie or to break a promise, it must be maintained that there is a difference between *prima facie* duty and actual or absolute duty. When we think ourselves justified in breaking, and indeed morally obliged to break, a promise in order to relieve some one's distress, we do not for a moment cease to recognize a *prima facie* duty to keep our promise, and this leads us to feel, not indeed shame or repentance, but certainly compunction, for behaving as we do; we recognize, further, that it is our duty to make up somehow to the promise for the breaking of the promise. We have to distinguish from the characteristic of being our duty that of tending to be our duty. Any act that we do contains various elements in virtue of which it falls under various categories. In virtue of being the breaking of a promise, for instance, it tends to be wrong; in virtue of being an instance of relieving distress it tends to be right. Tendency to be one's duty may be called a parti-resultant attribute, i.e., one which belongs to an act in virtue of some one component in its nature. *Being* one's duty is a toti-resultant attribute, one which belongs to an act in virtue of its whole nature and of nothing less than this. This distinction between parti-resultant and toti-resultant attributes is one which we shall meet in another context also. . . .

Something should be said of the relation between our apprehension of the *prima facie* rightness of certain types of act and our mental attitude towards particular acts. It is proper to use the word "apprehension" in the former case and not in the latter. That an act, *qua* fulfilling a promise, or *qua* effecting a just distribution of good, or *qua* returning services rendered, or *qua* promoting the good of others, or *qua* promoting the virture or insight of the agent, is *prima facie* right, is self-evident; not in the sense that it is evident from the beginning of our lives, or as soon as we attend to the proposition for the first time, but in the sense that when we have reached sufficient mental maturity and have given sufficient attention to the proposition is it evident without any need of proof, or of evidence beyond itself. It is self-evident just as a mathematical axiom, or the validity of a form of interference, is evident. The moral order expressed in these propositions is just as much part of the fundamental nature of the universe (and, we may add, of any possible universe in which there were moral agents at all) as is the spatial or numerical structure expressed in the axioms of geometry or arithmetic. In our confidence that these propositions are true there is involved the same trust in our reason that is involved in our confi-

dence in mathematics; and we should have no justification for trust-
ing it in the latter sphere and distrusting it in the former. In both
cases we are dealing with propositions that cannot be proved, but
that just as certainly need no proof. . . .

The general principles of duty are obviously not self-evident
from the beginning of our lives. How do they come to be so? The
answer is, that they come to be self-evident to us just as mathematical
axioms do. We find by experience that this couple of matches and
that couple make four matches, that this couple of balls on a wire
and that couple make four balls; and by reflection on these and
similar discoveries we come to see that it is of the nature of two and
two to make four. In a precisely similar way, we see the *prima facie*
rightness of an act which would be the fulfillment of a particular
promise, and of another which would be the fulfillment of another
promise, and when we have reached sufficient maturity to think in
general terms, we apprehend *prima facie* rightness to belong to the
nature of any fulfillment of promise. What comes first in time is the
apprehension of the self-evident *prima facie* rightness of an individual act of a particular type. From this we come by reflection to
apprehend the self-evident general principle of *prima facie* duty.
From this, too, perhaps along with the apprehension of the self-
evident *prima facie* rightness of the same act in virtue of its having
another characteristic as well, and perhaps is spite of the apprehension of its *prima facie* wrongness in virtue of its having some third
characteristic, we come to believe something not self-evident at all,
but an object of probable opinion, viz. that this particular act is
(not *prima facie* but) actually right.

In this respect there is an important difference between rightness and mathematical properties. A triangle which is isosceles necessarily has two of its angles equal, whatever other characteristics the
triangle may have—whatever, for instance, be its area, or the size of
its third angle. The equality of the two angles is a parti-resultant
attribute. And the same is true of all mathematical attributes. It is
true, I may add, of *prima facie* rightness. But no act is ever, in virtue
of falling under some general description, necessarily actually right;
its rightness depends on its whole nature [2] and not on any element
in it. The reason is that no mathematical object (no figure, for instance, or angle) ever has two characteristics that tend to give it
opposite resultant characteristics, while moral acts often (as every

[2] To avoid complicating unduly the statement of the general view I am putting forward,
I have here rather overstated it. Any act is the origination of a great variety of things
many of which make no difference to its rightness or wrongness. But there are always
many elements in its nature (i.e., in what it is the origination of) that make a difference to its rightness or wrongness, and no element in its nature can be dismissed
without consideration as indifferent.

one knows) and indeed always (as on reflection we must admit) have different characteristics that tend to make them at the same time *prima facie* right and *prima facie* wrong; there is probably no act, for instance, which does good to any one without doing harm to some one else, and *vice versa.*

Supposing it to be agreed, as I think on reflection it must, that no one *means* by "right" just "productive of the best possible consequences," or "optimific," the attributes "right" and "optimific" might stand in either of two kinds of relation to each other. (1) They might be so related that we could apprehend *a priori,* either immediately or deductively, that any act that is optimific is right and any act that is right is optimific, as we can apprehend that any triangle that is equilateral is equiangular and *vice versa.* Professor Moore's view is, I think, that the coextensiveness of "right" and "optimific" is apprehended immediately. He rejects the possibility of any proof of it. Or (2) the two attributes might be such that the question whether they are invariably connected had to be answered by means of an inductive inquiry. Now at first sight it might seem as if the constant connexion of the two attributes could be immediately apprehended. It might seem absurd to suggest that it could be right for any one to do an act which would produce consequences less good than those which would be produced by some other act in his power. Yet a little thought will convince us that this is not absurd. The type of case in which it is easiest to see that this is so is, perhaps, that in which one has made a promise. In such a case we all think that *prima facie* it is our duty to fulfill the promise irrespective of the precise goodness of the total consequences. And though we do not think it is necessarily our actual or absolute duty to do so, we are far from thinking that any, even the slightest, gain in the value of the total consequences will necessarily justify us in doing something else instead. Suppose, to simplify the case by abstraction, that the fulfillment of a promise to A would produce 1,000 units of good for him, but that by doing some other act I could produce 1,001 units of good for B, to whom I have made no promise, the other consequences of the two acts being of equal value; should we really think it self-evident that it was our duty to do the second act and not the first? I think not. We should, I fancy, hold that only a much greater disparity of value between the total consequences would justify us in failing to discharge our *prima facie* duty to A. After all, a promise is a promise, and is not to be treated so lightly as the theory we are examining would imply. What, exactly, a promise is, is not so easy to determine, but we are surely agreed that it constitutes a serious moral limitation to our freedom of action. To produce the 1,001 units of good for *B* rather than fulfill our promise to *A* would be to take, not perhaps our duty as philanthropists too seriously, but certainly our duty as makers of promises too lightly.

Or consider another phase of the same problem. If I have promised to confer on *A* a particular benefit containing 1,000 units of good, is it self-evident that if by doing some different act I could produce 1,001 units of good for *A* himself (the other consequences of the two acts being supposed equal in value), it would be right for me to do so? Again, I think not. Apart from my general *prima facie* duty to do *A* what good I can, I have another *prima facie* duty to do him the particular service I have promised to do him, and this is not to be set aside in consequence of a disparity of good of the order of 1,001 to 1,000, though a much greater disparity might justify me in so doing.

Or again, suppose that *A* is a very good and *B* a very bad man, should I then, even when I have made no promise, think it self-evidently right to produce 1,001 units of good for *B* rather than 1,000 for *A*? Surely not. I should be sensible of a *prima facie* duty of justice, i.e., of producing a distribution of goods in proportion to merit, which is not outweighed by such a slight disparity in the total goods to be produced.

Such instances—and they might easily be added to—make it clear that there is no self-evident connexion between the attributes "right" and "optimific." The theory we are examining has a certain attractiveness when applied to our decision that a particular act is our duty (though I have tried to show that it does not agree with our actual moral judgements even here). But it is not even plausible when applied to our recognition of *prima facie* duty. For if it were self-evident that the right coincides with the optimific, it should be self-evident that what is *prima facie* right is *prima facie* optimific. But whereas we are certain that keeping a promise is *prima facie* right, we are not certain that it is *prima facie* optimific (though we are perhaps certain that it is *prima facie* bonific). Our certainty that it is *prima facie* right depends not on its consequences but on its being the fulfillment of a promise. The theory we are examining involves too much difference between the evident ground of our conviction about *prima facie* duty and the alleged ground of our conviction about actual duty. . . .

To put the matter otherwise, utilitarians say that when a promise ought to be kept it is because the total good to be produced by keeping it is greater than the total good to be produced by breaking it, the former including as its main element the maintenance and strengthening of general mutual confidence, and the latter being greatly diminished by a weakening of this confidence. They say, in fact, that the case I put some pages back never arises—the case in which by fulfilling a promise I shall bring into being 1,000 units of good for my promisee, and by breaking it 1,001 units of good for some one else, the other effects of the two acts being of equal value. The other effects, they say, never are of equal value. By keeping my promise I am helping to strengthen the system of mutual confidence; by breaking it I am helping to weaken this; so that really the first act produces $1,000 + x$ units of good, and the second $1,001 - y$ units, and the difference between $+ x$ and $- y$ is enough to outweigh the slight superiority in the *immediate* effects of the second act. In answer to this it may be pointed out that there must be *some* amount of good that exceeds the difference between $+ x$ and $- y$ (i.e., exceeds $x + y$); say, $x + y + z$. Let us suppose the *immediate* good effects of the second act to be assessed not at 1,001 but at $1,000 + x + y + z$. Then its *net* good effects are $1,000 + x + z$, i.e., greater than those of the fulfillment of the promise; and the utilitarian is bound to say forthwith that the promise should be broken. Now, we may ask whether that is really the way we think about promises? Do we really think that the production of the slightest balance of good, no matter who will enjoy it, by the breach of a promise frees us from the obligation to keep our promise? We need not doubt that a system by which promises are made and kept is one that has great advantages for the general well-being. But that is not the whole truth. To make a promise is not merely to adapt an ingenious device for promoting the general well-being; it is to put oneself in a new relation to one person in particular, a relation which creates a specifically new *prima facie* duty to him, not reducible to the duty of promoting the general well-being of society. By all means let us try to foresee the net good effects of keeping one's promise and the net good effects of breaking it, but even if we assess the first at $1,000 + x$ and the second at $1,000 + x + z$, the question still remains whether it is not our duty to fulfill the promise. It may be suspected, too, that the effect of a single keeping or breaking of a promise in strengthening or weakening the fabric of mutual confidence is greatly exaggerated by the theory we are examining. And if we suppose two men dying together alone, do we think that the duty of one to fulfil before he dies a promise he has made to the other would be extinguished by the fact that neither act would have any effect on the general confidence? Any one who holds this may be suspected of not having reflected on what a promise is.

I conclude that the attributes "right" and "optimific" are not identical, and that we do not know either by intuition, by deduction, or by induction that they coincide in their application, still less that the latter is the foundation of the former. It must be added, however, that if we are ever under no special obligation such as that of fidelity to a promisee or of gratitude to a benefactor, we ought to do what will produce most good; and that even when we are under a special obligation the tendency of acts to promote general good is one of the main factors in determining whether they are right.

ROSS SELECTION

1.   Precisely what does Ross mean by the term *"prima facie* duty"? Is a *"prima facie* duty" a particular kind of duty? Why not?

2.   How do we know what are and are not *prima facie* duties? If two people disagree about whether a particular characteristic of an action is a *prima facie* duty, are there any procedures by which they can resolve their dispute? Would it make sense to cite the probable consequences of the action? To take a vote? To do sociological research about the patterns of beliefs in our society?

3.   Ross offers a list of classifications of *prima facie* duties. Do you think that list holds true for all persons at all times in all societies? What do you think Ross believes? What arguments can you give in favor of his view? What arguments can you give against it?

4.   Can some of an act's characteristics impose on us *prima facie* duties to *do* that act, while other characteristics impose on us the duty *not* to do it? Think up some examples of such acts, and see whether you can figure out how Ross would analyze them.

5.   How do we "add up" the weights of all the *prima facie* duties we have in a particular situation, so as to determine what we ought to do? Does Ross give us a rule to follow? Do you think he has a rule in mind?

6.   Ross compares the judgments we make about *prima facie* duties to our judgments about the fundamental axioms of mathematics. In what ways are they alike? Are there any ways in which they are different? If someone just doesn't *see* that equals added to equals makes equals, are there any arguments you can offer to help him or her? What can you say if someone just doesn't see that it is wrong to break promises?

(SELECTION 6)

EDWARD WESTERMARCK

The Relativity of Ethics

One of the most shattering discoveries we make as we grow up is that some other people—decent, nice, perfectly ordinary people—eat, work, pray, live, and die according to customs and rules totally different from those that we abide by. For some of us, that discovery comes early, when we meet a young boy or girl who worships at a different church, or doesn't worship at all. Or when we discover that some mothers and fathers get divorced, or don't get divorced, or never marry, or whatever. As we grow older, we learn about cultures in which the wise, respectable, solid citizens of the community own slaves, or kill their aged relatives, or treat women like property, or sacrifice children to their gods. And, what is perhaps even more unsettling, we discover that *they* consider us weird because we send our aging parents off to Golden Age Villages, or permit our sons and daughters to marry whomever they choose or practice birth control.

The easiest response to these discoveries is to stand fast by our own principles and conclude that the rest of the world is wicked or uncivilized or damned. A somewhat more sophisticated response is to look beneath the surfaces of local customs and try to find common underlying principles to which decent men and women of all cultures give their assent. A more complicated response still is to look for a developmental pattern in terms of which we can classify those who live their lives differently from us as "lower" on the scale of development or "earlier" in their historical evolution, rather than simply evil or benighted.

But perhaps the most unsettling response of all to the thoroughgoing inconstancy of social customs and modes is to conclude that *there are no universal, objectively valid moral principles at all!* This is a conclusion that is rejected by teleologists and deontologists of every sort, for each school of ethical theory, whatever its particular line, claims that its principle is universally binding, valid for all human beings (or even, as with Kant, for all rational agents whatsoever, whether human or nonhuman).

The doctrine of *ethical relativity*, as the denial of objective moral principles is sometimes called, is quite ancient. It was defended by the school of Greek philosophers known as Skeptics, and it figures in several of Plato's dialogues as a position to be refuted by Socrates. In the late nineteenth century, relativism received powerful new support from the young science of Anthropology, and in the twentieth century, the rediscovery by the West of Eastern and African cultures has weakened the appeal of various objectivist ethical theories and strengthened relativism. In this classic statement of the relativist position, the Finnish philosopher and anthropologist Edward Westermarck at-

tacks several of the philosophers we have read thus far in this and other chapters, arguing against the objectivity of moral judgments.

Ethics is generally looked upon as a "normative" science, the object of which is to find and formulate moral principles and rules possessing objective validity. The supposed objectivity of moral values, as understood in this treatise, implies that they have a real existence apart from any reference to a human mind, that what is said to be good or bad, right or wrong, cannot be reduced merely to what people think to be good or bad, right or wrong. It makes morality a matter of truth and falsity, and to say that a judgment is true obviously means something different from the statement that it is thought to be true. The objectivity of moral judgments does not presuppose the infallibility of the individual who pronounces such a judgment, nor even the accuracy of a general consensus of opinion; but if a certain course of conduct is objectively right, it must be thought to be right by all rational beings who judge truly of the matter and cannot, without error, be judged to be wrong.

In spite of the fervour with which the objectivity of moral judgments has been advocated by the exponents of normative ethics there is much diversity of opinion with regard to the principles underlying the various systems. This discord is as old as ethics itself. But while the evolution of other sciences has shown a tendency to increasing agreement on points of fundamental importance, the same can hardly be said to have been the case in the history of ethics, where the spirit of controversy has been much more conspicuous than the endeavour to add new truths to results already reached. Of course, if moral values are objective, only one of the conflicting theories can possibly be true. Each founder of a new theory hopes that it is he who has discovered the unique jewel of moral truth, and is naturally anxious to show that other theories are only false stones. But he must also by positive reasons make good his claim to the precious find.

These reasons are of great importance in a discussion of the question whether moral judgments really are objective or merely are supposed to be so; for if any one of the theories of normative ethics has been actually proved to be true, the objectivity of those judgments has *eo ipso* been established as an indisputable fact. I shall

From *Ethical Relativity* by Edward Westermarck. (London: Routledge & Kegan Paul Ltd., 1932. Reprinted by permission of the publisher.)

therefore proceed to an examination of the main evidence that has been produced in favour of the most typical of these theories.

I shall begin with hedonism, according to which actions are right in proportion as they tend to promote happiness, and wrong in proportion as they tend to produce the reverse of happiness. And by happiness is then meant "pleasure, and the absence of pain; by unhappiness, pain, and the privation of pleasure." [1] What is the evidence?

It has been said that the hedonistic principle requires no proof, because it is simply an analytic proposition, a mere definition. Because acts that are called right generally produce pleasure and acts that are called wrong generally produce pain, rightness and wrongness have been actually identified with the tendencies of acts to produce pleasure or pain. . . . Now the statement that a certain act has a tendency to promote happiness, or to cause unhappiness, is either true or false; and if rightness and wrongness are only other words for these tendencies, it is therefore obvious that the moral judgments also have objective validity. But it is impossible to doubt that anybody who sees sufficiently carefully into the matter must admit that the identification in question is due to a confusion between the meaning of terms and the use made of them when applied to acts on account of their tendencies to produce certain effects. Bentham himself seems to have felt something of the kind. For although he asserts that the rectitude of the principle of utility has been contested only by those who have not known what they have been meaning, he raises the question whether it is susceptible of any direct proof. And his answer is as follows—"It should seem not: for that which is used to prove everything else, cannot itself be proved: a chain of proofs must have their commencement somewhere." [2] The question and the answer suggest that Bentham, after all, hardly looked upon the principle of utility or, as he also calls it, the greatest happiness principle, as strictly speaking a mere definition of rightness. . . .

Now the utilitarian standard is not the agent's own greatest happiness, but the greatest amount of happiness altogether. It may be defined as the rules and precepts for human conduct by the observance of which happiness might be, to the greatest extent possible, secured to all mankind; "and not to them only, but, so far as the nature of things admits, to the whole sentient creation." [3] How can this be proved? Mill argues that "no reason can be given why the

---

[1] J. S. Mill, *Utilitarianism* (London, 1895), p. 10.
[2] J. Bentham, *An Introduction to the Principles of Morals and Legislation* (Oxford, 1879), p. 94.
[3] Mill, p. 16 *sq.*

general happiness is desirable, except that each person, so far as he believes it to be attainable, desires his own happiness. This, however, being a fact, we have not only all the proof which the case admits of, but all which it is possible to require, that happiness is a good: that each person's happiness is a good to that person, and the general happiness, therefore, a good to the aggregate of all persons." [4] But if a person desires his own happiness, and if what he desires is desirable in the sense that he ought to desire it, the standard of general happiness can only mean that each person ought to desire his own happiness. In other words, the premises in Mill's argument would lead to egotistic hedonism, not to utilitarianism or universalistic hedonism. . . .

It will perhaps be argued that even though this or that moral principle, or even all moral principles hitherto laid down, fail to be objectively valid or express a moral truth, there may nevertheless be in the human mind some "faculty" which makes the pronouncement of objectively valid moral judgments possible. There are so many "theoretical" truths which have never been discovered, and yet we have in our intellect a "faculty" enabling us to pronounce judgments that are true. So also moralists of different normative schools of ethics maintain that we possess a faculty which can pronounce true moral judgments. This faculty has been called by names like "moral sense," "conscience," or "practical" or "moral reason," or been simply included under the general terms "reason" or "understanding.". . .

Butler calls "the moral faculty" conscience, but as a synonym for it he frequently uses the term "principle of reflection." It has two aspects, a purely cognitive and an authoritative, and on its cognitive side it "pronounces determinately some actions to be in themselves evil, wrong, unjust." [5] Sometimes he even calls it reason. But his dominant view seems to be that which lays stress on the instinctive intuition rather than the reflection.[6] He says:—"In all common ordinary cases we see intuitively at first view what is our duty. . . . This is the ground of the observation, that the first thought is often the best. In these cases doubt and deliberation is itself dishonesty. . . . That which is called considering what is our duty in a particular case, is very often nothing but endeavouring to explain it away." [7] But how, then, is it that different consciences so often issue conflicting orders? This question is never raised by Butler. He gives us no

[4] Ibid., p. 53.
[5] J. Butler, Sermon II.—Upon Human Nature, § 8 (Works, i. [London, 1900], p. 45).
[6] Cf. J. Bonar, Moral Sense (London, 1930), p. 64.
[7] Butler, Sermon VII.—Upon the Character of Balaam, § 14 (Works, i. 100).

criterion of rightness and wrongness apart from the voice of conscience.[8]. . .

Since the days of Kant moral judgments have been referred to a special faculty or a part of the general faculty of reason, called "practical" or "moral" reason, as the source of the objective validity assigned to them; according to Kant the speculative and the practical reason "can ultimately be only one and the same reason which has to be distinguished merely in its application."[9] The very existence of this mysterious faculty presupposes that there really are self-evident or axiomatic moral propositions; hence if no such proposition can be shown to exist we have no right whatever to postulate that there is a faculty which ever could give us any. It is perfectly clear that Kant *assumed* the objectivity of duty, and that this assumption led him to the idea of a pure practical reason, not *vice versa*.[10] He needed a faculty to explain the moral law, which he regarded as a fact of pure reason, "of which we are *a priori* conscious, and which is apodictically certain," and the objective reality of which "cannot be proved by any deduction by any efforts of theoretical reason."[11]

The question to be answered, then, is whether any of the moral principles that have been regarded as self-evident really is so. If ethics is to be taken as the term for a normative science, I agree with Professor Moore's statement that "the fundamental principles of Ethics must be self-evident." I also agree with him when he says:— "The expression 'self-evident' means properly that the proposition so called is evident or true, *by itself* alone; that it is not an inference from some proposition other than *itself*. The expression does *not* mean that the proposition is true, because it is evident to you or me or all mankind, because in other words it appears to us to be true. That a proposition appears to be true can never be a valid argument

[8] Cf. J. M. Wilson and T. Fowler, *The Principles of Morals (Introductory Chapters)* (Oxford, 1886), p. 56; C. D. Broad, *Five Types of Ethical Theory* (London, 1930), p. 82 *sq.* Professor A. E. Taylor ("Some Features of Butler's Ethics," in *Mind*, N. S. xxxv. [London, 1926], p. 276 *sq.*) says that it is no fault of the *Sermons*, in which Butler's ethical doctrine is chiefly conveyed to us, that they did not consider the possibility of conflicting moral codes and the grounds on which a choice could be made between them, because the object of the preacher was to impress on his audience the necessity of conducting their lives virtuously, and they would be agreed, in all essentials, on the question what sort of conduct is right and wrong. But his disregard of the apparent or real variations in the deliverance of "conscience" certainly obscures his ethical theory in its most essential point.
[9] Kant, *Grundlegung zur Metaphysik der Sitten,* Vorrede (*Gesammelte Schriften;* iv [Berlin, 1911], p. 391; T. K. Abbott's translation in *Kant's Critique of Practical Reason and other Works on the Theory of Ethics* [London, 1898], p. 7).
[10] Cf. A. Hägerström, *Kants Ethik* (Uppsala, 1902), p. 594.
[11] Kant, *Kritik der praktischen Vernunft,* i. I. I. 8 (v. 47; Abbott, p. 136).

that true it really is." [12] Just as the statement "this proposition is true" does not mean the same as to say, "I consider this proposition to be true," so also the statement "this moral principle is self-evident" does not mean the same as to say, "this moral principle appears self-evident to me." But how, then, can I know if a proposition is really self-evident or only supposed to be so? In the case of theoretical truths no truth is considered to have a claim to self-evidence which is not generally accepted as self-evident or axiomatic by all those whose intellect is sufficiently developed to have an opinion on the matter worthy of any consideration at all. It is true, as Kant said, that universal assent does not prove the objective validity of a judgment [13]—indeed, there are mathematical axioms that have been called in question although they have passed current for centuries; but, to speak with Sidgwick, the absence of disagreement between experts must be an indispensable negative condition of the certainty of our beliefs. In the case of moral principles enunciated as self-evident truths disagreement is rampant.

The great variability of moral judgments does not of course *eo ipso* disprove the possibility of self-evident moral intuitions. It is incompatible with that cruder kind of intuitionism which maintains that some moral faculty directly passes true moral judgments on particular courses of conduct at the moment of action. But what about the differences of opinions as regards the great moral principles that are supposed to be self-evident? . . . How can there be such a great diversity of opinion among "moral specialists" with regard to propositions that are assumed to be axioms? Some of these specialists say it is an axiom that I ought not to prefer my own lesser good to the greater good of another; whilst others do not deny the self-evidence, but thoroughly disagree with the contents, of this proposition. According to Sidgwick the proposition that pleasure is the only rational ultimate end of action is an object of intuition; according to Dr. Moore, also a professor of moral philosophy, the untruth of this proposition is self-evident.[14]

There are no doubt moral propositions which really are certain and self-evident, for the simple reason that they are tautological, that the predicate is but a repetition of the subject; and moral philosophy contains a great number of such tautologies, from the days of Plato and Aristotle to the present times. But apart from such cases, which of course tell us nothing, I am not aware of any moral principle that could be said to be truly self-evident. The presumed self-evidence is only a matter of opinion; and in some cases one might even

[12] G. E. Moore, *Principia Ethica* (Cambridge, 1922), p. 143.
[13] Kant, *Kritik der praktischen Vernunft,* Vorrede (v. 12 *sq.;* Abbott, p. 98).
[14] Moore, *op. cit.,* pp. 75, 144.

be inclined to quote Mr. Bertrand Russell's statement that "if self-
evidence is alleged as a ground of belief, that implies that doubt has
crept in, and that our self-evident proposition has not wholly resisted
the assaults of scepticism." [15] None of the various theories of normative science can be said to have proved its case; none of them has
proved that moral judgments possess objective validity, that there is
anything good or bad, right or wrong, that moral principles express
anything more than the opinions of those who believe in them.

But what, then, has made moralists believe that moral judgments possess an objective validity which none of them has been
able to prove? What has induced them to construct their theories of
normative ethics? What has allured them to invent a science the
subject-matter of which—the objectively good or right—is not even
known to exist? The answer is not difficult to find. It has often been
remarked that there is much greater agreement among moralists on
the question of moral practice than on the question of theory. When
they are trying to define the ultimate end of right conduct or to find
the essence of right and wrong, they give us the most contradictory
definitions or explanations—as Leslie Stephen said, we find ourselves in a "region of perpetual antinomies, where controversy is
everlasting, and opposite theories seem to be equally self-evident to
different minds." [16] But when they pass to a discussion of what is
right and wrong in concrete cases, in the various circumstances of
life, the disagreement is reduced to a surprising extent. They all tell
us that we should be kind to our neighbour, that we should respect
his life and property, that we should speak the truth, that we should
live in monogamy and be faithful husbands or wives, that we should
be sober and temperate, and so forth. This is what makes books on
ethics, when they come to the particular rules of life, so exceedingly
monotonous and dull; for even the most controversial and pug-
nacious theorist becomes then quite tame and commonplace. And
the reason for this is that all ethical theories are as a matter of fact
based on the morality of common sense. . . . So also normative ethics
has adopted the common sense idea that there *is* something right and
wrong independently of what is thought to be right or wrong. People
are not willing to admit that their moral convictions are a mere
matter of opinion, and look upon convictions differing from their
own as errors. If asked why there is so much diversity of opinion on

[15] B. Russell, *The Analysis of Mind* (London, 1922), p. 263. See also H. H. Joachim,
The Nature of Truth (Oxford, 1906), p. 55.
[16] L. Stephen, *The Science of Ethics* (London, 1882), p. 2. *Cf.* H. Sidgwick, "My Station
and Its Duties," in *International Journal of Ethics,* iv. (Philadelphia, etc. 1893), p. 13,
sq.

moral questions, and consequently so many errors, they would probably argue that there *would be* unanimity as regards the rightness or
wrongness of a given course of conduct *if* everybody possessed a
sufficient knowledge of the case and all the attendant circumstances
and *if,* at the same time, everybody had a sufficiently developed
moral consciousness—which practically would mean a moral consciousness as enlightened and developed as their own. This characteristic of the moral judgments of common sense is shared by the
judgments of philosophers, and is at the bottom of their reasoned
arguments in favour of the objectivity of moral values.

The common sense idea that moral judgments possess objective
validity is itself regarded as a proof of their really possessing such
validity. It is argued that the moral judgment "claims objectivity,"
that it asserts a value which is found in that on which it is pro-
nounced. "This is the meaning of the judgment," says Professor
Sorley. "It is not about a feeling or attitude of, or any relation to,
the subject who makes the judgment." [17] . . . The whole argument is
really reduced to the assumption that an idea—in this case the idea
of the validity of moral judgments—which is generally held, or held
by more or less advanced minds, must be true: people claim objective validity for the moral judgment, therefore it must possess such
validity. The only thing that may be said in favour of such an argument is, that if the definition of a moral proposition implies the
claim to objectivity, a judgment that does not express this quality
cannot be a moral judgment; but this by no means proves that moral
propositions so defined are true—the predicated objectivity may be
a sheer illusion.

Well then, it might be argued, if you do not admit that there is
anything objectively right or wrong, you must not use these or any
other moral predicates, because if you do, you assign to them a meaning that they do not possess. But what about other predicates which
are also formally objective and yet, when we more carefully consider
the matter are admitted to be merely subjective estimates? The
aesthetic judgment makes claim to objectivity: when people say that
something is beautiful, they generally mean something more than
that it gives, or has a tendency to give, them aesthetic enjoyment;
and there are also many philosophers who uphold the objectivity of
beauty and maintain that the beauties of nature exist apart from a
beholding eye or a hearing ear. But even those who agree with
Hume that beauty is no quality in things themselves, but exists merely
in the mind which contemplates them,[18] do not hesitate to speak of

[17] W. R. Sorley, *Moral Values and the Idea of God* (Cambridge, 1924), p. 150.
[18] D. Hume, "Essay xxiii.—Of the Standard of Taste," in *Philosophical Works,* iii. (London, 1875), p. 268.

"beauty," and would consider it absurd to be taken to task for doing so. Sidgwick admits that if I say "the air is sweet" or "the food is disagreeable," it would not be exactly true that I mean no more than I like the one or dislike the other, although, if my statement is challenged, I shall probably content myself with affirming the existence of such feelings in my own mind. So also, if anybody calls a certain wine or cigar good, there is some objectivity implied in the judgment, and however willing he is to recognize that the so-called goodness is a mere matter of taste, he will certainly, even if he is a philosopher, continue to call the wine or cigar good, just as before. Or, to take an instance from the sphere of knowledge: Hume, in expounding his own view, still speaks with the man in the street of objects and processes in nature, although his very aim is to convince us that what we know is really limited to impressions and ideas. And every one of us makes use of the words sunrise and sunset, which are expressions from a time when people thought that the sun rose and set, though nobody now holds this view. Why, then, should not the ethical subjectivist be allowed to use the old terms for moral qualities, although he maintains that the objective validity generally implied in them is a mere illusion? . . .

There is thus a very general tendency to assign objectivity to our subjective experience, and this tendency is particularly strong and persistent with regard to our moral experience. Why we attribute validity to it is of course a matter that does not trouble the moral intuitionist any more than the mathematician looks for a ground for his axioms. He is not concerned with the question of origins. Professor Moore says that the questions as to the origin of people's moral feelings and ideas are of course "not without interest, and are subjects of legitimate curiousity," but "only form one special branch of Psychology or Anthropology." [19] And Professor Sorley remarks that when we ask, "Why do we assign validity to our moral approval and to moral ideas generally?" the history of their genesis gives us no anwser.[20] For my own part I maintain, on the contrary, that an examination into the history of the moral consciousness of mankind gives us a clue to its supposed objectivity, as well as to its other characteristics. . . .

The authority assigned to conscience is really only an echo of the social or religious sanctions of conduct: it belongs to the "public" or the religious conscience, *vox populi* or *vox dei*. In theory it may be admitted that every man ought to act in accordance with his

[19] G. E. Moore, *Ethics* (London, *s.d.*), p. 130 *sq*.
[20] Sorley, *op. cit.,* p. 64.

conscience. But this phrase is easily forgotten when, in any matter of importance, the individual's conscience comes into conflict with the common sense of his community; or doubt may be thrown upon the sincerity of his professed convictions, or he may be blamed for having such a conscience as he has. There are philosophers, like Hobbes and Hegel, who have denied the citizen the right of having a private conscience. The other external source from which authority has been instilled into the moral law is the alliance between morality and religion. . . . It has been pointed out by Schopenhauer and others [21] that Kant's categorical imperative, with its mysteriousness and awfulness, is really an echo of the old religious formula "Thou shalt," though it is heard, not as the command of an external legislator, but as a voice coming from within. Schiller wrote to Goethe, "There still remains something in Kant, as in Luther, that makes one think of a monk who has left his monastery, but been unable to efface all traces of it." [22]

The theological argument in favour of the objective validity of moral judgments, which is based on belief in an all-good God who has revealed his will to mankind, contains, of course, an assumption that cannot be scientifically proved. But even if it could be proved, would that justify the conclusion drawn from it? Those who maintain that they in such a revelation possess an absolute moral standard and that, consequently, any mode of conduct which is in accordance with it must be objectively right, may be asked what they mean by an all-good God. If God were not supposed to be all-good, we might certainly be induced by prudence to obey his decrees, but they could not lay claim to *moral* validity; suppose the devil were to take over the government of the world, what influence would that have on the moral values—would it make the right wrong and the wrong right? It is only the all-goodness of God than can give his commandments absolute moral validity. But to say that something is good because it is in accordance with the will of an all-good God is to reason in a circle; if goodness means anything, it must have a meaning which is independent of his will. God is called good or righteous because he is supposed to possess certain qualities that we are used to call so: he is benevolent, he rewards virtue and punishes vice, and so forth. For such reasons we add the attributes goodness and righteousness to his other attributes, which express qualities of an objective character,

[21] A. Schopenhauer, *Die Grundlage der Moral,* §§ 4, 6 (*Sämmtliche Werke,* iv.2 [Leipzig, 1916], pp. 124–26, 133 *sqq.*). F. Paulsen, *Immanuel Kant* (Stuttgart, 1899), p. 345 *sq.* J. Rehmke, *Grundlegung der Ethik als Wissenchaft* (Leipzig, 1925), p. 58. Cf. Kant, *Von der Einwohnung des bösen Princips neben dem guten,* Anmerkung (vi. 23 n.†; Abbott, p. 330 n.1), where he speaks of the majesty of the law "like that on Sinai."
[22] *Briefwechsel zwischen Schiller und Goethe in den Jahren 1794 bis 1805,* ii. (Stuttgart & Augsburg, 1856), p. 167.

and by calling him all-good we attribute to him perfect goodness. As a matter of fact, there are also many theologians who consider moral distinctions to be antecedent to the divine commands. Thomas Aquinas and his school maintain that the right is not right because God wills it, but that God wills it because it is right.

Before leaving this subject I must still mention a fact that has made moralists so anxious to prove the objectivity of our moral judgments, namely, the belief that ethical subjectivism is an extremely dangerous doctrine. In a little book called *Is Conscience an Emotion?* largely written to oppose views held either by Professor McDougall or myself, Dr. Rashdall remarks that "the scientific spirit does not require us to blind ourselves to the practical consequences which hang upon the solution of not a few scientific problems," and that "assuredly there is no scientific problem upon which so much depends as upon the answer we give to the question whether the distinction which we are accustomed to draw between right and wrong belongs to the region of objective truth like the laws of mathematics and of physical science, or whether it is based upon an actual emotional constitution of individual human beings." [23] He maintains that the emotionalist theory of ethics, which leads to a denial of the objective validity of moral judgments, "is fatal to the deepest spiritual convictions and to the highest spiritual aspirations of the human race," and that it therefore is "a matter of great practical as well as intellectual importance" that it should be rejected. "To deny the validity of the idea of duty," he says, "has a strong tendency to impair its practical influence on the individual's life"; and "the belief in the objectivity of our moral judgments is a necessary premise for any valid argument for the belief either in God, if by that be understood a morally good or perfect Being, or in Immortality." [24] The last statement is astounding. In another place Dean Rashdall argues that objective morality presupposes the belief in God, and now we are told that any valid argument for the belief in God presupposes objective morality. These two statements combined lead to the logical conclusion that there is no valid evidence *either* for the existence of God *or* for the objectivity of moral judgments.

It is needless to say that a scientific theory is not invalidated by the mere fact that it is likely to cause mischief. The unfortunate circumstance that there do exist dangerous things in the world, proves that something may be dangerous and yet true. Another question is whether the ethical subjectivism I am here advocating really is a danger to morality. It cannot be depreciated by the same infer-

23 H. Rashdall, *Is Conscience an Emotion?* (London, 1914), p. 109 *sq.*
24 *Ibid.*, pp. 126, 127, 194.

ence as was drawn from the teaching of the ancient Sophists, namely, that if that which appears to each man as right or good stands for that which is right or good, then everybody has the natural right to follow his caprice and inclinations and to hinder him doing so is an infringement on his rights. My moral judgments spring from my own moral consciousness; they judge of the conduct of other men not from their point of view but from mine, not in accordance with their feelings and opinions about right and wrong but according to my own. And these are not arbitrary. We approve and disapprove because we cannot do otherwise; our moral consciousness belongs to our mental constitution, which we cannot change as we please. Can we help feeling pain when the fire burns us? Can we help sympathizing with our friends? Are these facts less necessary or less powerful in their consequences, because they fall within the subjective sphere of our experience? So also, why should the moral law command less obedience because it forms a part of ourselves?

I think that ethical writers are often inclined to overrate the influence of moral theory upon moral practice, but if there is any such influence at all, it seems to me that ethical subjectivism, instead of being a danger, is more likely to be an advantage to morality. Could it be brought home to people that there is no absolute standard in morality, they would perhaps be on the one hand more tolerant and on the other hand more critical in their judgments. Emotions depend on cognitions and are apt to vary according as the cognitions vary; hence a theory which leads to an examination of the psychological and historical origin of people's moral opinions should be more useful than a theory which postulates moral truths enunciated by self-evident intuitions that are unchangeable. In every society the traditional notions as to what is good or bad, obligatory or indifferent, are commonly accepted by the majority of people without further reflection. By tracing them to their source it will be found that not a few of these notions have their origin in ignorance and superstition or in sentimental likes or dislikes, to which a scrutinizing judge can attach little importance; and, on the other hand, he must condemn many an act or omission which public opinion, out of thoughtlessness, treats with indifference. It will, moreover, appear that moral estimates often survive the causes from which they sprang. And what unprejudiced person can help changing his views if he be persuaded that they have no foundation in existing facts?

I have thus arrived at the conclusion that neither the attempts of moral philosophers or theologians to prove the objective validity of moral judgments, nor the common sense assumption to the same effect, give us any right at all to accept such a validity as a fact. So

far, however, I have only tried to show that it has not been proved;
now I am prepared to take a step further and assert that it cannot
exist. The reason for this is that in my opinion the predicates of all
moral judgments, all moral concepts, are ultimately based on emotions, and that, as is very commonly admitted,[25] no objectivity can
come from an emotion. It is of course true or not that we in a given
moment have a certain emotion; but in no other sense can the
antithesis of true and false be applied to it. The belief that gives rise
to an emotion, the cognitive basis of it, is either true or false; in the
latter case the emotion may be said to be felt "by mistake"—as when
a person is frightened by some object in the dark which he takes for
a ghost, or is indignant with a person to whom he imputes a wrong
that has been committed by somebody else; but this does not alter
the nature of the emotion itself. We may call the emotion of another
individual "unjustified," if we feel that we ourselves should not have
experienced the same emotion had we been in his place, or, as in
the case of moral approval or disapproval, if we cannot share his
emotion. But to speak, as Brentano does,[26] of "right" and "wrong"
emotions, springing from self-evident intuitions and having the same
validity as truth and error, is only another futile attempt to ob-
jectivize our moral judgments. . . .

   If there are no moral truths it cannot be the object of a science
of ethics to lay down rules for human conduct, since the aim of all
science is the discovery of some truth. Professor Höffding argues that
the subjectivity of our moral valuations does not prevent ethics from
being a science any more than the subjectivity of our sensations
renders a science of physics impossible, because both are concerned
with finding the external facts that correspond to the subjective
processes.[27] It may, of course, be a subject for scientific inquiry to
investigate the means which are conducive to human happiness or
welfare, and the results of such a study may also be usefully applied
by moralists, but it forms no more a part of ethics than physics is a
part of psychology. If the word "ethics" is to be used as the name for
a science, the object of that science can only be to study the moral
consciousness as a fact.

25 See, e.g., Rashdall, *The Theory of Good and Evil* (London, 1924), i. 145 *sq.* ii. 195;
Idem, Is Conscience an Emotion?, pp. 30, 36; Sorley, *op. cit.*, p. 54; H. Hebler, *Philo-
sophische Aufsätze* (Leipzig, 1869), p. 48; J. Watson, *Hedonistic Theories from Aristip-
pus to Spencer* (Glasgow, 1895), p. 135; H. Maier, *Psychologie des emotionalen Denkens*
(Tübingen, 1908), pp. 789, 790, 800; H. Münsterberg, *Philosophie der Werte* (Leipzig,
1908), p. 28; H. Höffding, *Etik* (Köbenhavn & Kristiania, 1913), p. 51; L. T. Hobhouse,
The Rational Good (London, 1921), p. 16; R. Müller-Freienfels, *Irrationalismus* (Leipzig,
1922), p. 226; *Idem, Metaphysik des Irrationalen* (Leipzig, 1927), p. 400; J. Laird, *The
Idea of Value* (Cambridge, 1929), pp. 247, 315.
26 F. Brentano, *Vom Ursprung sittlicher Erkenntnis* (Leipzig, 1921), p. 18 *sqq.*
27 Höffding, *op. cite.*, p. 68.

WESTERMARCK SELECTION

1. According to Westermarck, philosophers and theologians through the ages have disagreed about what is right and wrong, what is good and bad, while all the while claiming that there are objectively valid answers to those questions. Suppose that, as a matter of historical fact, all the philosophers and theologians had *agreed* with one another about questions of morality. Would that convince Westermarck that they were all correct? Why? Would it convince you?

2. If there are no objective truths of morality, then why does everyone think that there are? How would such a belief arise? What do you suppose Westermarck would say?

3. What does Westermarck consider proof of self-evidence? If there were a long history of fundamental disagreements about mathematics or physics, would that justify Westermarck's concluding that there are no objectively valid principles of mathematics and science? If some other culture rejects the principles of logic or of science, may we conclude that logic and science are not valid *for them?* If an entire society believes in astrology, does that make it true for them?

4. Do you think the doctrine of ethical relativity is dangerous? Is *any* moral philosophy likely to be either dangerous or beneficial? If a doctrine is dangerous, does that have anything to do with whether it is true? Is it sometimes justified to conceal the truth? If Westermarck is correct, then judgments about "dangerousness," since they are partially evaluative judgments, have no more objective validity than any other moral judgments. Does Westermarck, as an author, have an obligation to worry about the effects of his book on its readers? Why? What obligations has he?

(SELECTION 7)

W. D. HUDSON

On the Alleged Objectivity of Moral Judgments

In Chapter 3, we examined a variety of philosophical views concerning the role of reason in choice and evaluation. We saw there that the debate over the proper role of reason in the healthy personality turned into a debate over the nature of moral reasoning and the degree to which one could give reasons for moral judgments. In a very similar manner, the debate over the objectivity of moral judgments turns into an analysis of the possibility of giving reasons for those judgments, and the difference between the sorts of reasons one can give for moral judgments as opposed to mere expressions of taste or preference.

In this short journal article, W. D. Hudson undertakes to defend the subjectivist position against an argument concerning moral reasoning. His aim is to show that the same sorts of reasons *can* be given in support of our admittedly subjective tastes as are given in support of supposedly objective moral judgments. Hudson's argument, if successful, undercuts one widely used technique for distinguishing moral judgments from expressions of taste or preference.

We conclude this chapter on an indecisive note that is manifestly unsatisfactory. The unresolved issues of epistemology may perhaps await some new turn of argument or analysis in future years, but we are all forced by events to make moral judgments and to act on them every day of our lives. Whether in the minor crises of ordinary existence or in those moments of major decision when lives literally hang in the balance, we must act, and hence we must judge. Whether we calculate according to the Greatest Happiness principle, deduce particular moral rules from the categorical imperative, or embrace ethical relativism, the decision is ours and each of us bears the responsibility for his or her actions.

In this necessity for choice and action, we can see a coming together of the issues that we have already explored in Chapter 1, concerning the nature of persons, in Chapter 2, with regard to freedom and determinism, in Chapter 3, where the role of reason in these decisions was examined, and in the present chapter, which has taken a look at several of the substantive moral principles that have won support from philosophers over the years.

There is an oft-quoted passage of Bertrand Russell's in which he expresses his dissatisfaction with the subjectivist approach in ethics. Having argued that moral judgments simply express desires which one feels or wishes others to feel, he goes on:

> But what are "good" desires? Are they anything more than desires that you share? Certainly there *seems* to be something more. Suppose, for example, that some one were to advocate the introduction of bull-fighting in this country. In opposing the proposal, I should *feel*, not only that I was expressing my desires, but that my desires in the matter are *right*, whatever that may mean. As a matter of argument, I can, I think, show that I am not guilty of any logical inconsistency in holding to the above (sc. subjectivist) interpretation of ethics and at the same time expressing strong ethical preferences. But in feeling I am not satisfied, I can only say, while my own opinions as to ethics do not satisfy me, other people's satisfy me still less. ("Reply to Criticisms," in *The Philosophy of Bertrand Russell*, ed. Schilpp., p. 724.)

Most recent writers in ethics, whilst sharing in general Russell's subjectivist approach, do not share his dissatisfaction with it. This is not because they are simply tougher-minded subjectivists than he and so able to hold to their doctrine without experiencing deviationist doubts; what some, at least, of them claim, in effect, is that they are subtler-minded subjectivists and so able to show that a moral judgment is, in fact, what Russell would have liked to think it was, namely "something more" than an expression of feeling or taste.

What I wish to point out is that two lines of argument, which have recently been taken to establish the objectivity of moral judgments, do so only in an unusual, restricted sense of that word, and it is misleading to suggest otherwise.

One of these lines of argument concerns the *reasons* which are given for moral judgments. Professor Paul Edwards, with explicit reference to the passage from Russell quoted above, states it thus:

> My theory or Russell's own theory, supplemented by a consideration of the *reasons* for moral judgments, easily clears up the source of this dissatisfaction (sc. Russell's.) . . . "The introduction of bull-fighting in the United States would be a bad

From "On the Alleged Objectivity of Moral Judgments" by W. D. Hudson. First published in *Mind* in 1962. (Reprinted by permission of *Mind*.)

thing," in addition to expressing something concerning the speaker, makes some such objective claim as, "The introduction of bull-fighting would lead to avoidable pain for innocent animals. . . . " Russell's desire *is* objectively superior in the sense that its satisfaction would prevent the suffering of innocent animals . . . etc. The satisfaction of this opponent's desire would have altogether different consequences. This is, I think, what Russell means by "superior" in the sense of referent. It is certainly the sort of thing that I would mean. If the facts concerning bull-fighting are as I described them a moment ago it is clear that Russell is right. To the extent to which an advocate of bull-fighting means the same by "superior" he would be mistaken. If he means something different, then he may or may not be mistaken, but Russell's claim remains objective and true. (*The Logic of Moral Discourse,* p. 214.)

The other line of argument concerns the *universalisability* of moral judgments. Mr. Bernard Mayo says that, faced with the choice of calling moral judgments subjective or objective, he would choose the latter (*Ethics and the Moral Life,* p. 45). He is "against subjectivism" (*ibid.*). Moral judgments, in his view, are not quite statements of fact, but they are much more like statements of fact than like expressions of feeling or taste (*op. cit.* chap. v). Mayo finds the ground for this in the required universalisability of moral judgments, which he states thus:

A moral judgment must be universalisable, firstly, in the sense that it applies not to a particular action, but to a class of actions. . . . Secondly, . . . in the sense that it applies . . . to everybody. . . . And . . . thirdly, . . . in the sense that others besides the speaker are assumed to share it. (*op. cit.* p. 91.)

If Edwards and Mayo claimed simply to be explicating some of the conventions in accordance with which moral discourse proceeds, one could have no quarrel with them. But they claim more than this. Reason-giving and universalisability are taken to constitute a radical difference between moral judgments and expressions of feeling or taste, and, in Edwards at any rate, it is claimed that the ground for dissatisfaction with subjectivism, such as Russell felt, has been removed.

Factual reasons, however, can be given, not only for our moral judgments, but for our likes and dislikes also. Compare:

"Strawberries are nice."
"Why?"
"Because they are sweet."

with:

"Bull-fighting is wrong."
"Why?"
"Because it causes avoidable pain."

The reason-giving sentence, in each case, is factually true. Now, Edwards says: "If the facts concerning bull-fighting are as I described them . . . it is clear that Russell is right. . . . Russell's claim remains objective and true" (*op. cit.* p. 214). His point appears to be that the truth of the factual reasons which could be given for Russell's judgment confers upon it an objectivity which does not belong to expressions of feeling or taste. But, if the factual truth of "Bull-fighting causes pain" confers objectivity on the judgment, "Bull-fighting is wrong," then the factual truth of "Strawberries are sweet" must confer an exactly similar objectivity on the expression of taste, "Strawberries are nice."

Now consider universalisability. To say that "Bull-fighting is wrong" is universalisable is to say that there is a universal moral principle which, together with a true statement about certain of the non-moral characteristics of bull-fighting, entails this judgment. The non-moral characteristics may be explicated one by one in discussion thus:

A: "Bull-fighting is wrong."
B: "Why do you say that?"
A: "Because it causes pain."
B: "So you think acts which cause pain are wrong?"
A: "Yes."
B: "But you fought in the war. Why weren't you a conscientious objector?"
A: "That's different. I should have said that I think acts which cause pain that is avoidable are wrong."
B: "But surely the war was avoidable! The Allies could have given in to Hitler. Do you think they ought to have done so?"
A: "No. What I should have said is that acts, which cause pain that is avoidable with great harm resulting, are wrong. It would have done great harm to let Hitler have his way."

A's universal moral principle at last becomes clear: it is that all acts, which cause pain and are avoidable and, if left undone, would not result in great harm, are wrong. Notice what B is really pressing A to do in the above conversation: he is pressing him all the time to say *more precisely* what it is that he is morally for or against.

Now, it is surely possible to conceive of someone being pressed to say more precisely what he is for or against, not on a moral issue, but in a matter of taste.

C: "Strawberries are nice."

D: "Why do you say that?"

C: "Because they are sweet."

D: "So you consider sweet things nice?"

C: "Yes."

D: "But I just saw you refuse a humbug with a grimace. Surely you like humbugs, if you consider sweet things nice!"

C: "No. What I should have said is that I consider things which are sweet and succulent to be nice."

D: "Then you like grapes?"

C: "No. What I should have said is that I consider things which are sweet, succulent, and red in colour to be nice."

This conversation is eccentric but not inconceivable. If this way of talking gives A's judgment about bull-fighting objectivity in the former conversation, it must do the same for C's remark, "Strawberries are nice" in the latter conversation.

The differences in the way we talk about moral issues and the way we talk about matters of taste are empirical. When someone says, "Strawberries are nice," we do not normally press him for his reasons or insist that he show us how the niceness of strawberries is an instance of some more general niceness. It is not logically impossible to do so; it is just that we do not.

Why, then, are there these conventions of reason-giving and universalisability so far as moral judgments are concerned? The answer lies in the fact that these conventions make it, on the one hand, *possible always to open* an argument, when someone has delivered a moral judgment; and, on the other hand, *impossible to refuse to join* in argument, once one has delivered a moral judgment oneself.

In this connection, Mr. Jonathan Bennett recently made an important point about the universalisability principle. He said that it should be reformulated thus: a judgment is a moral judgment only if the person who makes it accepts some universal moral principle which, together with a true statement about *some but not all* of the non-moral characteristics of the act or state of affairs being judged, entails this judgment. If we read *"all,"* instead of *"some but not all,"* then the judgment will apply only to this particular act or state of affairs, and it will be just a logical trick to say that it passes the universalisability test. In favour of his more careful formulation, *"some but not all,"* Bennett points out that a moral judgment on X will then not apply only to X but to other acts or states, which have

certain non-moral characteristics in common with X, and consequently "there can be moral argument" ("Moral Argument," *Mind,*
vol. lxix (1960)). Where A has judged X to be right and stated the
non-moral characteristics of X because of which he thinks it right,
it is open to B to adduce some counter-instance, Y, which has the
relevant non-moral characteristics in common with, but which A does
not judge to be right. We saw this happening in the above conversation about bull-fighting. As long as the list of non-moral characteristics is not so complete that it will fit only X and nothing else, the
possibility of the counter-instance, and so of continued moral argument, remains open.

Matters which we discuss in the universe of moral discourse are
matters about which we want to be able to argue. Hence the rules
which make this possible. We have strong desires here and want
others to have them too. To make bull-fighting a subject of moral
discourse it to put oneself, and anyone who is prepared to discuss it
with one in these terms, in a position where a decision has to be
made, where this decision can be argued about, and where others
can be persuaded to make it also. This is certainly to differentiate it
from matters of feeling or taste in general. But does this make it
another kind of thing altogether, or simply a member of a sub-class
of matters of feeling or taste, to which certain rules apply? It is significant that many moral issues were originally matters of taste in
the accepted sense of that phrase. For example, there was a time
when it would have been considered a matter of personal inclination
whether or not one kept a slave; but a change in sentiment concerning their fellowmen who were slaves made some people begin to ask,
"But is it *right* to keep a slave?" They had a strong desire to stop
slavery and so they took the subject over into the universe of moral
discourse and began to talk about it in terms of right and wrong.
They passed verdicts and invited others to do so, gave and required
reasons for these, and, in short, began to argue and persuade in all
the ways which moral discourse makes possible.

If the alleged objectivity of moral judgments is taken to mean
simply that, once we have begun to talk about some matter of taste
in moral terms, we cannot say anything significant about it unless
we keep the rules of moral discourse, then this is indisputable. But
this is not to abandon the subjectivist position in ethics. It goes no
way at all towards what has traditionally been meant by the objectivity of moral judgments, namely, that they are statements of fact
known by a faculty of moral cognition. It is cold comfort to the
philosopher or plain man, dissatisfied, as Russell was dissatisfied,
with subjectivism, to tell him that, though he is merely expressing his

own feelings, he is doing so in accordance with certain linguistic conventions. It may be that there is no comfort for him. It may be that we should urge him to reconsider whether it is not enough that these matters which we call moral issues are ones about which he and others feel passionately. But this much is certain: if the objectivity which he would like to think his moral judgments have is to be established, it will have to be on grounds other than those which we have been considering.

HUDSON SELECTION

1. What are the two forms of argument that supposedly distinguish moral discussions from mere expressions of taste? Try to think up your own examples of reason-giving and of universalizing. Which philosophers in this chapter appeal to either of these modes of reasoning as supports for, or as especially relevant to, moral judgment?

2. If Hudson is correct, then I can always give the same sorts of reasons in support of my tastes and personal preferences that I can give in support of my moral convictions. How then does he distinguish between the two? What does he mean by saying that there are certain "linguistic conventions" governing moral discourse? In what sense, if any, am I bound to obey the linguistic conventions of my culture? Are "linguistic conventions" the conventions that govern correct use of a language (such as English), or simply the conventions that govern correct use of a language in certain social situations (such as the use of English in polite social gatherings)? How can I discover what linguistic conventions govern the use of my language? Who makes up linguistic conventions? Who changes them?

3. Have you ever really been argued out of doing something that you wanted to do by a moral argument? If the answer is yes, see whether you can reconstruct the argument in your mind; what would Hudson say about it? Was it an argument that appealed to the notion of universalizability? Were other sorts of reasons given?

1. Go all the way back to the example, in the Introduction, of the castaways and the flower, and try to figure out what each author in this section would say about it. Which authors would tell you to stay? Which would tell you to go? Why?

2. Some of the moral problems we face are personal problems concerning only ourselves and a few other persons close to us. Other moral problems are social problems, involving the state, social institutions, or many people. Which sorts of problems is utilitarianism most helpful in thinking about? Why? Which sorts of problems are the categorical imperative and the doctrine of *prima facie* duties most helpful in thinking about? Why?

3. Go back to the example of the sheriff and the innocent man in McCloskey's discussion. How would Bentham and Smart deal with that problem? How would Kant and Ross deal with it? Which side do you think is right? If you think both are wrong, what *is* the right way to answer McCloskey's problem? What would Westermarck say?

4. What are the most important moral principles that were taught to you as a child? Were any reasons given to you for accepting those principles? What were they? Do your principles conform more to utilitarian or to intuitionist moral theory? Have you changed any of your moral principles? Why? What led you to change your beliefs?

5. Do you think that there is one set of moral principles that ordinary citizens ought to obey, and a different set of principles that public officials ought to obey? Why? If so, what are they?

6. The discussion of moral principles in this chapter has proceeded pretty much without mention of religion, God, or an afterlife. How do you think religious beliefs relate to moral principles? Can someone be truly moral without believing in God? Can someone be truly moral if he or she *does* believe in God?

CHAPTER SIX

THE GOOD SOCIETY: DREAMS AND NIGHTMARES

(Focal Issues)

1. *If You Could Write a Blueprint of an Ideal Society, What Would It Look Like?*

2. *What Dangers Are There in Systematic Planning for the Good Society?*

3. *What Is the Major Obstacle to the Achievement of the Good Society?*

INTRODUCTION

In an essay with the sobering title, "Reflections on the Causes of Human Misery and upon Certain Proposals to Eliminate Them," the brilliant and gloomy social theorist, Barrington Moore, Jr., observes that it is exceedingly difficult to get human beings to agree on what constitutes happiness. But, he goes on, "matters stand otherwise with misery and suffering. . . . If human beings find it difficult to agree upon the meaning and causes of happiness, they find it much easier to know when they are miserable." Moore mentions, as universally acknowledged miseries, torture, death, starvation, illness, rotting in prison, the exactions of ruthless authorities who carry off the fruits of prolonged labor, and simply losing the means of livelihood for the expression of unpopular or heretical beliefs. His point is that, however men and women may argue over what would be an ideal society, they all agree that societies in which large numbers of people regularly suffer such evils are indisputably bad.

Despite the difficulty of formulating a universally acceptable conception of the good society, philosophers, politicians, priests and ordinary men and women go on debating the question with a fervor that often turns into violence. After all, one of the distinctive marks of the human condition is the ability to imagine a future different from the past, a future in which dreaded evils will be eliminated and longed-for fulfillments finally attained. Without that capacity, there would be very little point to life, and our existence would sink to the level of the nonrational brutes.

In 1516 Thomas More, the English statesman and author wrote a satire on conditions in the England of his day in which he described an imaginary island whose social, economic, and political arrangements were, by contrast, harmonious and peaceful. He called the island *Utopia,* which in Greek means *nowhere.* The name stuck, and to this day, portraits of ideal societies are called utopias.

Utopian literature characteristically springs from one of two motivations, as Barrington Moore's remarks suggest. Sometimes authors who are outraged or horrified by the miseries and evils of their own societies conjure up images of ideal alternatives as a way of showing their fellow citizens how those evils might be eliminated. This motivation, we might say, is negative. But at other times it is the thought of possibilities not yet realized, human potentiality waiting to be tapped, that fuels the imaginations of utopian writers. By contrast, we may call this motivation positive. There are very close connections between negative and positive utopian thinking, of course, for to some social critics, the greatest evil of their society is precisely its failure to provide opportunities for the development of slumbering human talents. Minds untaught, bodies undeveloped, creative abilities stifled—these, as well as actual pain and suffering, are human evils. In the most complex utopian speculations, quite subtle relationships are traced between the miseries suffered and the joys unfulfilled, and such diverse thinkers as Plato and Marx insist that the fulfillment of the one can be achieved only through the elimination of the other.

One philosopher's dream of the good society may be another's nightmare, and many of the most famous visions of ideal future societies have been violently condemned as blueprints for tyranny, misery, and destruction. Most often, the anti-utopians argue that in the rush to imagine away the evils of the present, utopian thinkers fail to foresee the new and even more horrible evils that would result from the establishment of one or another utopian scheme. As economists and sociologists are fond of pointing out, collective social actions sometimes have unanticipated consequences that are far worse than the problem that was originally being solved. Kill crop-eating bugs with DDT (a perfectly laudable and socially useful thing to do) and you may accidentally kill off a link in the ecological chain that costs ten times as much, in human misery, as was saved by the increased crop yield. Build a four-lane highway between two towns to relieve a traffic jam, and you end up encouraging more traffic, with disastrous results for the surrounding neighborhoods. Raise the minimum wage, and you may simply encourage capitalists to shift to labor-saving machinery, thereby eliminating jobs and increasing unemployment.

Most pessimistic, perhaps, are the warnings by the anti-utopians of the dangers that lie in giving great power to a small group of supposedly wise and well-intentioned rulers. Even if a society is fortunate at first in the goodness of its rulers, great power will attract corrupt men and women and will corrupt good men and women who hold it. The result may be not a better society, but one unimaginably worse than our present condition.

In this chapter we shall explore three of the most influential and widely discussed utopian dreams of the good society. In each case, after hearing from the leading proponent of the dream, we shall hear as well from one of its harshest critics. Since each of the three utopias typifies a certain kind of approach to the problem of defining the good society, it might be helpful in these introductory remarks to analyze the underlying assumptions of the approaches, so that we may understand better both what led their proponents to defend them and also what so violently alarms their critics.

One of the most common and persistent diagnoses of social ills is that they are the result of poor leadership. Those who rule, who make the great decisions, are ignorant, or unwise, or simply incompetent. If we can replace them with wise rulers, then at least the avoidable evils of human existence can be eliminated. Many utopian philosophers, therefore, concentrate on the problem of how to identify the truly wise among us and, once we have identified them, how to put them in positions of authority.

If we take this approach to improving society, several difficulties immediately come to the fore. First, we must ask whether there is such a thing as the *good* for man or for society, and whether it can be *known*. If there is no objectively good state of affairs for human beings, then it makes little sense to propose that we seek out men and women who know what it is! And even if there is some objective good, it will be no help to us unless it is knowable and unless there is some way to determine when someone knows it. Among utopian philosophers of this first sort, we therefore find considerable attention paid to the nature and grounds of ethical knowledge.

What sort of knowledge is it? Is it knowledge in the sense of knowing the truth of certain propositions (such as the categorical imperative), or in the sense of being acquainted with certain sorts of sense-experiences, or is it the sort of knowledge that consists in being wise, balanced, prudent, rationally in control of oneself? Is it technical knowledge that one could learn from books, or skill of the sort one acquires through experience and practice? Could I truly know the good for mankind and society and yet be an evil person, rather like a perverse doctor who puts his medical knowledge to wicked uses? Or does this sort of knowledge change those who acquire it, so that—like the wise gurus of Eastern religions—the knower becomes good through the knowing?

A second, subsidiary problem concerning the knowledge of human and social good is this: how many persons in a society must possess the knowledge in order for the society as a whole to be able to benefit from it? Is it enough that a single wise leader know the good, a single lawgiver whom all will follow? Or must the knowledge of the principles of justice spread throughout the entire society and be known by every rank and segment of the people? If only a few know the truth about the good for society, how will they persuade those who are ignorant? By force? By trickery? By lies?

Finally, once a society is ruled by wise men and women who know the good and seek to embody it in the institutions of government, what protection can there be against a falling away from truth? May those who are truly wise succumb to the great temptation to misuse their power for private gain? If they *are* truly wise, will they ever choose their successors unwisely? Are there any institutional safeguards that can permit the wise to rule and yet protect society from those who only seem wise?

When we reflect on these questions, it very quickly becomes obvious that utopian social philosophers who preach a doctrine of rule by the wise will be particularly concerned about the content and organization of the educational system in their ideal utopia. The proper education will be required for those—be they few or many—who are to achieve knowledge of the good and thereby earn the right to rule; and a different sort of education will be equally necessary for the rest of the people, to prepare them to accept the leadership of the wise. It is hardly surprising, therefore, that from the ancient Greek utopia of Plato, through the utopian reflections of Jean-Jacques Rousseau, to such modern social philosophies as those of Bertrand Russell and John Dewey, education has played a central role in planning for the good society. This tendency continues today in American society, where proposals for social change almost always include prescriptions for educational innovation.

A different approach to the study of the good society is taken by social critics who reject as too simplistic the notion that current social evils are the result of mere ignorance. They locate the real source in unresolved conflicts of the material interests of different segments of society, conflicts which are sometimes covered over by misleading platitudes about the common good. This diagnosis of society's evils takes four forms, roughly speaking. (*Very* roughly—this classification is not definitive, but you may find it useful.)

Some utopians view material conflicts of interest—conflicts over *who gets what*—as inevitable, so long as men and women concern themselves with the desires of the flesh. There is a long tradition, firmly rooted in the ascetic, otherwordly, Christian doctrine, that teaches us to turn away from the flesh, from a desire for worldly goods, for secular rewards, and for the gratification of our sensual desires, and to look instead to things of the spirit. Even in the writings of Plato, who is ordinarily very much a this-worldly philosopher, one sometimes encounters such a teaching. In the New Testament, of course, and also in much Christian political philosophy, it plays a major role.

A second analysis of interest conflict, superficially similar to the first but in fact quite different, teaches that social evils grow out of our egocentricity, our excessive concern with self rather than with those around us. This tradition of utopian theory gives rise to imaginative descriptions of ideal communities in which education to altruism eliminates the grounds of social disharmony. (Once again, we see the central importance of education in utopian thought.) In the nineteenth century a number of communities were actually organized, in England and America, on the basis of one or another version of this conception of the good society. Some lasted only a few years, but others flourished for decades, leaving behind such place names as New Harmony, Indiana, and New Hope, Pennsylvania. The central difference between these secular utopias and the other-worldly counsel of religious teachers is that the proponents of altruism sought to replace egoism with an equally this-worldly concern for others; the religious message, on the other hand, was that salvation for *oneself* lay in turning away from the things of this world, *including* other persons in their social relationships.

A third strain of interest-conflict theory, represented by our own Founding Fathers in Colonial America, held that conflicts of material interest were inevitable and impossible to eliminate; political institutions, therefore, should be designed to *use* those private interests for the public good, rather than seeking to suppress, eliminate, or supersede them. In our political system, for example, men and women run for public office in order to advance their own interests (by earning good salaries, by exercising power, and by gaining public recognition and esteem). But since they periodically run for re-election, they must be responsive to the will of their constituents or suffer defeat. In this way, they serve others *by* serving themselves, and so their private interests are made to advance the public good. On this analysis of social evil, the burden of progress falls not on education but on the set of political arrangements by which private interests are transmuted into public benefit. If significant segments of society (blacks, women, the poor) are excluded either in law or in fact from the political system, then it will cease to function properly as a protector of the public good.

The fourth version of the interest-conflict analysis of social ills is the one we shall be examining in this chapter. It holds that in the present condition of economy and society, deep-running and fundamental conflicts of material interests are inevitable and ineradicable. There is no way to transcend them, turn away from them, or devise a political system that will make them serve a public good. Instead, these conflicts must be brought to the surface and fought out, either violently or through militant political action, until one side is defeated and the other side rules supreme. Then, and only then, will it be possible to reconstruct our economic and social arrangements so that such peace-destroying oppositions are eliminated and collective social harmony can be achieved. The most famous proponent of this view of society is, of course, Karl Marx, the founder and leading theorist of the philosophy known variously as communism or historical materialism. In this chapter we shall read a well-known statement of the Marxist doctrine written by his lifelong collaborator and friend, Friedrich Engels.

We come finally to the third approach to the task of defining and planning for the good society. This approach emphasizes not education in the objective truths of social morality, not unremitting conflict between opposed interests, but the scientific manipulation of individual personalities, through psychological, political, and social techniques, in order to eliminate sources of anti-social behavior, strengthen socially productive tendencies, and thereby achieve social harmony through the adjustment of the individual to his social environment. Put in this way, such an approach to utopia sounds dangerously like what has come to be called brainwashing or thought-control, and many critics of this utopian doctrine make precisely that criticism of it. But as we shall see, such defenders of personality manipulation as the great American behavorial psychologist

B. F. Skinner can make their program sound very plausible indeed. In light of the persistent failures of more orthodox approaches to crime, violence, poverty, and human misery in America's recent past, we should perhaps not be quite so ready to reject the proposals of Skinner and others, however odd they may sound at first.

Utopia through personality manipulation obviously raises two fundamental questions: First, *can* it be done; and second, *should* it be done? Our attention tends to be focused on the second question, with the strong implications of totalitarian mind control, violation of civil rights, invasion of personal integrity, and the like. But it might be just as fruitful to reflect for a bit on the first question. Can psychologists really manipulate our thoughts and feelings? Do the techniques exist? Have we the knowledge that would be required actually to twist the desires, the aspirations, and the perceptions of an entire population?

Thus far, the evidence suggests that the answer is no. Tyrants can, to be sure, "break" a person by torture, or by enforced periods of wakefulness, or by starvation. And it would certainly appear that many men and women are susceptible to social pressure when it is exercised by the entire surrounding community. But there is a very great difference between the many coercing or pressuring the few, and the few manipulating and twisting the many!

So much for a brief overview of the subject of utopian speculation on the good society and how to achieve it. The first approach will be represented by Plato, who calls for rule by the philosophically wise. The second approach is represented by Engels, arguing the Marxist doctrine of class conflict leading to a communist society of the future. The last approach is taken by B. F. Skinner, the father of modern behavioral psychology, advocating "positive reinforcement" to eliminate anti-social behavior and produce a harmonious society of happy, well-adjusted people. Each author is paired with a vigorous critic, and it will be up to you to decide who gets the better of each debate.

(SELECTION 1)

PLATO

Philosophers Must Be Kings

Plato's *Republic* is the classic statement of the thesis that the wise must rule. Plato sketches for us a vision of a society in which the various fundamental socially necessary tasks are assigned to classes of citizens who have been chosen in accordance with their natural aptitudes. Each class consists of men and women in whose souls a particular set of talents predominate. As we might have guessed from the selection in Chapter 3, Plato assigns the leadership role to those citizens who, to the highest degree, exhibit the trait of rationality. In this case, rationality means not only intelligence or the capacity for theoretical reasoning, but also an internal order of personality in which desire is properly modulated and subordinated, in which warlike pride is held in check, and in which there is a full understanding of what is truly to be desired, what is truly to be feared, and what is truly to be valued.

Plato expresses his view in the slogan that philosophers must rule, and not at all surprisingly, professors of philosophy have tended to applaud this doctrine. But by "philosophers" Plato did not at all mean men and women who make their living by teaching a subject called "Philosophy" in colleges and universities. He meant, rather, that society should be led by the truly wise. Put that way, his doctrine has a very modern ring about it, for we in America tend to suppose that our collective life will be much improved if only we can find the right man to be President. (I say "man" because as of this writing, Americans seem unwilling to take seriously the idea that a woman be President. In that respect, Plato, who lived two thousand years ago, was far ahead of us. He insisted that women as well as men be tested and trained for leadership roles in the Republic.)

How can we guard against the danger of corrupt rulers? Despite what one might think from this selection, Plato was not terribly optimistic, either about the chances for instituting his ideal society or about the likelihood that it would last, once established. Nevertheless, he does have an answer to this crucial question. If those chosen as rulers are truly wise, they will be genuinely good persons, not merely highly trained experts. Because their souls, or personalities, will be internally harmonious and balanced, they will not fall prey to the temptations of desire or power. They will refuse to use their positions for personal gain because they will truly understand that such corruption does not lead to real happiness. They will no more seek to undermine the health of the state than a true artist would deliberately make an ugly painting.

Or so Plato says. If we ask how we

are to guard against rulers who are self-deluding, Plato's reply is that the knowledge of the Good is rational knowledge, akin to the knowledge of mathematical truths. Those who know the good by a rational grasp of fundamental principles know that they know, just as a mathematician who truly understands a proof knows that she understands it. Needless to say, this reply has not quieted the objections, as we shall see in the next selection.

Well, said I, let me begin by reminding you that what brought us to this point was our inquiry into the nature of justice and injustice.

True; but what of that?

Merely this: suppose we do find out what justice is, are we going to demand that a man who is just shall have a character which exactly corresponds in every respect to the ideal of justice? Or shall we be satisfied if he comes as near to the ideal as possible and has in him a larger measure of that quality than the rest of the world?

That will satisfy me.

If so, when we set out to discover the essential nature of justice and injustice and what a perfectly just and a perfectly unjust man would be like, supposing them to exist, our purpose was to use them as ideal patterns: we were to observe the degree of happiness or unhappiness that each exhibited, and to draw the necessary inference that our own destiny would be like that of the one we most resembled. We did not set out to show that these ideals could exist in fact.

That is true.

Then suppose a painter had drawn an ideally beautiful figure complete to the last touch, would you think any the worse of him, if he could not show that a person as beautiful as that could exist?

No, I should not.

Well, we have been constructing in discourse the pattern of an ideal state. Is our theory any the worse, if we cannot prove it possible that a state so organized should be actually founded?

Surely not.

That, then, is the truth of the matter. But if, for your satisfaction, I am to do my best to show under what conditions our ideal would have the best chance of being realized, I must ask you once more to admit that the same principle applies here. Can theory ever be fully realized in practice? Is it not in the nature of things that action should come less close to truth than thought? People may not think so; but do you agree or not?

I do.

Then you must not insist upon my showing that this construction we have traced in thought could be reproduced in fact down to the last detail. You must admit that we shall have found a way to

From *The Republic* by Plato. (trans. by Francis MacDonald Cornford, New York and London: Oxford University Press, 1941. Reprinted by permission of the publisher.)

meet your demand for realization, if we can discover how a state might be constituted in the closest accordance with our description. Will not that content you? It would be enough for me.

And for me too.

Then our next attempt, it seems, must be to point out what defect in the working of existing states prevents them from being so organized, and what is the least change that would effect a transformation into this type of government—a single change if possible, or perhaps two; at any rate let us make the changes as few and insignificant as may be. . . . There is one change which, as I believe we can show, would bring about this revolution—not a small change, certainly, nor an easy one, but possible.

What is it?

I have now to confront what we called the third and greatest wave. But I must state my paradox, even though the wave should break in laughter over my head and drown me in ignomity. Now mark what I am going to say.

Go on.

Unless either philosophers become kings in their countries or those who are now called kings and rulers come to be sufficiently inspired with a genuine desire for wisdom; unless, that is to say, political power and philosophy meet together, while the many natures who now go their several ways in the one or the other direction are forcibly debarred from doing so, there can be no rest from troubles, my dear Glaucon, for states, nor yet, as I believe, for all mankind; nor can this commonwealth which we have imagined ever till then see the light of day and grow to its full stature. This it was that I have so long hung back from saying; I knew what a paradox it would be, because it is hard to see that there is no other way of happiness either for the state or for the individual.

Socrates, exclaimed Glaucon, after delivering yourself of such a pronouncement as that, you must expect a whole multitude of by no means contemptible assailants to fling off their coats, snatch up the handiest weapon, and make a rush at you, breathing fire and slaughter. If you cannot find arguments to beat them off and make your escape, you will learn what it means to be the target of scorn and derision. . . .

Now, I continued, if we are to elude those assailants you have described, we must, I think, define for them whom we mean by these lovers of wisdom who, we have dared to assert, ought to be our rulers. Once we have a clear view of their character, we shall be able to defend our position by pointing to some who are naturally fitted to combine philosophic study with political leadership, while the rest of the world should accept their guidance and let philosophy alone.

Yes, this is the moment for a definition.

Here, then, is a line of thought which may lead to a satisfactory explanation. . . . A man will deserve to be called a lover of this or that, only if it is clear that he loves that thing as a whole, not merely in parts. . . . So the philosopher, with his passion for wisdom, will be one who desires all wisdom, not only some part of it. If a student is particular about his studies, especially while he is too young to know which are useful and which are not, we shall say he is no lover of learning or of wisdom; just as, if he were dainty about his food, we should say he was not hungry or fond of eating, but had a poor appetite. Only the man who has a taste for every sort of knowledge and throws himself into acquiring it with an insatiable curiosity will deserve to be called a philosopher. Am I not right?

That description, Glaucon replied, would include a large and ill-assorted company. It is curiosity, I suppose, and a delight in fresh experience that gives some people a passion for all that is to be seen and heard at theatrical and musical performances. But they are a queer set to reckon among philosophers, considering that they would never go near anything like a philosophical discussion, though they run round at all the Dionysiac festivals in town or country as if they were under contract to listen to every company of performers without fail. Will curiosity entitle all these enthusiasts, not to mention amateurs of the minor arts, to be called philosophers?

Certainly not; though they have a certain counterfeit resemblance.

And whom do you mean by the genuine philosophers?

Those whose passion it is to see the truth.

That must be so; but will you explain?

It would not be easy to explain to everyone; but you, I believe, will grant my permiss.

Which is ————?

That since beauty and ugliness are opposite, they are two things; and consequently each of them is one. The same holds of justice and injustice, good and bad, and all the essential Forms: each in itself is one; but they manifest themselves in a great variety of combinations, with actions, with material things, and with one another, and so each seems to be many.

That is true.

On the strength of this premiss, then, I can distinguish your amateurs of the arts and men of action from the philosophers we are concerned with, who are alone worthy of the name.

What is your distinction?

Your lovers of sights and sounds delight in beautiful tones and colours and shapes and in all works of art into which these enter; but they have not the power of thought to behold and to take delight in the nature of Beauty itself. That power to approach Beauty and behold it as it is in itself, is rare indeed.

Quite true.

Now if a man believes in the existence of beautiful things, but not of Beauty itself, and cannot follow a guide who would lead him to a knowledge of it, is he not living in a dream? Consider: does not dreaming, whether one is awake or asleep, consist in mistaking a semblance for the reality it resembles?

I should certainly call that dreaming.

Contrast with him the man who holds that there is such a thing as Beauty itself and can discern that essence as well as the things that partake of its character, without ever confusing the one with the other—is he a dreamer or living in a waking state?

He is very much awake.

So may we say that he knows, while the other has only a belief in appearances; and might we call their states of mind knowledge and belief?

Certainly.

But this person who, we say, has only belief without knowledge may be aggrieved and challenge our statement. Is there any means of soothing his resentment and converting him gently, without telling him plainly that he is not in his right mind?

We surely ought to try.

Come then, consider what we are to say to him. Or shall we ask him a question, assuring him that, far from grudging him any knowledge he may have, we shall be only too glad to find that there is something he knows? But, we shall say, tell us this: When a man knows, must there not be something that he knows? Will you answer for him, Glaucon?

My answer will be, that there must.

Something real or unreal?

Something real; how could a thing that is unreal ever be known?

Are we satisfied, then, on this point, from however many points of view we might examine it: that the perfectly real is perfectly knowable, and the utterly unreal is entirely unknowable?

Quite satisfied.

Good. Now if there is something so constituted that it both *is* and *is not,* will it not lie between the purely real and the utterly unreal?

It will.

Well then, as knowledge corresponds to the real, and absence of knowledge necessarily to the unreal, so, to correspond to this intermediate thing, we must look for something between ignorance and knowledge, if such a thing there be.

Certainly.

Is there not a thing we call belief?

Surely.

A different power from knowledge, or the same?

Different.

Knowledge and belief, then, must have different objects, answering to their respective powers.

Yes.

And knowledge has for its natural object the real—to know the truth about reality. However, before going further, I think we need a definition. Shall we distinguish under the general name of "faculties" those powers which enable us—or anything else—to do what we can do? Sight and hearing, for instance, are what I call faculties, if that will help you to see the class of things I have in mind.

Yes, I understand.

Then let me tell you what view I take of them. In a faculty I cannot find any of those qualities, such as colour or shape, which, in the case of many other things, enable me to distinguish one thing from another. I can only look to its field of objects and the state of mind it produces, and regard these as sufficient to identify it and to distinguish it from faculties which have different fields and produce different states. Is that how you would go to work?

Yes.

Let us go back, then, to knowledge. Would you class that as a faculty?

Yes; and I should call it the most powerful of all.

And is belief also a faculty?

It can be nothing else, since it is what gives us the power of believing.

But a little while ago you agreed that knowledge and belief are not the same thing.

Yes; there could be no sense in identifying the infallible with the fallible.

Good. So we are quite clear that knowledge and belief are different things?

They are.

If so, each of them, having a different power, must have a different field of objects.

Necessarily.

The field of knowledge being the real; and its power, the power of knowing the real as it is.

Yes.

Whereas belief, we say, is the power of believing. Is its object the same as that which knowledge knows? Can the same things be possible objects both of knowledge and of belief?

Not if we hold to the principles we agreed upon. If it is of the nature of a different faculty to have a different field, and if both knowledge and belief are faculties and, as we assert, different ones, it follows that the same things cannot be possible objects of both.

So if the real is the object of knowledge, the object of belief must be something other than the real.

Yes.

Can it be the unreal? Or is that an impossible object even for belief? Consider: if a man has a belief, there must be something before his mind; he cannot be believing nothing, can he?

No.

He is believing something, then; whereas the unreal could only be called nothing at all.

Certainly.

Now we said that ignorance must correspond to the unreal, knowledge to the real. So what he is believing cannot be real nor yet unreal.

True.

Belief, then, cannot be either ignorance or knowledge.

It appears not.

Then does it lie outside and beyond these two? Is it either more clear and certain that knowledge or less clear and certain than ignorance?

No, it is neither.

It rather seems to you to be something more obscure than knowledge, but not so dark as ignorance, and so to lie between the two extremes?

Quite so.

Well, we said earlier that if some object could be found such that it both *is* and at the same time *is not,* that object would lie between the perfectly real and the utterly unreal; and that the corresponding faculty would be neither knowledge nor ignorance, but a faculty to be found situated between the two.

Yes.

And now what we have found between the two is the faculty we call belief.

True.

It seems, then, that what remains to be discovered is that object which can be said both to be and not to be and cannot properly be called either purely real or purely unreal. If that can be found, we may justly call it the object of belief, and so give the intermediate faculty the intermediate object, while the two extreme objects will fall to the extreme faculties.

Yes.

On these assumptions, then, I shall call for an answer from our friend who denies the existence of Beauty itself or of anything that can be called an essential Form of Beauty remaining unchangeably in the same state for ever, though he does recognize the existence of beautiful things as a plurality—that lover of things seen who will not listen to anyone who says that Beauty is one, Justice is one, and so on. I shall say to him, Be so good as to tell us: of all these many beautiful things is there one which will not appear ugly? Or of these many just or righteous actions, is there one that will not appear unjust or un-righteous?

No, replied Glaucon, they must inevitably appear to be in some way both beautiful and ugly; and so with all the other terms your question refers to.

And again the many things which are doubles are just as much halves as they are doubles. And the things we call large or heavy have just as much right to be called small or light.

Yes; any such thing will always have a claim to both opposite designations.

Then, whatever any one of these many things may be said to be, can you say that it absolutely *is* that, any more than that it *is not* that?

They remind me of those punning riddles people ask at dinner parties, or the child's puzzle about what the eunuch threw at the bat and what the bat was perched on. These things have the same ambiguous character, and one cannot form any stable conception of them either as being or as not being, or as both being and not being, or as neither.

Can you think of any better way of disposing of them than by placing them between reality and unreality? For I suppose they will not appear more obscure and so less real than unreality, or clearer and so more real than reality.

Quite true.

It seems, then, we have discovered that the many conventional notions of the mass of mankind about what is beautiful or honour-able or just and so on are adrift in a sort of twilight between pure reality and pure unreality.

We have.

And we agreed earlier that, if any such object were discovered, it should be called the object of belief and not of knowledge. Fluc-tuating in that half-way region, it would be seized upon by the inter-mediate faculty.

Yes.

So when people have an eye for the multitude of beautiful things or of just actions or whatever it may be, but can neither behold Beauty or Justice itself nor follow a guide who would lead them to it, we shall say that all they have is beliefs, without any real knowledge of the objects of their belief.

That follows.

But what of those who contemplate the realities themselves as they are for ever in the same unchanging state? Shall we not say that they have, not mere belief, but knowledge?

That too follows.

And, further, that their affection goes out to the objects of knowledge, whereas the others set their affections on the objects of belief; for it was they, you remember, who had a passion for the spectacle of beautiful colours and sounds, but would not hear of Beauty itself being a real thing.

I remember.

So we may fairly call them lovers of belief rather than of wisdom—not philosophical, in fact, but philodoxical. Will they be seriously annoyed by that description?

Not if they will listen to my advice. No one ought to take offence at the truth.

The name of philosopher, then, will be reserved for those whose affections are set, in every case, on the reality.

By all means.

So at last, Glaucon, after this long and weary way, we have come to see who are the philosophers and who are not.

I doubt if the way could have been shortened.

Apparently not. I think, however, that we might have gained a still clearer view, if this had been the only topic to be discussed; but there are so many others awaiting us, if we mean to discover in what ways the just life is better that the unjust.

Which are we to take up now?

Surely the one that follows next in order. Since the philosophers are those who can apprehend the eternal and unchanging, while those who cannot do so, but are lost in the mazes of multiplicity and change, are not philosophers, which of the two ought to be in control of a state?

I wonder what would be a reasonable solution.

To establish as Guardians whichever of the two appear competent to guard the laws and ways of life in society.

True.

Well, there can be no question whether a guardian who is to

keep watch over anything needs to be keen-sighted or blind. And is not blindness precisely the condition of men who are entirely cut off from knowledge of any reality, and have in their soul no clear pattern of perfect truth, which they might study in every detail and constantly refer to, as a painter looks at his model, before they proceed to embody notions of justice, honour, and goodness in earthly institutions or, in their character of Guardians, to preserve such institutions as already exist?

Certainly such a condition is very like blindness.

Shall we, then, make such as these our Guardians in preference to me who, besides their knowledge of realities, are in no way inferior to them in experience and in every excellence of character?

It would be absurd not to choose the philosophers, whose knowledge is perhaps their greatest point of superiority, provided they do not lack those other qualifications.

What we have to explain, then, is how those qualifications can to combined in the same persons with philosophy.

Certainly.

The first thing, as we said at the outset, is to get a clear view of their inborn disposition. When we are satisfied on that head, I think we shall agree that such a combination of qualities is possible and that we need look no further for men fit to be in control of a commonwealth. One trait of the philosophic nature we may take as already granted: a constant passion for any knowledge that will reveal to them something of that reality which endures for ever and is not always passing into and out of existence. And, we may add, their desire is to know the whole of that reality; they will not willingly renounce any part of it as relatively small and insignificant, as we said before when we compared them to the lover and to the man who covets honour.

True.

Is there not another trait which the nature we are seeking cannot fail to possess—truthfulness, a love of truth and a hatred of falsehood that will not tolerate untruth in any form?

Yes, it is natural to expect that.

It is not merely natural, but entirely necessary that an instinctive passion for any object should extend to all that is closely akin to it; and there is nothing more closely akin to wisdom than truth. So the same nature cannot love wisdom and falsehood; the genuine lover of knowledge cannot fail, from his youth up, to strive after the whole of truth.

I perfectly agree.

Now we surely know that when a man's desires set strongly in one direction, in every other channel they flow more feebly, like a stream deverted into another bed. So when the current has set towards knowledge and all that goes with it, desire will abandon those pleasures of which the body is the instrument and be concerned only with the pleasure which the soul enjoys independently—if, that is to say, the love of wisdom is more than a mere pretence. Accordingly, such a one will be temperate and no lover of money; for he will be the last person to care about the things for the sake of which money is eagerly sought and lavishly spent.

That is true.

Again, in seeking to distinguish the philosophic nature, you must not overlook the least touch of meanness. Nothing could be more contrary than pettiness to a mind constantly bent on grasping the whole of things, both divine and human.

Quite true.

And do you suppose that one who is so high-minded and whose thought can contemplate all time and all existence will count this life of man a matter of much concern?

No, he could not.

So for such a man death will have no terrors.

None.

A mean and cowardly nature, then, can have no part in the genuine pursuit of wisdom.

I think not.

And if a man is temperate and free from the love of money, meanness, pretentiousness, and cowardice, he will not be hard to deal with or dishonest. So, as another indication of the philosophic temper, you will observe whether, from youth up, he is fair-minded, gentle, and sociable.

Certainly.

Also you will not fail to notice whether he is quick or slow to learn. No one can be expected to take a reasonable delight in a task in which much painful effort makes little headway. And if he cannot retain what he learns, his forgetfulness will leave no room in his head for knowledge; and so, having all his toil for nothing, he can only end by hating himself as well as his fruitless occupation. We must not, then, count, a forgetful mind as competent to pursue wisdom; we must require a good memory.

By all means.

Further, there is in some natures a crudity and awkwardness that can only trend to a lack of measure and proportion; and there is a close affinity between proportion and truth. Hence, besides our other requirements, we shall look for a mind endowed with measure and grace, which will be instinctively drawn to see every reality in its true light.

Yes.

Well then, now that we have enumerated the qualities of a mind destined to take its full part in the apprehension of reality, have you any doubt about their being indispensable and all necessarily going together?

None whatever. . . .

. . . But is there any existing form of society that you would call congenial to philosophy?

Not one. That is precisely my complaint: no existing constitution is worthy of the philosophic nature; that is why it is perverted and loses its character. As a foreign seed sown in a different soil yields to the new influence and degenerates into the local variety, so this nature cannot now keep its proper virtue, but falls away and takes on an alien character. If it can ever find the ideal form of society, as perfect as itself, then we shall see that it is in reality something divine, while all other natures and ways of life are merely human. No doubt you will ask me next what this ideal society is.

You are mistaken, he replied; I was going to ask whether you meant the commonwealth we have been founding.

Yes, in all points but one: our state must always contain some authority which will hold to the same idea of its constitution that you had before you in framing its laws. We did, in fact, speak of that point before, but not clearly enough; you frightened me with your objections, which have shown that the explanation is a long and difficult matter; and the hardest part is still to come.

What is that?

The question how a state can take in hand the pursuit of philosophy without disaster; for all great attempts are hazardous, and the proverb is only too true, that what is worth while is never easy.

All the same, this point must be cleared up to complete your account.

If I fail, it will not be for want of goodwill; "yourself shall see me do my uttermost." In proof of which I shall at once be rash enough to remark that the state should deal with this pursuit, not as it does now, but in just the opposite way. As things are, those who take it up at all are only just out of their childhood. In the interval before they set up house and begin to learn their living, they are introduced to the hardest part—by which I mean abstract discussions—and then, when they have done with that, their philosophic education is supposed to be complete. Later, they think they have done much if they accept an invitation to listen to such a discussion, which is, in their eyes, to be taken as a pastime; and as age draws on, in all but a very few the light is quenched more effectually than the sun of Heraclitus, inasmuch as it is never rekindled.

And what would be the right plan?

Just the opposite. Boys and youths should be given a liberal education suitable to their age; and, while growing up to manhood, they should take care to make their bodies into good instruments for the service of philosophy. As the years go on in which the mind begins to reach maturity, intellectual training should be intensified. Finally, when strength fails and they are past civil and military duties, let them range at will, free from all serious business but philosophy; for their is to be a life of happiness, crowned after death with a fitting destiny in the other world.

You really do seem to be doing your uttermost, Socrates. But I fancy most of your hearers will be even more in earnest on the other side. They are not at all likely to agree; least of all Trasymachus.

Don't try to make a quarrel between Thrasymachus and me, when we have just become friends—not that we were enemies before. You and I will spare no effort until we convince him and the rest of the company, or as least take them some way with us, against the day when they may find themselves once more engaged in discussions like ours in some future incarnation.

Rather a distant prospect!

No more than a moment in the whole course of time. However, it is no wonder that most people have no faith in our proposals, for they have never seen our words come true in fact. They have heard plenty of eloquence, not like our own unstudied discourse, but full of balanced phrases and artfully matched antitheses; but a man with a character so finely balanced as to be a match for the ideal of virtue in word and deed, ruling in a society as perfect as himself—that they have never yet seen in a single instance.

They have not.

Nor yet have they cared to listen seriously to frank discussion of the nobler sort that is entirely bent on knowing the truth for its own sake and leaves severely alone those tricks of special pleading in the law-court or the lecture-room which aim only at influencing opinion or winning a case.

Quite true.

These, then, were the obstacles I foresaw when, in spite of my fears, truth compelled me to declare that there will never be a perfect state or constitution, nor yet a perfect man, until some happy circumstance compels these few philosophers who have escaped corruption but are now called useless, to take charge, whether they like it or not, of a state which will submit to their authority; or else until kings and rulers or their sons are divinely inspired with a genuine passion for true philosophy. If either alternative or both were impossible, we might justly be laughed at as idle dreamers; but, as I maintain, there is no ground for saying so. Accordingly, if ever in the infinity of time, past or future, or even to-day in some foreign region far beyond our horizon, men of the highest gifts for philosophy are constrained to take charge of a commonwealth, we are ready to maintain that, then and there, the constitution we have described has been realized, or will be realized when once the philosophic muse becomes mistress of state. For that might happen. Our plan is difficult—we have admitted as much—but not impossible.

I agree to that.

But the public, you are going to say, think otherwise?

Perhaps.

My dear Adeimantus, you must not condemn the public so sweepingly; they will change their opinion, if you avoid controversy and try gently to remove their prejudice against the love of learning. Repeat our description of the philosopher's nature and of his pursuits, and they will see that you do not mean the sort of person they imagine. It is only ill-temper and malice in oneself that call out those qualities in others who are not that way inclined; and I will anticipate you by declaring that, in my belief, the public with a few exceptions is not of such an unyielding temper.

Yes, I agree with you there.

Will you also agree that, if it is ill-disposed towards philosophy, the blame must fall on that noisy crew of interlopers who are always bandying abuse and spiteful personalities—the last thing of which a philosopher can be guilty? For surely, Adeimantus, a man whose thoughts are fixed on true reality has no leisure to look downwards on the affairs of men, to take part in their quarrels, and to catch the infection of their jealousies and hates. He contemplates a world of unchanging and harmonious order, where reason governs and nothing can do or suffer wrong; and, like one who imitates an admired companion, he cannot fail to fashion himself in its likeness. So the philosopher, in constant companionship with the divine order of the world, will reproduce that order in his soul and, so far as man may, become godlike; though here, as everywhere, there will be scope for detraction.

Quite true.

Suppose, then, he should find himself compelled to mould other characters besides his own and to shape the pattern of public and private life into conformity with his vision of the ideal, he will not lack the skill to produce such counterparts of temperance, justice, and all the virtues as can exist in the ordinary man. And the public, when they see that we have described him truly, will be reconciled to the philosopher and no longer disbelieve our assertion that happiness can only come to a state when its lineaments are traced by an artist working after the divine pattern.

Yes, they will be reconciled when once they understand. But how will this artist set to work?

He will take society and human character as his canvas, and be-

gin by scraping it clean. That is no easy matter; but, as you know, unlike other reformers, he will not consent to take in hand either an individual or a state or to draft laws, until he is given a clean surface
to work on or has cleansed it himself.

Quite rightly.

Next, he will sketch in the outline of the constitution. Then, as
the work goes on, he will frequently refer to his model, the ideals of
justice, goodness, temperance, and the rest, and compare with them
the copy of those qualities which he is trying to create in human society. Combining the various elements of social life as a painter mixes
his colours, he will reproduce the complexion of true humanity,
guided by that divine pattern whose likeness Homer saw in the men
he called godlike. He will rub out and paint in again this or that
feature, until he has produced, so far as may be, a type of human
character that heaven can approve.

No picture could be more beautiful than that.

Are we now making any impression on those assailants who, you
said, would fall upon us so furiously when we spoke in praise of the
philosopher and proposed to give him control of the state? Will they
be calmer now that we have told them we mean an artist who will use
his skill in this way to design a constitution?

They ought to be, if they have any sense.

Yes, for what ground is left for dispute? It would be absurd to
deny that a philosopher is a lover of truth and reality; or that his
nature, as we have described it, is allied to perfection; or again, that
given the right training, no other will be so completely good and
enlightened. They will hardly give the preference to those impostors
whom we have ruled out.

Surely not.

So they will no longer be angry with us for saying that, until
philosophers hold power, neither states nor individuals will have rest
from trouble, and the commonwealth we have imagined will never
be realized.

Less angry perhaps.

I suggest that, if we go farther and assume them to be completely pacified and convinced, then, perhaps, they might agree with
us for very shame.

Certainly they might.

Granted, then, that they are convinced so far, no one will dispute our other point, that kings and hereditary rulers might have
sons with a philosophic nature, and these might conceivably escape
corruption. It would be hard to save them, we admit; but can anyone say that, in the whole course of time, not a single one could be
saved?

Surely not.

Well, one would be enough to effect all this reform that now seems so incredible, if he had subjects disposed to obey; for it is surely not impossible that they should consent to carry out our laws and customs when laid down by a ruler. It would be no miracle if others should think as we do; and we have, I believe, sufficiently shown that our plan, if practicable, is the best. So, to conclude: our institutions would be the best, if they could be realized, and to realize them, though hard, is not impossible.

Yes, that is the conclusion.

PLATO SELECTION

1. Socrates asks: what is the smallest change in existing states that would have any real chance of moving them in the direction of the ideal. What change does he propose? Once that change actually came about, what do you suppose the next steps would be? What problems do you see as standing in the way of a truly wise ruler making real progress toward a just state?

2. Would a great artist deliberately design and live in an ugly house? Would a great composer deliberately surround himself or herself with ugly music? Would a brilliant mathematician deliberately fill books with mistaken proofs? If the answers to those questions are no, then would a truly good ruler deliberately design and create evil political institutions? Could a ruler be truly good, in Plato's sense, but simply incompetent?

3. How are we to know the truly wise, according to Socrates? Can those who are *not* truly wise be trusted to choose the truly wise as their rulers? If not, then how are we to decide *who* shall rule? Even after we have decided that the wise shall rule, how are we to determine who are the wise? Can a person be wise and not know it? Can a person think he or she is wise and be mistaken?

4. Do those who rise to the top in our political system tend to be the wise? Why? Are there any changes that could be made in the system for choosing political rulers that would encourage choice of the wise? Does television raise or lower the level of wisdom of our political choices?

5. If the few are wise, and the many foolish, then what sense does it make to have our rulers chosen by the many? Does democracy require that the many be wise, or are there good reasons to put the power of choice in the hands of the many even though they may not be wise?

6. Plato's proposal is designed for a Greek city-state, roughly the size of a modern middle-sized city. Are there any reasons why the same proposal might be unworkable in a modern large-scale nation-state?

(SELECTION 2)

KARL POPPER

The Philosopher King

The most vigorous and thoroughgoing assault on Plato's political philosophy is to be found in a highly influential work by the prominent philosopher of science, Karl Popper. As you will see in this selection, Popper places great emphasis on certain of the less "philosophical" portions of Plato's utopian vision, including his scheme for eugenic breeding of citizens and his claim that the rulers shall have to tell "noble lies" to the common people in order to get them to accept the wise rule that is in their best interests. It would be easy to brush Popper's objections aside with the reply that they concern only minor matters of elaboration in Plato's scheme, matters that are not integrally related to the central epistemological and moral theses. But I think such a defense of Plato would be too quick.

Popper wrote at a time when the dominant political fact was the totalitarian fascism of Nazi Germany and the repressive regime of Stalinist Russia. Like virtually all of the leading intellectuals of the Thirties and Forties, Popper was horrified by the unspeakable acts committed by the Nazis and by the Russians in the name of high-sounding principles. Quite naturally—and perhaps also quite properly—he was unwilling to divorce philosophical principles from their concrete embodiments in the actual practices of existing states. If Plato can so easily call for controlled eugenic reproduction and a manipulation of public opinion that today would be called propaganda, then how sound can his philosophical theses really be?

By contrast, Popper's *ad hominem* attack on Plato himself (near the end of this selection) should perhaps be set to one side. It is a fact of life that the wisest men and women have mixed personal ambition with great theoretical contributions. Nevertheless, since Plato himself insists that true wisdom carries with it equanimity of soul and a freedom from misguided passion, we may perhaps permit Popper to ask whether Plato, in his discussion of the truly wise ruler, exhibits himself those traits of character that would mark him as a natural Philosopher King.

Plato, I have said, followed Socrates in his definition of the philosopher. "Whom do you call true philosophers?—Those who love truth," we read in the *Republic*. But he himself is not quite truthful when he makes this statement. He does not really believe in it, for he bluntly declares in other places that it is one of the royal privileges of the sovereign to make full use of lies and deceit: "It is the business of the rulers of the city, if it is anybody's, to tell lies, deceiving both its enemies and its own citizens for the benefit of the city; and no one else must touch this privilege."

"For the benefit of the city," says Plato. Again we find that the appeal to the principle of collective utility is the ultimate ethical consideration. Totalitarian morality overrules everything, even the definition, the Idea, of the philosopher. It need hardly be mentioned that, by the same principle of political expediency, the ruled are to be forced to tell the truth. "If the ruler catches *anyone else* in a lie . . . then he will punish him for introducing a practice which injures and endangers the city. . . ." Only in this slightly unexpected sense are the Platonic rulers—the philosopher kings—lovers of truth.

Plato illustrates this application of his principle of collective utility to the problem of truthfulness by the example of the physician. The example is well chosen, since Plato likes to visualize his political mission as one of the healer or saviour of the sick body of society. Apart from this, the role which he assigns to medicine throws light upon the totalitarian character of Plato's city where state interest dominates the life of the citizen from the mating of his parents to his grave. Plato interprets medicine as a form of politics, or as he puts it himself, he "regards Aesculapius, the god of medicine, as a politician." Medical art, he explains, must not consider the prolongation of life as its aim, but only the interest of the state. "In all properly ruled communities, each man has his particular work assigned to him in the state. This he must do, and no one has time to spend his life in falling ill and getting cured." Accordingly, the physician has "no right to attend to a man who cannot carry out his ordinary duties; for such a man is useless to himself and to the state." To this is added the consideration that such a man might have "children who would probably be equally sick," and who also would become a burden to the state. . . . Concerning the use of lies and deceit, Plato urges that these are "useful only as a medicine"; but the ruler of the state, Plato insists, must not behave like some of those "ordinary doctors" who

From "The Spell of Plato," vol. I, in *The Open Society and Its Enemies* by Karl R. Popper. (Princeton University Press, 5th rev. edn. 1966; Routledge and Kegan Paul, 5th edn. 1966, pp. 138–53. Reprinted by permission of the author and the publishers.)

have not the courage to administer strong medicines. The philosopher king, a lover of truth as a philosopher, must, as a king, be "a more courageous man," since he must be determined "to administer a great many lies and deceptions"—for the benefit of the ruled, Plato hastens to add. Which means . . . "for the benefit of the state." . . .

What kind of lies has Plato in mind when he exhorts his rulers to use strong medicine? Crossman rightly emphasizes that Plato means "propaganda, the technique of controlling the behaviour of . . . the bulk of the ruled majority." Certainly, Plato had these first in his mind; but when Crossman suggests that the propaganda lies were only intended for the consumption of the ruled, while the rulers should be a fully enlightened intelligentsia, then I cannot agree. I think, rather, that Plato's complete break with anything resembling Socrates' intellectualism is nowhere more obvious than in the place where he twice expresses his hope that even *the rulers themselves,* at least after a few generations, might be induced to believe his greatest propaganda lie; I mean his racialism, his Myth of Blood and Soil, known as the Myth of the Metals in Man and of the Earthborn. Here we see that Plato's utilitarian and totalitarian principles overrule everything, even the ruler's privilege of knowing, and of demanding to be told, the truth. The motive of Plato's wish that the rulers themselves should believe in the propaganda lie in his hope of increasing its wholesome effect, i.e., of strengthening the rule of the master race, and ultimately, of arresting all political change.

Plato introduces his Myth of Blood and Soil with the blunt admission that it is a fraud. "Well then," says the Socrates of the *Republic,* "could we perhaps fabricate one of those very handy lies which indeed we mentioned just recently? With the help of one single lordly lie we may, if we are lucky, persuade even the rulers themselves—but at any rate the rest of the city." It is interesting to note the use of the term "persuade." To persuade somebody to believe a lie means, more precisely, to mislead or to hoax him; and it would be more in tune with the frank cynicism of the passage to translate "we may, if we are lucky, hoax even the rulers themselves." But Plato uses the term "persuasion" very frequently, and its occurrence here throws some light on other passages. It may be taken as a warning that in similar passages he may have propaganda lies in his mind; more especially where he advocates that the statesman should rule "by means of both persuasion and force."

After announcing his "lordly lie," Plato, instead of proceeding directly to the narration of his Myth, first develops a lengthy preface, somewhat similar to the lengthy preface which precedes his discovery of justice; an indication, I think, of his uneasiness. It seems

that he did not expect the proposal which follows to find much favour with his readers. The Myth itself introduces two ideas. The first
is to strengthen the defence of the mother country; it is the idea that
the warriors of his city are autochthonous, "born of the earth of their
country," and ready to defend their country which is their mother.
This old and well-known idea is certainly not the reason for Plato's
hesitation (although the wording of the dialogue cleverly suggests it).
The second idea, however, "the rest of the story," is the myth of
racialism: "God . . . has put gold into those who are capable of ruling,
silver into the auxiliaries, and iron and copper into the peasants and
the other producing classes." These metals are hereditary, they are
racial characteristics. In this passage, in which Plato, hesitatingly, first
introduces his racialism, he allows for the possibility that children
may be born with an admixture of another metal than those of their
parents; and it must be admitted that he here announces the following rule: if in one of the lower classes "children are born with an admixture of gold and silver, they shall . . . be appointed guardians, and
. . . auxiliaries." But this concession is rescinded in later passages of
the *Republic* (and also in the *Laws*). . . .

Plato's opportunism and his theory of lies makes it, of course,
difficult to interpret what he says. How far did he believe in his
theory of justice? How far did he believe in the truth of the religious
doctrines he preached? Was he perhaps himself an atheist, in spite
of his demand for the punishment of other (lesser) atheists? Although
we cannot hope to answer any of these questions definitely, it is, I
believe, difficult, and methodologically unsound, not to give Plato at
least the benefit of the doubt. And especially the fundamental sincerity of his belief that there is an urgent need to arrest all change
can, I think, hardly be questioned. . . . On the other hand, we cannot doubt that Plato subjects the Socratic love of truth to the more
fundamental principle that the rule of the master class must be
strengthened.

It is interesting, however, to note that Plato's theory of truth is
slightly less radical than his theory of justice. Justice, we have seen,
is defined, practically, as that which serves the interest of his totalitarian state. It would have been possible, of course, to define the concept of truth in the same utilitarian or pragmatist fashion. The Myth
is true, Plato could have said, since anything that serves the interest
of my state must be believed and therefore must be called "true";
and there must be no other criterion of truth. . . . But Plato retained
enough of the Socratic spirit to admit candidly that he was lying. . . .

So much for the role played by the Idea of Truth in Plato's best
state. But apart from Justice and Truth, we have still to consider

some further Ideas, such as Goodness, Beauty, and Happiness. . . . An approach to the discussion of these Ideas, and also to that of Wisdom, which has been partly discussed in the last chapter, can be made by considering the somewhat negative result reached by our discussion of the Idea of Truth. For this result raises a new problem: Why does Plato demand that the philosophers should be kings or the kings philosophers, if he defines the philosophers as a lover of truth, insisting, on the hand, that the king must be "more courageous," and use lies?

The only reply to this question, of course, that Plato has, in fact, something very different in mind when he uses the term "philosopher." And indeed, . . . his philosopher is not the devoted seeker for wisdom, but its proud possessor. He is a learned man, a sage. What Plato demands, therefore, is the rule of learnedness—*sophocracy,* if I may so call it. In order to understand this demand, we must try to find what kind of functions make it desirable that the ruler of Plato's state should be a possessor of knowledge, a "fully qualified philosopher," as Plato says. The functions to be considered can be divided into two main groups, namely those connected with the *foundation* of the state, and those connected with its *preservation.*

The first and the most important function of the philosopher king is that of the city's founder and lawgiver. It is clear why Plato needs a philosopher for this task. If the state is to be stable, then it must be a true copy of the divine Form or Idea of the State. But only a philosopher who is fully proficient in the highest of sciences, in dialectics, is able to see, and to copy, the heavenly Original. This point receives much emphasis in the part of the *Republic* in which Plato develops his arguments for the sovereignty of the philosophers. Philosophers "love to see the truth," and a real lover always loves to see the whole, not merely the parts. Thus he does not love, as ordinary people do, sensible things and their "beautiful sounds and colours and shapes," but he wants "to see, and to admire the real nature of beauty"—the Form or Idea of Beauty. *In this way, Plato gives the term philosopher a new meaning,* that of a lover and a seer of the divine world of Forms or Ideas. As such, the philosopher is the man who may become the founder of a virtuous city: "The philosopher who has communion with the divine" may be "overwhelmed by the urge to realize . . . his heavenly vision," of the ideal city and of its ideal citizens. He is like a draughtsman or a painter who has "the divine as his model." Only true philosophers can "sketch the ground-plan of the city," for they alone can see the original, and can copy it, by "letting their eyes wander to and fro, from the model to the picture, and back from the picture to the model."

As "a painter of constitutions," the philosopher must be helped by the light of goodness and of wisdom. A few remarks will be added concerning these two ideas, and their significance for the philosopher in his function as a founder of the city.

Plato's *Idea of the Good* is the highest in the hierarchy of Forms. It is the sun of the divine world of Forms or Ideas, which not only sheds light on all the other members, but is the source of their existence. It is also the source or cause of all knowledge and all truth. The power of seeing, of appreciating, of knowing the Good is thus indispensable to the dialectician. Since it is the sun and the source of light in the world of Forms, it enables the philosopher-painter to discern his objects. Its function is therefore of the greatest importance for the founder of the city. But this purely formal information is all we get. Plato's Idea of the Good nowhere plays a more direct ethical or political role; never do we hear which deeds are good, or produce good, apart from the well-known collectivist moral code whose precepts are introduced without recourse to the Idea of Good. Remarks that the Good is the aim, that it is desired by every man, do not enrich our information. . . . In the *Republic,* Plato says frankly that he cannot explain what he means by "the Good." The only practical suggestion we ever get is the one mentioned at the beginning of Chapter 4—that good is everything that preserves, and evil everything that leads to corruption or degeneration. ("Good" does not, however, seem to be here the Idea of Good, but rather a property of things which makes them resemble the ideas.) Good is, accordingly, an unchanging, an arrested state of things; it is the state of things at rest.

This does not seem to carry us very far beyond Plato's political totalitarianism; and the analysis of Plato's *Idea of Wisdom* leads to equally disappointing results. Wisdom . . . does not mean to Plato the Socratic insight into one's own limitations; nor does it mean what most of us would expect, a warm interest in, and a helpful understanding of, humanity and human affairs. Plato's wise men, highly preoccupied with the problems of a superior world, "have no time to look down at the affairs of men . . . ; they look upon, and hold fast to, the ordered and the measured." It is the right kind of learning that makes a man wise: "Philosophic natures are lovers of that kind of learning which reveals to them a reality that exists for ever and is not harassed by generation and degeneration." It does not seem that Plato's treatment of wisdom can carry us beyond the ideal of arresting change.

Although the analysis of the functions of the city's founder has not revealed any new ethical elements in Plato's doctrine, it has shown that there is a definite reason why the founder of the city must be a philosopher. But this does not fully justify the demand for the permanent sovereignty of the philosopher. It only explains why the philosopher must be the first lawgiver, but not why he is needed as the permanent ruler, especially since none of the later rulers must introduce any change. For a full justification of the demand that the philosophers should rule, we must therefore proceed to analyse the tasks connected with the city's preservation.

We know from Plato's sociological theories that the state, once established, will continue to be stable as long as there is no split in the unity of the master class. The bringing up of that class is, therefore, the great preserving function of the sovereign, and a function which must continue as long as the state exists. How far does it justify the demand that a philosopher must rule? To answer this question, we distinguish again, within this function, between two different activities: the supervision of education, and the supervision of eugenic breeding.

Why should the director of education be a philosopher? Why is it not sufficient, once the state and its educational system are established, to put an experienced general, a soldier-king, in charge of it? The answer that the educational system must provide not only soldiers but philosophers, and therefore needs philosophers as well as soldiers as supervisors, is obviously unsatisfactory; for if no philosophers were needed as directors of education and as permanent rulers, then there would be no need for the educational system to produce new ones. The requirements of the educational system cannot as such justify the need for philosophers in Plato's state, or the postulate that the rulers must be philosophers. This would be different, of course, if Plato's education had an individualistic aim, apart from its aim to serve the interest of the state; for example, the aim to develop philosophical faculties for their own sake. But when we see . . . how frightened Plato was of permitting anything like independent thought; and when we now see that the ultimate theoretical aim of this philosophic education was merely a "Knowledge of the Idea of the Good" which is incapable of giving an articulate account of this Idea, then we begin to realize that this cannot be the explanation. . . . The great importance which Plato attaches to a philosophical education of the rulers must be explained by other reasons—by reasons which must be purely political.

The main reason I can see is the need for increasing of the utmost the authority of the rulers. If the education of the auxiliaries functions properly, there will be plenty of good soldiers. Outstanding military faculties may therefore be insufficient to establish an unchallenged and unchallengeable authority. This must be based on higher claims. Plato bases it upon the claims of supernatural, mystical powers which he develops in his leaders. They are not like other men. They belong to another world, they communicate with the divine. Thus the philosopher king seems to be, partly, a copy of a tribal priest-king. . . . Thus Plato's philosophical education has a definite political function. *It puts a mark on the rulers, and it establishes a barrier between the rulers and the ruled.* (This has remained a major function of "higher" education down to our own time.) Platonic wisdom is acquired largely for the sake of establishing a permanent political class rule. It can be described as political "medicine," giving mystic powers to its possessors, the medicine-men.

But this cannot be the full answer to our question of the functions of the philosopher in the state. It means, rather, that the question why a philosopher is needed has only been shifted, and that we would have now to raise the analogous question of the practical political functions of the shaman or the medicine-man. Plato must have had some definite aim when he devised his specialized philosophic training. We must look for a permanent function of the ruler, analogous to the temporary function of the lawgiver. The only hope of discovering such a function seems to be in the field of breeding the master race.

The best way to find out why a philosopher is needed as a permanent ruler is to ask the question: What happens, according to Plato, to a state which is not permanently ruled by a philosopher? Plato has given a clear answer to this question. If the guardians of the state, even of a very perfect one, are unaware of Pythagorean lore and of the Platonic Number, then the race of the guardians, and with it the state, must degenerate.

Racialism thus takes up a more central part in Plato's political programme than one would expect at first sight. Just as the Platonic racial or nuptial Number provides the setting for his descriptive sociology, . . . so it also provides the setting of Plato's political demand for the sovereignty of the philosophers. . . . The need for scientific, for mathematico-dialectical and philosophical breeding is not the least of the arguments behind the claim for the sovereignty of the philosophers.

. . . So far we have not met with any plausible reason why only a genuine and fully qualified philosopher should be a proficient and successful political breeder. And yet, as every breeder of dogs or horses or birds knows, rational breeding is impossible without a pattern, an aim to guide him in his efforts, an ideal which he may try to approach by the methods of mating and of selecting. Without such a standard, he could never decide which offspring is "good enough"; he could never speak of the difference between "good offspring" and "bad offspring." But this standard corresponds exactly to a Platonic Idea of the race which he intends to breed.

Just as only the true philosopher, the dialectician, can see, according to Plato, the divine original of the city, so it is only the dialectician who can see that other divine original—the Form or Idea of Man. Only he is capable of copying this model, of calling it down from Heaven to Earth, and of realizing it here. It is a kingly Idea, this Idea of Man. It does not, as some have thought, represent what is common to all men; it is not the universal concept "man." It is, rather, the godlike original of man, an unchanging superman; it is a super-Greek, and a super-master. The philosopher must try to realize on earth what Plato describes as the race of "the most constant, the most virile, and, within the limits of possibilities, the most beautifully formed men . . . : nobly born, and of awe-inspiring character." It is to be a race of men and women who are "godlike if not divine . . . sculptured in perfect beauty"—a lordly race, destined by nature to kingship and mastery.

We see that the two fundamental functions of the philosopher king are analogous: he has to copy the divine original of the city, and he has to copy the divine original of man. He is the only one who is able, and who has the urge, "to realize, in the individual as well as in the city, his heavenly vision."

Now we can understand why Plato drops his first hint that a more than ordinary excellence is needed in his rulers in the same place where he first claims that the principles of animal breeding must be applied to the race of men. We are, he says, most careful in breeding animals. "If you did not breed them in this way, don't you think that the race of your birds or your dogs would quickly degenerate?" When inferring from this that man must be bred in the same careful way, "Socrates" exclaims: "Good heavens! . . . What surpassing excellence we shall have to demand from our rulers, if the same principles apply to the race of men!" This exclamation is significant; it is one of the first hints that the rulers may constitute a class of "surpassing excellence" with status and training of their own; and it thus prepares us for the demand that they ought to be philosophers. But the passage is even more significant in so far as it directly leads to Plato's demand that it must be the duty of the rulers, as doctors of the race of men, to administer lies and deception. Lies are necessary, Plato asserts, "if your herd is to reach highest perfection"; for this needs "arrangements that must be kept secret from all but the rulers, if we wish to keep the herd of guardians really free from disunion." Indeed, the appeal . . . to the rulers for more courage in administering lies as a medicine is made in this connection; it prepares the reader for the next demand, considered by Plato as particularly important. He decrees that the rulers should fabricate, for the purpose of mating the young auxiliaries, "an ingenious system of balloting, so that the persons who have been disappointed . . . may blame their bad luck, and not the rulers," who are, secretly, to engineer the ballot. And immediately after this despicable advice for dodging the admission of responsibility (by putting it into the mouth of Socrates, Plato libels his great teacher), "Socrates" makes a suggestion which is soon taken up and elaborated by Glaucon and which we may therefore call the *Glauconic Edict.* I mean the brutal law which imposes on everybody of either sex the duty of submitting, for the duration of a war, to the wishes of the brave: "As long as the war lasts, . . . nobody may say "No" to him. Accordingly, if a soldier wishes to make love to anybody, whether male or female, this law will make him more eager to carry off the price of valour." The state, it is carefully pointed out, will thereby obtain two distinct benefits—more heroes, owing to the incitement, and again more heroes, owing to the increased numbers of children from heroes. (The latter benefit, as the most important one from the point of view of a long-term racial policy, is put into the mouth of "Socrates.")

No special philosophical training is required for this kind of breeding. Philosophical breeding, however, plays its main part in counteracting the dangers of degeneration. In order to fight these dangers, a fully qualified philosopher is needed, i.e., one who is trained in pure mathematics (including solid geometry), pure astronomy, pure harmonics, and, the crowning achievement of all, in dialectics. Only he who knows the secrets of mathematical eugenics, of the Platonic Number, can bring back to man, and preserve for him, the happiness enjoyed before the Fall. All this should be borne in mind when, after the announcement of the Glauconic Edict (and after an interlude dealing with the natural distinction between Greeks and Barbarians, corresponding, according to Plato, to that between masters and slaves), the doctrine is enunciated which Plato carefully marks as his central and most sensational political demand —the sovereignty of the philosopher king. This demand alone, he teaches, can put an end to the evils of social life; to the evil rampant in states, i.e., *political instability,* as well as to its more hidden cause, the evil rampant in the members of the race of men, i.e., *racial degeneration.*

Once this conclusion has been reached, many things which otherwise would remain unrelated become connected and clear. It can hardly be doubted, for instance, that Plato's work, full of allusions as it is to contemporary problems and characters, was meant by its author not so much as a theoretical treatise, but as a topical political manifesto. "We do Plato the gravest of wrongs," says A. E. Taylor, "if we forget that the *Republic* is no mere collection of theoretical discussions about government . . . but a serious project of practical reform put forward by an Athenian . . . , set on fire, like Shelley, with a 'passion for reforming the world.' " This is undoubtedly true, and we could have concluded from this consideration alone that, in describing his philosopher kings, Plato must have thought of some of the contemporary philosophers. But in the days when the *Republic* was written, there were in Athens only three outstanding men who might have claimed to be philosophers: Antisthenes, Isocrates, and Plato himself. If we approach the *Republic* with this in mind, we find at once that, in the discussion of the characteristics of the philosopher kings, there is a lengthy passage which is clearly marked out by Plato as containing personal allusions. It begins with an unmistakable allusion to a popular character, namely Alcibiades, and ends by openly mentioning a name (that of Theages), and with a reference of "Socrates" to himself. Its upshot is that only very few can be described as true philosophers, eligible for the post of philosopher king. The nobly born Alcibiades, who was of the right type, deserted philosophy, in spite of Socrates' attempts to save him. Deserted and defenceless, philosophy was claimed by unworthy suitors. Ultimately, "there is left only a handful of men who are worthy of being associated with philosophy." From the point of view we have reached, we would have to expect that the "unworthy suitors" are Antisthenes and Isocrates and their school (and that they are the same people whom Plato demands to have "suppressed by force," as he says in the key-passage of the philosopher king). And, indeed, there is some independent evidence corroborating this expectation. Similarly, we should expect that the "handful of men who are worthy" includes Plato and, perhaps, some of his friends (possibly Dio); and, indeed, a continuation of this passage leaves little doubt that Plato speaks here of himself: "He who belongs to this small band . . . can see the madness of the many, and the general corruption of all public affairs. The philosopher . . . is like a man in a cage of wild beasts. He will not share the injustice of the many, but his power does not suffice for continuing his fight alone, surrounded as he is by a world of savages. He would be killed before he could do any good, to his city or to his friends. . . . Having duly considered all these points, he will hold his peace, and confine his efforts to his own work. . . ." The strong resentment expressed in these sour and most un-Socratic words marks them clearly as Plato's own. For a full appreciation, however, of this personal confession, it must be compared with the following: "It is not in accordance with nature that the skilled navigator should beg the unskilled sailors to accept his command; nor that the wise man should wait at the doors of the rich. . . . But the true and natural procedure is that the sick, whether rich or poor, should hasten to the doctor's door. Likewise should those who need to be ruled besiege the door of him who can rule; and never should a ruler beg them to accept his rule, if he is any good at all." Who can miss the sound of an immense personal pride in this passage? Here am I, says Plato, your natural ruler, the philosopher king who knows how to rule. If you want me, you must come to me, and if you insist, I may become your ruler. But I shall not come begging to you.

Did he believe that they would come? Like many great works of literature, the *Republic* shows traces that its author experienced exhilarating and extravagant hopes of success, alternating with periods of despair. Sometimes, at least, Plato hoped that they would come; that the success of his work, the fame of his wisdom, would bring them along. Then again, he felt that they would only be incited to furious attacks; that all he would bring upon himself was "an uproar of laughter and defamation"—perhaps even death.

Was he ambitious? He was reaching for the stars—for god-likeness. I sometimes wonder whether part of the enthusiasm for Plato is not due to the fact that he gave expression to many secret dreams. Even where he argues against ambition, we cannot but feel that he is inspired by it. The philosopher, he assures us, is not ambitious; although "destined to rule, he is the least eager for it." But the reason given is —that his status is too high. He who has had communion with the divine may descend from his heights to the mortals below, sacrificing himself for the sake of the interest of the state. He is not eager; but as a natural ruler and saviour, he is ready to come. The poor mortals need him. Without him the state must perish, for he alone knows the secret of how to preserve it—the secret of arresting degeneration. . . .

I think we must face the fact that behind the sovereignty of the philosopher king stands the quest for power. The beautiful portrait of the sovereign is a self-portrait. When we have recovered from the shock of this finding, we may look anew at the awe-inspiring portrait; and if we can fortify ourselves with a small dose of Socrates' irony then we may cease to find it so terrifying. We may begin to discern its human, indeed, its only too human features. We may even begin to feel a little sorry for Plato, who had to be satisfied with establishing the first professorship, instead of the first kingship, of philosophy; who could never realize his dream, the kingly Idea which he had formed after his own image. Fortified by our dose of irony, we may even find, in Plato's story, a melancholy resemblance to that innocent and unconscious little satire on Platonism, the story of the

Ugly Dachshund, of Tono, the Great Dane, who forms his kingly Idea of "Great Dog" after his own image (but who happily finds in the end that he is Great Dog himself).

What a monument of human smallness is this idea of the philosopher king. What a contrast between it and the simplicity and humaneness of Socrates, who warned the statesman against the danger of being dazzled by his own power, excellence, and wisdom, and who tried to teach him what matters most—that we are all frail human beings. What a decline from this world of irony and reason and truthfulness down to Plato's kingdom of the sage whose magical powers raise him high above ordinary men; although not quite high enough to forgo the use of lies, or to neglect the sorry trade of every shaman— the selling of spells, of breeding spells, in exchange for power over his fellow-men.

POPPER SELECTION

1.   Popper focuses a great deal of his attention on Plato's proposals for eugenic breeding of the population, and on his recommendation that the rulers lie to the general public. Are these fundamental objections to Plato's theory, in your judgment? Why?

2.   If the rulers are wise and the general public is not, then how can the rulers avoid lying, or at least not telling the public everything they know? Would Popper object to the fact that doctors do not tell patients everything they know? Are there any safeguards in medicine that protect the patient against an unscrupulous doctor? Could the same safeguards be used in politics? How?

3.   Should the political leaders of a state be required to achieve a high level of education as a precondition of rulership? Why? Should the young boys and girls with the greatest natural intelligence and talent be given special education for leadership? How does this differ from Plato's scheme?

4.   Do you think it would corrupt a ruler to have to lie to his or her subjects? If the philosopher-rulers are truly wise, why can't they find ways of explaining their policies to the people that don't involve lying? Why do you suppose Plato thought that lying would be necessary? What does Popper think?

5.   In the modern world, much public policy is made by experts— economists, public health doctors, engineers, nuclear physicists, political scientists. Would Plato consider such experts to be philosopher kings? Why?

(SELECTION 3)

FRIEDRICH ENGELS

The Materialist Conception of History

The theory known today as Marxism was in fact the joint product of two nineteenth-century German thinkers, Karl Marx and Friedrich Engels. Engels is commonly viewed as the junior partner, and he is sometimes treated as no more than Marx's disciple and follower, but in fact, he was a man of considerable intellectual talents, the author of at least one truly classic work (*The Condition of the Working Class in England*), and a major force in the formation and advancement of the working-class movement known as socialism.

Marx and Engels were deeply influenced in their youth by the French utopian socialist literature of the first half of the nineteenth century, but eventually they turned strongly against it. In the books from which this selection is taken, Engels contrasts the doctrine of historical materialism with the teachings of such socialist philosophers as Saint-Simon, Fourier, and Proudhon, calling the teaching of himself and Marx "scientific" and condemning the others as mere "utopian" thinkers.

To Marx and Engels, "scientific" meant at least three things, in regard to each of which they believed their own theory to be superior to that of other, earlier socialists. First, "scientific" meant grounded in a correct analysis of the economic foundations of capitalist society. The bulk of Marx's mature work was devoted to a theoretical dissection of the workings of capitalism, and his central thesis was that capitalism rested on the systematic exploitation of workers by capitalists. Only a total transformation of the basic organization of production could eliminate that exploitation, he thought. Merely redistributing the products of capitalism more evenly among different sectors of society would have no lasting effect.

"Scientific" also meant descriptive instead of prescriptive and moralistic. Marx and Engels put little store by moral exhortation, either of workers or of capitalists. They were convinced that moral education would accomplish nothing so long as the objective structure of capitalism remained unaltered. Hence, they rejected the utopian proposals of the French and English reformers for ideal communities in which private interest would somehow be overcome and altruism be made to take its place. The only hope for the working class, they argued, was thoroughly self-interested collective action aimed at overthrowing capitalism as an economic and political order and replacing it with a different, socialist society.

Finally, to be "scientific" meant to be grounded in a correct theory of history. Unlike both the French socialists

447

and the English economists who preceded them, Marx and Engels believed that capitalism was a necessary but temporary historical stage in the ongoing development of advanced society. Only through a correct theoretical understanding (i.e., a "scientific" understanding) of the real direction and movement of history could a sound program for the future be formulated.

In light of this emphasis on the scientific character of historical materialism, it is only reasonable for Marx and Engels to submit their theory to the test of history and the empirical evidence. Whether the events of the last hundred years have tended to support or to contradict their theory is, needless to say, a subject of continuing debate.

The materialist conception of history starts from the proposition that the production of the means to support human life and, next to production, the exchange of things produced, is the basis of all social structure; that in every society that has appeared in history, the manner in which wealth is distributed and society divided into classes or orders is dependent upon what is produced, how it is produced, and how the products are exchanged. From this point of view the final causes of all social changes and political revolutions are to be sought, not in men's brains, not in man's better insight into eternal truth and justice, but in changes in the modes of production and exchange. They are to be sought, not in the *philosophy,* but in the *economics* of each particular epoch. The growing perception that existing social institutions are unreasonable and unjust, that reason has become unreason, and right wrong, is only proof that in the modes of production and exchange changes have silently taken place, with which the social order, adapted to earlier economic conditions, is no longer in keeping. From this it also follows the means of getting rid of the incongruities that have been brought to light must also be present, in a more or less developed condition, within the changed modes of production themselves. These means are not to be invented by deduction from fundamental principles, but are to be discovered in the stubborn facts of the existing system of production.

What is, then, the position of modern socialism in this connection?

The present structure of society—this is now pretty generally conceded—is the creation of the ruling class of today, of the bourgeoisie. The mode of production peculiar to the bourgeoisie, known, since Marx, as the capitalist mode of production, was incompatible with the feudal system, with the privileges it conferred upon individuals, entire social ranks and local corporations, as well as with the hereditary ties of subordination which constituted the framework of

From *Socialism, Utopian and Scientific* by Friedrich Engels. First published in this edition in 1935.

its social organization. The bourgeoisie broke up the feudal system and built upon its ruins the capitalist order of society, the kingdom of free competition, of personal liberty, of equality before the law of all commodity owners, and of all the rest of the capitalist blessings. Thenceforward the capitalist mode of production could develop in freedom. Since stream, machinery and the making of machines by machinery transformed the older manufacture into modern industry, the productive forces evolved under the guidance of the bourgeoisie developed with a rapidity and in a degree unheard of before. But just as the older manufacture, in its time, and handicraft, becoming more developed under its influence, had come into collision with the feudal trammels of the guilds, so now modern industry, in its more complete development, comes into collision with the bounds within which the capitalistic mode of production holds it confined. The new productive forces have already outgrown the capitalistic mode of using them. And this conflict between productive forces and modes of production is not a conflict engendered in the mind of man, like that between original sin and divine justice. It exists, in fact, objectively, outside us, independently of the will and actions even of the men that have brought it on. Modern socialism is nothing but the reflex, in thought, of this conflict in fact; its ideal reflection in the minds, first, of the class directly suffering under it, the working class.

Now, in what does this conflict consist?

Before capitalistic production, i.e., in the Middle Ages, the system of petty industry obtained generally, based upon the private property of the labourers in their means of production; in the country, the agriculture of the small peasant, freeman or serf; in the towns, the handicrafts organised in guilds. The instruments of labour—land, agricultural implements, the workshop, the tool—were the instruments of labour of single individuals, adapted for the use of one worker, and, therefore, of necessity, small, dwarfish, circumscribed. But for this very reason they belonged, as a rule, to the producer himself. To concentrate these scattered, limited means of production, to enlarge them, to turn them into the powerful levels of production of the present day—this was precisely the historic role of capitalist production and of its upholder, the bourgeoisie. In Part IV of *Capital* Marx has explained in detail, how since the fifteenth century this has been historically worked out through the three phases of simple co-operation, manufacture and modern industry. But the bourgeoisie, as is also shown there, could not transform these puny means of production into mighty productive forces, without transforming them, at the same time, from means of production of the individual into *social* means of production only workable by a collectivity of men. The spinning-wheel, the hand-loom, the blacksmith's hammer were replaced by the spinning machine, the power-loom, the steam-hammer; the individual workshop, by the factory, implying the co-operation of hundreds and thousands of workmen. In like manner, production itself changed from a series of individual into a series of social acts, and the products from individual to social products. The yarn, the cloth, the metal articles that now came out of the factory were the joint product of many workers, through whose hands they had successively to pass before they were ready. No one person could say of them: "I made that; this is *my* product."

But where, in a given society, the fundamental form of production is that spontaneous division of labour which creeps in gradually and not upon any preconceived plan, there the products take on the form of *commodities*, whose mutual exchange, buying and selling, enable the individual producers to satisfy their manifold wants. And this was the case in the Middle Ages. The peasant, e.g., sold to the artisan agricultural products and bought from him the products of handicraft. Into this society of individual producers, of commodity producers, the new mode of production thrust itself. In the midst of the old division of labour, grown up spontaneously and upon *no definite plan,* which had governed the whole of society, now arose division of labour upon *a definite plan,* as organised in the factory; side by side with *individual* production appeared *social* production. The products of both were sold in the same market, and, therefore, at prices at least approximately equal. But organisation upon a definite plan was stronger than spontaneous division of labour. The factories working with the combined social forces of a collectivity of individuals produced their commodities far more cheaply than the individual small producers. Individual production succumbed in one department after another. Socialised production revolutionised all the old methods of production. But its revolutionary character was, at the same time, so little recognised, that it was, on the contrary, introduced as a means of increasing and developing the production of commodities. When it arose, it found ready-made, and made liberal use of, certain machinery for the production and exchange of commodities; merchants' capital, handicraft, wage labour. Socialised production thus introducing itself as a new form of the production of commodities, it was a matter of course that under it the old forms of appropriation remained in full swing, and were applied to its products as well.

In the mediæval stage of evolution of the production of commodities, the question as to the owner of the product of labour could not arise. The individual producer, as a rule, had, from raw material belonging to himself, and generally his own handiwork, produced it with his own tools, by the labour of his own hands or of his family. There was no need for him to appropriate the new product. It belonged wholly to him, as a matter of course. His property in the product was, therefore, based *upon his own labour*. Even where external help was used, this was, as a rule, of little importance, and very generally was compensated by something other than wages. The apprentices and journeymen of the guilds worked less for board and wages than for education, in order that they might become master craftsmen themselves.

Then came the concentration of the means of production and of the producers in large workshops and manufactories, their transformation into actual socialised means of production and socialised producers. But the socialised producers and means of production and their products were still treated, after this change, just as they had been before, i.e., as the means of production and the products of individuals. Hitherto, the owner of the instruments of labour had himself appropriated the product, because as a rule it was his own product and the assistance of others was the exception. Now the owner of the instruments of labour always appropriated to himself the product, although it was no longer *his* product but exclusively the product of the *labour of others*. Thus, the products now produced socially were not appropriated by those who had actually set in motion the means of production and actually produced the commodities, but by the *capitalists*. The means of production, and production itself, had become in essence socialised. But they were subjected to a form of appropriation which presupposes the private production of individuals, under which, therefore, every one owns his own product and brings it to market. The mode of production is subjected to this form of appropriation, although it abolishes the conditions upon which the latter rests.

The contradiction, which gives to the new mode of production its capitalistic character, *contains the germ of the whole of the social antagonisms of today*. The greater the mastery obtained by the new mode of production over all important fields of production and in all manufacturing countries, the more it reduced individual production to an insignificant residuum, *the more clearly was brought out the incompatibility of socialised production with capitalistic appropriation*.

The first capitalists found, as we have said, alongside of other forms of labour, wage labour ready-made for them on the market. But it was exceptional, complementary, necessary, transitory wage labour. The agricultural labourer, though, upon occasion, he hired himself out by the day, had a few acres of his own land on which he could at all events live at a pinch. The guilds were so organised that the journeyman of today became the master of tomorrow. But all this changed, as soon as the means of production became socialised and concentrated in the hands of capitalists. The means of production, as well as the product of the individual producer became more and more worthless; there was nothing left for him but to turn wage worker under the capitalist. Wage labour, aforetime the exception and accessory, now became the rule and basis of all production; a foretime complementary, it now became the sole remaining function of the worker. The wage worker for a time became a wage worker for life. The number of these permanent wage workers was further enormously increased by the breaking up of the feudal system that occurred at the same time, by the disbanding of the retainers of the feudal lords, the eviction of the peasants from their homesteads, etc. The separation was made complete between the means of production concentrated in the hands of the capitalists on the one side, and the producers, possessing nothing but their labour power, on the other. *The contradiction between socialised production and capitalistic appropriation manifested itself as the antagonism of proletariat and bourgeoisie.*

We have seen that the capitalistic mode of production thrust its way into a society of commodity producers, of individual producers, whose social bond was the exchange of their products. But every society, based upon the production of commodities, has this peculiarity: that the producers have lost control over their own social interrelations. Each man produces for himself with such means of production as he may happen to have, and for such exchange as he may require to satisfy his remaining wants. No one knows how much of his particular article is coming on the market, nor how much of it will be wanted. No one knows whether his individual product will meet an actual demand, whether he will be able to make good his cost of production or even to sell his commodity at all. Anarchy reigns in socialised production.

But the production of commodities, like every other form of production, has its peculiar inherent laws inseparable from it; and these laws work, despite anarchy in and through anarchy. They reveal themselves in the only persistent form of social inter-relations, i.e., in exchange, and here they affect the individual producers as compulsory laws of competition. They are, at first, unknown to these producers themselves, and have to be discovered by them gradually and as the result of experience. They work themselves out, therefore, independently of the producers, and in antagonism to them, as inexorable natural laws of their particular form of production. The product governs the producers.

In mediæval society, especially in the earlier centuries, production was essentially directed towards satisfying the wants of the individual. It satisfied, in the main, only the wants of the producer and his family. Where relations of personal dependence existed, as in the country, it also helped to satisfy the wants of the feudal lord. In all this there was, therefore, no exchange; the products, consequently, did not assume the character of commodities. The family of the peasant produced almost everything they wanted: clothes and furniture, as well as means of subsistence. Only when it began to produce more than was sufficient to supply its own wants and the payments in kind to the feudal lord, only then did it also produce commodities. This surplus, thrown into socialised exchange and offered for sale, became commodities.

The artisans of the towns, it is true, had from the first to produce for exchange. But they, also, themselves supplied the greatest part of their own individual wants. They had gardens and plots of land. They turned their cattle out into the communal forest, which, also, yielded them timber and firing. The women spun flax, wool, and so forth. Production for the purpose of exchange, production of commodities was only in its infancy. . . .

But with the extension of the production of commodities, and especially with the introduction of the capitalist mode of production, the laws of commodity production, hitherto latent, came into action more openly and with greater force. The old bonds were loosened, the old exclusive limits broken through, the producers were more and more turned into independent, isolated producers of commodities. It became apparent that the production of society at large was ruled by absence of plan, by accident, by anarchy; and this anarchy grew to greater and greater height. But the chief means by aid of which the capitalist mode of production intensified this anarchy of socialised production was the exact opposite of anarchy. It was the increasing organisation of production, upon a social basis, in every individual productive establishment. By this, the old, peaceful, stable condition of things was ended. Wherever this organisation of production was introduced into a branch of industry, it brooked no other method of production by its side. . . .

Finally, modern industry and the opening of the world market made the struggle universal, and at the same time gave it an unheard-of virulence. Advantages in natural or artificial conditions of production now decide the existence or non-existence of individual capitalists, as well as of whole industries and countries. He that falls is remorsely cast aside. It is the Darwinian struggle of the individual for existence transferred from nature to society with intensified violence. The conditions of existence natural to the animal appear as the final term of human development. The contradiction between socialised production and capitalistic appropriation now presents itself as *an antagonism between the organisation of production in the individual workshop and the anarchy of production in society generally.* . . .

. . . It is the compelling force of anarchy in the production of society at large that more and more completely turns the great majority of men into proletarians; and it is the masses of the proletariat again who will finally put an end to anarchy in production. It is the compelling force of anarchy in social production that turns the limitless perfectibility of machinery under modern industry into a compulsory law by which every individual industrial capitalist must perfect his machinery more and more, under penalty of ruin. . . .

The fact that the socialised organisation of production within the factory has developed so far that it has become incompatible with the anarchy of production in society, which exists side by side with and dominates it, is brought home to the capitalists themselves by the violent concentration of capital that occurs during crises, through the ruin of many large, and a still greater number of small, capitalists. The whole mechanism of the capitalist mode of production breaks down under the pressure of the productive forces, its own creations. It is no longer able to turn all this mass of means of production into capital. They lie fallow, and for that very reason the industrial reserve army must also lie fallow. Means of production, means of subsistence, available labourers, all the elements of production and of general wealth, are present in abundance. But "abundance becomes the source of distress and want" (Fourier), because it is the very thing that prevents the transformation of the means of production and subsistence into capital. For in capitalistic society the means of production can only function when they have undergone a preliminary transformation into capital, into the means of exploiting human labour power. The necessity of this transformation into capital of the means of production and subsistence stands like a ghost between these and the workers. It alone prevents the coming together of the material and personal levers of production; it alone forbids the means of production to function, the workers to work and live. On the one hand, therefore, the capitalistic mode of production stands convicted to its own incapacity to further direct these productive forces. On the other, these productive forces themselves, with increasing energy, press forward to the removal of the existing contradiction, to the abolition of their quality as capital, to the *practical recognition of their character as social productive forces.*

This rebellion of the productive forces, as they grow more and more powerful, against their quality as capital, this stronger and stronger command that their social character shall be recognised, forces the capitalist class itself to treat them more and more as social productive forces, so far as this is possible under capitalist conditions. The period of industrial high pressure, with its unbounded inflation of credit, not less than the crash itself, by the collapse of great capitalist establishments, tends to bring about that form of the socialisation of great masses of means of production, which we meet with in the different kinds of joint-stock companies. Many of these means of production and of distribution are, from the outset, so colossal, that, like the railroads, they exclude all other forms of capitalistic exploitation. At a further stage of evolution this form also becomes insufficient. The producers on a large scale in a particular branch of industry in a particular country unite in a "trust" a union for the purpose of regulating production. They determine the total amount to be produced, parcel it out among themselves, and thus enforce the selling price fixed beforehand. But trusts of this kind, as soon as business becomes bad, are generally liable to break up, and, on this very account, compel a yet greater concentration of association. The whole of the particular industry is turned into one gigantic joint-stock company; internal competition gives place to the internal monopoly of this company. . . .

If the crises demonstrate the incapacity of the bourgeoisie for managing any longer modern productive forces, the transformation of the great establishments for production and distribution into joint-stock companies, trusts and state property, show how unnecessary the bourgeoisie are for that purpose. All the social functions of the capitalist are now performed by salaried employees. The capitalist has no further social function than that of pocketing dividends, tearing off coupons, and gambling on the Stock Exchange, where the different capitalists despoil one another of their capital. At first the capitalistic mode of production forces out the workers. Now it forces out the capitalists, and reduces them, just as it reduced the workers, to the ranks of the surplus population, although not immediately into those of the industrial reserve army.

But the transformation, either into joint-stock companies and trusts, or into state ownership, does not do away with the capitalistic nature of the productive forces. In the joint-stock companies and trusts this is obvious. And the modern state, again, is only the organisation that bourgeois society takes on in order to support the external conditions of the capitalist mode of production against the encroachments, as well of the workers as of individual capitalists. The modern state, no matter what its form, is essentially a capitalist machine, the state of the capitalists, the ideal personification of the total national capital. The more it proceeds to the taking over of productive forces, the more does it actually become the national capitalist, the more citizens does it exploit. The workers remain wage workers—proletarians. The capitalist relation is not done away with. It is rather brought to a head. But, brought to a head, it topples over. State ownership of the productive forces is not the solution of the conflict, but concealed within it are the technical conditions that form the elements of that solution.

This solution can only consist in the practical recognition of the social nature of the modern forces of production, and therefore in the harmonising of the modes of production, appropriation and exchange with the socialized character of the means of production. And this can only come about by society openly and directly taking possession of the productive forces which have outgrown all control except that of society as a whole. The social character of the means of production and of the products today reacts against the producers, periodically disrupts all production and exchange, acts only like a law of nature working blindly, forcibly, destructively. But with the taking over by society of the productive forces, the social character of the means of production and of the products will be utilised by the producers with a perfect understanding of its nature, and instead of being a source of disturbance and periodical collapse, will become the most powerful lever of production itself.

Active social forces work exactly like natural forces; blindly, forcibly, destructively, so long as we do not understand and reckon with them. But when once we understand them, when once we grasp their action, their direction, their effects, it depends only upon ourselves to subject them more and more to our own will, and by means of them to reach our own ends. And this holds quite especially of the mighty productive forces of today. As long as we obstinately refuse to understand the nature and the character of these social means of action—and this understanding goes against the grain of the capitalist mode of production and its defenders—so long these forces are at work in spite of us, in opposition to us, so long they master us, as we have shown above in detail.

But when once their nature is understood, they can, in the hands of the producers working together, be transformed from master demons into willing servants. The difference is as that between the destructive force of electricity in the lightning of the storm, and electricity under command in the telegraph and the voltaic arc; the difference between a conflagration, and fire working in the service of man. With this recognition at last of the real nature of the productive forces of today, the social anarchy of production gives place to a social regulation of production upon a definite plan, according to the needs of the community and of each individual. Then the capitalist mode of appropriation, in which the product enslaves first the producer and then the appropriator, is replaced by the mode of appropriation of the products that is based upon the nature of the modern means of production; upon the one hand, direct social appropriation, as means to the maintenance and extension of production—on the other, direct individual appropriation, as means of subsistence and of enjoyment.

Whilst the capitalist mode of production more and more completely transforms the great majority of the population into proletarians, it creates the power which, under penalty of its own destruction, is forced to accomplish this revolution. Whilst it forces on more and more the transformation of the vast means of production, already socialised, into state property, it shows itself the way to accomplishing this revolution. *The proletariat seizes political power and turns the means of production into state property.*

But, in doing this, it abolishes itself as proletariat, abolishes all class distinctions and class antagonisms, abolishes also the state as state. Society thus far, based upon class antagonisms, had need of the state. That is, of an organisation of the particular class which was *pro tempore* the exploiting class, an organisation for the purpose of preventing any interference from without with the existing conditions of production, and therefore, especially, for the purpose of forcibly keeping the exploited classes in the condition of oppression corresponding with the given mode of production (slavery, serfdom, wage labour). The state was the official representative of society as a whole; the gathering of it together into a visible embodiment. But it was this only in so far as it was the state of that class which itself represented, for the time being, society as a whole; in ancient times, the state of slave-owning citizens; in the Middle Ages, the feudal lords; in our own time, the bourgeoisie. When at last it becomes the real representative of the whole of society, it renders itself unnecessary. As soon as there is no longer any social class to be held in subjction; as soon as class rule and the individual struggle for existence based upon our present anarchy in production, with the collisions and excesses arising from these, are removed, nothing more remains to be repressed, and a special repressive force, a state, is no longer necessary. The first act by virtue of which the state really constitutes itself the representative of the whole of society—the taking possession of the means of production in the name of society—this is, at the same time, its last independent act as a state. State interference in social relations becomes, in one domain after another, superfluous, and then dies out of itself; the government of persons is replaced by the administration of things; and by the conduct of processes of production. The state is not "abolished." *It dies out. . . .*

Since the historical appearance of the capitalist mode of production, the appropriation by society of all the means of production has often been dreamed of, more or less vaguely, by individuals, as well as by sects, as the ideal of the future. But it could become possible, could become a historical necessity, only when the actual conditions for its realisation were there. Like every other social advance, it becomes practicable, not by men understanding that the existence of classes is in contradiction to justice, equality, etc., not by the mere willingness to abolish these classes, but by virtue of certain new economic conditions. The separation of society into an exploiting and an exploited class, a ruling and an oppressed class, was the necessary consequence of the deficient and restricted development of production in former times. So long as the total social labour only yields a produce which but slightly exceeds that barely necessary for the existence of all; so long, therefore, as labour engages all or almost all the time of the great majority of the members of society—so long, of necessity, this society is divided into classes. Side by side with the great majority, exclusively bond slaves to labour, arises a class freed from directly productive labour, which looks after the general affairs of society, the direction of labour, state business, law, science, art, etc. It is, therefore, the law of division of labour that lies at the basis of the division into classes. But this does not prevent this division into classes from being carried out by means of violence and robbery, trickery and fraud. It does not prevent the ruling class, once having the upper hand, from consolidating its power at the expense of the working class, from turning their social leadership into an intensified exploitation of the masses.

But if, upon this showing, division into classes has a certain historical justification, it has this only for a given period, only under given social conditions. It was based upon the insufficiency of production. It will be swept away by the complete development of modern productive forces. And, in fact, the abolition of classes in society presupposes a degree of historical evolution, at which the existence, not simply of this or that particular ruling class, but of any ruling class at all, and, therefore, the existence of class distinction itself has become an obsolete anachronism. It presupposes, therefore, the development of production carried out to a degree at which appropriation of the means of production and of the products, and, with this, of political domination, of the monopoly of culture, and of intellectual leadership by a particular class of society, has become not only superfluous, but economically, politically, intellectually a hindrance to development.

This point is now reached. Their political and intellectual bankruptcy is scarcely any longer a secret to the bourgeoisie themselves. Their economic bankruptcy recurs regularly every ten years.

In every crisis, society is suffocated beneath the weight of its own productive forces and products, which it cannot use, and stands helpless, face to face with the absurd contradiction that the producers have nothing to consume, because consumers are wanting. The expansive force of the means of production bursts the bonds that the capitalist mode of production had imposed upon them. Their deliverance from these bonds is the one precondition for an unbroken, constantly accelerated development of the productive forces, and therewith for a practically unlimited increase of production itself. Nor is this all. The socialised appropriation of the means of production does away not only with the present artificial restrictions upon production, but also with the positive waste and devastation of production forces and products that are at the present time the inevitable concomitants of production, and that reach their height in the crises. Further, it sets free for the community at large a mass of means of production and of products, by doing away with the senseless extravagance of the ruling classes of today, and their political representatives. The possibility of securing for every member of society, by means of socialised production, an existence not only fully sufficient materially, and becoming day by day more full, but an existence guaranteeing to all the free development and exercise of their physical and mental faculties —this possibility is now for the first time here, but *it is here*.

With the seizing of the means of production by society, production of commodities is done away with, and, simultaneously, the mastery of the product over the producer. Anarchy in social production is replaced by systematic definite organisation. The struggle for individual existence disappears. Then for the first time, man, in a certain sense, is finally marked off from the rest of the animal kingdom, and emerges from mere animal conditions of existence into really human ones. The whole sphere of the conditions of life which environ man, and which have hitherto ruled man, now comes under the dominion and control of man, who for the first time becomes the real, conscious lord of nature, because he has now become master of his own social organisation. The laws of his own social action, hitherto standing face to face with man as laws of nature foreign to and dominating him, will then be used with full understanding, and so mastered by him. Man's own social organisation, hitherto confronting him as a necessity imposed by nature and history, now becomes the result of his own free action. The extraneous objective forces that have hitherto governed history pass under the control of man himself. Only from that time will man himself, more and more consciously, make his own history—only from that time will the social causes set in movement by him have, in the main and in a constantly growing measure, the results intended by him. It is the ascent of man from the kingdom of necessity to the kingdom of freedom.

ENGELS SELECTION

1. What are the principal evils of bourgeois capitalism, according to Engels? Engels was writing in the nineteenth century. How, if at all, would he have changed his criticisms of capitalist society if he had been able to see modern capitalism?

2. Are we forced to accept whatever economic and social situation we find ourselves in, according to Engels, or can we change it? Can I, as an individual, alter my historical circumstances in any significant manner, or must many men and women work together to achieve a significant change? What are the significant groups in a society, according to Engels?

3. How would the seizure of the means of production by the working class alter society, according to Engels? If the capitalists legally own their property, then what right have the workers to take it away from them? What would happen to the state under socialism? Is there any historical evidence to suggest that Engels is right? That he is wrong?

4. What is to stop capitalists from reading this and other writings and then protecting themselves from the downfall that Engels predicts for them? In what ways might capitalists compromise with the workers, in order to avoid a class war or a revolution? Can such compromises work? Why?

5. In a different essay, Marx says that in a communist society each person will contribute whatever he or she can, and will receive whatever he or she needs. Is this a good rule for distributing society's goods and services? Is it workable? How does it differ from our present social and economic system?

(SELECTION 4)

FRIEDRICH HAYEK

The Conflict Between Socialism and Freedom

The central political fact of the twentieth century has been the continuing struggle between the Left and the Right, between socialism and fascism, in Europe, in Asia, and (under other names) in Africa and America as well. Or at least, that is what many political analysts *claim* to be the central political fact of the twentieth century. In the startling and provocative book from which this selection is taken, the Nobel Prize-winning economist Friedrich Hayek argues that in fact socialism and fascism are brothers under the skin. Both, he insists, preach collective, state control at the expense of individual liberty. It is no mere linguistic anomaly that Hitler's fascist movement called itself "National Socialism," or that the Stalinist repression in Russia cloaked itself in the doctrines and myths of Marxist socialism.

The key to Hayek's analysis is the problem of how we achieve large-scale social coordination of the economic behavior of millions of men and women in a modern industrial economy. Our economy has reached so advanced a stage of development that the parts are functionally interdependent, with agriculture providing food and raw materials to industry, industry in turn making the necessary tools of agriculture, and the so-called "service sector" producing es-

sential services to both. In such circumstances, there are only two ways in which coordination can be achieved so that the entire system does not simply grind to a halt in a tangle of shortages, bottlenecks, and stoppages. Either there must be top-down coordination through the exercise of highly concentrated, centralized political power; or else the impersonal and unguided marketplace must achieve a balance of supply and demand through the interaction of millions of private individuals each pursuing his or her private interest.

Socialism proposes central control and decision, in the interest of the public good, on the grounds that the marketplace is both inefficient and covertly biased in favor of the rich and the powerful. But Hayek replies that once decision-making power is concentrated in the hands of a few, it will inevitably follow that the desires of many are frustrated, *even if the few are conscientiously and honestly devoted to the public good.* The problem lies not in the motivations of those who rule, but in the necessarily dictatorial nature of centralized, top-down decision-making. Hence socialism, which rests on a system of centrally planned economy, will —according to Hayek—come to exhibit exactly the same loss of individual freedom as fascism, which also operates a centrally planned economy and society.

In reply to Hayek, there is one rather pessimistic question that we may pose: in this day of giant corporations, the annual sales of which may actually be larger than the total gross national products of small or medium-sized countries, is there really a possibility of a genuinely free and unplanned market economy under any political regime? Or aren't we forced, whether we like it or not, to choose either private planning for private interests or public planning for the public good?

The common features of all collectivist systems may be described, in a phrase ever dear to socialists of all schools, as the deliberate organization of the labors of society for a definite social goal. That our present society lacks such "conscious" direction toward a single aim, that its activities are guided by the whims and fancies of irresponsible individuals, has always been one of the main complaints of its socialist critics.

In many ways this puts the basic issue very clearly. And it directs us at once to the point where the conflict arises between individual freedom and collectivism. The various kinds of collectivism, communism, fascism, etc., differ among themselves in the nature of the goal toward which they want to direct the efforts of society. But they all differ from liberalism and individualism in wanting to organize the whole of society and all its resources for this unitary end and in refusing to recognize autonomous spheres in which the ends of the individuals are supreme. In short, they are totalitarian in the true sense of this new word which we have adopted to describe the unexpected but nevertheless inseparable manifestations of what in theory we call collectivism.

The "social goal," or "common purpose," for which society is to be organized is usually vaguely described as the "common good," the "general welfare," or the "general interest." It does not need much reflection to see that these terms have no sufficiently definite meaning to determine a particular course of action. The welfare and the happiness of millions cannot be measured on a single scale of less and more. The welfare of a people, like the happiness of a man, depends on a great many things that can be provided in an infinite variety of combinations. It cannot be adequately expressed as a single end, but only as a hierarchy of ends, a comprehensive scale of values in which every need of every person is given its place. To direct all our activities according to a single plan presupposes that every one of our needs is given its rank in an order of values which

From *The Road to Serfdom* by Friedrich Hayek. First published in 1944. (Reprinted by permission of the University of Chicago Press and Routledge & Kegan Paul Ltd., London.)

must be complete enough to make it possible to decide among all the different courses which the planner has to choose. It presupposes, in short, the existence of a complete ethical code in which all the different human values are allotted their due place.

The conception of a complete ethical code is unfamiliar, and it requires some effort of imagination to see what it involves. We are not in the habit of thinking of moral codes as more or less complete. The fact that we are constantly choosing between different values without a social code prescribing how we ought to choose does not surprise us and does not suggest to us that our moral code is incomplete. In our society there is neither occasion nor reason why people should develop common views about what should be done in such situations. But where all the means to be used are the property of society and are to be used in the name of society according to a unitary plan, a "social" view about what ought to be done must guide all decisions. In such a world we should soon find that our moral code is full of gaps.

We are not concerned here with the question whether it would be desirable to have such a complete ethical code. It may merely be pointed out that up to the present the growth of civilization has been accomplished by a steady diminution of the sphere in which individual actions are bound by fixed rules. The rules of which our common moral code consists have progressively become fewer and more general in character. From the primitive man, who was bound by an elaborate ritual in almost every one of his daily activities, who was limited by innumerable taboos, and who could scarcely conceive of doing things in a way different from his fellows, morals have more and more tended to become merely limits circumscribing the sphere within which the individual could behave as he liked. The adoption of a common ethical code comprehensive enough to determine a unitary economic plan would mean a complete reversal of this tendency.

The essential point for us is that no such complete ethical code exists. The attempt to direct all economic activity according to a single plan would raise innumerable questions to which the answer could be provided only by a moral rule, but to which existing morals have no answer and where there exists no agreed view on what ought to be done. People will have either no definite views or conflicting views on such questions, because in the free society in which we have lived there has been no occasion to think about them and still less to form common opinions about them.

Not only do we not possess such as all-inclusive scale of values: it would be impossible for any mind to comprehend the infinite variety of different needs of different people which compete for the available resources and to attach a definite weight to each. For our problem it is of minor importance whether the ends for which any person cares comprehend only his own individual needs, or whether they include the needs of his closer or even those of his more distant fellows—that is, whether he is egoistic or altruistic in the ordinary senses of these words. The point which is so important is the basic fact that it is impossible for any man to survey more than a limited field, to be aware of the urgency of more than a limited number of needs. Whether his interests center round his own physical needs, or whether he takes a warm interest in the welfare of every human being he knows, the ends about which he can be concerned will always be only an infinitesimal fraction of the needs of all men.

This is the fundamental fact on which the whole philosophy of individualism is based. It does not assume, as is often asserted, that man is egoistic or selfish or ought to be. It merely starts from the indisputable fact that the limits of our powers of imagination make it impossible to include in our scale of values more than a sector of the needs of the whole society, and that, since, strictly speaking, scales of value can exist only in individual minds, nothing but partial scales of values exist—scales which are inevitably different and often inconsistent with each other. From this the individualist concludes that the individuals should be allowed, within defined limits, to follow their own values and preferences rather than somebody else's that within these spheres the individual's system of ends should be supreme and not subject to any dictation by others. It is this recognition of the individual as the ultimate judge of his ends, the belief that as far as possible his own views ought to govern his actions, that forms the essence of the individualist position.

This view does not, of course, exclude the recognition of social ends, or rather of a coincidence of individual ends which makes it advisable for men to combine for their pursuit. But it limits such common action to the instances where individual views coincide; what are called "social ends" are for it merely identical ends of many individuals—or ends to the achievement of which individuals are willing to contribute in return for the assistance they receive in the satisfaction of their own desires. Common action is thus limited to the fields where people agree on common ends. Very frequently these common ends will not be ultimate ends to the individuals but means which different persons can use for different purposes. In fact, people are most likely to agree on common action where the common end is not an ultimate end to them but a means capable of serving a great variety of purposes.

When individuals combine in a joint effort to realize ends they have in common, the organizations, like the state, that they form for this purpose are given their own system of ends and their own means. But any organization thus formed remains one "person" among others, in the case of the state much more powerful than any of the others, it is true, yet still with its separate and limited sphere in which alone its ends are supreme. The limits of this sphere are determined by the extent to which the individuals agree on particular ends; and the probability that they will agree on a particular course of action necessarily decreases as the scope of such action extends. There are certain functions of the state on the exercise of which there will be practical unanimity among its citizens; there will be others on which there will be agreements of a substantial majority; and so on, until we come to fields where, although each individual might wish the state to act in some way, there will be almost as many views about what the government should do as there are different people.

We can rely on voluntary agreement to guide the action of the state only so long as it is confined to spheres where agreement exists. But not only when the state undertakes direct control in fields where there is no such agreement is it bound to suppress individual freedom. We can unfortunately not indefinitely extend the sphere of common action and still leave the individual free in his own sphere. Once the communal sector, in which the state controls all the means, exceeds a certain proportion of the whole, the effects of its actions dominate the whole system. Although the state controls directly the use of only a large part of the available resources, the effects of its decisions on the remaining part of the economic system become so great that indirectly it controls almost everything. Where, as was, for example, true in Germany as early as 1928, the central and local authorities directly control the use of more than half the national income (according to an official German estimate then, 53 per cent), they control indirectly almost the whole economic life of the nation. There is, then, scarcely an individual end which is not dependent for its achievement on the action of the state, and the "social scale of values" which guides the state's action must embrace practically all individual ends.

It is not difficult to see what must be the consequences when democracy embarks upon a course of planning which in its execution requires more agreement than in fact exists. The people may have agreed on adopting a system of directed economy because they have been convinced it will produce great prosperity. In the discussions leading to the decision, the goal of planning will have been described by some such term as "common welfare," which only conceals the absence of real agreement on the ends of planning. Agreement will in fact exist only on the mechanism to be used. But it is a mechanism which can be used only for a common end; and the question of the precise goal toward which all activity is to be directed will arise as soon as the executive power has to translate the demand for a single plan into a particular plan. Then it will appear that the agreement on the desirability of planning is not supported by agreement on the ends the plan is to serve. The effect of the people's agreeing that there must be central planning, without agreeing on the ends, will be rather as if a group of people were to commit themselves to take a journey together without agreeing where they want to go: with the result that they may all have to make a journey which most of them do not want at all. That planning creates a situation in which it is necessary for us to agree on a much larger number of topics than we have been used to, and that in a planned system we cannot confine collective action to the tasks on which we can agree but are forced to produce agreement on everything in order that any action can be taken at all, is one of the features which contributes more than most to determining the character of a planned system.

It may be the unanimously expressed will of the people that its parliament should prepare a comprehensive economic plan, yet neither the people nor its representatives need therefore be able to agree on any particular plan. The inability of democratic assemblies to carry out what seems to be a clear mandate of the people will inevitably cause dissatisfaction with democratic institutions. Parliaments come to be regarded as ineffective "talking shops," unable or incompetent to carry out the tasks for which they have been chosen. The conviction grows that if efficient planning is to be done, the direction must be "taken out of politics" and placed in the hands of experts—permanent officials or independent autonomous bodies. . . .

It is important clearly to see the causes of this admitted ineffectiveness of parliaments when it comes to a detailed administration of the economic affairs of a nation. The fault is neither with the individual representatives nor with parliamentary institutions as such but with the contradictions inherent in the task with which they are charged. They are not asked to act where they can agree, but to produce agreement on everything—the whole direction of the resources of the nation. For such a task the system of majority decision is, however, not suited. Majorities will be found where it is a choice between limited alternatives; but it is a superstition to believe that there must be a majority view on everything. There is no reason why there should be a majority in favor of any one of the different possible courses of positive action if their number is legion. Every member of the legislative assembly might prefer some particular plan for the direction of economic activity to no plan, yet no one plan may appear preferable to a majority to no plan at all. . .

It is the price of democracy that the possibilities of conscious control are restricted to the fields where true agreements exists and that in some fields things must be left to chance. But in a society which for its functioning depends on central planning this control cannot be made dependent on a majority's being able to agree; it will often be necessary that the will of a small minority be imposed upon the people, because this minority will be the largest group able to agree among themselves on the question at issue. Democratic government has worked successfully where, and so long as, the functions of government were, by a widely accepted creed, restricted to fields where agreement among a majority could be achieved by free discussion; and it is the great merit of the liberal creed that it reduce the range of subjects on which agreement was necessary to one on which it was likely to exist in a society of free men. It is now often said that democracy will not tolerate "capitalism." If "capitalism" means here a competitive system based on free disposal over private property, it is far more important to realize that only within this system is democracy possible. When it becomes dominated by a collectivist creed, democracy will inevitably destroy itself.

We have no intention, however, of making a fetish of democracy. It may well be true that out generation talks and thinks too much of democracy and too little of the values which it serves. It cannot be said of democracy, as Lord Acton truly said of liberty, that it "is not a means to a higher political end. It is itself the highest political end. It is not for the sake of a good public administration that it is required, but for the security in the pursuit of the highest objects of civil society, and of private life." Democracy is essentially a means, a utilitarian device for safeguarding internal peace and individual freedom. As such it is by no means infallible or certain. Nor must we forget that there has often been much more cultural and spiritual freedom under an autocratic rule than under some democracies—and it is at least conceivable that under the government of a very homogeneous and doctrinaire majority democratic government might be as oppressive as the worst dictatorship. Our point, however, is not that dictatorship must inevitably extirpate freedom but rather that planning leads to dictatorship because dictatorship is the most effective instrument of coercion and the enforcement of ideals and, as such, essential if central planning on a large scale is to be possible. The clash between planning and democracy arises simply from the fact that the latter is an obstacle to the suppression of freedom which the direction of economic activity requires. But in so far as democracy ceases to be a guaranty of individual freedom, it may well persist in some form under a totalitarian regime. A true "dictatorship of the proletariat," even if democratic in form, if it undertook centrally to direct the economic system, would probably destroy personal freedom as completely as any autocracy has ever done.

The fashionable concentration on democracy as the main value threatened is not without danger. It is largely responsible for the misleading and unfounded belief that, so long as the ultimate source of power is the will of the majority, the power cannot be arbitrary. The false assurance which many people derive from this belief is an important cause of the general unawareness of the dangers which we face. There is no justification for the belief that, so long as power is conferred by democratic procedure, it cannot be arbitrary; the contrast suggested by this statement is altogether false: it is not the source but the limitation of power which prevents it from being arbitary. Democratic control *may* prevent power from becoming arbitrary, but it does not do so by its mere existence. If democracy resolves on a task which necessarily involves the use of power which cannot be guided by fixed rules, it must become arbitrary power.

Nothing distinguishes more clearly conditions in a free country from those in a country under arbitrary government than the observance in the former of the great principles known as the Rule of Law. Stripped of all technicalities, this means that government in all its actions is bound by rules fixed and announced beforehand—rules which make is possible to foresee with fair certainty how the authority will use its coercive powers in given circumstances and to plan one's individual affairs on the basis of this knowledge. Though this ideal can never be perfectly achieved, since legislators as well as those to whom the administration of the law is intrusted are fallible men, the essential point, that the discretion left to the executive organs wielding coercive power should be reduced as much as possible, is clear enough. While every law restricts individual freedom to some extent by altering the means which people may use in the pursuit of their aims, under the Rule of Law the government is prevented from stultifying individual efforts by *ad hoc* action. Within the known rules of the game the individual is free to pursue his personal ends and desires, certain that the powers of government will not be used deliberately to frustrate his efforts.

The distinction we have drawn before between the creation of a permanent framework of laws within which the productive activity is guided by individual decisions and the direction of economic activity by a central authority is thus really a particular case of the more general distinction between the Rule of Law and arbitrary government. Under the first the government confines itself to fixing rules determining the conditions under which the available resources may be used, leaving to the individuals the decision for what ends they are to be used. Under the second the government directs the use of the means of production to particular ends. The first type of rules can be made in advance, in the shape of *formal rules* which do not aim at the wants and needs of particular people. They are intended to be merely instrumental in the pursuit of people's various individual ends. And they are, or ought to be, intended for such long periods that it is impossible to know whether they will assist particular people more than others. They could almost be described as a kind of instrument of production, helping people to predict the behavior of those with whom they must collaborate, rather than as efforts toward the satisfaction of particular needs.

Economic planning of the collectivist kind necessarily involves the very opposite of this. The planning authority cannot confine itself to providing opportunities for unknown people to make whatever use of them they like. It cannot tie itself down in advance to general and formal rules which prevent arbitrariness. It must provide for the actual needs of people as they arise and then choose deliberately between them. It must constantly decide questions which cannot be answered by formal principals only, and, in making these decisions, it must set up distinctions of merit between the needs of different people. When the government has to decide how many pigs are to be raised or how many buses are to be run, which coal mines are to operate, or at what prices shoes are to be sold, these decisions cannot be deduced from formal principles or settled for long periods in advance. They depend inevitably on the circumstances of the moment, and, in making such decisions, it will always be necessary to balance one against the other the interests of various persons and groups. In the end somebody's views will have to decide whose interests are more important; and these views must become part of the law of the land, a new distinction of rank which the coercive apparatus of government imposes upon the people. . . .

The Rule of Law was consciously evolved only during the liberal age and is one of its greatest achievements, not only as a safeguard but as the legal embodiment of freedom. As Immanuel Kant put it (and Voltaire expressed it before him in very much the same terms), "Man is free if he needs to obey no person but solely the laws." As a vague ideal it has, however, existed at least since Roman times, and during the last few centuries it has never been so seriously threatened as it is today. The idea that there is no limit to the powers of the legislator is in part a result of popular sovereignty and democratic government. It has been strengthened by the belief that, so long as all actions of the state are duly authorized by legislation, the Rule of Law will be preserved. But this is completely to misconceive the meaning of the Rule of Law. This rule has little to do with the question whether all actions of government are legal in the juridical sense. They may well be and yet not conform to the Rule of Law: The fact that someone has full legal authority to act in the way he does gives no answer to the question whether the law gives him power to act arbitrarily or whether the law prescribes unequivocally how he has to act . . .

To say that in a planned society the Rule of Law cannot hold is, therefore, not to say that the actions of the government will not be legal or that such a society will necessarily be lawless. It means only that the use of the government's coercive powers will no longer be limited and determined by pre-established rules. The law can, and to make a central direction of economic activity possible must, legalize what to all intents and purposes remains arbitrary action. If the law says that such a board or authority may do what it pleases, anything that board or authority does is legal—but its actions are certainly not subject to the Rule of Law. By giving the government unlimited powers, the most arbitrary rule can be made legal; and in this way a democracy may set up the most complete despotism imaginable.

HAYEK SELECTION

1. As clearly as you can, state what you think Hayek means by "freedom." In what ways does a socialist state restrict freedom? In what ways does a capitalist state restrict freedom? Why is more freedom better than less freedom?

2. Do men and women have a right to trade freedom for economic security? Does a minority have the right to make that choice for the majority? Does the majority have the right to make that choice for the minority? If we distinguish between freedom *from* restrictions, and freedom *to* fulfill our needs, which sort of freedom is Hayek more concerned with? Why?

3. According to Hayek, planning leads to dictatorship. Is there any way to make planning compatible with democracy in small groups? In large nations? Do we have economic planning of any sort in our country now? Does it get in the way of democracy, make democracy stronger, or have no effect on democracy? How?

4. What does Hayek mean by "the Rule of Law"? How does planning interfere with the Rule of Law? In what way does the Rule of Law support and enlarge freedom? Are there any ways in which the Rule of Law interferes with freedom?

5. Are there any social goods or social goals that ought to take precedence over freedom, in your judgment? What are they? Why are they more important than freedom? If you do *not* think anything is more important than freedom, then what price must you pay for that principle, according to Hayek?

(SELECTION 5)

B. F. SKINNER

Utopia Through Psychological Conditioning

It is unusual, although not unheard-of, for philosophy to be expounded in a literary form. (The ancient Epicurean metaphysician, Lucretius, after all, set forth his philosophy in the form of a lengthy poem, "On the Nature of Things.") But it is really rather startling to find a distinguished experimental behavioral psychologist choosing fiction as the medium in which to expound a utopian theory of man and society. This selection is taken from a novel entitled *Walden Two,* by B. F. Skinner. The title, of course, is in turn derived from one of the most famous works of nineteenth-century transcendentalist literature, *Walden,* by Henry David Thoreau.

The novel concerns an experimental community, run entirely in conformity with the principles of Skinner's "operant conditioning," in which ostensibly all the major social ills have been eliminated and men, women, and children are happy, fulfilled, harmonious, and at peace with one another. The major characters in this selection are the leader of the community, Frazier, who is pretty transparently Skinner himself; an extremely skeptical Professor of Philosophy, Castle, who quizzes Frazier about the community and criticizes its theoretical presuppositions; and the narrator (who simply refers to him(her?) rator (who simply refers to him(her?) self as "I"), who observes the debate and mediates.

In the Introduction to this chapter we raised the question: Could it be done? Are the techniques of psychology really powerful enough to bring about the personality transformations described in this selection? For the sake of argument, let us put that issue to one side and focus instead on the debate between Frazier and Castle, which really concerns the moral issue, *should* it be done.

One way to sharpen the issue is to ask an even more bizarre question based on even more hypothetically implausible technological assumptions. Suppose it were possible to plug people into a machine that would produce in their brains exactly the neural impulses that are now associated with happy, fulfilling, self-realizing experiences. These people would actually be lying flat on their backs in hospital beds, but they would think they were having all the wonderful experiences that the electrodes were feeding into their brains. Now, assuming no painful side effects, and assuming as well that they would continue to be taken care of for as long as they were on the machines, would this be a good way for them to spend their lives or not?

If your answer is no—if you reject the physical manipulation of a person's nervous system for the purpose of producing the subjective impression of meaningful, creative, happy, fulfilling experience—then what conclusions might we draw about psychological manipulation to the same end? Is it similar, or are there significant differences that would permit us to reject the first and yet accept the second? How do you think Skinner himself would respond to the idea of such an "experience machine"?

"The significant history of our times," Frazier began, "is the story of the growing weakness of the family. The decline of the home as a medium for prepetuating a culture, the struggle for equality for women including their right to select professions other than housewife or nursemaid, the extraordinary consequences of birth control and the practical separation of sex and parenthood, the social recognition of divorce, the critical issue of blood relationship or race— all these are parts of the same field. And you can hardly call it quiescent.

"A community must solve the problem of the family by revising certain established practices. That's absolutely inevitable. The family is an ancient form of community and the customs and habits which have been set up to perpetuate it are out of place in a society which isn't based on blood ties. Walden Two replaces the family not only as an economic unit, but to some extent as a social and psychological unit as well. What survives is an experimental question."

"What answer have you reached?" said Castle.

"No definite answer yet. But I can describe some of the family practices which were part of the plan of Walden Two and tell you the consequences to date. A few experimental questions have been answered to our satisfaction."

"Such as?"

"Oh, the advisability of separate rooms for husband and wife, for example. We don't insist on it, but in the long run there's a more satisfactory relation when a single room isn't shared. Many of our visitors suppose that a community means a sacrifice of privacy. On the contrary, we've carefully provided for much more personal privacy than is likely to be found in the world at large. You may be alone here whenever you wish. A man's room is his castle. And a woman's, too."

"But how could you *prove* that separate rooms were advisable?" said Castle.

"Very simply. We asked all husbands and wives who were willing to do so to accept separate or common rooms on the basis of a drawing of lots. That was in the early days. We did the same thing with new members. Our psychologists kept in close touch with all personal problems and at the end of eight years the troubles and satisfactions of our members were analyzed with respect to the factor of separate or common rooms. It's the sort of experiment that would be impossible, or next to impossible, anywhere except in Walden Two. The result was clear-cut. Living in a separate room not only made the individual happier and better adjusted, it tended to strengthen the love and affection of husband and wife. Most of our married couples have now changed to separate rooms. It's difficult to explain the advantages to the newly married, and I suspect it will become a sort of tradition to room together until the period of child-bearing is over. But the later advantages in point of health, convenience, and personal freedom are too great to be overlooked."

"But aren't you leaving the door wide open to promiscuity?" said Castle.

"On the contrary, we are perpetuating loyalty and affection. We can be sure that any continuing affection is genuine, and not the result of a police system, and hence it's something in which we take pride. We place abiding affection on a very high plane. . . .

"What about the children?" I said. "The group care we saw this morning must also weaken the relation between parent and child."

"It does. By design. We have to attenuate the child-parent relation for several reasons. Group care is better than parental care. In the old pre-scientific days the early education of the child could be left to the parents, and indeed almost certainly had to be left to them. But with the rise of a science of behavior all is changed. The bad repute into which scientific care has fallen is no reflection upon our technical knowledge of what should be done. The requirements of good child care are well established. Where we have failed is in getting good care in the average home. We have failed to teach the average parent even the simplest scientific principles. And that's not surprising. The control of behavior is an intricate science, into which the average mother could not be initiated without years of training. But the fact that most children today are badly raised isn't all the fault of a lack of technical skill, either. Even when the mother knows the right thing to do, she often can't do it in a household which is busy with other affairs. Home is not the place to raise children.

"Even when our young mothers and fathers become skilled nursery-school workers, we avoid a strong personal dependency. Our goal is to have every adult member of Walden Two regard all our children as his own, and to have every child think of every adult as his parent. To this end we have made it bad taste to single out one's own child for special favors. If you want to take your child on a picinic, the correct thing is to take several of his friends as well. If you want to give him a little present for his birthday, you are expected to give similar presents to the guests at his party. You may spend as much time as you like with your children, but to do so exclusively is taboo. The result is that a child never gets from its parents any services or favors which it does not also frequently get from others. We have untied the apron strings." . . .

"Don't many parents resent sharing their children?" I said.

"Why should they? What are they actually sharing? They see more of their children than the typical mother in most upper-class households—where the arrangement is also, by the way, from choice. And much more than the average father. Many parents are glad to be relieved of the awful responsibility of being a child's only source of affection and help. Here it's impossible to be an inadequate or unskillful parent, and the vigorous, happy growth of our children is enough to remove any last suspicion that we have been deprived of anything.

"The weakening of the relation between parent and child is valuable in other ways," Frazier continued, with sustained gentleness. "When divorce cannot be avoided, the children are not embarrassed by severe changes in their way of life or their behavior toward their parents. It's also easy to induce the unfit or unwell to forego parenthood. No stigma attaches to being childless, and no lack of affection. That's what I meant when I said that experiments in selective breeding would eventually be possible in Walden Two. The hereditary connection will be minimized to the point of being forgotten. Long before that, it will be possible to breed through artificial insemination without altering the personal relation of husband and wife. Our people will marry as they wish, but have children according to a genetic plan."

"It seems to me," said Castle, "that you're flying in the face of strong natural forces, just the same."

"What would you have said if I had proposed killing unwanted female babies?" said Frazier. "Yet that practice is condoned in some cultures. What do we really know about the *nature* of the parental relation? Anything? I doubt it." . . .

Frazier turned first to Castle.

"Have you ever taught a course in ethics, Mr. Castle?" he said.

"I have taught a course in ethics every year for thirteen years," said Castle in his most precise manner.

"Then you can tell us what the Good Life consists of," said Frazier.

"Oh, no, I can't," said Castle, "not by any means. You are thirteen years too late."

Frazier was delighted.

"Then let me tell you," he said. . . . "We all know what's good, until we stop to think about it. For example, is there any doubt that health is better than sickness?"

"There might be a time when a man would choose ill-health or death, even," said Castle. "And we might applaud his decision." . . .

"Yes, but . . . *other things being equal,* we choose health," Frazier continued. "The technical problem is simple enough. Perhaps we can find time tomorrow to visit our medical building.

"Secondly, can anyone doubt that an absolute minimum of unpleasant labor is part of the Good Life?" Frazier turned again to Castle, but he was greeted with a sullen silence.

"That's the millionaire's idea, anyway," I said.

"I mean the minimum which is possible without imposing on anyone. We must always think of the whole group. I don't mean that we want to be inactive—we have proved that idleness doesn't follow. But painful or uninteresting work is a threat to both physical and psychological health. Our plan was to reduce unwanted work to a minimum, but we wiped it out. Even hard work is fun if it's not beyond our strength and we don't have too much of it. A strong man rejoices to run a race or split wood or build a wall. When we're not being imposed on, when we choose our work freely, then we *want* to work. We may even search for work when a scarcity threatens. . . .

"The Good Life also means a chance to exercise talents and abilities. And we have to let it be so. We have time for sports, hobbies, arts and crafts, and most important of all, the expression of that interest in the world which is *science* in the deepest sense. It may be a casual interest in current affairs or in literature or the controlled and creative efforts of the laboratory—in any case it represents the unnecessary and pleasurably selective exploration of nature.

"And we need intimate and satisfying personal contacts. We must have the best possible chance of finding congenial spirits. Our Social Manager sees to that with many ingenious devices. And we don't restrict personal relations to conform to outmoded customs. We discourage attitudes of domination and criticism. Our goal is a general tolerance and affection.

"Last of all, the Good Life means relaxation and rest. We get that in Walden Two almost as a matter of course, but not merely because we have reduced our hours of work. In the world at large the leisure class is perhaps the least relaxed. The important thing is to satisfy our needs. Then we can give up the blind struggle to 'have a good time' or 'get what we want.' We have achieved a true leisure.

"And that's all, Mr. Castle—absolutely all. I can't give you a rational justification for any of it. I can't reduce it to any principle of 'the greatest good.' This *is* the Good Life. We know it. It's a fact, not a theory. It has an experimental justification, not a rational one. As for your conflict of principles, that's an experimental question, too. We don't puzzle our little minds over the outcome of Love versus Duty. We simply arrange a world in which serious conflicts occur as seldom as possible or, with a little luck, not at all."

Castle was gazing steadily across the evening landscape. There was no sign that he was listening. Frazier was not to be refused.

"Do you agree, Professor?" he said. There was obvious contempt for the honorific title.

"I don't think you and I are interested in the same thing," said Castle.

"Well, that's what *we* are interested in, and I think we've turned the trick," said Frazier, obviously disappointed. "Things are going well, at least."

"As I remember it, you made short shrift of perfectionism," I said. "Aren't you adopting a sort of perfectionist view yourself? You seem to imply that people will naturally be happy, active, affectionate, and so on, if you simply give them the chance. How do you keep these conditions in force?"

"There is no perfec—*In force!* Now there's an illuminating expression! You can't *enforce* happiness. You can't in the long run enforce anything. We don't *use* force! All we need is adequate behavioral engineering."

"Now we're getting somewhere," said Castle, looking up but still rather glum.

"I'll admit there's a special problem in the case of members who come to us as adults," said Frazier. "It's easier with members who are born into the community and pass through our school system. With new adult members we have to appeal to something like conversion."

"I should think so!" said Castle.

"It's not so difficult," said Frazier suspiciously. "The new member simply agrees to follow the customs of the community in return for the advantages of living among us. He may still thrive on motives which we carefully avoid in the design of our children. He may be the victim of emotions which we dispense with. But he agrees to hold himself in check, to live up to certain specifications, for the sake of the consequences. For example, he may be motivated very largely by a rejection of the outside world, a motive which is quite lacking in our children. But he agrees not to spend much time in invidious comparisons. Eventually, the adult members become very much like our properly educated second generation."

"That's all very fine as a program," said Castle. "It's more than that, it's beautiful. But here's the crux of the whole question of community life: how can you put such a program into effect?"

"It's really not so hard as the Philistines have supposed," said Frazier. "We have certain rules of conduct, the Walden Code, which are changed from time to time as experience suggests. Some of these, like the Ten Commandments, are rather fundamental, but many may seem trivial. Each member agrees to abide by the Code when he accepts membership. That's what he gives in return for his constitutional guarantee of a share in the wealth and life of the community. The Code acts as a memory aid until good behavior becomes habitual." . . .

"But why do you all continue to observe the Code?" I said. "Isn't there a natural drift away from it? Or simple disagreement?"

"As to disagreement, anyone may examine the evidence upon which a rule was introduced into the Code. He may argue against its inclusion and may present his own evidence. If the Managers refuse to change the rule, he may appeal to the Planners. But in no case must he argue about the Code with the members at large. There's a rule against that."

"I would certainly argue against the inclusion of *that* rule," said Castle. "Simple democracy requires public discussion of so fundamental a matter as a code."

"You won't find very much 'simple democracy' here," said Frazier casually, and he resumed his discussion as if he had referred to the absence of white flour in the Walden Two bread. "As to any drifting away from the Code, that's prevented by the very techniques which the Managers use to gain observance in the first place. The rules are frequently brought to the attention of the members. Groups of rules are discussed from time to time in our weekly meetings. The advantages for the community are pointed out and specific applications are described. In some cases simple rules are appropriately posted." . . .

. . . "I was going to ask you [I said] whether your techniques aren't already familiar to advertisers, politicians, and other kinds of applied psychologists. Is there anything very original about them?"

"Nothing original whatever. That's the point. Society already possesses the psychological techniques needed to obtain universal observance of a code—a code which would guarantee the success of a community or state. The difficulty is that these techniques are in the hands of the wrong people—or, rather, there aren't any right people. Our government won't accept the responsibility of building the sort of behavior needed for a happy state. In Walden Two we have merely created an agency to get these things done."

Castle had not been following much of this. As Frazier paused, he adopted a complete change of posture in his apparently uncomfortable deck chair and made several rustling noises preparatory to speaking.

"I am not satisfied with your Good Life," he said at last with a direct look at Frazier.

"You're not?"

"No. There's something lacking."

"Not the greatest good for the greatest number!" said Frazier.

"No. Something necessary to keep your exceptional people exceptional. Life here wouldn't challenge me—and I suspect it wouldn't challenge the dozen first-rate men who have gone through my classes during the past decade. As I remember them, they weren't interested in momentary tasks. They would have cared very little for something that could be finished tomorrow. What you lack, compared with the world at large, is the opportunity to make long-term plans. The scientist has them. An experiment which answers an isolated question is of little interest. Even the artist has them. If he's a good artist or a good composer, he isn't concerned with the single picture on his easel or the composition on his piano. He wants to feel that all his pictures, or compositions are saying something—are all part of a broader movement. The mere joy in running a race, or painting a picture, or weaving a rug, isn't enough. Your good man must be working on a theory or a new style or an improved technique."

"But don't think we all live from day to day!" said Frazier. "I can see why you might, because you have seen only our day-to-day life. We may seem to have some abiding preoccupation with the momentary enjoyment of happiness. That's by no means the case. But let me clear up another point first. You mentioned a dozen students who would be dissatisfied. What about the others?"

"Oh, you could take care of them well enough!" said Castle. "And you're welcome to do so."

"The difference between us, Mr. Castle, is greater than I supposed," said Frazier. "We not only have use for these people, we have respect. Most people do live from day to day, or, if they have any long-time plan it's little more than the anticipation of some natural course—they look forward to having children, to seeing the children grow up, and so on. The majority of people don't want to plan. They want to be free of the responsibility of planning. What they ask is merely some assurance that they will be decently provided for. The rest is a day-to-day enjoyment of life. That's the explanation of your Father Divines; people naturally flock to anyone they can trust for the necessities of life. People of that sort are completely happy here. And they pay their way. They aren't spongers and I don't see why you view them with contempt. They are the backbone of a community—solid, trustworthy, essential. But what about the highly intelligent few who must have distant and magnificent goals? In what sense would we interfere with their dreams?"

"It's just a feeling I have that these students would be quite out of water here. One of them might be interested in a social problem, for example."

"But do you think we have no social problems? Wouldn't your young friend enjoy a few months of apprenticeship with our Manager of Personal Behavior or Cultural Behavior or Public Relations? Wouldn't he find long-term ideas worth working for in educating our young—perhaps ways of interesting them in the very problems he holds so dear? Wouldn't he be an enthusiastic member of our newly formed Office of Information, which is to give an account of our experiment to the world? No, indeed, I don't think your young friend would lack distant goals. And the important thing is, we could show him how to *reach* these goals, or most of them, within a reasonable time. What can you do along that line?"

"Not much, I confess."

"Of course not. Because there are a thousand forces which prevent you and all the other men of good will from even starting toward your goal. What your young friend has, I'll wager, is a true spirit of experimentation, but like thousands of others he has no laboratory and no techniques. Shall we try an experiment right now? Send him here and let's see whether he will lack distant goals!"

This was not very subtle, and the excitement in Frazier's manner less so. But I could not tell whether he was simply out to recruit new material or whether he sincerely wanted to refute Castle's charge in the only way he knew—with a practical proof that Walden Two would challenge a good man.

"I wasn't thinking of any one man in particular," said Castle. "Merely of a certain type. Your answer is reasonable, but I happened to hit upon an easy case. What about the boy who wants to make a name for himself in some business? Let's say he has discovered some new process and wants to set up an industry."

"What does 'making a name for himself' mean?" asked Frazier. "Do you mean making a fortune? We have no need for fortunes, and until you can show me how a fortune can be made without making a few paupers in the bargain, it's one goal we're glad to do without."

"I suppose I was thinking more of fame than fortune," said Castle.

"Fame is also won at the expense of others. Even the well-deserved honors of the scientist or man of learning are unfair to many persons of equal achievement who get none. When one man gets a place in the sun, others are put in a denser shade. From the point of view of the whole group there's no gain whatsoever, and perhaps a loss."

"But is there anything wrong with admiring exceptional achievements, or being pleased to receive recognition?" I said.

"Yes," said Frazier flatly. "If it points up the unexceptional achievements of others, it's wrong. We are opposed to personal competition. We don't encourage competitive games, for example, with the exception of tennis or chess, where the exercise of skill is as important as the outcome of the game; and we never have tournaments even so. We never mark any member for special approbation. There must be some other source of satisfaction in one's work or play, or we regard an achievement as quite trivial. A triumph over another man is never a laudable act. Our decision to eliminate personal aggrandizement arose quite naturally from the fact that we were thinking about the whole group. We could not see how the group could gain from individual glory."

"But do you exclude simple personal gratitude?" asked Castle. "Suppose one of your doctors worked out a system of sanitation or medication so that none of you ever had colds. Wouldn't you want to honor him and wouldn't he want to be honored?"

"We don't need to talk about hypothetical cases," said Frazier. "Our people are constantly making contributions to the health, leisure, happiness, comfort, and amusement of the community. That's where your young friend with the new industrial process would find himself. But to single anyone out for citation would be to neglect all the others. Gratitude itself isn't wrong, it's the ingratitude or lack of gratitude which it involves."

"So you have just stopped being grateful," said Castle.

"On the contrary, we're all extraordinarily grateful. We overflow with gratitude—but to no one in particular. We are grateful to all and to none. We feel a sort of generalized gratitude toward the whole community—very much as one gives thanks to God for blessings which are more immediately due to a next-door neighbor or even the sweat of one's own brow."

"How is your generalized gratitude expressed?" I said.

"Well, what's gratitude, anyway?" said Frazier. He waited for an answer, but none came, and he went on. "Isn't it a readiness to do return favors? At least that's the sense in which we're all grateful here. There isn't one of us who wouldn't willingly enter upon the most difficult assignment if the need arose. We're ready to do something for all in return for what we've received from all." . . .

"What's left to motivate your workers? I said. "Take a Manager, for example. He doesn't work for money—that's out. He doesn't work for personal acclaim—that's forbidden. What's left? I suppose you'd say he works to avoid the consequences of failure. He has to keep going or he'll be held responsible for the resulting mess."

"I wouldn't say that. We don't condemn a man for poor work. After all, if we don't praise him, it would be unfair to blame him."

"You mean you would let an incompetent man continue to do a poor job?" said Castle.

"By no means. He would be given other work, and a competent man brought in. But he wouldn't be blamed."

"For heaven's sake, why not?" said Castle.

"Do you blame a man for getting sick?"

"Of course not."

"But poor work by a capable man is a form of illness."

"That sounds like *Erewhon*," said Castle, "and I confess that I find it absurd."

"I found *Erewhon* absurd when I first read it, too," said Frazier, and as Castle made a gesture of impatience he hastened to add, "I'm sorry. I didn't mean to imply that you hadn't thought the thing out. But you can't think these things all the way out; you have to *work* them out. 'Experience is the mother of all certainty.' We had no expectation of seeing Butler's little flight of fancy so beautifully confirmed. And, incidentally, we haven't confirmed his companion piece of cultural engineering. We don't throw a man into prison for illness. Butler was carried away by the Principle of Upside Down. A moral or ethical lapse, whether in explicit violation of the Code or not, needs treatment, not punishment."

"You merely offer your condolences for a mild case of larceny?" said Castle.

"No, condolences are out too. The doctor seldom expresses sympathy for his patient—and wisely, I think. We simply treat the illness as an objective fact."

"How do you treat a man for a bad case of 'poor work'?" I asked.

"With common sense! Take him off the job. If the boy who has charge of collecting eggs breaks too many, give him other work. And the same with a Manager. But why condemn him? Or blame him?"

"I should think you might encourage a sort of malingering," I said. "Wouldn't a man be tempted to do poor work in order to get an easier job?—Oh, well. Forgive me. I see the answer to that: you have no easier jobs, of course. And he could change jobs freely anyway. I'm sorry."

"But what if a man did poor work, or none at all, in every job you put him on?" said Castle.

"The disease would be judged quite serious, and the man would be sent to one of our psychologists. It's more likely that he would long since have gone of his own accord. This would happen before any very critical condition developed, and a cure would be quite possible. But compare the situation in the outside world. There the man would have stuck to his job in spite of his indisposition—that is, in spite of his desire not to work or work well—because he needed the wages, or was afraid of censure, or because another job wasn't available. The condition would have become critical. I think it's that kind of ultimate violent revolt that you're thinking about. It's quite unlikely here."

"But what would you do if it occurred?" Castle insisted. "Certainly you can conceive of a member refusing to work."

"We should deal with it somehow. I don't know. You might as well ask what we should do if leprosy broke out. We'd think of something. We aren't helpless." . . .

"You use the word 'experiment' a great deal," I said, "but do you really experiment at all? Isn't one feature of good scientific practice missing from all the cases you have described?"

"You mean the 'control.' " said Frazier.

"Yes," I said, rather surprised to have him get my point so quickly. "How do you know that the ethical training you give your young people is really responsible for their equanimity and happiness? Might these not be due to some of the other experimental conditions which you have set up? Why don't you divide your children into two groups? One could receive an ethical training, the other not."

"Probably," said Frazier, "because I am not offering Walden Two 'in partial fulfillment of the requirements for the degree of Doctor of Philosophy.' Besides, it wouldn't work. There would be too many cross-influences. We're too small to keep two groups of children separate. Some day it may be possible—we shall have controls to satisfy the most academic statistician. And by that time they may be necessary, too, for we shall have reached the point of dealing with very subtle differences. At present they aren't necessary. To go to all the trouble of running controls would be to make a fetish of scientific method. Even in the exact sciences we frequently don't ask for controls. If I touch a match to a mixture of chemicals and an explosion occurs, I don't set a second mixture aside to see if it will blow up without the help of the match. The effect of the match is obvious." . . .

I cannot recall that evening without remembering the grandeur of the slowly changing sky. It was not a picturesque sunset, for there were no clouds, but a strange pink light surrounded us, as if we were indeed looking at the world through rose-colored glasses. Eventually the sky faded and then darkened, and the stars came out.

It was now fairly late, as hours at Walden Two went. Most of the other occupants of the roof had gone, and the frogs and peepers had taken over all conversations but our own. Frazier indulged in a most conspicuous yawn.

"I find myself reminded of our cardinal piece of personal engineering," he said when he had composed his face again. He turned to me. "Have you ever studied sleep?"

"Not beyond the usual textbooks," I said. "It seems to be important in avoiding behavioral disorders in children."

"In adults, too," said Frazier. "It makes an enormous difference with me. I can take any frustration in my stride if I've had enough sleep. And give me a good night's sleep and I can do a day's work in a couple of hours."

"I thought that was the usual thing," said Castle.

"I mean intellectual work. Nowadays I can do more creative thinking or writing in a couple of hours than I used to do in a whole day, when I forced myself to keep going in spite of a distracting weariness. What folly that was! What an inefficient use of Man Thinking!"

"I'm sure many people never know what it's like to be rested," I said.

"Of course they don't," said Frazier, in exceptionally cordial agreement. "They never have a chance to discover how tired they really are, or how well they could work otherwise, or what brilliant flashes they might have."

"I get a glimpse of it at vacation time," I said.

"I dare say you do. But not the usual vacationer. He's so accustomed to a fast pace that he immediately looks about for something to do. Even the lucky ones who can relax, who don't feel that time is wasted if they sleep it away, seldom get beyond the drugged stage. The simple fact is, our civilization puts no value on rest.

"I'm sure it has a bearing on longevity, too," Frazier continued. "Many parts of *News from Nowhere* are ridiculous, but if Morris could convince me that he knew how to achieve his 'epoch of leisure,' I would grant him the fabulous youthfulness of his people." He rose and started to fold his chair. "Let us rejuvenate for a few hours," he said.

We rose and carried our chairs and cushions to neat piles along the rear edge of the roof.

"I suspect that 'Return your chairs' is to be found somewhere in the Code," I said.

Frazier smiled but said nothing. He led us down the ramp, saw us off safely in the direction of the Walk, and turned toward his room.

Castle and I were again soon deserted. We reached the hallway in front of our room and stood talking for a few moments as I indicated my intention of going outside. Castle was engaged in a bitter struggle with himself. He would clench his fist and slap it into the palm of his hand, and shake his head with an exaggerated sweep from side to side, in no apparent connection with our remarks. "Not for me!" he would interject "Not for me!" I said that I could see no fundamental flaw in Frazier's program and pointed to the apparently successful accomplished fact before our eyes. This was not exactly fair, for I was still in conflict myself, but I enjoyed Castle's struggle. And I was on Frazier's side on the main issue.

Finally, with a "Good night" which was less a farewell than a paraphrase of "The jig is up," Castle strode into our room and slammed the door.

SKINNER SELECTION

1. Would you like to live in Skinner's ideal community? Why? What would be the benefits of such living arrangements? What might be the problems? Are there any problems you think Skinner couldn't handle, given his techniques and theories?

2. Walden Two is a small community into which people have moved voluntarily. What problems might Skinner have in transferring his techniques to a large modern society into which people are born, with no choice whatsoever as to whether they are going to be part of it? Does Skinner's technique depend on the members of the community knowing one another personally? How? How do things change when the community gets too large for that sort of personal acquaintance?

3. At the end of this selection, Castle says "Not for me!" Can you put into words the sources of Castle's strong negative reaction to Frazier's arguments? Since all of us are profoundly influenced by our upbringing, by the standards of our parents, by the customs of our society, by the very language we speak, why should we be put off by Skinner's proposals for additional, rationally designed behavior modifications?

4. Skinner's arguments are based on the behavioral psychology to which he has made major scientific contributions. Would his argument be any better (or worse) if he were to employ a different theory of personality? How? Could there be a Walden Three based on Freudian theories of personality? How might it differ from Walden Two?

(SELECTION 6)

THOMAS SZASZ

The Myth of Mental Illness

The notion of virtue as rooted in a healthy personality, and of the good society as resting on the psychological health of the citizenry, is an ancient one. We find it clearly set forth in Plato's *Republic,* where repeated use is made of analogies between the health of the body, the health of the soul or psyche, and the health of the Body Politic. In the twentieth century the idea was given new life and force by the development of medical theories of personality. The leading figure in this development was the Austrian psychiatrist Sigmund Freud, and particularly in the United States, Freudian psychoanalysis, as it is called, has become a dominant force in our culture as well as in medical practice.

The significance of Freudian theory for social philosophy is simply this: if medicine can really provide us with a scientifically validated conception of the healthy personality, in terms of which we can explain a variety of anti-social behavior as a product of illness rather than moral failing, then we seem well on our way to discovering a scientific policy for producing emotionally healthy *and, therefore, socially acceptable* citizens. In short, we shall have the basis for a policy of social control that appears to rise above mere moral opinion to the level of medical truth. Just as we now have public health campaigns to

control epidemics of physical ailments, so we would (presumably) be able to devise public mental health campaigns to root out emotionally unhealthy behavior. Anyone who opposed such a campaign would be roughly in the position of a defender of smallpox or polio.

Thomas Szasz is a psychiatrist who abhors the idea of public policies devoted to the control and alteration of behavior. Striking at the theoretical foundation of all such policies, he denies the legitimacy of the analogy between physical and mental health. Strange as it may sound in the contemporary scene, Szasz rejects the core notion of mental illness. He insists that our judgment about personality and behavior are always partly evaluative, never purely descriptive.

Since Szasz wrote his essay, the issue has entered public political debate in the United States as part of the fight over the status of homosexuals in American society. The medical establishment, until recently, classified homosexuality as a form of mental illness. The clear implication was that public policy ought to encourage heterosexual behavior, just as public policy encourages good health habits through drug control laws, publicity campaigns, and mass inoculation procedures. If Szasz is correct, not only the condemnation of

homosexuals, but also the hospitaliza-
tion of thousands of men and women as
"insane" is simply the imposition by one part of the community of their value-
attitudes on others.

At the core of virtually all contemporary psychiatric theories and practices lies the concept of mental illness. A critical examination of this concept is therefore indispensable for understanding the ideas, institutions, and interventions of psychiatrists.

My aim in this essay is to ask if there is such a thing as mental illness, and to argue that there is not. Of course, mental illness is not a thing or physical object; hence it can exist only in the same sort of way as do other theoretical concepts. Yet, to those who believe in them, familiar theories are likely to appear, sooner or later, as "objective truths" or "facts." During certain historical periods, explanatory concepts such as deities, witches, and instincts appeared not only as theories but as *self-evident causes* of a vast number of events. Today mental illness is widely regarded in a similar fashion, that is, as the cause of innumerable diverse happenings.

As an antidote to the complacent use of the notion of mental illness—as a self-evident phenomenon, theory, or cause—let us ask: What is meant when it is asserted that someone is mentally ill? In this essay I shall describe the main uses of the concept of mental illness, and I shall argue that this notion has outlived whatever cognitive usefulness it might have had and that it now functions as a myth.

The notion of mental illness derives its main support from such phenomena as syphilis of the brain or delirious conditions—intoxication, for instance—in which persons may manifest certain disorders of thinking and behavior. Correctly speaking, however, these are diseases of the brain, not of the mind. According to one school of thought, *all* so-called mental illness is of this type. The assumption is made that some neurological defect, perhaps a very subtle one, will ultimately be found to explain all the disorders of thinking and behavior. Many contemporary physicians, psychiatrists, and other scientists hold this view, which implies that people's troubles cannot be caused by conflicting personal needs, opinions, social aspirations, values, and so forth. These difficulties—which I think we may simply call *problems in living*—are thus attributed to physicochemical processes that in due time will be discovered (and no doubt corrected) by medical research.

Mental illnesses are thus regarded as basically similar to other diseases. The only difference, in this view, between mental and bodily disease is that the former, affecting the brain, manifests itself by means of mental symptoms; whereas the latter, affecting other organ systems—for example, the skin, liver, and so on—manifests itself by means of symptoms referable to those parts of the body.

In my opinion, this view is based on two fundamental errors. In the first place, a disease of the brain, analogous to a disease of the skin or bone, is a neurological defect, not a problem in living. For example, a *defect* in a person's visual field may be explained by correlating it with certain lesions in the nervous system. On the other hand, a person's *belief*—whether it be in Christianity, in Communism, or in the idea that his internal organs are rotting and that his body is already dead—cannot be explained by a defect or disease of the nervous system. Explanations of this sort of occurrence—assuming that one is interested in the belief itself and does not regard it simply as a symptom or expression of something else that is more interesting—must be sought along different lines.

The second error is epistemological. It consists of interpreting communications about ourselves and the world around us as symptoms of neurological functioning. This is an error not in observation or reasoning, but rather in the organization and expression of knowledge. In the present case, the error lies in making a dualism between mental and physical symptoms, a dualism that is a habit of speech and not the result of known observations. Let us see if this is so.

In medical practice, when we speak of physical disturbances we mean either signs (for example, fever) or symptoms (for example, pain). We speak of mental symptoms, on the other hand, when we refer to a patient's communications about himself, others, and the world about him. The patient might assert that he is Napoleon or that he is being persecuted by the Communists. These would be considered mental symptoms only if the observer believed that the patient was *not* Napoleon or that he was *not* being persecuted by the Communists. This makes it apparent that the statement "X is a mental symptom" involves rendering a judgment that entails a covert comparison between the patient's ideas, concepts, or beliefs and those of the observer and the society in which they live. The notion of mental symptom is therefore inextricably tied to the social, and particularly the ethical, context in which it is made, just as the notion of bodily symptom is tied to an anatomical and genetic context.[1]

To sum up: For those who regard mental symptoms as signs of

[1] See T. S. Szasz, *Pain and Pleasure: A Study of Bodily Feelings* (New York: Basic Books, 1957), especially pp. 70–81; "The problem of psychiatric nosology." *Amer. J. Psychiatry*, 114:405–13 (Nov.), 1957.

brain disease, the concept of mental illness is unnecessary and misleading. If they mean that people so labeled suffer from diseases of
the brain, it would seem better, for the sake of clarity, to say that and
not something else.

The term "mental illness" is also widely used to describe something quite different from a disease of the brain. Many people today
take it for granted that living is an arduous affair. Its hardship for
modern man derives, moreover, not so much from a struggle for biological survival as from the stresses and strains inherent in the social
intercourse of complex human personalities. In this context, the notion of mental illness is used to identify or describe some feature of
an individual's so-called personality. Mental illness—as a deformity
of the personality, so to speak—is then regarded as the cause of human disharmony. It is implicit in this view that social intercourse
between people is regarded as something inherently harmonious, its
disturbance being due solely to the presence of "mental illness" in
many people. Clearly, this is faulty reasoning, for it makes the abstraction "mental illness" into a cause of, even though this abstraction
was originally created to serve only as a shorthand expression for,
certain types of human behavior. It now becomes necessary to ask:
What kinds of behavior are regarded as indicative of mental illness,
and by whom?

The concept of illness, whether bodily or mental, implies deviation from some clearly defined norm. In the case of physical illness,
the norm is the structural and functional integrity of the human
body. Thus, although the desirability of physical health, as such, is
an ethical value, what health is can be stated in anatomical and
physiological terms. What is the norm, deviation from which is regarded as mental illness? This question cannot be easily answered.
But whatever this norm may be, we can be certain of only one thing:
namely, that it must be stated in terms of psychosocial, ethical, and
legal concepts. For example, notions such as "excessive repression"
and "acting out an unconscious impulse" illustrate the use of psychological concepts for judging so-called mental health and illness.
The idea that chronic hostility, vengefulness, or divorce are indicative of mental illness is an illustration of the use of ethical norms
(that is, the desirability of love, kindness, and a stable marriage relationship). Finally, the widespread psychiatric opinion that only a
mentally ill person would commit homicide illustrates the use of a
legal concept as a norm of mental health. In short, when one speaks
of mental illness, the norm from which deviation is measured is a
psychosocial and ethical standard. Yet, the remedy is sought in terms

of *medical* measures that—it is hoped and assumed—are free from wide differences of ethical value. The definition of the disorder and the terms in which its remedy are sought are therefore at serious odds with one another. The practical significance of this covert conflict between the alleged nature of the defect and the actual remedy can hardly be exaggerated. . . .

While I maintain that mental illnesses do not exist, I obviously do not imply or mean that the social and psychological occurrences to which this label is attached also do not exist. Like the personal and social troubles that people had in the Middle Ages, contemporary human problems are real enough. It is the labels we give them that concern me, and, having labeled them, what we do about them. The demonologic concept of problems in living gave rise to therapy along theological lines. Today, a belief in mental illness implies—nay, requires—therapy along medical or psychotherapeutic lines.

I do not here propose to offer a new conception of "psychiatric illness" or a new form of "therapy." My aim is more modest and yet also more ambitious. It is to suggest that the phenomena now called mental illnesses be looked at afresh and more simply, that they be removed from the category of illnesses, and that they be regarded as the expressions of man's struggle with *the problem of how he should live*. This problem is obviously a vast one, its enormity reflecting not only man's inability to cope with his environment, but even more his increasing self-reflectiveness.

By problems in living, then, I refer to that explosive chain reaction that began with man's fall from divine grace by partaking of the fruit of the tree of knowledge. Man's awareness of himself and of the world about him seems to be a steadily expanding one, bringing in its wake an ever larger *burden of understanding*. This burden is to be expected and must not be misinterpreted. Our only rational means for easing it is more understanding, and appropriate action based on such understanding. The main alternative lies in acting as though the burden were not what in fact we perceive it to be, and taking refuge in an outmoded theological view of man. In such a view, man does not fashion his life and much of his world about him, but merely lies out his fate in a world created by superior beings. This may logically lead to pleading non-responsibility in the face of seemingly unfathomable problems and insurmountable difficulties. Yet, if man fails to take increasing responsibility for his actions, individually as well as collectively, it seems unlikely that some higher power or being would assume this task and carry this burden for him. Moreover, this seems hardly a propitious time in human history for obscuring the issue of man's responsibility for his actions by hiding

it behind the skirt of an all-explaining conception of mental illness. . . .

Science may be regarded as the sum total of human effort to
understand nature and thus gain a measure of control over it. The
process of naming, or symbolic identification, is perhaps the basic
building block of science. Classification is a refinement over naming,
as brick and concrete are over rock and timber. How does classification help us to master the world about us? By providing us with certain regularities: as a result, we are spared recurrent surprise over
various happenings about us. In temperate climates, the sequence of
the seasons is such an occurrence; at the seashore, the ebb and flow
of the tides. The naming of animals and plants, the ordering of elements, and the classification of human diseases are other, more complex patterns of regularities; each helps us to master certain aspects
of the world about us. In some cases, mastery is attained by having
the power to predict future events, and, hence, to prepare for and
adapt to them—for example, meteorology; in others, by having the
power to bring about certain future events by judiciously planned
action—for example, agriculture.

In broad outline, this has always been the attitude of rational
man toward the world of rocks, of plants, and of animals. Wherever
this attitude is most highly developed, man is most successful in "con-
quering" nature. This is the background against which we must
view the problems of psychiatric classification.

The aims of natural science, and the main criteria of the validity
of its assertions, are prediction and control. Naming and classification
—and the construction of hypotheses, theories, or so-called natural
laws—help to achieve these goals. But it is not enough for man to
understand and thus be able to plan for, or alter, the movement of
planets, the growth and decay of plants, and the behavior of animals.
There is another source of mystery and danger for man: other men.

Man's efforts to understand and control his fellow man have a
long and complicated history. Here I shall remark briefly on but one
part of the story—the past three hundred years. This period encom-
passes the development of most of modern physical science, and all
of modern social science. Of special interest is the scientist's attitude
toward the similarities and differences between describing, predicting, and controlling natural events and human behavior.

The idea of a "unified science" is not as new as we sometimes
think. In a sense, primitive man's view of the world is unified: his
attitude is the same toward animate and inanimate nature, toward
man, animals, and things. We call this *anthropomorphism:* the primitive tries to understand the physical world as if it were animated by

human spirits. Physical events, whether desired or disastrous, are viewed as the consequences of willed action. Consequently, the control of such events centers around efforts to propitiate the gods or spirits believed to have caused them.

Since the advent of modern science, beginning with men like Galileo and Newton, the image of nature as a harmoniously functioning mechanical machine inspired another view of man. Instead of "projecting" himself into nature, man now "introjects" nature into himself. Whereas primitive man personifies things, modern man "thingifies" persons. We call this *mechanomorphism:* modern man tries to understand man as if "it" were a machine. Thus, the student of man must take apart this machine and understand its parts and functions, so that he may predict and control its behavior as he would that of any other machine.

Is this the proper way to study man? The history of the dialogue between the yea-sayers and the nay-sayers to this question constitutes the history of social science. Since I cannot review or even summarize this dialogue here, a few remarks on its general nature must suffice.

Those who have considered the prediction and control of human behavior logically possible and morally desirable have, in general, tended to advocate its coercive social control. Their rank begins with Saint-Simon and Comte and extends to contemporary men like Harold D. Lasswell in political science and B. F. Skinner in psychology. In contrast, those who have been skeptical about the range of the predictability of human behavior, and about the moral desirability of making such predictions, have tended to advocate freedom from arbitrary or personal social restraints. Their rank begins with Locke and Jefferson and extends to contemporary figures like Ludwig von Mises in economics and Karl Popper in philosophy. . . .

As modern science progressed in its conquest of nature, it became clear—by the end of the nineteenth century and increasingly thereafter—that, among all the unpredictable events in the universe, human behavior was one of the most baffling. Nor is this surprising. Among all the objects and creatures in the world, man is the only one endowed with free will: his behavior is not only *determined* by antecedent events but is also *chosen* by him, in accordance with his view of himself and of the goals he seeks to attain. Or is this an illusion? Is personal freedom an ethical concept, unworthy of inclusion in the vocabulary of science?

I shall not engage in the futile controversy about the nature of "real science." Our interest in this problem lies in the concept of freedom it introduces. What is its import for psychiatric classification? The answer, it seems to me, may be briefly stated: *To classify human behavior is to constrain it.* Let me explain what I mean.

One of man's basic strivings is for order and harmony in a potentially chaotic universe. The classification of physical objects and of living but non-human things serves this need. It must be noted now that the behavior of these non-human objects is essentially independent of symbolic acts, and is, therefore, unaffected by the act of classification itself. A cow is a mammal regardless of what we call it or how we classify it. To affect the cow's behavior, we must act directly upon the animal: for example, by milking it or slaughtering it. This kind of separation between physical action and symbolic action exists in all realms where man acts upon non-human objects. However, in situations where man acts upon his fellow man, this separation is either absent or radically different in character: here language becomes a kind of action.

Viewed in this light, social role emerges as a classificatory prison, with personal identities as the cells in which men confine each other. This helps explain the persistent difficulties that psychiatric classifications pose for us. As a rule, medical diagnoses do not define an individual's personal identity, whereas psychiatric diagnoses do. What a difference there is between calling a person a "leukemic poet" and a "schizophrenic poet"! In other words, psychiatric diagnoses define personal identity in much the same way as descriptive adjectives like "existential," "Kantian," or "linguistic" define the noun "philosopher" and the person to whom it is applied.

It would be absurd for anyone, and especially for students of man, to disregard the ways in which men use language and respond to it. The expressions "hysterical mother" or "paranoid senator" differ fundamentally from "obese mother" or "diabetic senator." Again, Sartre has illuminated this issue. "The homosexual," he observed, "recognizes his faults, but he struggles with all his strength against the crushing view that his mistakes constitute for him a destiny. He does not wish to let himself be considered a thing. He has an obscure but strong feeling that a homosexual is not a homosexual as this table is a table or as this red-haired man is red-haired." [2]

It is precisely this defacing, this rendering of the person into a thing, that the psychiatric nosologist inflicts on his subject. Thus, according to the experts, the proper psychiatric method of treating a "patient" like Secretary of Defense Forrestal is to treat him like any

[2] J. P. Sartre, *Existential Psychoanalysis* [1953], trans. Hazel E. Barnes (Chicago: Regnery-Gateway, 1964), p. 193.

other patient—that is, as a non-human object bearing a psychiatric label.[3] Of course, when the "patient" is a Very Important Person, this is impossible, but the command to do so is revealing. For when the "patient" lacks the social power of an important personage, as is usually the case, he can be and is treated in this fashion.[4] Thus, when a hospital psychiatrist classifies a newly admitted patient as a paranoid schizophrenic, he does exactly what Sartre described. The diagnostic label imparts a defective personal identity to the patient. It will henceforth identify him to others and will govern their conduct toward him, and his toward them. The psychiatric nosologist thus not only *describes* his patient's so-called illness, but also *prescribes* his future conduct.

In short, we must choose between two radically different attitudes toward personal conduct. First, human behavior may be regarded as an event, essentially similar to other, non-human events; for example, as an astronomer can predict an eclipse of the sun, so a criminologist can predict the incidence of "recidivism" among discharged prisoners. Although this approach commits the investigator to treating people as essentially no different from things, it is not without merit. It is especially useful for certain kinds of statistical analyses and predictions of behavior.

Second, human behavior may be regarded as a unique achievement of which only man is capable. Personal conduct is based on the free choices of a sign-using, rule-following, and game-playing person whose *action* is often largely governed by his future goals rather than by his past experiences. This view of man casts efforts to predict his behavior in a new perspective. For, to the extent that man is free to act—that is, free to choose among alternative courses of action—his conduct is, and must be, unpredictable after all, this is what is meant by the word "free." Trying to predict human behavior is, therefore, likely to result in efforts to constrain it.

SZASZ SELECTION

1. Szasz rejects the notion that there is such a thing as mental health, or psychological health, analogous to physical health. What arguments does he give in support of that rejection? What does he mean by a "problem in living"?

2. If Szasz is correct, then what is the effect upon the arguments of Skinner and other psychological social planners? Are any of the laws or

[3] A. A. Rogow, *James Forrestal: A Study of Personality, Politics, and Policy* (New York: Macmillan, 1964).

[4] See, for example, E. Goffman, "The Moral Career of the Mental Patient," in E. Goffman, *Asylums: Essays on the Social Situation of Mental Patients and Other Inmates* (Garden City, N.Y.: Doubleday Anchor, 1961), pp. 125-70.

public policies now in force in our society based on the concept of "mental illness"? Which ones? How would Szasz have us alter those laws or policies? What would be the effects on society of the adoption of Szasz's point of view?

   3.   Are there any patterns of behavior or personality traits that would be considered "sick" in our society but "healthy" in some other society? Which ones? Are there any *physical* conditions that are considered unhealthy in one society and healthy in another? In the case of personality traits, is the disagreement between societies a disagreement in evaluations, or a disagreement over facts and causes? What is the difference between these two types of disagreements?

   4.   Szasz really has two objections to Skinner. The first is that it is a great deal more difficult to control human behavior than Skinner seems to suppose. The second is that even if we could control human behavior, it would be morally wrong to do so. In addition, Szasz argues that even trying to predict human behavior has the effect of constraining it. Why does Szasz think it is so hard to predict and control human behavior? Why does he think it is wrong to do so? Do you agree or disagree? Why?

1.   Although the selections in this chapter are paired, the arguments of the authors can be brought to bear on a number of different opponents. For example, what judgment do you think Hayek would make on Plato's proposal that society be ruled by philosopher kings? What might Popper say about Skinner's proposal for behavior modifications? How might Engels analyze the ideal society sketched by Plato?

2.   In what ways is Plato's Republic similar to Skinner's Walden Two? In what ways are they different? How does Plato's conception of the healthy personality compare with Skinner's notion of happiness? Do Plato and Skinner have similar or different conceptions of the role of reason in the good society? What are the similarities?

3.   Would Szasz consider Plato's educational and social proposals morally acceptable, or would he consider them "constraints" on human behavior? Suppose Plato could make his ideal society work without either "lies" or "eugenic breeding." Would that overcome Szasz's possible objections?

4.   Try to imagine your ideal society. What assumptions about human beings is it based on? What conception of happiness does it employ? What principles of human freedom does it attempt to adhere to? Which of the ideals presented in this chapter is closest to your own ideal? Which farthest? How would you reply to the objections that might be offered by the authors in this chapter to your own ideal society?

5.   Does it make any sense to think about ideal societies? Why? What is the relationship between conceptions of an ideal society and social or political action? Would we all be better off if we stopped thinking about ways in which our society could be made better? Does utopian literature raise our standards, or does it simply encourage unfulfillable hopes?

CHAPTER seven

GOD AND RELIGIOUS EXPERIENCE

(Focal Issues)

1. Is There a God?

2. Can We Prove the Existence of God?

3. What Is My Relationship to God?

4. Can God's Ways Be Morally Justified?

INTRODUCTION

If you spend much time browsing through bookstores, you may have noticed that Philosophy and Religion are very often grouped together on one shelf. I'm not sure, these days, whether that practice pleases either the theologian or the philosopher, but it reflects a very old association between the two. It is appropriate, therefore, that we should conclude this book of readings with a chapter devoted to what is usually called "the philosophy of religion."

Right away, we encounter a problem, for the term "philosophy of religion" applies to two great bodies of writings that may not seem to have much to do with one another. To some philosophers, the term calls to mind a large and long-standing literature devoted to proving the existence of a divine, infinite being called "God," and to analyzing His nature and His relationship to human beings and the world. But to other philosophers, the same term conjures up a wide and varied body of writings that explore religious *experience*— the experience of wonder, of doubt, of anxiety over the afterlife, of revelation, and of worship.

This duality in the study of the "philosophy of religion" is very nicely captured for us by a fundamental ambiguity in the familiar phrase, "faith in God." Some of you who are reading this book are, no doubt, deeply religious, while others either merely go through the motions of attending services (perhaps only when you are at home with your parents), or else engage in no religious practices at all. Let me ask all of you to reflect for a moment on what it means to say that someone "has faith."

When we say that a man or woman "has faith," we mean that he or she "believes in God," but there are two totally different things we may mean by "belief in God." These days, we are likely to mean that a person who believes in God believes *that there is a God*. So a believer is contrasted with a nonbeliever, an atheist, someone who says, "there is no god." But in the Judeo-Christian tradition to which most Americans belong, "belief in God" does not mean that at all! For traditional Christians, and for Jews as well, to believe in God means to believe that He will keep the promise He made and repeated, first to the Hebrews of Old Testament times, and then to all mankind through the birth, life, and death of Jesus Christ.

The promise takes different forms at different times. Sometimes it is God's promise to make His chosen people fruitful and numerous;

at other times, it is a promise of salvation, of life after death, of eternal blessedness. In the Old Testament, the promise is part of a contract, a "covenant." *If* Man obeys God's laws, *then* God will look after His chosen people. In the New Testament, this Divine care is offered as a free gift to all men and women. To receive it, and thereby to be taken up into God's bosom for all eternity, they need simply believe, freely and with all their hearts—believe, that is, that God will give them this gift. Those who lack faith are unable to believe that God will truly give them so infinitely valuable a gift freely, without constraint or condition. To "deny God" is, in this tradition, to turn away from Him, to refuse (or to be unable) to love Him; it is *not* to deny *that* He exists.

A great deal of the literature of religion, therefore, deals with the experience of faith or its loss. Sometimes the writing is joyous, overflowing with the happiness that is said to come from a full and unhesitating belief in the divine promise of an infinitely benevolent God. Sometimes the writing is desperate, unhappy, full of the misery that comes from not being able to believe that so good a God would ever bestow so great a gift on so sinful, so unworthy a subject. And often the writing is anguished, uncertain, doubtful as to whether one's faith is full, free, and unforced, whether it is truly the faith of one who has accepted God's promise and, therefore, will receive His gift.

This literature of religious experience is among the most moving of our culture. The feelings and thoughts that it voices find expression as well in the music, the painting, the sculpture, the poetry, and the fiction of the Western tradition. They continue today to inspire men and women to acts of faith and artistic creation.

It is doubtful that anyone has ever truly been *argued* into a faith of this sort. If you lay the facts before me, you can teach me that smoking cigarettes increases my chances of contracting lung cancer. If you go deeply enough into the theory of physics, you can persuade me that there are electrons, although I find them rather hard to imagine. And inconceivable, unimaginable though they may be, you can probably even convince me of the existence of millions of galaxies, each consisting of billions of stars. But does anyone suppose that you could produce a proof that would actually make me (or anyone else) believe in the existence of God if I did not *already* believe it?

From time to time, when I teach Introduction to Philosophy, I try a little experiment. First I ask how many students truly believe in the existence of God. Usually there is a pretty fair show of hands, perhaps a third to a half of the class. Then I trot out one of the standard proofs of the existence of God (proofs that you shall be reading in this chapter). I go through the steps of the proof, ask for questions or objections (there usually aren't any), and then ask how many people *now* believe in the existence of God. Well, as you might expect, there is *never* anyone who raises a hand and says: "Yes, you have persuaded me. Before I heard the proof, I was an atheist, but now I am a believer!" Men and women have been converted by fire, by sword, by oratory, by the threat of death, and by the wonder of birth, but surely no one has even been converted by a proof of God's existence!

That being so, why have so many philosophers spent so much time and such extraordinary ingenuity trying to find a proof? Contrary to what you might imagine, they are not simply being foolish or pigheaded. If we can become clearer about the role played by assertions of God's existence in philosophical systems, we shall be a good deal better prepared to confront the proofs of God's existence that occupy the first half of this chapter.

As we saw in the Introduction to Chapter 4, the traditional approach to problems of knowing and being that dominated philosophy from the fourth century B.C. through the beginning of the seventeenth century A.D. made ontology, or the study of Being, the foundation stone of all rational understanding of the universe. Although there were, of course, many approaches to the study of Being, one characteristic set of assumptions was widely accepted by the leading philosophers. It was thought—by Plato, by Aristotle, by St. Thomas Aquinas, and by many others as well—that the universe was at bottom rationally comprehensible because it had a rational structure. This structure was conceived either as inherent in the nature of things or as springing from a divine plan, but in either case philosophers argued that we human beings could know the fundamental order or structure of the universe because our own power of reason mirrored that structure. In effect, it was supposed that there was a fit between the inner, subjective structure of human reason and the outer, objective rational order of the universe. The rational objective order manifested itself in various ways: in patterns of regularities in the observable behavior of heavenly bodies and earthly objects; in the apparent purposiveness with which the parts of living things fitted together; in the stability and timeless order of the elements or building blocks of the universe.

This rational structure was reflected in certain features of human thought and language. Logical thought followed the order of rational nature, expressing itself in the form of laws of nature to which objects conformed. The very structure of language—the syntactical relationships of subject to predicate—seemed to echo the structure of reason and nature. Logic, the science of correct thought, was thus also a clue to ontology, the science of being.

In this vision of the parallel orders of being, of thought, and of language, God plays an absolutely fundamental role. As the Creator of all things, the necessary Being, the highest Being, the infinite Being, God is clearly the first and most important element in any rational ontology or science of being. And since our rational knowledge reflects the structure of being, our *knowledge of God* must similarly play a fundamental role in the system of human knowledge.

Just as God is the first Being, so the knowledge of God must be the rationally first knowledge, and the statement, "God is," must be the logically first proposition, the proposition best known, first established, and highest in the system of propositions constituting the expression of man's knowledge of the universe.

So, not from the point of view of the solitary, tortured Jew or Christian hungering after certainty and anxious for salvation, but from the point of view of the rational metaphysician searching for the logically fundamental basis on which to erect a sound system of knowledge of the universe, the establishment of the existence of God must take logical precedence over all other philosophical tasks. Just as the logician must be sure of his premises before he begins the deduction of his theorems, so the rational theologian or metaphysician must make certain his basic ontological premise before moving on to the subordinate examination of the nature of space and time, the laws of causation, the relation of God to the created universe, and the role of human beings in that universe.

The device employed by countless philosophers to establish the foundations of their ontology is a proof of the existence of an infinite and necessary being, or God. Enormous ingenuity has been lavished on these proofs by philosophers, from Aristotle in ancient Greece, to Spinoza in seventeenth-century Holland. No one, as we have seen, imagined that any of these proofs would create religious faith—an inner certainty in the trustworthiness of God's revealed promise—but many of the most powerful and creative philosophers believed that one or another of the proofs for the existence of God could serve as the starting place for the development of a rational metaphysical system of knowledge of the universe.

By and large, the proofs advanced by philosophers fall into two groups: those which begin from some fact or set of facts about the universe that are attested to by observation; and those which eschew all "empirical" or observational data and seek to develop a proof for the existence of God out of nothing more than an analysis of the *concept* or *idea* of a divine being. Now, you might think that proofs of the first sort put the cart before the horse. If the existence of God is to be the first, the fundamental, premise of all rational knowledge, then how can one possibly base a proof of that existence on *other* facts, facts whose certainty is presumably based in turn on the certainty of God's existence? Is this not merely reasoning in a circle?

Some philosophers have thought so, but many others have not. They have accepted Aristotle's argument that there is a difference between the order in which we come to know something and its place in the body of knowledge we thereby arrive at. The first things a doctor sees are the external symptoms of a disease. Only after many tests and long study does he come to recognize those symptoms as effects of some inner disorder. From the point of view of medical knowledge, the inner disorder is prior in the order of being, even though the symptoms are prior in the order of knowing (that is to say, the doctor knew about them before he understood their significance and causes). In an analogous way, philosophers have argued that even though a proof of God's existence begins with readily known facts of everyday experience, it may still establish a proposition (that God exists) that is absolutely first in the order of being.

Proofs of the second sort—proofs, that is, beginning merely with the idea of God—are among the most mysterious and challenging in all of philosophy. How, we might wonder, can one establish the *existence* of something with nothing more to work from than the mere *idea* of that thing? Surely a very powerful and special sort of argument will be needed to accomplish so unlikely a result! Not surprisingly, many philosophers have thought that such an enterprise was intrinsically impossible, but as you will discover in the readings in this chapter, the attempt is far from dead. The "Ontological Argument," as it is called, has had its defenders and its critics for a thousand years, and it seems still to be able to enlist sophisticated philosophers in its defense.

When we look at the subject of religion from the viewpoint of the individual believer, we find that there are an endless number of ways of being religious, and a wide variety of experiences that can legitimately be called "religious." Indeed, one of the perennial problems for the believer is precisely to distinguish between experiences that are truly encounters with the divine and experiences that are mere fantasies or counterfeit encounters. The use of drugs as a part of religious ceremonies is as ancient as religion itself, and in many cultures the priests or especially holy ones deliberately use hallucinogenic substances to induce states of consciousness that are believed to be encounters with, or true experiences of, the divine. Twenty years ago, when increasing numbers of Americans started to take such drugs, the old questions arose once more. Were the "trips" one took under the influence of drugs flights from reality or soaring ascensions to a higher and truer reality? We shall take a look at some answers to that question in this chapter.

Even more central to the religious experience of the Judeo-Christian tradition than drug-induced states of altered consciousness are the various "tests of faith" posed either by life or by religious doctrine. One of the most familiar and unsettling of these tests is the problem of reconciling the manifest evils of this world with the supposed goodness and omnipotence of God. For the believer, the existence of evil is a perpetually troubling mystery. If God loves us, and is infinitely powerful, could He not have arranged His universe so that the wicked did not so often flourish and the pious suffer? Are death and disfigurement, famine, plague, and the terrors of age really good and necessary elements of His plan for us? Can I truly love and worship a Being who creates such a universe? We shall grapple with that problem as well, although no one, I think, could promise to answer such questions to everyone's satisfaction.

But at the heart of all religious experience lies the question before all other questions: How do I stand with God? What is my relationship to the divine Being? What does He require of me, and how do I answer when He calls me? In the Old Testament, one of the most powerful presentations of that fateful question is to be found in the story of the patriarch Abraham and his response to God's command that he offer up his only son, Isaac, as a blood sacrifice to the Lord. In the moving exploration of the meaning of that event by the great Danish philosopher Søren Kierkegaard, we reach the most profound depths of the religious experience. It is, I think a fitting way to conclude this book.

(SELECTION 1)

ST. THOMAS AQUINAS

Five Ways to Prove That God Exists

The first formal *proof* of the existence of a Highest Being, in the strict sense of the word "proof," can be found in the writings of the ancient Greek philosopher Aristotle. Aristotle's proof takes the form of a demonstration that there must be a first or prime mover of things, given the fact that there manifestly is motion of various sorts in the world. He thus uses his proof as the philosophical basis for an explanation of the fact of change or motion.

Aristotle's philosophical works had a powerful influence on early medieval Arabic thought, which was, for many centuries, considerably more advanced than its Western European counterpart. Eventually, through the movement of Arabic philosophical works into European circles, Aristotle's philosophy was reintroduced into the mainstream of Christian theology, where it was taken up most systematically and fruitfully by St. Thomas Aquinas, the foremost rational theologian of Christianity.

As you can see from this selection, Aquinas starts with Aristotle's proof, and then moves on to develop four more proofs, all of which begin with some fact or facts about the world and then argue backwards to the existence of an infinite Being through whose nature we can explain the observed facts. Aquinas in this way follows Aristotle's suggestion that we begin with what is best known to us and reason ultimately to what is best known, or most fundamental, in itself.

Arguments of this sort have come to be called "Cosmological Arguments" for God's existence. Aquinas was aware of the "Ontological Argument," which takes as its starting point nothing more than the mere idea or concept of God, but he thought that argument was not valid and he did not include it in his list of proofs of the existence of God.

When you undertake to subject an argument to critical examination, there are at least three different questions that you must answer. Since Aquinas doesn't devote many words to each of his proofs, it may help you to keep these questions in mind as you read through this brief selection, testing each of the proofs to see whether it can provide answers to these questions.

First, ask whether the key terms in the argument are clear. Do we know what Aquinas means by "God," by "efficient cause," by the terms "possible" and "necessary"? Second, are the premises of the argument clear and do we agree that they are true? If the premises are questionable, then even the best argument will leave us uncertain as to the truth of the conclusion that God exists. Finally, are there gaps in the arguments, things assumed that are not actually spelled out?

Remember, if you understand the terms of the proof, and grant the truth of the premises, and acknowledge that the argument itself is sound, then by all rights you ought to accept the conclusion!

We proceed thus to the Third Article:—

Objection 1   It seems that God does not exist; because if one of two contraries be infinite, the other would be altogether destroyed. But the name *God* means that He is infinite goodness. If, therefore, God existed, there would be no evil discoverable; but there is evil in the world. Therefore God does not exist.

Objection 2   Further, it is superfluous to suppose that what can be accounted for by a few principles has been produced by many. But it seems that everything we see in the world can be accounted for by other principles, supposing God did not exist. For all natural things can be reduced to one principle, which is nature; and all voluntary things can be reduced to one principle, which is human reason, or will. Therefore there is no need to suppose God's existence.

On the contrary, It is said in the person of God: *I am Who am* (*Exod.* iii. 14).

I answer that, The existence of God can be proved in five ways.

The first and more manifest way is the argument from motion. It is certain, and evident to our senses, that in the world some things are in motion. Now whatever is moved is moved by another, for nothing can be moved except it is in potentiality to that towards which it is moved; whereas a thing moves inasmuch as it is in act. For motion is nothing else than the reduction of something from potentiality to actuality. But nothing can be reduced from potentiality to actuality, except by something in a state of actuality. Thus that which is actually hot, as fire, makes wood, which is potentially hot, to be actually hot, and thereby moves and changes it. Now it is not possible that the same thing should be at once in actuality and potentiality in the same respect, but only in different respects. For what is actually hot cannot simultaneously be potentially hot; but it is simultaneously potentially cold. It is therefore impossible that in the same respect and in the same way a thing should be both mover and moved, i.e., that it should move itself. Therefore, whatever is moved must be moved by another. If that by which it is moved be itself moved, then this also must needs be moved by another, and that by another again. But this cannot go on to infinity, because then there would be no first mover, and, consequently, no other mover,

From *Summa Theologica*, Part I, by St. Thomas Aquinas (in St. Thomas Aquinas, *Basic Writings,* ed. by Anton Pegis. New York: Random House, 1945. Reprinted by permission of Random House and Burns & Oates, London.)

seeing that subsequent movers move only inasmuch as they are moved by the first mover; as the staff moves only because it is moved by the hand. Therefore it is necessary to arrive at a first mover, moved by no other; and this everyone understands to be God.

The second way is from the nature of efficient cause. In the world of sensible things we find there is an order of efficient causes. There is no case known (neither is it, indeed, possible) in which a thing is found to be the efficient cause of itself; for so it would be prior to itself, which is impossible. Now in efficient causes it is not possible to go on to infinity, because in all efficient causes following in order, the first is the cause of the intermediate cause, and the intermediate is the cause of the ultimate cause, whether the intermediate cause be several, or one only. Now to take away the cause is to take away the effect. Therefore, if there be no first cause among efficient causes, there will be no ultimate, nor any intermediate, cause. But if in efficient causes it is possible to go on to infinity, there will be no first efficient cause, neither will there be an ultimate effect, nor any intermediate efficient causes; all of which is plainly false. Therefore it is necessary to admit a first efficient cause, to which everyone gives the name of God.

The third way is taken from possibility and necessity, and runs thus. We find in nature things that are possible to be and not to be, since they are found to be generated, and to be corrupted, and consequently, it is possible for them to be and not to be. But it is impossible for these always to exist, for that which can not be at some time is not. Therefore, if everything can not-be, then at one time there was nothing in existence. Now if this were true, even now there would be nothing in existence, because that which does not exist begins to exist only through something already existing. Therefore, if at one time nothing was in existence, it would have been impossible for anything to have begun to exist; and thus even now nothing would be in existence—which is absurd. Therefore, not all beings are merely possible, but here must exist something the existence of which is necessary. But every necessary thing either has its necessity caused by another, or not. Now it is impossible to go on to infinity in necessary things which have their necessity caused by another, as has been already proved in regard to efficient causes. Therefore we cannot but admit the existence of some being having of itself its own necessity, and not receiving it from another, but rather causing in others their necessity. This all men speak of as God.

The fourth way is taken from the gradation to be found in things. Among beings there are some more and some less good, true, noble, and the like. But *more* and *less* are predicated of different things according as they resemble in their different ways something which is the maximum, as a thing is said to be hotter according as it more nearly resembles that which is hottest; so that there is something which is truest, something best, something noblest, and, consequently, something which is most being, for those things that are greatest in truth are greatest in being. . . . Now the maximum in any genus is the cause of all in that genus, as fire, which is the maximum of heat, is the cause of all hot things. . . . Therefore there must also be something which is to all beings the cause of their being, goodness, and every other perfection; and this we call God.

The fifth way is taken from the governance of the world. We see that things which lack knowledge, such as natural bodies, act for an end, and this is evident from their acting always, or nearly always, in the same way, so as to obtain the best result. Hence it is plain that they achieve their end, not fortuitously, but designedly. Now whatever lacks knowledge cannot move towards an end, unless it be directed by some being endowed with knowledge and intelligence; as the arrow is directed by the archer. Therefore some intelligent being exists by whom all natural things are directed to their end; and this being we call God.

AQUINAS SELECTION

1. The key to Aquinas's first proof is the claim that the regress of movers "cannot go on to infinity." What does Aquinas mean by this statement? Why can't the backward tracing of movers go on to infinity?

2. The second proof, from the nature of "efficient causes," seems virtually the same as the first proof. What is an "efficient cause"? What difference is there between the first and second proofs? Is something that moves something else an efficient cause of that motion? If you do not think that there is a "first cause" of all things, then how do you explain the existence of the universe? Does the fact of the universe need an explanation? Why? Does it explain the fact of the universe to say that God created it?

3. The third proof, from possibility and necessity, is quite tricky. The key here is the assertion that "that which can not-be at some time is not." What does Aquinas mean by this assertion? How might he defend it? Can you think of a way of putting the same point in terms of probabilities? What does it mean to say that the existence of something is "necessary"?

4. The last proof, the so-called "argument from design," will be taken up at length in a later selection. Can you figure out what the argument is saying from Aquinas's very brief statement? Do things in the world seem to you to "act for an end"? What does that mean?

(SELECTION 2)

ST. ANSELM AND GAUNILO

The Ontological Argument

Well, here it is, probably the most notorious argument in the history of philosophy—the Ontological Argument for the Existence of God, as it is called. St. Anselm appears to have been the inventor or discoverer of this very special argument. Subsequently, it was taken up by the three great figures of seventeenth- and eighteenth-century Continental rationalism, Descartes, Spinoza, and Leibniz. It was subjected to brief but devasting criticism by David Hume and to extended and even more powerful attack by Immanuel Kant, who together appeared to have laid it permanently to rest. In recent decades, however, the Ontological Argument has made a dramatic comeback, thanks to some very sophisticated re-analyses of it by modern logicians. At the present time, I think it is fair to say that philosophers are fascinated by it, even mesmerized by it, but not really persuaded by it. In short, they are in precisely the same condition as St. Anselm's contemporaries.

The first stumbling block that we must overcome in attempting to understand the Ontological Argument is the notion of *existence* that St. Anselm is employing. God does not exist in the same way that created things exist. He exists eternally; He exists in total independence of all else; He neither came into existence nor can he go out of existence. These facts are sometimes summarized in the assertion that God exists necessarily, or—and this may or may not be the same thing—that He has *necessary existence.* Nothing else exists in the same way, and it is at least initially plausible, therefore, that a proof of God's existence will be quite unlike a proof of the existence of anything else.

The second difficulty with Anselm's proof is the claim that we all possess the concept of God with which Anselm is working. There is no doubt that we are all familiar with the word "God," whether we are believers or not, just as we are all familiar with the words "ghost" and "unicorn" and "man from Mars." But how do we go about determining whether we possess a *concept* or *idea* corresponding to that word? Anselm's argument depends on our actually having an idea of "that, than which nothing greater can be conceived." As you shall discover in reading these selections, it is extremely unclear whether we do indeed have such a concept, or whether we merely string the words together in what looks like a grammatical fashion.

There is one final question worth considering, even though it is not directly related to the debate over the Ontological Argument. This and other

508

proofs of the existence of God aim at establishing that there is an infinite Being, a Being greater than which none can be conceived, a Being that is necessarily existent, cause of all that occurs in the world, originator of all motion, etc. Is that Being God? Is that the Divine Person to whom the devout pray? What relation can we make out between the impersonal, metaphysically remote entity of formal philosophical theology and the God of Abraham, or Jesus upon the Cross?

St. Anselm's Ontological Argument

Truly there is a God, although the fool hath said in his heart, There is no God.

And so, Lord, do thou, who dost give understanding to faith, give me, so far as thou knowest it to be profitable, to understand that thou art as we believe; and that thou art that which we believe. And, indeed, we believe that thou art a being than which nothing greater can be conceived. Or is there no such nature, since the fool hath said in his heart, there is no God? (Psalm xiv. 1.) But, at any rate, this very fool, when he hears of this being of which I speak—a being than which nothing greater can be conceived—understands what he hears, and what he understands is in his understanding; although he does not understand it to exist.

For, it is one thing for an object to be in the understanding, and another to understand that the object exists. When a painter first conceives of what he will afterwards perform, he has it in his understanding, but he does not yet understand it to be, because he has not yet performed it. But after he has made the painting, he both has it in his understanding, and he understands that it exists, because he has made it.

Hence, even the fool is convinced that something exists in the understanding, at least, than which nothing greater can be conceived. For, when he hears of this, he understands it. And whatever is understood, exists in the understanding. And assuredly that, than which nothing greater can be conceived, cannot exist in the understanding alone. For, suppose it exists in the understanding alone: then it can be conceived to exist in reality; which is greater.

Therefore, if that, than which nothing greater can be conceived, exists in the understanding alone, the very being, than which nothing greater can be conceived is one, than which a greater can be conceived. But obviously this is impossible. Hence, there is no doubt that there exists a being, than which nothing greater can be conceived, and it exists both in the understanding and in reality.

From *The Basic Writings of Saint Thomas Aquinas*, Proslogian and In Behalf of the Fool. (ed. by Anton C. Pegis, New York: Random House, Inc., 1945.)

God cannot be conceived not to exist.—God is that, than which nothing greater can be conceived.—That which can be conceived not to exist is not God.

And it assuredly exists so truly, that it cannot be conceived not to exist. For, it is possible to conceive of a being which cannot be conceived not to exist; and this is greater than one which can be conceived not to exist. Hence, if that, than which nothing greater can be conceived, can be conceived not to exist, it is not that, than which nothing greater can be conceived. But this is an irreconcilable contradiction. There is, then, so truly a being than which nothing greater can be conceived to exist, that it cannot even be conceived not to exist; and this being thou art, O Lord, our God.

So truly, therefore, dost thou exist, O Lord, my God, that thou canst not be conceived not to exist; and rightly. For, if a mind could conceive of a being better than thee, the creature would rise above the Creator; and this is most absurd. And, indeed, whatever else there is, except thee alone, can be conceived not to exist. To thee alone, therefore, it belongs to exist more truly than all other beings, and hence in a higher degree than all others. For, whatever else exists does not exist so truly, and hence in a less degree it belongs to it to exist. Why, then, has the fool said in his heart, there is no God (Psalm xiv. 1), since it is so evident, to a rational mind, that thou dost exist in the highest degree of all? Why, except that he is dull and a fool?

How the fool has said in his heart what cannot be conceived. —A thing may be conceived in two ways: (1) when the word signifying it is conceived; (2) when the thing itself is understood. As far as the word goes, God can be conceived not to exist; in reality he cannot.

But how has the fool said in his heart what he could not conceive; or how is it that he could not conceive what he said in his heart? since it is the same to say in the heart, and to conceive.

But, if really, nay, since really, he both conceived, because he said in his heart; and did not say in his heart, because he could not conceive; there is more than one way in which a thing is said in the heart or conceived. For, in one sense, an object is conceived, when the word signifying it is conceived; and in other, when the very entity, which the object is, is understood.

In the former sense, then, God can be conceived not to exist; but in the latter, not at all. For no one who understands what fire and water are can conceive fire to be water, in accordance with the nature of the facts themselves, although this is possible according to the words. So, then, no one who understands what God is can conceive that God does not exist, although he says these words in his heart, either without any, or with some foreign, signification. For, God is that than which a greater cannot be conceived. And he who thoroughly understands this, assuredly understands that this being so truly exists, that not even in concept can it be non-existent. Therefore, he who understands that God so exists, cannot conceive that he does not exist.

I thank thee, gracious Lord, I thank thee; because what I formerly believed by thy bounty, I now so understand by thine illumination, that if I were unwilling to believe that thou dost exist, I should not be able not to understand this to be true.

Guanilo (dates unknown):
In Behalf of the Fool

1. If one doubts or denies the existence of a being of such a nature that nothing greater than it can be conceived, he receives this answer:

The existence of this being is proved, in the first place, by the fact that he himself, in his doubt or denial regarding this being, already has it in his understanding; for in hearing it spoken of he understands what is spoken of. It is proved, therefore, by the fact that what he understands must exist not only in his understanding, but in reality also.

And the proof of this is as follows.—It is a greater thing to exist both in the understanding and in reality than to be in the understanding alone. And if this being is in the understanding alone, whatever has even in the past existed in reality will be greater than this being. And so that which was greater than all beings will be less than some being, and will not be greater than all: which is a manifest contradiction.

And hence, that which is greater than all, already proved to be in the understanding, must exist not only in the understanding, but also in reality: for otherwise it will not be greater than all other beings.

2. The fool might make this reply:

This being is said to be in my understanding already, only because I understand what is said. Now could it not with equal justice be said that I have in my understanding all manner of unreal objects, having absolutely no existence in themselves, because I understand these things if one speaks of them, whatever they may be?

Unless indeed it is shown that this being is of such a character that it cannot be held in concept like all unreal objects, or objects whose existence is uncertain: and hence I am not able to conceive of it when I hear of it, or to hold it in concept; but I must understand it and have it in my understanding; because, it seems, I cannot conceive of it in any other way than by understanding it, that is, by comprehending in my knowledge its existence in reality.

But if this is the case, in the first place there will be no distinction between what has precedence in time—namely, the having of an object in the understanding—and what is subsequent in time—namely, the understanding that an object exists; as in the example of the picture, which exists first in the mind of the painter, and afterwards in his work.

Moreover, the following assertion can hardly be accepted: that this being, when it is spoken of and heard of, cannot be conceived not to exist in the way in which even God can be conceived not to exist. For if this is impossible, what was the object of this argument against one who doubts or denies the existence of such a being?

Finally, that this being so exists that it cannot be perceived by an understanding convinced of its own indubitable existence, unless this being is afterwards conceived of—this should be proved to me by an indisputable argument, but not by that which you have advanced: namely, that what I understand, when I hear it, already is in my understanding. For thus in my understanding, as I still think, could be all sorts of things whose existence is uncertain, or which do not exist at all, if some one whose words I should understand mentioned them. And so much the more if I should be deceived, as often happens, and believe in them: though I do not yet believe in the being whose existence you would prove.

3. Hence, your example of the painter who already has in his understanding what he is to paint cannot agree with this argument. For the picture, before it is made, is contained in the artificer's art itself; and any such thing, existing in the art of an artificer, is nothing but a part of his understanding itself. A joiner, St. Augustine says, when he is about to make a box in fact, first has it in his art. The box which is made in fact is not life; but the box which exists in his art is life. For the artificer's soul lives, in which all these things are, before they are produced. Why, then, are these things life in the living soul of the artificer, unless because they are nothing else than the knowledge or understanding of the soul itself?

With the exception, however, of those facts which are known to pertain to the mental nature, whatever, on being heard and thought out by the understanding, is perceived to be real, undoubtedly that real object is one thing, and the understanding itself, by which the object is grasped, is another. Hence, even if it were true that there is a being than which a greater in inconceivable: yet to this being, when heard of and understood, the not yet created picture in the mind of the painter is not analogous.

4. Let us notice also the point touched on above, with regard to this being which is greater than all which can be conceived, and which, it is said, can be none other than God himself. I, so far as actual knowledge of the object, either from its specific or general character, is concerned, am as little able to conceive of this being when I hear of it, or to have it in my understanding, as I am to conceive of or understand God himself: whom, indeed, for this very reason I can conceive not to exist. For I do not know that reality itself which God is, nor can I form a conjecture of that reality from some other like reality. For you yourself assert that that reality is such that there can be nothing else like it.

For, suppose that I should hear something said of a man absolutely unknown to me, of whose very existence I was unaware. Through that special or general knowledge by which I know what man is, or what men are, I could conceive of him also, according to the reality itself, which man is. And yet it would be possible, if the person who told me of him deceived me, that the man himself, of whom I conceived, did not exist; since that reality according to which I conceived of him, though a no less indisputable fact, was not that man, but any man.

Hence, I am not able, in the way in which I should have this unreal being in concept or in understanding, to have that being of which you speak in concept or in understanding, when I hear the word *God* or the words, *a being greater than all other beings.* For I can conceive of the man according to a fact that is real and familiar to me: but of God, or a being greater than all others, I could not conceive at all, except merely according to the word. And an object can hardly or never be conceived according to the word alone.

For when it is so conceived, it is not so much the word itself (which is, indeed, a real thing—that is, the sound of the letters and syllables) as the signification of the word, when heard, that is conceived. But it is not conceived as by one who knows what is generally signified by the word; by whom, that is, it is conceived according to a reality and in true conception alone. It is conceived as by a man who does not know the object, and conceives of it only in accordance with the movement of his mind produced by hearing the word, the mind attempting to image for itself the signification of the word that is heard. And it would be surprising if in the reality of fact it could ever attain to this.

Thus, it appears, and in no other way, this being is also in my understanding, when I hear and understand a person who says that there is a being greater than all conceivable beings. So much for the assertion that this supreme nature already is in my understanding.

5. But that this being must exist, not only in the understanding but also in reality, is thus proved to me:

If it did not so exist, whatever exists in reality would be greater than it. And so the being which has been already proved to exist in my understanding, will not be greater than all other beings.

I still answer: if it should be said that a being which cannot be even conceived in terms of any fact, is in the understanding, I do not deny that this being is, accordingly, in my understanding. But since through this fact it can in no wise attain to real existence also, I do not yet concede to it that existence at all, until some certain proof of it shall be given.

For he who says that this being exists, because otherwise the being which is greater than all will not be greater than all, does not attend strictly enough to what he is saying. For I do not yet say, no, I even deny or doubt that this being is greater than any real object. Nor do I concede to it any other existence than this (if it should be called existence) which it has when the mind, according to a word merely heard, tries to form the image of an object absolutely unknown to it.

How, then, is the veritable existence of that being proved to me from the assumption, by hypothesis, that it is greater than all other beings? For I should still deny this, or doubt yor demonstration of it, to this extent, that I should not admit that this being is in my understanding and concept even in the way in which many objects whose real existence is uncertain and doubtful, are in my understanding and concept. For it should be proved first that this being itself really exists somewhere; and then, from the fact that it is greater than all, we shall not hesitate to infer that it also subsists in itself.

6. For example: it is said that somewhere in the ocean is an island, which, because of the difficulty, or rather the impossibility, of discovering what does not exist, is called the lost island. And they say that this island has an inestimable wealth of all manner of riches and delicacies in greater abundance than is told of the Islands of the Blest; and that having no owner or inhabitant, it is more excellent than all other countries, which are inhabited by mankind, in the abundance with which it is stored.

Now if some one should tell me that there is such an island, I should easily understand his words, in which there is no difficulty. But suppose that he went on to say, as if by a logical inference: "You can no longer doubt that this island which is more excellent than all lands exists somewhere, since you have no doubt that it is in your understanding. And since it is more excellent not to be in the understanding alone, but to exist both in the understanding and in reality, for this reason it must exist. For if it does not exist, any land which really exists will be more excellent than it; and so the island already understood by you to be more excellent will not be more excellent."

If a man should try to prove to me by such reasoning that this island truly exists, and that its existence should no longer be doubted, either I should believe that he was jesting, or I know not which I ought to regard as the greater fool: myself, supposing that I should allow this proof; or him, if he should suppose that he had established with any certainty the existence of this island. For he ought to show first that the hypothetical excellence of this island exists as a real and indubitable fact, and in no wise as any unreal object, or one whose existence is uncertain, in my understanding.

7. This, in the mean time, is the answer the fool could make to the arguments urged against him. When he is assured in the first place that this being is so great that its non-existence is not even conceivable, and that this in turn is proved on no other ground than the fact that otherwise it will not be greater than all things, the fool may make the same answer, and say:

When did I say that any such being exists in reality, that is, a being greater than all others?—that on this ground it should be proved to me that it also exists in reality to such a degree that it cannot even be conceived not to exist? Whereas in the first place it should be in some way proved that a nature which is higher, that is, greater and better, than all other natures, exists; in order that from this we may then be able to prove all attributes which necessarily the being that is greater and better than all possesses.

Moreover, it is said that the non-existence of this being is inconceivable. It might better be said, perhaps, that its non-existence, or the possibility of its non-existence, is unintelligible. For according to the true meaning of the word, unreal objects are unintelligible. Yet their existence is conceivable in the way in which the fool conceived of the non-existence of God. I am most certainly aware of my own existence; but I know, nevertheless, that my non-existence is possible. As to that supreme being, moreover, which God is, I understand without any doubt both his existence, and the impossibiliy of his non-existence. Whether, however, so long as I am most positively aware of my existence, I can conceive of my non-existence, I am not sure. But if I can, why can I not conceive of the non-existence of whatever else I know with the same certainty? If, however, I cannot, God will not be the only being of which it can be said, it is impossible to conceive of his non-existence.

8. The other parts of this book are argued with such truth, such brilliancy, such grandeur; and are so replete with usefulness, so fragrant with a certain perfume of devout and holy feeling, that though there are matters in the beginning which, however rightly sensed,

are weakly presented, the rest of the work should not be rejected on this account. The rather ought these earlier matters to be reasoned more cogently, and the whole to be received with great respect and honor.

St. Anselm's Reply to Gaunilo

It was a fool against whom the argument of my Proslogium was directed. Seeing, however, that the author of these objections is by no means a fool, and is a Catholic, speaking in behalf of the fool, I think it sufficient that I answer the Catholic.

You say—whosoever you may be, who say that a fool is capable of making these statements—that a being than which a greater cannot be conceived is not in the understanding in any other sense than that in which a being that is altogether inconceivable in terms of reality, is in the understanding. You say that the inference that this being exists in reality, from the fact that it is in the understanding, is no more just than the inference that a lost island most certainly exists, from the fact that when it is described the hearer does not doubt that it is in his understanding.

But I say: if a being than which a greater is inconceivable is not understood or conceived, and is not in the understanding or in concept, certainly either God is not a being than which a greater is inconceivable, or else he is not understood or conceived, and is not in the understanding or in concept. But I call on your faith and conscience to attest that this is most false. Hence, that than which a greater cannot be conceived is truly understood and conceived, and is in the understanding and in concept. Therefore either the grounds on which you try to controvert me are not true, or else the inference which you think to base logically on those grounds is not justified.

But you hold, moreover, that supposing that a being than which a greater cannot be conceived is understood, it does not follow that this being is in the understanding; nor, if it is in the understanding, does it therefore exist in reality.

In answer to this, I maintain positively: if that being can be even conceived to be, it must exist in reality. For that than which a greater is inconceivable cannot be conceived except as without beginning. But whatever can be conceived to exist, and does not exist, can be conceived to exist through a beginning. Hence what can be conceived to exist, but does not exist, is not the being than which a greater cannot be conceived. Therefore, if such a being can be conceived to exist, necessarily it does exist.

Furthermore: if it can be conceived at all, it must exist. For no one who denies or doubts the existence of a being than which a greater is inconceivable, denies or doubts that if it did exist, its non-existence, either in reality or in the understanding, would be impossible. For otherwise it would not be a being than which a greater cannot be conceived. But as to whatever can be conceived, but does not exist—if there were such a being, its non-existence, either in reality or in the understanding, would be possible. Therefore if a being than which a greater is inconceivable can be even conceived, it cannot be non-existent.

But let us suppose that it does not exist, even if it can be conceived. Whatever can be conceived, but does not exist, if it existed, would not be a being than which a greater is inconceivable. If, then, there were a being a greater than which is inconceivable, it would not be a being than which a greater is inconceivable: which is most absurd. Hence, it is false to deny that a being than which a greater cannot be conceived exists, if it can be even conceived; much the more, therefore, if it can be understood or can be in the understanding.

Moreover, I will venture to make this assertion: without doubt, whatever an any place or at any time does not exist—even if it does exist at some place or at some time—can be conceived to exist nowhere and never, as at some place and at some time it does not exist. For what did not exist yesterday, and exists to-day, as it is understood not to have existed yesterday, so it can be apprehended by the intelligence that it ever exists. And what is not here, and is elsewhere, can be conceived to be nowhere, just as it is not here. So with regard to an object of which the individual parts do not exist at the same places or times: all it parts and therefore its very whole can be conceived to exist nowhere or never.

For, although time is said to exist always, and the world everywhere, yet time does not as a whole exist always, nor the world as a whole everywhere. And as individual parts of time do not exist when others exist, so they can be conceived never to exist. And so it can be apprehended by the intelligence that individual parts of the world exist nowhere, as they do not exist where other parts exist. Moreover, what is composed of parts can be dissolved in concept, and be non-existent. Therefore, whatever at any place or at any time does not exist as a whole, even if it is existent, can be conceived not to exist.

But that than which a greater cannot be conceived, if it exists, cannot be conceived not to exist. Otherwise, it is not a being than which a greater cannot be conceived: which is inconsistent. By no means, then, does it at any place or at any time fail to exist as a whole: but it exists as a whole everywhere and always.

Do you believe that this being can in some way be conceived or understood, or that the being with regard to which these things are understood can be in concept or in the understanding? For if it cannot, these things cannot be understood with reference to it. But if you say that it is not understood and that it is not in the understanding, because it is not thoroughly understood; you should say that a man who cannot face the direct rays of the sun does not see the light of day, which is none other than the sunlight. Assuredly a being than which a greater cannot be conceived exists, and is in the understanding, at least to this extent—that these statements regarding are understood.

I have said, then, in the argument which you dispute, that when the fool hears mentioned a being than which a greater is inconceivable, he understands what he hears. Certainly a man who does not understand when a familiar language is spoken, has no understanding at all, or a very dull one. Moreover, I have said that if this being is understood, it is in the understanding. Is that in no understanding which has been proved necessarily to exist in the reality of fact?

But you will say that although it is in the understanding, it does not follow that it is understood. But observe that the fact of its being understood does necessitate its being in the understanding. For as what is conceived, is conceived by conception, and what is conceived by conception, as it is conceived, so is in conception; so what is understood, is understood by understanding, and what is understood by understanding, as it is understood, so is in the understanding. What can be more clear than this?

After this, I have said that if it is even in the understanding alone, it can be conceived also to exist in reality, which is greater. If, then, it is in the understanding alone, obviously the very being than which a greater cannot be conceived is one than which a greater can be conceived. What is more logical? For if it exists even in the understanding alone, can it not be conceived also to exist in reality? And if it can be so conceived, does not he who conceives of this conceive of a thing greater than that being, if it exists in the understanding alone? What more consistent inference, then, can be made than this: that if a being than which a greater cannot be conceived is in the understanding alone, it is not that than which a greater cannot be conceived?

But, assuredly, in no understanding is a being than which a greater is conceivable a being that which a greater is inconceivable. Does it not follow, then, that if a being than which a greater cannot be conceived is in any understanding, it does not exist in the understanding alone? For if it is in the understanding alone, it is a being than which a greater can be conceived, which is inconsistent with the hypothesis.

But, you say, it is as if one should suppose an island in the ocean, which surpasses all lands in its fertility, and which, because of the difficulty, or rather the impossibility, of discovering what does not exist, is called a lost island; and should say that there can be no doubt that this island truly exists in reality, for this reason, that one who hears it described easily understands what he hears.

Now I promise confidently that if any man shall devise anything existing either in reality or in concept alone (except that than which a greater cannot be conceived) to which he can adapt the sequence of my reasoning, I will discover that thing, and will give him his lost island, not to be lost again.

But it now appears that this being than which a greater is inconceivable cannot be conceived not to be, because it exists on so assured a ground of truth; for otherwise it would not exist at all.

Hence, if any one says that he conceives this being not to exist, I say that at the time when he conceives of this either he conceives of a being than which a greater is inconceivable, or he does not conceive at all. If he does not conceive, he does not conceive of the non-existence of that of which he does not conceive. But if he does conceive, he certainly conceives of a being which cannot be even conceived not to exist. For if it could be conceived not to exist, it could be conceived to have a beginning and an end. But this is impossible.

He, then, who conceives of this being conceives of a being which cannot be even conceived not to exist; but he who conceives of this being does not conceive that it does not exist; else he conceives what is inconceivable. The non-existence, then, of that than which a greater cannot be conceived is inconceivable.

You say, moreover, that whereas I assert that this supreme being cannot be *conceived* not to exist, it might better be said that its non-existence, or even the possibility of its non-existence, cannot be *understood*.

But it was more proper to say, it cannot be conceived. For if I had said that the object itself cannot be understood not to exist, possibly you yourself, who say that in accordance with the true meaning of the term what is unreal cannot be understood, would offer the objection that nothing which is can be understood not to be, for the non-existence of what exists is unreal: hence God would not be the only being of which it could be said, it is impossible to understand its non-existence. For thus one of those beings which most certainly exist can be understood not to exist in the same way in which certain other real objects can be understood not to exist.

But this objection, assuredly, cannot be urged against the term *conception*, if one considers the matter well. For although no objects which exist can be understood not to exist, yet all objects, except that which exists in the highest degree, can be conceived not to exist. For all those objects, and those alone, can be conceived not to exist, which have a beginning or end or composition of parts: also, as I have already said, whatever at any place or at any time does not exist as a whole.

That being alone, on the other hand, cannot be conceived not to exist, in which any conception discovers neither beginning nor end nor composition of parts, and which any conception finds always and everywhere as a whole.

Be assured, then, that you can conceive of your own non-existence, although you are most certain that you exist. I am surprised that you should have admitted that you are ignorant of this. For we conceive of the non-existence of many objects which we know to exist, and of the existence of many which we know not to exist; not by forming the opinion that they so exist, but by imagining that they exist as we conceive of them.

And indeed, we can conceive of the non-existence of an object, although we know it to exist, because at the same time we can conceive of the former and know the latter. And we cannot conceive of the non-existence of an object, so long as we know it to exist, because we cannot conceive at the same time of existence and non-existence.

If, then, one will thus distinguish these two senses of this statement, he will understand that nothing, so long as it is known to exist, can be conceived not to exist; and that whatever exists, except that being than which a greater cannot be conceived, can be conceived not to exist, even when it is known to exist.

So, then, of God alone it can be said that it is impossible to conceive of his non-existence; and yet many objects, so long as they exist, in one sense cannot be conceived not to exist. But in what sense God is to be conceived not to exist, I think has been shown clearly enough in my book.

ANSELM AND GAUNILO SELECTION

1. Anselm's argument depends on two concepts, each of which is rather tricky and problematic. The first is the concept of that, than which nothing greater can be conceived. Explain this concept as clearly as you can. Do you have a mental picture of such a thing? If not, how do you form the concept? Could you state a rule for determining whether anything fits the concept?

2.   The second key concept is the notion of something that cannot be conceived not to exist. What does this mean? When we think of something, what is the difference between merely thinking of it and thinking of it as existing?

3.   Anselm insists that his proof depends only on our understanding the meanings of the word used. In what way does this differ from the proofs given by Aquinas? Could Anselm's proof be used to prove the existence of anything besides God? Why?

4.   State as clearly as you can Gaunilo's objections to the proof. Which objection do you think is the strongest? How does Anselm attempt to answer it? Does he succeed? Why?

(SELECTION 3)

CHARLES HARTSHORNE

The Necessarily Existent

In this selection from an even lengthier examination of the Ontological Argument, Charles Hartshorne undertakes to rebut a number of the objections that have been raised both by earlier philosophical critics of the eighteenth century and by contemporary critics. The key to his defense, as you might expect, is the claim that God's existence is unlike the existence of other beings. In effect, Hartshorne argues that we are guilty of a variety of faulty inferences in our attempts to draw conclusions about God's existence from an analysis of the existence of finite, created things.

This approach helps to keep us clear of one of the most common (and most clearly mistaken) objections to the Ontological Argument, namely that if it were valid, it could be used to prove the existence of all manner of things, such as a perfect mountain, a perfect horse, and so on. Hartshorne, following a very ancient tradition in rational theology, holds that there is and could be only *one* perfect being, call it or Him what you will. If there were two perfect beings, the existence of each would constitute a limitation on the other, and hence that other would not be perfect (for perfection is incompatible with limitation). It follows, therefore, that the Ontological Argument can be used to prove the existence of one being, at most.

There is a deeper problem posed by the uniqueness of God's mode of existence to which Hartshorne does not address himself. If God exists in a way utterly unlike that in which we or other created things exist, then surely our cognitive relationship to God must be different in kind from our cognitive relationship to ourselves or other created things. Do we fully understand what it is for us *to know that God exists,* given that He exists necessarily? The ordinary subject-object relationship on which knowledge is based seems not to obtain when the "object" is an infinite, necessarily existent being. Hence, it is at least possible that all our familiar modes of argument and categories of knowledge are inapplicable to this special case.

If the relationship between myself and God is not, in the ordinary sense, a relationship of knower to object known, then possibly the very attempt to provide a proof of the proposition, "God exists" must be given up as misguided. Later on, when we look at the religious thinking of Søren Kierkegaard, we shall find him saying something very much like this.

The ontological argument turns logically upon the unique relation between the possibility and the actuality, the "essence" and the "existence," of God. With ordinary finite ideas the task of knowledge is to decide among three cases: (1) the type of the thing conceived is impossible, and hence non-existent (e.g., a moral being totally without "freedom"); (2) the type of thing is possible, but there is no actual example (a Euclidean space?); (3) the thing is possible, and there is an example (a speaking animal). The ontological argument holds that with the idea of God only two of these three cases need be considered, since one of the three, (2), is meaningless. If, the argument holds, there exists no God, then there also can be no possibility of the existence of a God, and the concept is nonsense, like that of "round square." If, further, it can be shown that the idea of God is not nonsensical, that is must have an at least possible object, then it follows that it has an actual object, since a "merely possible" God is, if the argument is sound, inconceivable. *Where impossibility and mere unactualized possibility are both excluded, there nothing remains but actuality, if the idea has any meaning at all.*

The ontological argument itself does not suffice to exclude the impossibility or meaninglessness of God, but only to exclude his mere possibility. Or, as Leibniz said, it must assume that God is not impossible. (We shall consider presently whether the argument can be extended so as to justify this assumption.) The inventor of the argument, Anselm, took it for granted that the man with religious experience, to whom he addressed his discourse, though he may doubt God's existence, will not easily doubt that in hoping that there is a God he is at least hoping for something with a self-consistent meaning. Now, given a meaning, there must be something which is meant. We do not think just our act of thinking. What we think may not be actual, but can it be less than possible—unless it be a self-contradictory combination of factors, singly and separately possible? In short, when we think, can we fail to refer to something beyond our thought which, either as a whole or in its elements, is at least possible? Granting this, the ontological argument says that, with reference to God, "at least possible" is indistinguishable from "possible *and* actual" (though, as we shall see, "possible" here means simply "not impossible" and has no positive content different from actuality). Let us now present the reasons for the contention that "at least possible" and "actual" are indistinguishable in the case of the divine.

According to one theory of possibility, a given type of entity is possible if the most general features, the strictly generic characters, of existence or of the universe are compatible with the production of such an entity. Thus, there is no contradiction of the most general features of reality in the supposition that nature has really produced Mr. Micawber. There is contradiction of the details of nature (such as the detail that Micawber is a character in a novel written by a highly imaginative author), but these may be supposed otherwise without destroying the meaning, the generic content, of "existence." But the idea of God is the idea of a being everlasting in duration, and independent, in a certain aspect of his being (in his individual "essence"), from everything else. Such a being could not be produced, since he must then be both derivative and underivative, everlasting and yet not everlasting. To create the omniscient, one must endow him with a perfect memory of the past before he existed; to create the omnipotent, one must endow him with incomparably more power, a metaphysically different order of power, than that which created him. It is hardly necessary to prolong the discussion: no theologian holding either type-one or type-two theism has ever rejected that portion of the ontological argument which consists in the proof that *God could not be a mere possibility;* and (as we are about to show) it is demonstrable that in order to reject this proof one must construct a theory of possibility which would not be required for ordinary purposes, so that the tables may be turned upon those who accuse the argument of making God an exception to all principles of knowledge. The argument does make God an exception, but only in the sense that it *deduces* this exceptional status from a generally applicable theory of possibility together with the definition of God. Nothing else is required. The opposition, on the contrary, sets up a general principle which, but for God and the desire to avoid asserting his existence (as following from his possibility), would be without merit.

It might, however, be thought that "possible" need not mean the consistency of the supposition of the thing's being produced, or of its coming into existence due to some cause. Only with one type of thing, it may be held, does "possible" mean this. With another type, consisting of things with universal extent in time, a thing either just always exists or just always lacks existence, either status being possible, although no temporal cause could conceivably effect the difference.

I submit that this is a view so paradoxical that it would hardly be considered at all but for two reasons. One is that it invalidates the ontological argument. The other is that it lends color to the supposition that the laws of nature discoverable by science are eternal laws, although their non-existence is logically possible, and although, as eternal, they could never have been produced, constituting, as they do, the very machinery of all production, the presupposition of all events. The alternative to this supposition about laws is the idea that the laws of nature with which physics deals are themselves produced by the cosmic process, the most general principles of which are beyond "law" in this sense. (There must be some sort of law governing the production of laws, but this higher law is of another order, and may be conceived as the aesthetic principle of the value of order as such, and of the no less real value of a certain element of freedom and disorder, of surprise and novelty, as well as repetition and predictability.) On this view, nothing is possible and at the same time not actual unless at some stage of the cosmic evolution the forces were such that there is no contradiction in the idea of their having taken a turn which sooner or later would have led to the production of the thing in question. Thus, if nature had developed other habits—and who shall say she could not have?—other "laws" would have obtained. But clearly God could not be possible in this way, and he is the *only consistently conceivable object which must be conceived as unproduced,* a reality always existing or never existing or even capable of existing, either in essence uncaused or a mere nonentity. . . .

The question is, Can a possibility be real, unless it would, *if* actual, be an effect of a cause which is real, or the effect of a possible cause which, if actual, would itself be the effect of a cause which . . . (the series ultimately terminating in a cause which is real)? Otherwise, possibility is something wholly apart from actuality, something no experience could ever reveal or evidence support.

I may be told that "logical possibility" is simply self-consistency and that no further reality than this consistency is required. But the reply is that the meanings whose consistency is granted must mean something, and this referent of the meanings is not the consistency but the presupposition of there being any meanings, consistent or otherwise. If a consistent meaning means something, but something not even possible, then it means something very odd indeed. If it means only its own consistency, then it is really meaningless.

Let us be empirical. I may think of any object of any color I choose; will it be denied that an object of this color is consistently conceivable as a production of "nature"? In fact, of course, objects of at least approximately the same color have been actually given in my experience. The step "from thought to reality" is merely the reverse reading of the step from reality to thought without which there is no thought, as the very logicians who attack the ontological argument on the ground that it seeks to "derive existence from a mere idea" would be the first to grant. We are always in contact with the forces which produce realities, and hence we can think both actual and possible objects. Or, in other terms, we can distinguish, in the reality some portion of which is always given to us, between the essential or generic features and the details, and can see that this distinction implies that mutually incompatible details are both or all compatible (separately, though not together) with the generic features. But God is not a detail, and only contradiction results from trying to make his possibility conceivable in the fashion in which alone mere possibility is ever really conceived.

We may go further. The reason God is not a detail, whose existence would be one of two equally conceivable alternatives, is that he is really the content of "existence," the generic factor of the universe. To conceive God is not to conceive what might exist, but what "existence" itself must be—if the idea of God is not meaningless. Either God is nothing at all, or all else that exists exists in and through him, and therefore contingently, and he himself exists (in his essence, though not in his accidents) solely in and through himself, that is, necessarily. The cosmological argument showed that only "God" makes clearly conceivable the flexibility of the generic features of existence by which alternative details of existence can, as alternatives, be real. Alternativeness is one way of looking at creativeness, and the essential or cosmic creativeness is the divine, and nothing else.

Thus to make God's existence exceptional in relation to his conceivability is a result, not a violation, of the general principle of existence. Whatever is merely possible, this possibility as such is real, is other than nothing, only thanks to something which itself is not merely possible but is reality itself as self-identical, or as that which, being the ground of possibility, is more than merely possible. It is an implication of the idea of God that he is that ground.

At some point potentiality and actuality must touch, and at some point meaning must imply existence. God is the general, the cosmic and everlasting, the essential or a priori case of the unity of essence and existence, and he is this because he is supreme potentiality as existing power, a real agent who eternally does one or other of various pairs of alternatives which he "can" do. All meaning implicitly asserts God, because all meaning is nothing less than a reference to one or other of the two aspects of the cosmic reality, what it *has* done or what it *could* do—that is, to the consequent or primordial natures of God.

It has been objected to the ontological argument that existence is not a predicate, and hence cannot be implied by the predicate "perfection." But if existence is not a predicate, yet the *mode* of a thing's existence—its contingency or necessity of existence—is included in every predicate whatever. To be an atom is essentially to be a contingent product of forces which were also capable of not producing the atom, and doubtless for long ages did not do so. Again, contingent existence (the equal compatibility with existence or its negative) is implied by such predicates as those describing a man. His weaknesses imply that it is not true that he is the master of existence, able to exist through his own resources. The strength of God implies the opposite relation to existence. "Self-existence" is a predicate which necessarily and uniquely belongs to Gods, for it is part of the predicate divinity. It is part of the nature of ordinary causes that they are themselves effects of causes which antedate them. It is part of the nature of supreme causality that it is coextensive in time with all causal action. . . . To be God is essentially to be the supreme productive force itself, unproduced and unproducible (except in its accidents) by any force whatsoever. Hence either God is actual, or there is nothing which could be meant by his possible existence. Thus that God's essence should imply his existential status (as contingent or necessary) is not an exception to the rule, but an example of it, since the rule is that contingency or non-contingency of existence follows from the kind of thing in question.

There is another way in which the argument illustrates rather than violates general principles. The argument is not that God's individual nature implies his existence, while other individual natures do not. It may reasonably be held that every individual nature implies existence, and indeed is an existence. By regarding possibilities alone, one can never reach any truly individual character. Individuation and actualization are inseparable by any test, since individuals as such are known only by pointing. Description of contingent things gives always a class quality, unless in the description is included some reference to the space-time world which itself is identified as "this" world, not by description. But "perfection," as we shall see presently, is the one description which defines no class, not even a "one-membered" one, but either nothing or else an individual. If, then, it is true, as it seems to be, that mere possibility is always a matter of class, then the perfect being, which is no class, is either impossible or actual—there being no fourth status.

But if every individual quality implies existence, must not all individuals exist necessarily? The answer is that contingency is not a relation of existence to a thing, but of a thing to existence. To say a thing might not exist is not to say there might be the thing without existence. It is rather to say there might be existence without the thing. To pass from the actual to what might be is to generalize, ultimately to refer to the uttermost generalities. It is the world (in its generic features) which does not imply its contingent inhabitants, not the inhabitants which do not imply the world with themselves as its existing parts. They do imply it. Without it they, as individuals, would not be, even as possible. There is an unutilized possibility of individuals, but not an individuality of the unutilized possibility. Mr. Micawber is a quasi-individual, with some of the aesthetic properties of an individual, but not an individual in the strict sense. He is a class, specific enough to simulate an individual for the purposes of the aesthetic illusion or "make-believe."

The unique status of God is that no distinction can be drawn between any individual having perfection and any other. Every perfect being must have the same space-time locus (omnipresence), and must know the same things—all there are to know. If there had been another world, the God of this our world would have known it, for the very possibility of another world can be related to God only as something *he* (not some other God) could have done or can still do. Hence "the perfect" is no class of possibilities, all of which might be unactual, but only an individual character belonging to nothing, not even potentially (for the only individuality that could be involved is already involved), or else belonging to the one real perfect individual.

The necessary being is, then, that individual which existence implies, and which itself implies, not simply existence (for every individual does that), but implies, through the identity of its generic with its individual character, that (so far as its primordial nature is concerned) there is in its case no separation between possibility and actuality, the class and the individual. In other words, "perfection" implies that existence itself necessarily contains a real perfection, or that existence, in its cosmically essential features, *is* perfection as existent, as the unity of being and possibility. Or, perfection implies that exietence, any and all existence, implies the existence of perfection as its ground.

Again, to conceive a thing in two alternative states, actual and possible, is to conceive something common to these two states, as well as something different. But between the world with God and the world without God no common feature could be found. For the world with God is the world completely dependent upon the existence of God, for both its actuality and its possibility, and hence it follows that in the absence of God nothing of the world as it would be with God could be identified.

Doubtless these are all ways of construing the one simple principle: nothing but existent perfection could make perfection possible, or rather, perfection cannot have the dependent relation to other things implied by the status of mere possibility, but must have either the status of an impossible idea or pseudo-idea, or else must be simply actual, with no alternative of non-actual possibility at all.

If it be thought suspicious that the ontological argument argues from a unique relation of God to existence (though one deduced from the normal relation plus the definition of perfection), let it be remembered that, by definition, God's relation to every question is unique. He is the unique being, unique because maximal, the only unsurpassed and unsurpassable being. . . . Naturally, God's relation to existence is maximal also, that is, he exists under all possible circumstances, times, and places, in other words, necessarily. That which would exist, if at all, necessarily, cannot be non-existent and yet possible, for this would mean having existence as a contingent alternative, and a contingent alternative cannot be necessary. To object to this is to object to the idea of God, and not merely to the affirmation, "There is a being corresponding to the idea."

If all individuals are contingent, then the whole of existence is contingent, and it might be that nothing existed, or it might be true (though nonsensical) that there was nothing of which any proposition would be true. Furthermore, what could constitute the identity of existence as such, if not eternal and necessary individual manifested in all individuals? We human beings tend to carry our own personality with us in all our hypotheses, in so far as we say to ourselves, Suppose *I* were to experience so and so. This gives an aspect of identity by which we might try to define existence as such. But the definition would be solipsistic. Hence there must be some further aspect of identity, like ourselves in being a concrete existent, but unlike us in being able to constitute the unity, the all-embracing register of existence itself, without limitation upon conceivable variety and independence. This is what God is, the all-embracing register of existence, perfect in his flexible and tolerant ("merciful") sensitivity to all experiences, who can see things as they see themselves, also as other things see them, and also as they are related without distinct awareness on the part either of themselves or of other imperfect things.

It is to the credit of the ontological argument that it has to be opposed by making an absolute disjunction between meaning and its referent, reality, or between universals and individuals, a disjunction *at no point* mediated by a higher principle. Only if there is *one* actual individual whose presence is universal, have universals an intelligible ground in actuality. Otherwise we have to relate mere universals and mere individuals by—what? Ordinary individuals, being non-universal in their relevance, cannot explain the identity of the universals as such. Aristotelian objections to disembodied universals can be sustained only if there be a universal embodiment, a "concrete" universal so far as present actuality is concerned, though a universal which is also (contrary to Hegelianism) abstract so far as the future and potentiality are involved.

Thus there is not from any point of view good reason to object to the exceptional status of God's existence, every reason to welcome it as the completion of the theory of meaning. . . .

That the ontological argument is hypothetical we have admitted. It says, "*If* 'God' stands for something conceivable, it stands for something actual." But this hypothetical character is often distorted out of all recognition. We are told that the only logical relation brought out by the argument is this: The necessary being, if it exists, exists necessarily. Thus to be able to use the argument in order to conclude "God exists necessarily," we should have to know the premise "God exists." This makes the argument seem ludicrous enough, but it is itself based on a self-contradictory assumption, which says, "If the necessary being happens to exist, that is, if as mere contingent fact, it exists, then it exists not as contingent fact, but as necessary truth." Instead of this nonsense, we must say, "If the phrase 'necessary being' has a meaning, then what it means exists necessarily, and if it exists necessarily, then, a fortiori, it exists." The "if" in the statement, "if it exists, it exists necessarily," cannot have the force of making the existence of the necessary being contingent —except in the sense that the argument leaves it open to suppose that the phrase "necessary being" is nonsense, and of course nonsense has no objective referent, possible or actual. Thus, what we should maintain is, "that which exists, if at all, necessarily," is the same as "that which is conceivable, if at all, only if it exists." Granting that it is conceivable, it then follows that it exists because it could not, being an object of thought at all, be a non-actual object. Or once more, the formula might be this: The necessary being, if it is not nothing, and therefore the object of no possible positive idea, is actual. . . .

It is said by logicians to be absurd to say, "The such and such (or the perfect) exists." We must say, There is an x, an individual, such that it has a certain property. Thus: there is an x such that x is perfect (omniscient, etc.). Now the ontomological argument merely holds that if this proposition is false, *then perfection is imperfection*. For if there is no perfect x, then perfection is either a meaningless term, or it means the mere possibility of perfection; but the mere possibility of perfection implies that perfection could come into being, or be produced or have its being derivatively from whatever it is that constitutes its "possibility," and this amounts to saying that perfection could come into being as imperfection.

Why have logicians denied that we could ever infer from a predicate that something embodies that predicate? The ground appears to be the inductive one that most predicates do not imply existence; therefore we may suppose that none do. Such an inference obviously could not be conclusive. To clarify the matter we should consider carefully the relation between essence and existence in the most widely contrasting cases. By considering "redness" alone we certainly never could discover what things in the world are in fact red. But it may be going too far to say that the predicate redness is conceivable in complete detachment from red objects. If we imagine red, at least our psychological, and perhaps our physiological, state is somehow qualified by redness, and it is a moot point in philosophy whether redness literally does ever qualify anything except minds-and-bodies endowed with color vision. The quantitative properties ascribed by physics to things which we experience as red are distinguishable from redness as given. To ask whether anything is really red means in science whether anything really has these quantitative properties. And while these properties do not in the mere conception imply the reality of external objects precisely embodying them, it is nevertheless true that if we know what we mean by wave lengths and the like it is because we have experiences, and are organisms, which do illustrate in principle though not necessarily in detail what such quantitative aspects are like. In other words, the more fundamental aspects of predicates are always actualized somehow in the experience which refers to them.

The problem is not, whatever logicians may sometimes like to imagine, that of getting from mere disembodied predicates to actualities, but of getting from actualities, such as actual experiences (which include some portions of the actual environment as experienced), to other real or possible experiences or portions of the environment. This is done by following the tracks of universals, generic features of actuality and possibility alike. By this means, predicates can be approximately (though only so) defined, even though they are not actualized. But if nothing like redness were actual here and now, say as the memory of a real red object, I could not here and now speak of the possibility of redness somewhere else. Nor could I do so unless the idea of a "place" were illustrated by the here and now. Logicians may claim that it is only a psychological, not a logical, necessity that essences should be illustrated in actuality. But the making of such a verbal distinction seems to correspond to no actual evidence.

HARTSHORNE SELECTION

1. According to Hartshorne, the Ontological Argument depends on (among other things) the uniqueness of God. In what ways is God unique? Why, according to Hartshorne, must God be unique? How is God's uniqueness related to the connection between His possibility and His actuality?

2.   What, according to Hartshorne, is the relationship between the possibility and actuality of ordinary things? How does this relationship explain the notion of contingent existence?

3.   In what sense is the Ontological Argument "hypothetical"? Does this hypothetical character rob the argument of its force? In what way are arguments for the existence of ordinary things hypothetical? How do these arguments differ from the Ontological Argument for God's existence?

4.   Is Anselm's argument clearer to you after reading Hartshorne? What problems or objections remain? In what way does Hartshorne's analysis illuminate the relationship between God and human beings? Is our knowledge of God different from our knowledge of all other things? How?

(SELECTION 4)

WILLIAM PALEY

The Argument from Design

Despite the fact that the Cosmological and Ontological Arguments for the existence of God have considerable interest for the professional philosopher or theologian, their conceptual difficulty makes them relatively inaccessible to the laymen. There is another classic argument, however, that is so natural, so plausible, that devout men and women frequently hit upon it simply as an expression of their religious sense of God's presence. The argument, whose official name is the Argument from Design, goes something like this: Everywhere we look in the world around us, we find an order and regularity, a fittingness of part to part and means to end, that cannot possibly have come about by sheer chance. The intricacies of construction of a beehive, the majestic orderly sweep of the planets in their endless travels around the sun, the subtle adjustments of the metabolism of even the simplest one-celled animals—surely these are the products of an intelligence, a mind, a power of reason capable of suiting means to ends and part to whole in a manner analogous to that of the intelligent human craftsman. And if it requires the ingenuity of the most gifted men and women to design the poor artifacts of human life, what immeasurable intelligence and power must be reflected in the incomprehensible order of the universe!

Although this argument has an ancient lineage, it came especially to prominence in the philosophical and religious writings of the eighteenth century. Countless writers of both prose and poetry expanded on the notion of God's design, drawing on the most recent discoveries of biology and physics for examples of the purposive order of nature. The two most famous statements of the argument are to be found in Alexander Pope's stately poem, "An Essay on Man," and in William Paley's book-length exposition of the doctrine, *Natural Theology*. The present selection is taken from Paley's work.

Philosophers have found it relatively easy to poke holes in the Argument from Design, as we shall see in the selection by David Hume following this one. But before you start to pick it apart, you might pause for a moment really to reflect on what it says. When we look at the orderliness of nature—when we *really* think for a bit about the workings of the human eye, as Paley asks us to—can we honestly brush aside any suggestion of intelligent purpose and explain it all by "chance" or "evolution" or "natural selection"? I do not mean, is it *logically possible* to explain the universe by mere chance? Paley himself might have agreed to that minimal claim. I mean, can we *believe* such an explanation? It is surely no

accident that some of the most devout
believers in the modern world are precisely those scientists who are most in-
timately acquainted with the order and
complexity of nature.

In crossing a heath, suppose I pitched my foot against a *stone* and
were asked how the stone came to be there, I might possibly answer
that for anything I knew to the contrary it had lain there forever;
nor would it, perhaps, be very easy to show the absurdity of this
answer. But suppose I had found a *watch* upon the ground, and it
should be inquired how the watch happened to be in that place, I
should hardly think of the answer which I had before given, that for
anything I knew the watch might have always been there. Yet why
should not this answer serve for the watch as well as for the stone;
why is it not as admissible in the second case as in the first? For this
reason, and for no other, namely, that when we come to inspect the
watch, we perceive—what we could not discover in the stone—that
its several parts are framed and put together for a purpose, e.g., that
they are so formed and adjusted as to produce motion, and that
motion so regulated as to point out the hour of the day; that if the
different parts had been differently shaped from what they are, or
placed after any other manner or in any other order than that in
which they are placed, either no motion at all would have been
carried on in the machine, or none which would have answered the
use that is now served by it. To reckon up a few of the plainest of
these parts and of their offices, all tending to one result: we see a
cylindrical box containing a coiled elastic spring, which, by its
endeavor to relax itself, turns round the box. We next observe a
flexible chain—artificially wrought for the sake of flexure—communicating the action of the spring from the box to the fusee. We
then find a series of wheels, the teeth of which catch in and apply
to each other, conducting the motion from the fusee to the balance
and from the balance to the pointer, and at the same time, by the
size and shape of those wheels, so regulating that motion as to
terminate in causing an index, by an equable and measured pro-
gression, to pass over a given space in a given time. We take notice
that the wheels are made of brass, in order to keep them from rust;
the springs of steel, no other metal being so elastic; that over the
face of the watch there is placed a glass, a material employed in no
other part of the work, but in the room of which, if there had been
any other than a transparent substance, the hour could not be seen
without opening the case. This mechanism being observed—it requires indeed an examination of the instrument, and perhaps some

From *Natural Theology* by William Paley. First published in 1802.

previous knowledge of the subject, to perceive and understand it; but being once, as we have said, observed and understood—the inference we think is inevitable, that the watch must have had a maker—that there must have existed, at some time and at some place or other, an artificer or artificers who formed it for the purpose which we find it actually to answer, who completely comprehended its construction and designed its use.

Nor would it, I apprehend, weaken the conclusion, that we had never seen a watch made—that we had never known an artist capable of making one—that we were altogether incapable of executing such a piece of workmanship ourselves, or of understanding in what manner it was performed; all this being no more than what is true of some exquisite remains of ancient art, of some lost arts, and, to the generality of mankind, of the more curious productions of modern manufacture. Does one man in a million know how oval frames are turned? Ignorance of this kind exalts our opinion of the unseen and unknown artist's skill, if he be unseen and unknown, but raises no doubt in our minds of the existence and agency of such an artist, at some former time and in some place or other. Nor can I perceive that it varies at all the inference, whether the question arise concerning a human agent or concerning an agent of a different species, or an agent possessing in some respects a different nature.

Neither, secondly, would it invalidate our conclusion, that the watch sometimes went wrong or that it seldom went exactly right. The purpose of the machinery, the design, and the designer might be evident, and in the case supposed, would be evident, in whatever way we accounted for the irregularity of the movement, or whether we could account for it or not. It is not necessary that a machine be perfect in order to show with what design it was made: still less necessary, where the only question is whether it were made with any design at all.

Nor, thirdly, would it bring any uncertainty into the argument, if there were a few parts of the watch, concerning which we could not discover or had not yet discovered in what manner they conduced to the general effect; or even some parts, concerning which we could not ascertain whether they conduced to that effect in any manner whatever. . . .

Nor, fourthly, would any man in his senses think the existence of the watch with its various machinery accounted for, by being told that it was one out of possible combinations of material forms; that whatever he had found in the place where he found the watch, must have contained some internal configuration or other; and that this configuration might be the structure now exhibited, namely, of the works of a watch, as well as a different structure.

Nor, fifthly, would it yield his inquiry more satisfaction, to be answered that there existed in things a principle of order, which had disposed the parts of the watch into their present form and situation. He never knew a watch made by the principle of order; nor can he even form to himself an idea of what is meant by a principle of order distinct from the intelligence of the watchmaker. . . .

Neither, lastly, would our observer be driven out of his conclusion or from his confidence in its truth by being told that he knew nothing at all about the matter. He knows enough for his argument; he knows the utility of the end; he knows the subserviency and adaptation of the means to the end. These points being known, his ignorance of other points, his doubts concerning other points affect not the certainty of his reasoning. The consciousness of knowing little need not beget a distrust of that which he does know.

Suppose, in the next place, that the person who found the watch should after some time discover that, in addition to all the properties which he had hitherto observed in it, it possessed the unexpected property of producing in the course of its movement another watch like itself—the thing is conceivable; that it contained within it a mechanism, a system of parts—a mold, for instance, or a complex adjustment of lathes, files, and other tools—evidently and separately calculated for this purpose; let us inquire what effect ought such a discovery to have upon his former conclusion.

The first effect would be to increase his admiration of the contrivance, and his conviction of the consummate skill of the contriver. Whether he regarded the object of the contrivance, the distinct apparatus, the intricate, yet in many parts intelligible mechanism by which it was carried on, he would perceive in this new observation nothing but an additional reason for doing what he had already done—for referring the construction of the watch to design and to supreme art. If that construction *without* this property, or, which is the same thing, before this property had been noticed, proved intention and art to have been employed about it, still more strong would the proof appear when he came to the knowledge of this further property, the crown and perfection of all the rest.

He would reflect that, though the watch before him were *in some sense* the maker of the watch which was fabricated in the course of its movements, yet it was in a very different sense from that in which a carpenter, for instance, is the maker of a chair—the author of its contrivance, the cause of the relation of its parts to their use. With respect to these, the first watch was no cause at all to the second; in no such sense as this was it the author of the constitution and order, either of the parts which the new watch contained, or of the parts by the aid and instrumentality of which it was produced. We might possibly say, but with great latitude of expression, that a stream of water ground corn; but no latitude of expression would allow us to say, no stretch of conjecture could lead us to think that the stream of water built the mill, though it were too ancient for us to know who the builder was. What the stream of water does in the affair is neither more nor less than this: by the application of an unintelligent impulse to a mechanism previously arranged, arranged independently of it and arranged by intelligence, an effect is produced, namely, the corn is ground. But the effect results from the arrangement. The force of the stream cannot be said to be the cause or the author of the effect, still less of the arrangement. Understanding and plan in the formation of the mill were not the less necessary for any share which the water has in grinding the corn; yet is this share the same as that which the watch would have contributed to the production of the new watch, upon the supposition assumed in the last section. Therefore,

Though it be now no longer probable that the individual watch which our observer had found was made immediately by the hand of an artificer, yet this alteration does not in anywise affect the inference that an artificer had been originally employed and concerned in the production. The argument from design remains as it was. Marks of design and comtrivance are no more accounted for now than they were before. In the same thing, we may ask for the cause of different properties. We may ask for the cause of the color of a body, of its hardness, of its heat; and these causes may be all different. We are now asking for the cause of that subserviency to a use, that relation to an end, which we have remarked in the watch before us. No answer is given to this question by telling us that a preceding watch produced it. There cannot be design without a designer; contrivance without a contriver; order without choice; arrangement without anything capable of arranging; subserviency and relation to a purpose without that which could intend a purpose; means suitable to an end, and executing their office in accomplishing that end, without the end ever having been contemplated or the means accommodated to it. Arrangement, disposition of parts, subserviency of means to an end, relation of instruments to a use imply the presence of intelligence and mind. No one, therefore, can rationally believe that the insensible, inanimate watch, from which the watch before us issued, was the proper cause of the mechanism we so much admire in it—could be truly said to have constructed the instrument, disposed its parts, assigned their office, determined their order, action, and mutual dependency, combined their several motions into one result, and that also a result connected with the utilities of other beings. All thse properties, therefore, are as much unaccounted for as they were before.

Nor is anything gained by running the difficulty farther back, that is, by supposing the watch before us to have been produced from another watch, that from a former, and so on indefinitely. Our going back ever so far brings us no nearer to the least degree of satisfaction upon the subject. Contrivance is still unaccounted for. We still want a contriver. A designing mind is neither supplied by this supposition nor dispensed with. If the difficulty were diminished the farther we went back, by going back indefinitely we might exhaust it. And this is the only case to which this sort of reasoning applies. Where there is a tendency, or, as we increase the number of terms, a continual approach toward a limit, *there,* by supposing the number of terms to be what is called infinite, we may conceive the limit to be attained; but where there is no such tendency or approach, nothing is effected by lengthening the series. There is no difference as to the point in question, whatever there may be as to many points, between one series and another—between a series which is finite and a series which is infinite. A chain composed of an infinite number of links can no more support itself than a chain composed of a finite number of links. And of this we are assured, though we never *can* have tried the experiment; because, by increasing the number of links, from ten, for instance, to a hundred, from a hundred to a thousand, etc., we make not the smallest approach, we observe not the smallest tendency toward self-support. There is no difference in this respect—yet there may be a great difference in several respects—between a chain of a greater or less length, between one chain and another, between one that is finite and one that is infinite. This very much resembles the case before us. The machine which we are inspecting demonstrates, by its construction, contrivance and design. Contrivance must have had a contriver, design a designer, whether the machine immediately proceeded from another machine or not. That circumstance alters not the case. That other machine may, in like manner, have proceeded from a former machine: nor does that alter the case; the contrivance must have had a contriver. That former one from one preceding it: no alteration still; a contriver is still necessary. No tendency is perceived, no approach toward a diminution of this necessity. It is the same with any and every succession of these machines—a succession of ten, of a hundred, of a thousand; with one series, as with another—a series which is finite, as with a series which is infinite. In whatever other respects they may differ, in this they do not. In all equally, contrivance and design are unaccounted for.

The question is not simply, how came the first watch into

existence?—which question, it may be pretended, is done away by supposing the series of watches thus produced from one another to have been infinite, and consequently to have had no such *first* for which it was necessary to provide a cause. This, perhaps, would have been nearly the state of the question, if nothing had been before us but an unorganized, unmechanized substance, without mark or indication of contrivance. It might be difficult to show that such substance coud not have existed from eternity, either in succession—if it were possible, which I think it is not, for unorganized bodies to spring from one another—or by individual perpetuity. But that is not the question now. To suppose it to be so is to suppose that it made no difference whether he had found a watch or a stone. As it is, the metaphysics of that question have no place; for, in the watch which we are examining are seen contrivance, design, an end, a purpose, means for the end, adaptation to the purpose. And the question which irresistibly presses upon our thoughts is, whence this contrivance and design? The thing required is the intending mind, the adapted hand, the intelligence by which that hand was directed. This question, this demand is not shaken off by increasing a number or succession of substances destitute of these properties; nor the more, by increasing that number to infinity. If it be said that, upon the supposition of one watch being produced from another in the course of that other's movements and by means of the mechanism within it, we have a cause for the watch in my hand, namely, the watch from which it proceeded; I deny that for the design, the contrivance, the suitableness of means to an end, the adaptation of instruments to a use, all of which we discover in the watch, we have any cause whatever. It is in vain, therefore, to assign a series of such causes or to allege that a series may be carried back to infinity; for I do not admit that we have yet any cause at all for the phenomena, still less any series of causes either finite or infinite. Here is contrivance but no contriver; proofs of design, but no designer.

Our observer would further also reflect that the maker of the watch before him was in truth and reality the maker of every watch produced from it: there being no difference, except that the latter manifests a more exquisite skill, between the making of another watch with his own hands, by the mediation of files, lathes, chisels, etc., and the disposing, fixing, and inserting of these instruments, or of others equivalent to them, in the body of the watch already made, in such a manner as to form a new watch in the course of the movements which he had given to the old one. It is only working by one set of tools instead of another.

The conclusion which the *first* examination of the watch, of its works, construction, and movement, suggested, was that it must have had, for cause and author of the construction, an artificer who understood its mechanisms and designed its use. This conclusion is invincible. A *second* examination presents us with a new discovery. The watch is found, in the course of its movement, to produce another watch similar to itself; and not only so, but we perceive in it a system or organization separately calculated for that purpose. What effect would this discovery have or ought it to have upon our former inference? What, as has already been said, but to increase beyond measure our admiration of the skill which had been employed in the formation of such a machine? Or shall it, instead of this, all at once turn us round to an opposite conclusion, namely, that no art or skill whatever has been concerned in the business, although all other evidences of art and skill remain as they were, and this last and supreme piece of art be now added to the rest? Can this be maintained without absurdity? Yet this is atheism.

This is atheism; for every indication of contrivance, every manifestation of design which existed in the watch, exists in the words of nature, with the difference on the side of nature of being greater and more, and that in a degree which exceeds all computation. I mean that the contrivances of nature surpass the contrivances of art in the complexity, subtlety, and curiosity of the mechanisms; and still more, if possible, do they go beyond them in number and variety; yet, in a multitude of cases, are not less evidently mechanical, not less evidently contrivances, not less evidently accommodated to their end or suited to their office than are the most perfect productions of human ingenuity.

I know no better method of introducing so large a subject than that of comparing a single thing with a single thing: an eye, for example, with a telescope. As far as the examination of the instrument goes, there is precisely the same proof that the eye was made for vision as there is that the telescope was made for assisting it. They are made upon the same principles, both being adjusted to the laws by which the transmission and refraction of rays of light are regulated. I speak not of the origin of the laws themselves; but such laws being fixed, the construction in both cases is adapted to them. For instance, these laws require, in order to produce the same effect, that rays of light in passing from water into the eye should be refracted by a more convex surface than when it passes out of air into the eye. Accordingly, we find that the eye of a fish, in that part of it called the crystalline lens, is much rounder than the eye of terrestrial animals. What plainer manifestation of design can there be than this difference? What could a mathematical instrument maker have done more to show his knowledge of his principle, his application of that knowledge, his suiting of his means to his end—I will not say to display the compass or excellence of his skill and art, for in these all comparison is indecorous, but to testify counsel, choice, consideration, purpose?

To some it may appear a difference sufficient to destroy all similitude between the eye and the telescope, that the one is a perceiving organ, the other an unperceiving instrument. The fact is that they are both instruments. And as to the mechanism, at least as to the mechanism being employed, and even as to the kind of it, this circumstance varies not the analogy at all. For observe what the constitution of the eye is. It is necessary, in order to produce distinct vision, that an image or picture of the object be formed at the bottom of the eye. Whence this necessity arises, or how the picture is connected with the sensation or contributes to it, it may be difficult, nay, we will confess, if you please, impossible for us to search out. But the present question is not concerned in the inquiry. It may be true that in this and in other instances we trace mechanical contrivance a certain way, and that then we come to something which is not mechanical, or which is inscrutable. But this affects not the certainty of our investigation, as far as we have gone. The difference between an animal and an automatic statue consists in this, that in the animal we trace the mechanism to a certain point, and then we are stopped, either the mechanism being too subtle for our discernment, or something else beside the known laws of mechanism taking place; whereas, in the automaton, for the comparatively few motions of which it is capable, we trace the mechanism throughout. But, up to the limit, the reasoning is as clear and certain in the one case as in the other. In the example before us it is a matter of certainty, because it is a matter which experience and observation demonstrate, that the formation of an image at the bottom of the eye is necessary to perfect vision. The formation then of such an image being necessary—no matter how—to the sense of sight and to the exercise of that sense, the apparatus by which it is formed is constructed and put together not only with infinitely more art, but upon the selfsame principles of art as in the telescope or the camera obscura. The perception arising from the image may be laid out of the question; for the production of the image, these are instruments of the same kind. The end is the same, the means are the same. The purpose in both is alike, the contrivance for accomplishing that purpose is in both alike. The lenses of the telescopes and humors of the eye bear a complete resemblance to one another, in their figure, their position, and in their power over the rays of light, namely, in bringing each pencil to a point at the right distance from the lens; namely, in the eye, at the exact place where the membrane is spread to receive it.

How is it possible, under circumstances of such close affinity, and under the operation of equal evidence, to exclude contrivance from the one, yet to acknowledge the proof of contrivance having been employed, as the plainest and clearest of all propositions, in the other?

The resemblance between the two cases is still more accurate, and obtains in more points than we have yet represented, or than we are, on the first view of the subject, aware of. In dioptric telescopes there is an imperfection of this nature. Pencils of light in passing through glass lenses are separated into different colors, thereby tinging the object, especially the edges of it, as if it were viewed through a prism. To correct this inconvenience had been long a desideratum in the art. At last it came into the mind of a sagacious optician to inquire how this matter was managed in the eye, in which there was exactly the same difficulty to contend with as in the telescope. His observation taught him that in the eye the evil was cured by combining lenses composed of different substances, that is, of substances which possessed different refracting powers. Our artist borrowed thence his hint and produced a correction of the defect by imitating, in glasses made from different materials, the effects of the different humors through which the rays of light pass before they reach the bottom of the eye. Could this be in the eye without purpose which suggested to the optician the only effectual means of attaining that purpose?

But further, there are other points not so much perhaps of strict resemblance between the two as of superiority of the eye over the telescope, yet of a superiority which, being founded in the laws that regulate both, may furnish topics of fair and just comparison. Two things were wanted to the eye, which were not wanted, at least in the same degree, to the telescope; and these were the adaptation of the organ, first, to different degrees of light, and secondly, to the vast diversity of distance at which objects are viewed by the naked eye, namely, from a few inches to as many miles. These difficulties present not themselves to the maker of the telescope. He wants all the light he can get; and he never directs his instrument to objects near at hand. In the eye, both these cases were to be provided for; and for the purpose of providing for them, a subtle and appropriate mechanism is introduced. . . .

Were there no example in the world of contrivance except that of the *eye*, it would be alone sufficient to support the conclusion which we draw from it, as to the necessity of an intelligent Creator. It could never be got rid of, because it could not be accounted for by any other supposition which did not contradict all the principles we possess of knowledge—the principles according to which things do, as often as they can be brought to the test of experience, turn out to be true or false. Its coats and humors, constructed as the lenses of a telescope are constructed, for the refraction of rays of light to a point, which forms the proper action of the organ; the provision in its muscular tendons for turning its pupil to the object, similar to that which is given to the telescope by screws, and upon which power of direction in the eye the exercise of its office as an optical instrument depends; the further provision for its defense, for its constant lubricity and moisture, which we see in its socket and its lids, in its glands for the secretion of the matter of tears, its outlet or communication with the nose for carrying off the liquid after the eye is washed with it; these provisions compose altogether an apparatus, a system of parts, a preparation of means, so manifest in their design, so exquisite in their contrivance, so successful in their issue, so precious, and so infinitely beneficial in their use, as, in my opinion, to bear down all doubt that can be raised upon the subject. And what I wish, under the title of the present chapter, to observe is that, if other parts of nature were inaccessible to our inquiries, or even if other parts of nature presented nothing to our examination but disorder and confusion, the validity of this example would remain the same. If there were but one watch in the world, it would not be less certain that it had a maker. If we had never in our lives seen any but one single kind of hydraulic machine, yet if of that one kind we understood the mechanism and use, we should be as perfectly assured that it proceeded from the hand and thought and skill of a workman, as if we visited a museum of the arts and saw collected there twenty different kinds of machines for drawing water, or a thousand different kinds for other purposes. Of this point each machine is a proof independently of all the rest. So it is with the evidences of a divine agency. The proof is not a conclusion which lies at the end of a chain of reasoning, of which chain each instance of contrivance is only a link, and of which, if one link fail, the whole fails; but it is an argument separately supplied by every separate example. An error in stating an example affects only that example. The argument is cumulative in the fullest sense of that term. The eye proves it without the ear; the ear without the eye. The proof in each example is complete; for when the design of the part and the conduciveness of its structure to that design is shown, the mind may set itself at rest; no future consideration can detract anything from the force of the example.

PALEY SELECTION

1. Exactly *what* do the order and causal interconnectedness of things in nature prove, according to Paley? Can you think of other examples of the apparant purposiveness of the arrangement of nature?

2.   We are now able to make machines whose complexity far exceeds anything Paley could ever have imagined. Consider a television set, or a modern computer. Does man's ability to create such machines weaken Paley's argument, or strengthen it? Why?

3.   Advances in biochemical genetics seem to be bringing us closer to the day when we will be able to "create life in a test tube." Suppose we are able to synthesize a living thing. Will that show that Paley's argument fails? Or will it provide further support for Paley's argument? Why?

4.   If you were to encounter a functioning computer on a distant planet, would you be absolutely sure that some sort of intelligent life had been there? If the answer is yes, then how—save by admitting the existence of God—can you explain the unimaginable complexity and precision of the physical structure of the universe?

5.   If we accept Paley's argument, what can we conclude from it about the *nature* of the God who has created the universe? What relationship, if any, must there be between such a God and the God of the Bible?

(SELECTION 5)

DAVID HUME

A Refutation of the Argument from Design

In the 1750s, when he was beginning to earn a substantial reputation as an essayist and historian, David Hume undertook to write a series of twelve dialogues exploring the various arguments for the existence of God, with special attention to the Argument from Design in all its forms. The results, while brilliant, were so devastating to all the familiar proofs of established theology that Hume's friends, including the economist Adam Smith, persuaded him not to publish what he had written. Hume had already acquired notoriety through the skeptical force of his epistemological works, and it was feared that the anti-religious line of the Dialogues would ruin his literary reputation. Consequently, the Dialogues were not published until 1779, three years after Hume's death. (Notice that even though Hume might seem to be writing with Paley specifically in mind, he actually composed the Dialogues fully half a century before Paley published *Natural Theology*.)

Hume's attack on the Argument from Design draws heavily on the skeptical critique of causal reasoning that he had set forth in his first and most important work, *A Treatise of Human Nature*. The Argument from Design is, Hume points out, an extension of ordinary causal inferences. It reasons backwards from the effect (the order of regularity in nature) to the cause (an intelligent creator of the universe). Such an argument suffers from two weaknesses, in Hume's view. First of all, it is vulnerable to all the objections that can be brought against causal reasoning of any sort, objections which can be summarized by noting that nothing in logic or observation guarantees that events as yet unexamined will exhibit the same patterns that we have noticed in the past.

But the Argument from Design has a second weakness peculiar to it alone. Most causal inferences reason from one sort of event that we have observed in the past (such as the touching of a lighted match to paper) to other events that have also been observed in the past (such as the bursting into flames of the paper). Since the touching of the lighted match to the paper has on past occasions been followed by the burning of the paper, we make an inferential leap to the conclusion that the next time we touch a lighted match to a piece of paper, it too will burn. Hence, we conclude that "Paper burns when lit."

In the case of the Argument from Design, however, we reason backwards from the effect to a cause (namely, the purposive creation of an orderly world) that we have *never* before observed.

There has been at most one creation, and by the nature of the case none of us was here to see it. So, Hume concludes, even if we accept causal inference in general within the world—a move about which Hume has the gravest doubts— we have no warrant to extend that mode of reasoning beyond the world to some unique act of creation outside of time and space.

Hume's central criticism is thus rather simple. Much of the fun of the Dialogues comes from the imaginativeness with which Hume embellishes both the Argument from Design and his refutations of it.

Not to lose any time in circumlocutions, said Cleanthes, addressing himself to Demea, much less in replying to the pious declamations of Philo; I shall briefly explain how I conceive this matter. Look round the world: contemplate the whole and every part of it: you will find it to be nothing but one great machine, subdivided into an infinite number of lesser machines, which again admit of subdivisions, to a degree beyond what human senses and faculties can trace and explain. All there various machines, and even their most minute parts, are adjusted to each other with an accuracy, which ravishes into admiration all men, who have ever contemplated them. The curious adapting of means to ends, throughout all nature, resembles exactly, though it much exceeds the productions of human contrivance; of human design, thought, wisdom, and intelligence. Since therefore the effects resemble each other, we are led to infer, by all rules of analogy, that the causes also resemble; and that the Author of Nature is somewhat similar to the mind of men; though possessed of much larger faculties, proportioned to the grandeur of the work, which he has executed. By this argument *a posteriori*, . . . and by this argument alone, do we prove at once the existence of a Deity, and his similarity to human mind and intelligence.

I shall be so free, Cleanthes, said Demea, as to tell you, that from the beginning, I could not approve of your conclusion concerning the similarity of the Deity to men; still less can I approve of the mediums, by which you endeavor to establish it. What! No demonstration of the being of a God! No abstract arguments! No proofs *a priori!* . . . Are these which have hitherto been so much insisted on by philosophers, all fallacy, all sophism? Can we reach no farther in this subject than experience and probability? I will not say, that this is betraying the cause of a deity: but surely, by this affected candor, you give advantage to atheists, which they never could obtain, by the mere dint of argument and reasoning.

What I chiefly scruple in this subject, said Philo, is not so much, that all religious arguments are by Cleanthes reduced to

From *Dialogues Concerning Natural Religion* by David Hume. Written in the 1750s and first published in 1779.

experience, as that they appear not to be even the most certain and irrefragable of that inferior kind. That a stone will fall, that fire will burn, that the earth has solidity, we have observed a thousand and a thousand times; and when any new instance of this nature is presented, we draw without hesitation the accustomed inference. The exact similarity of the cases gives us a perfect assurance of a similar event; and a stronger evidence is never desired nor sought after. But wherever you depart, in the least, from the similarity of the cases, you diminish proportionably the evidence; and may at last bring it to a very weak *analogy,* which is confessedly liable to error and uncertainty. After having experienced the circulation of the blood in human creatures, we make no doubt that it takes place in Titius and Maevius: but from its circulation in frogs and fishes, it is only a presumption, though a strong one, from analogy, that it takes place in men and other animals. The analogical reasoning is much weaker, when we infer the circulation of the sap in vegetables from our experience, that the blood circulates in animals, and those, who hastily followed that imperfect analogy are found, by more accurate experiments, to have been mistaken.

If we see a house, Cleanthes, we conclude, with the greatest certainty, that it had an architect or builder; because this is precisely that species of effect, which we have experienced to proceed from that species of cause. But surely you will not affirm, that the universe bears such a resemblance to a house, that we can with the same certainty infer a similar cause, or that the analogy is here entire and perfect. The dissimilitude is so striking, that the utmost you can here pretend to is a guess, a conjecture, a presumption concerning a similar cause; and how that pretension will be received in the world, I leave you to consider.

It would surely be very ill received, replied Cleanthes; and I should be deservedly blamed and detested, did I allow, that the proofs of a Deity amounted to no more than a guess or conjecture. But is the whole adjustment of means to ends in a house and in the universe so slight a resemblance? The economy of final causes? The order, proportion, and arrangement of every part? Steps of a stair are plainly contrived, that human legs may use them in mounting; and this inference is certain and infallible. Human legs are also contrived for walking and mounting; and this inference, I allow, is not altogether so certain, because of the dissimilarity which you remark; but does it, therefore, deserve the name only of presumption or conjecture?

Good God! cried Demea, interrupting him, where are we? Zealous defenders of religion allow, that the proofs of a Deity fall short of perfect evidence! And you, Philo, on whose assistance I depended, in proving the adorable mysteriousness of the Divine Nature, do you assent to all these extravagant opinions of Cleanthes? For what other name can I give them? Or why spare my censure, when such principles are advanced, supported by such an authority, before so young a man as Pamphilus?

You seem not to apprehend, replied Philo, that I argue with Cleanthes in his own way; and by showing him the dangerous consequences of his tenets, hope at last to reduce him to our opinion. But what sticks most with you, I observe, is the representation which Cleanthes has made of the argument a posteriori; and finding, that the argument is likely to escape your hold and vanish into air, you think it so disguised, that you can scarcely believe it to be set in its true light. Now, however much I may dissent, in other respects, from the dangerous principles of Cleanthes, I must allow, that he has fairly represented that argument; and I shall endeavor so to state the matter to you, that you will entertain no farther scruples with regard to it.

Were a man to abstract from everything which he knows or has seen, he would be altogether incapable, merely from his own ideas, to determine what kind of scene the universe must be, or to give the preference to one state or situation of things above another. For as nothing which he clearly conceives, could be esteemed impossible or implying a contradiction, every chimera of his fancy would be upon an equal footing; nor could he assign any just reason, why he adheres to one idea or system, and rejects the others, which are equally possible.

Again; after he opens his eyes, and contemplates the world, as it really is, it would be impossible for him, at first, to assign the cause of any one event; much less, of the whole of things or of the universe. He might set his fancy a rambling; and she might bring him in an infinite variety of reports and representations. These would all be possible; but being all equally possible, he would never, of himself, give a satisfactory account for his preferring one of them to the rest. Experience alone can point out to him the true cause of any phenomenon.

Now, according to this method of reasoning, Demea, it follows (and is, indeed, tacitly allowed by Cleanthes himself) that order, arrangement, or the adjustment of final causes is not, of itself, any proof of design; but only so far as it has been experienced to proceed from that principle. For aught we can know a priori, matter may contain the source or spring of order originally, within itself, as well as mind does; and there is no more difficulty in conceiving, that the several elements, from an internal unknown cause, may fall into the most exquisite arrangement, than to conceive that their ideas, in the great, universal mind, from a like internal, unknown cause, fall into that arrangement. The equal possibility of both these suppositions is allowed. But by experience we find (according to Cleanthes), that there is a difference between them. Throw several pieces of steel togther, without shape or form; they will never arrange themselves so as to compose a watch: stone, and mortar, and wood, without an architect, never erect a house. But the ideas in a human mind, we see, by an unknown, inexplicable economy, arrange themselves so as to form the plan of a watch or house. Experience, therefore, proves, that there is an original principle of order in mind, not in matter. From similar effects we infer similar causes. The adjustment of means to ends is alike in the universe, as in a machine of human contrivance. The causes, therefore, must be resembling.

I was from the beginning scandalized, I must own, with this resemblance, which is asserted, between the Deity and human creatures; and must conceive it to imply such a degradation of the Supreme Being as no sound theist could endure. With your assistance, therefore, Demea, I shall endeavor to defend what you justly called the adorable mysteriousness of the Divine Nature, and shall refute this reasoning of Cleanthes, provided he allows, that I have made a fair representation of it.

When Cleanthes had assented, Philo, after a short pause, proceeded in the following manner.

That all inferences, Cleanthes, concerning fact, are founded on experience, and that all experimental reasonings are founded on the supposition, that similar causes prove similar effects, and similar effects similar causes; I shall not, at present, much dispute with you. But observe, I entreat you, with what extreme caution all just reasoners proceed in the transferring of experiments to similar cases. Unless the cases be exactly similar, they repose no perfect confidence in applying their past observation to any particular phenomenon. Every alteration of circumstances occasions a doubt concerning the event; and it requires new experiments to prove certainly, that the new circumstances are of no moment or importance. A change in bulk, situation, arrangement, age, disposition of the air, or surrounding bodies; any of these particulars may be attended with the most unexpected consequences: and unless the objects be quite familiar to us, it is the highest temerity to expect with assurance, after any of these changes, an event similar to that which before fell under our observation. The slow and deliberate steps of philosophers, here, if anywhere, are distinguished from the precipitate march of the vulgar, who, hurried on by the smallest similitudes, are incapable of all discernment or consideration.

But you can think, Cleanthes, that your usual phlegm and philosophy have been preserved in so wide a step as you have taken, when you compared to the universe, houses, ships, furniture, machines; and from their similarity in some circumstances inferred a similarity in their causes? Thought, design, intelligence, such as we discover in men and other animals, is no more than one of the springs and principles of the universe, as well as heat or cold, attraction or repulsion, and a hundred others, which fall under daily observation. It is an active cause, by which some particular parts of nature, we find, produce alterations on other parts. But can a conclusion, with any propriety, be transferred from parts to the whole? Does not the great disproportion bar all comparison and inference? From observing the growth of a hair, can we learn anything concerning the generation of a man? Would the manner of a leaf's blowing, even though perfectly known, afford us any instruction concerning the vegetation of a tree?

But allowing that we were to take the *operations* of one part of nature upon another for the foundation of our judgment concerning the *origin* of the whole (which never can be admitted), yet why select so minute, so weak, so bounded a principle as the reason and design of animals is found to be upon this planet? What peculiar privilege has this little agitation of the brain which we call *thought,* that we must thus make it the model of the whole universe? Our partiality in our own favor does indeed present it on all occasions; but sound philosophy ought carefully to guard against so natural an illusion.

So far from admitting, continued Philo, that the operations of a part can afford us any just conclusion concerning the origin of the whole, I will not allow any one part to form a rule for another part, if the latter be very remote from the former. Is there any reasonable ground to conclude, that the inhabitants of other planets possess thought, intelligence, reason, or anything similar to these faculties in men? When Nature has so extremely diversified her manner of operation in this small globe; can we imagine, that she incessantly copies herself throughout so immense a universe? And if thought, as we may well suppose, be confined merely to this narrow corner, and has even there so limited a sphere of action; with what propriety can we assign it for the original cause of all things? The narrow views of a peasant, who makes his domestic economy the rule for the government of kingdoms, is in comparison a pardonable sophism.

But were we ever so much assured, that a thought and reason, resembling the human, were to be found throughout the whole universe, and were its activity elsewhere vastly greater and more commanding than it appears in this globe; yet I cannot see, why the operations of a world, constituted, arranged, adjusted, can with any propriety be extended to a world, which is in its embryo state, and is advancing towards that constitution and arrangement. By observation, we know somewhat of the economy, action, and nourishment of a finished animal; but we must transfer with great caution that observation to the growth of a fetus in the womb, and still more, to the formation of an animalcule in the loins of its male parent. Nature, we find, even from our limited experience, possesses an infinite number of springs and principles, which incessantly discover themselves on every change of her position and situation. And what new and unknown principles would actuate her in so new and unknown a situation as that of the formation of a universe, we cannot, without the utmost temerity, pretend to determine.

A very small part of this great system, during a very short time, is very imperfectly discovered to us; and do we thence pronounce decisively concerning the origin of the whole?

Admirable conclusion! Stone, wood, brick, iron, brass, have not, at this time in this minute globe of earth, an order or arrangement without human art and contrivance: therefore the universe could not originally attain its order and arrangement, without something similar to human art. But is a part of nature a rule for another part very wide of the former? Is it a rule for the whole? Is a very small part a rule for the universe? Is nature in one situation, a certain rule for nature in another situation, vastly different from the former?

And can you blame me, Cleanthes, if I here imitate the prudent reserve of Simonides, who, according to the noted story, being asked by Hiero, *What God was?* desired a day to think of it, and then two days more; and after that manner continually prolonged the term, without ever bringing in his definition or description? Could you even blame me, if I had answered at first *that I did not know,* and was sensible that this subject lay vastly beyond the reach of my faculties? You might cry out sceptic and rallier as much as you pleased: but having found, in so many other subjects, much more familiar, the imperfections and even contradictions of human reason, I never should expect any success from its feeble conjectures, in a subject, so sublime, and so remote from the sphere of our observation. When two species of objects have always been observed to be conjoined together, I can infer, by custom, the existence of one wherever I see the existence of the other: and this I call an argument from experience. But how this argument can have place, where the objects, as in the present case, are single, individual, without parallel, or specific resemblance, may be difficult to explain. And will any man tell me with a serious countenance, that an orderly universe must arise from some thought and art, like the human; because we have experience of it?

To ascertain this reasoning, it were requisite that we had experience of the origin of worlds; and it is not sufficient surely, that we have seen ships and cities arise from human art and contrivance. . . .

But to show you still more inconveniences, continued Philo, in your anthropomorphism; please to take a new survey of your principles. *Like effects prove like causes.* This is the experimental argument; and this, you say too, it the sole theological argument. Now it is certain, that the liker the effects are, which are seen, and the liker the causes, which are inferred, the stronger is the argument. Every departure on either side diminishes the probability, and renders the experiment less conclusive. You cannot doubt of the principle: neither ought you to reject its consequences.

All the new discoveries in astronomy, which prove the immense grandeur and magnificence of the works of nature, are so many additional arguments for a Deity, according to the true system of theism: but according to your hypothesis of experimental theism, they become so many objections, by removing the effect still farther from all resemblance to the effects of human art and contrivance.

And what say you to the discoveries in anatomy, chemistry, botany? . . . These surely are no objections, replied Cleanthes: they only discover new instances of art and contrivance. It is still the image of mind reflected on us from innumerable objects. Add, a mind *like the human,* said Philo. I know of no other, replied Cleanthes. And the liker the better, insisted Philo. To be sure, said Cleanthes.

Now, Cleanthes, said Philo, with an air of alacrity and triumph, mark the consequences. *First,* By this method of reasoning, you renounce all claim to infinity in any of the attributes of the Deity. For as the cause ought only to be proportioned to the effect, and the effect, so far as it falls under our cognizance, is not infinite; what pretensions have we, upon your suppositions, to ascribe that attribute to the Divine Being? You will still insist, that, by removing him so much from all similarity to human creatures, we give in to the most arbitrary hypothesis, and at the same time weaken all proofs of his existence.

Secondly, You have no reason, on your theory, for ascribing perfection to the Deity, even in his finite capacity; or for supposing him free from every error, mistake, or incoherence in his undertakings. There are many inexplicable difficulties in the works of nature, which if we allow a perfect author to be proved *a priori,* are easily solved, and become only seeming difficulties, from the narrow capacity of man, who cannot trace infinite relations. But according to your method of reasoning, there difficulties become all real; and perhaps will be insisted on, as new instances of likeness to human art and contrivance. At least, you must acknowledge, that it is impossible for us to tell, from our limited views, whether this system contains any great faults, or deserves any considerable praise, if compared to other possible, and even real systems. Could a peasant, if the *Aeneid* were read to him, pronounce that poem to be absolutely faultless, or even assign to it its proper rank among the productions of human wit; he, who had never seen any other production?

But were this world ever so perfect a production, it must still remain uncertain, whether all the excellences of the work can justly be ascribed to the workman. If we survey a ship, what an exalted idea must we form of the ingenuity of the carpenter, who framed so complicated, useful, and beautiful a machine? And what surprise must we feel, when we find him a stupid mechanic, who imitated others, and copied an art, which, through a long succession of ages, after multiplied trials, mistakes, corrections, deliberations, and controversies, had been gradually improving? Many worlds might have been botched and bungled, throughout an eternity, ere this system was struck out: much labor lost: many fruitless trials made: and a slow, but continued improvement carried on during infinite ages in the art of world-making. In such subjects, who can determine, where the truth; nay, who can conjecture where the probability lies; amidst a great number of hypotheses which may be proposed, and a still greater number which may be imagined?

And what shadow of an argument, continued Philo, can you produce, from your hypothesis, to prove the unity of the Deity? A great number of men join in building a house or ship, in rearing a city, in framing a commonwealth: why may not several deities combine in contriving and framing a world? This is only so much greater similarity to human affairs? By sharing the work among several, we may so much further limit the attributes of each, and get rid of that extensive power and knowledge, which must be supposed in one deity, and which, according to you, can only serve to weaken the proof of his existence. And if such foolish, such vicious creatures as man can yet often unite in framing and executing one plan; how much more those deities or demons, whom we may suppose several degrees more perfect?

To multiply causes, without necessity, is indeed contrary to true philosophy: but this principle applies not to the present case. Were one deity antecedently proved to your theory, who were possessed of every attribute, requisite to the production of the universe; it would be needless, I own (though not absurd) to suppose any other deity existent. But while it is still a question, whether all these attributes are united in one subject, or dispersed among several independent beings: by what phenomena in nature can we pretend to decide the controversy? Where we see a body raised in a scale, we are sure that there is in the opposite scale, however concealed from sight, some counterpoising weight equal to it: but it is still allowed to doubt, whether that weight be an aggregate of several distinct bodies, or one uniform united mass. And if the weight requisite very much exceeds anything which we have ever seen conjoined in any single body, the former supposition becomes still more probable and natural. An intelligent being of such vast power and capacity, as is necessary to produce the universe, or, to speak in the language of ancient philosophy, so prodigious an animal, exceeds all analogy, and even comprehension.

But farther, Cleanthes; men are mortal, and renew their species by generation; and this is common to all living creatures. The two great sexes of male and female, says Milton, animate the world. Why must this circumstance, so universal, so essential, be excluded from those numerous and limited deities? Behold then the theogony of ancient times brought back upon us.

And why not become a perfect anthropomorphite? Why not assert the deity or deities to be corporeal, and to have eyes, nose, mouth, ears, etc.? Epicurus maintained, that no man had ever seen reason but in a human figure; therefore the gods must have a human figure. And this argument, which is deservedly so much ridiculed by Cicero, becomes, according to you, solid and philosophical.

In a word, Cleanthes, a man, who follows your hypothesis, is able, perhaps, to assert, or conjecture, that the universe, sometime, arose from something like design: but beyond that position he cannot ascertain one single circumstance, and is left afterwards to fix every point of his theology, by the utmost license of fancy and hypothesis. This world, for aught he knows, is very faulty and imperfect, compared to a superior standard; and was only the first rude essay of some infant deity, who afterwards abandoned it, ashamed of his lame performance; it is the work only of some dependent, inferior deity; and is the object of derision to his superiors: it is the production of old age and dotage in some superannuated deity; and even since his death, has run on at adventures, from the first impulse and active force, which it received from him. You justly give signs of horror, Demea, at these strange suppositions: but these, and a thousand more of the same kind, are Cleanthes's suppositions, not mine. From the moment the attributes of the Deity are supposed finite, all these have place. And I cannot, for my part, think, that so wild and unsettled a system of theology is, in any respect, preferable to none at all.

These suppositions I absolutely disown, cried Cleanthes: they strike me, however, with no horror; especially, when proposed in that rambling way in which they drop from you. On the contrary, they give me pleasure, when I see, that, by the utmost indulgence of your imagination, you never get rid of the hypothesis of design in the universe; but are obliged, at every turn, to have recourse to it. To this concession I adhere steadily; and this I regard as a sufficient foundation for religion.

But here, continued Philo, in examining the ancient system of the soul of the world, there strikes me, all on a sudden, a new idea, which, if just, must go near to subvert all your reasoning, and destroy even your first inferences, on which you repose such confidence. If the universe bears a greater likeness to animal bodies and to vegetables, than to the works of human art, it is more probable that its cause resembles the cause of the former than that of the latter, and its origin ought rather to be ascribed to generation or vegetation than to reason or design. Your conclusion, even according to your own principles, is therefore lame and defective.

Pray open up this argument a little farther, said Demea. For I do not rightly apprehend it, in that concise manner, in which you have expressed it.

Our friend, Cleanthes, replied Philo, as you have heard, asserts, that since no question of fact can be proved otherwise than by experience, the existence of a Deity admits not of proof from any other medium. The world, says he, resembles the works of human contrivance: therefore its cause must also resemble that of the other. Here we may remark, that the operation of one very small part of nature, to wit man, upon another very small part, to wit that inanimate matter lying within his reach, is the rule, by which Cleanthes judges of the origin of the whole; and he measures objects, so widely disproportioned, by the same individual standard. But to waive all objections drawn from this topic; I affirm, that there are other parts of the universe (besides the machines of human invention) which bear still a greater resemblance to the fabric of the world, and which therefore afford a better conjecture concerning the universal origin of this system. These parts are animals and vegetables. The world plainly resembles more an animal or a vegetable, than it does a watch or a knitting-loom. Its cause, therefore, it is more probable, resembles the cause of the former. The cause of the former is generation or vegetation. The cause, therefore, of the world, we may infer to be some thing similar or analogous to generation or vegetation.

But how is it conceivable, said Demea, that the world can arise from anything similar to vegetation or generation?

Very easily, replied Philo. In like manner as a tree sheds its seed into the neighboring fields, and produces other trees; so the great vegetable the world, or this planetary system, produces within itself certain seeds, which, being scattered into the surrounding chaos, vegetate into new worlds. A comet, for instance, is the seed of a world; and after it has been fully ripened, by passing from sun to sun, and star to star, it is at last tossed into the unformed elements, which everywhere surround this universe, and immediately sprouts up into a new system.

Or if, for the stake of variety (for I see no other advantage), we should suppose this world to be an animal; a comet is the egg of this animal; and in like manner as an ostrich lays its egg in the sand, which, without any further care, hatches the egg, and produces a new animal, so. . . .

I understand you, says Demea: but what wild, arbitrary suppositions are these? What *data* have you for such extraordinary conclusions? And is the slight, imaginary resemblance of the world to a vegetable or an animal sufficient to establish the same inference with regard to both? Objects, which are in general so widely different; ought they to be a standard for each other?

Right, cries Philo: this is the topic on which I have all along insisted. I have still asserted, that we have no *data* to establish any system of cosmogony. Our experience, so imperfect in itself, and so limited both in extent and duration, can afford us no probable conjecture concerning the whole of things. But if we must needs fix on some hypothesis; by what rule, pray ought we to determine our choice? Is there any other rule than the greater similarity of the objects compared? And does not a plant or an animal, which springs from vegetation or generation, bear a stronger resemblance to the world, than does any artificial machine, which arises from reason and design?

But what is this vegetation and generation of which you talk? said Demea. Can you explain their operations, and anatomize that fine internal structure, on which they depend?

As much, at least, replied Philo, as Cleanthes can explain the operations of reason, or anatomize that internal structure, on which *it* depends. But without any such elaborate disquisitions, when I see an animal, I infer, that it sprang from generation; and that with as great certainty as you conclude a house to have been reared by design. These words, *generation, reason,* mark only certain powers and energies in nature, whose effects are known, but whose essence is incomprehensible; and one of these principles, more than the other, has no privilege for being made a standard to the whole of nature.

In reality, Demea, it may reasonably be expected, that the larger the views are which we take of things, the better will they conduct us in our conclusions concerning such extraordinary and such magnificent subjects. In this little corner of the world alone, there are four principles, *reason, instinct, generation, vegetation,* which are similar to each other, and are the causes of similar effects. What a number of other principles may we naturally suppose in the immense extent and variety of the universe, could we travel from planet to planet and from system to system, in order to examine each part of this mighty fabric? Any one of these four principles above mentioned (and a hundred others which lie open to our conjecture) may afford us a theory, by which to judge of the origin of the world; and it is a palpable and egregious partiality, to confine our view entirely to that principle, by which our own minds operate. Were this principle more intelligent on that account, such a partiality might be somewhat excusable. But reason, in its internal fabric and structure, is really as little known to us as instinct or vegetation; and perhaps even that vague, undeterminate word, *Nature,* to which the vulgar refer everything, is not at the bottom more explicable. The effects of these principles are all known to us from experience: but the principles themselves, and their manner of operation, are totally unknown: nor is it less intelligible, or less conformable to experience to say, that the word arose by vegetation from a seed shed by another world, than to say that it arose from a divine reason or contrivance, according to the sense in which Cleanthes understands it.

But methinks, said Demea, if the world had a vegetative quality, and could sow the seeds of new worlds into the infinite chaos, this power would be still an additional argument for design in its author. For whence could arise so wonderful a faculty but from design? Or how can order spring from anything, which perceives not that order which it bestows?

You need only look around you, replied Philo, to satisfy yourself with regard to this question. A tree bestows order and organization on that tree which springs from it, without knowing the order: an animal, in the same manner, on its offspring: a bird, on its nest: and instances of this kind are even more frequent in the world, than those of order, which arise from reason and contrivance. To say, that all this order in animals and vegetables proceeds ultimately from design, is begging the question; nor can that great point be ascertained otherwise than by proving *a priori,* both that order is, from its nature, inseparably attached to thought, and that it can never, of itself, or from original unknown principles, belong to matter.

But farther, Demea; this objection, which you urge, can never be made use of by Cleanthes, without renouncing a defense, which he has already made against one of my objections. When I inquired concerning the cause of that supreme reason and intelligence, into which he resolves everything; he told me, that the impossibility of satisfying such inquiries could never be admitted as an objection in any species of philosophy. *We must stop somewhere, says he; nor is it ever within the reach of human capacity to explain ultimate causes, or show the last connections of any objects. It is sufficient, if our steps, so far as we go, are supported by experience and observation.* Now, that vegetation and generation, as well as reason, are experienced to be principles of order in nature, is undeniable. If I rest my system of cosmogony on the former, preferably to the latter, 'tis at my choice. The matter seems entriely arbitrary. And when Cleanthes asks me what is the cause of my great vegetative or generative faculty, I am equally entitled to ask him the cause of his great reasoning principle. These questions we have agreed to forebear on both sides; and it is chiefly his interest on the present occasion to stick to this agreement. Judging by our limited and imperfect experience, generation has some privileges above reason: for we see every day the latter arise from the former, never the former from the latter.

Compare, I beseech you, the consequences on both sides. The world, say I, resembles an animal, therefore it is an animal, therefore it arose from generation. The steps, I confess, are wide; yet there is some small appearance of analogy in each step. The world, says Cleanthes, resembles a machine, therefore it is a machine, therefore it arose from design. The steps are here equally wide, and the analogy less striking. And if he pretends to carry on *my* hypothesis a step farther, and to infer design or reason from the great principle of generation, on which I insist; I may, with better authority, use the same freedom to push farther *his* hypothesis, and infer a divine generation or theogony from his principle of reason. I have at least some faint shadow of experience, which is the utmost that can ever be attained in the present subject. Reason, in innumerable instances, is observed to arise from the principle of generation, and never to arise from any other principle.

Hesiod, and all the ancient mythologists, were so struck with this analogy, that they universally explained the origin of nature from an animal birth, and copulation. Plato too, so far as he is intelligible, seems to have adopted some such notion in his *Timaeus*.

The Brahmins assert, that the world arose from an infinite spider, who spun this whole complicated mass from his bowels, and annihilates afterwards the whole or any part of it, by absorbing it again, and resolving it into his own essence. Here is a species of cosmogony, which appears to us ridiculous; because a spider is a little contemptible animal, whose operations we are never likely to take for a model of the whole universe. But still here is a new species of analogy, even in our globe. And were there a planet wholly inhabited by spiders (which is very possible), this inference would there appear as natural and irrefragable as that which in our planet ascribes the origin of all things to design and intelligence, as explained by Cleanthes. Why an orderly system may not be spun from the belly as well as from the brain, it will be difficult for him to give a satisfactory reason.

I must confess, Philo, replied Cleanthes, that of all men living, the task which you have undertaken, of raising doubts and objections, suits you best, and seems, in a manner, natural and unavoidable to you. So great is your fertility of invention, that I am not ashamed to acknowledge myself unable, on a sudden, to solve regularly such out-of-the-way difficulties as you incessantly start upon me: though I clearly see, in general, their fallacy and error. And I question not, but you are yourself, at present, in the same case, and have not the solution so ready as the objection; while you must be sensible, that common sense and reason are entirely against you, and that such whimsies as you have delivered, may puzzle, but never can convince us.

HUME SELECTION

1. In this selection, the character called Cleanthes defends the Argument from Design. Does his statement of it differ in any significant way from Paley's statement?

2. Philo does not directly dispute the use of causal arguments, but he suggests that there are a variety of limitations on their use, limitations that make them unsuitable for proofs of the existence of God. What are the limitations on the use of causal arguments, according to Philo? How do these limitations undermine the Argument from Design? How might Cleanthes answer this line of objection, in your view?

3. Philo uses a variety of arguments to show that the Argument from Design cannot prove the existence of the God of the Scriptures and of Religion. What are the problems he points to? How could a devout Christian, Jew, or Moslem answer Philo's rather irreverent objections? What *can* we learn about God the Creator from an examination of His

Creation? If God is infinitely powerful and infinitely wise and infinitely good, couldn't He have arranged things a bit better in this world? Did He really have to include mosquitos?

4.   What is the point—aside from having some fun—in Philo's wild hypotheses about the Divine Creation being like the laying of an egg or the dropping of seeds? How might Cleanthes answer these fanciful arguments?

5.   Do you think Hume gives the Argument from Design a fair shake? Does he load the deck against it by making Philo's speeches so extravagant and humorous? Can you rewrite some of Cleanthes's speeches so as to give him a stronger position?

(SELECTION 6)

HUSTON SMITH

Do Drugs Have Religious Import?

Many drug users seek an escape from reality, either because reality is so painful or because their drug-induced fantasies are so pleasant. Some men and women, however, in cultures as varied as those of the ancient Greeks and the American Indians, have used consciousness-altering drugs as a pathway to experiences that they firmly believed to be *religious.*

If we are interested in religion sociologically, as a virtually universal feature of human social life, then it seems merely parochial and small-minded to deny that drug-induced experiences can be genuinely religious in character. Indeed, there are some religions in which the use of such drugs plays an essential, publically defined role. But what if we are concerned to distinguish true from false religion? What, indeed, if we wish to determine whether there is any true religion at all? How then shall we evaluate the reports of those who have had visions? Indeed, how are we to evaluate our own "visions," assuming we have used LSD or some other hallucinogen to induce them?

The most natural reply, perhaps, is to say that if we can deliberately, planfully, foresightedly induce a vision by ingesting small bits of a mushroom or traces of a drug, then that "vision" can-

not possibly be reliable evidence of the existence of a realm beyond the reach of the ordinary senses. Somehow, knowing the mechanism by which the experience is produced robs it of its power as a revelation of the supernatural.

But is such an evaluation sound? Let us reflect, after all, that the way to induce visual experiences is to arrange for light to strike the retina of the eye. Does the fact that we can deliberately produce a visual experience deprive that experience of all epistemic value? Is it reasonable to reject the realm of the visual as imaginary or unreal merely because we have managed to discover the mechanisms by which light generates visual experiences in our minds?

To be sure, if we have doubts about the very existence of God and the realm of the divine, then "visions," whether drug-induced or not, are scarcely likely to resolve those doubts. But then, if we have skeptical doubts about the reality of the physical world, visual experiences will not resolve those doubts either! So drug-induced religious experiences seem to have as much, or as little, epistemological standing as visual experiences. Each is insufficient, by itself, to assure us of the reality of its supposed objects, and each is a perfectly acceptable bit of evidence concerning the supernatural or the visible,

assuming we are already convinced on   But there is something wrong with
other grounds that the supernatural or   that argument, isn't there? Or is there?
the visible exists.

Until six months ago, if I picked up my phone in the Cambridge
area and dialed KISS-BIG, a voice would answer, "If-if." There were
coincidences: KISS-BIG happened to be the letter equivalents of an
arbitrarily assigned telephone number, and I.F.I.F. represented the
initials of an organization with the improbable name of the International Federation for Internal Freedom. But the coincidences were
apposite to the point of being poetic. "Kiss big" caught the euphoric,
manic, life-embracing attitude that characterized this most publi-
cized of the organizations formed to explore the newly synthesized
conscious-changing substances; the organization itself was surely one
of the "iffy-est" phenomena to appear on our social and intellectual
scene in some time. It produced the first firings in Harvard's history,
an ultimatum to get out of Mexico in five days, and "the miracle of
Marsh Chapel," in which, during a two-and-one-half-hour Good
Friday service, ten theological students and professors ingested psilocybin and were visited by what they generally reported to be the
deepest religious experiences of their lives.

Despite the last of these phenomena and its numerous if less
dramatic parallels, students of religion appear by and large to be
dismissing the psychedelic durgs that have sprung to our attention
in the '60s as having little religious relevance. The position taken
in one of the most forward-looking volumes of theological essays to
have appeared in recent years—*Soundings*, edited by A. R. Vidler [1]
—accepts R. C. Zaehner's *Mysticism Sacred and Profane* as having
"fully examined and refuted" the religious claims for mescalin which
Aldous Huxley sketched in *The Doors of Perception*. This closing
of the case strikes me as premature, for it looks as if the drugs have
light to throw on the history of religion, the phenomenology of
religion, the philosophy of religion, and the practice of the religious
life itself.

1. *Drugs and Religion Viewed Historically*

In his trial-and-error life explorations man almost everywhere
has stumbled upon connections between vegetables (eaten or brewed)
and actions (yogi breathing exercises, whirling-dervish dances, flagel-

---

[1] *Soundings: Essays Concerning Christian Understandings*, A. R. Vidler ed. (Cambridge:
University Press, 1962). The statement cited appears on page 72, in H. A. Williams's
essay on "Theology and Self-awareness."

From "Do Drugs Have Religious Import?", first published in *The Journal of Philosophy* (Vol. LXI, no. 18, October 1, 1964). Reprinted by permission of the author
and *The Journal of Philosophy*.

lations) that alter states of consciousness. From the psychopharmacological standpoint we now understand these states to be the products of changes in brain chemistry. From the sociological perspective we see that they tend to be connected in some way with religion. If we discount the wine used in Christian communion services, the instances closest to us in time and space are the peyote of The Native American [Indian] Church and Mexico's 2000-year-old "sacred mushrooms," the latter rendered in Aztec as "God's Flesh"—striking parallel to "the body of our Lord" in the Christian eucharist. Beyond these neighboring instances lie the *soma* of the Hindus, the *haoma* and hemp of the Zoroastrians, the Dionysus of the Greeks who "everywhere . . . taught men the culture of the vine and the mysteries of his worship and everywhere [was] accepted as a god," [2] the *benzoin* of Southeast Asia, Zen's tea whose fifth cup purifies and whose sixth "calls to the realm of the immortals," [3] the *pituri* of the Australian aborigines, and probably the mystic *kykeon* that was eaten and drunk at the climactic close of the sixth day of the Eleusinian mysteries.[4] There is no need to extend the list, as a reasonably complete account is available in Philippe de Félice's comprehensive study of the subject, *Poisons sacrés, ivresses divines.*

More interesting than the fact that consciousness-changing devices have been linked with religion is the possibility that they actually initiated many of the religious perspectives which, taking root in history, continued after their psychedelic origins were forgotten. Bergson saw the first movement of Hindus and Greeks toward "dynamic religion" as associated with the "divine rapture" found in intoxicating beverages; [5] more recently Robert Graves, Gordon Wasson, and Alan Watts have suggested that most religions arose from such chemically induced theophanies. Mary Barnard is the most explicit proponent of this thesis. "Which . . . was more likely to happen first," she asks,[6] "the spontaneously generated idea of an afterlife in which the disembodied soul, liberated from the restrictions of time and space, experiences eternal bliss, or the accidental discovery of hallucinogenic plants that give a sense of euphoria, dislocate the center of consciousness, and distort time and space, making them balloon outward in greatly expanded vistas?" Her own answer is that "the [latter] experience might have had . . . an almost explosive effect on the largely dormant minds of men, causing them to think of things they had never thought of before. This, if

[2] Edith Hamilton, *Mythology* (New York: Mentor, 1953), p. 55.
[3] Quoted in Alan Watts, *The Spirit of Zen* (New York: Grove Press, 1958), p. 110.
[4] George Mylonas, *Eleusis and the Eleusinian Mysteries* (Princeton, N.J.: Princeton University Press, 1961), p. 284.
[5] *Two Sources of Morality and Religion* (New York: Holt, 1935), pp. 206–212.
[6] "The God in the Flowerpot," *The American Scholar* **32,** 4 (Autumn 1963): 584, 586.

you like, is direct revelation." Her use of the subjunctive "might" renders this formulation of her answer equivocal, but she concludes her essay on a note that is completely unequivocal: "Looking at the matter coldly, unintoxicated and unentranced, I am willing to prophesy that fifty theobotanists working for fifty years would make the current theories concerning the origins of much mythology and theology as out-of-date as pre-Copernican astronomy."

This is an important hypothesis—one which must surely engage the attention of historians of religion for some time to come. But as I am concerned here only to spot the points at which the drugs erupt onto the field of serious religious study, not to ride the geysers to whatever heights, I shall not pursue Miss Barnard's thesis. Having located what appears to be the crux of this historical question, namely the extent to which drugs not merely duplicate or simulate theologically sponsored experiences but generate or shape theologies themselves, I turn to phenomenology.

2. *Drugs and Religion Viewed Phenomenologically*

Phenomenology attempts a careful description of human experience. The question the drugs pose for the phenomenology of religion, therefore, is whether the experiences they induce differ from religious experiences reached naturally, and if so how.

Even the Bible notes that chemically induced psychic states bear *some* resemblance to religious ones. Peter had to appeal to a circumstantial criterion—the early hour of the day—to defend those who were caught up in the Pentecostal experience against the charge that they were merely drunk: "These men are not drunk, as you suppose, since it is only the third hour of the day" (Acts 2:15); and Paul initiates the comparison when he admonishes the Ephesians not to "get drunk with wine . . . but [to] be filled the spirit" (Ephesians 5:18). Are such comparisons, paralleled in the accounts of virtually every religion, superficial? How far can they be pushed?

Not all the way, students of religion have thus far insisted. With respect to the new drugs, Prof. R. C. Zaehner has drawn the line emphatically. "The importance of Huxley's *Doors of Perception*," he writes, "is that in it the author clearly makes the claim that what he experienced under the influence of mescalin is closely comparable to a genuine mystical experience. If he is right, . . . the conclusions . . . are alarming." [7] Zaehner thinks that Huxley is not right, but I fear that it is Zaehner who is mistaken.

There are, of course, innumerable drug experiences that have no religious feature; they can be sensual as readily as spiritual, trivial

---

[7] *Mysticism, Sacred and Profane* (New York: Oxford, 1961), p. 12.

as readily as transforming, capricious as readily as sacramental. If there is one point about which every student of the drugs agrees, it is that there is no such thing as the drug experience *per se*—no experience that the drugs, as it were, merely secrete. Every experience is a mix of three ingredients: drug, set (the psychological make-up of the individual), and setting (the social and physical environment in which it is taken). But given the right set and setting, the drugs can reduce religious experiences indistinguishable from experiences that occur spontaneously. Nor need set and setting be exceptional. The way the statistics are currently running, it looks as if from one-fourth to one-third of the general population will have religious experiences if they take the drugs under naturalistic conditions, meaning by this conditions in which the researcher supports the subject but does not try to influence the direction his experience will take. Among subjects who have strong religious inclinations to begin with, the proportion of those having religious experiences jumps to three-fourths. If they take the drugs in settings that are religious too, the ratio soars to nine in ten.

How do we know that the experiences these people have really are religious? We can begin with the fact that they say they are. The "one-fourth" to one-third of the general population" figure is drawn from two sources. Ten months after they had had their experiences, 24 per cent of the 194 subjects in a study by the California psychiatrist Oscar Janiger characterized their experiences as having been religious.[8] Thirty-two per cent of the 74 subjects in Ditman and Hayman's study reported, looking back on their LSD experience, that it looked as if it had been "very much" or "quite a bit" a religious experience; 42 per cent checked as true the statement that they "were left with a greater awareness of God, or a higher power, or ultimate reality." [9] The statement that three-fourths of subjects having religious "sets" will have religious experiences comes from the reports of sixty-nine religious professionals who took the drugs while the Harvard project was in progress.[10]

In the absence of (a) a single definition of religious experience acceptable to psychologists of religion generally and (b) foolproof ways of ascertaining whether actual experiences exemplify any definition, I am not sure there is any better way of telling whether the experiences of the 333 men and women involved in the above studies were religious than by noting whether they seemed so to them. But if

[8] Quoted in William H. McGlothlin, "Long-lasting Effects of LSD on Certain Attitudes in Normals," printed for private distribution by the RAND Corporation, May 1962, p. 16.
[9] *Ibid.*, pp. 45, 46.
[10] Timothy Leary, "The Religious Experience: Its Production and Interpretation," *The Psychedelic Review*, **1,** 3 (1964): 325.

more rigorous methods are preferred, they exist; they have been utilized, and they confirm the conviction of the man in the street that drug experiences can indeed be religious. In his doctoral study at Harvard University, Walter Pahnke worked out a typology of religious experience (in this instance of the mystical variety) based on the classic cases of mystical experiences as summarized in Walter Stace's *Mysticism and Philosophy*. He then administered psilocybin to ten theology students and professors in the setting of a Good Friday service. The drug was given "double blind," meaning that neither Dr. Pahnke not his subjects knew which ten were getting psilocybin and which ten placebos to constitute a control group. Subsequently the reports the subjects wrote of their experiences were laid successively before three college-graduate housewives who, without being informed about the nature of the study, were asked to rate each statement as to the degree (strong, moderate, slight, or none) to which it exemplified each of the nine traits of mystical experience enumerated in the typology of mysticism worked out in advance. When the test of significance was applied to their statistics, it showed that "those subjects who received psilocybin experienced phenomena which were indistinguishable from, if not identical with . . . the categories defined by our typology of mysticism." [11]

With the thought that the reader might like to test his own powers of discernment on the question being considered, I insert here a simple test I gave to a group of Princeton students following a recent discussion sponsored by the Woodrow Wilson Society:

Below are accounts of two religious experiences. One occurred under the influence of drugs, one without the influence. Check the one you think *was* drug-induced.

I

Suddenly I burst into a vast, new, indescribably wonderful universe. Although I am writing this over a year later, the thrill of the surprise and amazement, the awesomeness of the revelation, the engulfment in an overwhelming feeling-wave of gratitude and blessed wonderment, are as fresh, and the memory of the experience is as vivid, as if it had happened five minutes ago. And yet to concoct anything by way of description that would even hint at the magnitude, the sense of ultimate reality . . . this seems such an impossible task. The knowledge which has infused and affected every aspect of my life came instan-

[11] "Drugs and Mysticism: An Analysis of the Relationship between Psychedelic Drugs and the Mystical Consciousness," a thesis presented to the Committee on Higher Degree in History and Philosophy of Religion, Harvard University, June 1963.

taneously and with such complete force of certainty that it was impossible, then or since, to doubt its validity.

II

All at once, without warning of any kind, I found myself wrapped in a flame-colored cloud. For an instant I thought of fire . . . the next, I knew that the first was within myself. Directly afterward there came upon me a sense of exultation, of immense joyousness accompanied or immediately followed by an intellectual illumination impossible to describe. Among other things, I did not merely come to believe, but I saw that the universe is not composed of dead matter, but is, on the contrary, a living Presence; I became conscious in myself of eternal life. . . . I saw that all men are immortal: that the cosmic order is such that without any preadvanture all things work together for the good of each and all; that the foundation principle of the world . . . is what we call love, and that the happiness of each and all is in the long run absolutely certain.

On the occasion referred to, twice as many students (46) answered incorrectly as answered correctly (23). I bury the correct answer in a footnote to preserve the reader's opportunity to test himself.[12]

Why, in the face of this considerable evidence, does Zaehner hold that drug experiences cannot be authentically religious? There appear to be three reasons:

1. His own experience was "utterly trivial." This of course proves that not all drug experiences are religious; it does not prove that no drug experiences are religious.

2. He thinks the experiences of others that appear religious to them are not truly so. Zaehner distinguishes three kinds of mysticism: nature mysticism, in which the soul is united with the natural world; monistic mysticism, in which the soul merges with an impersonal absolute; and theism, in which the soul confronts the living, personal God. He concedes that drugs induce the first two species of mysticism, but not its supreme instance, the theistic. As proof, he analyzes Huxley's experience as recounted in *The Doors of Perception* to show that it produced at best a blend of nature and monistic mysticism. Even if we were to accept Zaehner's evaluation of the

[12] The first account is quoted anonymously in "The Issue of the Consciousness-expanding Drugs," *Main Currents in Modern Thought*, **20,** 1 (September–October, 1963): 10–11. The second experience was that of Dr. R. M. Bucke, the author of *Cosmic Consciousness*, as quoted in William James, *The Varieties of Religious Experience* (New York: Modern Library, 1902), pp. 390–391. The former experience occurred under the influence of drugs; the latter did not.

three forms of mysticism, Huxley's case, and indeed Zaehner's entire book, would prove only that not every mystical experience induced by the drugs is theistic. Insofar as Zaehner goes beyond this to imply that drugs do not and cannot induce theistic mysticism, he not only goes beyond the evidence but proceeds in the face of it. James Slotkin reports that the peyote Indians "see visions, which may be of Christ Himself. Sometimes they hear the voice of the Great Spirit. Sometimes they become aware of the presence of God and of those personal shortcomings which must be corrected if they are to do His will." [13] And G. M. Carstairs, reporting on the use of psychedelic *bhang* in India, quotes a Brahmin as saying, "It gives good bhakti. . . . You get a very good bhakti with bhang," *bhakti* being precisely Hinduism's theistic variant.[14]

3. There is a third reason why Zaehner might doubt that drugs can induce genuinely mystical experiences. Zaehner is a Roman Catholic, and Roman Catholic doctrine teaches that mystical rapture is a gift of grace and as such can never be reduced to man's control. This may be true; certainly the empirical evidence cited does not preclude the possibility of a genuine ontological or theological difference between natural and drug-induced religious experiences. At this point, however, we are considering phenomenology rather than ontology, description rather than interpretation, and on this level there is no difference. Descriptively, drug experiences cannot be distinguished from their natural religious counterpart. When the current philosophical authority on mysticism, W. T. Stace, was asked whether the drug experience is similar to the mystical experience, he answered, "It's not a matter of its being *similar* to mystical experience; it *is* mystical experience."

What we seem to be witnessing in Zaehner's *Mysticism Sacred and Profane* is a reenactment of the age-old pattern in the conflict between science and religion. Whenever a new controversy arises, religion's first impulse is to deny the disturbing evidence science has produced. Seen in perspective, Zaehner's refusal to admit that drugs can induce experiences descriptively indistinguishable from those which are spontaneously religious is the current counterpart of the seventeenth-century theologians' refusal to look through Galileo's telescope or, when they did, their persistence on dismissing what they saw as machinations of the devil. When the fact that drugs can trigger religious experiences becomes incontrovertible, discussion will move to the more difficult question of how this new fact is to

[13] James S. Stotkin, *Peyote Religion* (New York: Free Press of Glencoe, 1956).
[14] "Daru and Bhang," *Quarterly Journal of the Study of Alcohol,* **15** (1954): 229.

be interpreted. The latter question leads beyond phenomenology into philosophy.

3. *Drugs and Religion Viewed Philosophically*

Why do people reject evidence? Because they find it threatening, we may suppose. Theologians are not the only professionals to utilize this mode of defense. In his *Personal Knowledge,*[15] Michael Polanyi recounts the way the medical profession ignored such palpable facts as the painless amputation of human limbs, performed before their own eyes in hundreds of successive cases, concluding that the subjects were imposters who were either deluding their physicians or colluding with them. One physician, Esdaile, carried out about 300 major operations painlessly under mesmeric trance in India, but neither in India nor in Great Britain could he get medical journals to print accounts of his work. Polanyi attributes this closed-mindedness to "lack of a conceptual framework in which their discoveries could be separated from specious and untenable admixtures."

The "untenable admixture" in the fact that psychotomimetic drugs can induce religious experience is its apparent implicate: that religious disclosures are no more veridical than psychotic ones. For religious skeptics, this conclusion is obviously not untenable at all; it fits in beautifully with their thesis that *all* religion is at heart an escape from reality. Psychotics avoid reality by retiring into dream worlds of make-believe; what better evidence that religious visionaries do the same than the fact that identical changes in brain chemistry produce both states of mind? Had not Marx already warned us that religion is the "opiate" of the people?—apparently he was more literally accurate than he supposed. Freud was likewise too mild. He "never doubted that religious phenomena are to be understood only on the model of the neurotic symptoms of the individual." [16] He should have said "psychotic symptoms."

So the religious skeptic is likely to reason. What about the religious believer? Convinced that religious experiences are not fundamentally delusory, can he admit that psychotomimetic drugs can occasion them? To do so he needs (to return to Polyanyi's words) "a conceptual framework in which [the discoveries can] be separated from specious and untenable admixtures," the "untenable admixture" being in this case the conclusion that religious experiences are in general delusory.

[15] Chicago: University of Chicago Press, 1958.
[16] *Totem and Taboo* (New York: Modern Library, 1938).

One way to effect the separation would be to argue that, despite phenomenological similarities between natural and drug-induced religious experiences, they are separated by a crucial *ontological* difference. Such an argument would follow the pattern of theologians who argue for the "real presence" of Christ's body and blood in the bread and wine of the Eucharist despite their admission that chemical analysis, confined as it is to the level of "accidents" rather than "essences," would not disclose this presence. But this distinction will not appeal to many today, for it turns on an essence-accident metaphysics which is not widely accepted. Instead of fighting a rear-guard action by insisting that if drug and non-drug religious experiences cannot be distinguished empirically there must be some transempirical factor that distinguishes them and renders the drug experience profane, I wish to explore the possibility of accepting drug-induced experiences as religious without relinquishing confidence in the truth-claims of religious experience generally.

To begin with the weakest of all arguments, the argument from authority: William James did not discount *his* insights that occurred while his brain chemistry was altered. The paragraph in which he retrospectively evaluates his nitrous oxide experiences has become classic, but it is so pertinent to the present discussion that it merits quoting once again.

> One conclusion was forced upon my mind at that time, and my impression of its truth has even since remained unshaken. It is that our normal waking consciousness, rational consciousness as we call it, is but one special type of consciousness, whilst all about it, parted from it by the filmiest of screens, there lie potential forms of consciousness entirely different. We may go through life without suspecting their existence; but apply the requisite stimulus, and at a touch they are there in all their completeness, definite types of mentality which probably somewhere have their field of application and adaptation. No account of the universe in its totality can be final which leaves these other forms of consciousness quite disregarded. How to regard them is the question—for they are so discontinuous with ordinary consciousness. Yet they may determine attitudes though they cannot furnish formulas, and open a region though they fail to give a map. At any rate, they forbid a premature closing of our accounts with reality. Looking back on my own experiences, they all converge toward a kind of insight to which I cannot help ascribing some metaphysical significance (*op. cit.*, 378–379).

To this argument from authority, I add two arguments that try to provide something by ways of reasons. Drug experiences that assume a religious cast tend to have fearful and/or beatific features, and each of my hypotheses relates to one of these aspects of the experience.

Beginning with the ominous, "fear of the Lord," awe-ful features, Gordon Wasson, the New York banker-turned-mycologist, describes these as he encountered them in his psilocybin experience as follows: "Ecstasy! In common parlance . . . ecstasy in fun. . . . But ecstasy is not fun. Your very soul is seized and shaken until it tingles. After all, who will choose to feel undiluted awe? . . . The unknowing vulgar abuse the word; we must recapture its full and terrifying sense." [17] Emotionally the drug experience can be like having forty-foot waves crash over you for several hours while you cling desperately to a life-raft which may be swept from under you at any minute. It seems quite possible that such an ordeal, like any experience of a close call, could awaken rather fundamental sentiments respecting life and death and destiny and trigger the "no atheists in foxholes" effect. Similarly, as the subject emerges from the trauma and realizes that he is not going to be insane as he had feared, there may come over him an intensified appreciation like that frequently reported by patients recovering from critical illness. "I happened on the day when my bed was pushed out of doors to the open gallery of the hospital," reads one such report:

> I cannot now recall whether the revelation came suddenly or gradually; I only remember finding myself in the very midst of those wonderful moments, beholding life for the first time in all its young intoxication of loveliness, in its unspeakable joy, beauty, and importance. I cannot say exactly what the mysterious change was. I saw no new thing, but I saw all the usual things in a miraculous new light—in what I believe is their true light. I saw for the first time how wildly beautiful and joyous, beyond any words of mine to describe, is the whole of life. Every human being moving across that porch, every sparrow that flew, every branch tossing in the wind, was caught in and was a part of the whole mad ecstasy of loveliness, of joy, of importance, of intoxication of life.[18]

---

[17] "The Hallucinogenic Fungi of Mexico: An Inquiry into the Origins of the Religious Idea among Primitive Peoples," *Harvard Botanical Museum Leaflets,* **19,** 7 (1961).
[18] Margaret Prescott Montague, *Twenty Minutes of Reality* (St. Paul, Minn.: Macalester Park, 1947), pp. 15, 17.

If we do not discount religious intuitions because they are prompted by battlefields and *physical* crises; if we regard the latter as "calling us to our senses" more often than they seduce us into delusions, need comparable intuitions be discounted simply because the crises that trigger them are of an inner, *psychic* variety?

Turning from the hellish to the heavenly aspects of the drug experience, *some* of the latter may be explainable by the hypothesis just stated; that is, they may be occasioned by the relief that attends the sense of escape from high danger. But this hypothesis cannot possibly account for *all* the beatific episodes, for the simple reason that the positive episodes often come first, or to persons who experience no negative episodes whatever. Dr. Sanford Unger of the National Institute of Mental Health reports that among his subjects "50 to 60% will not manifest any real disturbance worthy of discussion," yet "around 75% will have at least one episode in which exaltation, rapture, and joy are the key descriptions." [19] How are we to account for the drug's capacity to induce peak experiences, such as the following, which are *not* preceded by fear?

> A feeling of great peace and contentment seemed to flow through my entire body. All sound ceased and I seemed to be floating in a great, very very still void or hemisphere. It is impossible to describe the overpowering feeling of peace, contentment, and being a part of goodness itself that I felt. I could feel my body dissolving and actually becoming a part of the goodness and peace that was all around me. Words can't describe this. I feel an awe and wonder that such a feeling could have occurred to me.[20]

Consider the following line of argument. Like every other form of life, man's nature has become distinctive through specialization. Man has specialized in developing a cerebral cortex. The analytic powers of this instrument are a standing wonder, but the instrument seems less able to provide man with the sense that he is meaningfully related to his environment: to life, the world, and history in their wholeness. As Albert Camus describes the situation, "If I were . . . a cat among animals, this life would have a meaning, or rather this problem would not arise, for I should belong to this world. I would *be* this world to which I am now opposed by my whole consciousness." [21] Note that it is Camus' consciousness that opposes him to

[19] "The Current Scientific Status of Psychedelic Drug Research," read at the Conference on Methods in Philosophy and the Sciences, New School for Social Research, May 3, 1964, and scheduled for publication in David Solomon, ed., *The Conscious Expanders* (New York: Putnam, fall of 1964).
[20] Quoted by Dr. Unger in the paper just mentioned.
[21] *The Myth of Sisyphus* (New York, Vintage, 1955), p. 38.

his world. The drugs do not knock this consciousness out, but while they leave it operative they also activate areas of the brain that normally lie below its threshold of awareness. One of the clearest objective signs that the drugs are taking effect is the dilation they produce in the pupils of the eyes, and one of the most predictable subjective signs is the intensification of vsual perception. Both of these responses are controlled by portions of the brain that lie deep, further to the rear than the mechanisms that govern consciousness. Meanwhile we know that the human organism is interlaced with its world in innumerable ways it normally cannot sense—through gravitational fields, body respiration, and the like: the list could be multiplied until man's skin began to seem more like a thoroughfare than a boundary. Perhaps the deeper regions of the brain which evolved earlier and are more like those of the lower animals—"If I were . . . a cat . . . I should belong to this world"—can sense this relatedness better than can the cerebral cortex which now dominates our awareness. If so, when the drugs rearrange the neurohumors that chemically transmit impulses across synapses between neurons, man's consciousness and his submerged, intuitive, ecological awareness might for a spell become interlaced. This is, of course, no more than a hypothesis, but how else are we to account for the extraordinary incidence under the drugs of that kind of insight the keynote of which James described as "invariably a reconciliation"? "It is as if the opposites of the world, whose contradictoriness and conflict make all our difficulties and troubles, were melted into one and the same genus, but *one of the species,* the nobler and better one, *is itself the genus, and so soaks up and absorbs its opposites into itself*" (*op. cit.,* 379).

4. *The Drugs and Religion Viewed "Religiously"*

Suppose that drugs can induce experiences indistinguishable from religious experiences and that we can respect their reports. Do they shed any light, not (we now ask) on life, but on the nature of the religious life?

One thing they may do is throw religious experiences itself into perspective by clarifying its relation to the religious life as a whole. Drugs appear able to induce religious experiences; it is less evident that they can produce religious lives. It follows that religion is more than religious experiences. This is hardly news, but it may be a useful reminder, especially to those who incline toward "the religion of religious experience"; which is to say toward lives bent on the acquisition of desired states of experience irrespective of their relation to life's other demands and components.

Despite the dangers of faculty psychology, it remains useful to regard man as having a mind, a will, and feelings. One of the lessons of religious history is that, to be adequate, a faith must rouse and involve all three components of man's nature. Religions of reason grow arid; religions of duty, leaden. Religions of experience have their comparable pitfalls, as evidenced by Taoism's struggle (not always successful) to keep from degenerating into quietism, and the vehemence with which Zen Buddhism has insisted that once students have attained *satori,* they must be driven out of it, back into the world. The case of Zen is especially pertinent here, for it pivots on an enlightenment experience—*satori,* or *kensho*—which some (but not all) Zennists say resembles LSD. Alike or different, the point is that Zen recognizes that unless the experience is poined to discipline, it will come to naught:

> Even the Buddha . . . had to sit . . . Without *joriki,* the partic-
> ular power developed through *zazen* [seated meditation], the
> vision of oneness attained in enlightenment . . . in time be-
> comes clouded and eventually fades into a pleasant memory
> instead of remaining an omnipresent reality shaping our daily
> life. . . . To be able to live in accordance with what the
> Mind's eye has revealed through *satori* requires, like the puri-
> fication of character and the development of personality, a
> ripening period of *zazen.*[22]

If the religion of religious experience is a snare and a delusion, it follows that no religion that fixes its faith primarily in substances that induce religious experiences can be expected to come to a good end. What promised to a short cut will prove to be a short circuit; what began as a religion will end as a religion surrogate. Whether chemical substances can be helpful *adjuncts* to faith is another ques-tion. The peyote-using Native American Church seems to indicate that they can be; anthropologists give this church a good report, noting among other things that members resist alcohol and alco-holism better than nonmembers.[23] The conclusion to which evidence currently points would seem to be that chemicals *can* aid the religious life, but only where set within a context of faith (meaning by this the conviction that what they disclose is true) and discipline (mean-ing diligent exercise of the will in the attempt to work out the impli-cations of the disclosures for the living of life in the everyday, com-mon-sense world).

Nowhere today in Western civilization are these two conditions jointly fulfilled. Churches lack faith in the sense just mentioned;

[22] Philip Kapleau, *Zen Practice and Attainment,* a manuscript in process of publication.
[23] Slotkin, *Peyote Religion.*

hipsters lack discipline. This might lead us to forget about the drugs, were it not for one fact: the distinctive religious emotion and the emotion that drugs unquestionably can occasion—Otto's *mysterium tremendum, majestas, mysterium fascinans;* in a phrase, the phenomenon of religious awe—seems to be declining sharply. As Paul Tillich said in an address to the Hillel Society at Harvard several years ago:

> The question our century puts before us [is]: Is it possible to regain the lost dimension, the encounter with the Holy, the dimension which cuts through the world of subjectivity and objectivity and goes down to that which is not world but is the mystery of the Ground of Being?

Tillich may be right; this may be the religious question of our century. For if (as we have insisted) religion cannot be equated with religious experiences, neither can it long survive their absence.

SMITH SELECTION

1. Have you ever had drug-induced visions? (You may answer silently, if you wish!) Have you ever heard firsthand descriptions of drug-induced visions? Do they sound anything like religious experiences? What do you suppose a religious vision is like? What were the visions of St. Joan or St. Theresa like? Do you think you could tell the difference between a genuine vision and a mere hallucination? How?

2. There are really two quite different questions mixed up together in this subject of drugs and religious experiences. The first question is: Can drug-induced experiences provide conclusive evidence of the existence of the Divine? The second question is: Assuming the existence of the Divine, can drug-induced experiences put us in touch with it? Is there any relation between these two questions? If I answer "no" to the first, must I in all consistency answer "no" to the second?

3. If God wants to communicate with human beings, He has to accommodate Himself in some way to our limitations. He may appear as a burning bush, or as a voice in the clouds, or as a shining light. Why shouldn't He appear through the intermediation of drugs? Are some modes of Divine Appearance more plausible, more believable, more probable, than others? Why?

4. If it is possible to give a consistent explanation of drug-induced "religious" experiences without assuming the existence of a Divine realm, and if it is also possible to give a consistent "religious" interpretation of those same experiences, is there any fruitful debate possible between believers and nonbelievers? Is religious belief susceptible to rational debate? Why?

(SELECTION 7)

JOHN L. MACKIE

The Problem of Evil

By a curious paradox, it is the inescapable miseries of human existence that serve both as the most powerful impetus to religious faith and as the greatest obstacle to that faith. By and large, men and women turn to God when they are afflicted with disease, with suffering, and with death, rather than when all is going well with the affairs of this world. In the Judeo-Christian tradition, at least, and in many other religions as well, a belief in the existence of God, and in His shepherd-like concern for our well-being, serves as a comfort when we are unable to cope with life.

But the very afflictions that drive us *to* God also drive us *from* Him. We are taught that God is powerful, God is good. And yet the wicked flourish, the just are brought low. Innocent children die of cruel diseases, and for countless millions of human beings life fits all too well Thomas Hobbes's bleak description of the breakdown of social order as "solitary, poor, nasty, brutish, and short." What sort of God can it be that would create such a world and permit it to continue in this way? Has he infinite power? Then surely He could right injustice and relieve needless suffering if only He cared! Is He infinitely good? Then surely He must lack that infinite power we call omnipotence, for if He had it, He would use it for the benefit of His creatures. Are these evils then not *really* evil? Is there some higher understanding, from whose wisdom we would see that the sufferings of the innocent are truly good?

To say that the existence of evil is a "paradox" states the problem too tamely. It is an affront to reason, an outrage to moral sentiment, an absurdity rather than a mere paradox, to insist that there is an omnipotent, benevolent God who looks upon this world and says, "It is good!"

In this essay, the British philosopher John Mackie examines the "problem of evil," as it has come to be known, and analyzes in turn the major attempts by theologians and philosophers to resolve it. Mackie's conclusions are largely negative, as you shall see, but he does not confine himself simply to the problem of evil. Through an examination of its complexities, he hopes to throw light on our notions of omnipotence and causality, in order to suggest certain weaknesses in our notion of God. By this point in the chapter, it should be clear that merely formulating an adequate definition of the word "God" is a philosophical task of great difficulty. Whether for purposes of testing the Ontological Argument, or as a prelude to a consideration of the significance of drug-induced experiences, or in the present context of the problem of evil, it is both essential and extremely difficult to decide exactly what we mean when we use the word "God."

The traditional arguments for the existence of God have been fairly thoroughly criticised by philosophers. But the theologian can, if he wishes, accept this criticism. He can admit that no rational proof of God's existence is possible. And he can still retain all that is essential to his position, by holding that God's existence is known in some other, non-rational way. I think, however, that a more telling criticism can be made by way of the traditional problem of evil. Here it can be shown, not that religious beliefs lack rational support, but that they are positively irrational, that the several parts of the essential theological doctrine are inconsistent with one another, so that the theologian can maintain his position as a whole only by a much more extreme rejection of reason than in the former case. He must now be prepared to believe, not merely what cannot be proved, but what can be *disproved* from other beliefs that he also holds.

The problem of evil, in the sense in which I shall be using the phrase, is a problem only for someone who believes that there is a God who is both omnipotent and wholly good. And it is a logical problem, the problem of clarifying and reconciling a number of beliefs: it is not a scientific problem that might be solved by further observations, or a practical problem that might be solved by a decision or an action. These points are obvious; I mention them only because they are sometimes ignored by theologians, who sometimes parry a statement of the problem with such remarks as "Well, can you solve the problem yourself?" or "This is a mystery which may be revealed to us later" or "Evil is something to be faced and overcome, not to be merely discussed."

In its simplest form the problem is this: God is omnipotent; God is wholly good; and yet evil exists. There seems to be some contradiction between these three propositions, so that if any two of them were true the third would be false. But at the same time all three are essential parts of most theological positions: the theologian, it seems, at once *must* adhere and *cannot consistently* adhere to all three. (The problem does not arise only for theists, but I shall discuss it in the form in which it presents itself for ordinary theism.)

However, the contradiction does not arise immediately; to show it we need some additional premises, or perhaps some quasi-logical rules connecting the terms "good," "evil," and "omnipotent." These additional principles are that good is opposed to evil, in such

From "Evil and Omnipotence" by John L. Mackie. First published in *Mind* in 1955. (Reprinted by permission of *Mind*.)

a way that a good thing always eliminates evil as far as it can, and that there are no limits to what an omnipotent thing can do. From these it follows that a good omnipotent thing eliminates evil completely, and then the proposition that a good omnipotent thing exists, and that evil exists, are incompatible.

A. *Adequate Solutions*

Now once the problem is fully stated it is clear that it can be solved, in the sense that the problem will not arise if one gives up at least one of the propositions that constitute it. If you are prepared to say that God is not wholly good, or not quite omnipotent, or that evil does not exist, or that good is not opposed to the kind of evil that exists, or that there are limits to what an omnipotent thing can do, then the problem of evil will not arise for you.

There are, then, quite a number of adequate solutions of the problem of evil, and some of these have been adopted, or almost adopted, by various thinkers. For example, a few have been prepared to deny God's omnipotence, and rather more have been prepared to keep the term "omnipotence" but severely to restrict its meaning, recording quite a number of things that an omnipotent being cannot do. Some have said that evil is an illusion, perhaps because they held that the whole world of temporal, changing things is an illusion, and that what we call evil belongs only to this world, or perhaps because they held that although temporal things *are* much as we see them, those that we call evil are not really evil. Some have said that what we call evil is merely the privation of good, that evil in a positive sense, evil that would really be opposed to good, does not exist. Many have agreed with Pope that disorder is harmony not understood, and that partial evil is universal good. Whether any of these views is *true* is, of course, another question. But each of them gives an adequate solution of the problem of evil in the sense that if you accept it this problem does not arise for you, though you may, of course, have *other* problems to face.

But often enough these adequate solutions are only *almost* adopted. The thinkers who restrict God's power, but keep the term "omnipotence," may reasonably be suspected of thinking, in other contexts, that his power is really unlimited. Those who say that evil is an illusion may also be thinking, inconsistently, that this illusion is itself an evil. Those who say that "evil" is merely privation of good may also be thinking, inconsistently, that privation of good is an evil. (The fallacy here is akin to some forms of the "naturalistic fallacy" in ethics, where some thnk, for example, that "good" is just what contrbutes to evolutionary progress, and that evolutionary progress is itself good.) If Pope meant what he said in the first line of his couplet, that "disorder" is only harmony not understood, the "partial evil" of the second line must, for consistency, mean "that which, taken in isolation, falsely appears to be evil," but it would more naturally mean "that which, in isolation, really is evil." The second line, in fact, hesitates between two views, that "partial evil" isn't really evil, since only the universal quality is real, and that "partial evil" is really an evil, but only a little one.

In addition, therefore, to adequate solutions, we must recognise unsatisfactory inconsistent solutions, in which there is only a half-hearted or temporary rejection of one of the propositions which together constitute the problem. In these, one of the constituent propositions is explicitly rejected, but it is covertly re-asserted or assumed elsewhere in the system.

B. *Fallacious Solutions*

Besides these half-hearted solutions, which explicitly reject but implicitly assert one of the constituent propositions, there are definitely fallacious solutions which explicitly maintain all the constituent propositions, but implicitly reject at least one of them in the course of the argument that explains away the problem of evil.

There are, in fact, many so-called solutions which purport to remove the contradiction without abandoning any of its constituent propositions. These must be fallacious, as we can see from the very statement of the problem, but it is not so easy to see in each case precisely where the fallacy lies. I suggest that in all cases the fallacy has the general form suggested above: in order to solve the problem one (or perhaps more) of its constituent propositions is given up, but in such a way that it appears to have been retained, and can therefore be asserted without qualification in other contexts. Sometimes there is a further complication: the supposed solution moves to and fro between, say, two of the constituent propositions, at one point asserting the first of these but covertly abandoning the second, at another point asserting the second but covertly abandoning the first. These fallacious solutions often turn upon some equivocation with the words "good" and "evil," or upon some vagueness about the way in which good and evil are opposed to one another, or about how much is meant by "omnipotence." I propose to examine some of these so-called solutions, and to exhibit their fallacies in detail. Incidentally, I shall also be considering whether an adequate solution could be reached by a minor modification of one or more of the constituent propositions, which would, however, still satisfy all the essential requirements of ordinary theism.

1. "Good cannot exist without evil" or "Evil is necessary as a counterpart to good."

It is sometimes suggested that evil is necessary as a counterpart to good, that if there were no evil there could be no good either, and that this solves the problem of evil. It is true that it points to an answer to the question "Why should there be evil?" But it does so only by qualifying some of the propositions that constitute the problem.

First, it sets a limit to what God can do, saying that God *cannot* create good without simultaneously creating evil, and this means either that God is not omnipotent or that there are *some* limits to what an omnipotent thing can do. It may be replied that these limits are always presupposed, that omnipotence has never meant the power to do what is logically impossible, and on the present view the existence of good without evil would be a logical impossibility. This interpretation of omnipotence may, indeed, be accepted as a modification of our original account which does not reject anything that is essential to thesim, and I shall in general assume it in the subsequent discussion. It is, perhaps, the most common theistic view, but I think that some theists at least have maintained that God can do what is logically impossible. Many theists, at any rate, have held that logic itself is created or laid down by God, that logic is the way in which God arbitrarily chooses to think. (This is, of course, parallel to the ethical view that morally right actions are those which God arbitrarily chooses to command, and the two views encounter similar difficulties.) And *this* account of logic is clearly inconsistent with the view that God is bound by logical necessities—unless it is possible for an omnipotent being to bind himself, an issue which we shall consider later, when we come to the Paradox of Omnipotence. This solution of the problem of evil cannot, therefore, be consistently adopted along with the view that logic is itself created by God.

But, secondly, this solution denies that evil is opposed to good in our original sense. If good and evil are counterparts, a good thing will not "eliminate evil as far as it can." Indeed, this view suggests that good and evil are not strictly qualities of things at all. Perhaps the suggestion is that good and evil are related in much the same way as great and small. Certainly, when the term "great" is used relatively as a condensation of "greater than so-and-so," and "small" is used correspondingly, greatness and smallness are counterparts and cannot exist without each other. But in this sense greatness is not a quality, not an intrinsic feature of anything; and it would be absurd to think of a movement in favour of greatness and against smallness in this sense. Such a movement would be self-defeating, since relative greatness can be promoted only by a simultaneous promotion of relative smallness. I feel sure that no theists would be content to regard God's goodness as analogous to this—as if what he supports were not the *good* but the *better,* and as if he had the paradoxical aim that all things should be better than other things.

This point is obscured by the fact that "great" and "small" seem to have an absolute as well as a relative sense. I cannot discuss here whether there is absolute magnitude or not, but if there is, there could be an absolute sense for "great," it could mean of at least a certain size, and it would make sense to speak of all things getting bigger, of a universe that was expanding all over, and therefore it would make sense to speak of promoting greatness. But in *this* sense great and small are not logically necessary counterparts: either quality could exist without the other. There would be no logical impossibility in everything's being small or in everything's being great.

Neither in the absolute nor in the relative sense, then, of "great" and "small' do these terms provide an analogy of the sort that would be needed to support this solution of the problem of evil. In neither case are greatness and smallness *both* necessary counterparts *and* mutually opposed forces or possible objects for support and attack.

It may be replied that good and evil are necessary counterparts in the same way as any quality and its logical opposite: redness can occur, it is suggested, only if non-redness also occurs. But unless evil is merely the privation of good, they are not logical opposites, and some further argument would be needed to show that they are counterparts in the same way as genuine logical opposites. Let us assume that this could be given. There is still doubt of the correctness of the metaphysical principle that a quality must have a real opposite: I suggest that it is not really impossible that everything should be, say, red, that the truth is merely that if everything were red we should not notice redness, and so we should have no word "red"; we observe and give names to qualities only if they have real opposites. If so, the principle that a term must have an opposite would belong only to our language or to our thought, and would not be an ontological principle, and, correspondingly, the rule that good cannot exist without evil would not state a logical necessity of a sort that God would just have to put up with. God might have made everything good, though *we* should not have noticed it if he had.

But, finally, even if we concede that this *is* an ontological principle, it will provide a solution for the problem of evil only if one is prepared to say, "Evil exists, but only just enough evil to serve as the counterpart of good." I doubt whether any theist will accept this. After all, the *ontological* requirement that non-redness should occur would be satisfied even if all the universe, except for a minute speck, were red, and, if there were a corresponding requirement for evil as a counterpart to good, a minute dose of evil would presumably do. But theists are not usually willing to say, in all context, that all the evil that occurs is a minute and necessary dose.

2. "Evil is necessary as a means to good."

It is sometimes suggested that evil is necessary for good not as a counterpart but as a means. In its simple form this has little plausibility as a solution of the problem of evil, since it obviously implies a severe restriction of God's power. It would be a *causal* law that you cannot have a certain end without a certain means, so that if God has to introduce evil as a means to good, he must be subject to at least some causal laws. This certainly conflicts with what a theist normally means by omnipotence. This view of God as limited by causal laws also conflicts with the view that causal laws are themselves made by God, which is more widely held than the corresponding view about the laws of logic. This conflict would, indeed, be resolved if it were possible for an omnipotent being to bind himself, and this possibility has still to be considered. Unless a favourable answer canbe given to this question, the suggestion that evil is necessary as a means to good solves the problem of evil only by denying one of its constituent propositions, either that God is omnipotent or that "omnipotent" means what it says.

3. "The universe is better with some evil in it than it could be if there were no evil."

Much more important is a solution which at first seems to be a mere variant of the previous one, that evil may contribute to the goodness of a whole in which it is found, so that the universe as a whole is better as it is, with some evil in it, than it would be if there were no evil. This solution may be developed in either of two ways. It may be supported by an aesthetic analogy, by the fact that contrasts heighten beauty, that in a musical work, for example, there may occur discords which somehow add to the beauty of the work as a whole. Alternatively, it may be worked out in connexion with the notion of progress, that the best possible organisation of the universe will not be static, but progressive, that the gradual overcoming of evil by good is really a finer thing than would be the eternal unchallenged supremacy of good.

In either case, this solution usually starts from the assumption that the evil whose existence gives rise to the problem of evil is primarily what is called physical evil, that is to say, pain. In Hume's rather half-hearted presentation of the problem of evil, the evils that he stresses are pain and disease, and those who reply to him argue that the existence of pain and disease makes possible the existence of sympathy, benevolence, heroism, and the gradually successful struggle of doctors and reformers to overcome these evils. In fact, theists often seize the opportunity to accuse those who stress the problem of evil of taking a low, materialistic view of good and evil, equating these with pleasure and pain, and of ignoring the more spiritual goods which can arise in the struggle against evils.

But let us see exactly what is being done here. Let us call pain and misery "first order evil" or "evil (1)." What contrasts with this, namely, pleasure and happiness, will be called "first order good" or "good (1)." Distinct from this is "second order good" or "good (2)" which somehow emerges in a complex situation in which evil (1) is a necessary component—logically, not merely causally, necessary. (Exactly *how* it emerges does not matter: in the crudest version of this solution good (2) is simply the heightening of happiness by the contrast with misery, in other versions it includes sympathy with suffering, heroism in facing danger, and the gradual decrease of first order evil and increase of first order good.) It is also being assumed that second order good is more important than first order good or evil, in particular that it more than outweighs the first order evil it involves.

Now this is a particularly subtle attempt to solve the problem of evil. It defends God's goodness and omnipotence on the ground that (on a sufficiently long view) this is the best of all logically possible worlds, because it includes the important second order goods, and yet it admits that real evils, namely first order evils, exist. But does it still hold that good and evil are opposed? Not, clearly, in the sense that we set out originally: good does not tend to eliminate evil in general. Instead, we have a modified, a more complex pattern. First order good (e.g., happiness) *contrasts with* first order evil (e.g., misery): these two are opposed in a fairly mechanical way; some second order goods (e.g., benevolence) try to maximise first order good and minimise first order evil; but God's goodness is not this, it is rather the will to maximise *second* order good. We might, therefore, call God's goodness an example of a third order goodness, or good (3). While this account is different from our original one, it might well be able to be an improvement on it, to give a more accurate description of the way in which good is opposed to evil, and to be consistent with the essential theist position.

There might, however, be several objections to this solution.

First, some might argue that such qualities as benevolence—and *a fortiori* the third order goodness which promotes benevolence—have a merely derivative value, that they aren not higher sorts of good, but merely means to good (1), that is, to happiness, so that it would be absurd for God to keep misery in existence in order to make possible the virtues of benevolence, heroism, etc. The theist who adopts the present solution must, of course, deny this, but he can do so with some plausibility, so I should not press this objection.

Secondly, it follows from this solution that God is not in our sense benevolent or sympathetic: he is not concerned to minimise evil (1), but only to promote good (2); and this might be a disturbing conclusion for some theists.

But, thirdly, the fatal objection is this. Our analysis shows clearly the possibility of the existence of a *second* order evil, an evil (2) contrasting with good (2) as evil (1) contrasts with good (1). This would include malevolence, cruelty, callousness, cowardice, and states in which good (1) is decreasing and evil (1) increasing. And just as good (2) is held to be the important kind of good, the kind that God is concerned to promote, so evil (2) will, by analogy, be the important kind of evil, the kind which God, if he were wholly good and omnipotent, would eliminate. And yet evil (2) plainly exists, and indeed most theists (in other contexts) stress its existence more than that of evil (1). We should, therefore, state the problem of evil in terms of second order evil, and again this form of the problem the present solution is useless.

An attempt might be made to use this solution again, at a higher level, to explain the occurrence of evil (2): indeed the next main solution that we shall examine does just this, with the help of some new notions. Without any fresh notions, such a solution would have little plausibility: for example, we could hardly say that the really important good was a good (3), such as the increase of benevolence in proportion to cruelty, which logically required for its occurrence the occurrence of some second order evil. But even if evil (2) could be explained in this way, it is fairly clear that there would be third order evils contrasting with this third order good: and we should be well on the way to an infinite regress, where the solution of a problem of evil, stated in terms of evil (n), indicated the existence of an evil $(n + 1)$, and a further problem to be solved.

4. "Evil is due to human freewill."

Perhaps the most important proposed solution of the problem of evil is that evil is not to be ascribed to God at all, but to the independent actions of human beings, supposed to have been endowed by God with freedom of the will. This solution may be combined with the preceding one: first order evil (e.g., pain) may be justified as a logically necessary component in second order good (e.g., sympathy) while second order evil (e.g., cruelty) is not *justified,* but is so ascribed to human beings that God cannot be held responsible for it. This combination evades my third criticism of the preceding soilution.

The freewill solution also involves the preceding solution at a higher level. To explain why a wholly good God gave men freewill although it would lead to some important evils, it must be argued that it is better on the whole that men should act freely, and sometimes err, than that they should be innocent automata, acting rightly in a wholly determined way. Freedom, that is to say, is now treated as a third order good, and as being more valuable than second order goods (such as sympathy and heroism) would be if they were deterministically produced, and it is being assumed that second order evils, such as cruelty, are logically necessary accompaniments of freedom, just as pain is a logically necessary pre-condition of sympathy.

I think that this solution is unsatisfactory primarily because of the incoherence of the notion of freedom of the will: but I cannot discuss this topic adequately here, although some of my criticisms will touch upon it.

First I should query the assumption that second order evils are logically necessary accompaniments of freedom. I should ask this: if God has made men such that in their free choices they sometimes prefer what is good and sometimes what is evil, why could he not have made men such that they always freely choose the good? If there is no logical impossibility in a man's freely choosing the good on one, or on several, occasions, there cannot be a logical impossibility in his freely choosing the good on every occasion. God was not, then, faced with a choice between making innocent automata and making beings who, in acting freely, would sometimes go wrong: there was open to him the obviously better possibility of making beings who would act freely but always go right. Clearly, his failure to avail himself of this possibility is inconsistent with his being both omnipotent and wholly good.

If it is replied that this objection is absurd, that the making of some wrong choices is logically necessary for freedom, it would seem that "freedom" must here mean complete randomness or indeterminacy, including randomness with regard to the alternatives good and evil, in other words that men's choices and consequent actions can be "free" only if they are not determined by their characters. Only on this assumption can God escape the responsibility for men's actions; for if he made them as they are, but did not determine their wrong choices, this can only be because the wrong choices are not determined by men as they are. But then if freedom is randomness, how can it be a characteristic of *will?* And, still more, how can it be the most important good? What value or merit would there be in free choices if these were random actions which were not determined by the nature of the agent?

I conclude that to make this solution plausible two different senses of "freedom" must be confused, one sense which will justify the view that freedom is a third order good, more valuable than other goods would be without it, and another sense, sheer randomness, to prevent us from ascribing to God a decision to make men such that they sometimes go wrong when he might have made them such that they would always freely go right.

This criticism is sufficient to dispose of this solution. But besides this there is a fundamental difficulty in the notion of an omnipotent God creating men with free will, for if men's wills are really free this must mean that even God cannot control them, that is, that God is no longer omnipotent. It may be objected that God's gift of freedom to men does not mean that he *cannot* control their wills, but that he always *refrains* from controlling their wills. But why, we may ask, should God refrain from controlling evil wills? Why should he not leave men free to will rightly, but intervene when he sees them beginning to will wrongly? If God could do this, but does not, and if he is wholly good, the only explanation could be that even a wrong free act of will is not really evil, that its freedom is a value which outweighs its wrongness, so that there would be a loss of value if God took away the wrongness and the freedom together. But this is utterly opposed to what theists say about sin in other contexts. The present solution of the problem of evil, then, can be maintained only in the form that God has made men so free that he *cannot* control their wills.

This leads us to what I call the Paradox of Omnipotence: can an omnipotent being make things which he cannot subsequently control? Or, what is practically equivalent to this, can an omnipotent being make rules which then bind himself? (These are practically equivalent because any such rules could be regarded as setting certain things beyond his control, and *vice versa*.) The second of these formulations is relevant to the suggestions that we have already met, that an omnipotent God creates the rules of logic or causal laws, and is then bound by them.

It is clear that this is a paradox: the questions cannot be answered satisfactorily either in the affirmative or in the negative. If we answer "Yes," it follows that if God actually makes things which he cannot control, or makes rules which bind himself, he is not omnipotent once he has made them: there are *then* things which he cannot do. But if we answer "No," we are immediately asserting that there are things which he cannot do, that is to say that he is already not omnipotent.

It cannot be replied that the question which sets this paradox is not a proper question. It would make perfectly good sense to say that a human mechanic has made a machine which he cannot control: if there is any difficulty about the question it lies in the notion of omnipotence itself.

This, incidentally, shows that although we have approached this paradox from the free will theory, it is equally a problem for a theological determinist. No one thinks that machines have free will, yet they may well be beyond the control of their makers. The determinist might reply that anyone who makes anything determines its ways of acting, and so determines its subsequent behaviour: even the human mechanic does this by his *choice* of materials and structure for his machine, though he does not know all about either of these: the mechanic thus determines, though he may not foresee, his machine's actions. And since God is omniscient, and since his creation of things is total, he both determines and foresees the ways in which his creatures will act. We may grant this, but it is beside the point. The question is not whether God *originally* determined the future actions of his creatures, but whether he can *subsequently* control their actions, or whether he was able in his original creation to put things beyond his subsequent control. Even on determinist principles the answers "Yes" and "No" are equally irreconcilable with God's omnipotence.

Before suggesting a solution of this paradox, I would point out that there is a parallel Paradox of Sovereignty. Can a legal sovereign make a law restricting it own future legislative power? For example, could the British parliament make a law forbidding any future parliament to socialise banking, and also forbidding the future repeal of this law itself? Or could the British parliament, which was legally soverign in Australia in, say, 1899, pass a valid law, or series of laws, which made it no longer sovereign in 1933? Again, neither the affirmative nor the negative answer is really satisfactory. If we were to answer "Yes," we should be admitting the validity of a law which, if it were actually made, would mean that parliament was no longer sovereign. If we were to answer "No," we should be admitting that there is a law, not logically absurd, which parliament cannot validly make, that is, that parliament is not now a legal sovereign. This paradox can be solved in the following way. We should distinguish between first order laws, that is laws governing the actions of individuals and bodies other than the legislature, and second order laws, that is laws about laws, laws governing the actions of the legislature itself. Correspondingly, we should distinguish two orders of sovereignty, first order sovereignty (sovereignty (1)) which is unlimited authority to make first order laws, and second order sovereignty (sovereignty (2)) which is unlimited authority to make second order laws. If we say that parliament is sovereign we might mean that any parliament at any time has sovereignty (1), or we might mean that parliament has both sovereignty (1) and sovereignty (2) at present, but we cannot without contradiction mean both that the present parliament has sovereignty (2) and that every parliament at every time has sovereignty (1), for if the present parliament has sovereignty (2) it may use it to take away the sovereignty (1) of later parliaments. What the paradox shows is that we cannot ascribe to any continuing institution legal sovereignty in an inclusive sense.

The analogy between omnipotence and sovereignty shows that the paradox of omnipotence can be solved in a similar way. We must distinguish between first order omnipotence (omnipotence (1)), that is unlimited power to act, and second order omnipotence (omnipotence (2)), that is unlimited power to determine what powers to act things shall have. Then we could consistently say that God all the time has omnipotence (1), but if so no beings at any time have powers to act independently of God. Or we could say that God at one time had omnipotence (2), and used it to assign independent powers to act to certain things, so that God thereafter did not have omnipotence (1). But what the paradox shows is that we cannot consistently ascribe to any continuing being omnipotence in an inclusive sense.

An alternative solution of this paradox would be simply to deny that God is a continuing being, that any times can be assigned to his actions at all. But on this assumption (which also has difficulties of its own) no meaning can be given to the assertion that God made men with wills so free that he could not control them. The paradox of omnipotence can be avoided by putting God outside time, but the freewill solution of the problem of evil cannot be saved in this way, and equally it remains impossible to hold than an omnipotent God *binds himself* by causal or logical laws.

Conclusion

Of the proposed solutions of the problem of evil which we have examined, none has stood up to criticism. There may be other solutions which require examination, but this study strongly suggests that there is no valid solution of the problem which does not modify at least one of the constituent propositions in a way which would seriously affect the essential core of the theistic position.

Quite apart from the problem of evil, the paradox of omnipotence has shown that God's omnipotence must in any case be restricted in one way or another, that unqualified omnipotence cannot be ascribed to any being that continues through time. And if God and his actions are not in time, can omnipotence, or power of any sort, be meaningfully ascribed to him?

MACKIE SELECTION

1.   What is "the problem of evil"? State it as clearly and precisely as you can. What, according to Mackie, would be "adequate" solutions of the problem? What is the difficulty with these various solutions?

2.   Mackie considers four "solutions," each of which has been advanced at some time or other. Which of these solutions is the best, in your judgment? How would you reply to Mackie's objections?

3.   What *is* evil, and what is good? Where do we get our standards of good and evil from? What sorts of evil pose the greatest problem for a believer in an omnipotent and good God?

4.   In what way does our freedom of will seem to interfere with God's infinite goodness and power? What would prompt a perfect God to create a universe, anyway? Having decided to create a universe, would God necessarily create the best possible universe? Why? Must the best possible universe be a perfect universe? If not, why not?

THE OLD TESTAMENT (Genesis 22:1–19)

The Trial of Abraham's Faith

One of the most terrifying passages in the Old Testament is the brief but moving account of the testing of Abraham's faith in the Book of Genesis. Perhaps one would have to be a parent to appreciate in all its awfulness God's command to Abraham that he kill his only son, Isaac, and offer him up as a burnt offering to the Lord. Abraham has no doubt that it is God himself who has spoken. Although we might use the story to illustrate the difficulty in telling when a voice is really from God and when it is a mere hallucination, the Bible has no interest in such refined epistemological puzzles. The testing of Abraham is nothing less than a stark confrontation between our most deeply rooted moral convictions and the un-questioning demands of absolute faith. The proof of Abraham's faith is his will-ingness to do what he *knows* to be wrong by all human standards of con-duct. In a sense, the real sacrifice of-fered up by Abraham to God is not his son Isaac, but his own conscience.

Søren Kierkegaard, the brilliant Danish religious philosopher who is usually accounted the first existentialist, elaborates on the laconic Biblical ac-count of Abraham and Isaac with con-summate literary skill. He makes us feel in all its pathos the situation in which God puts Abraham. And he makes us see, in a way that the few lines in Gene-sis cannot, how much was at stake in Abraham's response to God's command.

Behind the discourse upon the case of Abraham lies Kierkegaard's more systematic view of the relationship between what he called the ethical and the religious stages of human existence. Unlike the religious thinkers in the mainstream of Western theology, Kier-kegaard rejects the view that the ra-tional, this-worldly demands of morality can be made to cohere with the non-rational, otherworldly demands of reli-gious faith. Like the Church Father Ter-tullian, who said of his faith, "I believe *because* it is absurd!" Kierkegaard holds that to have true faith is to be in an ontologically different condition from the secular man or woman whose ac-tions are guided by principles of moral-ity. He does not deny the validity of those principles. He simply asserts that to be religious is to have gone *beyond* morality. Abraham did not decide to sacrifice Isaac because he had con-cluded, after a rationally reflective phil-osophical examination, that the act was, taking all in all, the right thing to do. He undertook to sacrifice Isaac because God had commanded him to do so. He withheld the knife because God told him to. Just that, nothing more. It is that sublime submission to the will of God, Kierkegaard believes, that constitutes Abraham's faith.

The Trial of Abraham's Faith

And it came to pass after these things, that God did tempt Abraham, and said unto him, Abraham: and he said, Behold, *here* I *am*. And he said, Take now thy son, thine only *son* Isaac, whom you lovest, and get thee into the land of Moriah; and offer him there for a burnt offering upon one of the mountains which I will tell thee of. And Abraham rose up early in the morning, and saddled his ass, and took two of his young men with him, and Isaac his son, and clave the wood for the burnt offering, and rose up, and went unto the place of which God had told him. Then on the third day Abraham lifted up his eyes, and saw the place afar off. And Abraham said unto his young men, Abide ye here with the ass; and I and the lad will go yonder and worship, and come again to you. And Abraham took the wood of the burnt offering, and laid *it* upon Isaac his son; and he took the fire in his hand, and a knife; and they went both of them together. And Isaac spake unto Abraham his father, and said, My father: and he said, Here *am* I, my son. And he said, Behold the fire and the wood: but where *is* the lamb for a burnt offering? And Abraham said, My son, God will provide himself a lamb for a burnt offering: so they went both of them together.

And they came to the place which God had told him of; and Abraham built an altar there, and laid the wood in order, and bound Isaac his son, and laid him on the altar upon the wood. And Abraham stretched forth his hand, and took the knife to slay his son. And the Angel of the Lord called unto him out of heaven, and said, Abraham, Abraham: and he said, Here *am* I. And he said, Lay not thine hand upon the lad, neither do thou any thing unto him: for now I know that thou fearest God, seeing thou hast not withheld thy son, thine only *son*, from me. And Abraham lifted up his eyes, and looked, and behold behind *him* a ram caught in a thicket by his horns: and Abraham went and took the ram, and offered him up for a burnt offering in the stead of his son. And Abraham called the name of that place Jehovah-jireh: as it is said *to* this day, In the mount of the Lord it shall be seen. And the Angel of the Lord called unto Abraham out of heaven the second time, And said, By myself have I sworn, saith the Lord, for because thou hast done this thing, and hast not withheld they son, thine only *son*, That in

The Old Testament, Genesis 22: 1–19. (King James version)

blessing I will bless thee, and in multiplying I will multiply thy seed as the stars of the heaven, and as the sand which *is* upon the seashore; and they seed shall possess the gate of his enemies; And in thy seed shall all the nations of the earth be blessed; because thou hast obeyed my voice. So Abraham returned unto his young men, and they rose up and went together to Beer-sheba; and Abraham dwelt at Beer-sheba.

(SELECTION 9)

SØREN KIERKEGAARD

A Panegyric upon Abraham

If there were no eternal consciousness in a man, if at the foundation of all there lay only a wildly seething power which writhing with obscure passions produced everything that is great and everything that is insignificant, if a bottomless void never satiated lay hidden beneath all—what then would life be but despair? If such were the case, if there were no sacred bond which united mankind, if one generation arose after another like the leafage in the forest, if the one generation replaced the other like the song of birds in the forest, if the human race passed through the world as the ship goes through the sea, like the wind through the desert, a thoughtless and fruitless activity, if an eternal oblivion were always lurking hungrily for its prey and there was no power strong enough to wrest it from its maw—how empty then and comfortless life would be! But therefore it is not thus, but as God created man and woman, so too He fashioned the hero and the poet or orator. The poet cannot do what that other does, he can only admire, love and rejoice in the hero. Yet he too is happy, and not less so, for the hero is as it were his better nature, with which he is in love, rejoicing in the fact that this after all is not himself, that his love can be admiration. He is the genius of recollection, can do nothing except call to mind what has been done, do nothing but admire what has been done; he contributes nothing of his own, but is jealous of the intrusted treasure. He follows the option of his heart, but when he has found what he sought, he wanders before every man's door with his song and with his oration, that all may admire the hero as he does, be proud of the hero as he is. This is his achievement, his humble work, this is his faithful service in the house of the hero. If he thus remains true to his love, he strives day and night against the cunning of oblivion which would trick him out of his hero, then he has completed his work, then he is gathered to the hero, who has loved him just as faithfully, for the poet is as it were the hero's better nature, powerless it may be as a memory is, but also transfigured as a memory is. Hence no one shall be forgotten who was great, and though time tarries long, though a cloud of misunderstanding takes the hero away, his lover comes nevertheless, and the longer the time that has passed, the more faithfully will he cling to him.

No, not one shall be forgotten who was great in the world. But each was great in his own way, and each in proportion to the greatness of that was he *loved*. For he who loved himself became great by himself, and he who loved other men became great by his selfless devotion, but he who loved God became greater than all. Everyone shall be remembered, but each became great in proportion to his *expectation*. One became great by expecting the possible, another by expecting the eternal, but he who expected the impossible became greater than all. Everyone shall be remembered, but each was great in proportion to the greatness of that with which he *strove*. For he who strove with the world became great by overcoming the world, and he who strove with himself became great by overcoming himself, but he who strove with God became greater than all. So there was strife in the world, man against man, one against a thousand, but he who strove with God was greater than all. So there was strife upon earth: there was one who overcame all by his power, and there was one who overcame God by his impotence. There was one who relied upon himself and gained all, there was one who secure in his strength sacrificed all, but he who believed God was greater than all. There was one who was great by reason of his power, and one who was great by reason of his wisdom, and one who was great by reason of his hope, and one who was great by reason of his love; but Abraham was greater than all, great by reason of his power whose strength is impotence, great by reason of his wisdom whose secret is foolishness, great by reason of his hope whose form is madness, great by reason of the love which is hatred of oneself.

By faith Abraham went out from the land of his fathers and became a sojourner in the land of promise. He left one thing behind, took one thing with him: he left his earthly understanding behind and took faith with him—otherwise he would not have wandered forth but would have thought this unreasonable. By faith he was a stranger in the land of promise, and there was nothing to recall what was dear to him, but by its novelty everything tempted his soul to melancholy yearning—and yet he was God's elect, in whom the Lord was well pleased! Yea, if he had been disowned, cast off from God's grace, he could have comprehended it better; but now it was like a mockery of him and of his faith. There was in the world one too who lived in banishment from the fatherland he loved. He is not forgotten, nor his Lamentations when he sorrowfully sought and found what he had lost. There is no song of Lamentations by Abraham. It is human to lament, human to weep with them that weep, but it is greater to believe, more blessed to contemplate the believer.

By faith Abraham received the promise that in his seed all races of the world would be blessed. Time passed, the possibility was there, Abraham believed; time passed, it became unreasonable, Abraham believed. There was in the world one who had an expectation, time passed, and evening drew nigh, he was not paltry enough to have forgotten his expectation, therefore he too shall not be forgotten. Then he sorrowed, and sorrow did not deceive him as life had done, it did for him all it could, in the sweetness of sorrow he possessed his delusive expectation. It is human to sorrow, human to sorrow with them that sorrow, but it is greater to believe, more blessed to contemplate the believer. There is no song of Lamentations by Abraham. He did not mournfully count the days while time passed, he did not look at Sarah with a suspicious glance, wondering whether she was growing old, he did not arrest the course of the sun, that Sarah might not grow old, and his expectation with her. He did not sing lullingly before Sarah his mournful lay. Abraham became old, Sarah became a laughingstock in the land, and yet he was God's elect and inheritor of the promise that in his seed all the races of the world would be blessed. So were it not better if he had not been God's elect? What is it to be God's elect? It is to be denied in youth the wishes of youth, so as with great pains to get them fulfilled in old age. But Abraham believed and held fast the expectation. If Abraham had wavered, he would have given it up. If he had said to God, "Then perhaps it is not after all Thy will that it should come to pass, so I will give up the wish. It was my only wish, it was my bliss. My soul is sincere, I hide no secret malice because Thou didst deny it to me"—he woud not have been forgotten, he would have saved many by his example, yet he would not be the father of faith. For it is great to give up one's wish, but it ie greater to hold it fast after having given it up, it is great to grasp the eternal, but it is greater to hold fast to the temporal after having given it up.

Then came the fulness of time. If Abraham had not believed, Sarah surely would have been dead of sorrow, and Abraham, dulled by grief, would not have understood the fulfilment but would have smiled at it as at a dream of youth. But Abraham believed, therefore he was young; for he who always hopes for the best becomes old, and he who is always prepared for the worst grows old early, but he who believes preserves an eternal youth. Praise therefore to that story! For Sarah, though stricken in years, was young enough to desire the pleasure of motherhood, and Abraham, though gray-haired was young enough to wish to be a father. In an outward respect the marvel consists in the fact that it came to pass according to their expectation, in a deeper sense the miracle of faith consists in the fact that Abraham and Sarah were young enough to wish, and that faith had preserved their wish and therewith their youth. He accepted the fulfilment of the promise, he accepted it by faith, and it came to pass according to the promise and according to his faith—for Moses smote the rock with his rod, but he did not believe.

Then there was joy in Abraham's house, when Sarah became a bride on the day of their golden wedding.

But it was not to remain thus. Still once more Abraham was to be tried. He had fought with that cunning power which invents everything, with that alert enemy which never slumbers, with that old man who outlives all things—he had fought with Time and preserved his faith. Now all the terror of the trife was concentrated in one instant. "And God tempted Abraham and said unto him, Take Isaac, thine only son, whom thou lovest, and get thee into the land of Moriah, and offer him there for a burnt offering upon the mountain which I will show thee."

So all was lost—more dreadfully than if it had never come to pass! So the Lord was only making sport of Abraham! He made miraculously the preposterous actual, and now in turn He would annihilate it. It was indeed foolishness, but Abraham did not laugh at it like Sarah when the promise was announced. All was lost! Seventy years of faithful expectation, the brief joy at the fulfilment of faith. Who then is he that plucks away the old man's staff, who is it that requires that he himself shall break it? Who is he that would make a man's gray hairs comfortless, who is it that requires that he himself shall do it? Is there no compassion for the venerable oldling, none for the innocent child? And yet Abraham was God's elect, and it was the Lord who imposed the trial. All would now be lost. The glorious memory to be preserved by the human race, the promise in Abraham's seed—this was only a whim, a fleeting thought which the Lord had had, which Abraham should now obliterate. That glorious treasure which was just as old as faith in Abraham's heart, many, many years older than Isaac, the fruit of Abraham's life, sanctified by prayers, matured in conflict—the blessing upon Abraham's lips, this fruit was now to be plucked prematurely and remain without significance. For what significance had it when Isaac was to be sacrificed? That sad and yet blissful hour when Abraham was to take leave of all that was dear to him, when yet once more he was to lift up his head, when his countenance would shine like that of the Lord, when he would concentrate his whole soul in a blessing which was potent to make Isaac blessed all his days—this time would not come! For he would indeed take leave of Isaac, but in such a way that he himself would remain behind; death would separate them, but in such a way that Isaac remained its prey. The old man would not be joyful in death as he laid his hands in blessing upon Isaac, but he would be weary of life as he laid violent hands upon Isaac. And it was God who tried him. Yea, woe, woe unto the messenger who had come before Abraham with such tidings! Who would have ventured to be the emissary of this sorrow? But it was God who tried Abraham.

Yet Abraham believed, and believed for this life. Yea, if his faith had been only for a future life, he surely would have cast everything away in order to hasten out of this world to which he did not belong. But Abraham's faith was not of this sort, if there be such a faith; for really this is not faith but the furthest possibility of faith which has a presentiment of its object at the extremest limit of the horizon, yet is separated from it by a yawning abyss within which despair carries on its game. But Abraham believed precisely for this life, that he was to grow old in the land, honored by the people, blessed in his generation, remembered forever in Isaac, his dearest thing in life, whom he embraced with a love for which it would be a poor expression to say that he loyally fulfilled the father's duty of loving the son, as indeed is evinced in the words of the summons, "the son whom thou lovest." Jacob had twelve sons, and one of them he loved; Abraham had only one, the son whom he loved.

Yet Abraham believed and did not doubt, he believed the preposterous. If Abraham had doubted—then he would have done something else, something glorious; for how could Abraham do anything but what is great and glorious! He would have marched up to Mount Moriah, he would have cleft the fire-wood, lit the pyre, drawn the knife—he would have cried out to God, "Despise not this sacrifice, it is not the best thing I possess, that I know well, for what is an old man in comparison with the child of promise; but it is the best I am able to give Thee. Let Isaac never come to know this, that he may console himself with his youth." He would have plunged the knife into his own breast. He would have been admired in the world, and his name would not have been forgotten; but it is one thing to be admired, and another to be the guiding star which saves the anguished.

But Abraham believed. He did not pray for himself, with the hope of moving the Lord—it was only when the righteous punishment was decreed upon Sodom and Gomorrha that Abraham came forward with his prayers.

We read in those holy books: "And God tempted Abraham, and said unto him, Abraham, Abraham, where art thou? And he said, Here am I." Thou to whom my speech is addressed, was such the case with thee? When afar off thou didst see the heavy dispensation of providence approaching thee, didst thou not say to the mountains, Fall on me, and to the hills, Cover me? Or if thou wast stronger, did not they foot move slowly along the way, longing as it were for the old path? When a call was issued to thee, didst thou answer, or didst thou not answer perhaps in a low voice, whispering? Not so Abraham: joyfully, buoyantly, confidently, with a loud voice, he answered, "Here am I." We read further: "And Abraham rose early in the morning"—as though it were to a festival, so he hastened, and early in the morning he had come to the place spoken of, to Mount Moriah. He said nothing to Sarah, nothing to Eleazar. Indeed who could understand him? Had not the temptation by its very nature exacted of him an oath of silence? He cleft the wood, he bound Issaac, he lit the pyre, he drew the knife. My hearer, there was many a father who believed that with his son he lost everything that was dearest to him in the world, that he was deprived of every hope for the future, but yet there was none that was the child of promise in the sense that Isaac was for Abraham. There was many a father who lost his child; but then it was God, it was the unalterable, the unsearchable will of the Almighty, it was His hand took the child. Not so with Abraham. For him was reserved a harder trial, and Isaac's fate was laid along with the knife in Abraham's hand. And there he stood, the old man, with his only hope! But he did not doubt, he did not look anxiously to the right or to the left, he did not challenge heaven with his prayers. He knew that it was God the Almighty who was trying him, he knew that it was the hardest sacrifice that could be required of him; but he knew also that no sacrifice was too hard when God required it—and he drew the knife.

Who gave strength to Abraham's arm? Who held his right hand up so that it did not fall limp at his side? He who gazes at this becomes paralyzed. Who gave strength to Abraham's soul, so that his eyes did not grow dim, so that he saw neither Isaac nor the ram? He who gazes at this becomes blind.—And yet rare enough perhaps is the man who becomes paralyzed and blind, still more rare one who worthily recounts what happened. We all know it—it was only a trial.

If Abraham when he stood upon Mount Moriah had doubted, if he had gazed about him irresolutely, if before he draw the knife he had by chance discovered the ram, if God had permitted him to offer it instead of Isaac—then he would have betaken himself home, everything would have been the same, he has Sarah, he retained Isaac, and yet how changed! For his retreat would have been a flight, his salvation an accident, his reward dishonor, his future perhaps perdition. Then he would have borne witness neither to his faith nor to God's grace, but would have testified only how dreadful it is to march out to Mount Moriah. Then Abraham would not have been forgotten, nor would Mount Moriah, this mountain would then be mentioned, not like Ararat where the Ark landed, but would be spoken of as a consternation, because it was here that Abraham doubted.

Venerable Father Abraham! In marching home from Mount Moriah thou hadst no need of a panegryic which might console thee for they loss; for thou didst gain all and didst retain Isaac. What it not so? Never again did the Lord take him from thee, but thou didst sit at table joyfully with him in they tent, as thou dost in the beyond to all eternity. Venerable Father Abraham! Thousands of years have run their course since those days, but thou hast need of no tardy lover to snatch the memorial of thee from the power of all oblivion, for every language calls thee to remembrance—and yet thou dost reward thy lover more gloriously than does any other; hereafter thou dost make him blessed in they bosom; here thou dost enthral his eyes and his heart by the marvel of thy deed. Venerable Father Abraham! Second Father of the human race! Thou who first wast sensible of and didst first bear witness to that prodigious passion which disdains the dreadful conflict with the rage of the elements and with the powers of creation in order to strive with God; thou who first didst know that highest passion, the holy, pure and humble expression of the divine madness which the pagans admired—forgive him who would speak in praise of thee, if he does not do it fittingly. He spoke humbly, as if it were the desire of his own heart, he spoke briefly, as it becomes him to do, but he will never forget that thou hadst need of a hundred years to obtain a son of old age against expectation, that thou didst have to draw the knife before retaining Isaac; he will never forget that in a hundred and thirty years thou didst not get further than to faith.

BIBLE AND KIERKEGAARD SELECTIONS

1. What is the background and setting of the story of Abraham and Isaac? Who is Abraham? What is the significance of Isaac, beyond simply the fact that he is Abraham's son?

2. Why does Kierkegaard repeat the refrain that Abraham would have been remembered had he acted differently?

3. Do you think Kierkegaard believes that Abraham did the *morally* right thing? Is there some higher condition, some higher law, than morality, according to Kierkegaard? What is it? What does it command?

4. In the story, as Kierkegaard points out, Abraham does not tell his wife or his kinsmen what he is going to do. What does this tell us about the connection (or lack of connection) between our relationship to one another and our relationship to God?

5. Does it ever occur to Abraham to doubt that it is God who is speaking to him? Why not? In exactly what way is this experience a test of Abraham's faith?

1. Does it make sense to try to prove the existence of God? Is Aquinas attempting to convert unbelievers? Is Anslem? Is Paley? If you were presented with a proof of God's existence with which you could find nothing wrong, and if nevertheless you did not believe, would you take that as evidence that something was wrong with the proof, or as evidence that something was wrong with your powers of reason?

2. What view do you suppose Kierkegaard would take of proofs for the existence of God? Is it God's existence that he is concerned with in the selection you have read, or something else? What?

3. On the basis of his selection in this chapter, how do you suppose Kierkegaard would deal with the "problem of evil"? How would Mackie analyze Kierkegaard's position?

4. Would Hume accept drug-induced experiences as evidence of the existence of a Divine Being? Why? Would Aquinas, do you suppose?

5. Does it make sense to suspend belief in God until adequate evidence or a really sound proof is discovered? What do you risk if you suspend belief?

6. In your own experience, do arguments for or against God's existence play an important role? Why? If you *are* a believer, what (so far as you can tell) is the source of your belief? If you are not a believer, what (if anything) would make you a believer? Which of the authors in this chapter comes closest to your own conception of religious belief?

bibliography

CHAPTER ONE

ANDERSON, A. R., ed., *Minds and Machines.* Englewood Cliffs, N.J.: Prentice-Hall, 1964.

BROAD, C. D., *The Mind and Its Place in Nature.* London: Routledge, 1925.

DREYFUS, HUBERT L., *What Computers Can't Do: A Critique of Artificial Intelligence.* New York: Harper and Row, 1973.

FLEW, ANTHONY, ed., *Body, Mind, and Death.* New York: Macmillan, 1964.

GRICE, H. P., "Personal Identity," *Mind,* vol. 50, 1941.

HOOK, SIDNEY, ed., *Dimensions of Mind.* New York: New York University Press, 1960.

HUME, DAVID, *A Treatise of Human Nature,* Book I, Part iv, Section 6.

JAMES, WILLIAM, *The Principles of Psychology.* New York: Henry Holt, 1890.

PARFIT, DEREK, "Personal Identity," *Philosophical Review,* vol. 80, 1971.

PENELHUM, TERENCE, "Hume on Personal Identity," *Philosophical Review,* vol. 64, 1955.

REID, THOMAS, *Essays on the Intellectual Powers of Man.* New York: Garland Pub., 1971.

RYLE, GILBERT, *The Concept of Mind.* New York: Barnes and Noble, 1949.

SAYRE, KENNETH, M., *Consciousness: A Philosophic Study of Minds and Machines.* New York: Random House, 1969.

SHOEMAKER, SIDNEY, *Self-Knowledge and Self-Identity.* Ithaca, N.Y.: Cornell University Press, 1962.

VESEY, G. N. A., ed., *Body and Mind.* London: George Allen and Unwin, 1964.

WISDOM, JOHN, *Other Minds.* Oxford: Basil Blackwell, 1952.

————, *Problems of Mind and Matter.* Cambridge: Cambridge University Press, 1934.

CHAPTER TWO

BERGSON, HENRI, *Time and Free Will.* New York: Macmillan, 1921.

BERLIN, ISAIAH, *Historical Inevitability.* London: Oxford University Press, 1954.

BEROFSKY, BERNARD, ed., *Free Will and Determinism.* New York: Harper and Row, 1966.

CAMPBELL, C. A., *In Defense of Free Will.* Glasgow: Glasgow University Press, 1924.

DAVIDSON, DONALD, "Actions, Reasons, and Causes," *Journal of Philosophy,* vol. 60, 1963.

DWORKIN, GERALD, ed., *Determinism, Free Will, and Moral Responsibility.* Englewood Cliffs, N.J.: Prentice-Hall, 1970.

FOOT, PHILIPPA, "Free Will as Involving Determinism," *Philosophical Review,* vol. 66, 1957.

HAMPSHIRE, STUART, *Freedom of the Individual.* New York: Harper and Row, 1965.

HART, H. L. A., "The Ascription of Rights and Responsibilities," in *Essays in Logic and Language, First Series,* ed. A. Flew. New York: Philosophical Library, 1951.

HOBBES, THOMAS, *Leviathan,* chap. 21, [many editions].

HOOK, SIDNEY, ed., *Determinism and Freedom in the Age of Modern Science.* New York: New York University Press, 1961.

HOSPERS, JOHN, "Free-Will and Psychoanalysis," pp. 560–575 in *Readings in Ethical Theory,* ed. W. Sellers and J. Hospers. New York: Appleton-Crofts, 1952.

JAMES, WILLIAM, "The Dilemma of Determinism" in *Essays on Pragmatism*, New York: Hafner, 1948.

LAIRD, JOHN, *On Human Freedom*. London: G. Allen, 1947.

LAMONT, CORLISS, *Freedom of Choice Affirmed*. New York: Horizon Press, 1967.

LEHRER, KEITH, ed., *Freedom and Determinism*. New York: Random House, 1966.

MELDEN, A. I., *Free Action*. London: Routledge and Kegan Paul, 1961.

MILL, JOHN STUART, *A System of Logic*, Book 6. London: Longmans, Green, 1959.

NOWELL-SMITH, P. H., "Free-Will and Moral Responsibility," *Mind*, vol. 57, 1948.

SPINOZA, BENEDICT, *Ethics*, Book III.

TAYLOR, RICHARD, *Action and Purpose*. Englewood Cliffs, N.J.: Prentice-Hall, 1966.

CHAPTER THREE

ARISTOTLE, *Nichomachean Ethics*, trans. W. D. Ross. Oxford: Oxford University Press, 1915.

BAIER, KURT, *The Moral Point of View: A Rational Basis for Ethics*. Ithaca, N.Y.: Cornell University Press, 1958.

BRANDT, R. B., *Ethical Theory: The Problems of Normative and Critical Ethics*. Englewood Cliffs, N.J.: Prentice-Hall, 1959.

CAREY, S., ed., *Morality and Moral Reasoning*. London: Methuen, 1971.

DEWEY, JOHN, *Theory of the Moral Life*. New York: Holt, Rinehart and Winston, 1960.

EDWARDS, PAUL, *The Logic of Moral Discourse*. New York: Free Press, 1955.

FOOT, PHILIPPA, "Moral Beliefs," *Proceedings of the Aristotelian Society*, 1958–59.

FRANKENA, WILLIAM, *Ethics*. Englewood Cliffs, N.J.: Prentice-Hall, 1963.

GAUTHIER, DAVID, *Practical Reasoning*. London: Oxford University Press, 1963.

HARE, R. M., *The Language of Morals*. Oxford: Clarendon Press, 1952.

LEWIS, C. I., *An Analysis of Knowledge and Valuation.* La Salle, Ill.: Open Court Publishing Company, 1946.

NOWELL-SMITH, P. H., *Ethics.* Baltimore: Penguin Books, 1954.

PLATO, *Gorgias,* trans. W. C. Helmbold. Indianapolis: Bobbs-Merrill, 1952.

———, *The Apology,* trans. F. J. Church, rev. R. D. Cumming. New York: Liberal Arts Press, 1956.

SANTAYANA, GEORGE, *The Life of Reason,* Vol. I. New York: Charles Scribner's Sons, 1918.

SEARLE, J. R., "How to Derive 'Ought' from 'Is,'" *Philosophical Review,* vol. 73, 1964.

STEVENSON, CHARLES L., *Ethics and Language.* New Haven: Yale University Press, 1944.

URMSON, J. O., *The Emotive Theory of Ethics.* London: Hutchinson, 1968.

———, "On Grading," *Mind,* vol. 59, 1950.

CHAPTER FOUR

AUSTIN, J. L., *Sense and Sensibilia.* Oxford: Clarendon Press, 1962.

AYER, A. J., *The Problem of Knowledge,* chap. 3. Harmondsworth: Publican Books, 1956.

BROAD, C. D., *Perception, Physics, and Reality.* Cambridge: Cambridge University Press, 1914.

CHISHOLM, R. M., *Perceiving: A Philosophical Study.* Ithaca, N.Y.: Cornell University Press, 1957.

HARDIE, W. F. R., "The Paradox of Phenomenalism," *Proceedings of the Aristotelian Society,* vol. 46, 1945.

HUME, DAVID, *A Treatise of Human Nature,* Book I. (many editions)

KANT, IMMANUEL, *Critique of Pure Reason,* Transcendental Aesthetic and Transcendental Analytic, New York: St. Martin's Press, 1961.

LEWIS, CLARENCE IRVING, *Mind and the World Order.* New York: Charles Scribner's Sons, 1929.

LOCKE, D., *Perception and Our Knowledge of the External.* London: Allen & Unwin, 1968.

LOCKE, JOHN, *An Essay Concerning the Human Understanding.* (many editions)

MILL, JOHN STUART, *An Examination of Sir William Hamilton's Philosophy.* London: Longmans, Green, 1872.

MOORE, G. E., "The Refutation of Idealism," in *Philosophical Studies.* London: Kegan Paul, 1922.

PAUL, G. A., "Is There a Problem About Sense-Data?" *Proceedings of the Aristotelian Society, Supplementary Volumes 15,* 1936.

PITCHER, GEORGE, *A Theory of Perception.* Princeton, N.J.: Princeton University Press, 1971.

PRICE, H. H., *Hume's Theory of the External World.* Oxford: Clarendon Press, 1940.

PRICHARD, H. A., "The Sense-Datum Fallacy," *Proceedings of the Aristotelian Society, Supplementary Volumes 17,* 1938.

RUSSELL, BERTRAND, *Human Knowledge.* London: Allen & Unwin, 1927.

————, *The Problems of Philosophy.* London: Oxford University Press, 1912.

SELLARS, R. W., *The Philosophy of Physical Realism.* New York: Macmillan, 1932.

SIBLEY, F. H., ed., *Perception: A Philosophical Symposium.* London: Methuen, 1971.

SWARTZ, ROBERT J., ed., *Perceiving, Sensing, and Knowing.* Garden City, N.Y.: Doubleday, 1965.

CHAPTER FIVE

ARISTOTLE, *Nichomachean Ethics.* (various translations)

BAYLES, MICHAEL, ed., *Contemporary Utilitarianism.* New York: Doubleday, 1968.

BECK, LEWIS WHITE, *A Commentary on Kant's Critique of Practical Reason.* Chicago: University of Chicago Press, 1960.

BROAD, C. D., *Five Types of Ethical Theory.* New York: Humanities Press, 1956.

BUTLER, JOSEPH, "On Self-Love," in *Fifteen Sermons Upon Human Nature.* (many editions)

EWING, A. C., *The Morality of Punishment.* London: Kegan Paul, 1929.

FRANKENA, WILLIAM K., *Ethics.* Englewood Cliffs, N.J.: Prentice-Hall, 1963.

GAUTIER, D. P., ed., *Morality and Rational Self-Interest*. Englewood Cliffs, N.J.: Prentice-Hall, 1970.

HODGSON, D. G., *Consequences of Utilitarianism*. Oxford: Clarendon Press, 1967.

KANT, IMMANUEL, *Critique of Practical Reason*, trans. Lewis White Beck. New York: Liberal Arts Press, 1956.

LYONS, DAVID, *Forms and Limits of Utilitarianism*. Oxford: Clarendon Press, 1965.

MELDON, A. I., *Ethical Theories*. Englewood Cliffs, N.J.: Prentice-Hall, 1955.

MILL, JOHN STUART, *Utilitarianism*. (many editions)

NAGEL, THOMAS, *The Possibility of Altruism*. Oxford: Clarendon Press, 1970.

RAWLS, JOHN, "Two Concepts of Rules," *Philosophical Review*, vol. 64, 1955.

SIDGWICK, HENRY, *The Methods of Ethics*. London: Macmillan & Co., 1922.

SINGER, MARCUS G., *Generalization in Ethics*. New York: Alfred A. Knopf, 1961.

SUMNER, W. G., *Folkways*. Boston, Ginn & Co., 1934.

WOLFF, ROBERT PAUL, *The Autonomy of Reason*. New York: Harper & Row, 1973.

CHAPTER SIX

BELLAMY, EDWARD, *Looking Backward*. New York: Random House, 1951.

BETTLEHEIM, BRUNO, *The Children of the Dream*. New York: Avon Books, 1969.

ERIKSON, ERIK H., *Childhood and Society*. New York: W. W. Norton, 1950.

FREUD, SIGMUND, *Civilization and Its Discontents*. New York: Norton, 1962.

FRIEDMAN, MILTON, *Capitalism and Freedom*. Chicago: University of Chicago Press, 1962.

FROMM, ERICH, *Escape from Freedom*. New York: Holt, Rinehart and Winston, 1941.

———, *Marx's Concept of Man*. New York: Fredrick Unger, 1961.

GOODMAN, PAUL, and PERCIVAL GOODMAN, *Communitas*. New York: Random House, 1947.

HERTZLER, J. O., *The History of Utopian Thought*. New York: Macmillan, 1923.

KAMENKA, EUGENE, *The Ethical Foundations of Marxism*. New York: Frederick A. Praeger, 1962.

MARCUSE, HERBERT, *An Essay on Liberation*. Boston: Beacon Press, 1969.

———, *One-Dimensional Man*. Boston: Beacon Press, 1955.

MARX, KARL, and FRIEDERICK ENGELS, *Basic Writings on Politics and Philosophy*. New York: Doubleday, 1959.

MORE, THOMAS, *Utopia*. (many editions)

ORWELL, GEORGE, *1984*. New York: Harcourt Brace Jovanovich, 1949.

RAND, AYN, *The Virtue of Selfishness*. New York: Signet Books, 1969.

RANDALL, JOHN HERMAN, JR., *Plato: Dramatist of the Life of Reason*. New York: Columbia University Press, 1970.

ROSZAK, THEODORE, *The Making of a Counter Culture*. New York: Doubleday, 1969.

SPIRO, MELFORD E., *Kibbutz: Venture in Utopia*. Cambridge: Harvard University Press, 1956.

YOUNG, MICHAEL, *The Rise of Meritocracy*. Harmondsworth: Penguin Books, 1961.

CHAPTER SEVEN

BROAD, C. D., *Religion, Philosophy, and Psychical Research*. New York: Harcourt, 1953.

BUIRELL, DONALD R., ed., *The Cosmological Arguments*. New York: Anchon Books, 1967.

DESCARTES, RENÉ, *Meditations on First Philosophy*. Meditations III and V. (many editions)

FEUERBACK, LUDWIG, *The Essence of Christianity* (2d ed.), trans. Marian Evans. Boston: Houghton Mifflin, 1881.

FREUD, SIGMUND, *The Future of an Illusion,* trans. W. D. Robson-Scott. Garden City, N.Y., Doubleday, 1957.

HICK, JOHN, *Philosophy of Religion*. Englewood Cliffs, N.J.: Prentice-Hall, 1963.

HOOK, SIDNEY, ed., *Religious Experience and Truth*. New York: New York University Press, 1961.

JAMES, WILLIAM, *The Varieties of Religious Experience*. (many editions)

———, *The Will to Believe*. London: Longmans, Green, 1897.

JOHNSON, H. A., and H. THULSTRUP, eds., *A Kierkegaard Critique*. Chicago: Regnery, 1962.

KANT, IMMANUEL, *Critique of Pure Reason*, "The Ideal of Pure Reason," trans. Norman Kemp Smith. New York: St. Martin's Press, 1961.

LAIRD, JOHN, *Theism and Cosmology*. London: Allen & Unwin, 1940.

MACINTYRE, A. and A. FLEW, eds., *New Essays in Philosophical Theology*. London: SCM Press, 1955.

MALCOLM, NORMAN, "Anselm's Ontological Arguments," *Philosophical Review,* vol. 69, 1960

MILL, JOHN STUART, *Three Essays in Religion*. Holt, Rinehart and Winston, 1874.

PENELHUM, T., *Religion and Rationality*. New York: Random House, 1971.

PIKE, NELSON, ed., *God and Evil*. Englewood Cliffs, N.J.: Prentice-Hall, 1964.

PLANTINGA, ALVIN, *God and Other Minds*. Ithaca, N.Y.: Cornell University Press, 1967.

RUSSELL, BERTRAND, *Why I Am Not a Christian and Other Essays*. London: Oxford University Press, 1935.

SIWEK, PAUL, *The Philosophy of Evil*. New York: Ronald, 1956.

TAYLOR, A. E., *Does God Exist?* London: Macmillan, 1947.